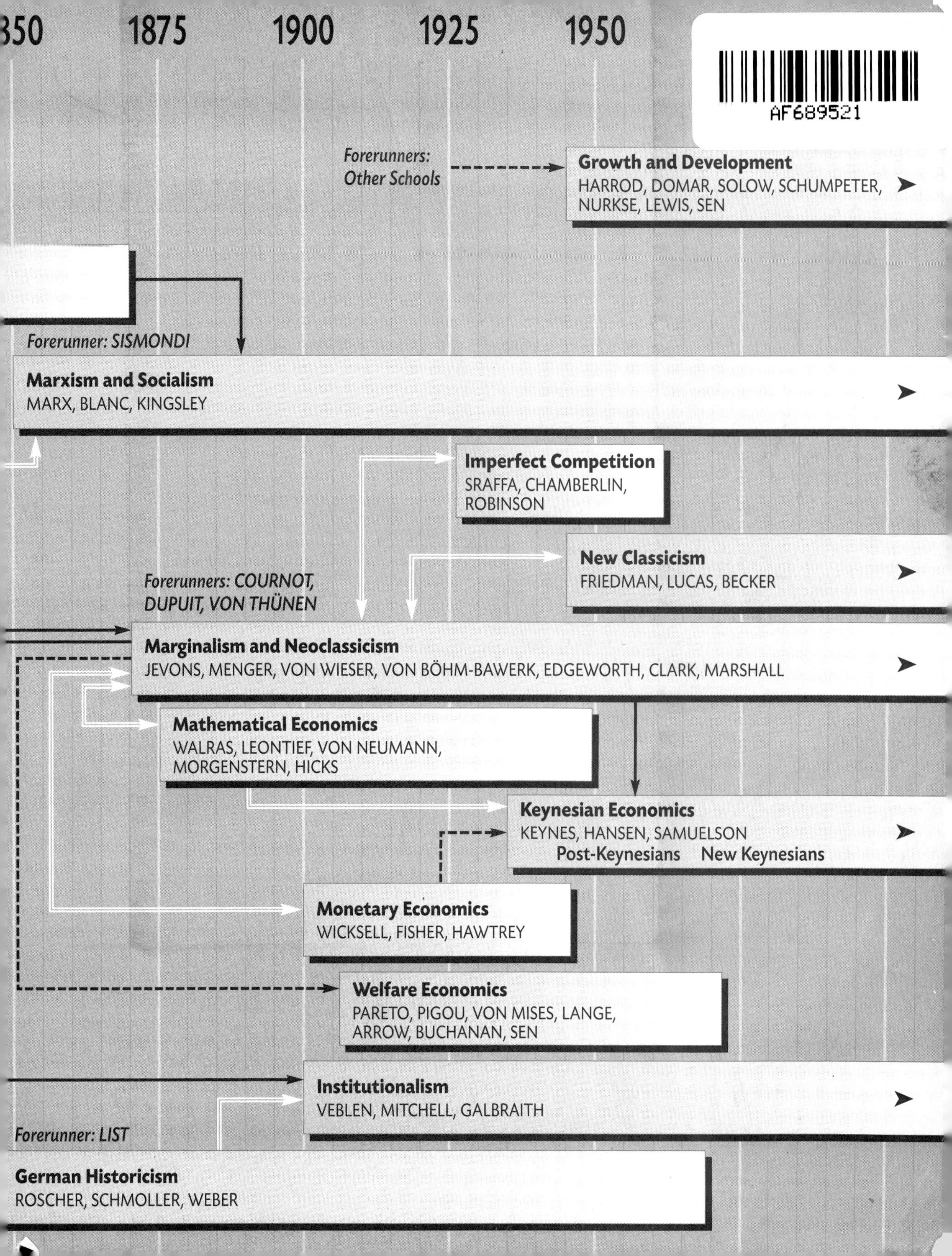

1850
1875
1900
1925
1950
Forerunners: Other Schools
Growth and Development
HARROD, DOMAR, SOLOW, SCHUMPETER, NURKSE, LEWIS, SEN
Forerunner: SISMONDI
Marxism and Socialism
MARX, BLANC, KINGSLEY
Imperfect Competition
SRAFFA, CHAMBERLIN, ROBINSON
New Classicism
FRIEDMAN, LUCAS, BECKER
Forerunners: COURNOT, DUPUIT, VON THÜNEN
Marginalism and Neoclassicism
JEVONS, MENGER, VON WIESER, VON BÖHM-BAWERK, EDGEWORTH, CLARK, MARSHALL
Mathematical Economics
WALRAS, LEONTIEF, VON NEUMANN, MORGENSTERN, HICKS
Keynesian Economics
KEYNES, HANSEN, SAMUELSON
Post-Keynesians
New Keynesians
Monetary Economics
WICKSELL, FISHER, HAWTREY
Welfare Economics
PARETO, PIGOU, VON MISES, LANGE, ARROW, BUCHANAN, SEN
Institutionalism
VEBLEN, MITCHELL, GALBRAITH
Forerunner: LIST
German Historicism
ROSCHER, SCHMOLLER, WEBER

THE EVOLUTION OF ECONOMIC THOUGHT

STANLEY L. BRUE
Pacific Lutheran University

•

RANDY R. GRANT
Linfield College

Seventh Edition

THOMSON
SOUTH-WESTERN

Australia · Brazil · Canada · Mexico · Singapore · Spain · United Kingdom · United States

THOMSON
SOUTH-WESTERN

The Evolution of Economic Thought, Seventh Edition
Stanley Brue and Randy Grant

VP/Editorial Director:
Jack W. Calhoun

Editor-in-Chief:
Alex von Rosenberg

Associate Acquisitions Editor:
Sarah Dorger

Developmental Editor:
Katie Yanos

Marketing Manager:
Jennifer Garamy

Production Project Manager:
Stephanie Schempp

Manager of Technology, Editorial:
Vicky True

Technology Project Manager:
Dana Cowden

Web Coordinator:
Karen Schaffer

Manufacturing Coordinator:
Sandee Milewski

Production House:
International Typesetting and Composition

Printer:
RR Donnelley
Crawfordsville, IN

Art Director:
Michelle Kunkler

Internal and Cover Designer:
Joe Pagliaro

Cover Images:
© Getty Images, Inc.

Printed in the United States of America
2 3 4 5 10 09 08 07 06

Student Edition:
ISBN-13: 978-0-324-32145-6
ISBN-10: 0-324-32145-7

Library of Congress Control Number: 2006901299

For more information about our products, contact us at:

Thomson Learning Academic Resource Center

1-800-423-0563

Thomson Higher Education
5191 Natorp Boulevard
Mason, OH 45040
USA

Brief Contents

Contents

Preface

THE SEVENTH EDITION

The primary purpose of this book is to tell the story of the history of economics in a clear, scholarly, balanced, and interesting fashion. It is, after all, a story of great importance—one that sharpens our understanding of contemporary economics and provides a unique perspective not found in other fields of the discipline.

The study of the history of economic thought continues to grow as the discipline of economics matures. New ideas, new evidence, new problems, and new values call for a reconsideration of basic disputes and major contributions of the past. Although the basic features of previous editions are retained, this edition has been substantially updated and revised. The most significant changes are listed next.

New Web Site

This edition introduces a new web site that is integrated with the text. Access this new web site at brue.swlearning.com. Features of the web site include:

- **New chapters on economic thought before 1500.** Chapters on Greek philosophy, Judeo-Christian contributions from the Bible through the Protestant Reformation, and Medieval Arab-Islamic economic thought illuminate early ideas in economics, some of which can be found in modern times.
- **New economists.** Biographies and contributions of additional economists have been added for many of the chapters. George Stigler, Abba Lerner, and many others have been added in downloadable files.
- **Links to other web sites.** Links to other important history of thought web sites are provided for students who want to learn more about famous characters in the evolution of economic thought story.
- **Instructor support.** Pedagogical suggestions and additional questions for study and discussion are provided for instructors looking for new ways to enhance their courses.

Newly Featured Economist

One economist is newly featured in this edition:

- **Amartya Sen** Chapter 20 now includes a section on Amartya Sen and his contributions to social choice theory and the economics of inequality. Although Sen employs mainstream methodology, his emphasis on normative economics sets him apart from many other modern contributors.

To make room for the new content on this Nobel laureate, the sections on Theodore Schultz and Joseph Schumpeter's discussion on "The Decay of Capitalism," in Chapter 23, have been moved to the new web site that accompanies the text.

New Past as Prologue Sections

This edition contains five new or significantly revised Past as Prologue sections. These "boxes" connect earlier ideas, sometimes addressed only briefly, to subsequent or contemporary economic contributions or issues. In some cases the particular link of ideas spans many decades; in other cases it spans only a few years. Sometimes the sections look toward the future; other times they look toward the past. But in all instances they involve original ideas and their impact on subsequent economic theory, issues, or events.

The Past as Prologue sections should help students recognize historical and logical connections between ideas. After reading these sections, students perhaps will begin to link historical ideas in other areas of their studies. Also, these sections occasionally serve as a vehicle for introducing important ideas or issues that are somewhat tangential to the main flow of the text, and thus they are best treated separately.

The new Past as Prologue titles are:

- Franklin and Bastiat on Opportunity Cost (Chapter 13)
- Rational Economic Behavior and Prospect Theory (Chapter 15)
- Advances in Econometrics (Chapter 18)
- The Mundell-Fleming Contribution to IS-LM (Chapter 22)
- Human Capital Formation? Or Signaling and Screening? (Chapter 24)

The table of contents contains a complete list of the Past as Prologue sections. To ensure that these boxes do not interrupt the logical flow of the chapter, we have placed an indication in the margin to alert the reader when to read each section.

Augmented End-of-Chapter Elements

The end-of-chapter Questions for Study and Discussion have been augmented with questions relating to the new content. Also, the Selected Readings section lists have been expanded and updated with current references.

Product Differentiation

The distinguishing features of this textbook include:

- **Five Major Questions** As each important school of economic thought is introduced, five major questions are considered: What was the historical background of the school? What were the major tenets of the school? Whom did the school benefit or seek to benefit? How was the school valid, useful, or correct in its time? Which tenets of the school became lasting contributions?

  The answers to these questions provide a concise summary of each school. Discussion then focuses on the major contributors within each broadly defined school. This approach is not only sound intellectually, but also makes sense educationally by presenting the history of economic thought in a way that fosters student retention of knowledge.

- **Extensive Quotations** Extensive quotations from original sources are used to acquaint readers firsthand with the flavor and substance of history's major economic works. Ideally, these passages will whet students' appetites so they will turn to the original works for further reading.
- **Intellectual History** This edition continues the liberal-arts orientation of previous editions. It is more than a treatise on the emergence of modern, formalistic economic theory; it also addresses the development of broader economic thought and its relationship to other portions of intellectual history. A broad, liberal-arts orientation, of course, does not preclude—and in many instances demands—rigorous, in-depth treatment of both orthodox and unorthodox economic theory. Thus, careful attention is given to the emergence of the technical aspects of major textbook models of modern economics.
- **Clarity of Exposition** This book continues to emphasize clarity in exposition. *The Evolution of Economic Thought* is designed to be understandable and accessible not only to those who have taken numerous courses in economics, but also to those undergraduates who have taken just a reasonably rigorous principles-of-economics course sequence.
- **Time Scale of Economic Ideas** The inside front cover of this book contains the Time Scale of Economic Ideas. Each rectangle in the time scale represents a major school or approach, and the names within each rectangle are those of economists most important or representative in the development of that school or set of ideas. The particular type of arrow (white or black) linking two schools indicates the nature of the relationship that existed between them. The relevant part of the time scale is enlarged and presented at the beginning of each chapter to remind the reader where the ideas to be discussed fit within the overall development of economic thought.
- **Appendix on Information Sources** Chapter 1 contains an appendix summarizing the major information sources in the field, including those found on the Internet.
- **Study Questions** Questions for study and discussion are found at the end of each chapter. These questions review the chapter content, entice students to "stretch" their understanding, and interconnect past, present, and upcoming material.
- **Figures with Legends** A carefully written explanatory legend accompanies each figure. Many of these legends have been revised for completeness and clarity in this edition.

Acknowledgments

Longtime adopters of this textbook will recognize Jacob Oser's legacy within it. Although Professor Oser was not alive to participate in the past four editions, it retains the features, style, and, in many places, the actual words of the early editions. It has been an honor for us to carry on Professor Oser's work.

In revising this book, we have benefited greatly from the help provided by reviewers and would like to thank them publicly. They are Syad Ahman, McMaster University; Ernest Ankrim, Frank Russell Company; Benjamin Balak, Rollins College;

Richard Ballman, Augustana College in Illinois; Les Carson, Augustana College in South Dakota; Karl W. Einolf, Mount Saint Mary's University in Maryland; Maxwell O. Eseonu, Virginia State University; Tawni Hunt Ferrarini, Northern Michigan University; Peter Garlick, SUNY-New Paltz; David E. R. Gay, University of Arkansas; Geoffrey Gilbert, Hobart and William Smith Colleges; Ching-Yao Hsieh, George Washington University; Robert Jensen, Pacific Lutheran University; John Larrivee, Mount Saint Mary's University in Maryland; Charles G. Leathers, University of Alabama in Tuscaloosa; Mary H. Lesser, Iona College; Andrea Maneschi, Vanderbilt University; John A. Miller, Wheaton College in Massachusetts; Tracy Miller, Baylor University; Clair E. Morris, U.S. Naval Academy; Laurence Moss, Babson College; Norris Peterson, Pacific Lutheran University; Michael Reed, University of Nevada in Reno; Thomas Reinwald, Shippensburg University; Teresa M. Riley, Youngstown State University; Robert P. Rogers, Ashland University; and Neil T. Skaggs, Illinois State University. Numerous students in History of Economic Thought courses have also eagerly identified errors and suggestions for improvement.

Also, our thanks go to the following highly talented people at Thomson/South-Western and Interactive Composition Corporation for their expert handling of the revision from conception to final product: Sarah Dorger, acquisitions editor; Katie Yanos, developmental editor; Stephanie Schempp, production project manager; Jennifer Garamy, marketing manager; Kay Mikel, copy editor; Michelle Kunkler, art director; John Hill, photo/permission manager; Sandee Milewski, senior manufacturing manager; Dana Cowden, technology project editor; Karen Schaffer, web coordinator; and Sam RC, project manager.

Finally, we are grateful for the support of our families who pick up the slack at home while we get to have all the fun.

Chapter 1

INTRODUCTION AND OVERVIEW

Early strands of economic thinking can be linked to antiquity. For example, the word *economics* traces its roots to ancient Greece, where *oeconomicus* meant "management of the household." Aristotle (384–322 B.C.) engaged in economic thinking by distinguishing between "natural and unnatural arts of acquisition." Natural acquisition, he wrote, includes such activities as farming, fishing, and hunting, which produce goods for life's necessities. Unnatural acquisition, of which he disapproved, involves acquiring goods beyond one's needs. Plato (427–347 B.C.) wrote of the benefits of human specialization within the ideal city-state. Such specialization foreshadowed the later ideas of Adam Smith on the division of labor. The Bible contains several thoughts on economics, including those in opposition to lending at interest. In the Middle Ages, St. Thomas Aquinas (1225–1274) advanced the idea of a just price: one in which neither the buyer nor the seller takes advantage of the other.

The period before A.D. 1500 represented an epoch far different from the 1500s to the present. There was little trade before 1500, and most goods were produced for consumption in the community that produced them without first being sent to market. Money and credit were, therefore, not widely used, although they existed even in ancient times. Strong national states and integrated national economies had not yet fully evolved, nor had any schools of economic thought been formed.

In contrast, markets and trade expanded rapidly after 1500, with the great geographical explorations both resulting from this process and accelerating it. The money economy superseded the natural or self-sufficient economy. National states with unified economies became dominant forces. Economic schools arose, representing systematic bodies of thought and policy formation.

In the 1500s the "age of political economy" began to supplant the "age of moral philosophy." The focus on political economy brought with it a more coherent organization of economic thinking, turning fragments of economic ideas into systematic theories. We recognize, however, the seminal nature of these earlier fragments, so on the web site that accompanies this book (http://brue.swlearning.com) we include chapters on Ancient Greece and the influence of religious ideas from biblical times through the Protestant Reformation. Although we will occasionally refer to earlier ideas, we begin our story of the evolution of economic thought in the sixteenth century with mercantilism.

A TIME SCALE OF ECONOMIC IDEAS

Economic thinking has displayed a significant degree of continuity over the centuries. The founders of a new theory may draw on the ideas of their predecessors and develop them further, or they may react in opposition to earlier ideas that stimulate their own thinking in new directions. These relations among different schools of thought are depicted in the Time Scale of Economic Ideas, shown on the inside front cover of this book. When viewing this scale, keep in mind that any organizing schema that maps influences and links schools requires some arbitrary decisions about what fits where.

Each rectangle in the Time Scale represents a major school or approach. The names in each rectangle are economists who were most important or most typical in developing that school or approach. The names immediately above each rectangle are forerunners of the school. A white arrow linking two rectangles shows that the later group was generally friendly to the group from which it grew or that it superseded. A black arrow shows that the later group was antagonistic to or rose in opposition to the earlier group. A dashed arrow indicates groups in which some contributors were friendly to predecessors, but others were antagonistic.

Thus you will discover, for example, that the physiocrats were completely opposed to the doctrines of the mercantilists (black arrow), whereas Adam Smith and the classical school were friendly toward the physiocrats (white arrow). The marginalists showed a break with the classical school from which they sprang, while John Maynard Keynes in turn rejected the macroeconomic ideas of marginalism. Therefore, black arrows appear in these sequences, although it could be argued that the similarities in both cases were greater than the differences. Certainly, however, the marginalists had close and friendly relations with the monetary economists (white arrow). Alternatively, some welfare economists advanced marginalist ideas, whereas others challenged those ideas. Therefore, the arrow from the marginalist school to the welfare economists is dashed.

Numerous modern ideas bear some similarity to never-adopted or long-repudiated concepts of past epochs. For example, some supply-side economists writing in the United States in the 1980s advocated a return to the domestic gold standard, an idea that was promoted by economists and adopted by nations in the 1800s but that fell out of favor following the depression of the 1930s. The idea of human capital stated by Adam Smith and John Stuart Mill lay dormant until it was revitalized and expanded by Theodore Schultz and Gary Becker in the post-1960 period. The gloomy pronouncements of Thomas Robert Malthus in 1798 were heard in a modified form in the voices of the handful of economists in the 1970s who predicted that shortages of resources would soon cause the world economy to collapse. The emergence of new classical macroeconomics in the 1980s and 1990s as a challenge to prevailing Keynesian views repackaged some of the old classicism of the previous century.

This is not to suggest that history moves in circles and that we move back to where we were in earlier periods. Rather, the history of economic thought seems to move in spirals. Economic theories and policies frequently *do* return to similar ones of an earlier era, but they are on different planes under very different conditions. The differences are as significant as the similarities, and both are worth examining closely. This we do as we progress through the Time Scale.

Refer to the Time Scale often as you progress through the book, because it will help identify where the economists and ideas being studied fit within the larger historical flow of doctrines.

Finally, you will see many Past as Prologue sections throughout the book. These numbered sections demonstrate that past ideas, sometimes in fragmentary form, are precursors of later, more developed and formalized ideas or economic policies. A symbol in the page margin indicates the best place to pause and read these sections. It will also remind you where to once again begin your reading after the pause.

THE FIVE MAJOR QUESTIONS

As each important school of economic thought is introduced, five major questions about it will be considered. This method will provide perspective on the school and the social background that produced it. This concise summary at the outset will help clarify the main points as we study the ideas of the leading economists. The study of the economists will illustrate the characteristics of the schools with which they have been linked, and quotations from their writings will indicate the flavor of their thinking.

What Was the Historical Background of the School?

Here we examine the historical background to ascertain whether it may have nurtured a particular system of thought. Economic theory often develops in response to changes in the environment that draw attention to new problems. Some knowledge of the times is essential to understand why people thought and acted the way they did. It is true, of course, that many systems of thought exist simultaneously in the minds of many individuals. Intellects tend to develop a wide multiplicity of ideas, ranging from the most sensible to the wildly fantastic. Ideas irrelevant to society at the time they are presented tend to wither and die, whereas those that are useful and effective in answering at least some questions and in solving some problems are disseminated and popularized, thereby contributing to the stature of their authors. Adam Smith contributed much to economic thinking; but can anyone doubt that, had he never lived, the same ideas would have come somewhat later? Perhaps they would not have been expressed so well or so clearly. Then scholars would have stumbled about a bit more before they found themselves on the intellectual path that he so clearly laid out.

Smith made a great contribution precisely because his ideas answered the requirements of his time. If, for example, David Ricardo's theory of comparative advantage in international trade had been discovered in the feudal epoch, it would have been without major significance in a world of local self-sufficiency with a minimum of trade. The dispute over the corn laws in England in the early 1800s brought forth the theory of rent. Had Keynes published *The General Theory of Employment, Interest and Money* in 1926 instead of 1936, it may have attracted much less attention than it did. Clearly the social milieu in which ideas grow is important.

In fact some economists assign *primary* importance to the social, political, and economic environment for shaping the nature of the questions economists ask, and hence the content of the economic theories that emerges during a particular period. For example, according to John Kenneth Galbraith, "Ideas are inherently conservative. They yield not to the attack of other ideas, but to the massive onslaught of circumstances with which they cannot contend."[1] Restated, new ideas supplant widely accepted economic theories only when the events of the day render the old theories clearly inadequate. For example, some would argue that the long-held notion that a market economy automatically produces full employment did not yield to the logic of Keynes's *General Theory* but rather to the worldwide depression and massive unemployment of the 1930s.

A similar point was made by Wesley C. Mitchell, who wrote:

> Economists are prone to think their work is the outcome of a play of free intelligence over logically formulated problems. They may acknowledge that their ideas have been influenced by their reading and the teaching which they were wise enough to choose, but they seldom realize that their free intelligence has been molded by the circumstances in which they have grown up; that their minds are social products; that they cannot in any serious sense transcend their environment.
>
> To realize all this about themselves is important if students are to become properly self-critical; that is, if they are to realize the limits to which their vision is subject. But it is exceedingly difficult for a mind which has been shaped by a given environment not to take that environment as a matter of course, or to see that it is itself the product of transitory conditions and so subject to a variety of limitations.[2]

Many other economists, however, would disagree with—or at least greatly qualify—the idea that environmental forces are primary shapers of economic theory. They argue that internal factors within a discipline, such as the discovery and explanation of unresolved paradoxes, account for most theoretical advances. George J. Stigler may be allowed to speak for them:

> Every major development in economic theory in the last hundred years, I believe, could have come much earlier if appropriate environmental conditions were all that were needed. Even Keynes's *General Theory* could have found an evident empirical basis in the post–Napoleonic period or the 1870s or the 1890s. Perhaps this amounts only to saying—what is surely true and almost tautological—that the elements of an economic system which economists believe to be basic have been present for a long time. The nature of economic systems has changed relatively little since Smith's time.
>
> Thus I assign a minor, and even an accidental, role to the contemporary environment in the development of economic theory since it has become a professional discipline. Even where the original environmental stimulus to a particular analytical development is fairly clear, as in Ricardo's theory of rent, the profession soon appropriates the problem and reformulates it in a manner that becomes increasingly remote from current events, until finally its origin bears no recognizable relationship to its nature or uses.[3]

---

[1] John Kenneth Galbraith, *The Affluent Society* (Boston: Houghton Mifflin, 1958), 20.

[2] Wesley C. Mitchell, *Types of Economic Theory,* ed. Joseph Dorfman, vol. 1 (New York: A. M. Kelley, 1967), 36–37.

[3] George J. Stigler, *Essays in the History of Economics* (Chicago: University of Chicago Press, 1965), 23.

Which of these two alternative perspectives is correct? Both perspectives contain elements of the truth. Some theories clearly emerge directly as a consequence of burning issues of the day; other advancements in economics arise from the ongoing search for knowledge, quite independent of current events.

What Were the Major Tenets of the School?

Broad generalizations about the ideas of successive economic schools are provided under this heading. The strength of this procedure is that it enables a concise presentation of the essence of the school. The weakness is that there are always exceptions to the generalization that cannot be examined in detail until later. A succinct summary presents patterns of uniformity in ideas of groups of economists, but the exceptions may contain the seeds of ideas that eventually will triumph. Thus we will generalize that mercantilists favored the accumulation of gold and silver, yet there were some among them who took an antibullionist position. These people were overwhelmed and hardly heard at first, but their ideas were ultimately vindicated. Similarly, the classical school believed in free trade among nations; yet Malthus, a classical economist, favored tariffs on imported goods.

Whom Did the School Benefit or Seek to Benefit?

The type of economic questions that are dominant in the thoughts of one group may be insignificant to another. Theologians in the Middle Ages, for example, were very much concerned about the morality of charging interest on money lent out. With the passage of time this problem seemed less important. A group of thinkers and practitioners called mercantilists asked, "How can a country best accumulate gold and silver?" The classical economists were more concerned with "How can we increase production?" Keynes inquired how a market-based economy could avoid depressions and high unemployment. Monetarists pondered the causes of inflation. To be popularized, a system of ideas must either fit the needs of all of society or at least be acceptable to an element of society that will defend, extend, and apply it.

Most economic theorists assume that the self-interest of the individual is dominant and guides the economic process. Yet individual self-interest does not result in the chaotic conditions of individuals going their own way in opposition to the rest of society; individuals are guided by market, social, political, and ethical forces to cooperate with others in organizing a reasonable working relationship with society. Furthermore, they coalesce into groups because of social pressures, common interests and ideas, and natural gregariousness. Thus there are religious, political, aesthetic, social, and economic groups, each of which represents a unified outlook and program in its sphere of special interest. We are concerned here with groups of people who develop common ideas based partly on self-interest and partly on other considerations that help shape their concept of how an economy should be organized and in what direction it should move. We will try to identify the groups that supported each school of thought and the groups to which each school appealed for support, either successfully or unsuccessfully.

How Was the School Valid, Useful, or Correct in Its Time?

Here a way must be found between two opposing dangers. One is the erroneous idea that thinkers of the past were wrong, naive, ignorant, or foolish and that we, being wiser, have discovered the final truth. Thus J. B. Say, writing more than 150 years ago, asked, "What useful purpose can be served by the study of absurd opinions and doctrines that have long ago been exploded and deserved to be? It is mere useless pedantry to attempt to revive them. The more perfect a science becomes the shorter becomes its history."

This view applies more to the physical sciences than to the social sciences. Because the physical universe has not changed perceptibly during recent centuries, the laws under which it operates have not changed much either. As our scientific knowledge has grown, we have come closer to the truth. Even so, the history of physical science is meaningful. But society *has* changed, and therefore it is not surprising that new theories have emerged to explain the new developments. Plausible theories or policies in the seventeenth century may be of little relevance 400 years later.

The other extreme is to find every dominant idea of the past right, just, and good in its time. The possible validity of economic theories must, of course, be related to their time and place, but they may have been wrong or deficient even when first presented. Thus, for example, Karl Marx's labor theory of value must be evaluated not only in relationship to the earlier labor theories of Smith and Ricardo but also by the standards of contemporary value theory. This critical approach, of course, must be applied to current thinking also. Concepts that are widely accepted today are often inapplicable to earlier times, and they may become inappropriate in the future.

Which Tenets of the School Became Lasting Contributions?

This section identifies the ideas presented by a school that have been of lasting significance and thus can still be found in current economics textbooks. Here those contributions that "have stood the test of time" will be sorted out from those that, although perhaps valid in their day, outlived their usefulness as new evidence emerged or as social conditions changed.

THE VALUE OF STUDYING ECONOMICS AND ITS HISTORY

Students about to struggle over the difficult intellectual terrain ahead may well wonder, "Will it be worth the effort? Why study economic theory? Why study its history?"

Many answers come to mind. Two major reasons, other than the personal advantages that might be gained, justify the study of economic *theory*. First, such study allows us to gain an understanding of how an economy works; that is, what makes it hang together and function? Second, economic theory helps society reach the economic goals that it has selected for itself. Society can progress faster in achieving economic goals through a knowledge of economics.

But, why study the *history* of economic thought? First, such a study enhances one's understanding of contemporary economic thought. As just one example, the historical development of the numerous intricate concepts that underlie contemporary supply-and-demand analysis will be traced. More specifically, we will see how such ideas as diminishing returns and returns to scale paved the way for modern short- and long-run supply analysis, and how marginal utility and indifference curve models led to the emergence of modern demand theory. You will discover that, as stated by Mark Blaug, "contemporary theory wears the scars of yesterday's problems now resolved, yesterday's blunders now corrected, and cannot be fully understood except as a legacy handed down from the past."[4]

Second, the vast amounts of analysis and evidence that economists have generated over the decades can provide a closer check on irresponsible generalizations. This should enable us to make fewer errors than in the past when making personal decisions and when formulating national and local economic policies. Yet numerous unsolved problems and unanswered questions remain in economics. Our understanding of past successes, errors, and dead ends will be useful in solving these problems and answering these questions.

Finally, and above all, the study of the history of economic thought provides perspective and understanding of our past, of changing ideas and problems, and of our direction of movement. It helps us appreciate that no group has a monopoly on the truth and that many groups and individuals have contributed to the richness and diversity of our intellectual, cultural, and material inheritance. A study of the evolution of economic thought and the changing social background associated with it can illuminate changes in other areas of concern to us, such as politics, art, literature, music, philosophy, and science. A reciprocal relationship, of course, exists here—a better understanding of these areas of knowledge can help explain changing economic ideas.

Unfortunately the accumulation of knowledge and understanding does not *necessarily* lead to a better world. Even if all people were perfectly well-informed on economic matters, disagreements and conflicts would continue because of different ideas about what is good and what is bad, which goals should be adopted and which rejected, and what the priority of each goal should be. Even if we agree on the goals for the economy, we will disagree on their relative importance. But economic analysis helps us devise systems through which the common good can be individually and socially defined and through which people can pursue their own interests while simultaneously enhancing the well-being of others.

In certain combinations of circumstances, the desperately evil qualities of people rise to the surface. It is hoped that as our economic understanding grows

[4] Mark Blaug, *Economic Theory in Retrospect*, 4th ed. (London: Cambridge University Press, 1985), vii.

and our mastery over social problems increases, as our material well-being rises, as our appreciation of the cultural, aesthetic, and intellectual facets of life enlarges, we will become more civilized, more humane, and more considerate of each other. If the study of economic theories and problems of the past and present contributes to the achievement of these goals, it will have been worth the effort.

Questions for Study and Discussion

1. According to the authors, how do the contributions made to economic thought prior to A.D. 1500 differ from those made since that time?
2. Explain the meaning of the white and black arrows that connect schools of economic thought in the Time Scale. How are forerunners of a school distinguished in the diagram from the actual members of the school? Speculate as to why it is sometimes difficult to place a particular economist in a specific school of economic thought.
3. List the five major questions used in this book to organize discussion of schools of economic thought. Briefly explain why each question is important to understanding and assessing the major schools.
4. List five contemporary economic issues or problems that have recently been reported or discussed by the media. As you progress through the book, note the instances in which economists have developed ideas that relate to these issues.
5. Of what value is it to know something about the social, political, and economic setting in which a particular economist lived and wrote?
6. Evaluate this quote: "The danger of arrogance toward the writers of the past is certainly a real one—but so too is ancestor worship." (Mark Blaug)
7. What are the benefits of studying economics and its history?

Selected Readings

Books

Blaug, Mark. *The Methodology of Economics, or How Economists Explain*. London: Cambridge University Press, 1980.

———, ed. *The Historiography of Economics*. Brookfield, VT: Edward Elgar, 1991.

Colander, David, and A. W. Coats, eds. *The Spread of Economic Ideas*. New York: Cambridge University Press, 1989.

Mackie, Christopher D. *Canonizing Economic Theory: How Theories and Ideas Are Selected in Economics*. Armonk, NY: M. E. Sharpe, 1998.

Meeks, Ronald L. *Economics and Ideology and Other Essays: Studies in the Development of Economic Thought*. London: Chapman and Hall, 1967.

Mitchell, Wesley C. *Types of Economic Theory*. Introduction by Joseph Dorfman. 2 vols. New York: Kelly, 1967, 1969.

Rogin, Leo. *The Meaning and Validity of Economic Theory*. New York: Harper, 1956.

Stigler, George J. *Essays in the History of Economics*. Chicago: University of Chicago Press, 1965.

Journal Articles

Cesarano, Filippo. "On the Role of the History of Economic Analysis." *History of Political Economy* 15 (Spring 1983): 63–82.

Dillard, Dudley. "Revolutions in Economic Theory." *Southern Economic Journal* 44 (April 1978): 705–721.

Ekelund, R. B., and R. W. Ault. "The Problems of Unnecessary Originality in Economics." *Southern Economic Journal* 53 (January 1987): 650–661.

Stigler, George J. "The Influence of Events and Policies on Economic Theory." *American Economic Review* 50 (May 1960): 36–45.

APPENDIX

History of Economic Thought: Information Sources

The purpose of this appendix is to provide a concise summary of types of sources available for gathering information about the history of economic thought. Students doing term papers or wishing to explore topics in greater depth will benefit by examining the large and growing literature in this field.

Primary Sources

Primary sources consist of the full writings of the economist discussed in the text. These are cited in the Selected Readings section at the end of each chapter.

Books of Readings

In addition to full works, there are several excellent books of readings that contain selected excerpts from the original sources. Examples include the following:

Abbott, Leonard Dalton, ed. *Masterworks of Economics.* 3 vols. New York: McGraw-Hill, 1973.

Needy, Charles W., ed. *Classics of Economics.* Oak Park, IL: Moore, 1980.

Newman, Philip C., Arthur D. Gayer, and Milton H. Spencer, eds. *Source Readings in Economic Thought.* New York: W. W. Norton, 1954.

Treatises on the History of Economic Thought

A number of significant treatises on the history of economic methods and theory merit listing. These volumes are not normally used as textbooks at the undergraduate level because of their great length, minute detail, or rigorous content. They nevertheless are good sources for extending and intensifying one's knowledge. Four examples of books of this genre are:

Blaug, Mark. *Economic Theory in Retrospect.* 5th ed. London: Cambridge University Press, 1997.

Pribram, Karl. *A History of Economic Reasoning.* Baltimore: Johns Hopkins University Press, 1983.

Schumpeter, Joseph A. *History of Economic Analysis.* New York: Oxford University Press, 1954.

Spiegel, Henry W. *The Growth of Economic Thought.* 3d ed. Durham, NC: Duke University Press, 1991.

Theses of Scientific Change

By developing broad theories of the factors that produce scientific change, the following provide useful frameworks for studying the history of economics:

Kuhn, Thomas. *Structure of Scientific Revolutions.* 3d ed. Chicago: University of Chicago Press, 1996.

Lakatos, Imre. *The Methodology of Scientific Research Programmes.* London: Cambridge University Press, 1978.

Popper, Karl. *The Logic of Scientific Discovery.* 2d ed. London: Hutchinson and Co., 1968.

Books on Individual Economists

Numerous biographies examine the lives and times of the great economists, and several monumental works examine the contributions of specific economists. Most books of major significance are listed as Selected Readings at the end of the appropriate text chapters. Be advised that these listings are not exhaustive; new volumes appear frequently. The reference system at an academic library is the place to begin a search for these books.

Journal Articles

Scholarly journals in economics are the outlet that economists use to advance new knowledge about the history of economic thought. Several journal articles are cited in chapter footnotes and at the end of each chapter, but these references are only a small fraction of the many articles written on the various aspects of the topics discussed in the chapter. Journals are of two types: (1) general journals, which contain articles covering the wide spectrum of subfields within economics, and (2) specialized journals, which are specific to an area of economics, such as public finance, labor economics, or the history of economic thought.

General journals. Articles on the history of economic thought occasionally appear in general economic journals such as the *American Economic Review, Oxford Economic Papers, Journal of Political Economy, Southern Economic Journal, Economica*, and the like. The following two important indexes are instrumental in searching for articles of interest:

American Economic Association. *Index of Economic Articles.* Homewood, IL: Richard D. Irwin, Inc. This series is updated through periodic new volumes and contains citations to articles from more than 250 economics journals. Each volume covers a specific period. The volumes, however, are not current, and therefore recently published articles need to be found by employing the source that follows.

American Economic Association. *Journal of Economic Literature (JEL).* Quarterly. This publication lists the most recent journal articles, indexed topically, and abstracts of selected articles, also categorized by topic. The B1, B2, and B3 categories (formerly 030) in the classification system define topics in the history of economic thought. The *JEL* listings are also available via EconLit (DIALOG Information Retrieval Service: File 139). This electronic file is available at many academic libraries and can be searched by author, journal, subject, and *JEL* index number.

Special mention also should be made of the *Scandinavian Journal of Economics*, which annually contains intellectual biographies of Nobel Prize winners in economics.

Specific journals. Five noteworthy journals are devoted exclusively to the history of economic thought: *History of Political Economy*, *Journal of the History of Economic Thought*, *History of Economics Review* (published in Australia), *The European Journal of the History of Economic Thought* (published in Great Britain), and *History of Economic Ideas* (published in Rome).

Collections of Journal Articles

Several superb multivolume collections of journal articles are available. Here are three recent collections arranged by specific economists and schools of economic thought:

Blaug, Mark, ed. *Schools of Thought in Economics*. 11 vols. Brookfield, VT: Edward Elgar, 1990.

———, ed. *Pioneers in Economics*. 46 vols. Brookfield, VT: Edward Elgar, 1991.

Wood, John C. *Contemporary Economists: Critical Assessments*. continuing series. London: Routledge, 1990.

Internet Sites

The Internet provides much useful information relating to the history of economic thought. Links to these and other sites of interest can be found on the text web site (http://brue.swlearning.com). Three sites of particular significance are:

History of economic thought web site

http://cepa.newschool.edu/het

This excellent Internet site contains detailed information on contributors to the history of economic thought, listed alphabetically and grouped into broad schools of economic thought. It also provides links to many other Internet sites relating to the development of economic ideas.

Archives of primary sources

http://www.economics.mcmaster.ca/ugcm/3ll3/

The McMaster University Archive for the History of Economic Thought provides primary text readings for more than 200 scholars important to the evolution of economic ideas, and new materials are added regularly. It also offers links to mirror sites in the United Kingdom and Australia.

Economic journals on the web

http:www.oswego.edu/~economic/journals.htm

This site contains an index to the Internet locations of numerous economic journals.

(Each of these Internet addresses was current at the time of publication, but Internet addresses sometimes change. If these addresses do not work, try linking through the text web site or finding them using standard Internet search aids such as AltaVista, Excite, Google, or Yahoo!.)

Chapter 2

THE MERCANTILIST SCHOOL

The economic doctrine known as mercantilism appeared between the Middle Ages and the period of the triumph of laissez-faire. Mercantilism can be dated roughly from 1500 to 1776. These dates vary, however, in different countries and regions.

In this chapter we first use the "five major questions" to provide an overview of mercantilism and then examine four individuals who expressed mercantilist ideas: Mun, Malynes, Davenant, and Colbert. We also discuss Sir William Petty, a mercantilist who developed some concepts that foreshadowed classical economics.

OVERVIEW OF MERCANTILISM

The Historical Background of the Mercantilist School

The self-sufficiency of the feudal community slowly gave way to the new system of merchant capitalism. Cities, which had been growing gradually during the Middle Ages, became increasingly important. Trade flourished both within each country and between countries, and the use of money expanded. The discovery of gold in the Western Hemisphere facilitated the growing volume of commerce and stimulated theorizing about precious metals. Great geographical discoveries, based in part on the development of navigation, were extending the sphere of commerce. Production was small scale, but increasingly the merchant interceded between the producer and the consumer. Although they remained "contemptible tradesmen" in the eyes of the "landed aristocracy," the merchant capitalists were becoming key figures in the world of business.

National states were rising, and the most powerful of them were acquiring colonies and spheres of influence. Economic rivalries between nations were intensified. It is not surprising, then, that a body of doctrine evolved that superseded feudal concepts, promoted nationalism, gave new dignity and importance to the merchant, and justified a policy of economic and military expansion. This body of doctrine became the mercantilist school.

Major Tenets of the Mercantilist School

The main principles of this school are as follows:

- Gold and silver the most desirable form of wealth. Mercantilists tended to equate the wealth of a nation with the amount of gold and silver bullion it possessed. A few early mercantilists even believed that these precious metals were the only type of wealth worth pursuing. All of them valued bullion as the way to achieve power and riches. A surplus of exports from a country was therefore necessary to generate payments in hard money. Even when at war, nations would export goods to the enemy as long as the products were paid for in gold.

- Nationalism. All countries could not simultaneously export more than they imported. Therefore one's own country should promote exports and accumulate wealth at the expense of its neighbors. Only a powerful nation could capture and hold colonies, dominate trade routes, win wars against rivals, and compete successfully in international trade. According to this static concept of economic life, there was a fixed quantity of economic resources in the world; one country could increase its resources only at the expense of another. The French essayist Michel de Montaigne wrote in 1580, "The profit of one man is the damage of another. . . . No profit whatever can possibly be made but at the expense of another."

  Mercantilist nationalism quite naturally led to militarism. Strong navies and merchant fleets were an absolute requirement. Because fisheries were "nurseries for seamen," that is, because they were training grounds for naval personnel, the mercantilists imposed "political Lent" on England in 1549. People were forbidden by law to eat meat on certain days of the week to ensure a domestic market for fish and hence a derived demand for sailors. This enactment was vigorously maintained for about a century, and it did not disappear from the statute books until the nineteenth century.

- Duty-free importation of raw materials that could not be produced domestically, protection for manufactured goods and raw materials that could be produced domestically, and export restriction on raw materials. This emphasis on exports and a reluctance to import has been called "the fear of goods." The interests of the merchant took precedence over those of the domestic consumer. Merchants received inflows of gold in return for their exports, while the restrictions on imports reduced the availability of goods for consumption at home. Consequently, gold and silver accumulated, supposedly enhancing the country's wealth and power.

  Prohibitions against the outward movement of raw materials helped keep the prices of finished exports low. For example, a law passed in 1565–1566 during Queen Elizabeth's reign forbade the export of live sheep. The penalties for violating this law were the confiscation of property, a year in prison, and the cutting off of the left hand. The death penalty was prescribed for a second offense. The export of raw wool was prohibited, and the same penalties were applied in a law enacted during the reign of Charles II (1660–1685).

- Colonization and monopolization of colonial trade. Merchant capitalists favored colonization and wanted to keep the colonies eternally dependent upon and subservient to the mother country. Any benefits that spilled over to the colonies from the home country's growth and military power were an accidental by-product of the policy of exploitation.

  The English Navigation Acts of 1651 and 1660 are good examples of this policy. Goods imported into Great Britain and the colonies had to move in English or colonial ships or in ships of the country where the goods originated.

Certain colonial products had to be sold only to England, and others had to land in England before being shipped to foreign countries. Foreign imports into the colonies were restricted or prohibited. Colonial manufacturing was curbed or in some cases outlawed, so that dependent territories would remain suppliers of low-cost raw materials and importers of English manufactured goods.

- Opposition to internal tolls, taxes, and other restrictions on the movement of goods. Mercantilist writers and practitioners recognized that tolls and taxes could throttle business enterprise and drive up the price of a country's exports. An extreme example of this is the situation on the Elbe River in 1685. A shipment of sixty planks from Saxony to Hamburg required the payment of fifty-four planks at toll stations along the way! Consequently, only six planks arrived at the destination.

  It is important to point out, however, that mercantilists did not favor free internal trade in the sense of allowing people to engage in any trade that they wished. On the contrary, mercantilists preferred monopoly grants and exclusive trading privileges whenever they could acquire them.

- Strong central government. A strong central government was needed to promote mercantilist goals. The government granted monopoly privileges to companies engaged in foreign trade. It restricted free entry into business at home to limit competition. Agriculture, mining, and industry were promoted with subsidies from the government and protected from imports via tariffs. Furthermore, the government closely regulated the methods of production and the quality of goods so that a country would not gain a bad reputation for its products in foreign markets, thereby hampering exports. In other words, mercantilists placed little trust in their own judgment and honesty, believing that the common interest of merchants required that the government prohibit poor workmanship and shoddy materials. The result was a bewildering maze of regulations governing the production of goods.

  A strong national government was therefore required to ensure uniform national regulation. Central governments were also necessary to achieve the goals discussed previously: nationalism, protectionism, colonialism, and internal trade unhampered by tolls and excessive taxes.

- Importance of a large, hard-working population. Not only would a sizable, industrious population provide an abundance of soldiers and sailors ready to fight for the glory and the wealth of the nation, but also it would keep labor supply high and wages therefore low. The advantage? These low wages would (1) enable lower prices on exports, thereby increasing the inflow of gold, and (2) reduce idleness and promote greater participation in the labor force.

  Idleness and begging by able-bodied people were dealt with mercilessly, and thievery was severely punished. During the reign of Henry VIII in Great Britain (1509–1547), 7,200 thieves were hanged. In 1536 it was decreed that "sturdy vagabonds" should have their ears cut off, and death was the penalty for the third offense of vagabondage. In 1547 those who refused to work were condemned to be the slaves of whoever denounced them. A law passed during Queen Elizabeth's reign in 1572 decreed that unlicensed beggars of fourteen years or older were to be flogged and branded unless someone was willing to employ them; for a second offense they were to be executed unless someone would take them into service; for a third offense they were to be considered as felons and executed without mercy.

Bernard de Mandeville (1670?–1733), the Dutch philosopher, satirist, and medical doctor who settled in London, wrote:

> In a free Nation where Slaves are not allow'd of, the surest Wealth consists in a Multitude of laborious Poor. . . . As they ought to be kept from starving, so they should receive nothing worth saving. . . . It is the Interest of all rich Nations, that the greatest part of the Poor should almost never be idle, and yet continually spend what they get. . . . The Poor should be kept strictly to Work, and that it was Prudence to relieve their wants, but Folly to cure them. . . . To make the Society happy and People easy under the meanest Circumstances, it is requisite that great Numbers of them should be Ignorant as well as Poor.[1]

William Temple, in his *Essay on Trade and Commerce,* published in 1770, gave thoughtful consideration to full employment for children:

> When these children are four years old, they shall be sent to the country workhouse and there taught to read two hours a day and be kept fully employed the rest of their time in any of the manufactures of the house which best suits their age, strength and capacity. If it be objected that at these early years, they cannot be made useful, I reply that at four years of age there are sturdy employments in which children can earn their living; but besides, there is considerable use in their being, somehow or other, constantly employed at least twelve hours in a day, whether they earn their living or not; for by these means, we hope that the rising generation will be so habituated to constant employment that it would at length prove agreeable and entertaining to them.[2]

Refer to 2-1 PAST AS PROLOGUE

Whom Did the Mercantilist School Benefit or Seek to Benefit?

This doctrine obviously benefited the merchant capitalists, the kings, and government officials. It especially benefited those who were most powerful and entrenched and had the most favored monopolies and privileges. Some historians of economic thought suggest that mercantilism can best be understood as an extreme example of *rent seeking behavior.*[3] As applicable here, *economic rent* is defined as profits beyond those that would be just necessary to keep the merchant capitalists engaged in their present activities, that is, just sufficient to compensate

[1] Bernard de Mandeville, *Fable of the Bees,* ed. F. B. Kay (London: Oxford University Press, 1924), 193–194, 248, 287–288.

[2] Edgar S. Furniss, *The Position of the Laborer in a System of Nationalism* (Boston: Houghton Mifflin, 1920), 114–115.

[3] B. Baysinger, R. B. Ekelund Jr., and R. D. Tollison, "Mercantilism as a Rent-Seeking Society," in *Towards a Theory of the Rent-Seeking Society,* ed. J. M. Buchanan et al. (College Station, TX: Texas A&M University Press, 1980), 235–268.

2-1 PAST AS PROLOGUE

Mercantilism and the Supply of Labor

Some mercantilists contended that low wages were necessary to reduce idleness and promote participation in the labor force. They believed that increases in the wage rate, enabling workers to earn more income per hour, would allow them to reduce their hours of work. Some secondary workers, including children, might even exit the labor force if their parents could earn more income per hour.

In modern terminology, the mercantilists emphasized the *income effect* of a wage rate increase. Because higher wage rates raise hourly income, workers can afford to "buy" additional leisure. They purchase more leisure by reducing the number of hours they work.

But the mercantilists overlooked a potentially offsetting *substitution effect* of a wage rate increase. In a classic 1930 article, British economist Lionel Robbins (1898–1984) explains that a higher wage rate reduces the "price of income." Less work time is required to obtain $1 worth of goods. For example, the "price" of $1 of income is half an hour of work time when the wage rate is $2 per hour. But, when the wage rate increases to $3 per hour, the "price" of $1 of income falls to one-third of an hour of work. Because income is cheaper in terms of work hours, workers will buy more income. They purchase this income by working more hours and taking less leisure.*

Robbins's substitution effect can be explained differently. A wage rate increase means that workers must give up more income (goods) for each hour of leisure consumed, implying that the price or opportunity cost of leisure rises. When the price of a good increases, people buy less of it. Here, workers will purchase less leisure and work more hours; they will substitute work for the now more expensive leisure.

Because the income and substitution effects of a wage rate increase operate in opposite directions, it is not clear how workers will respond. If the income effect dominates the substitution effect, work hours and labor force participation will fall; the aggregate labor supply curve will have a downward slope. If the substitution effect dominates the income effect, a wage hike will increase work hours and participation; the labor supply curve will slope upward.

What evidence has been gathered on this issue? Contemporary studies of the United States indicate that income and substitution effects roughly offset each other. Yet, historically, higher wage rates *have* resulted in shorter workweeks.† Since the mercantilist era, income effects of wage rate increases have exceeded substitution effects.

Are shorter workweeks bad, as the mercantilists believed? Contemporary economists would disagree. The purpose of the economy is to maximize the well-being of the participants, not to maximize the amount of gold and silver in the government's treasury. If society values an hour of added leisure more than an hour's worth of added income (goods), then working fewer hours enhances society's well-being.

---

*Lionel Robbins, "On the Elasticity of Demand for Income in Terms of Effort," *Economica* 10 (June 1930): 123–129.

†Since 1945 the length of the workweek in the United States has remained relatively stable.

them for their opportunity costs. Rent seeking activities are simply attempts by private parties to increase their profits by securing favorable laws and regulations from government.

In this case, such laws took the form of grants of monopoly status, prohibitions against imports, and regulations that made it difficult for new producers and merchants to compete successfully against the established ones. According to this line of reasoning, the government officials in power were willing to make these laws and regulations—to dispense economic rent—as a way to secure benefits for themselves and for the royalty at whose pleasure they served. In England, for example, the wool interest saw to it that importing printed cottons, substitutes for woolens called "calicoes," was prohibited. In 1721 the use of printed calicoes was outlawed, but production and export were permitted. In the late 1600s the law required the dead to be buried in woolen shrouds even though religious traditions required linens.

In France mercantilism had a stronger feudal flavor, and the entrenched monopolistic interests were even more successful in getting the government to intervene on their behalf. From 1686 to 1759 the production, import, and use of printed calicoes were prohibited. In armed conflicts and executions arising from the enforcement of these measures, an estimated 16,000 people died, and many more were sent to the galley ships.

As yet another example, the rules published in France from 1666 to 1730 on textiles alone required seven huge volumes. The dyeing manual, alleged to be the best set of instructions on dyeing techniques at the time, contained 317 articles. These regulations prevented inferior methods from being used, but they also seriously impeded experimentation and the development of new techniques, possibly by producers who could have competed with the existing firms.

A host of government officials, inspectors, judges, and enforcement officers also gained from mercantilist regulations. The French government (but not the English) received significant revenue from fines, concessions, and monopoly privileges sold to business interests. Officials kept a percentage of the fines levied against violators of the many government regulations. Also, the inflow of gold and silver that resulted from mercantilist policies enhanced general tax collections and improved a country's ability to achieve economic gain through the fighting of wars.

How Was the Mercantilist School Valid, Useful, or Correct in Its Time?

The arguments for bullionism, although exaggerated, made some sense in a period of transition between the predominantly self-sufficient economy of the Middle Ages and the money and credit economy of modern times. The rapid growth of commerce required more money in circulation, and banking was insufficiently developed to produce it. Wars were fought on a pay-as-you-go basis, and bullion provided a reserve that could be used to hire and maintain soldiers, build ships, buy allies, and bribe enemies.

British trade with the Baltic region and the East Indies required international liquidity by way of precious metals. Great Britain produced little that could have been exported to these areas, and the latter would not accept paper sterling because of the underdeveloped international money market. The British colonies were therefore tapped to yield silver and gold that could be used in payment for Baltic and East Indian wares. Before the development of international finance and multilateral trade, bullion was of major significance in making international payments.

Mercantilists were also aware that an influx of precious metals made tax collection easier. They knew that prices would rise, or at least would not fall, if the quantity of money increased as trade expanded. Not only was the volume of output expanding, but also the self-sufficient household was being drawn into the market economy. More money was therefore needed to buy and sell the same volume of output. Some mercantilists were also aware that increases in the amount of gold and silver in circulation reduced interest rates and promoted business.

Which Tenets of the Mercantilist School Became Lasting Contributions?

The mercantilists made a lasting contribution to economics by emphasizing the importance of international trade. In that context, they also developed the economic and accounting notion of what today is termed the balance of payments between a nation and the remainder of the world. But beyond these contributions, the mercantilists (excluding Petty and perhaps Mun) contributed little to economic theory as we know it today. Most of them failed to grasp that a country could become richer not only by impoverishing its neighbors but also by discovering a greater quantity of natural resources, producing more capital goods, and using labor more efficiently. They also did not comprehend that all nations can enrich themselves simultaneously through specialization and trade and that higher wages for workers need not lead to idleness and reduced labor force participation.

But although the mercantilists made few *direct* contributions to economic theory, they did *indirectly* contribute to economics and economic development. First, they permanently influenced attitudes toward the merchant. The medieval aristocracy had classed people engaged in business as contemptible second-class citizens who were immersed in the muck of merchandising and the exchange of money. The mercantilists gave respectability and importance to merchants by arguing that, when their activities were properly channeled by government, merchants enriched not only themselves but also the king and the kingdom. The landed aristocrats eventually began to participate in business ventures without losing their status and dignity. Ultimately they gave their children in marriage to the offspring of business families, thereby merging aristocratic lineages with great commercial fortunes.

Second, mercantilism made an indirect impact on economics by promoting nationalism, a force that is very much alive today. Central government regulation is necessary when uniform weights, measures, coinage, and laws are needed; when production and trade have not yet developed sufficiently to permit reliance on competition to provide consumers a wide choice of goods; and when the financial risks of trade are so high that monopoly privileges are necessary to induce more risk taking than would otherwise occur.

Third, the privileged chartered trading companies, ancestors of the modern corporation, helped transform the economic organization of Europe by bringing in

Refer to 2-2 PAST AS PROLOGUE

new products, providing outlets for manufactured goods, and furnishing incentives for the growth of capital investment. Finally, mercantilism made a permanent contribution to economic development by expanding the internal market, promoting the free movement of goods unhampered by tolls, establishing uniform laws and taxes, and protecting people and goods in transit within and between countries.

THOMAS MUN

Thomas Mun (1571–1641), the son of a British dealer in textiles, acquired his wealth and reputation while he was a merchant in the Italian and Near Eastern trade. After he was elected a director of the East India Company, Mun became involved in a controversy over that company's policy of exporting gold and published a tract in its defense. In 1621 Mun published *A Discourse of Trade from England unto the East Indies,* in which he argued that as long as total exports exceeded total imports, the drain of species from a country in any one trade area did not matter.

Around 1630 Mun wrote his famous exposition of mercantilist doctrine in *England's Treasure by Forraign Trade,* published posthumously by his son in 1664. The title of Chapter 2, "The means to enrich the Kingdom, and to encrease our Treasure," posed a key problem. How was the kingdom to be enriched? According to Mun, the answer lay neither in production nor in the accumulation of capital goods, but rather in a surplus of exports. Of course, one must produce in order to export, but production is subservient to the final goal—the accumulation of gold. The first page of the two-page chapter on this issue reads as follows:

> Although a Kingdom may be enriched by gifts received, or by purchase taken from some other Nations, yet these are things uncertain and of small consideration when they happen. The ordinary means therefore to encrease our wealth and treasure is by *Forraign Trade,* wherein wee must ever observe this rule; to sell more to strangers yearly than wee consume of theirs in value. For suppose that when this Kingdom is plentifully served with the Cloth, Lead, Tinn, Iron, Fish and other native commodities, we doe yearly export the overplus to forraign Countries to the value of twenty two hundred thousand pounds; by which means we are enabled beyond the Seas to buy and bring a forraign wares for our use and Consumptions, to the value of twenty hundred thousand pounds; By this order duly kept in our trading, we may rest assured that the Kingdom shall be enriched yearly two hundred thousand pounds, which must be brought to us in so much Treasure; because that part of our stock which is not returned to us in wares must necessarily be brought home in treasure.[4]

Mun argued that although England was rich, it could be still richer if it used wasteland to grow hemp, flax, lumber, tobacco, and other things "which now we fetch from strangers to our great impoverishing." Exports should be carried in English ships to gain insurance and freight charges.

[4] Thomas Mun, *England's Treasure by Forraign Trade* (New York: Macmillan, 1903), 7–8.

2-2 PAST AS PROLOGUE

Lingering Mercantilism

Some of the doctrines of mercantilism have not completely disappeared; a few ideas and policies present in the twentieth and twenty-first centuries resemble the ideas of 200 to 300 years ago.

For example, during the worldwide Great Depression of the 1930s, nations enacted high tariffs and devalued their currencies to restrict imports and promote exports. The tariffs were designed to reduce imports, so that idle domestic labor and capital resources could be employed to satisfy the demand for the previously imported goods. Ideally, that would expand domestic output and income. It was also thought that currency devaluation would reduce a nation's imports by making imports more expensive in terms of the national currency. Moreover, a nation's currency devaluation supposedly would increase its exports, because foreigners would need fewer units of their own currency to buy goods produced abroad.

Unfortunately, these mercantilist policies do not work as designed if trading partners retaliate with tariff increases and devaluations of their own. Such retaliation is exactly what happened in the Great Depression. Nation after nation enacted higher tariffs and devalued their currency. The overall outcome was loss of the gains from international specialization and trade and the collapse of the international monetary system.

In the late 1980s and early 1990s many Americans expressed great concern over very large U.S. balance of trade deficits. This "fear of goods" was legitimate to the extent that these large deficits reflected domestic and international conditions that sooner or later needed correction. This fear, however, produced proposals to enact tariffs, to impose import quotas, to grant subsidies to exporters, to require "domestic content" on some imported products, and to allow antitrust exemptions for U.S. firms engaged in export. Economists pointed out that such a set of policies, if enacted, would constitute a return to the outmoded precepts of mercantilism.

Japan, too, has been accused of adhering to a policy of promoting exports and restricting imports. Its continuing large trade surpluses throughout the 1980s and 1990s partly reflected a "fear of goods" from abroad. It also reflected a desire to "capture" lucrative international markets. In running such large trade surpluses, Japan's consumers were denied some of the potential consumption benefits from international specialization and trade.

Some developing nations still promote nationalism as a way of overcoming tribalism and local loyalties that impede economic development. They also frequently offer monopoly grants to encourage new investments and erect trade barriers to protect infant domestic industries.

Mercantilism lingers well into the 2000s. In the United States, "offshoring," the practice of domestic firms moving operations to nations with cheaper labor,

2-2 PAST AS PROLOGUE (continued)

has drawn considerable attention. Added to the "fear of goods" is now a "fear of services." Even while manufacturing jobs were moving overseas, workers in U.S. service industries felt reasonably secure. However, because of technological advances that significantly reduce the cost of global communication, operations such as customer call centers for financial services and computer technical support have been relocated from the United States to India. The realized and potential loss of jobs due to offshoring has prompted calls for protection.

Environmental and labor standards as a trade issue have also come to the forefront, with advanced economies calling for tighter regulations in developing nations. They claim that the weaker standards in developing nations provide an unfair trade advantage by keeping costs lower at the expense of the environment and exploited workers. In the most recent negotiations of the World Trade Organization (WTO), developing nations joined together to resist attempts by advanced economies to impose tighter restrictions.

China's strategy for economic growth in the 2000s includes maintaining large trade surpluses by keeping exports cheap and imports expensive and by holding down the value of the Chinese yuan in international exchange markets. China's mercantilist approach has supported strong economic growth, but it has also drawn international criticism and calls for trade barriers to offset what 2004 Democratic U.S. presidential candidate John Kerry called "predatory currency manipulation."*

In short, mercantilist ideas are still alive and well. It is important to realize, however, that ideas and policies reflect only selected aspects of the overall doctrine of mercantilism. Furthermore, nations are applying these ideas today in different circumstances, for different reasons, and in the context of social policies different from those of the mercantilist era.

*John Kerry, "Kerry Statement on the U.S.-China Economic and Security Review Commissions' Report," June 15, 2004 (www.johnkerry.com/pressroom/releases/pr_2004_0615b.html).

In defending the East India Company's export of gold to pay for goods, Mun argued for multilateral, rather than bilateral, trade:

> In some Countreys we sell our commodities and bring away their wares, or part in mony; in other Countreys we sell our goods and take their mony, because they have little or no wares that fits our turns: again in some places we have need of their commodities, but they have little use of ours: so they take our mony which we get in other Countreys: And thus by a course of traffick (which changeth according to the accurrents of time) the particular members do accommodate each other, and all accomplish the whole body of the trade.[5]

[5] Mun, *Treasure*, 46–47.

Mun analyzed England's overall balance of trade rather than its separate account with each foreign country. He thought that increasing imports would increase England's stock of precious metal if the wares were exported to some other country at a profit. Mun reasoned, therefore, that the export of gold should be allowed to pay for the import of goods, which in turn would increase the total volume of goods exported:

> Why should we then doubt that our monys sent out in trade, must not necessarily come back again in treasure; together with the great gains which it may procure. . . . If we only behold the actions of the husbandman in the seed-time when he casteth away much good corn into the ground, we will rather accompt him a mad man than a husbandman: but when we consider his labours in the harvest which is the end of his endeavours, we find the worth and plentiful encrease of his actions.[6]

But Mun's emphasis was on purchase and sale at a profit rather than on the processing of imported raw materials into manufactured goods, although the latter was mentioned in the case of textiles.

This emphasis on importing treasure led to the strange conclusion that trade at home could not enrich a country. Mun wrote, "We may exchange either amongst our selves, or with strangers; if amongst our selves, the Commonwealth cannot be enriched thereby; for the gain of one subject is the loss of another. And if we exchange with strangers, then our profits is the gain of the Commonwealth."

In looking at the total balance of payments, Mun was sufficiently astute to include invisible items. Writing more than three and a half centuries ago, Mun listed the invisible items that should be included in an overall balance if it were to show whether "we prosper or decline in this great and weighty business." He included in the balance of payments the freight charges for shipping goods; ships lost at sea; insurance; money paid out in supporting foreign wars; international payment of bribes and funds for espionage "the receipt whereof notwithstanding is plain Treachery"; expenses of travelers; gifts to foreigners and ambassadors; interest on money; smuggling to evade tariffs; and contributions to religious orders that secretly sent the money abroad. On this last point Mun added, "If this mischief cannot be prevented, yet it must be esteemed [estimated] and set down as a cleer loss to the Kingdom."

GERARD MALYNES

Gerard Malynes (died 1641) was born in Antwerp, Belgium, of English parents. He returned to England and became a merchant in foreign trade. Not being very successful in this occupation, he spent a short term in a debtor's prison. He also served as the English commissioner of trade in Belgium, a government advisor on trade matters, an assay master of the mint, and commissioner of mint affairs.

In *Lex Mercatoria: or, The Ancient Law-Merchant,* published in 1622 and reissued in 1686, Malynes expressed several mercantilist ideas. For example, he noted

[6] Mun, *Treasure*, 26–27.

that trade once was considered to be too low for the aristocracy. But Malynes defended the merchants:

> For the maintenance of Traffick and Commerce is so pleasant, amiable and acceptable unto all Princes and Potentates, that Kings have been and at this day are of the Society of Merchants: And many times, notwithstanding their particular differences and quarrels, they do nevertheless agree in this course of Trade; because Riches is the bright Star, whose height Traffick takes to direct it self by, whereby Kingdoms and Commonweals do flourish; Merchants being the means and instruments to perform the same, to the Glory, Illustration, and benefit of their Monarchies and States. Questionless therefore the State of a Merchant is of great dignity, and to be cherished; for by them Countries are discovered, familiarity between Nations is procured, and politick experience is attained.[7]

Malynes also advanced the idea that regulation of goods by government was necessary to ensure high-quality exports. He stated:

> The Cloth being truly made, will be more vendible beyond the Seas, where many complaints are daily made of the false making thereof; . . . hereby traffick will increase for the general good of the Realm, and his Majesties Custom will be duly payed, according to the said Statute, and all will tend to the glory of God, and honour of the King, in all Equity and Justice to be observed in all well-Governed Commonweals.[8]

The mercantilist notion that more money in a country would raise prices and stimulate business was developed by Malynes as follows:

> Plenty of Mony maketh generally all things dear, and scarcity of Mony maketh generally things good cheap. Whereas particularly Commodities are also dear or good cheap, according to plenty or scarcity of the Commodities themselves, and the use of them. Mony then (as the blood in the body) constraineth the Soul which infuseth life: for if Mony be wanting, Traffique doth decrease, although Commodities be abundant and good cheap: And on the contrary, If Monies be plentiful Commerce increaseth, although Commodities be scarce, and the price thereof is thereby more advanced.[9]

CHARLES DAVENANT

Charles Davenant (1656–1714), the son of poet and dramatist Sir William Davenant, spent much of his life in various government posts that dealt with taxes, imports, and exports. He was also a member of Parliament.

Davenant has been called an enlightened mercantilist, an eclectic who tried to blend the old and the new, a man who foreshadowed more of the argument of laissez-faire than any other influential mercantilist. So he was. But an examination of his writings indicates that, in some respects, Davenant was an orthodox mercantilist.

[7] Gerard Malynes, *Lex Mercatoria: or, The Ancient Law-Merchant* (1622), a.

[8] Malynes, *Lex Mercatoria*, 43.

[9] Malynes, *Lex Mercatoria*, 176.

He developed the following bullionist argument in *An Essay on the East-India Trade* (1696):

> I have often wonder'd upon what Grounds the Parliament proceeded in the Act for Burying in Woollen: It Occasions indeed a Consumption of Wooll, but such a Consumption, as produces no advantage to the Kingdom. For were it not plainly better, that this Wooll made into Cloth, were Exported, paid for, and worn by the Living abroad, than laid in the Earth here at home. And were it not better, That the Common People (who make up the Bulk and are the great Consumers) should be bury'd in an old Sheet, fit for nothing else, as formerly, than is so much new Wooll, which is thereby utterly lost . . . . For it is the Interest of all Trading Nations whatsoever, that their Home-Consumption should be little, of a Cheap and Foreign Growth, and that their own Manufactures should be sold at the highest Markets, and spent Abroad; since by what is Consum'd at Home, one loseth only what another gets, and the Nation in General is not at all Richer; but all Foreign Consumption is a clear and certain Profit.[10]

In *An Essay on the Probable Means of Making the People Gainers in the Balance of Trade* (1699), Davenant argued that a kingdom can reap the benefit of the entire value of an exported product if it is made from domestic raw materials. If raw materials are imported and the product exported, then the net profit is the difference between the two values.

In *Discourses on the Publick Revenues, and on the Trade of England* (1698), Davenant expressed a preference for wars fought within a country rather than abroad, citing economics as the underlying reason:

> A Foreign War must needs drein a Kingdom of its Treasure. . . . *France,* from the time of *Charles* IX to the Reign of *Harry* IV, had a continual Civil War in its Bowels, and was often ravag'd by Armies from *Spain* and *Germany*; but this War exporting no Treasure, did not Impoverish the Kingdom.[11]

In the same work Davenant called for government regulation of business because merchants were not to be trusted:

> There is hardly a Society of Merchants, that would not have it thought the whole Prosperity of the Kingdom depends upon their single Traffick. So that at any time, when they come to be Consulted, their Answers are dark and partial; and when they deliberate themselves in Assemblies, 'tis generally with a byass, and a secret Eye to their own Advantage. . . . And 'tis now to be apprehended, That they who stand possess'd of the ready Cash, when they discover the Necessities of other People, will, in all likelihood, prompted by their Avarice, make a use of it very destructive to their Fellow-Subjects, and to the King's Affairs, if not prevented by the Care and Wisdom of the State.[12]

Davenant *was* sufficiently enlightened to say that the wealth of a country is what it produces, not its gold or silver. Trade governs money rather than the other

[10] Charles Davenant, *An Essay on the East-India Trade* (1696), 26, 30.

[11] Charles Davenant, *Discourses on the Publick Revenues, and on the Trade of England* (1698), 12.

[12] Davenant, *Publick Revenues,* 30, 45–46.

way around. Wealth invested in ships, building, manufacturing, furniture, apparel, and so forth constitutes riches as much as coin and bullion do. Davenant favored a trade surplus because he believed that when the quantity of money increases, interest rates fall, land values rise, and taxes increase. But too much gold and silver can be detrimental, as it was in Spain, where affluence caused neglect of the arts and manufacturing. Davenant defended both the Navigation Acts and multilateral trade. In other words, he maintained that, whenever possible, a nation should enforce bilateralism between itself and its colonies, excluding foreigners from trading there, but that multilateral trade is desirable among equals.

JEAN BAPTISTE COLBERT

Jean Baptiste Colbert (1619–1683) represents the heart and soul of mercantilism, which is called Colbertism in France. He was the French minister of finance from 1661 to 1683 under Louis XIV. In spite of his modest origin (he came from a family of dry-goods merchants), he rose to a position of great power, often by unscrupulous means. Matching his unbounded ambition was a tremendous capacity for work and attention to the minutest details of his office.

Colbert was a bullionist who believed that the strength of a state depends on its finances, its finances rest on its collection of taxes, and tax revenues in turn are greatest if money is abundant. He favored expanded exports, reduced imports, and laws preventing the outflow of bullion from the country.

As an arch-nationalist and militarist, Colbert held that four professions are useful for great purposes. He cited these professions as "agriculture, trade, war on land, and from the sea." He believed that colonies were desirable as markets for French goods and as sources of raw materials and that a big navy and merchant marine were essential. Colbert felt that one nation could become richer only at the expense of another, because the volume of trade, the number of ships engaged in commerce, and the production of manufactured goods were all relatively fixed. Commerce was therefore a continual and bitter war among nations for economic advantage.

Colbert did his best to facilitate internal trade. He tried to give France a uniform system of weights and measures but was rebuffed by feudal provincialism and tradition and the vested interest of the church and the nobility. He unsuccessfully opposed tolls on the movement of goods, internal customs barriers, and excessive local taxes. Colbert subsidized the construction of the Canal of Languedoc, which joined the Atlantic and the Mediterranean. By enforcing the feudal system of compulsory labor of peasants on the roads (called the *corvée*), he made himself thoroughly hated; but 15,000 miles of roads were surfaced.

Government regulation of business, which had a strong feudal flavor in France, was an important feature of Colbert's policies. Reflecting the prevailing feudal contempt for businessmen, Colbert considered them a shortsighted, selfish, grasping lot who sacrificed the national interests to their own profit. The quality of goods and methods of production were thus closely regulated to attain uniformity, protect the consumer, and earn a good name for French goods in foreign markets.

Monopoly privileges and subsidies were offered for new industries, especially those that were difficult and expensive to establish. But the system could be abused, and some monopolies were granted to raise money for the state or to endow favorite courtiers. Many businesses were declared to be "royal manufacturers," thus ensuring sales of their products to the royal court.

Despite his contempt for men of business, Colbert had laws passed that permitted aristocrats to participate in commerce without losing their status and privileges. An edict of 1669 declared, "We desire that a gentleman shall have the right to participate in a company and take a share in merchant vessels, so long as he does not sell at retail."

Colbert favored a large, hard-working, and poorly paid population. No child, he thought, was too young to enter industry, and the state should enforce child labor. Colbert remarked in 1665 that "experience has always certainly shown that idleness in the first years of a child's life is the real source of all the disorders in later life." In a decree of 1668 he commanded that all the inhabitants of Auxerre send their children into the lace industry at the age of six, or pay a penalty of 30 sous per child.

Colbert regarded monks, nuns, lawyers, and officials as unproductive idlers, and he tried to reduce their number. Attempts were made to curb religious feeling and limit religious institutions. He canceled seventeen holy days, leaving only twenty-four (in addition to Sundays) when work ceased.

In an edict of 1666, people were exempted from taxes for a number of years if they married early. Every father of ten living children was also exempted from taxes. Interestingly enough, sons who died in the armed forces were counted as living, but priests, nuns, and monks were not counted. This law was revoked in 1683 because of widespread fraud.

It remained for the French Revolution of 1789 to abolish feudal rights, internal tolls and tariffs, special privileges, and local power. The practice of openly selling offices was discontinued, taxes were equalized, and weights and measures were standardized on the basis of the metric system. These steps opened the way for great advances in French commerce, industry, and agriculture.

SIR WILLIAM PETTY

Sir William Petty (1623–1687) was a mercantilist who offered some new ideas that foreshadowed classical economics.

Before he was sixteen, Petty had mastered Latin, Greek, French, mathematics, astronomy, and navigation. The son of a poor clothier, he achieved great wealth, fame, and honor. This is an example of the upward mobility that was slowly becoming possible in seventeenth-century Britain. During his busy life Petty was a sailor, a physician, a professor of anatomy, an inventor, a surveyor, a member of Parliament, a promoter of iron and copper works, an experimental shipbuilder, an author, a statistician, and a large landowner.

We shall first discuss Petty's mercantilist views and then those of his ideas that anticipated Adam Smith's.

Petty's Mercantilist Views

Petty's economic views were set forth in several important works: *A Treatise of Taxes and Contributions* (1662), *Verbum Sapienti* (1664), "The Political Anatomy of Ireland" (written in 1672 and published in 1691), and *Political Arithmetick* (written from 1672 to 1676 and first published in 1690). Petty favored freer foreign trade than many of the mercantilists, partly because he felt it would circumvent the widespread smuggling that was occurring. He wanted imported goods taxed so that they "may be made somewhat dearer than the same things grown or made at home, if the same be feasible." Imports of raw materials ought to be "gently dealt with," that is, only lightly taxed. Petty opposed laws prohibiting the export of money, but in *Political Arithmetick* he deplored the money paid to foreigners for shipping, the money paid to Hollanders for their fishing trade "practised upon our Seas," and the money spent on imported commodities that could be manufactured in England.

As did other mercantilists, Petty favored a large population. But Petty based his position on the concept of increasing returns to government, which would reduce unit costs of governing a larger population. "Fewness of people, is real poverty; and a Nation wherein are Eight millions of people, are more than twice as rich as the same scope of Land wherein but Four; For the same Governours which are the great charge, may serve near as well, for the greater, as the lesser number."[13]

In *A Treatise of Taxes and Contributions* Petty expressed his enthusiasm for the mercantilist vision of "full employment." His argument for a poll (per person) tax was succinct: "It seems to be a spur unto all men, to set their Children to some profitable employment upon their first capacity, out of the proceed whereof, to pay each childe his own Poll-money."

Petty also was against hanging thieves, but hardly from humanitarian motives:

> Why should not insolvent Thieves be rather punished with slavery than death? so as being slaves they may be forced to as much labour, and as cheap fare, as nature will endure, and thereby become as two men added to the Commonwealth, and not as one taken away from it; for if *England* be under-peopled (suppose by half) I say that next to the bringing in of as many more as now are, is the making these that are, to do, double the work which now they do; that is, to make some slaves.[14]

Petty felt that those out of work should be employed by the state working on roads, dredging rivers, planting trees, building bridges, mining minerals, and manufacturing various goods. In this sense he was a predecessor to those contemporary economists who advocate public service employment to reduce structural and cyclical unemployment. But true mercantilist that he was, Petty added that this employment should be "without expence of Foreign Commodities, and then 'tis no matter if it be employed to build a useless Pyramid upon *Salisbury Plain,* bring the Stones at *Stonehenge* to *Tower-Hill,* or the like." Thus Petty was a harbinger of Keynes's theory that in both ancient and modern times building pyramids—or their equivalent—was an antidote to unemployment!

---

[13] Sir William Petty, "A Treatise of Taxes and Contributions," in *Economic Writings*, ed. Charles H. Hull, vol. 1 (Cambridge: The University Press, 1899), 34.

[14] Petty, *Taxes and Contributions* 1: 69.

How would these public works be financed? For Keynes, it was by printing money or borrowing from the public, but for Petty it was by taxes. Because people were concerned with their relative incomes as compared with their neighbors', a proportional tax would not matter so long as the money was spent within the country:

> Let the Tax be never so great, if it be proportional unto all, then no man suffers the loss of any Riches by it. For men (as we said but now) if the Estates of them all were either halfed or doubled, would in both cases remain equally rich. For they would each man have his former state, dignity and degree; and moreover, the Money leavied not going out of the Nation, the same also would remain as rich in comparison of any other Nation.[15]

Petty as a Forerunner of Classical Economics

Petty was a pioneer statistician. In the preface of *Political Arithmetick* he stated, "Instead of using only comparative and superlative Words, and intellectual Arguments, I have taken the course . . . to express my self in Terms of Number, Weight, or Measure; to use only Arguments of Sense, and to consider only such Causes, as have visible Foundations in Nature," leaving "those that depend on the mutable minds, opinions, appetites and passions of particular men to the consideration of others."[16] Many of his calculations were crude, and some rested on weak assumptions. For example, Petty concluded that because there were one-third more oxen, sheep, butter, and beef exported from England in 1664 than in 1641, there were also one-third more people in 1664! But lapses such as these do not detract from the fact that Petty was one of the founders of the science of statistics. Today statistical analysis is a significant feature of the discipline of economics.

Petty stated in fragmentary form several other ideas that classical economists later developed in detail. These included the notion of velocity, the division of labor, rent as the surplus from land, the importance of capital goods, and a labor theory of value. Let's briefly examine each.

- Velocity. In *Verbum Sapienti,* Petty recognized that the velocity of circulation—the rate at which money changes hands—can be as important as the quantity of money. If payments are made weekly rather than quarterly, less money will do the same work. He suggested even that there could be too much money as well as too little. "For Money is but the Fat of the Body-politick, whereof too much doth as often hinder its agility as too little makes it sick." He recommended the sale of surplus gold abroad to prevent harm at home.
- Division of labor. Although not developing this idea in detail, Petty recognized the economies associated with the specialization of labor and division of tasks. For instance, he stated that "clothe must be cheaper when one cards, another spins, and another weaves . . . than when all the operations above were clumsily performed by the same hand." Adam Smith later discussed and developed this idea in great depth.

[15] Petty, *Taxes and Contributions* 1: 32.

- Rent theory. Petty arrived at a primitive theory of rent:

> Suppose a man could with his own hands plant a certain scope of Land with Corn, that is, could Digg, or Plough, Harrow, Weed, Reap, Carry home, Thresh, and Winnow so much as the Husbandry of this Land requires; and had withal Seed wherewith to sowe the same, I say, that when this man hath subducted his seed out of the proceed of his Harvest, and also, what himself hath both eaten and given to others in exchange for Clothes, and other Natural necessaries; that the remainder of Corn is the natural and true Rent of the Land for that year.[17]

This analysis of rent as the surplus from land was an advance in economic thinking. But Petty did not separate the return to capital from the return to land—an error easy to commit in the 1600s when capital investments in tools and fertilizer were insignificant. Nor did he show rent to be a differential return arising at the extensive and intensive margin of cultivation. But Petty did realize that land near the market yielded a higher rent because the cost of transporting the produce was lower.

- Importance of capital. In "The Political Anatomy of Ireland," published in 1691, Petty wrote:

> We must make a Par and Equation between Art and Simple Labour; for if by such Simple Labour I could dig and prepare for Seed a hundred Acres in a thousand days; suppose then, I spend a hundred days in studying a more compendious way, and in contriving Tools for the same purpose; but in all that hundred days dig nothing, but in the remaining nine hundred days I dig two hundred Acres of Ground; then I say, that the said Art which cost but one hundred days Invention is worth one Mans labour for ever, because the new Art, and one Man, perform'd as much as two Men could have done without it.[18]

This emphasis on capital and production would increasingly become appropriate with the emergence of the industrial revolution in the 1700s. Petty's attention to these topics was very unmercantilist!

- Labor theory of value. According to Petty, labor is the father, and land the mother, of wealth. In *A Treatise of Taxes and Contributions* he said that the value of a bushel of corn will be equal to that of an ounce of silver if the labor necessary to produce each is the same.

Petty's interest in production and his groping for a theory of value that determines price initiated new lines of reasoning. His ideas were to be extended and improved by economists who followed.

Questions for Study and Discussion

1. Briefly identify and state the significance of each of the following to the history of economic thought: Thomas Mun, *England's Treasure by Forraign Trade,* Gerard Malynes, Charles Davenant, Jean Baptiste Colbert, Sir William Petty, and *Political Arithmetick.*

[16] Petty, "Political Arithmetic," in *Economic Writings* 1: 244.

[17] Petty, *Taxes and Contributions* 1: 43.

[18] Petty, "The Political Anatomy of Ireland," in *Economic Writings* 1: 182.

2. Comment on the following statement: Mercantilism is as much a set of observed policies as it is a truly unified economic doctrine set forth by major scholars.
3. Why are mercantilists sometimes referred to as bullionists? Incorporate each of the following in your answer: exports, imports, colonies, war, tariffs, state-chartered monopolies, colonialism, large populations, free internal trade.
4. Why did the mercantilists favor large populations and low wages? How does the mercantilists' position on this issue relate to income and substitution effects of a wage rate increase? What advantages did Petty ascribe to large populations?
5. What is meant by the term *fear of goods* as it relates to international trade? Is it consistent to favor the free exchange of goods within a nation but to support trade restrictions on imported products? Who benefits from such restrictions? Who loses?
6. Compare and contrast modern arguments for protectionism (Past as Prologue 2-2) with those of the Mercantilist era.
7. Mercantilists realized that (a) a surplus of exports would cause gold and silver to flow in from other countries, and (b) increases in the stock of money can drive up a nation's prices. Are these outcomes compatible with one another in the long run?
8. On what basis did the mercantilist Thomas Mun defend the practice of shipping some gold abroad?
9. Match the following persons with their ideas or contributions. Explain each match.

______	Malynes	a. Wars fought at home are better than wars fought abroad.
______	Davenant	b. compulsory labor on roads
______	Petty	c. strong defense of merchants
______	Colbert	d. *Political Arithmetick*

10. In what respects did Petty's economic analysis extend beyond the typical mercantilist views?

Selected Readings

Books

Blaug, Mark, ed. *The Early Mercantilists.* Brookfield, VT: Edward Elgar, 1991.

Cole, Charles W. *Colbert and a Century of French Mercantilism.* 2 vols. New York: Columbia University Press, 1939.

Davenant, Charles. *Discourses on the Publick Revenues, and on the Trade in England.* 1698.

Furniss, Edgar S. *The Position of Labor in a System of Nationalism.* Boston: Houghton Mifflin, 1920.

Heckscher, Eli F. *Mercantilism.* 2d ed. 2 vols. London: Allen and Unwin, 1955.

Johnson, E. A. J. *Predecessors of Adam Smith.* New York: Prentice-Hall, 1937.

Magnusson, Lars. *Mercantilism: The Shaping of an Economic Language.* London: Routledge, 1994.

Malynes, Gerard. *Lex Mercatoria: or, The Ancient Law-Merchant.* 1686. [Written in 1622.]

Mun, Thomas. *England's Treasure by Forraign Trade.* New York: Macmillan, 1903. [Written in 1630.]

Petty, William. *Economic Writings.* Edited by Charles H. Hull. 2 vols. Cambridge: The University Press, 1899.

Roncaglia, Alessandro. *Petty: The Origin of Political Economy.* Armonk, NY: M. E. Sharpe, 1985.

Viner, Jacob. *Studies in the Theory of International Trade.* New York: Harper, 1937.

Journal Articles

Allen, W. R. "Modern Defenders of Mercantilist Theory." *History of Political Economy* 2 (Fall 1970): 381–397.

Aspromourgos, Tony. "The Life of William Petty in Relation to His Economics: A Tercentenary Interpretation." *History of Political Economy* 20 (Fall 1988): 337–356.

Ekelund, R. B., Jr., and R. D. Tollison. "Economic Regulation in Mercantile England: Heckscher Revisited." *Economic Inquiry* 18 (October 1980): 567–599.

Officer, Lawrence H. "The Purchasing-Power Parity Theory of Gerard de Malynes." *History of Political Economy* 14 (Summer 1982): 256–259.

Chapter 3

The Physiocratic School

The physiocrats appeared in France toward the end of the mercantilist epoch. The beginning of this school can be dated at 1756 when Quesnay published his first article on economics in the *Grande Encyclopédie.* The school ended in 1776 when Turgot lost his high position in the French government and Smith published his *Wealth of Nations.* But the influence of the physiocrats lasted well beyond the two decades during which they led the world in economic thinking. After presenting an overview of the school, we will examine the economic contributions of the two most prominent physiocrats—Quesnay and Turgot.

OVERVIEW OF THE PHYSIOCRATS

The Historical Background of the Physiocratic School

Physiocracy was a reaction to mercantilism and to the feudal characteristics of the old regime in France, yet it could not completely escape the medieval concepts that pervaded French society.

The detailed government regulation of production, even specifying the required threads per inch of cloth, may once have promoted high quality, but it certainly imprisoned production in a straightjacket that did not allow for experimentation, improvement of production methods, or changing consumer tastes. A corrupt and extravagant government made equitable enforcement of the rules impossible, and the growth of business enterprise and increasing competition made such rules unnecessary.

French industry was retarded in its development by the local authorities who imposed internal tolls, taxes, and tariffs, thereby impeding the movement of goods. French agriculture was burdened by the conditions enforced by the landowning nobility. Peasants were subjected to taxes on land and on the profits of farming, but the nobility and the clergy were exempt from such taxes. Taxes varied from year to year, depending on the whim of the tax collector and the wealth of the peasants. In fact, franchises were sold to "tax farmers," allowing them to collect for themselves as much in taxes as they could squeeze from the inhabitants of a given area. Tax farmers paid a fixed annual fee to the government at the beginning of each tax year, and they kept everything they collected above that. Incentives for individuals to accumulate wealth and expand investment were thus seriously impaired. Peasants had to pay dues to the lord when they inherited a holding or when they transferred it through sale. They had to do business with and pay heavy charges to the lord's millers, bakers, and winepressers. The nobles had the right to hunt game across the cultivated fields of their peasants, and game laws prohibited weeding and hoeing if it disturbed young partridges. The hated *corvée,* revived by Colbert and perpetuated after him, forced the peasants and their draft animals to work without pay on the public roads, largely for the benefit of others.

For centuries the French government and the authorities in the towns had subjected the grain trade to a bewildering maze of regulations. Even the little freedom allowed the other kinds of trade was denied to the grain trade. The export of grain from France was prohibited; the authorities were more concerned with maintaining adequate supplies than with promoting the interests of agriculture. But exceptions were granted in years of plenty. Special permits to individuals might be issued indicating the quantity and kind of grain to be exported and frequently its destination. Within the kingdom, grain and flour could not be moved from one province to another without permission. To receive a license to sell grain between provinces, a merchant had to submit all details of the enterprise to an inspector; after the grain had been transported, a certificate had to be produced showing that the consignment had actually reached the prescribed destination. Grain was subject to further restriction within each province. Laws specified the price of grain and where it was to be sold. In times of shortage, selling was made compulsory to prevent hoarding. Tolls as well as regulations impeded the grain trade, so that in one area surpluses might glut the warehouses while a few miles away people starved.

Merchant and craft guilds, which arose during the medieval period, persisted longer in France than in England. Merchant guilds controlled the right to carry on a trade in a town; craft guilds—composed of apprentices, journeymen, and masters within a craft—dictated the production and marketing methods of the town's workshops. The character of these guilds changed as national authorization and regulation of guilds replaced the authority of town or feudal lords. But until 1789 guilds impeded the free entry of labor into certain occupations, restricted and regulated output, fixed prices, and opposed competition from other towns and from abroad. Jurisdictional quarrels and litigation between guilds dragged on for generations and centuries at great cost in time and money. The annual cost of legal battles to the Paris guilds during the mid-1700s was 800,000 to one million livres (a unit of French money that was replaced by the franc, and more recently by the euro). Gooseroasters and poulterers quarreled for half a century until the latter were finally restricted to the sale of uncooked game. The successful roasters then turned on the cooks, who had won a triumph over the sauce-makers. A 300-year litigation between the secondhand-clothes dealers and the tailors in Paris had not been resolved by 1789 when the Revolution destroyed the guilds. It was through this corrupt and decayed society that physiocratic ideas swept like a fresh breeze.

Major Tenets of the Physiocratic School

The concepts of the physiocratic school may be summarized as follows:

- Natural order. The physiocrats introduced the idea of natural order to economic thinking. The term *physiocrat* itself means "rule of nature." According to this idea, laws of nature govern human societies just as those discovered by Newton govern the physical world. All human activities therefore should be brought into harmony with these natural laws. The object of all scientific study was to discover the laws to which all the phenomena of the universe were subject. In the economic sphere the laws of nature conferred to individuals the natural right to enjoy the fruits of their own labor, provided that such enjoyment was consistent with the rights of others.

- Laissez-faire, laissez-passer. This phrase, credited to Vincent de Gournay (1712–1759), in effect means "let people do as they please without government interference." Governments should never extend their interference in economic affairs beyond the minimum absolutely essential to protect life and property and to maintain freedom of contract. Thus physiocrats were opposed to almost all feudal, mercantilist, and government restrictions, favoring freedom of business enterprise at home and free trade abroad. Gournay was one of several high functionaries of the mercantilist system whose experience led him to become an adherent of laissez-faire.
- Emphasis on agriculture. The physiocrats thought that industry, trade, and the professions were useful but sterile, simply reproducing the value consumed in the form of raw materials and subsistence for the workers. Only agriculture (and possibly mining) was productive, because it produced a surplus, a net product above the value of the resources used in production.
- Taxation of the landowner. Physiocrats thought that because only agriculture produced a surplus, which the landowner received in the form of rent, only the landowner should be taxed. All taxes imposed on others would be passed on to the landowner anyway. A direct tax on the landowner was preferable to indirect taxes, which increased as they were passed along to others.
- Interrelatedness of the economy. Quesnay, in particular, and the physiocrats, in general, analyzed the circular flow of goods and money within the economy.

Whom Did the Physiocratic School Benefit or Seek to Benefit?

The peasants ultimately would gain from the ideas of the physiocrats because onerous obligations to the landowners would end. But if the physiocrats had had their way, the peasants would have become wage laborers on large farms. Business interests stood to gain from the prescription to remove all restrictions on production and the movement of goods. By advocating the doctrine of laissez-faire, the physiocrats were promoting industry, even though this was not their intention; they were interested in encouraging freer internal grain trade and in stimulating the export of farm products and the import of manufactured goods.

The physiocrats especially favored capitalistic farms employing wage labor and advanced techniques. These progressive farms could be found mostly in northern France. Big producers having surpluses for sale would be helped by the physiocratic emphasis on agriculture and free internal trade in grain. The tax on the surplus produced in agriculture would have lowered land values and hurt the landowning nobility instead of the current or prospective farm entrepreneurs who paid rent. The nobility and clergy were exempt from the multiplicity of taxes that burdened the commoner landowners, and a single tax applicable to all land in production would have helped spread the tax burden in the society.

The physiocrats tried to placate the nobility by genuinely defending their right to own land and receive rent. Unlike the American Henry George who, in the 1880s, wanted to tax away all rent, the physiocrats thought that a tax taking one-third of the economic surplus would be sufficient. This, they believed, would not redistribute wealth from the rich to the poor, because the landowners paid all taxes in any case; rather, converting the taxes from an indirect to a direct basis would lower the overall burden. In this view the nobility would be aided if the physiocrat program were enacted. But this belief was erroneous; it was based on the faulty analysis that all taxable surpluses could come only from land.

How Was the Physiocratic School Valid, Useful, or Correct in Its Time?

Before the industrial revolution, industry was characterized by extremely low productivity. This was particularly true of the handicraft economy of France during the last decades of the *ancien régime*. Production of luxury items for the nobility in a miserably poor country, therefore, could easily appear to be "sterile." Farming, on the other hand, sometimes produced bountiful harvests in spite of the primitive methods of cultivation. Agriculture often provided the surpluses that could be saved and reinvested to initiate a rising state of economic growth and industrial development not only in France but also in the United States, Germany, Japan, Russia, and other countries.

In promoting laissez-faire, the physiocrats were opposing obstacles to capitalistic economic development. They unwittingly promoted the French Revolution of 1789, which swept away the numerous obstacles to progress. By emphasizing the productivity of agriculture, they were getting away from the older concept that only commerce produces and augments wealth; the physiocrats emphasized production rather than exchange as a source of wealth. Their support for direct taxes was a valid reaction to the indirect taxes that pervaded and corroded French society of their time. They argued for capital accumulation through reduced consumption by the wealthy.

Which Tenets of the Physiocratic School Became Lasting Contributions?

Several of the ideas of the physiocrats clearly were incorrect. The school was wrong to consider industry and trade as sterile; the more industry and trade developed in France, the more conspicuously inaccurate the physiocratic analysis became. This fault led to another error—the belief that only landowners should be taxed because only land could yield a surplus. Wealthy industrialists could smile as they endorsed the doctrine that they should not be made to pay taxes because they added nothing to wealth. This physiocratic tax concept left a long legacy. John Stuart Mill, writing in the mid-1800s, proposed that future increases in rent be taxed by the state as a way to take all capital gains accruing from increases in the price of land. Henry George, writing in the United States more than one hundred years after the physiocrats, founded a "single tax" movement, the purpose of which was to confiscate all rent.

The physiocrats extolled the capitalistic farmer as the key figure in French economic development but were wrong on two counts. First, industrialists and laborers became the most important figures in the economic growth of the country, whereas the relative importance of agriculture declined. Second, the small peasant farmer rather than the large farm entrepreneur became typical in France. Had the land remained in the hands of the nobility, a tax on land ownership would have curbed luxury consumption. But when the small peasants got the land after the Revolution, they would have borne the bulk of the tax burden.

Nevertheless, the physiocrats made several lasting contributions to economics. First, by examining society as a whole and analyzing the laws that governed the circulation of wealth and goods, they founded economics as a social science. We will discover that Quesnay's economic table is a precursor to two items found in modern economics texts: the economic flow diagram and national income accounting. Second, the law of diminishing returns—usually credited to Malthus and Ricardo—actually was stated earlier by the physiocrat Turgot. Third, the physiocrats originated the analysis of tax shifting and incidence that today is an important part of applied microeconomics. Finally, by advocating laissez-faire, the physiocrats turned the attention of economists to the question of the proper role of government in the economy.

FRANÇOIS QUESNAY

François Quesnay (1694–1774), the son of a landed proprietor, was the founder and leader of the physiocratic school. Trained to be a physician, he made a fortune through his skill in medicine and surgery. Quesnay rose to be the court physician of Louis XV and Madame de Pompadour. In 1750 he met Gournay and soon became more interested in economics than in medicine. Quesnay and his cohorts hoped to transform the king into an "enlightened despot" as the instrument of peaceful reform. In an encyclopedia article in 1757 Quesnay noted that small farms were incapable of using the most productive methods; he favored large farms managed by "entrepreneurs," thereby anticipating the large agricultural enterprises that have emerged in our time.

To Quesnay, society was analogous to the physical organism. The circulation of wealth and goods in the economy was like the circulation of blood in the body. Both conformed to the natural order, and both could be understood through thoughtful analysis.

Quesnay believed that laws made by people should be in harmony with natural laws. The dauphin of France once bemoaned to Quesnay the difficulties of the office of king (which he was not destined to live to assume). "I do not see," said Quesnay, "that it is so troublesome." "What then," asked the dauphin, "would you do if you were king?" Said Quesnay, "Nothing." Asked who would govern, Quesnay replied cryptically, "The Law." He clearly meant the natural law.

His famous *Tableau Economique,* constructed for the king of France in 1758 and revised in 1766, depicted the circular flow of goods and money in an ideal, freely competitive economy. This was the first systematic analysis of the flow of wealth on what later came to be called a macroeconomic basis. Economists such as Smith, Marx, and Keynes, who also described economic activities in terms of large aggregates, paid tribute to Quesnay for originating this approach.

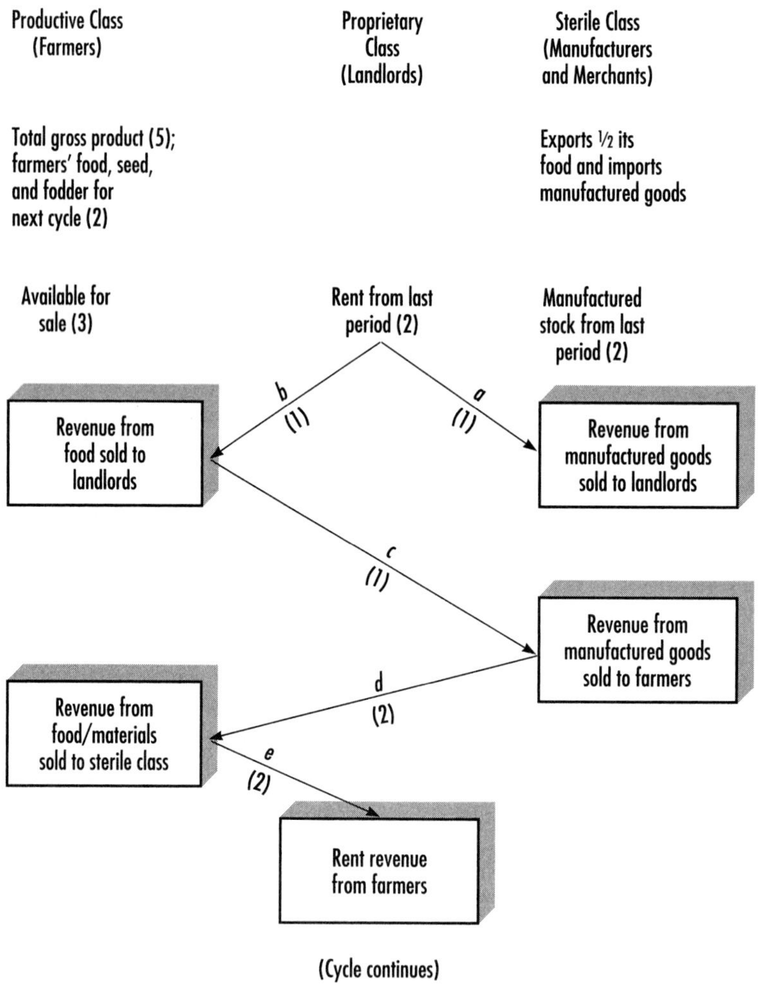

Figure 3-1 Quesnay's Tableau Economique
Quesnay's table traces spending, and thus revenue received, by farmers, landlords, and manufacturers/merchants. Landlords use rent from the previous period to buy goods from the manufacturers/merchants (flow *a*) and food from the farmers (flow *b*), thus creating revenue for these two classes. The revenue to the farmers, in turn, enables them to purchase manufactured goods from the manufacturers/merchants (flow *c*). The manufacturers/merchants use that revenue to buy food from farmers (flow *d*), which creates revenue for farmers. Farmers pay rent out of their farm revenues (flow *e*), and the cycle repeats.

A simplified account of Quesnay's *Tableau Economique* is presented in Figure 3–1. Quesnay assumed that the land is owned by landlords but is cultivated by tenant farmers, who are therefore the only really productive class. The product that the tenant farmers create has to satisfy not only their own needs but also the needs of the landowners (including the king, the church, the public servants, and others who depend on the income of the landowners). In addition, the output of the farmers provides for the needs of the sterile class (manufacturers and merchants). The *Tableau* shows how the net product circulates among the three classes and how it is reproduced each year.

Suppose that the farmers start with an annual gross product of 5 billion livres. Of this, 2 billion livres are immediately deducted as necessary expenses of production to provide food, seed, and fodder for the farmers themselves. As seen in the left column, this leaves 3 billion livres' worth of food for sale. The landlords (middle column) start with 2 billion livres in rent paid by the farmers during the preceding cycle. Finally, the manufacturers and merchants (right column) start with 2 billion livres' worth of goods manufactured during the previous cycle.

The landlord class uses its 2 billion livres to buy 1 billion in manufactured goods from the sterile class (arrow *a*) and 1 billion in food from the farmers (arrow *b*). The farmers then use the 1 billion in revenue from their sale of food to the landlords to buy 1 billion livres' worth of manufactured goods (arrow *c*). This spending by the farmers, of course, represents an equal amount of revenue to the manufacturer and merchants. The sterile class now has 1 billion livres of revenue from sales of goods to the landlords and another 1 billion from sales to the farmers. The sterile class then purchases from the farmers food and raw materials worth 2 billion livres (arrow *d*).

After the transaction shown by arrow *d*, the cycle repeats itself. At this stage the farmers have 2 billion livres in food, seed, and fodder, which they will use to produce another 5 billion livres' worth of farm products in the next year. The landlords have food, manufactured goods, and a claim for 2 billion livres in rent from the farmers' next harvest (arrow *e*). The sterile class has 2 billion livres' worth of food and raw materials, which it will use to produce manufactured goods worth 2 billion livres.

Some observers have noted that Quesnay's table implies that the manufacturing class is left with no manufactured goods for its own consumption. Ronald L. Meek has a solution to this problem. He finds that the physiocratic writings imply that the size of the sterile class is only one-half that of the productive class. Therefore, it does not need the entire 2 billion livres of food and raw materials that it buys from the farmers (arrow *d*). Instead it exports some of the food as a way to pay for imported manufactured goods.[1]

Quesnay's *Tableau Economique* foreshadowed national income analysis and laid the foundation for statistical work to describe an economy. Quesnay himself tried to estimate the values of annual output and other aggregates. The table also explicitly conveyed the concept of equilibrium within the economy as a whole, because if one of the interdependent variables changed, others would change also. Furthermore, Quesnay's table is a predecessor of the input-output analysis (Chapter 18), which Leontief introduced in the 1930s and which economists still widely use today.

It is important to note that although Quesnay called nonagricultural production "sterile," he did not question the right of the proprietors to receive rent. Nature, not the worker, produces the surplus, he said. The landowner therefore has a right to the surplus product, which goes with the title to the land. Because their

[1] Ronald L. Meek, *The Economics of Physiocracy* (Cambridge, MA: Harvard University Press, 1963), 282–283.

class makes the original capital investment required to make the land productive, they are entitled to the surplus product. Thus Quesnay felt that he was a defender of the rights of the landlords. Yet his proposal to tax only landowners was seen by them as an attack on their interests.

Quesnay argued that "an excess of luxury in the way of decoration may quickly ruin with magnificence an opulent Nation." He preferred spending on raw materials. This was the language of economic growth at a time when the aristocracy was wasteful in its consumption and industry was far less important than agriculture and mining as a means to accumulate wealth for further investment.

Refer to 3-1 PAST AS PROLOGUE

Quesnay's thinking, however, also had somewhat of a medieval flavor. This is apparent in his glorification of agriculture and in his belief—contrary to the other physiocrats—that the government should fix the rate of interest.[2] Quesnay also favored the idea of a "just price," but he felt that a free market rather than regulation by authority would best achieve it.[3]

ANNE ROBERT JACQUES TURGOT

Anne Robert Jacques Turgot (1727–1781) was born of a noble family of Normandy that for several generations had furnished the state with able administrative officials. As a younger son he was educated for the church, but after receiving his theological degree he decided instead to enter the judicial and administrative service. Turgot rose in the ranks of government service until he became the finance minister of France in 1774; this had been Colbert's office one hundred years earlier. After less than two years in office he introduced antifeudal and antimercantilist measures in keeping with physiocratic ideas. Freedom of internal grain trade was ordered, and guilds and privileged trading corporations were abolished. He ended the oppressive *corvée*, the twelve or fifteen days of unpaid labor required of peasants yearly to maintain roads, bridges, and canals; in its place he enacted a tax that all landowners had to pay. Turgot cut government spending drastically. The credit of the government was so improved that he was able to borrow a huge sum from the Dutch at an interest rate of 4 percent instead of the previous 7 to 12 percent. Annual government interest payments were reduced by almost two-thirds. Turgot advocated a tax on the nobility, freedom of all people to choose their occupations, universal education, religious liberty, and the creation of a central bank, which Napoleon would later establish in 1800.

Turgot's edicts and plans aroused the most determined opposition from all kinds of people. The nobility hated him because he wanted to levy all taxes upon the land. The clergy distrusted him as an unbeliever who not only rarely went to mass but also urged religious liberty. The financiers resented his getting loans abroad at lower rates of interest than they charged. The members of the king's entourage were angered by Turgot's opposition to their extravagance, their sinecures, and their pensions. The tax farmers who paid lump sums to the government for the right to collect as much taxes

---

[2] For a history of early thinking on lending at interest, see Barry Gordon, "Lending at Interest: Some Jewish, Greek, and Christian Approaches, 800 BC–AD 100," *History of Political Economy* 14 (Fall 1982): 406–426.

[3] The ethical notion of a "just price" was advanced by Saint Thomas Aquinas in the 1200s.

3-1 PAST AS PROLOGUE

Quesnay and the Circular Flow Diagram

Quesnay's *Tableau Economique* (Figure 3–1) is a predecessor to the circular flow diagram often found in the early chapters of textbooks on contemporary principles of economics. Quesnay's table traces spending or revenue flows among three classes: farmers, landlords, and manufacturers and merchants. His table clearly implies counterflows of real goods and services. For example, manufacturers and merchants receive revenue, a monetary flow, in exchange for goods, a real flow that is moving in the opposite direction.

The modern circular flow diagram traces its immediate roots, however, to economist Frank Knight, who developed his "wheel of wealth" while teaching at the University of Chicago in the early 1930s.* The current diagram (see the accompanying figure) traces both monetary and real flows. Also, it divides the economy into two sectors (households and businesses) rather than three classes (farmers, landlords, and manufacturers and merchants). Finally, this diagram shows two markets: the resource market and the product market. In the resource market, households supply resources and businesses demand resources. In the product market, households demand products and businesses supply them.

Like Quesnay's table, the modern circular flow diagram implies an interrelated web between economic decision making and economic activity.

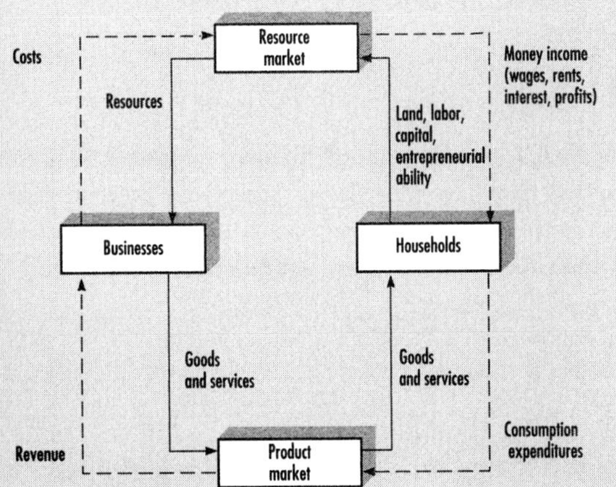

*For a fascinating discussion of the origins of Knight's diagram, see Don Patinkin, *Essays On and In the Chicago Tradition* (Durham, NC: Duke University Press, 1981), 53–72.

as they could were infuriated because he wanted to replace them with government tax collectors. The rich and entrenched bourgeoisie objected to his interference with their monopolies. Louis XVI dismissed Turgot because of the protests of the court, Marie Antoinette, and the other powerful people who were losing privileges because of his policies. His reforms were canceled at once, not to be reintroduced until the French Revolution of 1789. In fact, it is possible that Turgot's downfall made the Revolution inevitable; his experience proved that the old regime could not reform itself.

Turgot, like other physiocrats, believed in an enlightened absolutism, and he looked to the king to carry through all reforms. He opposed the interference of parliaments in legislation. A plan that he submitted to the king would have allowed only land proprietors to form the electorate. The elected parliament would have had no legislative powers but would have administered taxation, education, and relief to the poor. Obviously Turgot and the other physiocrats had their roots in the old feudalistic regime of France; they were reformers rather than revolutionaries. But the reactionary French regime could not tolerate their reforms.

In *Reflections on the Formation and the Distribution of Riches,* written in 1766, Turgot developed a theory of wages in which he held that competition among workers lowers the wage to the minimum subsistence level. This was an early statement of what was later called the "iron law of wages." Only farmers produce a surplus, which is used to feed and provide raw materials for all society.

> He [the farmer] is, therefore, the sole source of the riches, which, by their circulation, animate all the labors of the society; because he is the only one whose labor produces over and above the wages of the labor.[4]

Turgot said that the rich capitalist tenant farmers are most capable of efficient farming because they have the capital to invest in the soil. They receive profits and the return of their investment with interest. Entrepreneurs reinvest most of their profits and savings, but the landlords do not.

> It is even generally true that, although the proprietors have a greater superfluity, they save less because as they have more leisure, they have more desires and more passions; they regard themselves as more assured of their fortunes; they think more about enjoying it agreeably than about increasing it: luxury is their inheritance.[5]

In a 1767 letter to David Hume, Turgot stated that taxes imposed on other groups were passed on to the landowner. A tax on wage earners would be shifted only if it were above the minimum subsistence level, but this was a temporary deviation. Wages at the minimum subsistence level could not be lowered by taxes because workers had to earn enough to survive. A direct tax on the landowners was therefore preferable to indirect taxes, which were passed on to them. This inevitable incidence of taxes was also best for economic development, as implied previously, because the landlords wasted their share of the revenue.

Turgot was a persistent advocate of economy in government. In an earlier letter to Hume he wrote:

---

[4] Anne Robert Jacques Turgot, *Reflections on the Formation and the Distribution of Riches* (New York: Macmillan, 1898), 9.

[5] Turgot, *Reflections,* 97.

> You know, also, as well as I do what is the great end of all governments on earth: obedience and money. The object is as the saying goes to pluck the hen without making it cry out; now it is the proprietors [landlords] who cry out, and the government has always preferred to attack them indirectly, because then they do not perceive the harm until after the matter has become law.[6]

In a memorandum connected with his government duties, Turgot presented an argument for free trade:

> To persist in opposing . . . [free trade] from a narrowminded political viewpoint which thinks it is possible to grow everything at home, would be to act like the proprietors of Brie who thought themselves thrifty by drinking bad wine from their own vineyards, which really cost them more in the sacrifice of land suited for good wheat than they would have paid for the best Burgandy, which they could have bought from the proceeds of their wheat.[7]

Turgot's greatest contribution in the realm of economic theory was in correctly presenting the law of diminishing returns. This appeared in his *Observation sur un Mémoire de M. de Saint-Péravy,* probably written in 1767. It never can be imagined, he said, that a doubling of expenditure in agriculture will double the product.

> The earth's fertility resembles a spring that is being pressed downwards by the addition of successive weights. If the weight is small and the spring not very flexible, the first attempts will leave no results. But when the weight is enough to overcome the first resistance then it will give to the pressure. After yielding a certain amount it will again begin to resist the extra force put upon it, and weights that formerly would have caused a depression of an inch or more will now scarcely move it by a hair's breadth. And so the effect of additional weights will gradually diminish.[8]

Curiously, Adam Smith—who traveled to France, where he met Turgot and became familiar with his work—did not apply the law of diminishing returns to agriculture. The doctrine was later used in the analysis of rent by Ricardo, Malthus, and Edward West; but none of them recognized, as Turgot did, that when successive units of a variable factor of production are added to land (the fixed factor), increasing returns may initially precede diminishing returns.

Questions for Study and Discussion

1. Briefly identify and state the significance of each of the following to the history of economic thought: merchant guilds, craft guilds, natural order, laissez-faire, Quesnay, *Tableau Economique,* Turgot, and sterile class.
2. When did the physiocratic school begin? When did it end? Why was the school so short-lived?

---

[6] Turgot, *Reflections,* 103.

[7] Anne Robert Jacques Turgot, "Letter on the Marque des fers," in Peter Groenewegen, "Turgot's Place in the History of Economic Thought: A Bicentenary Estimate," *History of Political Economy* 15 (Winter 1983): 591.

[8] Anne Robert Jacques Turgot, *Observation sur un Mémoire de M. de Saint-Péravy* (1767), ed. Gustave Schelle, *Œuvres de Turgot et Documents le Concernant,* vol. 2 (Paris: Librairie Félix Alcan, 1914), 644.

3. In what respects was the physiocratic school a reaction to mercantilism? Why did it develop in France?
4. Briefly summarize the key elements of Quesnay's *Tableau Economique*. In what way did this table foreshadow the contemporary circular flow diagram and national income accounting? Could one table be derived from the other? Explain.
5. What do Colbert (Chapter 2) and Turgot have in common, other than their reputation as French economic thinkers? Contrast their general economic perspectives.
6. What concept did Turgot have in mind in his analogy of successive weights being applied to a spring? Use what you have learned in previous economics courses to graph this concept, drawing a production function with one variable input. Label the vertical axis "agricultural output" and the horizontal axis "variable input." (Check your graph against the top one in Figure 14–3.)
7. What sector of the economy did the physiocrats emphasize? Why? What were the implications for tax policy?
8. Discuss the major shortcomings and contributions of physiocratic thought.
9. Attempt to resolve the following paradox: The physiocrats spoke of the natural order and favored laissez-faire yet strongly supported the absolute authority of the monarchy.

Selected Readings

Books

Beer, Max. *An Inquiry into Physiocracy.* London: Allen and Unwin, 1939.

Blaug, Mark, ed. *Francois Quesnay.* 2 vols. Brookfield, VT: Edward Elgar, 1991.

Groenewegen, Peter D. *The Economics of A. R. J. Turgot.* The Hague: Martinus Nijhoff, 1977.

Higgs, Henry. *The Physiocrats.* New York: Langland Press, 1952. [Originally published in 1897.]

Meek, Ronald L. *The Economics of Physiocracy.* Cambridge, MA: Harvard University Press, 1963.

Turgot, Anne Robert Jacques. *Reflections on the Formation and the Distribution of Riches.* New York: Macmillan, 1898. [Originally published in 1766.]

Vaggi, Gianni. *The Economics of Francois Quesnay.* Durham, NC: Duke University Press, 1987.

Journal Articles

Brewer, Anthony A. "Turgot: Founder of Classical Economics." *Economica* 54 (November 1987): 417–428.

Groenewegen, Peter. "Turgot's Place in the History of Economic Thought." *History of Political Economy* 15 (Winter 1983): 585–616.

Phillips, Almarin. "The Tableau Economique as a Simple Leontief Model." *Quarterly Journal of Economics* 69 (February 1955): 137–144.

Pressman, Steven. "Quesnay's Theory of Taxation." *Journal of the History of Economic Thought* 16 (Spring 1994): 86–105.

Ware, Norman J. "The Physiocrats: A Study in Economic Rationalization." *American Economic Review* 21 (December 1931): 607–619.

Chapter 4

The Classical School—Forerunners

The classical school began in 1776 when Adam Smith published his *Wealth of Nations.* It ended in 1871 when W. Stanley Jevons, Carl Menger, and Leon Walras independently published works expounding neoclassical theories. In this chapter, we first provide an overview of the classical school and then examine the contributions of several of the school's forerunners. (Their names are listed directly above the classical school in the Time Scale of Economic Ideas.) In Chapter 5, we take a detailed look at Adam Smith's ideas.

OVERVIEW OF THE CLASSICAL SCHOOL

The Historical Background of the Classical School

Two "revolutions," one relatively mature and the other just beginning, were of particular significance to classical economic thought.

The scientific revolution. In 1687 Isaac Newton (1642–1727) greatly advanced Kepler's earlier scientific laws of planetary motion and Galileo's mathematical laws of the movement of bodies on earth. In his *Mathematical Principles of Natural Philosophy,* Newton set forth the law of universal gravitation: The attractive force between any two bodies in the universe varies proportionally as the product of the masses of the two, and inversely as the square of the distance between them. This law explains, among other things, the motion of the planets.

The revolution in science associated with Newton and others had three major aspects that merit mention. First, these scientists relied heavily on experimental evidence. Newton and his contemporaries did not believe in innate knowledge derived from reason alone without reliance on experience. Second, Newton popularized the already existing idea that the universe is governed by natural laws. The third aspect of Newton's system was a static view of the universe: Space, time, and matter are independent of each other. Nothing changes over time; the motion and relationships in the universe continue in endless repetition.

Newton's impact can be seen in the ideas of the classical school. According to the classicists, the lingering feudal institutions and the restrictive controls of mercantilism were no longer necessary. For them Newtonian science furnished a nature fully as effective as the earlier will of God. If the Divine Will had created a mechanism that worked harmoniously and automatically without interference, then laissez-faire was the highest form of wisdom in social affairs. Natural laws would guide the economic system and the actions of people.

These ideas were revolutionary in their time. No longer would people unquestioningly accept ancient truths, such as that interest is sinful or that people inherited their station in life. Society would be best served if people were free to follow the natural law of self-interest. Newtonian thinking in classical economics provided an ideology that justified property incomes. As natural law is best left unobstructed, and as private thrift and prudence contribute to the good of society, then rent, interest, and profits are just rewards for the ownership and productive use of wealth.

The industrial revolution. In 1776 the industrial revolution was just beginning, but it intensified over the period in which the later classical economists wrote. In the seventeenth century England trailed Holland in commerce and lagged behind France in manufacturing. But by the middle of the eighteenth century, England gained supremacy in both commerce and industry. Both the industrial revolution and classical political economy developed first in England. Smith and his contemporaries, living during the early stages of the industrial revolution, could not adequately identify the significance of this phenomenon and the direction its development would take. Such wisdom is usually displayed through hindsight; but they were aware of the substantial growth of manufacturing, trade, inventions, and the division of labor. This growth of industry led to increased emphasis on the industrial aspect of economic life in current thinking.

By 1776 England, the most industrially efficient and powerful country in the world, stood to benefit greatly by free international trade. As English entrepreneurs became stronger, they no longer had to rely on government subsidies, monopoly privileges, and tariff protection. And with entrepreneurs becoming sufficiently numerous to make monopoly agreements difficult to achieve and enforce, competition could increasingly be relied on to ensure moderate prices and product quality. Many mercantilist practices were breaking down under the upsurge of business activity that was spreading in every direction.

A free, mobile, low-paid, and hardworking labor force also was emerging. Before the final triumph of classical political economy, national and local governments had regulated labor and working conditions. Sometimes labor was protected, but more frequently employers were favored. Local justices of the peace had regulated wages in England for centuries, usually imposing wage ceilings. This practice had died out by 1762, however, because conditions of labor supply and demand were dictating low market-determined wages. Enclosure acts passed by Parliament authorized the use of fences, hedges, and walls to enclose the common lands and unfenced open fields where peasants formerly had raised crops, grazed cattle or pigs, and gathered fuel. These laws brought land under a strict regime of private ownership and encouraged larger scale, more capital-intensive agriculture. This raised the productivity of farm labor and land but also turned peasants into wage laborers who sought employment from landlords, merchants, and manufacturers. Furthermore, handicraftsmen tended to lose their competitive advantage as the factory system developed, driving an increasing number of them into the labor market as wage workers. A high birthrate and a falling death rate increased the population, and child laborers and bankrupt Irish peasants arriving in England also augmented the labor supply. Government steps to keep wages low were therefore no longer necessary, hence making it easier for businessmen to subscribe to the new doctrine of laissez-faire. Now it was the workers' turn to try, unsuccessfully, to invoke government regulation to establish minimum wages.

Major Tenets of the Classical School

Classical doctrine is frequently called economic liberalism. Its bases are personal liberty, private property, individual initiative, private enterprise, and minimal government interference. The term *liberalism* should be considered in its historical context: Classical ideas were liberal in contrast to feudal and mercantilist restrictions on choice of occupations, land transfers, trade, and so forth. It is a testament to historical change that today we might call a person who advocates economic liberalism a "conservative."

The major features of this body of thought can be summarized as follows. A fuller development of these notions appears throughout the next several chapters.

- Minimal government involvement. The first principle of the classical school was that the best government governs the least. The forces of the free, competitive market would guide production, exchange, and distribution. The economy was held to be self-adjusting and tending toward full employment without government intervention. Government activity should be confined to enforcing property rights, providing for the national defense, and providing public education.
- Self-interested economic behavior. The classical economists assumed that self-interested behavior is basic to human nature. Producers and merchants provided goods and services out of a desire to make profits; workers offered their labor services to obtain wages, and consumers purchased products as a way to satisfy their wants.
- Harmony of interests. With the important exception of Ricardo, the classicists emphasized the natural harmony of interest in a market economy. By pursuing their own individual interests, people served the best interests of society.
- Importance of all economic resources and activities. The classicists pointed out that all economic resources—land, labor, capital, and entrepreneurial ability—as well as all economic activities—agriculture, commerce, production, and international exchange—contribute to a nation's wealth. The mercantilists had said that wealth was derived from commerce; the physiocrats had viewed land and agriculture as the source of all wealth.
- Economic laws. The classical school made tremendous contributions to economics by focusing analysis upon explicit economic theories or "laws." Examples include the law of comparative advantage, the law of diminishing returns, the Malthusian theory of population, the law of markets (Say's law), the Ricardian theory of rent, the quantity theory of money, and the labor theory of value. The classicists believed that the laws of economics are universal and immutable.

Whom Did the Classical School Benefit or Seek to Benefit?

In the long run classical economics served all society because the application of its theories promoted capital accumulation and economic growth. It gave businesspeople respectability in a world that previously had directed honors and income toward the nobility and the gentry. Merchants and industrialists achieved a new status and dignity as promoters of the nation's wealth, and entrepreneurs were assured that by seeking profit they were serving society. These doctrines ultimately led to more material benefits for owners and managers of businesses, because the classical ideas helped promote the political, social, and economic climate that encouraged industry, trade, and profit.

But not all people shared equally from the concepts of classicism; there were costs along with the benefits of industrialization. In Great Britain the wage earners in particular bore the heaviest share of costs through long hours of work at low pay. But ultimately economic progress enabled workers to enhance their own position, and in this sense classical economics benefited them too. Today, wages and salaries typically constitute two-thirds of the total national income in the industrial market economies.

How Was the Classical School Valid, Useful, or Correct in Its Time?

Classical economics rationalized the practices being engaged in by enterprising people. It justified the overthrow of mercantilist restrictions, which had outlived their usefulness. Competition was a growing phenomenon, and reliance upon it as the great regulator of the economy was a tenable viewpoint. Governments were notoriously wasteful and corrupt, and under the circumstances, the less government intervention, the better. By helping to remove the remnants of the feudal system, classical economics promoted business enterprise. For example, when feudal land laws were abolished and land could serve as security for credit, landowners were able to raise large sums for investment in agriculture or industry.

When industrialization was beginning, society's greatest need was to concentrate resources on the maximum possible expansion of production. The elevation of the private sector over the public sector served this end admirably. Because consumers were generally poor and investment opportunities were seemingly unlimited, capitalists had a strong incentive to reinvest a substantial portion of their profits. The outcome was a rapid expansion of output. Continued growth of the public sector would have required increased taxation, thereby diverting resources from private capital formation.

Classical economics and those who endorsed it enlarged the market not only by achieving freer international trade but also by promoting an urban labor force. Subsistence farmers would consume much of their own product while buying little in the market; urban laborers of the late 1700s, by contrast, purchased their foodstuffs in the market. Hence agriculture entered more directly into the monetary sector of the economy, and the merchant and processor found a niche between the farmer and the consumer.

Which Tenets of the Classical School Became Lasting Contributions?

The classical economists gave the best analysis of the economic world up to their time, far surpassing the analyses of the mercantilists and physiocrats. They laid the foundation of modern economics as a social science, and generations who followed built upon their insights and achievements. Several of the classical "laws" are now taught as "principles" of economics in standard economics textbooks. Tenets that became lasting contributions include, but are not limited to, the following: (1) the law of diminishing returns, (2) the law of comparative advantage, (3) the notion of consumer sovereignty, (4) the importance of capital accumulation to economic growth, and (5) the market as a mechanism for reconciling the interests of individuals with those of society.

This is not to suggest that classical economics was without its weaknesses and errors. History and subsequent economic theorists were to show that laissez-faire was inadequate as a public policy to deal with, among other things, economic depressions, monopolies (whether natural or not), monopsony power, external effects of private actions, and provisions of goods whose benefits were indivisible (public goods). Some advocates of classical economics carried their call for laissez-faire to absurd extremes. To cite just one example, the London *Economist* criticized the "sanitary movement," which urged that the government require a pure water supply and proper sewage disposal. Even after sewage lines were built, owners of houses were not required at first to hook up to them. The *Economist* declared that poor housing and high urban death rates

> spring from two causes, both of which will be aggravated by these new laws. The first is the poverty of the masses, which, if possible, will be increased by the taxation inflicted by the new laws. The second is that the people have never been allowed to take care of themselves. They have always been treated as serfs or children, and they have to a great extent become in respect to those objects which the government has undertaken to perform for them, imbecile. . . . There is a worse evil than typhus or cholera or impure water, and that is mental imbecility.[1]

In addition to its overemphasis on laissez-faire, classical economics was ambiguous, deficient, or wrong in several areas of economic analysis. For example, we will discover that the classical prediction that rental income would rise and profits would fall as the economy advanced failed to consider the role of technological change and the relationship between rising productivity and wages. As a second example, the labor theory of value advanced by some of the classicists failed to fully incorporate the role of utility and demand in establishing product value. But this is not the place for elaboration of such points. Let's instead turn to three forerunners of the classical school.

SIR DUDLEY NORTH

Sir Dudley North (1641–1691), living during the height of the mercantilist period, struck hard at the heart of mercantilist doctrine. He was a wealthy merchant in the Turkish trade who later became commissioner of customs and then a treasury official. North has been called the world's first prominent free trader.

[1] *Economist,* London, July 13, 1850.

His brief tract, *Discourses upon Trade,* was North's only published work, appearing anonymously in 1691. Such caution was understandable in a merchant and high government official whose views did not conform to prevailing ideas. Decades later his brother hinted that the publication was deliberately suppressed. When Ricardo read a reprinted edition, he wrote: "I had no idea that any one entertained such correct opinions, as are expressed in this publication, at so early a period."

North emphasized that trade is not a one-sided benefit to whichever country realizes a surplus of exports but rather is an act of mutual advantage to both sides. Its object is not to accumulate specie but to exchange surpluses. A division of labor and international trade would promote wealth even if no gold or silver existed:

> Trade is nothing else but a Commutation of Superfluities; for instance: I give of mine, what I can spare, for somewhat of yours, which I want, and you can spare. . . . He who is most diligent, and raiseth most Fruits, or maketh most of Manufactory, will abound most in what others make, or raise; and consequently be free from Want, and enjoy most Conveniences, which is truly to be Rich, altho' there were no such thing as Gold, Silver, or the like amongst them.[2]

North repudiated the concept that wealth should be measured by a country's stock of precious metals. His emphasis was on business enterprise and accumulation. Here he struck at the theory rather than the practice of the mercantilists. But, understandably for his time, he did not include manufacturing in his list of productive activities. Even taking its original meaning to "making by hand," manufacturing was relatively unimportant in the seventeenth century.

> No Man is richer for having his Estate all in Money, Plate, etc. lying by him, but on the contrary, he is for that reason the poorer. That man is richest, whose Estate is a growing condition, either in Land at Farm, Money at Interest, or Goods in Trade: If any man, out of an humour, should turn all his Estate into Money, and keep it dead, he would soon be sensible of Poverty growing upon him, whilst he is eating out the quick stock.
>
> But to examine the matter closer, what do these People want, who cry out for Money? I will begin with the Beggar: he wants, and importunes for Money: What would he do with it if he had it? buy Bread, etc. Then in truth it is not Money, but Bread, and other Necessaries of Life that he wants.[3]

Some people have not mastered the profound truth of the last paragraph even today: We want money only to part with it, because what we truly want are goods and services. What then is the wealth of a nation?

North observed that commerce among nations distributes the money supply according to the needs of trade. He wrote,

---

[2] Sir Dudley North, *Discourses upon Trade* (1691), ed. Jacob H. Hollander (Baltimore, MD: Johns Hopkins Press, 1907), 2.

[3] North, *Discourses,* 11, 12.

> For it hath been observed that where no Mints were, Trade hath not wanted a full supply of Money; because if it be wanted, the Coyn of other Princes will become currant, as in *Ireland,* and the *Plantation.* . . . Then let not the care of Specifick Money torment us so much; for a People that are rich cannot want it, and if they have none, they will be supplied with the Coyn of other Nations.[4]

North argued for laissez-faire as the way to achieve the maximum gains from both intra- and international trade. This was bold theorizing in an age of rampant nationalism.

> Now it may appear strange to hear it said, That the whole World as to Trade is but as one Nation or People, and therein Nations are as Persons. That the loss of Trade with one Nation, is not that only, separately considered, but so much of the Trade of the World rescinded and lost, for all is combined together. That there can be no Trade unprofitable to the Publick; for if any prove so, men leave it off; and whenever the Traders thrive, the Publick, of which they are a part, thrives also. That to force Men to deal in any prescrib'd manner, may profit such as happen to serve them; but the Publick gains not, because it is taking from one Subject, to give to another. . . . In short, That all favour to one Trade or Interest against another, is an Abuse, and cuts so much of Profit from the Publick.[5]

Although North believed that free trade would help both the traders and the country, he did not profess a harmony of interests doctrine such as that later stated by Smith. Indeed North saw that many special interests were profiting at the expense of the public by using the power of government to acquire special privileges. His idea that the authorities therefore should not support narrow private interests was quite contrary to mercantilist doctrine. Again he presents an insight that has relevance to contemporary trade issues:

> Whenever Men consult for the Publick Good, as for the advancement of Trade, wherein all are concerned, they usually esteem the immediate Interest of their own to be the common Measure of Good and Evil. And there are many, who to gain a little in their own Trades, care not how much others suffer; and each Man strives, that all other may be forc'd, in their dealings, to act subserviently for his Profit, but under the covert of the Publick.
>
> So clothiers would have men be forc'd to buy their Manufacture; and I may mention such as sell Wool, they would have men forc'd to buy of them at an high price, though the Clothier loseth. . . . And in general all those who are lazy, and do not, or are not active enough, and cannot look out, to vent the Product of their Estates, or to Trade with it themselves, would have all Traders forc'd by Laws, to bring home to them sufficient Prizes, whether they [the traders] gain or lose by it.[6]

Finally, North disagreed with the mercantilist concept that war and conquest enrich a country. He wrote, "Money Exported in Trade is an increase to the Wealth of the

---

[4] North, *Discourses,* 16, 17.

[5] North, *Discourses,* B1, B2.

[6] North, *Discourses,* B.

Nation; but spent in War, and Payments abroad, is so much Impoverishment." By "payments abroad" he probably meant payments made without receiving an equivalent return of imports, as in the case of military subsidies to allies. This is an antimercantilist view of the strongest kind, but one that itself is open to criticism: A nation's wealth consists of the value of services rendered in addition to the value of domestic and imported goods that are available.

RICHARD CANTILLON

Richard Cantillon (1680?–1734) was born in Ireland. He spent many years in Paris, becoming a wealthy banker and a successful speculator in stocks and foreign currencies. In 1734 Cantillon was robbed and murdered and his house was set afire, probably by a cook he had dismissed ten days earlier. His only book, *Essai sur la Nature du Commerce en Général,* was written between 1730 and 1734 and published in French in 1755. Cantillon himself may have translated it from his English manuscript, which was never found.

Cantillon predated the physiocrats in two ways. First, he used the term *entrepreneur* and emphasized the role of this figure in economic life. Businesspeople, Cantillon said, commit themselves to definite payments in expectation of uncertain receipts; this risk taking is remunerated by profit, which competition tends to reduce to the normal value of the entrepreneurs' services. Second, writing a generation before Quesnay constructed his *Tableau Economique,* Cantillon stated:

> Cash is therefore necessary, not only for the Rent of the Landlord . . . but also for the City merchandise consumed in the Country. . . . The circulation of this money takes place when the Landlords spend in detail in the City the rents which the Farmers have paid them in lump sums, and when the Entrepreneurs of the Cities, Butchers, Bakers, Brewers, etc. collect little by little this same money to buy from the Farmers in lump sums Cattle, Wheat, Barley, etc.[7]

Cantillon developed a theory of value and price. His emphasis on the role of land and labor, on supply and demand, and on the fluctuations of price around intrinsic value makes him a direct forerunner of classical economics.

> The Villagers come to Town on Market-Days to sell their produce and to buy the things they need. Prices are fixed by the proportion between the produce exposed for sale and money offered for it. . . . When the price has been settled between a few the others follow without difficulty and so the Market-price of the day is determined. . . .
>
> The Price or intrinsic value of a thing is the measure of the quantity of Land and Labour entering into its production, having regard to the fertility or produce of the Land and to the quantity of the Labour. But it often happens that many things which have actually this intrinsic value are not sold in the Market according to that value; that will depend on the Humours and Fancies of men and on their consumption. . . .

[7] Richard Cantillon, *Essai sur la Nature du Commerce en Général,* ed. Henry Higgs (London: Macmillan, 1931), 125–126. Reprinted by permission of the publisher.

> If the Farmers in a State sow more corn than usual, much more than is needed for the year's consumption, the real and intrinsic value of the corn will correspond to the Land and Labour which enter into its production; but as there is too great an abundance of it and there are more sellers than buyers the Market Price of the Corn will necessarily fall below the intrinsic price or Value. If on the contrary the Farmers sow less corn than is needed for consumption there will be more buyers than sellers and the Market Price of corn will rise above its intrinsic value.
>
> There is never a variation in intrinsic values, but the impossibility of proportioning the production of merchandise and produce in a State to their consumption causes a daily variation, and a perpetual ebb and flow in Market Prices.[8]

Cantillon anticipated classical economic thought in several other ways. For example, he stated, "Men multiply like Mice in a barn if they have unlimited Means of Subsistence." The classical economist Thomas Malthus held a similar view. Also, Cantillon analyzed interest as a reward for the risk taken in lending, based on profits that the entrepreneurs can make by borrowing and investing. Bankers, he pointed out, create credit, because if 100,000 ounces of gold are deposited with them, as much as 90,000 can be lent out; such loans will not, of course, diminish the ability of the depositor to use the bank-issued demand deposit to purchase goods from others. In addition, Cantillon focused on the productivity of a nation's resources. He regretted that both nobles and monks did not work to produce goods. But nobles are a great ornament to the country, he pointed out, and during wartime they will at least use their retinues and horses for victory, "while Monks are, as people say, neither useful nor ornamental in peace or war on this side of heaven." Furthermore, Cantillon said, in Catholic countries there are too many holy days, "which diminish the labour of the People by about an eight part of the year."

With one foot in the mercantilist camp, Cantillon opted for a surplus of exports as being good for business. But he did not believe that gold and silver mined at home would serve the same purpose. His emphasis was on the production of goods and their sale abroad, so that business would flourish. But he believed that an export surplus could not be maintained indefinitely; subsequent events would wipe it out. Cantillon's analysis of the forces that prevent a perpetual export surplus and his emphasis on the sale of goods rather than on the accumulation of gold came close to classical thinking.

Cantillon held that the discovery and exploitation of rich mines of gold and silver would raise domestic prices, rents, and wages. These increased costs would in turn promote imports to the detriment of domestic workers and manufacturers because money would flow out of the country. "The great circulation of Money, which was general at the beginning, ceases; poverty and misery follow and the labour of the Mines appears to be only to the advantage of those employed upon them and the Foreigners who profit thereby." This is what happened in Spain, he said.

But if the increase in money comes from a surplus of exports of goods, it enriches merchants and entrepreneurs and gives employment to workers. However, as money flows into the country and business prospers, consumption and prices rise, spending

[8] Cantillon, *Commerce,* 29–30.

on imported luxury items grows, and the export surplus dwindles. The state begins to lose some branches of its profitable trade, and workers leave the country.

> This will gradually impoverish the State and cause it to pass from great power into great weakness. When a State has arrived at the highest point of wealth (I assume always that comparative wealth of States consists principally in the respective quantities of money which they possess) it will inevitable fall into poverty by the ordinary course of things. The too great abundance of money, which so long as it lasts forms the power of States, throws them back imperceptibly but naturally into poverty. Thus it would seem that when a State expands by trade and the abundance of money raises the price of Land and Labour, the Prince or the Legislator ought to withdraw money from circulation.[9]

Notice that there is no reliance on natural law or the automatic reestablishment of equilibrium here! It is David Hume who takes this line of reasoning a step further.

DAVID HUME

David Hume (1711–1776) was born in Scotland twelve years before his fellow national and friend, Adam Smith. Hume entered the University of Edinburgh at the age of twelve and left at fifteen without taking a degree. Later, eminent as a philosopher, Hume was twice refused a chair in philosophy at Edinburgh because of his skeptical spirit and unorthodox thinking. In fact Adam Smith was once nearly expelled from Oxford University because a copy of Hume's *A Treatise of Human Nature* was found in his room.

Hume spent his life as a tutor to a marquis and as a minor government official. Upon retirement he returned to his inherited estate, where he wrote prolifically. His fame as a historian derived from his multivolume *History of England,* which went through numerous editions; his reputation as an economist was established by his economic essays in *Political Discourses,* published in 1752. Of all the forerunners of classical economics, Hume came closest to the ideas of Smith. Had he written a complete and systematic treatise on economics, he would have ranked near the top as one of the founders of the science.

Hume's greatest contribution as an economist was in presenting what has since been called the *price specie-flow mechanism.* The mercantilists wanted to promote a surplus of exports in order to accumulate specie. In the somber view of Cantillon, this tactic was self-defeating because if more specie were available, prices would go up and imports would increase. But to pay for the imports, money would be shipped abroad, leaving poverty and bankruptcy behind; therefore, the government should prevent an excess of money. The physiocrats were basically unconcerned with foreign trade, except that they wished to permit the free flow of grain abroad. But Hume, who like Cantillon accepted John Locke's quantity theory of money (the price level is determined by the quantity of money available, given the velocity and quantity of output), analyzed the mechanism of international equilibrium that would operate without government intervention. Laissez-faire could prevail with happy results. In his essay, "Of the Balance of Trade" (1752), Hume wrote:

---

[9] Cantillon, *Commerce,* 185.

> Suppose four-fifths of all the money in GREAT BRITAIN to be annihilated in one night, and the nation reduced to the same condition, with regard to specie, as in the reigns of the HARRYS and EDWARDS, what would be the consequence? Must not the price of all labour and commodities sink in proportion, and everything be sold as cheap as they were in those ages? What nation could then dispute with us in any foreign market, or pretend to navigate or to sell manufactures at the same price, which to us would afford sufficient profit? In how little time, therefore, must this bring back the money which we had lost, and raise us to the level of all the neighboring nations? Where, after we have arrived, we immediately lose the advantage of the cheapness of labour and commodities; and the farther flowing in of money is stopped by our fulness and repletion.
>
> Again, suppose, that all the money of GREAT BRITAIN were multiplied fivefold in a night, must not the contrary effect follow? Must not all labour and commodities rise to such an exorbitant height, that no neighbouring nations could afford to buy from us; while their commodities, on the other hand, became comparatively so cheap, that, in spite of all the laws which could be formed, they would be run in upon us, and our money flow out; till we fall to a level with foreigners, and lose that great superiority of riches, which had laid us under such disadvantages?[10]

Hume did not believe these price-level adjustments (either upward or downward) would occur instantaneously. In his "Of Money" and "Of Interest," he stated that price-level changes initially would lag behind the changes in money. For a time an increase in money would boost spending, production, and employment. But eventually the influx of money would be fully absorbed as an increase in the price level. Likewise a decrease in the supply of money would first depress spending, output, and employment before it lowered the price level.[11]

Hume's price specie-flow mechanism is natural law thinking; it proceeds from the assumption of an equilibrium. Once the economy moves away from equilibrium, events automatically occur to restore it. Hume's mechanism, of course, no longer works well in the international economy. Because the full gold standard has been abandoned everywhere, the quantity of money in a particular economy no longer depends on the flow of gold. Central banks control the supply of money in their economies largely independent of the balance of trade. Nor are prices and wages as flexible downward as Hume assumed. But Hume was also aware of a second factor that would promote equilibrium in international trade—a factor that precedes price changes and gold movements. When exchange rates between nations' currencies are free to fluctuate, an imbalance of trade tends to correct itself. In a footnote to "Of the Balance of Trade," Hume wrote:

> There is another cause, though more limited in its operation, which checks the wrong balance of trade, to every particular nation to which the kingdom trades. When we import more goods than we export, the exchange turns against us, and this becomes a new encouragement to export.[12]

[10] David Hume, *Writings on Economics,* ed. Eugene Rotwein (Surrey, Eng.: Thomas Nelson and Sons, 1970), 62, 63. Reprinted by permission of the publisher.

[11] Hume, *Economics,* 37–38.

[12] Hume, *Economics,* 64.

Restated, if a nation, say England, imports more than it exports, eventually it will experience a decline in the value of its currency relative to others. Why is this so? The reason for the depreciation in the pound relative to the currencies of other nations is that England needs more foreign currency to finance its imports than it is earning through its sales abroad. This shortage of foreign currencies will drive up their prices; that is, the pound price of foreign currencies will rise. This means that the pound depreciates while other world currencies appreciate. British goods therefore are cheaper to other nations, and consequently British exports rise. And because foreign goods are now more expensive (a pound will buy less of them), England reduces its imports. The initial net import surplus in England vanishes.

In "Of the Jealousy of Trade" (1758), Hume disputed the mercantilist concept that trading states are rivals, with one gaining only at the expense of the other:

> In opposition to this narrow and malignant opinion, I will venture to assert, that the encrease of riches and commerce in any one nation, instead of hurting, commonly promotes the riches and commerce of all its neighbours; and that a state can scarcely carry its trade and industry very far where all the surrounding states are buried in ignorance, sloth, and barbarism.[13]

In the parlance of modern game theory (Chapter 18), Hume is saying that international trade is a positive sum game, one in which the payoffs sum to a positive number. This is to be contrasted to the zero-sum of the mercantilists, where the gain to one party is exactly offset by a loss to the other.

But won't international trade simply perpetuate the advantages that rich nations enjoy relative to poor ones? After all, rich nations have extensive commerce, great capital, developed industries, skilled labor, and so forth. In a letter for Lord Kames in 1758, Hume answered "No." Provisions and labor become more expensive in the wealthy nations, he argued. The poorer countries can then compete successfully in the coarser manufactures and later in the more elaborate ones.

More than 200 years of hindsight indicate that Hume's optimism was justified in some cases and unjustified in others. Rich nations attract capital and talent, which the poorer countries cannot always do successfully. Wealth leads to improvements in health and education, increased social overhead capital, larger markets, and other benefits, which in turn result in the further expansion of wealth and income. Poverty, in contrast, often leads to conditions that perpetuate poverty. In many cases, therefore, the gap between rich and poor nations has widened, but in other cases Hume's prediction has proved to be accurate. South Korea, Taiwan, Singapore, and Japan are a few examples of nations whose reliance on international trade has enabled them to improve their standards of living relative to England, the Netherlands, and France since Hume's time. But the idea of an international equilibrium in which all nations eventually become equally wealthy thus far seems too optimistic. Hume clearly exaggerated the international harmony of interest, but this was a healthy antidote to the suspicion and the economic warfare between countries during the eighteenth century.

---

[13] Hume, *Economics,* 78.

Hume treated several other topics of interest. For example, he showed an awareness of the concept of elasticity of demand, which was not formally incorporated into economic analysis until far later. You may recall that this idea concerns the responsiveness of buyers of a product to changes in price. Hume said that if duties on wine are lowered, the government will collect *more* revenue, apparently assuming that the increase in revenue from greater sales abroad will exceed the loss of revenue from the lower price per unit. But he did not extend this concept to international equilibrium. He contended that an increase in imports would stimulate exports. But he did not realize that with an inelastic demand (lower percentage quantity change than the percentage price change) for a country's products abroad, a surplus of imports that would cause a price drop at home would not stimulate enough exports to produce equilibrium.

In a letter to Turgot in 1766, Hume opposed the physiocratic idea that taxes imposed on workers get passed on to the landowner in the form of higher wages and reduced rent. Labor, he pointed out, is more expensive in Switzerland, where there are no taxes, than it is in France, where there are many. There are almost no taxes in the English colonies, yet labor is three times more expensive there than in any European country. Wages of labor depend, he said, on the supply and demand for labor, not on taxes. When a tax is laid on the products that workers consume, the immediate consequence is that these people consume less or work more; the tax is not simply passed on to the landowner.

Refer to 4-1 PAST AS PROLOGUE

Hume and Adam Smith were good friends. When the latter published *The Theory of Moral Sentiments,* Hume, using sardonic humor, wrote a letter complimenting him:

> I proceed to tell you the melancholy news that your book has been very unfortunate, for the public seem disposed to applaud it extremely. It was looked for by the foolish people with some impatience; and the mob of literati are beginning already to be very loud in its praises. . . . Millar [the publisher] exults and brags that two-thirds of the edition are already sold, and that he is now sure of success. You see what a son of the earth that is, to value books only by the profit they bring him. In that view, I believe, it may prove a very good book.[14]

Hume displayed insight into Ricardian rent theory in a letter to Smith. On April 1, 1776, having read Smith's *Wealth of Nations,* Hume wrote:

> I am much pleas'd with your Performance. . . . If you were here at my Fireside, I should dispute some of your Principles. I cannot think, that the Rent of Farms makes any part of the Price of the Produce, but that the Price is determined altogether by the Quantity and the Demand. . . . But these and a hundred other Points are fit only to be discussed in Conversation; which, till you tell me the contrary, I shall still flatter myself with soon. I hope it will be soon: For I am in a very bad state of Health and cannot afford a long Delay.[15]

Less than five months later Hume was dead, but Smith had visited him during the last days of his illness.

[14] John Rae, *Life of Adam Smith* (London: Macmillan, 1895), 143–144.

[15] Hume, *Economics,* 216–217.

4-1 PAST AS PROLOGUE

Hume and Cooperation

Recently, the analysis of "repeated games" in game theory has been of great interest to economists. What is game theory, and what are repeated games? And how does David Hume fit into this picture?

In 1944 John von Neumann and Oskar Morgenstern published their *Theory of Games and Economic Behavior*, a contribution discussed in Chapter 18. Game theory is applicable in situations where firms, in making their own pricing, production, advertising, and related decisions, assess the likely counteractions of their rivals. The traditional assumption has been that the best strategy in such "games" is to take advantage of profit opportunities presented by the "moves" of rivals.

One well-known scenario is called the prisoner's dilemma game, which assumes that two people—Adams and Benson—have committed a crime and are being detained as suspects. Unknown to the suspects, the outside evidence of their guilt is weak. The police place the suspects in separate rooms and offer them each a deal: confess to the crime and obtain a reduced sentence. Thus each detainee faces a dilemma: If Adams holds his tongue and Benson confesses, Adams will be found guilty and receive a lengthy sentence. The same situation holds for Benson. What happens? Both prisoners confess, even though they would be better off if both had remained silent. Each party worries that the other party will confess first!

The concept of the prisoner's dilemma has been applied to the tendency of duopolists (the firms in a two-firm industry) to cheat on a price fixing agreement. Upon consummating such an agreement, each firm fears that the other firm will take advantage of the high price by secretly giving slight price concessions to buyers. This will allow the cheater to increase its profits and market share at the expense of the other conspirator. Fearing that the other firm will cheat, each firm decides to cheat, and the price fixing agreement erodes.

Questions for Study and Discussion

1. Briefly identify and state the significance of each of the following to the history of economic thought: economic liberalism, enclosure laws, Newton, industrial revolution, North, Cantillon, intrinsic value, entrepreneur, Hume, and price specie-flow mechanism.
2. What relationship, if any, do you see between the scientific revolution associated with Newton and others and Hume's most significant contribution to economics? Explain.
3. Compare the list of major tenets of the classical school with those of the physiocratic school (Chapter 3). Which are similar? Which are dissimilar? Based on this comparison, would you characterize the physiocrats as forerunners to the classical school? Explain.

But the prisoner's dilemma and duopolist behavior may not be comparable. It is unlikely that the prisoners intend to work together over the remainder of their lifetimes. In contrast, the duopolists may compete with one another into perpetuity. The prisoner's dilemma thus is a "one-time game"; the duopoly situation, a "repeated game."

In 1984 political scientist Robert Axelrod demonstrated that the optimal strategy for repeated games is to cooperate so long as the other side reciprocates.* If Ajax takes advantage of Acme today, Acme will take advantage of Ajax in a future "game" where there is a different set of circumstances. If Ajax cooperates with Acme now, Ajax can expect Acme to cooperate later.

Axelrod's contribution to game theory has promoted much new theorizing and research on cooperation as an optimal strategy. But just how new is this idea? Writing in 1740 in *A Treatise on Human Nature,* David Hume stated:

> [W]e can better satisfy our appetites in an oblique and artificial manner, than by their headlong and impetuous notion. I learn to do a service to another, without bearing him any real kindness; because I foresee that he will return my service, in expectation of another of the same kind, and in order to maintain the same correspondence of good offices with me or with others. And accordingly, after I have served him, and he is in possession of the advantage arising from my action, he is induced to perform his part, as foreseeing the consequences of his refusal.†

In short, Hume recognized that a strategy of cooperation may be optimal in situations where future interactions among two parties are likely. The economic implication of this idea is that some price fixing agreements may be more durable than we might otherwise surmise.

---

* Robert Axelrod, *The Evolution of Cooperation* (New York: Basic Books, 1984).

† David Hume, as quoted by James W. Friedman in *Game Theory with Applications to Economics,* 2d ed. (New York: Oxford University Press, 1990), 110.

4. Why, according to North, do people desire money?
5. Relate the following statement by North to contemporary international trade issues: "Whenever Men consult for the Publick Good . . . they usually esteem the immediate Interest of their own to be the common Measure of Good and Evil."
6. What, according to Cantillon, determines the intrinsic value of a good? Why might the market price differ from this intrinsic price?
7. Elaborate on the following statement: A rise in the British pound price of U.S. dollars necessarily implies a fall in the dollar price of pounds. Which currency has appreciated? Which has been devalued? What trade factors, according to Hume, might cause this change in the relative value of the two currencies? How might the change in the exchange rate eventually correct the situation?
8. Use the following mathematical identity (the equation of exchange) to explain Hume's price specie-flow mechanism: $MV = PT$, where $M =$ the stock of money,

V = velocity, P = price level, and T = quantity of goods transacted. Assume that V and T are constant.

9. Discuss: Classical economists viewed economic laws as immutable, not to be tampered with or thwarted. They and their followers could not understand that economic laws, which are generalizations about tendencies, can be curbed, overcome, or redirected—that people can control economic life.

Selected Readings

Books

Blaug, Mark, ed. *Richard Cantillon and Jacques Turgot.* Brookfield, VT: Edward Elgar, 1991.

Brewer, Anthony. *Richard Cantillon: Pioneer of Economic Theory.* London: Routledge, 1992.

Cantillon, Richard. *Essai sur la Nature du Commerce en Général.* Edited by Henry Higgs and printed in French and English. London: Macmillan, 1931. [Originally published in 1775.]

Irwin, Douglas A. *Against the Tide: An Intellectual History of Free Trade.* Princeton, NJ: Princeton University Press, 1996. Chapter 3.

Murphy, Antoin E. *Richard Cantillon: Entrepreneur and Economist.* Oxford: Clarendon Press, 1986.

North, Dudley. *Discourses upon Trade.* Edited by Jacob H. Hollander. Baltimore: Johns Hopkins Press, 1907. [Originally published in 1691.]

Rotwein, Eugene. *David Hume: Writings on Economics.* Madison, WI: University of Wisconsin Press, 1970.

Journal Articles

Aspromourgos, Tony. "The Theory of Production and Distribution in Cantillon's *Essai.*" *Oxford Economic Papers* 41 (April 1989): 356–373.

Brems, H. "Cantillon versus Marx: The Land Theory and the Labor Theory of Value." *History of Political Economy* 10 (Winter 1978): 669–678.

Duke, M. I. "David Hume and Monetary Adjustment." *History of Political Economy* 11 (Winter 1979): 572–587.

Hebért, Robert F. "Richard Cantillon's Early Contribution to Spatial Economics." *Economica* 48 (February 1981): 71–77.

Perlman, Morris. "Of a Controversial Passage in Hume." *Journal of Political Economy* 95 (April 1987): 274–289.

Spengler, J. J. "Richard Cantillon: First of the Moderns." *Journal of Political Economy* 62 (August and October 1954): 281–295, 406–424.

Chapter 5

The Classical School—Adam Smith

In this chapter we present the economic contributions of Adam Smith, who was not only the founder of the classical school but also its most noted member. In subsequent chapters we discuss other important classical economists.

In the discussion of Smith we initially look at some of the details of his life and note several key influences on him. Next, we examine Smith's first book, *The Theory of Moral Sentiments,* to explore the relationship between his thinking on moral philosophy and on political economy. Then, we dissect his monumental *Wealth of Nations,* highlighting Smith's views on (1) laissez-faire and the harmony of interests, (2) the division of labor, and (3) the economic laws of a competitive economy.

BIOGRAPHICAL DETAILS

Adam Smith (1723–1790), the kindly, brilliant founder of the classical school, was born in the seaport and manufacturing town of Kirkcaldy, Scotland. His father, comptroller of customs in the town, died before his son was born. Margaret Douglas Smith provided a home for her son until her death in 1784 in her ninetieth year.

Young Smith attended Glasgow College at fourteen years of age; he later studied moral and political science and languages at Balliol College, Oxford. He then returned to his mother's home to continue independent study for two years. After that Smith moved to Edinburgh, where he gave lectures on rhetoric and literature. He was elected professor of logic at Glasgow College in 1751, and in the following year he was given the chair of moral philosophy, which he held for nearly twelve years. In 1759 he published *The Theory of Moral Sentiments,* after which his lectures concentrated less on ethical doctrines and more on jurisprudence and political economy.

Smith resigned his professorship to become the tutor to the stepson of Charles Townsend, chancellor of the exchequer, who later came to prominence in America on the issue of the colonial tea tax. Smith spent more than two years with his charge in France, where he established close personal friendships with the physiocrats, including Quesnay and Turgot. After returning to Scotland, Smith retired on an annual pension of £300, which his tutorship paid him for the rest of his life.

In 1776 Smith published *An Inquiry into the Nature and Causes of the Wealth of Nations,* which he had begun in France ten years earlier. Its fame was immediate, and it established Smith's reputation forever.

After the publication of his book, Smith spent two years in London, where he mingled with the leading intellectuals of the day. Then, on being appointed commissioner of customs in Scotland, he went to live in Edinburgh with his mother.

It is believed that much of his income was spent secretly on charities. He was always happy to receive his friends at dinner, even without the formality of an invitation, and his Sunday suppers were long celebrated in Edinburgh. Among the honors bestowed on Smith was his election as lord rector of Glasgow College. Shortly before he died in 1790 most of his unpublished manuscripts were destroyed according to his wish and without explanation.

IMPORTANT INFLUENCES

There were several key influences on Smith's thinking. First and perhaps foremost was the general intellectual climate of his time. This was the period known as the Enlightenment. This intellectual movement was built upon two pillars: people's reasoning ability and the concept of the natural order. As indicated in Chapter 4, the scientific revolution associated with Newton established that order and harmony characterize the physical universe. Through systematic reasoning, people could discover not only these physical laws but also those that govern the society. Enlightenment thinkers therefore were optimists; they generally believed that human thought and energy could produce virtually unlimited progress.

Second, but definitely related, Smith was influenced by the physiocrats, particularly Quesnay and Turgot. He praised the physiocratic system "with all its imperfections" as "perhaps the nearest approximation to the truth that has yet been published on the subject of Political Economy." The physiocrats' attack on mercantilism and their proposals to remove trade barriers won his admiration. From these thinkers he drew the theme of wealth as "the consumable goods annually reproduced by the labour of society," the desirability of minimal government interference in the economy, and the concept of the circular process of production and distribution. He had planned to dedicate his *Wealth of Nations* to Quesnay, had the latter lived until the book was completed.

Francis Hutcheson, Smith's instructor at Glasgow College, was a third significant influence on Smith. Hutcheson felt that people themselves could discover what is ethically good—the will of God—by discovering the actions that serve the good of humankind.

Finally, Smith was influenced by his friend David Hume, who through his letters and personal conversations contributed to Smith's intellectual development and economic ideas.

THE THEORY OF MORAL SENTIMENTS

The Theory of Moral Sentiments was published seventeen years before *Wealth of Nations.* It went through six editions during Smith's lifetime, the last in the final year of his life, so it cannot be said that this book represented only his earlier ideas and *Wealth of Nations* his later ideas. The books stand side by side, presenting different but complementary facets of his thinking. *Moral Sentiments* discussed the moral forces that restrain selfishness and bind people together in a workable society; *Wealth of Nations* assumed the existence of a just society and showed how the individual is guided and limited by economic forces.

Moral Sentiments opens with a chapter titled "Of Sympathy." Sympathy, said Smith, overcomes even selfishness. Sympathy (or "empathy" or "fellow-feeling") interests us in the fortune of others and makes their happiness necessary to us. This is true in spite of the fact that we derive nothing from another's happiness except the pleasure of seeing it. Grief and joy in others arouse similar emotions in ourselves. If we place ourselves in another person's position, our imaginations can evoke sympathy for a situation of which the other person is unaware. Persons who go mad may laugh and sing and be entirely insensible of any misery. Thus the anguish we feel in observing such persons comes not from their suffering but from our awareness of their situation through our own powers of reason and judgment. This is sympathy. We sympathize even with the dead, because we imagine our own living souls in their inanimate bodies and then conceive what our emotions would be under such circumstances. The dread of death poisons our happiness but restrains the injustice of humankind; this dread afflicts and mortifies the individual, but it guards and protects society.

There are, according to Smith, unsocial and social passions. Examples of the former are hatred and resentment. With regard to such passions, we divide our sympathy between the person who feels them and the person who is the object of them, because the interests of these two individuals are contradictory. The social passions are generosity, humanity, kindness, compassion, and mutual friendship and esteem. These please indifferent spectators on almost every occasion, because their sympathy with the person who feels these passions coincides exactly with their concern for the person who is the object of them. We always have the strongest sympathy for the benevolent passions, because they appear in every respect agreeable to us.

Because people are disposed to identify more with our joy than with our sorrow, we parade our riches and conceal our poverty. Much of the toil and bustle of this world is undertaken not to supply our necessities but to gratify our vanity. We want to be observed, to be attended to, to be noticed with sympathy and approval. The rich glory in their riches because they draw upon them the attention of the world; the poor are ashamed of their poverty, which leaves them in obscurity. Smith stated:

> This disposition to admire, and almost to worship, the rich and powerful, and to despise, or, at least, to neglect, persons of poor and mean condition, though necessary both to establish and to maintain the distinction of ranks and the order of society, is, at the same time, the great and most universal cause of the corruption of our moral sentiments. . . .
>
> We frequently see the respectful attentions of the world more strongly directed toward the rich and the great, than toward the wise and the virtuous. We see frequently the vices and follies of the powerful much less despised than the poverty and weakness of the innocent. To deserve, to acquire, and to enjoy the respect and admiration of mankind, are the great objects of ambition and emulation. Two different roads are presented to us, equally leading to the attainment of this so much desired object; the one, by the study of wisdom and the practice of virtue; the other, by the acquisition of wealth and greatness. . . .
>
> To attain to this envied situation, the candidates for fortune too frequently abandon the paths of virtue; for unhappily, the road which leads to the one and that which leads to the other, lie sometimes in very opposite directions. But the ambitious man flatters himself that, in the splendid situation to which he advances, he will have so many

> means of commanding the respect and admiration of mankind, and will be enabled to act with such superior propriety and grace, that the lustre of his future conduct will entirely cover, or efface, the foulness of the steps by which he arrived at that elevation.[1]

People, said Smith, can exist only in society; they are exposed to mutual injuries, and they need one another's assistance. When the necessary assistance is reciprocally offered out of love, gratitude, friendship, and esteem, the society flourishes and is happy. Even if mutual love and affection are absent, however, the society may continue to exist because of its utility, though it will be less happy and agreeable. But it cannot exist among those who are at all times ready to hurt and injure one another. Therefore a system of justice is required.

> Beneficence, therefore, is less essential to the existence of society than justice. Society may subsist, though not in the most comfortable state, without beneficence; but the prevalence of injustice must utterly destroy it.[2]

Smith then considered the disturbing problem of our own selfishness and how it could be curbed and controlled.

> To the selfish and original passions of human nature, the loss or gain of a very small interest of our own appears to be of vastly more importance, excites a much more passionate joy or sorrow, a much more ardent desire or aversion, than the greatest concern of another with whom we have no particular connection. His interest, as long as they are surveyed from his station, can never be put into the balance with our own, can never restrain us from doing whatever may tend to promote our own, how ruinous soever to him. . . .
>
> Let us suppose that the great empire of China, with all its myriads of inhabitants, was suddenly swallowed up by an earthquake, and let us consider how a man of humanity in Europe, who had no sort of connection with that part of the world, would be affected upon receiving intelligence of this dreadful calamity. He would, I imagine, first of all express very strongly his sorrow for the misfortune of that unhappy people, he would make many melancholy reflections upon the precariousness of human life, and the vanity of all the labours of man, which could thus be annihilated in a moment. He would, too, perhaps, if he was a man of speculation, enter into many reasonings concerning the effects which this disaster might produce upon the commerce of Europe, and the trade and business of the world in general. And when all this fine philosophy was over, when all these humane sentiments had been once fairly expressed, he would pursue his business or his pleasure, take his repose or his diversion, with the same ease and tranquility as if no such accident had happened. The most frivolous disaster which could befall himself would occasion a more real disturbance. If he was to lose his little finger tomorrow, he would not sleep tonight; but provided he never saw them, he will snore with the most profound security over the ruin of a hundred millions of his brethren, and the destruction of that immense multitude seems plainly an object less interesting to him than this paltry misfortune of his own. . . . When we are always so much more deeply affected by whatever concerns ourselves than by whatever concerns

---

[1] Adam Smith, *The Theory of Moral Sentiments,* 10th ed. (London: Strahan and Preston, 1804), 119–122, 126–127. [Originally published in 1759.]

[2] Smith, *Moral Sentiments,* 175.

> other men; what is it which prompts the generous upon all occasions, and the mean upon many, to sacrifice their own interest to the greater interests of others? It is not the soft power of humanity, it is not that feeble spark of benevolence which Nature has lighted up in the human heart, that is thus capable of counteracting the strongest impulses of self-love. It is a stronger power, a more forcable motive, which exerts itself upon such occasions. It is reason, principle, conscience, the inhabitant of the breast, the man within, the great judge and arbiter of our conduct. . . .
>
> When the happiness or misery of others depends in any respect upon our conduct, we dare not, as self-love might suggest to us, prefer the interest of one to that of many. The man within immediately calls to us, that we value ourselves too much and other people too little, and that, by so doing, we render ourselves the proper object of the contempt and indignation of our brethren.[3]

Smith is saying that our moral faculties prescribe rules of conduct that restrain our actions of selfishness. These rules can be regarded as commands and laws of the deity. If we violate God's rules, we will be punished by the torments of inward shame and self-condemnation. If we obey God's wishes, we will be rewarded with tranquility of mind, contentment, and self-satisfaction. Thus God promotes the happiness of human beings.

In a passage that resembles a more famous one in the *Wealth of Nations,* Smith states that the rich tend to save and reinvest, therefore consuming little more than the workers. The rich inadvertently share the produce of all their improvements with the poorer workers, "though they mean only their own conveniency, though the sole end which they propose from the labours of all the thousands whom they employ be the gratification of their own vain and insatiable desires." He continued this idea with the following:

> [The business owners] . . . are led by an invisible hand to make nearly the same distribution of the necessaries of life which would have been made had the earth been divided into equal portions among all its inhabitants; and thus, without intending it, without knowing it, advance the interest of the society, and afford the means to the multiplication of the species.[4]

Both *Moral Sentiments* and *Wealth of Nations* reconcile the individual with the social interest through the principle of the invisible hand, or natural harmony, and the principle of natural liberty of the individual, or the right to justice. In *Moral Sentiments,* sympathy and benevolence restrain selfishness; in *Wealth of Nations,* competition channels economic self-interest toward the social good.

WEALTH OF NATIONS

Smith's 900-page economic treatise, *An Inquiry into the Nature and Causes of the Wealth of Nations,* appeared in 1776, the year of the American Revolution. This was the book that established him as one of the premier economic thinkers in the

---

[3] Smith, *Moral Sentiments,* 274–280.

[4] Smith, *Moral Sentiments,* 386.

history of economic thought. The insights contained in *Wealth of Nations* therefore require careful scrutiny.

The Division of Labor

The first chapter of *Wealth of Nations* is titled "Of the Division of Labour," an unfamiliar phrase in Smith's time. The first sentence reads as follows: "The greatest improvement in the productive powers of labour, and the greater part of the skill, dexterity, and judgment with which it is any where directed or applied, seem to have been the effects of the division of labour."[5]

Recognizing its importance to his overall theme, Smith applied this concept in a detailed description of a pin factory:

> To take an example, therefore, from a very trifling manufacture; but one in which the division of labour has been very often taken notice of, the trade of the pin-maker; a workman not educated to this business (which the division of labour had rendered a distinct trade), nor acquainted with the use of the machinery employed in it (to the invention of which the same division of labour has probably given occasion), could scarce, perhaps, with his utmost industry, make one pin in a day, and certainly could not make twenty. But in the way in which this business is now carried on, not only the whole work is a peculiar trade, but it is divided into a number of branches, of which the greater part are likewise peculiar trades. One man draws out the wire, another straights it, a third cuts it, a fourth points it, a fifth grinds it at the top for receiving the head; to make the head requires two or three distinct operations; to put it on, is a peculiar business, to whiten the pins is another; it is even a trade by itself to put them into the paper; and the important business of making a pin is, in this manner, divided into about eighteen distinct operations, which in some manufactories, are all performed by distinct hands, though in others the same man will sometimes perform two or three of them. I have seen a small manufactory of this kind where ten men only were employed, and where some of them consequently performed two or three distinct operations. But though they were poor, and therefore but indifferently accommodated with the necessary machinery, they could, when they exerted themselves, make among them about twelve pounds of pins in a day. There are in a pound upwards of four thousand pins of a middling size. Those ten persons, therefore, could make among them upwards of forty-eight thousand pins in a day. Each person, therefore, making a tenth part of forty-eight thousand pins might be considered as making four thousand eight hundred pins a day. But if they had all wrought separately and independently, and without any of them having been educated to this peculiar business, they certainly could not each of them have made twenty, perhaps not one pin in a day.[6]

The division of labor, said Smith, increases the quantity of output produced for three reasons. First, each worker develops increased dexterity in performing one single task repeatedly. Second, time is saved if the worker need not go from one kind of work to another. Third, machinery can be invented to increase productivity once tasks have

[5] Adam Smith, *An Inquiry into the Nature and Causes of the Wealth of Nations* (New York: G. P. Putnam's Sons, 1877), 19. [Originally published in 1776.]

[6] Smith, *Wealth of Nations,* 20.

been simplified and made routine through the division of labor. Notice the emphasis on manufacturing production and the productivity of labor here. Recall that mercantilists were concerned mainly with how the exchange of goods, once produced, could add to the nation's well-being. The physiocrats, on the other hand, focused on agricultural output. By beginning his book with a discussion of how the same number of workers could produce substantially more output by dividing their labor, Smith immediately made it clear that *Wealth of Nations* was a break from the prominent economic notions then in existence.[7]

The Harmony of Interests and Limited Government

Smith pointed out that participants in the economy tend to pursue their own personal interests. The person of business pursues profit: "It is not from the benevolence of the butcher, the brewer, or the baker, that we expect our dinner, but from their regard to their own interest."[8] The consumer looks to find the lowest price for a good, given its quality. The worker tries to find the highest pay, given the nonwage aspects of the job. But hidden within the apparent chaos of economic activity is a natural order. There is an invisible hand that channels self-interested behavior in such a way that the social good emerges. Listen to Smith:

> Every individual necessarily labours to render the annual revenue of the society as great as he can. He generally, indeed, neither intends to promote the public interest, nor knows how much he is promoting it. By preferring the support of domestic industry to that of foreign industry, he intends only his own security; and by directing that industry in such a manner as its produce may be of the greatest value, he intends only his own gain, and he is in this, as in many other cases, led by an invisible hand to promote an end which was no part of his intention. Nor is it always the worse for the society that it was no part of it. By pursuing his own interest he frequently promotes that of the society more effectually than when he really intends to promote it. I have never known much good done by those who affected to trade for the public good. It is an affectation, indeed, not very common among merchants, and very few words need be employed in dissuading them from it.[9]

The key to understanding Smith's invisible hand is the concept of competition. The action of each producer or merchant who is attempting to garner profit is restrained by the other producers or merchants who are likewise attempting to make money. Competition drives down the prices of goods and in so doing reduces the profit received by each seller. In situations in which there is initially only a single seller, extraordinary profit attracts new competitors who increase supply and erase the excessive profit. In an analogous way, employers compete with one another for the best workers, workers compete with each other for the best jobs, and consumers

[7] It is instructive to note that productivity in pin manufacturing has expanded greatly since Smith's time, a fact that would be of no surprise to Smith. In 1980 daily pin production in England was 800,000 pins per worker, a 167-fold increase over the 4,800 per worker estimated by Smith for his time. Most of this increase can be traced to improved capital equipment. See Clifford F. Pratten, "The Manufacture of Pins," *Journal of Economic Literature* 18 (March 1980): 93–96.

[8] Smith, *Wealth of Nations,* 27.

[9] Smith, *Wealth of Nations,* 354.

compete with one another for the right to consume products. Stated in contemporary economic terms, the result is that resources get allocated to their highest valued uses; economic efficiency prevails. Furthermore, because businesspersons save and invest—again out of their self-interest—capital accumulates and the economy grows. The pursuit of self-interest, restrained by competition, thus tends to produce Smith's social good—maximum output and economic growth.

This harmony of interests implies that intrusion by government into the economy is unneeded and undesirable. According to Smith, governments are wasteful, corrupt, inefficient, and the grantors of monopoly privileges to the detriment of the society as a whole.

> [E]very individual, it is evident, can, in his local situation judge [his own economic interest] much better than any statesman or lawgiver can do for him. The statesman, who should attempt to direct private people in what manner they ought to employ their capitals, would not only load himself with a most unnecessary attention, but assume an authority which could safely be trusted, not only to no single person, but to no council or senate whatever, and which would nowhere be so dangerous as in the hands of a man who had folly and presumption enough to fancy himself to exercise it.[10]

Smith's distrust of government is further reflected in his references to his own government, a regime that most historians judge to be one of the most honest and efficient ones in the world at that time.

> But though the profusion of government must, undoubtedly, have retarded the progress of England towards wealth and improvement, it has not been able to stop it. The annual produce of its land and labour is, undoubtedly, much greater at present than it was either at the restoration or at the revolution. The capital, therefore, annually employed in cultivating land, and in maintaining this labour, must likewise be much greater. In the midst of all the exactions of government, this capital has been silently and gradually accumulated by the private frugality and good conduct of individuals, by their universal, continual, and uninterrupted effort to better their own condition. It is this effort, protected by law and allowed by liberty to exert itself in the manner that is most advantageous, which has maintained the progress of England towards opulence and improvement in almost all the former times, and which, it is to be hoped, will do so in all future times. England, however, has never been blessed with a very parsimonious government, so parsimony has at no time been the characteristic virtue of its inhabitants. It is the highest impertinence and presumption, therefore, in kings and ministers, to pretend to watch over the economy of private people, and to restrain their expence, either by sumptuary laws, or by prohibiting the importation of foreign luxuries. They are themselves always, and without any exception, the greatest spendthrifts in the society. Let them look well after their own expence, and they may safely trust private people with theirs. If their own extravagance does not ruin the state, that of their subjects never will.[11]

---

[10] Smith, *Wealth of Nations,* 354.

[11] Smith, *Wealth of Nations,* 277–278.

Smith extended his belief in the harmony of interests and laissez-faire to international trade:

> The wealth of a neighboring nation, however, though dangerous in war and politics, is certainly advantageous in trade. In a state of hostility it may enable our enemies to maintain fleets and armies superior to our own; but in a state of peace and commerce it must likewise enable them to exchange with us to a greater value, and to afford a better market, either for the immediate produce of our own industry, or for whatever is purchased with that produce. As a rich man is likely to be a better customer to the industrious people in his neighborhood, than a poor, so is likewise a rich nation.[12]

In a direct attack on mercantilism, Smith argued that government should not interfere in international trade. Nations, like individuals and private families, should specialize in producing goods for which they have an advantage and trade for goods for which other nations have an advantage.

> To give the monopoly of the home market to the produce of domestic industry, in any particular art or manufacture, is in some measure to direct people in what manner they ought to employ their capitals, and must, in almost all cases, be either a useless or a harmful regulation. If the produce of domestic [industry] can be brought here as cheap as that of foreign industry, the regulation is evidently useless. If it cannot, it must generally be harmful. It is the maxim of every prudent master of a family, never to attempt to make at home what it will cost him more to make than to buy. The taylor does not attempt to make his own shoes, but buys them of the shoemaker. The shoemaker does not attempt to make his own clothes, but employs a taylor. The farmer attempts to make neither the one nor the other, but employs those artificers. All of them find it for their interest to employ their whole industry in a way in which they have some advantage over their neighbours, and to purchase with a part of its produce, or what is the same thing, with the price of a part of it, whatever else they have occasion for.
>
> What is prudence in the conduct of every private family, can scarce be folly in that of a great kingdom. If a foreign country can supply us with a commodity cheaper than we can make it, better buy it of them with some part of the produce of our own industry, employed in a way in which we have some advantage.[13]

Elsewhere Smith speaks about how foreign trade can promote greater division of labor by overcoming the narrowness of the home market. Exports also remove surplus products for which there is no demand at home and bring back products for which there is a domestic demand. He also condemned bounties (subsidies) on exports:

> Whatever extension of the foreign market can be occasioned by the bounty, must, in every particular year, be altogether at the expense of the home market; as every bushel of corn which is exported by means of the bounty, and which would not have been exported without the bounty, would have remained in the home market to increase the consumption, and to lower the price of that commodity. The corn bounty, it is to be observed, as well as is every other bounty upon exportation, imposes two different taxes upon the people; first, the tax which they are obliged to contribute, in order to pay the

[12] Smith, *Moral Sentiments,* 386.

[13] Smith, *Wealth of Nations,* 354–355.

> bounty; and secondly, the tax which arises from the advanced price of the commodity in the home market, and which, as the whole body of the people are purchasers of corn, must, in this particular commodity, be paid by the whole body of the people. On this particular commodity, therefore, this second tax is by much the heaviest of the two.[14]

It is tempting to label Smith as an advocate of laissez-faire; we have seen his dislike for government involvement in the economy. But unlike some of the more extreme advocates of that view, Smith did see a significant albeit limited role for the state. Specifically, he saw three major functions of government: (1) to protect society from foreign attack, (2) to establish the administration of justice, and (3) to erect and maintain the public works and institutions that private entrepreneurs cannot undertake profitably.

At scattered points throughout his book, Smith favors a variety of state interventions that fit into the preceding three categories or that enlarge the scope of acceptable government action. He thought the law should enforce the performance of contracts. Control over the issue of paper money by bankers is necessary even though it might be considered a violation of natural liberty. Legal control over interest rates is acceptable; but the rate should be somewhat (though not much) above the lowest market rate to promote sound projects rather than frivolous, wasteful, and speculative ones, which high interest rates might permit. Laws ensuring the security of the agricultural tenant are good because they promote improvements and investments in the land. Smith approved of patents and copyrights of limited duration. He even favored two kinds of protectionist tariffs: (1) those that protect a domestic industry essential to the national defense and (2) those that equalize the tax burden on a particular domestic industry by imposing a tariff on imports of that good. Otherwise, free trade is in order. But if free trade is to be introduced after a long period of protectionism, stated Smith, it should be done gradually to avoid suddenly throwing many people out of work and entrepreneurs into bankruptcy. Among the public works that a government should support are those that promote commerce and education, including canals, roads, harbors, post offices, coinage, schools, and churches. Free public education for the common people is essential as a way to, among other things, counteract the stultifying effects of the division of labor:

> The man whose whole life is spent in performing a few simple operations, of which the effects too are, perhaps, always the same, or very nearly the same, has no occasion to exert his understanding, or to exercise his invention in finding out expedients for removing difficulties which never occur. He naturally loses, therefore, the habit of such exertion, and generally becomes as stupid and ignorant as it is possible for a human creature to become. . . . His dexterity at his own particular trade seems, in this manner, to be acquired at the expense of his intellectual, social, and marital virtues. But in every improved and civilized society this is the state into which the labouring poor, that is, the great body of the people, must necessarily fall, unless government takes some pains to prevent it.[15]

To finance these government activities Smith recommended taxation. His four maxims for good taxes are as follows: First, taxes should be proportional to the revenue

[14] Smith, *Wealth of Nations,* 396.

[15] Smith, *Wealth of Nations,* 616–617.

enjoyed under the protection of the state. This was a drastic departure from the regressive taxes prevalent at the time. Second, taxes should be predictable and uniform as to the time of payment, the manner of payment, and the amount to be paid. Third, taxes should be levied at the time and in the manner most convenient to the contributor. Finally, taxes should be collected at minimum cost to the government.

THE ECONOMIC LAWS OF A COMPETITIVE ECONOMY

In analyzing the market economy, Smith developed several ideas that later economists classify as economic laws. We have already discussed three such ideas—the division of labor, the law of self-interested behavior, and the law of absolute advantage in international trade. Other laws include those dealing with value and price; wages, profits, and rents; the role of money and debt; and economic development.

Value

In a statement in which he poses the "water-diamond paradox," Smith observed that there are two kinds of value.

> The word VALUE, it is to be observed, has two different meanings, and sometimes expresses the utility of some particular object, and sometimes the power of purchasing other goods which the possession of that object conveys. The one may be called "value in use;" the other, "value in exchange." The things which have the greatest value in use have frequently little or no value in exchange; those which have the greatest value in exchange have frequently little or no use value. Nothing is more useful than water: but it will purchase scarce any thing; scarce any thing can be had in exchange for it. A diamond, on the contrary, has scarce any value in use; but a very great quantity of other goods may frequently be had in exchange for it.[16]

Smith did not solve the paradox of value. This had to await later economists who clearly saw the distinction between a good's total utility and its marginal utility. Smith directed his attention toward exchange value, the power that the possession of a commodity provides to purchase other goods—its "natural" price. The question of what determines the exchange value of a good, or simply its relative price, has been one of the central interests of economists since the market economy developed. Posed differently by later economists, "Do pearls have value because people dive for them, or do people dive for pearls because pearls have value?"

Smith basically answered that pearls (goods) have value because people need to dive to get them; that is, that the costs of production determine a good's exchange value or relative price. Smith first examined exchange value in an economy in "an early and rude" state, which he defined as one in which labor is the only scarce resource (capital and land are either nonexistent or are free goods). Then he developed a theory

[16] Smith, *Wealth of Nations,* 37.

of value for an advanced economy, in which capital had accumulated, and both it and land commanded a positive price.

Labor theory of value in a primitive society. Smith argued that in a society in which labor was the only resource, the relative value of a good would be determined by the amount of labor necessary to produce it. This is an elaboration of the "labor cost theory of value" first presented by Petty (Chapter 2). Smith wrote:

> In that early and rude state of society which precedes both the accumulation of stock [of capital] and the appropriation of land, the proportion between the quantities of labour necessary for acquiring different objects seems to be the only circumstance which can afford any rule for exchanging them for one another. If among a nation of hunters, for example, it usually costs twice the labour to kill a beaver which it does to kill a deer, one beaver should naturally exchange for or be worth two deer.[17]

This can be viewed in another way, according to Smith. The value of any commodity to a person who possesses it, *if he wishes to exchange it for other commodities,* "is equal to the quantity of labour which it enables him to purchase or command. Labour, therefore, is the real measure of the exchangeable value of all commodities." This version of Smith's value theory sometimes is referred to as his "labor commanded theory of value." Using Smith's deer-beaver example, suppose that it took two hours to trap a beaver and one hour to hunt and shoot a deer. What is the value in exchange of the beaver? Answer: two deer or two hours of labor. That is, a person could either exchange the beaver for two deer (because each deer requires only one hour of labor to harvest) or could use the beaver to command two hours of labor services. In a primitive economy, according to Smith, labor is both the source (labor cost theory) and the measure (labor commanded theory) of exchange value.

Value theory in an advanced economy. Smith realized that the growth of capital would invalidate a simple labor cost theory of value. To see why, imagine two commodities made from labor of equal skill. Suppose we add up all the time required to make each commodity, including the labor necessary to produce the raw materials and the labor required to make capital goods used in production. Let us assume that each commodity takes two hours to produce. But commodity *A*—say, potatoes grown where good land is abundant—requires virtually no capital to produce. Commodity *B*—cotton yarn—on the other hand requires intricate and expensive machinery in the production process. If one pound of cotton yarn and ten pounds of potatoes, each containing two hours of labor, could be exchanged for each other in the market, which would people produce? Potatoes, of course, because they could avoid investing large amounts of capital, and they would get the same return for their labor. This dilemma will again come up when we discuss labor theories of value presented by Ricardo and Marx.

In a society where capital investments and land resources become important, said Smith, goods will normally be exchanged for other goods, for money, or for

---

[17] Smith, *Wealth of Nations,* 51.

labor at a figure high enough to cover wages, rent, and profits. Moreover, profits will depend on the whole value of the capital advanced by the employer. The real value of commodities can no longer be measured by the labor contained in them. They still, however, can be measured by "the quantity of labour which they can, each of them, purchase or command." The quantity of labor that a commodity can buy exceeds the quantity of labor embodied in its production by the total profits and rents.

Demand, according to Smith, does not influence the value of commodities; the cost of production—wages, rent, and profits—are the only determinants of value in the long run. This is a reasonable proposition if we base it on Smith's implicit assumption that production will expand or shrink at constant cost per unit of output. Competition will drive prices down to costs, including a normal profit. Any increase in demand will not increase value because the costs of producing each unit of the commodity remain unchanged. However, if we assume either increasing or decreasing costs, Smith's principle becomes untenable. If the demand for the product rises, and if as the industry expands it produces the good at higher costs, then the long-run price (value) of the item will rise. If rising output results in falling costs per unit, then an increase in demand will cause the long-run price of the good to fall.

Market Price

Like Cantillon, Smith distinguished between the intrinsic or natural price of a good and its short-run market price. According to Smith, there are ordinary, or average, rates of wages, rent, and profit in every society or neighborhood. He called these the natural rates of each. When a commodity is sold for its natural price, there will be exactly enough revenue to pay these natural rates of wages, rent, and profit. The *natural price* is the long-run price below which the entrepreneurs no longer would continue to sell their goods. In a desperate situation they would sell goods more cheaply, but this would not continue. They could always go out of business or enter another line of production.

The actual price at which any commodity is sold is called its *market price*. It may be above, below, or exactly the same as its natural price. The market price depends on the aberrations of short-run supply and demand, and it will tend to fluctuate around the natural price. If it is above the natural price, more goods will come to market, depressing the price. If it is below the natural price, some productive factors will be withdrawn, the quantity supplied will fall, and the market price will rise toward the natural price. Restated, short-run supply and demand are not fundamental determinants of prices (exchange values), but instead simply cause fluctuations in market prices around the natural prices or values of commodities.

Smith also distinguished between the real price of a product and its money, or nominal price. Here he was simply echoing Hume and others by pointing out that increases in the stock of money in the society can cause the money price of products and resources to rise. Smith reminded the reader that the real price of a commodity is its command over labor, not its command over money. A doubling of prices will not increase a commodity's command over labor if wages also double.

Wages

Smith addressed three facets of wages: the aggregate level of wages, the growth of wages over time, and the wage structure. With respect to the first two, he employed the wages fund theory:

> It seldom happens that the person who tills the ground has wherewithal to maintain himself till he reaps the harvest. His maintenance is generally advanced to him from the stock of a master, the farmer who employs him, and who would have no interest to employ him, unless he was to share in the produce of his labour, or unless his stock was to be replaced to him with a profit.[18]

The wages fund idea implies that there is a stock of circulating capital out of which present wages are paid. This stock consists of the savings of the capitalists and is dependent on the revenue from previous production and sales. Consequently this fund is fixed in the short run, but it can be increased from one year to the next. As seen in Equation 5–1, the average annual wage depends on the size of the wages fund in relationship to the number of laborers.

$$\text{Average annual wage} = \frac{\text{Wages fund}}{\text{Number of laborers}} \tag{5-1}$$

The minimum rate of wages must be that which will enable a worker with a family to survive and perpetuate the labor supply. But when the demand for labor rises, wages will rise above this minimum. The rate of increase of national wealth determines the demand for labor and the wage by influencing the size of the wages fund. If the wealth of a country were great but stationary, population and thus labor supply would eventually multiply beyond the employment opportunities, and wages would fall. This explains Smith's emphasis on capital accumulation and economic growth. Smith applauded the rise of wages that accompanied economic growth, thus opposing the low wage doctrine of mercantilism.

> Is this improvement in the circumstances of the lower ranks of the people to be regarded as an advantage or as an inconveniency to the society? The answer seems at first sight abundantly plain. Servants, labourers and workmen of different kinds, make up the far greater part of every great political society. But what improves the circumstances of the greater part can never be regarded as an inconveniency to the whole. No society can surely be flourishing and happy, of which the far greater part of the members are poor and miserable. It is but equity, besides, that they who feed, clothe, and lodge the whole body of the people, should have such a share of the produce of their own labour as to be themselves tolerably well fed, cloathed and lodged.[19]

Refer to 5-1 PAST AS PROLOGUE

Furthermore, Smith said that high wages increase the health and strength of the workers, animating them to do their best work because high wages give hope for an improved life. In contemporary terms, this concept is known as *economies of high wages*, or *efficiency wages*.

---

[18] Smith, *Wealth of Nations*, 65.

[19] Smith, *Wealth of Nations*, 78.

5-1 PAST AS PROLOGUE

Adam Smith and Efficiency Wages

In *Wealth of Nations* Adam Smith linked the wages paid to workers with worker productivity. He stated:

> The liberal reward for labour, as it encourages the propagation, so it increases the industry of the common people. The wages of labour are the encouragement of industry, which like every other human quality, improves in proportion to the encouragement it receives. A plentiful subsistence increases the bodily strength of the labourer, and the comfortable hope of bettering his position, and of ending his days perhaps in ease and plenty, animates him to exert that strength to the utmost. Where wages are high, accordingly, we shall always find the workmen more active, diligent, and expeditious, than where they are low.*

Later, Smith pointed out that goldsmiths and jewelers receive high pay "on account of the precious metals with which they are entrusted."† Smith implies that their pay must be sufficient to dissuade them from running off with the gold and jewels!

Smith's association between pay and job performance has found its modern expression in a group of contemporary *efficiency wage theories.*‡ One set of these theories suggests that some employers pay higher than market-clearing wages—*efficiency wages*—to reduce employee shirking and labor turnover, both of which lower productivity and the firms' profitability. Workers avoid neglecting or evading work to ensure that they retain their high-paying jobs. This reduced shirking raises each worker's productivity. Also, workers receiving efficiency pay are less likely to quit their jobs to take new ones. The resulting reduced labor turnover increases the average productivity of the firm's workforce because of the lower proportion of new trainees.

Efficiency wage theories purportedly help explain frictional and cyclical unemployment. Efficiency wages attract more job applicants than employers want to hire. But rather than taking different jobs, these applicants choose to remain unemployed until jobs paying efficiency wages become available through normal attrition. Therefore, *wait unemployment* occurs, and frictional unemployment rises.

Also, efficiency wages may contribute to downward wage inflexibility. When the demand for their products falls, firms paying efficiency wages are reluctant to reduce pay—these wage cuts may not only encourage shirking but also could increase the number of job resignations. Included in this turnover are more-skilled workers in whom firms have invested large sums for job training. The increased shirking and higher turnover induced by wage cuts will dampen productivity.

Efficiency wages therefore may help channel declines in aggregate demand to declines in real output. That is, such wages may help explain why employment and output, rather than prices, typically fall during recessions. Facing slack demand,

5-1 PAST AS PROLOGUE (continued)

firms cut back production and lay off less-skilled, low-seniority employees rather than reduce efficiency wages for their still-employed workers. Thus, major declines in aggregate demand can produce recessions and widespread unemployment. Ironically, Smith's fragmentary ideas on efficiency wages have been extended in ways that question Smith's broader idea of the self-regulating, fully employed economy.

* Smith, *Wealth of Nations,* 78.

† Smith, *Wealth of Nations,* 96.

‡ George A. Akerlof and Janet L. Yellen, eds., summarize these theories in *Efficiency Wage Models of the Labor Market* (Cambridge: Cambridge University Press, 1986).

Smith also recognized that bargaining plays a role in the process through which wages are determined:

> What are the common wages of labour depends every where upon the contract usually made between [workers and employers] whose interest are by no means the same. The workmen desire to get as much, the masters to give as little as possible. The former are disposed to combine in order to raise, the latter in order to lower the wages of labour.[20]

Smith assumed a society with perfect liberty, a society in which all were free to choose and change their occupations. Consequently, he argued that the advantages and disadvantages of every type of employment would be equal or tend toward equality. Under this theory of "equalizing differences," or what contemporary economists call *compensating wage differentials,* actual wage rates for different jobs—the wage structure—would vary according to five factors.[21]

- Agreeableness of the occupation. Smith argued that the harder, the dirtier, the more disagreeable, and the more dangerous the work, the higher the wages paid, all else being equal.
- Cost of acquiring the necessary skills and knowledge. Smith pointed out that an expensive machine has to yield a return that covers both its initial cost and profits on the investment. Similarly, he said, people's income must pay for the cost of their education and training and still provide a rate of return on that

[20] Smith, *Wealth of Nations,* 66.

[21] Greg J. Duncan and Bertil Holmlund provide an interesting discussion of equalizing wage differences in their article, "Was Adam Smith Right After All? Another Test of the Theory of Compensating Wage Differentials," *Journal of Labor Economics* 1 (October 1983): 366–379. Also see R. F. Elliot and R. Sandy, "Adam Smith May Have Been Right After All: A New Approach to the Analysis of Compensating Differentials," *Economic Letters* 59 (April 1998): 127–131.

investment. Those jobs that require more education and training will pay higher wages than jobs for which no such education and training is necessary. This embryonic *theory of human capital* is yet another one of Smith's contributions to contemporary economic thought.[22]

- Regularity of employment. Smith held that the less regular the employment, the higher the wage. Because most workers prefer regular to irregular work, employers must pay a compensating wage premium to workers who face substantial unemployment and employment risk.
- Level of trust and responsibility. Those individuals, such as goldsmiths, jewelers, physicians, and attorneys, in whom much trust is given will receive higher pay than persons who have jobs that entail little responsibility and accountability to others.
- Probability or improbability of success. Those who are successful in occupations in which there is great risk of failure will receive higher wages than persons who are employed in occupations characterized by low failure rates.

Profit

Because every investment, said Smith, is exposed to the risk of loss, the lowest rate of profit must be high enough to compensate for such losses and still leave a surplus for the entrepreneur. The gross profit includes compensation for any loss *and* the surplus. Net or clear profit is the surplus alone or, in other words, the net revenue of the business.

In countries that are advancing rapidly in wealth, competition among businesses lowers the rate of profit.

> When the stocks of many rich merchants are turned into the same trade, their mutual competition naturally tends to lower its profit; and when there is an increase in stock in all the different trades carried on in the same society, the same competition must produce the same effect in all.[23]

The low rate of profit in rapidly advancing economies may offset high wages. Thriving countries therefore may sell goods as cheaply as their less fortunate neighbors who may have lower wage rates.

Classical economists generally did not treat interest as a separate distributive share; it was handled simply as a deduction from profit. The lowest rate of interest must be a little higher than the losses that sometimes occur through lending. The interest that the borrower can afford to pay is proportional to the net or clear profit only, and the rate must generally be lower than the rate of profit in order to induce borrowing. As profits rise, borrowers seek more money, and interest rates rise, and as profits fall, interest rates decline along with them.

[22] For an elaboration of this point, see Joseph J. Spengler, "Adam Smith on Human Capital," *American Economic Review* 67 (February 1977): 32–36.

[23] Smith, *Wealth of Nations,* 83.

Rent

Smith presents several theories of rent, none of which is complete or entirely accurate. Recall that David Hume had criticized Smith's statement that the rent of the land enters into the price of the goods produced from the land. But in that discussion Smith was examining the components of the price of commodities in general. When commodities are sold, the revenue received must cover wages, rent, and profit. Where else could rent come from?

But in other parts of his book, Smith adhered to Petty's (and Hume's) perspective that prices of agricultural produce determine the rent that the landlord can charge. Rent, said Smith, "is the price paid for the use of land." It is the highest price the tenant can afford to pay after deducting wages, the wear and tear of capital, average profits, and other expenses of production. Rent therefore is a surplus or a residual. High prices of produce yield high rents, and low prices yield low rents. In these statements Smith was on the same analytical path that Ricardo later took to develop his differential theory of rent. But Ricardo's theory rested on the law of diminishing returns, which Smith did not apply to agriculture. This is surprising because Petty and Turgot had stated the concept earlier, and Smith himself evidenced a rudimentary understanding of it in a discussion of the price of fish. Instead Smith traveled several other avenues in attempting to explain rent, including viewing it as a monopoly return and as an opportunity cost of using the land for one purpose rather than another. None of these attempts produced a complete, accurate, and unified theory of rent akin to the one that Ricardo later offered.

Taken together, Smith's views on wages, profits, and rents constitute an attempt to formulate a theory of the functional (factor share) distribution of income. Although incomplete, Smith's analysis certainly was far superior to the distribution theories presented by the physiocrats.

The Role of Money and Debt

Smith established the classical tradition of deemphasizing the importance of money. Money is vital as a means of payment, to be sure, because without it business would be shackled with a barter system. But money itself does not add to the output or the wealth of a society. It facilitates the circulation of goods, but the production of the latter is what constitutes the wealth. Although the gold and silver coins that circulate are a valuable part of the capital of the country, they are dead stock, producing nothing. This latter insight is a lasting contribution. Modern economists exclude money from their list of economic resources because, as such, money is not productive.

Smith's views on money clearly were in opposition to the mercantilists. If money's function is to serve as a medium of exchange, then paper money would do equally well as gold and silver and would require less effort to produce. Gold and silver, said Smith, are like a highway that enables goods to be brought to market without being itself productive. Banking would save the labor of producing gold by providing paper money, just as a highway through the air would save land that might be used for other things. As long as paper money was redeemable in gold, a small reserve of metal would be sufficient.

The mercantilists argued that consumable commodities are soon destroyed, whereas gold and silver are more durable. Smith asked if we would consider the exchange of English hardware for French wines to be disadvantageous: We could augment our supply of pots and pans to an incredible degree, but we need only a limited supply of utensils. So it is with coin. We require only a certain amount to circulate goods, and an excess is unnecessary and will be exported rather than left idle at home. Smith's refutation of the mercantilist overemphasis on gold, however, ignored the special qualities of this metal. By being a universally acceptable medium of exchange, it can, unlike pots and pans, be spent for any number of purposes.

Smith deplored the growth of public debt and the taxes required to pay interest on it. The view among many contemporary economists that an internally held debt is of little economic consequence because we owe it to ourselves was voiced in Smith's time. He answered in the following terms:

> In the payment of the interest of the public debt, it has been said, it is the right hand which pays the left. The money does not go out of the country. It is only a part of the revenue of one set of the inhabitants which is transferred to another; and the nation is not a farthing the poorer. This apology is founded altogether in the sophistry of the mercantile system.[24]

Smith was afraid that the heavy taxes needed to pay the interest on the debt would induce merchants and manufacturers to invest their capital abroad to the detriment of the home country. Writing before the development of recurring business cycles, he did not envision the contemporary practice of deficit spending as a way to counteract recessions. Assuming full employment, Smith felt that government debt and interest charges represented resources that might have been used productively by private individuals if government had not diverted them to its own purpose. With militaristic, corrupt, and wasteful governments far removed from the people and partial to special interests, such a diversion of resources would not serve society.

Smith gloomily forecasted that growing debts would in the long run probably ruin all the great nations of Europe. The British debt that troubled him so was 129 million British pounds, each pound today being worth approximately one and a half U.S. dollars.

Economic Development

Smith viewed the economy as a whole and emphasized growth and economic development. Figure 5-1 summarizes the various elements constituting Smith's theory of economic growth.

As indicated by the top two boxes in the diagram, Smith viewed the division of labor and the accumulation of capital as the primary factors that promote a growing stock of the nation's wealth. In this regard, first note arrow *a* that connects these two boxes. Smith discovered the truth that the division of labor makes possible the introduction of machinery to increase people's productivity. When an individual worker made a complete pair of shoes himself, there could be no single

[24] Smith, *Wealth of Nations,* 742.

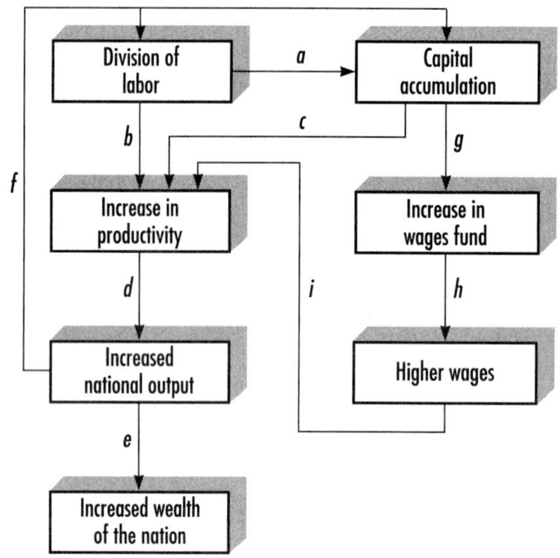

Figure 5-1 Smith's Theory of Economic Development
Smith contended that the division of labor spurs capital accumulation (arrow *a*) and that both work together to increase labor productivity (arrows *b* and *c*). The rise in labor productivity increases national output (arrow *d*), which widens the market and justifies further division of labor and capital accumulation (arrow *f*). As a result of the capital accumulation, the wages fund increases (arrow *g*) and wages rise (arrow *h*). Higher wages motivate further productivity growth (arrow *i*). The rise in national output increases the goods available for consumption, which, for Smith, constitutes the wealth of a nation (arrow e).

machine to do the work because it was too complicated. But when shoemaking was broken down into a series of simple operations, tools and machines could be invented to replace hand labor. Arrow *a* points only in one direction because Smith failed to recognize that new technology often creates new tools and equipment that themselves *cause* the division of labor. Smith saw the introduction of capital as mainly being a *result* of the division of labor.

Increased specialization of labor acts together with an enlargement of the capital stock to increase productivity (arrows *b* and *c*), which in turn increases national output (arrow *d*). Greater national output enables higher levels of consumption within the society, and the latter, according to Smith, constitutes a rise in the true wealth of the nation (arrow *e*).

As indicated by arrow *f*, the rise in national output widens or extends the market, permitting more labor specialization. It is for this reason, not the reason given by the mercantilists, that international trade is important, said Smith. The higher level of national output also permits the greater accumulation of capital, because not all the output consists of consumer goods. Notice that the cycle of events promoting economic growth then repeats itself.

And how does the common person fare in this process? Arrows *g* and *h* to the far right in Figure 5–1 provide Smith's answer. As we noted earlier in Equation 5–1, capital accumulation enlarges the wages fund from which labor is paid. If this increase in the wages fund exceeds the increase in the number of laborers, average wages rise. Furthermore, higher wages may enhance the health and vitality of workers, further increasing their productivity (arrow *i*). Later classical economists assumed that workers tend to receive the minimum of subsistence and therefore have nothing to gain from economic development. This clearly was not Smith's view!

Smith spoke of one additional factor that might give rise to increased productivity and growth. That was "a more proper distribution of employment." Here Smith made a distinction between productive labor, which adds value to a product, and unproductive labor, which does not. Productive employment stores up labor in a tangible commodity that has market value. Unproductive labor is that invested in offering services; it does not result in tangible goods available in the marketplace. According to Smith, unproductive laborers include kings, soldiers, churchmen, lawyers, doctors, writers, players, buffoons, musicians, opera singers, dancers, and so forth. Among the productive workers are "artificers, manufacturers and merchants."

To contemporary economists it seems odd that Smith would say that the person who gives a public piano recital is unproductive but that the one who prints the tickets is productive. To Smith it would have seemed strange that we, in our national income accounting, say that payments to servants, military personnel, advertisers, and physicians are additions to national income. He would have considered such expenditures as deductions. But to understand Smith, we should look at the problem through his approach to capital accumulation and economic growth. For him, material goods can be accumulated and therefore are a potential means of increasing wealth. Even consumer goods produced today can be used to support workers in the future, thereby enabling them to work and produce goods. But services are of the moment only; they vanish in the simultaneous acts of production and consumption, and they cannot be accumulated. From this point of view they are unproductive, although they indeed are useful. Nevertheless, in the modern meaning of the term *productive,* Smith obviously was in error. This error in thinking is still common today. For example, some observers of the contemporary scene appear to lament the secular decline in manufacturing employment relative to employment within the service industries. Often implicit to their concern is the idea that the service workers are not productive, whereas those who make goods are. Both sets of workers are productive; both are helping to produce something of value. The increase in the service proportion of domestic output simply reflects a relatively greater increase in society's demand for services than for manufactured goods.

Smith's confusion on productive versus unproductive labor does not, however, tarnish the splendor of his contribution to an understanding of the factors that lead to greater wealth of nations. Smith, writing at a time when investment and production were burgeoning, laid out an optimistic scenario for economic growth and human progress. Business cycles, overproduction, unemployment, and redundant capital still lay in the future. The harmony of interest prevailed, with a free and competitive market forcing each individual to serve society while he served himself. Smith was clearly more optimistic about the future than Thomas Malthus, the subject of our next chapter.

Questions for Study and Discussion

1. Briefly identify and state the significance of each of the following to the history of economic thought: the Enlightenment, *The Theory of Moral Sentiments, The Wealth of Nations,* invisible hand, division of labor, law of absolute advantage in international trade, water-diamond paradox, labor cost theory of value, labor commanded theory of value, wages fund doctrine, equalizing wage differences, widening of the market, and capital accumulation.
2. What is the general theme of Smith's *Theory of Moral Sentiments*? How does it relate to his *Wealth of Nations*?
3. How does the title of Smith's treatise on economics relate to his criticism of mercantilism? How does Smith define the wealth of a nation? What factors interact to cause increases in a nation's wealth?
4. State the major point that Smith was attempting to make through his description of a pin factory. How does his description relate to his call for public education?
5. In what respects might Smith rightly be called an advocate of laissez-faire? On what basis might one challenge this label?
6. How, according to Smith, can the social good result from the pursuit of individual self-interest? Relate this notion to the short- and long-run graphical models of a perfectly competitive product market. (Review a principles of economics text, if necessary.)
7. What, according to Smith, determines exchange value in a primitive economy? What determines exchange value in an advanced economy? Why did Smith use "labor commanded" rather than simply "money commanded" as a measure of the value of a good?
8. Is Smith's natural price determined by supply, demand, or both? Explain carefully.
9. Why does the division of labor give rise to capital accumulation (arrow *a* in Figure 5-1), according to Smith? Today's economists would also include a reverse arrow from capital accumulation to the division of labor. Explain, citing current examples.
10. What is an efficiency wage? What role do these wages play in Smith's theory of economic development? How might efficiency wages contribute to high rates of frictional unemployment and to recessions, according to modern efficiency wage theorists?
11. Discuss the following statement: Adam Smith appeals to many contemporary economists precisely because they, like Smith, have a conception of human nature that is entirely too narrow.

Selected Readings

Books

Blaug, Mark, ed. *Adam Smith.* Brookfield, VT: Edward Elgar, 1991.

Campbell, R. H., and A. S. Skinner. *Adam Smith.* New York: St. Martin's Press, 1982.

Fry, Michael, ed. *Adam Smith's Legacy.* London: Routledge, 1992.

Hollander, Samuel. *The Economics of Adam Smith.* Toronto: University of Toronto Press, 1973.

Rae, John. *Life of Adam Smith.* London: Macmillan, 1895.
Raphael, David D. *Adam Smith.* London: Oxford University Press, 1985.
Smith, Adam. *An Inquiry into the Nature and Causes of the Wealth of Nations.* New York: G. P. Putnam's Sons, 1877. [Originally published in 1776.]
———. *The Theory of Moral Sentiments.* Edited by D. D. Raphael and A. L. Macfie. Oxford: Clarendon Press, 1976. [Originally published in 1759.]

Journal Articles

Anspach, Ralph. "The Implications of the *Theory of Moral Sentiments* for Adam Smith's Economic Thought." *History of Political Economy* 4 (Spring 1972): 176–206.
Evensky, Jerry. "The Evolution of Adam Smith's Views on Political Economy." *History of Political Economy* 21 (Spring 1989): 123–145.
Gherity, James A. "Adam Smith and the Glasgow Merchants." *History of Political Economy* 24 (September 1992): 357–368.
Levy, David. "Adam Smith's Case for Usury Laws." *History of Political Economy* 19 (Fall 1987): 387–400.
Recktenwald, H. C. "An Adam Smith Renaissance *anno* 1976? The Bicentenary Output—A Reappraisal of His Scholarship." *Journal of Economic Literature* 16 (March 1978): 56–83.
Stigler, George G. "The Successes and Failures of Professor Smith." *Journal of Political Economy* 84 (December 1976): 1199–1214.
West, E. G. "The Burdens of Monopoly: Classical versus Neo-Classical." *Southern Economic Journal* 44 (April 1978): 829–845.
Willis, Kirk. "The Role in Parliament of the Economic Ideas of Adam Smith, 1776–1800." *History of Political Economy* 11 (Winter 1979): 505–544.

Chapter 6

THE CLASSICAL SCHOOL—THOMAS ROBERT MALTHUS

Thomas Robert Malthus (1766–1834) is an important, although controversial, figure in classical economic thought. He addressed such topics as population growth, the methodology of GDP accounting, value theory, diminishing returns, land rent, and aggregate demand. We shall discover, however, that several of his conclusions were at variance with those of other members of the classical school.

Malthus was born the son of Daniel Malthus, a distinguished country gentleman and a close friend of such leading intellects as Jean-Jacques Rousseau and David Hume. The younger Malthus graduated from Jesus College, Cambridge, in 1788 and was ordained a minister of the Church of England. His *An Essay on the Principle of Population* appeared in 1798, and an expanded version followed in 1803. This work established his enduring fame; it went through six editions during twenty-eight years. His most significant other volume was *Principles of Political Economy,* which was published in 1820.

Our discussion of Parson Malthus proceeds as follows. First, we look at the historical and intellectual setting that influenced his thinking. Then we examine Malthus's major economic theories, directing the spotlight toward his law of population and his theory of general gluts. Finally, we critically assess his contributions to economics.

HISTORICAL AND INTELLECTUAL SETTING

Historical Setting

Two major controversies in England attracted Malthus's attention during the period in which he wrote. The first was an increase in poverty and the controversy over what to do about it. By 1798 some of the negative effects of the industrial revolution as well as growing urbanization were beginning to appear. Unemployment and poverty were increasingly visible problems, creating calls for remedial treatment. The latest of a series of English "poor laws"—the Speenhamland law of 1795—liberalized previous law by providing that the poor should have a minimum income irrespective of their earnings. The law linked family income to the price of bread, and if earnings fell below the prescribed level, allowances would be granted to make up the difference. This system, which prevailed in most of the rural parishes and in some manufacturing districts, quite naturally sparked heated debate. Even though the ferment of the French Revolution was spreading outward to the poorer classes in other countries, the British propertied class denied any responsibility for poverty and actively opposed laws that would redistribute income.

The second controversy of note was over the so-called corn laws. These laws placed tariffs on imported grain and effectively placed a minimum price on grain imported to England from abroad. The landlords favored these tariffs but were under attack as people who, as Smith had phrased it, loved to reap where they had not sown. Their political power was under challenge by the rising merchant class, industrial capitalists, and followers of each group. Growing population, documented by the census of 1801, was placing pressure on England's food supply. As early as 1790, England had found it necessary to import food. But the Napoleonic wars had kept these imports relatively low, and the results were extremely high domestic grain prices and land rents. When Napoleon was captured in 1813, the English landlords, who dominated Parliament, became greatly concerned that a new surge of imported grain would depress the price of agricultural commodities and greatly reduce rental income. Thus they demanded that the existing price floors on imported grain be raised. The business interests, on the other hand, spoke against higher tariffs on grain and argued for the total repeal of the corn laws.

Intellectual Setting

Malthus's father, Daniel, subscribed to the optimistic belief of the perfectibility of people and society. This faith in progress was based in part on the works of Godwin and Condorcet. In a sense these thinkers were key influences on the younger Malthus in that he purposely set about to challenge their theories. A reasonably detailed discussion of their ideas therefore will be useful.

William Godwin (1756–1836), father-in-law of the poet Shelley, was a minister, novelist, and political philosopher who turned anarchist and atheist and whose doctrines resembled those of the French revolutionaries. In 1793 he published his influential book, *An Enquiry Concerning Political Justice and Its Influence on General Virtue and Happiness.* This work was among the first to formulate the philosophy of anarchism. Godwin was an extreme individualist who opposed not only all coercive action by the state but also collective action by the citizenry. He relied entirely on the voluntary goodwill and sense of justice of the individual guided by the ultimate rule of reason. According to Godwin, the human race is perfectible through a continuous advance toward higher rationality and increased well-being. Because a person's character depends on the social environment instead of being immutable and determined by heredity, a perfect society will produce perfect people. The major obstacles to progress, Godwin said, are private property, economic and political inequality, and the coercive state. Population growth, he believed, would not be a problem. When the population limit is reached, humanity will refuse to propagate itself further. Godwin later regretted that his optimism helped to evoke what he thought was the evil genius of Malthusian pessimism about overpopulation and the hopelessness of the human condition.

The Marquis de Condorcet (1743–1794), an eminent French mathematician of an aristocratic family, was elected to the Academy of Sciences at age twenty-six and to the French Academy at age thirty-nine. He was a skeptic in religion, a democrat in politics, a physiocrat in economics, and a pacifist. Among his friends were Turgot, Voltaire, Thomas Paine, Thomas Jefferson, Benjamin Franklin, and Adam Smith. After the outbreak of the French Revolution, which he greeted with enthusiasm, he and Paine founded the journal *Le Républicain*.

Condorcet favored universal suffrage for men and women. He vigorously opposed the provisions of the French Constitution in 1791 that established property qualifications for voting and election to office. The fierce party strife of the Revolution left him isolated, and his arrest was ordered in 1793. Friends hid him for nine months, after which he deliberately left his refuge in order not to endanger further the woman who sheltered him. After several days of wandering in disguise, he was arrested as a suspect and imprisoned; the morning after his arrest he was found dead from either exposure to the elements or from suicide by poison.

While in hiding, Condorcet wrote his most important work, *Sketch of the Intellectual Progress of Mankind*. In spite of his persecution by the Revolution he had welcomed so ardently, his theme was the idea of social progress based on three fundamental principles: (1) equality among nations, (2) equality of individuals within nations, and (3) the perfectibility of humanity. Ultimately the equality of nations, he wrote, would abolish war "as the greatest of plagues and as the greatest of crimes." A permanent league of nations would maintain peace and the independence of every nation. The equality of individuals would be won when differences in wealth, inheritance, and education were eliminated. Condorcet favored the wide distribution of property, social security, and universally free education for women and men. He believed that the natural order tends toward economic equality but that existing laws and institutions encourage inequalities. Equality would overcome the social evils of the day and lead to perfection. The only inequalities that should be permitted, he thought, are those that derive from natural abilities. Population would increase as a result of these beneficent reforms, but the food supply would increase even more rapidly. If the problem of subsistence could eventually no longer be solved this way, Condorcet favored birth control to limit the population.

These were the ideas against which young Malthus rebelled. The vices and misery that plague society are due, he said, not to evil human institutions but rather to the prolific fertility of the human race. The abolition of war for which Condorcet dreamed would merely remove one of the essential remedies of overpopulation. The French thinker's welfare programs would only counter a second factor limiting population—hunger. Godwin's egalitarian, communistic society would mean more food for the masses and therefore a more rapid growth of population. Godwin and Condorcet seemed to stand for all the excesses of the French Revolution, whereas Malthus's voice appealed to conservatives as a sane and able defense of the status quo.

MALTHUS'S POPULATION THEORY

In the first edition of *An Essay on the Principle of Population*, Malthus set out "to account for much of that poverty and misery observable among the lower classes of every nation." Here he presented his law of population: Population, when unchecked, increases geometrically; subsistence increases at best only arithmetically. That is, population tends to increase at the rate of 1, 2, 4, 8, 16, 32, and so forth, whereas the rate of increase of subsistence is at best only 1, 2, 3, 4, 5, 6.[1] He pointed to the rapid population growth in America (the India of its day) for proof of his propositions.

Some observers have argued that in 1798 Malthus was a rash young man, overly enthusiastic and too extreme in presenting his theory; in his more mature writing he supposedly relinquished the idea of mathematical ratios. Let us look, therefore, at *A Summary View of the Principle of Population,* which appeared in 1830. This work was published even later than the last edition of *An Essay on the Principle of Population.* In *A Summary View,* published thirty-two years after the first edition of the *Essay* and four years before his death, Malthus wrote:

> It may be safely asserted, therefore, that population, when unchecked, increases in a geometrical progression of such a nature as to double itself every twenty-five years. . . . If, setting out from a tolerably well peopled country such as England, France, Italy, or Germany, we were to suppose that, by great attention to agriculture, its produce could be permanently increased every twenty-five years by a quantity equal to that which it at present produces, it would be allowing a rate of increase decidedly beyond any probability of realization. . . . Yet this would be an arithmetical progression, and would fall short, beyond all comparison, of the natural increases of population in a geometrical progression.[2]

Malthus identified two types of checks to population growth: those he called "preventive checks" and those he called "positive checks."

Preventive Checks to Population

Preventive checks to population growth are those that reduce the *birth* rate. The preventive check of which Malthus approved was termed moral restraint. People who could not afford children should either postpone marriage or never marry; conduct before marriage should be strictly moral. The preventive check of which Malthus disapproved he called vice. This included prostitution and birth control, both of which reduced the birth rate. During Malthus's lifetime, the English reformer Francis Place and others were popularizing mechanical birth control. In 1817, in the appendix to the fifth edition of his *Essay,* Malthus wrote:

> Indeed I should always particularly reprobate any artificial and unnatural modes of checking population, both on account of their immorality and their tendency to remove a necessary stimulus to industry. If it were possible for each married couple to limit by a wish the number of their children, there is certainly reason to fear that the indolence [laziness] of the human race would be very greatly increased; and that neither the population of individual countries, nor of the whole earth, would ever reach its natural and proper extent.[3]

[1] Such geometric progressions advance with remarkable speed. The interested reader should use a pocket calculator or computer to confirm that, beginning with the number one, forty progressions produce roughly the number one trillion!

[2] Thomas Malthus, "A Summary View of the Principle of Population," in *Introduction to Malthus,* ed. D. V. Glass (London: Watts, 1953), 119. "A Summary View" first appeared as an article written for the 1830 edition of the *Encyclopedia Britannica.*

[3] Thomas Malthus, *An Essay on the Principle of Population,* 5th ed. (London: 1817), Appendix.

This reference to the laziness of the human race has led some scholars to wonder whether Malthus was more interested in maintaining a large, hard-working, poorly paid population than he was in establishing really effective measures of limiting human reproduction.

Positive Checks to Population

Malthus also recognized certain positive checks to population—those that increase the *death* rate. These were famine, misery, plague, and war. Malthus elevated these to the position of natural phenomena or laws; they were unfortunate evils required to limit the population. These positive checks represented punishments for people who had not practiced moral restraint. If the positive checks could somehow be overcome, people would face starvation because a rapidly growing population would press upon a food supply that at best would grow slowly. In the sixth edition of his *Essay,* Malthus pictured the positive checks to population as follows:

> It is an evident truth that, whatever the increase in the means of subsistence, the increase in population must be limited by it, at least after the food has once been divided into the smallest shares that will support life. All the children born, beyond what would be required to keep up the population to this level, must necessarily perish, unless room be made for them by the deaths of grown persons. . . . To act consistently therefore, we should facilitate, instead of foolishly and vainly endeavoring to impede, the operations of nature in producing this mortality; and if we dread the too frequent visitation of the horrid form of famine, we should sedulously encourage the other forms of destruction, which we compel nature to use. Instead of recommending cleanliness to the poor, we should encourage contrary habits. In our towns we should make the streets narrower, crowd more people into the houses, and court the return of the plague. In the country, we should build our villages near stagnant pools, and particularly encourage settlements in all marshy and unwholesome situations. But above all, we should reprobate specific remedies for ravaging diseases; and those benevolent, but much mistaken men, who have thought they were doing a service to mankind by projecting schemes for the total extirpation of particular disorders. If by these and similar means the annual mortality were increased . . . we might probably every one of us marry at the age of puberty, and yet few be absolutely starved.[4]

Policy Implication: The Poor Laws

According to Malthus, then, poverty and misery are the natural punishment for the failure by the "lower classes" to restrain their reproduction. From this view followed a highly significant policy conclusion: There must be no government relief for the poor. To give them aid would cause more children to survive, thereby

[4] Malthus, *An Essay,* 6th ed., 465–466. (Orig. pub. 1826.)

ultimately worsening the problem of hunger. This is the way he phrased it in the second edition of his *Essay* in 1803:

> A man who is born into a world already possessed, if he cannot get subsistence from his parents on whom he has a just demand, and if the society do not want his labour, has no claim of *right* to the smallest portion of food, and, in fact has no business to be where he is. At nature's mighty feast there is no vacant cover for him. She tells him to be gone, and will quickly execute her own orders, if he do not work upon the compassion of some of her guests. If these guests get up and make room for him, other intruders immediately appear demanding the same favour. . . . The order and harmony of the feast is disturbed, the plenty that before reigned is changed into scarcity.[5]

Malthus withdrew that harsh statement from later editions of the *Essay,* but he offered a specific proposal concerning the poor laws in the sixth edition:

> I have reflected much on the subject of the poor-laws, and hope therefore that I shall be excused in venturing to suggest a mode of their gradual abolition. . . . We are bound in justice and honour formally to disclaim the *right* of the poor to support.
>
> To this end, I should propose a regulation to be made, declaring that no child born from any marriage, taking place after the expiration of a year from the date of the law, and no illegitimate child born two years from the same date, should ever be entitled to parish assistance. . . .
>
> With regard to illegitimate children, after proper notice had been given, they should not be allowed to have any claim to parish assistance, but be left entirely to the support of private charity. If the parents desert their child, they ought to be made answerable for the crime. The infant is, comparatively speaking, of little value to society, as others will immediately supply its place.[6]

Some of Malthus's ideas were adopted in the harsh Poor Law Amendment of 1834. The law abolished all relief for able-bodied people outside workhouses. A man applying for relief had to pawn all his possessions and then enter a workhouse before assistance was granted; his wife and children either entered a workhouse or were sent to work in the cotton mills. In either case the family was broken up and treated harshly to discourage it from becoming a public charge. The workhouse was invested with a social stigma, and entering it imposed high psychological costs. The law aimed at making public assistance so unbearable that most people would rather starve quietly than submit to its indignities. This system was to be the basis of English poor law policy until early in the twentieth century. Malthus, who died four months after the Poor Law Amendment was passed, must have regarded it as a vindication of his idea that there is not room enough at nature's feast for everyone. No wonder Thomas Carlyle, after reading Malthus, called political economy the "dismal science"!

Malthus enjoyed a warm, close friendship with David Ricardo (Chapter 7) in spite of the fact that they disagreed about almost every aspect of political economy

---

[5] Malthus, *An Essay,* 2nd ed., 532.

[6] Malthus, *An Essay,* 6th ed., 485, 486, 487.

except Malthus's analysis of population.[7] Even on the latter topic Ricardo tended to be far less dogmatic. In this regard Ricardo wrote in *On the Principles of Political Economy and Taxation:*

> It has been calculated, that under favourable circumstances population may be doubled in twenty-five years; but under the same favourable circumstances, the whole capital of a country might possibly be doubled in a shorter period. In that case, wages during the whole period would have a tendency to rise, because the demand for labour would increase still faster than the supply.[8]

In a lighter vein Ricardo wrote the following in a letter:

> Now that I am a grandfather I should be puzzled, even with the assistance of Mr. Malthus, . . . to calculate the accelerated ratio at which my progeny is increasing. I am sure that it is neither arithmetical nor geometrical. I have some notion of consulting Mr. Owen [Chapter 9] on the best plan of establishing one of his villages for me and my descendants, admitting only in addition a sufficient number of families to prevent the necessity of celibacy.[9]

Malthus, who married at thirty-eight, had three children but no grandchildren. Ricardo, who married at twenty-one, had eight children and twenty-five grandchildren. Had this progression continued, England would have been overrun with Ricardos!

Refer to 6-1 PAST AS PROLOGUE

THE THEORY OF MARKET GLUTS

In Book II of *Principles of Political Economy,* Malthus developed his theory of the potential insufficiency of effective demand. He assumed that workers receive a subsistence wage. Employers hire these workers because they produce a value greater than that which they receive as wages; that is, the employer makes a profit. Because the workers cannot buy back the total output, others must. The profit cannot be returned to the workers in the form of higher wages because the disappearance of profits causes production and employment to cease. So who will purchase the extra output? Capitalists will buy some of it in the form of capital goods. Spending on capital goods stimulates production and employment, as does spending on consumption goods. But, said Malthus, the consumption by workers employed in productive labor can never alone furnish a sufficient motive to the continued accumulation and employment of capital. Investment is undertaken in the final analysis only to provide consumption, and if the final products cannot be sold, no investment will be forthcoming. To be sure, capitalists have the power to consume their profit, but it is not their habit to do so. The central

[7] Robert Dorfman chronicles this relationship in "Thomas Malthus and David Ricardo," *Journal of Economic Perspectives* 3 (Summer 1989): 153–164.

[8] David Ricardo, *The Works and Correspondence of David Ricardo,* ed. Piero Sraffa, 10 vols. (Cambridge: University Press, 1962), 1: 98. Copyrighted by and reprinted with the permission of the publisher.

[9] Ricardo, *Works and Correspondence,* 7: 177.

6-1 PAST AS PROLOGUE

Malthus, Sen, and Modern-Day Famine

In the 1980s and early 1990s the world was shocked to see television and newspaper pictures of emaciated, starving children in such African nations as Ethiopia, Sudan, and Somalia. An estimated one million people died from starvation in Africa in the mid-1980s. Before food aid arrived in Somalia in late 1992, severe famine had caused an estimated 2,000 deaths each day. Three hundred thousand Somali children under the age of five are believed to have died.

Population growth averaging about 3 percent annually has contributed to famine in parts of Africa. In some places, the food supply at times has simply not grown fast enough to accommodate the rising population. This was particularly true in the 1980s in sub-Saharan Africa, when per-capita income fell by 25 percent.

Population growth has also caused ecological degradation in parts of Africa. Forests that once served as barriers to the encroachment of the desert have been cut to expand crop production. The desert winds in turn have blown away the fragile topsoil, reducing the capacity of the land to grow crops and absorb rainfall and retain moisture. Because of the ultimate scarcity of wood caused by the deforestation, farmers increasingly have been forced to use animal dung as fuel rather than as fertilizer. All of these factors have hindered the growth of agricultural productivity.

However, famine in Africa has far more complex causes than simply population growth. Drought and warfare are even greater contributors to famine. Rainfall decreased dramatically in the sub-Saharan nations in the 1980s, and historically poor crop yields became even poorer. Drought is particularly catastrophic in Africa because of the lack of facilities available there for crop storage. Surplus grain from "wet" years is often lost to rats, insects, and spoilage and thus is unavailable during dry periods.

War has also caused famine in Africa. Regional rebellion and prolonged civil wars have devastated several African nations. The 1992 Somalian famine mainly resulted from a violent civil war that destroyed the nation's power plants and major cities. More than one million Somalis fled the country for refugee camps in neighboring, but equally impoverished, African nations. Devastating battles between rebels and Nigerian-led troops displaced thousands of Sierra Leoneans from their homes in 1999, causing widespread hunger. Armed conflicts in Africa have destroyed infrastructure, diverted needed resources to military use, and hindered

object of their lives is to amass a fortune, and they are too busy in the counting-house to consume it all:

> There must therefore be a considerable class of persons who have both the will and power to consume more material wealth than they produce, or the mercantile classes could not continue profitably to produce so much more than they consume. In this class the landlords no doubt stand pre-eminent; but if they were not assisted by the great mass of individuals engaged in personal services, whom they maintain, their own

relief efforts. Governments have frequently denied food aid to areas controlled by antigovernment forces. Also, the military has often secretly or brazenly diverted donated food and medical supplies.

Thus, the ghost of Malthus still haunts parts of Africa. In some relatively recent years, the vagaries of nature and the realities of war have joined with population growth to threaten the survival of many of its inhabitants.

Amartya Sen (Chapter 20), while acknowledging these Malthusian causes of famine, offers additional explanations, including the notion that Malthus himself is an unwitting accomplice in the promotion of hunger and starvation. According to Sen, Malthus's population theory oversimplified the problem by putting all of the attention on food output per capita, a mistake repeated by modern policymakers and analysts. As long as per-capita food output rises or remains constant, no imminent threat of famine is perceived ("Malthusian optimism"), and remedial action may come too late. What Malthus failed to address in *Essay** was what Sen refers to as the "acquirement problem," the processes by which people obtain food and other commodities. Food can be acquired either through direct production (farmers growing their own crops) or indirectly through the production of income that is converted into food through exchange (wage laborers). If a segment of the population lacks adequate income to purchase food, famine may result even though food is available.

Sen separates famines into two broad categories: boom famines and slump famines. In a boom famine (Bengal famine of 1943), a large segment of the population fails to benefit from rapid but uneven economic growth. They suffer a decline in real income (due either to falling nominal wages or inflation), and their worsening absolute and relative position prevents them from competing successfully for available food. Slump famines result from an economic downturn, but not necessarily in the production of food.

According to Sen, famine prevention and relief efforts often fail because of overreliance on the Malthusian warning signal of food output per capita. By neglecting the processes by which people acquire food, famines occur in places where food is, if not abundant, at least adequate to sustain the population.[†]

*According to Sen, Malthus addresses the acquirement problem, but in one of his lesser read works, *An Investigation of the Cause of the Present High Price of Provisions* (1800).

†Amartya Sen, "Food, Economics, and Entitlements," *The Political Economy of Hunger,* eds. Jean Dreze, Amartya Sen, and Athar Hussain. (Oxford: Oxford University Press, 1995): 50–68; see also Amartya Sen, *Poverty and Famines.* (Oxford: Oxford University Press, 1981).

consumption would of itself be insufficient to keep up and increase the value of the produce, and enable the increase of its quantity more than to counterbalance the fall of its price. Nor could the capitalist in that case continue with effect the same habits of savings.[10]

[10] Thomas Malthus, *Principles of Political Economy,* 2nd ed. (1951; reprint, New York: A. M. Kelley, 1986), 400. (2nd ed. org. pub. 1836; 1st ed. org. pub. 1820.) Reprinted by permission of the publisher.

The Need for Unproductive Consumption

Spending by landlords is essential to avoid a glut of goods on the market that in turn would produce economic stagnation.[11] Rent, said Malthus, is a surplus based on the difference between the price of agricultural produce and the costs of production (wages, interest, and profits). Its expenditure therefore adds to effective demand without adding to the cost of production. The other forms of income—wages, interest, and profit—increase purchasing power but also raise production costs, and costs must be kept down if a nation is to maintain its competitive position in world markets.

Policy Implications

This theory of market gluts and the need for unproductive consumption had several policy implications. The most important one, according to Malthus, was that the corn laws must be retained. These tariffs on imported grain enrich the landlords and consequently promote unproductive consumption. The latter is necessary to avoid economic stagnation.

Although Malthus favored unproductive consumption by landlords, including the hiring of large numbers of menial servants, he opposed excessive unproductive consumption financed by the government. Government officials, soldiers, sailors, and those who live from interest on the national debt necessitate higher taxes, which might impede the increase of wealth. Society should consider private property sacred, and it should not allow the redistribution of wealth through excessive taxation. Nor is a growing government debt desirable, because the inflation it promotes will hurt those on fixed incomes.

In his *Principles of Political Economy,* Malthus implied that war offered another stimulus that could eliminate gluts:

> England and America . . . suffered the least by the [Napoleonic wars], or rather were enriched by [them], and they are now suffering the most by the peace. It is certainly a very unfortunate circumstance that any period should ever have occurred in which peace should appear to have been, in so marked a manner, connected with distress.[12]

For times of acute economic distress, Malthus recommended government spending on public works:

> It is also of importance to know that, in our endeavors to assist the working classes in a period like the present, it is desirable to employ them in those kinds of labour, the results of which do not come for sale into the market, such as roads and public works. The objection to employing a large sum in this way, raised by taxes, would not be its tendency to diminish the capital employed in productive labour; because this, to a certain extent is exactly what is wanted; but it might, perhaps, have the effect of concealing too

---

[11] Even so, said Malthus, a general glut may occur if the wants of consumers become satiated. See Salim Rashid, "Malthus' Model of General Gluts," *History of Political Economy* 9 (Fall 1977): 55–79.

[12] Malthus, *Political Economy,* 2nd ed., 422.

> much the failure of the national demand for labour, and prevent the population from gradually accommodating itself to a reduced demand. This however might be, in a considerable degree, corrected by the [low] wages given.[13]

We will discover, in Chapter 7, that Ricardo denied the possibility of long-term unemployment, responding to Malthus as follows:

> A body of unproductive labourers are just as necessary and as useful with a view to future production, as a fire, which should consume in the manufacturers warehouse the goods which those unproductive labourers would otherwise consume. . . . In what way can a man's consuming my produce, without making me any return whatever, enable me to make a fortune? I should think my fortune would be more likely to be made, if the consumer of my produce returned me an equivalent value.[14]

ASSESSMENT OF MALTHUS'S CONTRIBUTIONS

Malthus's theories were well received by wealthy landlords, a group that had long been dominant but was rapidly losing its political power and social prestige. His population theory absolved the wealthy from any responsibility for poverty; the poor had only themselves to blame for their position. He opposed the poor laws, which, if abolished, would have effectively reduced taxes on property at a time when property ownership was concentrated among relatively few people. His defense of the corn laws and unproductive consumption likewise served the interests of landlords. It was with some amazement that he wrote in his *Principles of Political Economy:* "It is somewhat singular that Mr. Ricardo, a considerable receiver of rents, should have so much underrated their national importance; while I, who never received, nor expect to receive any, should probably be accused of overrating their importance."[15]

Malthus did indeed overrate the significance of rents and spending by the landlords. His distinction between productive and unproductive consumption is inaccurate. Spending by all groups in the economy is productive in the sense that such spending creates a demand for goods and services and therefore causes them to be produced. Nevertheless, the theory of gluts did show an awareness of the potential problem of unemployment resulting from a lack of aggregate demand. In this respect it was a significant insight into what history has shown to be an occasional problem of a capitalistic economy. This insight was acknowledged and greatly expanded by Keynes in the 1930s.

Not only did Malthus overrate the significance of rents, but also he overrated the rate of growth of population relative to that of subsistence. The widespread poverty of his day required an explanation, and Malthus developed what appeared to be a plausible theory. But subsequent evidence has not supported the predictions of the theory. Although world population has increased dramatically—from about

---

[13] Malthus, *Political Economy,* 2nd ed., 429–430.

[14] Ricardo, *Works and Correspondence,* 2: 421–422.

[15] Malthus, *Political Economy,* 2nd ed., 216–217n.

one billion in 1800 to three billion in 1960 to six billion in 2000—it has done so at a far lower than twenty-five-year geometric progression. And, more important, the world's output has increased even faster. The result has been growth of per-capita world output and income.

Malthus developed a theory of diminishing returns in agriculture based on a view that the improvements made to a fixed amount of land would provide increasingly smaller rises in yields: "When acre has been added to acre till all the fertile land is occupied, the yearly increase of food must depend upon the melioration [improvement] of the land already in possession. This is a fund which, from the nature of all soils, instead of increasing, must be gradually diminishing."[16] But Malthus underestimated the possibilities of enlarging agricultural production. Today, as a result of technological innovation and capital accumulation, fewer workers in agriculture produce more food than ever. Rather than being driven to a biological subsistence, wages in the industrial economies have risen sharply since the period during which Malthus wrote.

As to population growth, Malthus tended to assert and moralize rather than to analyze, and he failed to recognize that views of morality are subject to change. (For example, lending at interest was once considered a sin.) Malthus ruled out birth control as a vice, and as a result, his population predictions did not allow for the reality of the widespread use of contraception. Indeed, increases in national output may *reduce* the birth rate in those societies in which methods for controlling births are widely available. The opportunity costs of having children rise when real hourly wages increase, and many people respond by limiting the size of their families.[17]

In recognizing these criticisms, however, we must also emphasize that Malthus's population theory still has considerable relevance in today's world. Seventy percent of the world's inhabitants live in the developing nations, and nine out of every ten people added to the world population during the 2000–2010 period will live in these countries. Twenty percent of the world's population lives on less than $1 per day. For some of the world's poorer inhabitants the Malthusian predictions of famine, malnutrition, and disease are all too real. But today we view these realities as production and distribution problems demanding solutions rather than as inevitable and largely unavoidable results of natural law.

Finally, it must be acknowledged that population and market gluts were but two of several topics of political economy of interest to Malthus. His formulation of value theory is particularly noteworthy. Although fragmentary, it was based on both supply and demand rather than simply on the costs of production. In a letter to Ricardo, Malthus wrote:

> [W]hen you reject the consideration of demand and supply in the price of commodities and refer only to the means of supply, you appear to me to look only at half of your subject. No wealth can exist unless the demand, or the estimation in which the commodity is held exceeds the cost of production: and with regard to a vast mass of

[16] Malthus, *An Essay,* 6th ed., 4.

[17] The theory underlying this tendency can be found in Gary Becker, *The Economic Approach to Human Behavior* (Chicago: University of Chicago Press, 1976), part 6.

> commodities does not demand actually determine the cost? How is the price of corn, and the quality of the last land taken into cultivation determined but by the state of population and the demand? How is the price of metals determined?[18]

Ricardo countered that he had fully recognized the role of demand in determining the value of goods that are not reproducible (in today's language, goods for which supply is perfectly inelastic). For reproducible goods, said Ricardo, the long-term cost of production will determine the value of the commodity. Malthus, however, was "on the trail of a theory not fully expressed until the end of the century, the neoclassical theory of value."[19]

Questions for Study and Discussion

1. Briefly identify and state the significance of each of the following to the history of economic thought: Malthus, *An Essay on the Principle of Population*, Speenhamland law, Godwin, Condorcet, preventive checks to population, positive checks to population, the poor laws, theory of market gluts, unproductive consumption, and corn laws.
2. Compare and contrast the implication for wages of the theory of population presented by Thomas Malthus with the wage theory provided by Adam Smith (Chapter 5).
3. Succinctly summarize Malthus's theory of population and relate it to his position on the poor laws. How does this theory relate to his notion of diminishing returns associated with "meliorations" to the soil?
4. How does Malthus's theory of population help explain famines? In what ways does it fall short or even distort understanding so as to contribute to modern famines?
5. What, according to Malthus, are market gluts? How and why do they come about? How can they be avoided? What is the significance of the corn laws to all of this?
6. Explain the following: Although the Malthusian theory of gluts was the first attempt to explain unemployment, it was not a theory of business cycles.
7. Illustrate, using a contemporary supply and demand graph, the following: Malthus's population theory implied a subsistence wage. Increases in labor demand would be fully offset by eventual increases in labor supply. Explain.
8. Contrast Malthus's reasons for favoring tariffs on imported grain with the reasons cited earlier by the mercantilists.
9. Debate the following: The way to improve living standards in poor countries is not to reduce population growth but rather to promote growth of output. Once real output and wages begin to rise, the population growth rate will fall.
10. Relate the following statement by Mark Blaug to Malthus's population theory: "If we are given a prediction which is not falsifiable within a specific period of time, we can never falsify the theory because at every moment of time we will be told to 'wait and see.'"

---

[18] Ricardo, *Works and Correspondence,* 8: 286.

[19] Everett J. Burtt Jr., *Social Perspectives in the History of Economic Theory* (New York: St. Martin's, 1972), 87.

Selected Readings

Books

Blaug, Mark, ed. *Robert Malthus and John Stuart Mill.* Brookfield, VT: Edward Elgar, 1991.

Godwin, William. *An Enquiry Concerning Political Justice and Its Influence on General Virtue and Happiness.* 2 vols. New York: Knopf, 1926. [Originally published in 1793.]

Hollander, Samuel. *Economics of Thomas Robert Malthus.* Toronto: Toronto University Press, 1997.

Malthus, Thomas R. *An Essay on the Principle of Population.* London: 1798.

———. *An Inquiry into the Nature and Progress of Rent.* Edited by Jacob H. Hollander. Baltimore, MD: Johns Hopkins Press, 1903. [Originally published in 1815.]

———. *Principles of Political Economy.* 2d ed. New York: Kelley, 1951. [Second edition originally published in 1836; first edition published in 1820.]

Oser, Jacob. *Must Men Starve? The Malthusian Controversy.* London: Cape, 1956; New York: Abelard-Schuman, 1957.

Schapiro, J. Salwyn. *Condorcet and the Rise of Liberalism.* New York: Harcourt, Brace & World, 1934.

Smith, Kenneth. *The Malthusian Controversy.* London: Routledge and Kegan Paul, 1951.

Winch, Donald. *Malthus.* New York: Oxford University Press, 1987.

Journal Articles

Bonar, James, C. R. Fay, and J. M. Keynes. "A Commemoration of Thomas Robert Malthus." *Economic Journal* 45 (June 1935): 221–234.

Dorfman, Robert. "Thomas Malthus and David Ricardo." *Journal of Economic Perspectives* 3 (Summer 1989): 153–164.

Gilbert, G. N. "Economic Growth and the Poor in Malthus' *Essay on Population.*" *History of Political Economy* 12 (Spring 1980): 83–96.

Hollander, Samuel. "Malthus's Vision of the Population Problem in the *Essay on Population.*" *Journal of History of Economic Thought* 12 (Spring 1990): 1–26.

Levy, David. "Some Normative Aspects of the Malthusian Controversy." *History of Political Economy* 10 (Summer 1978): 271–285.

Minisymposium: Malthus at 200 (papers and comments by Neil de Marchi, A. M. C. Waterman, Samuel Hollander, John Pullen, and Donald Winch). *History of Political Economy* 30 (Summer 1998): 289–364.

Pullen, J. M. "Malthus on Agricultural Protection: An Alternative View." *History of Political Economy* 27 (Fall 1995): 517–530.

Rashid, Salim. "Malthus' Model of General Gluts." *History of Political Economy* 9 (Fall 1977): 366–383.

———. "Malthus' *Principles* and British Economic Thought, 1820–35." *History of Political Economy* 13 (Spring 1981): 55–79.

Chapter 7

THE CLASSICAL SCHOOL—DAVID RICARDO

Although Smith was the founder of the classical school and set its dominant tone, David Ricardo (1772–1823), a contemporary of Malthus, was the leading figure in further developing the ideas of the school. Ricardo demonstrated the possibilities of using the abstract method of reasoning to formulate economic theories. He also extended the scope of economic inquiry to the distribution of income. Around Ricardo rallied an ardent band of scholars who enthusiastically disseminated his ideas. These followers amended and extended his theories, moving them toward neoclassical positions.

After presenting important details of Ricardo's life, we discuss his views on the currency question in England. Then we develop his theory of land rent and related theory of diminishing returns. These two theories are relevant to the two important topics that follow: first, the theory of exchange value, and second, the theory of the distribution of income. The chapter continues with sections on Ricardo's law of comparative advantage, his views on the possibility of unemployment, and a brief assessment of his overall contribution.

BIOGRAPHICAL DETAILS

Ricardo, the third of seventeen children, was born of Jewish immigrants who had migrated to England from Holland. He was trained for his father's stock brokerage business, which he entered at the age of fourteen. At twenty-one he married a Quaker woman and left the Jewish faith to become a Unitarian. As a result of this act, his father disowned him, although they later reconciled. Using funds advanced by bankers who knew and trusted him, young Ricardo entered the stock market on his own. In a few years he had accumulated more wealth than his father, and at forty-three he retired from business. Nevertheless, he continued to look after his business interests for the rest of his life. Ricardo died when he was fifty-one from an ear infection, leaving a large fortune, two-thirds of it in landed estates and mortgages.

Ricardo's principles for making money on the stock exchange may be as interesting to many as his abstract economic theorizing. He said that he had made all his money by observing that people generally exaggerated the importance of events. If there was reason for a small advance in stock values, he bought because of his certainty that an unreasonable advance would occur. When stocks were falling, he sold on the conviction that alarm and panic would produce a decline not warranted by circumstances.

Ricardo also credited his financial success to his contentment with small profits, never holding commodities or securities too long when small profits could be made quickly. Ricardo had his eye on every new road, bank, or other joint stock enterprise, and when he deemed the prospect of success to be fair he bought shares. The shares of new undertakings, he claimed, soon rose above their long-run price, and he sold quickly in order to invest elsewhere. His high reputation as a judicious speculator led others to buy when he bought. He was quoted as saying, "In this state of things, it must be manifest that I may often have created that very demand which enabled me to dispose of the article purchased, with a small profit, only a very short time afterward."

As a person of firm conviction and high principles, Ricardo frequently advocated policies that conflicted with his own personal interests. He argued against the excessive gains of the Bank of England, although he was a stockholder of that institution. He defended the cause of investors in British government bonds when he had ceased to be an investor himself. Even after Ricardo had become a large landowner, he put forward theories that, according to his critics, would ruin the landlords. Parliamentary reform, which he supported with enthusiasm, would have deprived him of the seat he had bought representing an Irish constituency in which he had never lived nor visited. He advocated a levy on capital to liquidate the national debt although he was one of the richest people in England. Other reforms that he favored included voting by secret ballot, legalizing the right to discuss religious opinions freely, reducing the number of offenses subject to capital punishment, abolishing flogging as a court punishment, and ending discriminatory laws against Roman Catholics. Only after Ricardo's death was an act passed (in 1829) that gave Catholics the right to sit in Parliament and to hold some public offices.

Ricardo, without any formal schooling beyond the age of fourteen, turned to the systematic study of political economy rather late in life. During his spare time in his youth, Ricardo worked rather diligently at physical science and mathematics. When he was twenty-seven he came across Smith's *Wealth of Nations,* and it was this fortunate event that fixed his attention on economics. His first "published work"—a letter to a newspaper on currency problems—did not appear until ten years later. Within the next decade, however, he had completed his major works, including his *Principles of Political Economy and Taxation* (1817). Writing was difficult and painful for Ricardo, despite his keen analytical mind. "Oh that I were capable of writing a book!" he wrote to his friend James Mill. Mill encouraged Ricardo, writing, "For as you are already the best *thinker* on political economy, I am resolved you shall also be the best writer." Mill read and criticized Ricardo's writing, always driving him to produce when Ricardo felt that writing was impossible for him.

Ricardo was an outstanding example of a deductive thinker. He began with basic premises and then used logic to deduce generalizations. Ricardo called his broad generalizations economic laws, and he considered their operation to be as valid in economics as are the laws of physics in the natural sciences. For example, there were laws that regulated the distribution of precious metals throughout the world, laws that governed the international exchange of goods, laws that regulated the distribution of income, and so forth. Although Ricardo was very well acquainted with the facts of business and economic life through his personal experience, he did not use the inductive method of reasoning. That is, he did not gather historical or experimental data; nor did he reason from the part to the whole, from particulars to the general, from facts to theories. Instead he formulated sweeping laws and then sometimes drew upon facts to illustrate their operation. His tendency to use restrictive assumptions to bolster his arguments was referred to by Schumpeter (Chapter 23) as the "Ricardian vice." Yet the theoretical questions that interested Ricardo had a significant bearing on the practical problems of both his own and later times.

THE CURRENCY QUESTION

In 1797 in the midst of more than two decades of warfare between England and France, a panic and a run on gold dangerously depleted the reserves in the Bank of England. When the government suspended cash payments, England found itself on an irredeemable paper standard. In other words, people holding paper money could not redeem it for gold. The price of gold gradually rose from its mint parity price of about 3.17 pound sterling per ounce to a market price of 5.10 in 1813. This was accompanied by a general price inflation. Instead of gold being brought to the mint where only 3.17 pound sterling could be received, it was sold privately in the domestic or foreign market. Worried citizens wondered why the market price of gold was rising and how it could be stopped.

Because Ricardo had transactions with the Bank of England involving great sums of money, he began to reflect and write on this topic. His conclusion on this so-called currency question reaffirmed the quantity theory of money noted previously by Locke, Hume, and Smith. The bank, said Ricardo, was overissuing paper currency because it no longer was checked by the requirement to pay gold on demand. Printing and lending bank notes were profitable operations that helped finance government spending but were hardly conducive to stable prices for gold or commodities. It was analogous to the feudal practice of clipping coins whereby, as a way to finance their excessive spending, princes would shave gold from the coins that came through the treasury. By increasing the money supply, the Bank of England drove up prices of commodities, thereby reducing the value of the currency.

The problem, according to Ricardo, was not the high price of gold but rather the low value of the pound sterling. Put simply, more pounds were now necessary to buy an ounce of gold. The remedy that Ricardo called for was a return to the gold standard. Then, if the price of gold in the market rose, currency would be redeemed for gold at the bank at the mint price. Every overissue of bank notes would be automatically canceled by the flow of paper to the bank. The restoration of the gold standard would curb inflation.

The directors of the Bank of England and their friends argued that the market price of gold rose because of its increased scarcity; gold, not paper, had changed value. If the gold standard were restored, every gold guinea would be withdrawn from the bank and sold abroad.

Ricardo replied that there was evidence that it was paper, not gold, that had changed value. An ounce of gold would buy as many commodities as it had previously. But the paper that gold represented at the mint parity price would buy far less, because inflation of prices was in terms of money. As for gold leaving the country, it was already happening except for that held in the coffers of the bank. The gold standard could be restored safely if the bank reduced its note circulation first. To eliminate the cost of coinage and to economize on gold that would otherwise circulate as coins, Ricardo proposed a gold bullion standard. The bank should buy and sell gold bullion rather than coin on demand, with at least 20 ounces as the minimum transaction.

Ricardo's plan was adopted in 1819 by Parliament; the Bank of England was ordered to resume gold payments in ingots of 60 ounces. In 1821 a law was passed requiring payment in coin. The gold standard served for more than a century thereafter, except during major wars and financial crises.

THE THEORY OF DIMINISHING RETURNS AND RENT

Ricardo's law of diminishing returns and theory of rent developed in response to the debate over the corn laws (Chapter 6). Recall that the concept of diminishing returns in agriculture dates back to Turgot, the French government official and physiocrat.[1] But in 1815 Ricardo, Malthus, West, and Torrens reformulated the principle and applied it to land rent. Ricardo modestly credited Malthus and West for the discovery. But it was Ricardo who developed the notion most clearly and completely. In using this concept to develop his theory of rent, Ricardo became the first economist to formulate a marginal principle in economic analysis. His theory of rent, therefore, is seminal to the later rise of the marginalist school.

"Rent," said Ricardo, "is that portion of the produce of the earth, which is paid to the landlord for the use of the original and indestructible powers of the soil." He modified this definition by including as rent the return on long-run capital investments that are amalgamated with the land and increase its productivity. According to Ricardo, rent arises at both the extensive and intensive margins of cultivation.

Rent at the Extensive Margin of Cultivation

No one pays rent in a newly settled country in which fertile soil is abundant. But:

> When in the progress of society, land of the second degree of fertility is taken into cultivation, rent immediately commences on that of the first quality, and the amount of that rent will depend on the difference in quality of these two portions of land.
>
> When land of the third quality is taken into cultivation, rent immediately commences on the second, and it is regulated as before, by the difference in their productive powers. At the same time, the rent of the first quality will rise, for that must always be above the rent of the second, by the difference between the produce which they yield with a given quantity of capital and labour. With every step in the progress of population, which shall oblige a country to have recourse to land of a worse quality, to enable it to raise its supply of food, rent, on all the more fertile lands, will rise.[2]

[1] The idea was again stated in 1777 by Scottish economist James Anderson.

[2] David Ricardo, *The Works and Correspondence of David Ricardo,* ed. Piero Sraffa, vol. 1 (Cambridge: University Press, 1962), 70. Copyrighted by and reprinted with the permission of the publisher.

Table 7-1
Rent Measured from the Extensive Margin of Cultivation

PRICE OF WHEAT PER BUSHEL	RENT DERIVED FROM EACH GRADE OF LAND A	B	C	D	E
Input:	$10	$10	$10	$10	$10
Yield: (bu/acre)	20	15	10	5	4
$.50	0*				
.66⅔	$ 3.33	0*			
1.00	10.00	$ 5.00	0*		
2.00	30.00	20.00	$10.00	0*	
2.50	40.00	27.50	15.00	$2.50	0*

*Price at which $10 input is made.

The produce from marginal land will bring in enough revenue to cover all the expenses of production plus the average rate of profit on the investment in labor and capital. The value of farm produce depends on the labor required per unit of output on the least productive land in use. The better land produces a surplus that is taken by the landowner as rent.

Table 7-1 illustrates Ricardo's theory of rent by showing how rent is measured from the *extensive* margin of cultivation. The table shows five grades of land (highest *A* to lowest *E*). Investing $10 per acre gives us the greatest return from *A*, 20 bushels per acre, because it is the best land, whereas the worst land, *E*, returns only 4 bushels per acre. The left column shows various prices of wheat. If the price of wheat were less than $.50 per bushel, none would be produced, because the yield on even the best grade of land would be insufficient to justify the $10 worth of input. At $.50 per bushel it pays to invest the $10 per acre on land *A*, because the yield of 20 bushels provides $10 (20 × $.50) of revenue, and this is sufficient to cover labor and capital costs, including the average rate of profit. But note that rent is zero here; revenues just match the input costs. If the price of wheat rises to $.66⅔, it pays to invest $10 per acre on both land *A* and *B*. At $.66⅔ per bushel, land *B* brings in $10 (15 × $.66⅔) of revenue, while land *A* produces $13.33 (20 × $.66⅔).

So what will be the rent on land *B*? On land *A*? The answers are shown in the respective columns in the table. Land *B* garners rent of zero ($10 – $10), while using *B* allows for rent of $3.33 ($13.33 – $10) on *A*. The rent on land *A* occurs because a $10 return is sufficient for the tenant to cover labor and capital expenses, including an average profit. Competition among tenants causes them to bid $3.33 per acre for the right to farm land *A*, and the landlord receives this sum in the form of rent. If the price of wheat rises to $1 per bushel, land C becomes the zero-rent marginal land, *B* yields rent of $5 per acre, and *A* yields $10. If the price of wheat rises to $2, land *D* will be brought into production, and the rent on *A*, *B*, and *C*

Table 7-2
Rent Measured from the Intensive Margin of Cultivation

	LAND GRADE A			
	Marginal			
Price of Wheat per Bushel	Input	Output	Δ Output	Rent
$ .50	$10	20		0
.66⅔	20	35	15	$ 3.33
1.00	30	45	10	15.00
2.00	40	50	5	60.00
2.50	50	54	4	85.00

	LAND GRADE B				LAND GRADE C			
	Marginal				Marginal			
	Input	Output	Δ Output	Rent	Input	Output	Δ Output	Rent
.66⅔	$10	15		0				
1.00	20	25	10	$ 5.00	$10	10		0
2.00	30	30	5	30.00	20	15	5	$10.00
2.50	40	34	4	45.00	30	19	4	17.50

will rise to $30, $20, and $10. The reader is urged to confirm these numbers using the aforementioned method for deriving them.

Rent at the Intensive Margin of Cultivation

Because of the law of diminishing returns, rent also arises from the *intensive* cultivation of land. If successive units of labor and capital are added to a piece of land while technology remains constant, each added unit of investment will add less to the output than previous units. If this were not so, food for the entire world could be grown in a flower pot! The last unit of labor and capital must pay for itself and provide an average rate of profit as well. Earlier units yield a surplus return, which is rent.

Table 7-2 displays hypothetical data for three separate acres of land of declining grade and analyzes rent at the intensive margin. Here, as before, the revenue received from the marginal output must be compared with the labor and capital cost of producing that extra output. The principle of diminishing returns is reflected in the columns labeled "Marginal Output" in the table. Our assumption again is that we add inputs in increments of $10. Notice that as more $10 increments are added, that is, as one moves down the input columns for each grade of land, output rises at a diminishing rate. Thus the marginal or extra output falls.

Our next task is to determine rent. We will initially focus our attention exclusively on the highest grade of land, *A*. At a price of \$.50 per bushel, an expenditure of \$10 is forthcoming, and rent is zero (output of 20 × \$.50 = \$10 of revenue, which covers labor and capital costs, including an average profit). What happens if the price per bushel rises, say, to \$1? Again, looking only at the acre of grade *A* land, we see that rent is now \$15. The 45 bushels of output sell for \$1 each, bringing in \$45 of revenue. But labor and capital costs (input column) are only \$30. The landlord charges the \$15 difference as rent. Similarly, if the price of wheat rises to \$2.50 per bushel, rent climbs to \$85 on the acre of land *A*. Notice that higher prices justify the use of more inputs, even though the added inputs do not increase total output by as much as did the previous additions.

It is a relatively easy matter to extend the analysis to more than one grade of land. At \$2.50 per bushel for wheat, it not only would pay to invest \$50 on grade *A* land, but it also would be profitable to employ \$40 of inputs on land *B* and \$30 on *C*. The total labor and capital costs would be \$120 (\$50 + \$40 + \$30), while the total yield would be 107 bushels (54 + 34 + 19). Total revenue would be \$267.50 (107 × \$2.50), yielding a total rent of \$147.50 (\$267.50 – \$120) on the three acres of land.[3]

It is obvious that every increase in the price of wheat, whether through tariffs on imported grain or through population growth, raises rent. Every fall in the price of grain, whether through lowered tariffs or technological improvements or reduced population, lowers rents. Note also that rent is both a differential return and surplus above labor and capital costs. Rent is price determined but not price determining. That is, high rents are explained by high grain prices; high prices cannot be explained by high rents. These important points need to be kept in mind as we examine Ricardo's theories of exchange value and distribution.

THE THEORY OF EXCHANGE VALUE AND RELATIVE PRICES

Exchange Value

Ricardo was concerned with relative values, not with absolute value; he wanted to discover the basis for the ratio of exchange between commodities. This would enable him to determine the causes of changes in these relative values over time.

In his *Principles of Political Economy and Taxation* (1817), Ricardo wrote that for a commodity to have exchange value, it must have use value. Utility (subjective want satisfying power) is not the measure of exchangeable value, although it is essential to it. Possessing utility, or use value, commodities derive their exchange

[3] Ricardo was also aware that rent can originate through differences in location. If lands of equal fertility are situated at varying distances from the market, the farthest land worked must pay the normal returns to labor and capital. The more favorably located land will yield extra returns because of smaller transport costs, and the landlord will capture these returns as land rent.

value from two sources: (1) their scarcity and (2) the quantity of labor required to obtain them. The value of *nonreproducible* commodities, such as rare works of art, classic books, and old coins, is determined by their scarcity alone. For these items, supply is fixed, and therefore demand will be the primary factor in determining exchange value: "Their value is wholly independent of the quantity of labour originally necessary to produce them, and varies with the varying wealth and inclinations of those who are desirous to possess them." But most commodities are *reproducible,* and Ricardo assumed that they are produced without restraint under conditions of competition. It was these goods to which Ricardo applied his labor theory of value.

Recall that Smith stated a labor theory of value for a primitive society in which neither capital nor land resources were used (or where their relative abundance was so great that they could be obtained freely). Smith then abandoned this approach when he analyzed an advanced economy, instead developing a "labor commanded" theory of exchange value. Unlike Smith, Ricardo applied his labor theory of value to an advanced economy. In fact, he felt that Smith's distinction between the two types of economies was artificial. In reference to Smith's deer-beaver example, Ricardo pointed out that "without some weapon neither the beaver nor the deer could be destroyed; and therefore their value would be regulated not solely by the time and labour necessary for their destruction, but also by the time and labour necessary for providing the hunter's capital, the weapon by the aid of which their destruction was effected."

According to Ricardo, the exchange value of a commodity depends on the labor time necessary to produce it. The labor time includes not only the work done in making the commodity itself but also the work embodied in the raw materials and capital goods used up in the process of production. The advantage of this approach, said Ricardo, is that it could be used to determine the causes of changes in exchange values over time. If, for example, the ratio of exchange of one beaver for two deer rose over the years to five beaver for two deer, we could determine whether this occurred because it required less labor time to trap a beaver, more labor time to harvest a deer, or some combination of the two.

The problem with this simple theory of value is that, among other things, it does not seemingly account for such factors as differences in capital-labor ratios among industries, differences in the combinations of skilled and unskilled workers among various industries, and variations in wages, profit rates, and rent among producers. Ricardo recognized all of these potential complications and tried to address each of them.

Differing capital-labor ratios. Recall that Smith had noted that differing capital–labor ratios between industries meant that if all commodities sold at their value as measured by labor, rates of return to capital would vary across industries. This, of course, could not happen in a competitive economy because capital would be attracted toward the high-return industries and away from the low-return ones until profits equalized. As evidenced by the following illustration, paraphrased from the third edition of his *Principles,* Ricardo also noted this complication.

Suppose a farmer employs 100 workers for a year to grow grain, and a cotton manufacturer employs 100 workers for a year to make a machine to produce yarn.

The machine will have the same value as the grain. Now assume that during the second year the farmer again employs 100 workers, and the cotton manufacturer uses 100 laborers to work the machine to produce the yarn. Disregarding the wear and tear on the machine, we see that the 100 workers growing grain during the second year will produce commodities of less value than the 100 workers spinning yarn, because the latter use capital and the former do not. If wage rates were \$50 per year per worker and profits were 10 percent, the value of the grain produced each year and the value of the machine would each be \$5,500 [(100 × \$50) + (\$5,000 × .10)]. The yarn produced during the second year would be worth \$6,050 [\$5,500 + (\$5,500 × .10)], because 10 percent would have to be earned on the investment in the machine. Otherwise, such capital investment would not occur. Here then are two capitalists employing the same quantity of labor in the production of their commodities, and yet the goods they produce differ in value because of the different quantities of fixed capital used by each.

How did Ricardo handle this problem? The answer is that he simply stated that this cause of variation in the value of commodities is slight in its effect. A commodity will sell at more than its labor-time value if more-than-average capital is invested in its production; conversely, a commodity will sell at less than its labor-time value if less-than-average capital is invested in its production. Much more important in determining the value of a commodity is the labor time required to produce it.

Differences in labor quality. Ricardo recognized that not all labor is of equal quality. Highly skilled workers can obviously produce more in an hour of work than low-skilled workers. Different commodities get produced with wide variations in the combinations of grades of labor employed. So how can it be that the relative value of two goods is determined by the respective labor time necessary to produce each? Ricardo's answer was that if labor of type *A* is twice as productive as labor of type *B*, then we can simply think of an hour of labor *A* as being twice the labor time as *B*. Differences in combinations of grades of labor among industries, therefore, will not affect exchange values. Put differently, substituting one worker of type *A* labor for two workers of type *B* will leave unaffected the total labor time required to make the product. Hence the relative exchange value will also remain the same.

Wages, profits, and rents. Exchange value does not depend on wages; it depends on the quantity of labor. Skilled workers naturally will receive higher wages than unskilled. But this is of no consequence for exchange value, said Ricardo, because the skilled labor actually represents more labor than does the unskilled labor. Furthermore, wages and profits vary inversely (for reasons we will explore later). An increase in the wages paid for a specific grade of labor will reduce profits by an equal amount. Therefore, a change in the wage rate will affect only the ratio of profits to wages, not the exchange value of a good.

Nor do profit variations present an insurmountable problem. Regardless of whether profits rise or fall, they do not influence the relative values of goods. If a pair of shoes embodying five hours of labor exchanges for a dress also made with five hours, a rise in wages and a decline in profit or vice versa will not affect the one-to-one ratio of exchange.[4] An important point emerges here: Labor does not have to receive the whole product simply because the amount of labor is the measure and source of value. There is no hint of exploitation in Ricardo's analysis; in fact, he defended the institution of private property. It was Marx who later modified and drew revolutionary implications from Ricardo's labor theory of value.

Finally, Ricardo pointed out that rent does not figure into the exchange value of a commodity. Recall from our previous discussion that, in the Ricardian system, rent payments do not influence the prices of goods. On the contrary, the prices of goods (which tend to reflect their value) are one of the elements that determine rent.

Relative Prices

Although labor is the foundation of the value of commodities, market prices deviate from value or natural price because of accidental or temporary fluctuations of supply and demand. If the market price rises above the natural price, profits rise, and more capital is used to produce the commodity. If the market price falls, capital flows out of the industry. The actions of individuals seeking maximum advantage tend to equalize the rates of profit and to keep market prices proportional to values. Short-run prices depend on supply and demand, but long-run values depend on the real costs of production, and the relative real costs of production of two commodities are nearly proportional to the total quantity of labor required for the entire production process.

> However abundant the demand it can never permanently raise the price of a commodity above the expence of its production, including in that expence the profits of the producers. It seems natural therefore to seek for the cause of the variation of permanent price in the expences of production. Diminish these and the commodity must finally fall, increase them and it must certainly rise. What has this to do with demand?[5]

Refer to 7-1 PAST AS PROLOGUE

This is an interesting contrast to the value theory introduced later by marginalist economists such as Jevons and Menger. But let's not get ahead of our story.

THE DISTRIBUTION OF INCOME

In a letter to Malthus in 1820, Ricardo stated:

> Political economy you think is an enquiry into the nature and causes of wealth—I think it should rather be called an enquiry into the laws which determine the division of the produce of industry amongst the classes who concur in its formation. No law can be laid down respecting quantity, but a tolerably correct one can be laid down respecting proportions.[6]

[4] Ricardo did recognize that profit rates will be a larger proportion of product price in capital-intensive industries than in labor-intensive ones but concluded that the influence of these differences was quantitatively insignificant.

[5] Ricardo, *Works and Correspondence*, 7: 250–251.

[6] Ricardo, *Works and Correspondence*, 8: 278.

7-1 PAST AS PROLOGUE

The Ricardian Equivalence Theorem

Conventional macroeconomic theory suggests that an increase in government spending will have a greater expansionary effect on GDP when financed by borrowing rather than by a tax increase. Unlike borrowing, a tax increase will reduce consumption spending, partly offsetting the increase in government spending.

A handful of prominent contemporary economists have challenged this view, claiming that debt financing has the same limited effect on GDP as financing a deficit with a tax increase.* Because David Ricardo first raised the possibility of the equivalency of debt financing and tax financing, this idea is known as the Ricardian equivalence theorem. In 1820 Ricardo stated:

> Suppose a country to be free from debt, and a war to take place, which should involve it in an annual additional expenditure of twenty millions. There are [two] modes by which this expenditure may be provided; first, taxes may be raised to the amount of twenty millions per annum, from which the country would be totally freed on the return of peace; or secondly, the money might be annually borrowed and funded; in which case, if the interest agreed upon was 5 percent, a perpetual charge of one million per annum taxes would be incurred for the first year's expence, from which there would be no relief during peace, or in any future war; of an additional million for the second year's expence, and so on for every year that the war might last. At the end of twenty years, if the war lasted so long, the country would be perpetually encumbered with taxes of twenty million per annum. . . .
>
> In point of economy, there is no real difference in either of the modes; for twenty millions in one payment [and] one million per annum for ever are precisely of the same value.†

The modern version of the Ricardian equivalence theorem hypothesizes that debt financing of new government spending is matched by an equal increase in private saving. According to this view, people conclude that today's deficit spending will require higher future taxes to pay the added interest expense. In anticipation of these taxes, people will increase their present saving by reducing their present consumption. A debt-financed increase in government spending, therefore, will not increase aggregate expenditures and GDP by the amounts predicted by standard macroeconomic theory. Fiscal policy is allegedly either completely ineffective or severely weakened.

Ricardo himself questioned whether people would actually view debt and tax financing equivalently.‡ Most contemporary economists also are skeptical of this claim. They point out the implausibility of people today increasing their saving as

7-1 PAST AS PROLOGUE (continued)

a way to help their children, grandchildren, and great-grandchildren pay the interest on a rising public debt. Also, critics note that by most measures the rate of national saving in the United States *declined* in the 1980s, a period during which the federal government incurred record-high deficits.

*Robert Barro, "Are Government Bonds Net Wealth?" *Journal of Political Economy* 82 (December 1974): 1095–1117.

†David Ricardo, "Funding System," *Works and Correspondence*, 4: 185–186.

‡Gerald O'Driscoll, "The Ricardian Nonequivalence Theorem," *Journal of Political Economy* 85 (February 1977): 207–210.

Ricardo's reference is to factor shares or what today we call the *functional distribution of income*. His concern was for understanding the forces that determine the shares of the national income accruing as wages, profits, and rents (interest was combined with profits). We first examine his thinking on each share, then summarize his analysis through a simple graphical representation, and finally discuss the policy implications that he drew from his analysis.

Wages

Labor, said Ricardo, like all other things that are bought and sold, has its natural price and its market price. The *natural* price of labor is that price that, given the habits and customs of the people, enables workers to subsist and to perpetuate themselves without a change in their numbers. The natural price of labor depends on the price of the necessities of life required by the laborers and their families. If the cost of necessities rises, nominal wages will rise so that the workers can maintain their real wages and continue to buy enough to perpetuate the labor force. If the price of commodities falls, nominal wages fall. The *market* price of labor depends on supply and demand, but as with commodities, the market price fluctuates around the natural price.

In the long run, both the natural price of labor and nominal wages tend to rise, said Ricardo, because of the increased difficulty and cost of producing food for growing numbers of people. Improvements in agriculture and imports of food counteract this tendency by lowering the cost of living, but the forces raising the cost of living remain predominant. Ultimately, therefore, nominal wages must rise to meet the increasing costs of food.

Ricardo's idea that in the long run the worker gets only a minimum wage came to be known as "the iron law of wages." When the market price of labor rises above the natural price, a worker can rear a large and healthy family. As population increases, wages fall to their natural price or even below. When the market price of labor is below the natural price, misery reduces the working population and wages rise. The long-run tendency is, therefore, for workers to receive the subsistence minimum. This pessimistic analysis was modified in two ways. First, in an industrialized society with expanding capital, the wages fund (Chapter 5) may rise faster than population, and hence wages may remain above the subsistence wage for an indefinite period. Second, Ricardo apparently did not view this natural wage as necessarily being a *biologically* subsistence wage in the same sense as did Malthus. Rather, this wage depended on the habits and customs of the people and what they consider to be the minimum acceptable subsistence.

Profits

We have seen that Ricardo felt that the rates of profit in different fields of enterprise within a country tend to equalize. Entrepreneurs seek the maximum rate of profit, after allowing for the advantages or disadvantages that one business offers as compared to another. Price movements influence rates of profit that in turn direct the flow of capital. The moneyed class in particular can quickly shift funds to the most profitable business. The free, competitive market and the actions of individuals tend to produce rates of profit that are equal or equally advantageous, on balance, for all types of businesses. In fact, suggested Ricardo, the rate of profit on marginal land (where rent is zero) governs the rate of profit in the whole economy. If the rate of profit is higher in industry than in the farming of marginal land, capital will flow from agriculture to industry, and a better grade of land will become the new marginal land. If agriculture is more profitable than industry, capital will flow toward agriculture, and the next worse grade of land will become the marginal land cultivated.

Recall that Ricardo emphasized that profits and wages vary inversely; one increases at the expense of the other. Why must higher wages come out of profits instead of being passed on in higher prices? The answer lies in the equation of exchange and in the international balance of payments. If prices rise, more money will be required to sell a given quantity of goods. Where will the money come from? Instead of gold flowing in from abroad, gold will leave the country because prices abroad would be lower than at home. With a shrinking money supply, prices cannot rise. Therefore, employers themselves must bear the higher costs of production; the wage increases simply reduce profits. Conversely, if wages fall, prices will not fall. If they do, gold will flow into the country, and prices will rise again. Therefore a fall in wages will result in a rise in profits.

And what will be the long-run trend for the profit rate and the profit share of national income? Recall that Adam Smith thought that the rate of profit would fall because of growing competition among entrepreneurs, and he welcomed this development. Ricardo thought that the rate of profit would fall because of the increasing difficulty of growing food for an expanding population, and this concerned him. Falling profit rates, he thought, would curb the accumulation and investment of capital and ultimately produce a stationary state. This state would be reached when new investment ceased, when population could no longer expand because the limits of food production had been reached, and when every available surplus had been appropriated as rent. For Ricardo, however, this stationary state was seen as a theoretical outcome of his theory and not as a near-term reality.

Rents

As stated in the previous section, Ricardo saw a conflict between the interests of workers and capitalists. An even more basic conflict exists, he said, between landlords and the rest of society. As population increases, the increased demand for food will raise its price. We know from our previous discussions that this will bring poorer land into cultivation and will cause better land to be worked more intensively. Rents, therefore, will rise. Nominal wages, we have seen, will also rise to maintain the natural, or subsistence, wage. Thus, profit rates and the profit share of the national income will fall.

Contemporary Representation

Contemporary economists summarize the simplest features of Ricardo's distribution by way of a graphical representation.[7] In Figure 7-1 we measure the size of the labor force horizontally while measuring the level of total output, rent, profit, and wages vertically. As population and the labor force increase, diminishing marginal returns within agriculture mean that total product increases at a diminishing rate. The curve "Total product minus rent" flattens out even faster than the "Total product" curve, producing a growing vertical distance between the two curves. Thus, total rent received by landlords rises with population. Straight line *OS* measures total wages (measured on the vertical axis). Its constant slope reflects a constant real wage rate that remains at the subsistence level as the labor force grows. That is, although total wages *do* rise, subsistence wages remain constant.

Suppose initially that the size of the labor force is *A*. There, total wages, total profits, and total rents are shown as vertical distances *W*, *P*, and *R*, respectively. The relatively high profits increase the size of the wages fund, allowing a temporary rise (not shown) of the real wage. This higher real wage enables population growth and increases the labor force to, say, *B*, which drives the real wage back to its subsistence level. But at labor force size *B* the profit share is lower than at *A*, while the rent share is higher.

The process repeats because, though smaller, profits are still positive at labor force size *B*. Population and the size of the labor force once again expand. Eventually the economy reaches labor force size *C*, where profits are eliminated and no further capital investment is forthcoming. Population and labor force growth end, with the economy reaching a stationary state. Specifically, the stationary state occurs at labor force size *C*, where total wages are *W′*, profits are zero, and rent is *R′*.

[7] William J. Baumol, *Economic Dynamics*, 3d ed. (New York: Macmillan, 1970), chap. 2. Thomas M. Humphrey has nicely demonstrated this analysis using average product and marginal product curves. See his "Algebraic Production Functions and Their Uses before Cobb-Douglas," *Economic Quarterly* 83 (Federal Reserve Bank of Richmond, Winter 1997): 60.

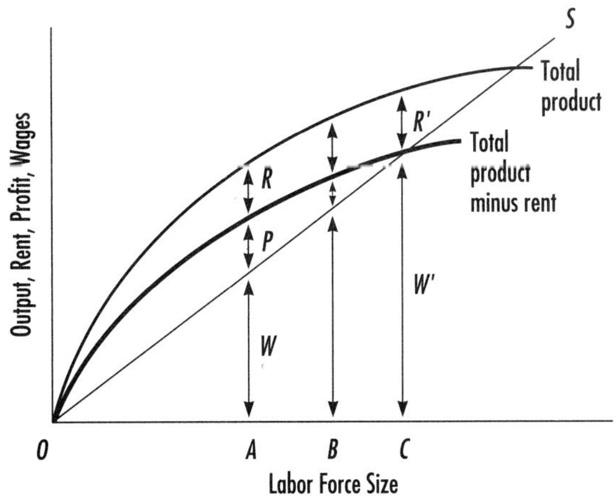

Figure 7-1 A Modern Representation of Ricardo's Theory of Income Distribution
According to Ricardo, increases in labor force size interact with fixed land and diminishing returns in agriculture to cause total product to increase at a diminishing rate. An increase in labor force size from *A* to *C* raises total wages from *W* to *W'*, reduces profits from *P* to zero, and increases rents from *R* to *R'*. At labor force size *C* the economy reaches a stationary state, at which no additional capital accumulation occurs. Because real wages, measured by the slope of *S*, remain at a subsistence level and profits are eliminated, the landlords are the sole beneficiaries of the long-run growth process.

Because wages remain at the subsistence level while profits are squeezed out, the landlords are the sole beneficiaries of the long-run expansion process. Their numbers remain constant, and their rents grow. Large rents continue even when the economy reaches the stationary state.

POLICY IMPLICATIONS

Ricardo drew several important conclusions from his analysis of the components of the national income. First, he felt that wages should not be regulated, nor should relief be given to the indigent:

> Like all other contracts, wages should be left to the fair and free competition of the market, and should never be controlled by the interference of the legislature.
>
> The clear and direct tendency of the poor laws, is in direct opposition to those obvious principles: it is not, as the legislature benevolently intended, to amend the condition of the poor, but to deteriorate the condition of both poor and rich; instead of making the poor rich, they are calculated to make the rich poor.[8]

[8] Ricardo, *Works and Correspondence,* 1: 105–106.

Second, Ricardo concluded (as had the physiocrats) that a tax on rent would affect only rent. Such a tax would fall wholly on landlords and could not be shifted to anyone else. The landlords could not raise rents to pay for the tax, because marginal land would pay no rent and therefore no tax. The tax on rent would leave undisturbed the difference in productivity between marginal and better land. The tax would not raise the price of farm produce, nor would it discourage the cultivation of land. In the United States, this was the analysis that led to Henry George's idea of a single tax, a tax that took all the land rent. This was not Ricardo's idea of justice.

Finally, disagreeing with Malthus, Ricardo strongly opposed the corn laws. By the repeal of the tariffs and other restrictions on the import of grain, society's interest would be promoted at the expense of the landlords. Why? The answer, of course, follows from his distribution theory. Lower grain prices will reduce rent and increase profits, thereby increasing capital accumulation, bolstering the wages fund, and delaying the arrival of a stationary state.

Ricardo opposed the corn laws for a second reason: They reduced the gains from international trade. It is to this topic we now turn.

The Theory of Comparative Costs

Ricardo made a strong argument for free trade based on the efficiency gains that it confers:

> Under a system of perfectly free commerce, each country naturally devotes its capital and labour to such employments as are most beneficial to each. This pursuit of individual advantage is admirably connected with the universal good of the whole. By stimulating industry, by rewarding ingenuity, and by using most efficaciously the peculiar powers bestowed by nature, it distributes labour most effectively and most economically: while, by increasing the general mass of productions, it diffuses general benefit, and binds together by one common tie of interest and intercourse, the universal society of nations throughout the civilized world. It is this principle which determines that wine shall be made in France and Portugal, that corn shall be grown in America and Poland, and that hardware and other goods shall be manufactured in England.[9]

Smith advocated foreign trade without impediments in order to widen markets and remove surpluses; trade was based on differences in absolute costs. Ricardo made a brilliant and lasting contribution to economic thought by showing that even if one country is more efficient than another in producing all commodities, trade between the two nevertheless can be of mutual benefit. His theory of comparative costs is now known as the *law of comparative advantage*.

Ricardo *explicitly* assumed in his theoretical proof of the gains from trade that capital and labor did not flow between countries. He *implicitly* assumed that cost remained constant as output increased. Otherwise, specialization would not be carried on to its fullest extent. All costs were measured in terms of labor hours, an approach consistent with the labor theory of value.

---

[9] Ricardo, *Works and Correspondence*, 1: 133–134.

Table 7-3
Illustration of Comparative Advantage
(Hypothetical Output per Unit of Labor Employed)

	WINE	CLOTH
PORTUGAL	3	6
ENGLAND	1	5
Total	4	11

Ricardo based his explanation of the law of comparative costs on the number of units of labor necessary to produce a specific quantity of cloth and wine in two countries: England and Portugal. To say that it takes a certain amount of labor to produce each unit of cloth or wine is also to say that a certain quantity of wine or cloth can be produced with each unit of labor. That is, if it takes, say, two units of labor to produce each unit of output, then obviously each unit of labor can produce one-half unit of output. We will employ this later terminology to illustrate Ricardo's law of comparative advantage.

Table 7-3 shows that Portugal has an absolute cost advantage over England in producing both wine and cloth. Portugal can produce three units of wine with each unit of labor; England can produce only one unit of wine. Similarly, Portugal can produce more units of cloth (6) from a unit of labor than can England (5). Would Portugal be better off foregoing trade with England? Ricardo answered with an emphatic "No." Each nation should produce the product for which it has a relative advantage; that is, the product for which it has the lowest domestic opportunity cost. Portugal's opportunity cost of producing one unit of wine is two units of cloth (6/3). England's opportunity cost of producing one unit of wine is five units of cloth (5/1). It is relatively less costly for Portugal to specialize in producing wine. Alternatively, Portugal's opportunity cost of producing one unit of clothing is one-half unit of wine (3/6); England's is one-fifth unit of wine. England should therefore specialize in clothing because it has a lower opportunity cost than Portugal.

Now suppose that Portugal transfers one unit of labor out of the manufacture of cloth and into the production of wine. As summarized in Table 7-4, wine production in Portugal rises by three units (1 × 3), and cloth output falls by six units

Table 7-4
The Gains from Specialization and Trade
(Hypothetical Output per Unit of Labor Employed)

	WINE	CLOTH
PORTUGAL	+3	−6
ENGLAND	−2	+10
Total Gain	+1	+4

(1 × 6). Meanwhile, suppose that England transfers two units of labor (one isn't sufficient to show the gain) from wine production to cloth manufacture. The result? Cloth production increases by 10 units (2 × 5), and wine output falls by 2 units (2 × 1). Specialization has increased the output of both wine and cloth! Ricardo emphasized that the corn laws reduced efficiency gains such as these.

Ricardo also inquired as to the impact that an improved English manufacture of wine might have on the equilibrium of trade between England and Portugal. Suppose, he said, that this improvement made it no longer profitable for Portugal to ship wine to England but that it still paid for Portugal to import cloth from England. The Portuguese importer would no longer have British pounds sterling received as payment for wine and would have to use gold and silver to acquire them. This would drive up the price of pound sterling and might even cut off imports of cloth entirely. But if the premium on British currency were less than the profit from importing cloth, gold or silver would flow to England in payment for the British currency required to buy cloth. The declining money supply in Portugal would cause falling prices there, and the rising money supply in England would cause rising prices in that country. This would bring about a new equilibrium in foreign trade. Here is Hume's price species-flow mechanism once again.

Ricardo did not specify clearly how the gains shown in Table 7-4 would get divided between England and Portugal. Although his theory defines the limits within which the ratios of exchange between internationally traded commodities could fluctuate, it does not attempt to explain what determines the ratios. John Stuart Mill (Chapter 8) later presented a theory of reciprocal demand that addressed this question.

RICARDO ON UNEMPLOYMENT

Recall that Malthus argued that capitalists satiate their wants and hence save large sums. Unless countered by spending by landlords, effective demand will be insufficient to purchase all of the output. The resulting glut of goods will force producers to reduce their production and discharge workers. Ricardo agreed that a temporary glut could occur but argued that full production and employment normally would prevail. He invoked what today is known as Say's law of markets to defend his position.[10] This law is that "supply creates its own demand." According to this perspective, the process of producing goods generates sufficient wage, profit, and rental income to buy the goods. Furthermore, the *will* to purchase either consumption or capital goods matches the *ability* to do so. Overproduction of a particular commodity might occur due to poor foresight, but such a circumstance would automatically correct itself. The product would sell at a loss, and resources would be shifted to the production of other commodities for which there evidently must now be greater demand. Moreover, capitalists' savings give rise to investment expenditures that create demand for factors of production and therefore income to the suppliers of these resources. Consequently, effective demand would always be present at a level sufficient to purchase the output.

[10] We will see in Chapter 8 that his law actually had its origins in Smith and was developed by Ricardo's friend, James Mill. J. M. Keynes credited J. B. Say—who also expressed the idea—and consequently it became known as Say's law.

In the third edition of *Principles of Political Economy and Taxation*, Ricardo inserted a new chapter titled "On Machinery" in which he raised the possibility of technological unemployment. Ricardo claimed that he had erred in supporting the view that the introduction of machinery would help all three major classes of income receivers. Their money incomes, he once thought, would remain the same while their real incomes would rise, because goods could be produced more cheaply with machinery. Even workers would gain because the same labor would be demanded as before mechanization, and therefore nominal wages would not fall. Even if the number of workers in one industry became excessive, capital would shift to some other industry and increase employment there. The only inconvenience would be the temporary maladjustment that occurs when capital and labor move from one employment to another.

Ricardo's revised argument was that the introduction of machinery would benefit the landlord and the capitalist, as he had believed in the past, but would frequently be very injurious to labor. If more capital were invested in machinery (fixed capital), less circulating capital would be available for the wages fund out of which wages are paid. In other words, capital is scarce, and the portion that is diverted to machinery represents a deduction from that allocated to wages: "The opinion entertained by the labouring class, that the employment of machinery is frequently detrimental to their interests, is not founded on prejudice and error, but is conformable to the correct principles of political economy."[11]

Ricardo thought that the long-run effect of the introduction of machinery might be more favorable than the short-run effect. Even if the money profit of the capitalist remains the same after an increased investment in machinery, more can be saved because the cost of producing consumer goods falls. Thus the capitalist can invest more, ultimately reemploying the redundant population. Technological unemployment is therefore likely to be only a short-run problem for the workers, but nonetheless a very real one.

In any case, said Ricardo, government should never discourage the use of machinery. The capitalist who is not permitted to receive the greatest possible profit from the use of machinery at home will invest capital abroad. The demand for labor will be reduced if machinery is introduced at home, but it will disappear altogether if the capital is invested abroad. In addition, because new machinery lowers the cost of producing goods, it enables a country to remain competitive with foreign countries that are permitting new and better machines to be used.

ASSESSMENT

Ricardo made several lasting contributions to economic analysis. Of particular significance were his contributions to the use of abstract reasoning, his theory of comparative advantage, his employment of marginal analysis, his presentation of the law of diminishing returns in agriculture, and his widening of the scope of economic analysis to include the distribution of income.

[11] Ricardo, *Works and Correspondence*, 1: 392.

On the other hand, his analysis was weak or inaccurate in several respects. Like Malthus, he tended to overemphasize the law of diminishing returns in agriculture. Technological advance and capital accumulation historically have increased output per unit of labor in the advanced nations. In Figure 7-1, this can be shown by upward movements of the "Total product" and "Total product minus rent" curves. Nor was Ricardo correct in emphasizing that landlords as a whole had no interest in increased productivity in agriculture. Land that cannot support the people to work on it will not be tilled. Improvements made by the landlord permit poorer land to be worked, increasing the surplus available for rent on more productive land. Rent will fall only if improvements in agriculture are unaccompanied by increased demand for farm products.

Ricardo also may be faulted for unrealistically assuming that land has a single use. This enabled him to conclude that rent is not a cost of production. In reality, there are competing uses for most parcels of land, just as there are competing uses for labor and capital. A parcel of land will be used where it is the most productive and therefore will command a payment to cover its opportunity cost (output forgone from the next best use). In this respect, rent *is* a cost of production and not simply a residual available after wages and profits are subtracted from revenue.

Ricardo's thinking with respect to the impact of additions of new machinery on employment was also misleading. The introduction of new capital can just as well increase the demand for labor as decrease it; capital and labor are often complementary resources.

Finally, most scholars of Ricardo contend that his theory of value did not place sufficient emphasis on the role of demand. In this respect, it is argued that his labor theory of value represented a detour from the line of reasoning that eventually produced contemporary value theory. But in the 1980s one or two prominent scholars challenged this conventional wisdom. Their reinterpretation of Ricardo's analysis of exchange value places it squarely within the tradition of value theory associated with Alfred Marshall and other neoclassical economists.[12] Although the resulting debate over Ricardo's proper "fit" in the history of economic thought has been spirited, all scholars agree that Ricardo is an extremely important figure in the development of economic analysis.

Questions for Study and Discussion

1. Briefly identify and state the significance of each of the following to the history of economic thought: currency question, law of diminishing returns, extensive margin of cultivation, intensive margin of cultivation, nonreproducible commodities, reproducible commodities, functional distribution of income, stationary state, and theory of comparative costs.

[12] Samuel Hollander makes this latter case in his *The Economics of David Ricardo* (Toronto: University of Toronto Press, 1979). This book has generated controversy. For example, see D. O'Brien, "Ricardian Economics and the Economics of David Ricardo," *Oxford Economic Papers* 33 (November 1981): 352–386; S. Hollander, "The Economics of David Ricardo: A Response to Professor O'Brien," *Oxford Economic Papers* 34 (March 1982): 224–246; and A. Roncaglia, "Hollander's Economics," *Journal of Post-Keynesian Economics* 4 (Spring 1982): 339–359.

2. Relate Ricardo's position on the corn laws to his (a) theory of distribution and (b) theory of comparative costs.
3. Compare and contrast the views of Ricardo and Malthus on each of the following topics: (a) corn laws, (b) subsistence wage, and (c) market gluts.
4. Use the following data to determine which nation should specialize in the production of shoes and which in the production of wheat. Suppose that nation *A* transfers five units of labor toward the commodity for which it has a comparative advantage while nation *B* transfers one unit of labor to the commodity for which it has a comparative advantage. By how many units will the total output of wheat rise? By how many units will the total output of shoes rise? Explain your conclusions.

	WHEAT	SHOES
	(PER UNIT OF LABOR INPUT)	
NATION A	1	1
NATION B	4	8

5. Suppose that the prices in the column labeled "Price of Wheat per Bushel" in Table 7-2 (land grade *A*) were twice those shown. Derive the new values for rent. What is the implication of these price increases for rent measured at the *extensive* margin of cultivation?
6. How did Ricardo's labor theory for an advanced economy differ from Smith's? Use a contemporary supply and demand graph to demonstrate Ricardo's notion that an increase in product demand will not increase the value (price) of reproducible goods that are produced at a constant average cost. Hint: Remember from previous courses that a product supply curve is a marginal cost curve.
7. Discuss the statement: Adam Smith looked at the economy and saw a grand concert; Ricardo looked at it and saw something quite different.
8. What impact would an improvement in agricultural technology have on the "Total product" and "Total product minus rent" curves shown in Figure 7-1? Show this on the diagram and state the implication with respect to the arrival of the stationary state.
9. Use Hume's price species-flow mechanism to explain why Ricardo thought that increases in nominal wages paid to workers would reduce firms' profits.

Selected Readings

Books

Blaug, Mark. *Ricardian Economics.* New Haven, CT: Yale University Press, 1958.

———, ed. *David Ricardo.* Brookfield, VT: Edward Elgar, 1991.

Dobb, Maurice. "Ricardo and Adam Smith." In *Essays on Adam Smith.* Edited by A. S. Skinner and Thomas Wilson. London: Clarendon Press, 1975.

Hollander, Samuel. *The Economics of David Ricardo.* Toronto: University of Toronto Press, 1979.

Peach, Terry. *Interpreting Ricardo.* Cambridge: Cambridge University Press, 1993.

Ricardo, David. *Works and Correspondence.* Edited by Piero Sraffa. 10 vols. Cambridge: The University Press, 1951–1955.

Journal Articles

Barkai, Haim. "Ricardo's Volte-Face on Machinery," *Journal of Political Economy* 94 (June 1986): 595–613.

Fetter, Frank W. "The Rise and Decline of Ricardian Economics," *History of Political Economy* 1 (Spring 1969): 370–387.

Hollander, Samuel. "The Reception of Ricardian Economics," *Oxford Economic Papers* 29 (July 1977): 221–257.

Peach, Terry. "Samuel Hollander's 'Ricardian Growth Theory': A Critique," *Oxford Economic Papers* 42 (October 1990): 751–764.

Roncaglia, Alessandro. "Hollander's Ricardo," *Journal of Post-Keynesian Economics* 4 (Spring 1982): 339–359.

Stigler, George J. "Ricardo and the 93% Labor Theory of Value," *American Economic Review* 48 (June 1958): 357–367.

———. "Ricardo or Hollander?" *Oxford Economic Papers* 42 (October 1990): 765–768.

Chapter 8

THE CLASSICAL SCHOOL—BENTHAM, SAY, SENIOR, AND MILL

Several important thinkers in addition to Smith, Malthus, and Ricardo contributed to classical economic analysis. We examine four of them in this chapter. Of this group, it is generally agreed that the last, John Stuart Mill, made the most significant contributions to economics.

JEREMY BENTHAM

The life span of Jeremy Bentham (1748–1832) overlapped the publication of David Hume's economic essays, Adam Smith's *Wealth of Nations,* the works of David Ricardo and Thomas Malthus, and the early writings of John Stuart Mill. Not only was Bentham an enthusiastic adherent of the classical school, but also he made some original contributions to its philosophy and economics. Bentham boasted, "I was the spiritual father of [James] Mill, and Mill was the spiritual father of Ricardo: so that Ricardo was my spiritual grandson."

Bentham, a precocious child, read history and studied Latin at the age of four. He matriculated Queen's College, Oxford, at twelve and took his degree at fifteen. After that he studied law as his father wished. He soon deserted the legal profession for a scholarly life, relying on his indulgent and admiring father for support. Bentham gathered around him a circle of congenial friends and ardent disciples who promoted his ideas, but most of his prolific writings were not published until well over a century after his death.

In accordance with his wishes, Bentham's body was dissected for the benefit of science. He left his entire estate to University College, London, with the stipulation that his remains be present at all meetings of its board. His skeleton, padded and dressed, is on public display in a glass case. The skeleton is seated in a chair, with cane in gloved hand. The head of the body is wax, but Bentham's actual head, preserved in the manner of South American headhunters, rests on a plate between his feet.

Utilitarianism

The central theme of Bentham's thought has been called utilitarianism, or the principle of the greatest happiness. Its underlying philosophy—hedonism—dates back to the Greeks of antiquity.[1] This notion is that people pursue things that provide pleasure and avoid things that produce pain; all individuals seek to maximize their total pleasure. Utilitarianism superimposed on hedonism the ethical doctrine that conduct should be directed toward promoting the greatest happiness of the greatest number of people. Thus, by recognizing a positive role for society, utilitarianism tempered the extremely individualistic outlook of hedonism. If an individual pursues only personal pleasure, will this action promote the general happiness? Not necessarily, thought Bentham. Society, however, has its own methods of compelling individuals to promote the general happiness. The rule of law establishes sanctions to punish individuals who in their own pursuit of pleasure harm others excessively. Moral or social sanctions also exist, of which ostracism is an example. Even theological sanctions, such as fear of punishment in the hereafter, would help reconcile the individualistic self-interest of hedonism with the utilitarian principle of the greatest happiness for the greatest number of people.

Using utilitarianism as his foundation, Bentham developed a systematic set of philosophical and economic doctrines pointing toward reform. We can let Bentham speak for himself on the principle of utility, as he did in the first chapter of *An Introduction to the Principles of Morals and Legislation*, first printed in 1780:

> Nature has placed mankind under the governance of two sovereign masters, *pain* and *pleasure*. It is for them alone to point out what we ought to do, as well as to determine what we shall do. On the one hand the standard of right and wrong, on the other the chain of causes and effects, are fastened to their throne. They govern us in all we do, in all we say, in all we think: every effort we make to throw off our subjection, will serve but to demonstrate and confirm it. In words a man may pretend to abjure their empire: but in reality he will remain subject to it all the while. The principle of utility recognizes this subjection, and assumes it for the foundation of that system, the object of which is to rear the fabric of felicity by the hands of reason and law. . . .
>
> By the *principle of utility* is meant that principle which approves or disapproves of every action whatsoever, according to the tendency which it appears to have to augment or diminish the happiness of the party whose interest is in question: or, what is the same thing in other words, to promote or to oppose that happiness. I say of every action whatsoever; and therefore not only of every action of a private individual, but of every measurement of government.
>
> By utility is meant that property in any object, whereby it tends to produce benefit, advantage, pleasure, good, or happiness . . . or . . . to prevent the happening of mischief, pain, evil, or unhappiness to the party whose interest is considered: if that party be the community in general, then the happiness of the community: if a particular individual, then the happiness of that individual.
>
> The community is a fictitious body, composed of the individual persons who are considered as constituting as it were its *members*. The interest of the community then is, what?—the sum of the interests of the several members who compose it.
>
> It is vain to talk of the interest of the community, without understanding what is the interest of the individual. A thing is said to promote the interest . . . of an individual,

[1] For example, S. Todd Lowry shows that the theory of quantitative subjective value was detailed in Plato's *Protagoras*. See Lowry's "The Roots of Hedonism: An Ancient Analysis of Quantity and Time," *History of Political Economy* 13 (Winter 1981): 812–823.

when it tends to add to the sum total of his pleasures; or, what comes to the same thing, to diminish the sum total of his pains.

An action then may be said to be comformable to the principle of utility . . . when the tendency it has to augment the happiness of the community is greater than any it has to diminish it.

A measure of government . . . may be said to be comformable to or dictated by the principle of utility, when in the like manner the tendency which it has to augment the happiness of the community is greater than any which it has to diminish it.[2]

Diminishing Marginal Utility

In *The Philosophy of Economic Science,* Bentham argued that wealth is a measure of happiness but that wealth has diminishing marginal utility as it increases:

> Of two persons having unequal fortunes, he who has most wealth must by a legislator be regarded as having most happiness. But the quantity of happiness will not go on increasing in anything near the same proportion as the quantity of wealth:—ten thousand times the quantity of wealth will not bring with it ten thousand times the quantity of happiness. It will even be matter of doubt, whether ten thousand times the wealth will in general bring with it twice the happiness. The effect of wealth in the production of happiness goes on diminishing, as the quantity by which the wealth of one man exceeds that of another goes on increasing: in other words, the quantity of happiness produced by a particle of wealth (each particle being of the same magnitude) will be less at every particle; the second will produce less than the first, the third than the second, and so on.[3]

Here Bentham introduced the idea of the marginal utility of money, just as Ricardo introduced the idea of marginal productivity in his theory of rent.

Implications of Bentham's Ideas

In their time, Bentham's ideas promoted progress, reform, wider democracy, and the amelioration of undesirable social conditions. Bentham lived and wrote during a period when common people, the "labouring poor," had little voice and no vote in the management of social and political affairs. They were expected to be subservient, docile, and hardworking. Their toil and sacrifices enhanced the power of the nation, the glory of its rulers, the wealth of industrialists and merchants, and the indolent ease of the aristocrats. Yet here was a philosopher who said that people are people regardless of their social position. Thus, if something adds to a commoner's pleasure more than it detracts from the pleasure of an aristocrat, it is commendable; if government intervention enhances the happiness of a community more than it diminishes it, the intervention is justified.

Bentham emphasized that legislators ought actively to augment the total happiness of the community. Instead of people serving the state, the state should serve the people. Individuals themselves, not government, are generally the best judge of what

---

[2] Jeremy Bentham, *An Introduction to the Principles of Morals and Legislation* (New York: Hafner, 1948), 1–3. (Orig. pub. 1780.)

[3] W. Stark, *Jeremy Bentham's Economic Writings,* 3 vols. (New York: Franklin, 1952), 1: 113.

most effectively promotes their own well-being. He concluded that most existing state controls and regulations were harmful, and his slogan for government was "Be quiet." But he did not worship laissez-faire as a principle to be accepted blindly. Bentham advocated the philosophy that if special reasons exist the government ought to intervene. For example, he thought the state should monopolize the issue of paper money, thereby saving interest on its borrowing. It should also operate life and annuity insurance and tax inheritance, monopolies, and so forth. Where people's interests are not naturally harmonious, the state should establish an artificial harmony of interests that promotes the greatest happiness of the greatest number.

The utilitarian philosophers hoped to make morals an exact science. In their view, if only pleasure and pain could be measured quantitatively and compared among different individuals, every law and act could be judged by balancing the total pleasure produced against the total pain. Bentham concluded that money is the instrument that measures the quantity of pleasure or pain. "Those who are not satisfied with accuracy of this instrument must find out some other that shall be more accurate, or bid adieu to politics and morals."[4]

Bentham's idea of diminishing marginal utility of money supported an argument for the redistribution of income. If government takes income from someone who has an income of $10,000 per year and gives it to someone who earns only $1,000, more happiness will be gained by the poor person than will be lost by the wealthy one. But Bentham did not suggest that this theory be put into practice. By marshaling counterarguments against the redistribution of income, he was able to repudiate the conclusions of his own theory. Equalizing incomes, he thought, would destroy happiness by alarming the rich and depriving them of a feeling of security, by taking away their enjoyment of the fruits of their work, and by destroying the incentive to work. When security and equality are in opposition, said Bentham, equality should give way.

Bentham's devotion to the greatest good for the greatest number led him to study and advocate many democratic reforms. He supported universal (male) suffrage, equal electoral districts, annual parliaments, and the secret ballot. He opposed the monarchy and the House of Lords, arguing that only in a democracy do the interests of the governors and the governed become identical. At a time when there was little enthusiasm for education, Bentham urged a system of national education, even for pauper children. Frugality Banks, he suggested, should be organized to stimulate saving by the poor. Public works should provide jobs for unemployed workers during slack times. He endorsed lending at interest, free trade, competition, and legal reforms. He designed an elaborate plan for a model prison that would reform criminals rather than punish them. No wonder Bentham and his circle of intellects (including James Mill, John Stuart Mill, and Ricardo) were called "philosophic radicals."

Refer to 8-1 PAST AS PROLOGUE

Criticisms

Despite their positive aspects, however, Bentham's economics and philosophy have been widely criticized on both economic as well as philosophical and ethical grounds.

[4] Stark, *Jeremy Bentham's Economic Writings,* 1: 117.

8-1 PAST AS PROLOGUE

Aquinas, Bentham, and Fisher on Usury

Although lending money at interest is now commonplace, it once was called "usury" and thought to be sinful.* The medieval theologian Saint Thomas Aquinas (1225–1274) reached that conclusion based on the Bible, citing Luke 6:35, where Jesus says, "Lend freely, hoping nothing thereby." For Christians, said Aquinas, lending should be charitable, not exploitative. Charging interest on loans is sinful because it reflects avarice: lust for earthly things. Also, according to Aquinas, usury increases income inequality. Those who borrow are poor, and those who lend are wealthy, so interest transfers income from the poor to the wealthy.

Strict legal prohibition against lending at interest became commonplace in Europe during the Middle Ages (roughly 500–1500). Gradually, however, this outright prohibition was replaced with usury laws setting maximum interest rates on loans. These laws had widespread support, with even Adam Smith approving of the existing British usury law that limited interest rates to 5 percent.

Jeremy Bentham, in contrast, strongly opposed any such government restrictions on interest rates. In his *Defense of Usury* (1778), he supported a "liberty of making one's own terms in money-bargains."

> In a word, the proposition I have been accustomed to lay down to myself on this subject is the following one, viz. that *no man of ripe years and sound mind, acting freely, and with his eyes wide open ought to be hindered, with a view to his advantage, from making such bargain, in the way of obtaining money, as he thinks fit: nor* (what is a necessay consequence) *any body hindered from supplying him, upon any terms he thinks proper to accede to.*
>
> This proposition, were it to be received, would level, you see, at one stroke, all the barriers which law, either statute or common, have in their limited wisdom set up . . . against the crying sin of Usury.†

Bentham argued that no legislator could judge the worth of money to an individual as well as could that individual himself or herself. Moreover, he pointed out that "laws against usury may do mischief" by precluding many from getting loans altogether, exposing lenders to unmerited disgrace and encouraging ingratitude among borrowers.

Although Bentham defended usury, it was left for subsequent economists to analyze the true nature of interest. One such economist was Irving Fisher (1867–1947), whose theory of interest is discussed in Chapter 16. The following story told by Fisher previews that discussion.

In the process of a massage, a masseur told Fisher he was a socialist and believed that "interest is the basis of capitalism, and is robbery." Following the massage, Fisher asked, "How much do I owe you?"

The masseur replied, "Thirty dollars."

8-1 PAST AS PROLOGUE (continued)

"Very well," said Fisher, "I will give you a note payable a hundred years hence. I suppose you have no objections to taking this note without any interest. At the end of that time you, or perhaps your grandchildren can redeem it."

"But I cannot afford to wait that long," said the masseur.

"I thought you said that interest was robbery. If interest is robbery, you ought to be willing to wait indefinitely for the money. If you are willing to wait ten years, how much would you require?"

"Well, I would have to get more than thirty dollars."

With a gleam in his eye, Fisher replied, "That is interest."‡

---

*Today, *usury* implies lending money at *excessive* interest, but as used earlier, it simply meant lending money at any interest rate.

†Stark, *Jeremy Bentham's Economic Writings,* 1: 129.

‡Irving Fisher, as quoted in Irving Norton Fisher, *My Father Irving Fisher* (New York: Comet, 1956), 77.

Economic criticisms. Bentham recognized that assessments of pleasure and pain are subjective; they vary from person to person. But his goal of promoting the greatest happiness for the greatest number of people required the making of interpersonal utility comparisons. Such comparisons necessitate the precise measurement of utility in cardinal terms. That is, utility must be measured in units that can be added, subtracted, multiplied, and divided, just like the cardinal numbers 1 through 10.

Bentham chose money as his unit of cardinal measurement. But how does one determine the monetary value of pleasurable things? To be sure, many things are exchanged in the market, and the prices paid for them provide information about subjective value. When a buyer pays $10 for an item we can reasonably assume that the person expects it to provide at least $10 worth of pleasure. But, as Dupuit and Marshall later showed, many purchases at market prices are made by people who are willing to pay more than those amounts rather than forego the products. They receive what economists call a *consumer surplus*—utility in excess of price. How does one measure this surplus? Similarly, what procedure should be used to measure the monetary value of the utility derived from public goods (for example, national defense) whose benefits are received independently of payment for them? Conclusion: People have different subjective valuations of the value of things; to measure and to compare these valuations in a meaningful way are extremely difficult, if not impossible.

Philosophical and ethical criticisms. Many critics of utilitarianism claim that it is deficient as a philosophy. Bentham, abjuring all value judgments on the quality of pleasure, stated that the "quantity of pleasure being equal, push-pin is as good as poetry." He playfully described the difference between prose and poetry: "*Prose* is where all the lines but the last go on to the margin—poetry is where some of them fall short of it." If, in a recent decade, a quarterback for a professional football team provided more joy to more people than Shakespeare's dramas, Bentham would say that the quarterback's contribution to humanity during that time was greater. Yet critics point out that qualitative and long-term aspects of happiness may be more significant than quantitative ones. Shakespeare's insights into the human condition and his ability to inspire generation after generation, these people argue, surely count more in the human scheme of things than the collective pleasure resulting from the quarterback's touchdown passes.

According to this perspective, our value judgments in aesthetics and our philosophy of the good life aim at more than a narrow definition of happiness. As John Stuart Mill said, "It is better to be a human being dissatisfied than a pig satisfied; better to be Socrates dissatisfied than a fool satisfied." Or as George Bernard Shaw said, "Happiness is not the object of life: life has no object: it is an end in itself: and courage consists in the readiness to sacrifice happiness for an intenser quality of life."

Detractors of utilitarianism also point to alternative explanations of human behavior that dispute the hedonistic view that people are motivated solely by the desire to maximize pleasure and minimize pain. For example, behaviorists in psychology talk of conditioned reflexes. Freudian psychiatry claims that the fundamental driving force governing human behavior is the conflict between opposing forces deep within the personality. Students of cultural anthropology point out that, in one way or another, society imposes on the individual its system of ideas, patterns of behavior, and way of living. These ideas all challenge the pleasure-pain principle as the guiding force of human behavior.

Finally, several rival ethical systems also have challenged Bentham's utilitarianism. Many people deny the idea that every society and every government should promote the greatest happiness for the greatest number of people. Plato taught that pleasure is subordinate in value to knowledge and that it should be a by-product of effective achievement. The Stoics favored disciplining the sensual appetites of the body, because they considered passion and desire morbid conditions of the soul. Various religions preached resignation to the inescapable suffering of this world as the key to the good and worthy life, mortification and self-denial as the means of overcoming impulses to sin, or the performance of duty as the way to salvation. Thomas Hobbes (1588–1679) held that humans have a fundamentally depraved nature that drives them toward war, strife, and the selfish appropriation of all that they can lay their hands on; therefore, a strong and absolute government is required to keep them in check. John Locke (1632–1704), who did not think every good is a moral good, found in people a social bent and sense of obligation that would bind them together where no restraint of law existed. Modern fascists glorify the strong state as the supreme good, and communists place the advancement of class interests above the individual quest for happiness. All such systems of thought or belief claim that they, too, seek the greatest happiness of the greatest number of people. The difference, of course, is that these other systems would approach this goal indirectly, either in this world or in the next, either in the present or in some vague undefined future.

Bentham's Legacy to Economics

Bentham's concept of human nature—although not his utilitarianism—became the foundation for the economic systems of Ricardo, John Stuart Mill, and the early marginalists, especially William Stanley Jevons. The concepts of utility maximization, which assumed that each person would compare the intensity of satisfactions received from a great variety of goods, and diminishing marginal utility are at the heart of the marginalist theory of demand. People were assumed to be perfectly rational and carefully calculating. Labor was believed to be "painful" and therefore requiring "compensation." To achieve maximum happiness, people would work the number of hours at which the marginal utility of their earnings just equaled the marginal disutility of their labor. The entrepreneurs, in determining volume of output, would try to maximize their profits (utility) by comparing revenues and costs.

As we proceed through the history of economic thought, we will discover that contemporary economic analysis does not depend on Bentham's narrow "felicific calculus" (pain-pleasure calculus) as a philosophical base. Today, economic theory takes other motives and other behavior patterns into account. Also, most modern economists reject interpersonal utility comparisons. Yet few observers would deny that a great deal of contemporary economic thought, with its emphasis on rational choice made by comparing costs and benefits, has its roots planted firmly in the concept of human behavior developed by Jeremy Bentham. For better or worse, most modern economists view human behavior as being purposeful activity. In fact, one recent trend in the discipline has been to search out and analyze rationality in such unusual areas as discrimination, marriage, crime, and addiction. Bentham was correct when he stated: "But I have planted the tree of utility. I have planted it deep and spread it wide."

JEAN-BAPTISTE SAY

Jean-Baptiste Say (1767–1832) was a Frenchman who popularized Adam Smith's ideas on the Continent. His major work, *A Treatise on Political Economy,* was published in 1803. Say's career was temporarily blocked because Napoleon was displeased with his extreme laissez-faire views. Some time after Napoleon's defeat at Waterloo, Say became a professor of political economy, after having spent numerous years in business.

Value Theory, Costs of Monopoly, and Entrepreneurship

Say opposed the labor theory of value of the classical school, replacing it with supply and demand, which in turn are regulated by costs of production and utility. Thus in some respects his analysis was more advanced than that of Ricardo. Say's discussion of supply and demand, however, did not include development of schedules showing price-quantity relationships as did that of Marshall. Instead the terms *supply* and *demand* were used quite loosely and imprecisely.

Say contributed to the modern theory of the costs of monopoly by pointing out that monopolists not only create what today we call *efficiency losses* (or *deadweight losses*) but also use scarce resources in their competition to obtain and protect their monopoly positions.

Refer to 8-2 PAST AS PROLOGUE

Finally, Say contributed to economic thought by emphasizing entrepreneurship as a fourth factor of production along with the more traditional ones of land, labor, and capital. Recall that Cantillon first used the term *entrepreneur.*

8-2 PAST AS PROLOGUE

Say and Rent Seeking*

Ricardo defined rent as "that portion of the produce of the earth, which is paid to the landlord for the use of the original and indestructible powers of the soil." Because the total quantity of land is fixed (its supply curve is perfectly inelastic), increases in the demand for food will raise food prices and increase the demand for the use of land. Rents therefore will rise. Although they serve to ration land use, these higher rents have no incentive function; they do not bring forth more land. Thus, rents are payments that are not necessary to ensure the availability of land to the economy as a whole.

Since Ricardo's time, economists have expanded the definition of economic rent to include payments above those funds necessary to keep *any* resource in its present employment. For example, firms earning economic profits (those above a normal profit) are said to be receiving economic rents.

James Buchanan (Chapter 20), Gordon Tullock, and other contemporary economists have pointed out that government is often a major dispenser of economic rent. To get re-elected, politicians curry favor by providing something of value to their constituents. Public goods and services are one such set of items. Another set is laws, rules, and regulations that enable people or firms to obtain or maintain economic rent. The behavior of those producers (or consumers or workers) competing to get such government favors is called "rent seeking." This behavior may be privately rewarding, but it is socially unproductive.

Formalization of the idea of rent seeking is relatively new, but it is clear from the following four quotations that J.-B. Say understood this idea.[†] Writing in 1803, he stated:

> [Participants in the activity of requesting and granting state monopoly privileges are] those engaged in any particular branch of trade who are so anxious to have themselves made the subject of regulation; and the public authorities are commonly, on their part, very ready to indulge them in what offers so fair an opportunity of raising a revenue.[‡]

> If one individual, or one class, can call in the aid of authority to ward off the effects of competition, it acquires a privilege to the prejudice and at the cost of the whole community; it can then make sure of profits not altogether due to the productive services rendered, but composed in part of an actual tax upon consumers for its private profit; which tax it commonly shares with the authority that thus unjustly lends its support.[§]

> When printed calicos [imported from abroad] first came into fashion, all the chambers of commerce were up in arms; meetings, discussions everywhere took place; memorial and deputations poured in from every quarter, and great sums were spent in opposition.[||]

> Who then are the classes of the community so importunate for prohibitions of heavy import duties? The producers of the particular commodity, that applies for protection from foreign competition, not the consumers of that commodity. . . . Whatever profit

8-2 PAST AS PROLOGUE (continued)

> is acquired in this manner is so much taken out of the pockets of a neighbor and fellow-citizen and, if the excess of charge thrown upon consumers could be correctly computed, it would be found, that the loss of the consumer exceeds the gain of the monopolist.[#]

Clearly, Say viewed the cost of government-granted or government-protected monopoly as having two components: the traditional efficiency loss *plus* society's opportunity cost of rent-seeking activity.

---

*Based on Patricia J. Euzent and Thomas L. Martin, "Classical Roots in the Emerging Theory of Rent Seeking: The Contribution of Jean-Baptiste Say," *History of Political Economy* (Summer 1984): 255–262.

†Adam Smith also addressed this idea. See E. G. West, "The Burdens of Monopoly: Classical Versus Neoclassical," *Southern Economic Journal* (April 1978): 829–845.

‡J.-B. Say, *A Treatise on Political Economy* (Philadelphia: Claxton, Remsen & Haffelfinger, 1880), 176–177. (Orig. pub. 1803.)

§Say, *Treatise,* 161–162.

‖Say, *Treatise,* 147.

#Say, *Treatise,* 161–162.

Say's Law of Markets

But Say's chief claim to fame rests on his theory that general overproduction is impossible. As indicated in the previous chapter, this came to be known as Say's law of markets.

The earliest statement of this idea can be found in the writings of Smith's instructor, Francis Hutcheson. Smith himself implied such a law and specifically stated, "A particular merchant, with abundance of goods in his warehouse, may sometimes be ruined by not being able to sell them in time, [but] a nation is not liable to the same accident." The idea was put most succinctly by James Mill in 1808: "If a nation's power of purchasing is exactly measured by its annual produce . . . the more you increase the annual produce, the more by that very act you extend the national market, the power of purchasing and the actual purchases of the nation." But Say also expressed this idea, and Keynes later attributed it to him. As a result it became Say's law, as opposed to the Smith-Mill law.[5] Let us listen to Say:

> Should a tradesman say, "I do not want other products for my woolens, I want money," . . . he may be told, . . . "You say, you only want money; I say, you want other commodities, and not money. For what, in point of fact, do you want money? Is it not for the purchase of raw materials or stock for your trade, or of victuals for your support? Wherefore, it is products that you want, and not money."[6]

---

[5] William O. Thweatt, "Early Formulators of Say's Law," *Quarterly Review of Economics and Business* 19 (Winter 1978): 79–96.

[6] J.-B. Say, *A Treatise on Political Economy* (Philadelphia: Claxton, Remsen & Haffelfinger, 1880), 133. (Orig. pub. 1803.)

Furthermore, Say added a cheerful footnote:

> Even when money is obtained with a view to hoard or bury it, the ultimate object is always to employ it in a purchase of some kind. The heir of the lucky finder uses it in that way, if the miser do not: for money, as money, has no other use than to buy with.[7]

And even more to the point.

> It is worth while to remark, that a product is no sooner created, than it, from that instance, affords a market for other products to the full extent of its own value. When the producer has put the finishing hand to his product, he is most anxious to sell it immediately, lest its value should vanish in his hands. Nor is he less anxious to dispose of the money he may get for it; for the value of money is also perishable. But the only way of getting rid of money is in the purchase of some product or other. Thus, the mere circumstance of the creation of one product immediately opens a vent for other products.[8]

Although challenged by Malthus, Sismondi, and Marx, Say's law continued to dominate economic thinking until Keynes highlighted its weaknesses in 1936. Uncritical acceptance of this law of markets appears to have delayed the study of business cycles for many decades. But although Smith, James Mill, and Say were wrong in assuming that the economy always tends toward full employment, there is a certain long-run validity to this doctrine. Underdeveloped economies are characterized by low output and corresponding low income payments to people. As an economy grows, it simultaneously generates an increased supply of goods and increased payments to the factors of production, which in turn generate an increased demand for goods. Similarly, in international trade as a country produces more, it can export more, and it can therefore afford to import more. Both in domestic and in foreign trade, "supply creates its own demand" in the long run. This principle does not hold true, however, in the short run in market-based economies. Even though payments to factors of production would be enough to buy all the goods produced, there is no guarantee that the recipients of these income payments will spend them on the existing output.

NASSAU WILLIAM SENIOR

Nassau William Senior (1790–1864) was the oldest son of a country clergyman who had ten children. In 1825 Senior became the first professor of political economy at Oxford. The government appointed him a member of several royal commissions that investigated important social problems. In his economic thinking he departed significantly from classical economics and moved toward the neoclassical position that triumphed after 1870.

Positive Economics

Senior wished to separate the science of political economy from all value judgments, all policy pronouncements, and all efforts to promote welfare. Today we refer to this

[7] Say, *Treatise,* 133.

[8] Say, *Treatise,* 134–135.

suggested type of analysis as *positive economics,* in contrast to *normative economics,* which concerns itself with the "ought to be" and uses economics to champion public policies. According to Senior, economists should concern themselves with analyzing the production and distribution of wealth, not the promotion of happiness. Senior stated:

> But [the economist's] conclusions, whatever be their generality and their truth, do not authorize him in adding a single syllable of advice. That privilege belongs to the writer and statesman who has considered all the causes which may promote or impede the general welfare of those whom he addresses, not to the theorist who has considered only one, though among the most important, of those causes. The business of a Political Economist is neither to recommend nor to dissuade, but to state general principle.[9]

Senior's Four Propositions

Senior stated four principles of economics that he felt are empirically verifiable and from which an integrated theory of economics could be deduced.

> (1) That man desires to obtain additional wealth with as little sacrifice as possible. [*Principle of income or utility maximization.*]
>
> (2) That the Population of the world, in other words, the number of persons inhabiting it, is limited only by moral or physical evil, or by fear of a deficiency of those articles of wealth which the habits of each class of its inhabitants lead them to require. [*Principle of population.*]
>
> (3) That the powers of Labour and of the other instruments which produce wealth, may be indefinitely increased by using their Products as means of further production. [*Principle of capital accumulation.*]
>
> (4) That agricultural skill remaining the same, additional Labour employed on the land within a given district produces in general a less proportionate return, or, in other words, that though, with every increase of the labour bestowed, the aggregate return is increased, the increase of the return is not in proportion to the increase of the labour. [*Principle of diminishing returns.*][10]

Abstinence

The exchange value of goods, according to Senior, depends on demand and supply. Underlying demand is the concept of the diminishing marginal utility of goods as more units are acquired. This was an important insight that later was expanded by the marginalists. Supply depends on the costs of production. But cost, said Senior, is *subjective*—the sum of sacrifices required in order to use nature's agents to produce useful goods. The costs of production are the labor of the workers and the abstinence of the capitalists. *Abstinence* was a new term that Senior contributed to the lexicon of political economy, as follows:

---

[9] Nassau William Senior, *An Outline of the Science of Political Economy* (New York: Kelley, 1951), 3. (Orig. pub. 1836.)

[10] Senior, *Outline,* 26.

> But although Human Labour, and the Agency of Nature, independently of that of man, are the primary Productive Powers, they require the concurrence of a Third Productive Principle to give them complete efficiency. . . . To the Third Principle, or Instrument of Production, without which the two others are inefficient, we shall give the name of *Abstinence:* a term by which we express the conduct of a person who either abstains from the unproductive use of what he can command, or designedly prefers the production of remote to that of immediate results. . . . *By the word Abstinence, we wish to express that agent, distinct from labour and the agency of nature, the concurrence of which is necessary to the existence of Capital, and which stands in the same relation to Profit as Labour does to Wages.*[11]

Senior's use of the term *abstinence* implied a value judgment about the sacrifices undertaken by the capitalist in postponing (or foregoing forever) the consumption of wealth. Marx and the German state socialist Ferdinand Lassalle made great sport of this concept. The latter wrote scornfully of the abstinence of a Baron Rothschild and the profligate wastefulness of the English laborer who squandered all his income of a few shillings a week on consumption. Alfred Marshall later redesignated the function of savings as *waiting*—that is, postponing consumption. This term was both less colorful and less controversial than *abstinence;* it did not imply any suffering or sacrifice by the rich while they were accumulating wealth.

The socialist critics who ridiculed the concept of the irksomeness of saving overlooked one crucial point: The sacrifice is not the *total* amount of saving, but rather the sacrifice *at the margin*—the point of change at which decisions are made. It is likely that a millionaire could save $10,000 with far less agony per dollar than a poor man would incur in saving $100. Let us consider, however, that portion of the savings that is made at the borderline of uncertainty—the point at which one decides whether to save an extra sum or spend it on consumption. At those margins—the 10,000th dollar and the 100th dollar—the sacrifices of postponing consumption may well be equal. They also may be sufficiently large to require remuneration in the form of interest.

An interesting implication long associated with classical economics derives from this definition of saving. Saving is the activity that produces new investment spending. When the reward—the interest rate (i)—paid for abstaining from consumption rises, then more saving (S) occurs. Stated mathematically, $S = f(i)$. On the other hand, investment spending (I)—the purchase of capital goods—varies positively with the opportunity cost of investing, the interest rate (i). That is, $I = g(i)$. Thus, an extension of Say's law emerges: Because saving is a positive function of the interest rate and investment a negative function of the interest rate, the rate will adjust to a level at which all the savings will be invested. If for some reason the pool of savings rises (consumption falls), the equilibrium interest rate will fall, which in turn will increase borrowing and purchases of capital goods. The decline in spending on consumer goods will be exactly offset by increased spending on capital goods. Thus, according to this classical perspective, no deficiency of total demand will occur; Say's law is not invalidated by the act of saving.

---

[11] Senior, *Outline,* 58–59.

Productive Labor

Senior disagreed with Smith, who thought that the producers of services are all unproductive. Lawyers, doctors, and teachers, Senior said, are productive because they promote the increase of wealth. Where a soldier must protect the farmers, both are productive. Suppose a thousand people are employed forging bars and bolts to keep out thieves; if a hundred of them can achieve the same purpose by becoming security workers instead, is wealth diminished by this conversion from "productive" to "unproductive" workers? To Senior the proper distinction was not between productive and unproductive labor but rather between productive and unproductive consumption. The latter category includes consumption of lace, embroidery, jewelry, tobacco, gin, and beer, all of which diminish the mass of commodities without adding to the workers' capacity to produce.

Policy Positions

Senior did not heed his own prescription that economists should never offer a single syllable of advice. In his long career in public life, he made numerous pronouncements on policy issues, never explaining whether his recommendations were offered with all the weight of his economic theories behind them or not.

Poor laws. Senior served on the Poor Law Commission appointed in 1832. He wrote the bulk of the report resulting in the harsh Poor Law Amendment of 1834, which sought to discourage application for relief by people physically able to work. The act established the principle that the living conditions of those receiving welfare should be worse than those of the poorest-paid laborers. These poor laws were in force for seventy years.

Trade unions. As a passionate champion of limited government, economic freedom (as he viewed it), and mobility of labor, Senior was unequivocally opposed to the trade union movement. Among his proposals were prohibition of all conspiracies and restraints of trade by labor, severe punishment for all solicitations to form unions, prohibition of and severe punishment for all picketing, confiscation of funds owned by unions, and compensation from public funds for people who were injured while resisting unions.

Factory Acts. In 1837 Senior published a pamphlet opposing the English Factory Acts, which at the time limited the working day to 12 hours in factories where children were employed. Although he endorsed the principle of regulating child labor, he opposed laws limiting the hours of adults. In calculating the economic effect of a shorter working day, he made no allowance for reduced outlays for raw materials, heating, lighting, depreciation, and so forth. He also ignored the probability of increased output per hour that might result from a shorter working day. His confused and erroneous reasoning led to the conclusion that all profit is derived from the last hour of work. If the working day were shortened by more than an hour, capitalists would fail to earn profits, and England would be ruined in competition with foreign producers. His major concern was to attack the rising agitation for a 10-hour workday.

JOHN STUART MILL

Life and Influences

John Stuart Mill (1806–1873) was the last great economist of the classical school, undoubtedly the greatest since Ricardo's death in 1823. Mill made some significant original contributions, and he systematized and popularized the whole body of economic thought of his predecessors. The classical school was already in decline during Mill's mature years, and he departed from some of the key concepts built into the classical structure by Smith and Ricardo. Before his death neoclassical economics had appeared on the scene, ultimately to displace its classical forebears. Mill's great *Principles of Political Economy,* first published in 1848 and reprinted in the United States as late as 1920, was the leading textbook in the field, at least until the publication of Alfred Marshall's *Principles of Economics* in 1890.

Mill reported his amazing upbringing in his *Autobiography,* published shortly after his death. His father, James Mill, was the man who urged Ricardo to write, publish, and sit in Parliament; James popularized Bentham's ideas and helped found the group known as philosophical radicals, which pushed for political reforms in Great Britain. James Mill also offered the earliest clear statement of Say's law of markets. A strict disciplinarian, he himself supervised the education of John, the oldest of nine children. The elder Mill was strongly committed to the idea that all people are born alike, with little or no significant variation in their innate genetic potential for learning. Any child could be molded into what mistakenly appeared to be a genius. Therefore, John was to be raised to carry on the great work of his predecessors in utilitarian economics and politics. The boy began to learn Greek at three, but as he wrote apologetically, "I learnt no Latin until my eighth year." By then he was reading the Greek philosophers in the original but not always understanding them. At eleven he read proofs of his father's *History of India* and was greatly impressed. He mastered algebra and elementary geometry and began to study differential calculus by the time he was twelve; he had by then written a history of the Roman government, which was not published. John then began to study logic, and at thirteen he began the study of political economy. Between the ages of fifteen and eighteen Mill edited and published five volumes of Bentham's manuscripts. At nineteen he was publishing original scholarly articles, and at twenty he had a well-earned nervous breakdown.

John Stuart Mill wrote in his *Autobiography* that his father made him read and give verbal accounts of books in which he had no interest. He was permitted few toys or children's books, he was not allowed to take holidays or associate much with other children lest the habit for work be broken and a taste for idleness acquired. "But my father, in all his teaching, demanded of me not only the utmost that I could do, but much that I could by no possibility have done." No wonder John Mill wrote of his father that "the element which was chiefly deficient in his moral relation to his children was that of tenderness."

Refer to 8-3 PAST AS PROLOGUE

Although raised in the Benthamite tradition, Mill rejected the latter's narrow and dogmatic utilitarianism, because Mill regarded as too limited Bentham's view that human beings are motivated in their conduct by nothing more than self-love

8-3 PAST AS PROLOGUE

Mill, Taylor, and the Rights of Women

John Stuart Mill met Mrs. Harriet Taylor (1807–1858) when he was twenty-four years old. A warm friendship and association between them followed; they even took vacations together on the Continent and in the English countryside. Twenty years later, after her husband died, John and Harriet were married. Mill attributed to his wife his humanitarianism, hope for and faith in human progress, love of liberty, and passionate defense of the rights of women.

The views of Harriet and John Stuart Mill on the economic rights of women are interesting, particularly in view of the intense interest in this topic today. In the essay "Enfranchisement of Women," first published in 1851, the Mills deplored the exclusion of women from certain fields that were considered "unfeminine"; they repudiated the idea that the "proper sphere" of women is not politics or publicity but private and domestic life. They denied the right of any people to decide for others what is and what is not their "proper sphere."

> Let every occupation be open to all, without favour or discouragement to any, and employments will fall into the hands of those men and women who are found by experience to be most capable of worthily exercising them. There need be no fear that women will take out of the hands of men any occupation which men perform better than they. Each individual will prove his or her capacities, in the only way in which capacities can be proved—by trial; and the world will have the benefit of the best faculties of all its inhabitants. But to interfere beforehand by an arbitrary limit, and declare that whatever be the genius, talent, energy, or force of mind of an individual of a certain sex or class, those faculties shall not be exerted, or shall be exerted only in some few of the many modes in which others are permitted to use theirs, is not

and the desire for self-gratification. He charged Bentham with neglecting the human search for perfection, honor, and other ends entirely for their own sakes. Mill did not abandon the utilitarian ideas but rather modified them. He was concerned, for example, with the quality of enjoyment as well as the quantity.

Mill's *Principles of Political Economy* is divided into five books: "Production," "Distribution," "Exchange," "Influence of the Progress of Society on Production and Distribution," and "Of the Influence of Government." These topics will provide the structure for the remainder of the chapter.

Production

In the first book, Mill analyzed three productive factors: land, labor, and capital. Wealth is defined as including all useful things that possess exchange value; only material objects are included because only they can be accumulated. Productive

> only an injustice to the individual, and a detriment to society, which loses what it can ill spare, but is also the most effectual mode of providing that, in the sex or class so fettered, the qualities which are not permitted to be exercised shall not exist.*

In "The Subjection of Women" (published in 1869), Mill pursued the idea that equal rights for women would also benefit men. Think what it is to a boy, he said, to grow up believing that without any merit or exertion of his own, although he may be empty and ignorant, but the mere fact of being born a male he is superior to every woman on earth. His feeling is similar to that of a hereditary king. The relation between husband and wife is comparable to that between a lord and vassal. "However the vassal's character may have been affected, for better or worse, by his subordination, who can help seeing that the lord's was affected greatly for the worse?"†

Although women's rights and their role in the labor force have expanded greatly since the mid-1800s, contemporary studies continue to find gender discrimination in pay.‡ Also, women are overrepresented in the relatively low-paying fields of teaching, nursing, child care, and clerical and secretarial work. Does this pattern reflect free choice, or sexism and discrimination? Where firms *do* have women managers, do they also have "glass ceilings" preventing women from reaching the executive suites? Are government requirements that companies take affirmative action to hire more women efficient and equitable? These contemporary issues would surely be of great interest to the Mills.

---

*John Stuart Mill, "Enfranchisement of Women," *Dissertations and Discussions,* 2 vols. (London, 1859), 2: 423.

†John Stuart Mill and Harriet Taylor Mill, *Essays on Sex Equality,* ed. Alice S. Rossi (Chicago: University of Chicago Press, 1970), 219.

‡For a summary of this literature, see Francine D. Blau and Marianne A. Ferber, "Discrimination: Empirical Evidence from the United States," *American Economic Review* 77 (May 1987): 316–320; and Glen G. Cain, "The Economics of Discrimination: A Survey," in *Handbook of Labor Economics,* eds. Orley Ashenfelter and Richard Layard (Amsterdam: North Holland Press, 1986), 693–785.

labor includes only those kinds of exertions that produce utilities embodied in material objects. But labor that yields a material product only indirectly is also held to be productive. Thus, educators and government officials are productive because their services create the conditions required for the output of material goods. Unproductive labor is that which does not terminate in the creation of material wealth. For example, labor that ends in immediate enjoyment without any increase of the accumulated stock or permanent means of enjoyment is unproductive; saving a friend's life is unproductive unless the friend is a productive laborer of greater production than consumption; and missionaries or clergymen are unproductive unless they teach the arts of civilization in addition to religious doctrines. Unproductive labor may nevertheless be useful.

Capital, the result of saving, is the accumulated stock of the produce of labor, and its aggregate amount limits the extent of industry. Every increase of capital is capable of giving additional employment to labor without limit. This tendency eliminates the need for unproductive expenditure by the rich to give employment to the poor. Mill assumed that everything saved through the abstinence of the capitalist would be invested. If capitalists spent less on luxury consumption and more on investment, the wages fund and demand for labor would rise. If population increased, the increased demand for necessities by wage earners would offset the decreased demand for luxuries by capitalists. If population did not increase in proportion to the growth of capital, wages would rise, and luxury consumption by workers would supplant luxury consumption by their employers. This is the optimistic world of full employment. "Thus the limit of wealth is never deficiency of consumers, but of producers and productive power. Every addition to capital gives to labour either additional employment, or additional remuneration; enriches either the country, or the labouring class."[12]

What are the obstacles to increasing production? Lack of labor is not one of them, said Mill, because population could increase geometrically. That it does not is due to impulses superior to mere animal instincts. People do not propagate like swine but are restrained by prudence from multiplying beyond the means of subsistence. Population is limited by *fear of want* rather than by want itself.

The increase of capital depends on two things: (1) the surplus product after the necessities are supplied to all engaged in production and (2) the disposition to save. The greater the profit that can be made from capital, the stronger the motive for its accumulation. The inclination to save also varies from person to person and from country to country.

The limited extent of land and its limited productiveness are the real barriers to increases of production. Mill recognized *increasing* returns to scale in manufacturing; that is, within certain limits, the larger the enterprise, the more efficient it becomes. He thought that agriculture exhibits *decreasing* returns to scale; larger farm size is not matched with commensurate increases in farm output. He applied the short-run law of diminishing returns only to agriculture. That is, if the supply of land is constant, adding labor will not add to the product in the same proportion. Mill did not concern himself with whether the same proposition would hold true in industry if capital were kept constant. His reason for differentiating between the two was his assumption that the supply of capital can be increased easily, whereas the supply of land cannot. Mill's implicit distinction between the short-run law of diminishing returns and the long-run concept of returns to scale was an important insight upon which later neoclassical theorists built the theory of the firm.

Distribution

In Book II, "Distribution," Mill began with his famous, far-reaching pronouncement:

> The laws and conditions of the production of wealth, partake of the character of physical truths. There is nothing optional or arbitrary in them. . . . It is not so with the Distribution of Wealth. That is a matter of human institutions solely. The things once there, mankind, individually or collectively, can do with them as they like.[13]

[12] John Stuart Mill, *Principles of Political Economy,* 7th ed. (London: Longmans, Green, 1896), 43. (Orig. pub. 1848.)

[13] Mill, *Principles,* 123.

Mill failed to recognize that production and distribution are interrelated and that interference with one involves interference with the other. The "things" are not there as a mass of goods already produced. They appear as a continuous flow that gets produced through the incentives provided by payments to the factors of production. The flow can get reduced or completely interrupted if the distribution of income is unfavorable to the maintenance of production. Although both of his propositions in the quotation are exaggerations, they allowed Mill to raise the prospect of a greater role for the political process in determining the proper income distribution. It can be said, to Mill's credit, that he abandoned Ricardo's idea of inexorable "laws of distribution," under whose rule humanity is helpless. Mill flung a challenge at the classical school's belief in the universality and permanence of natural law. This rationalized his defense of limitations on inheritance for distant relatives and his support for other measures that would promote a broader diffusion of ownership of wealth. Although he was basically committed to a private enterprise, profit-oriented economy, he welcomed "profit sharing" and "producer cooperatives" as methods through which workers could enhance their wealth.

Mill on the Wages Fund

Mill, like Senior, Ricardo, James Mill, and Smith before him, accepted the wages fund notion. Wages, he said, depend mainly upon labor demand and supply. The demand for labor depends on that part of the capital set aside for the payments of wages. The supply of labor depends on the number of people seeking work. Under the rule of competition, wages cannot be affected by anything but the relative amounts of capital and population. Wage rates cannot rise except by an increase of the aggregate funds employed in hiring laborers or by a decrease in the number of workers employed. Nor can wage rates fall except by a decline of the funds devoted to paying for labor or by an increase in the number of laborers to be paid. This theory presupposes a *unitary* elasticity of demand for labor; no matter what the wage rate, the same sum is expended for labor.

It follows then, according to Mill, that government cannot increase total wage payments by fixing a minimum wage above the equilibrium level. Given a wages fund of a fixed size, the higher wage income that some workers would receive would be offset entirely by the lost wage income of those who became unemployed. To remedy this condition, the government can increase the size of the wages fund by instituting forced saving through taxation, using the proceeds to overcome the unemployment created by minimum wage laws. Mill recognized that this would have the side effect of removing the restraining influence on the procreation of the poor. "But no one has a right to bring creatures into life, to be supported by other people."

The wages fund doctrine provided a basis for opposing unionism, although Mill did not use it for this purpose. Workers cannot raise their incomes through collective action. If one group raises its wage rate, wages must fall elsewhere. Mill, passionately devoted to liberty, argued that workers should have the right to combine to raise wages even though he considered unions seldom effectual, and when effectual, seldom desirable.

The wages fund concept was erroneous because there is no predetermined proportion of capital that must go to labor. The idea of a fund arose because the harvest of one season was used to provide subsistence for labor for the following year. But once a business gets established, wages are paid not from an advance fund of so-called circulating capital but rather from a current flow of revenue derived from the sale of the output. Later economists pointed out that the decision to hire a worker is based not on the availability of *past* revenue but rather on the *prospective* revenue that the firm will receive by selling the output that the worker helps produce.

Mill supposedly repudiated the wages fund notion in 1869 in a book review he published in *Fortnightly Review*. We say "supposedly" because there is considerable dispute on this point. Some historians of economic thought claim that he indeed tried to repudiate the idea but actually failed to do what he thought he had accomplished.[14] Others contend that what he set out to repudiate was not the concept of the fund but rather the notion that, given the fund, unions are incapable of raising wages.[15] Unions *could* raise the general level of wages, said Mill. Their own higher wages might bolster the ranks of the morally fittest workers who had fewer children, and the resulting unemployment might increase the mortality of the class of workers who would tend to have larger families. If this were the case, population would fall relative to the size of the wages fund, and the overall level of wages would rise. In any event, Mill came to the conclusion that the real limit to increases in wages comes at the point at which the employer would be ruined financially or driven to abandon the business if wages were increased further.

Two additional ideas presented by Mill merit mention before concluding our discussion of his book on distribution. Profit, he said, resolves itself into three parts: interest, insurance, and the wages of superintendence. These are the rewards for abstinence, risk, and exertion implied in the employment of capital. Allowing for differences in risk, attractiveness of different employments, and natural or artificial monopolies, the rate of profit in all spheres of the employment of capital tends toward equality.

Second, like Smith before him, Mill noted that expenditures on education and training partly represent present investments justified by later wage returns. Today we refer to these expenditures as investments in human capital. Mill stated:

> If an artisan must work several years at learning his trade before he can earn anything, and several years more before becoming sufficiently skilful for its finer operations, he must have a prospect of at last earning enough to pay the wages of all this past labour, with compensation for the delay of payment, and an indemnity for the expenses of his education. His wages, consequently, must yield, over and above the ordinary amount, an annuity sufficient to repay these sums, with the common rate of profit, within the number of years he can expect to live and be in working condition.[16]

[14] R. B. Ekelund Jr., "A Short-Run Classical Model of Capital and Wages: Mill's Recantation of the Wages Fund," *Oxford Economic Papers* 28 (March 1976): 22–37.

[15] E. G. West and R. W. Hafer, "J. S. Mill, Unions and the Wages Fund Recantation: A Reinterpretation," *The Quarterly Journal of Economics* 92 (November 1978): 603–619. This view is challenged in R. B. Ekelund Jr. and William F. Kordsmeier, "J. S. Mill, Unions, and the Wages Fund Recantation: A Reinterpretation—Comment," *Quarterly Journal of Economics* 96 (August 1981): 532–541.

[16] Mill, *Principles*, 236–237.

Exchange

In the portion of his *Principles* titled "Exchange," Mill confidently stated the following:

> Happily there is nothing in the laws of Value which remains for the present or any future writer to clear up; the theory of the subject is complete: the only difficulty to overcome is that of so stating it as to solve by anticipation the chief perplexities which occur in applying it.[17]

Price expresses the value of a thing in relation to money; the value of a commodity is measured by its general power to purchase other commodities. There can be a rise of prices but not a general rise of values, because in relative terms all things cannot rise in value simultaneously.

The value of a commodity cannot rise higher than its estimated use value to the buyer. Effectual demand—desire plus purchasing ability—is therefore one determinant of value. But differing quantities are demanded at different values. If demand depends partly on value and value depends on demand, is this not a contradiction, asked Mill. He resolved it by introducing the concept of a demand *schedule* (a relationship between price and the quantity demanded), and by so doing greatly advanced value theory. The quantity demanded is what varies according to the value (or price). The market value gets determined through the interaction of supply and demand, and once this value is established, the quantity demanded gets determined.

Mill had a definite understanding of supply and demand schedules, elasticity of supply and demand, and their influence on prices. These were significant concepts on which Alfred Marshall built further in his elaboration of marginalist principles. With respect to elasticity of supply, Mill classified goods into three categories. The first is "of things absolutely limited in quantity, such as ancient sculptures or pictures." We would call this a perfectly inelastic supply; price changes do not result in changes in the quantity supplied. Demand and supply, said Mill, regulate the value of such goods, with demand being of greatest consequence. The second category of goods is those for which supply is perfectly elastic, and Mill said that the majority of all things bought and sold fit into this category. Production can be expanded without limit at constant cost per unit of output, and values of such commodities depend on supply, or costs of production. The third category of goods is those with a relative elastic supply—those that fall between the two extremes. As Mill put it, "Only a limited quantity can be produced at given cost; if more is wanted, it must be produced at greater cost." This is especially the case in agriculture and mineral products, which have rising costs of production. Their value depends on "the costs necessary for producing and bringing to market the most costly portion of the supply required," or, as we would say, the marginal cost.

The preceding analysis, of course, applies to commodities in the long run. In the short run, prices fluctuate around values according to the relationship of supply and demand; prices rise as demand rises, and prices fall as supply increases.

---

[17]Mill, *Principles,* 265.

Mill stated his concept of equilibrium price and elasticity as follows:

> Let us suppose that the demand at some particular time exceeds the supply, that is, there are persons ready to buy, at the market value, a greater quantity than is offered for sale. Competition takes place on the side of the buyers, and the value rises: but how much? In the ratio (some may suppose) of the deficiency: if the demand exceeds the supply by one-third, the value rises by one-third. By no means: for when the value has risen one-third, the demand may still exceed the supply; there may, even at that higher value, be a greater quantity wanted than is to be had; and the competition of buyers may still continue. If the article is a necessary of life, which, rather than resign, people are willing to pay for at any price, a deficiency of one-third may raise the price to double, triple, or quadruple. Or, on the contrary, the competition may cease before the value has risen in even the proportion of the deficiency. A rise, short of one-third, may place the article beyond the means, or beyond the inclinations, of purchasers to the full amount. At what point, then, will the rise be arrested? At that point, whatever it be, which equalizes the demand and supply.[18]

The Law of International Value

Mill endorsed Ricardo's advocacy of free international trade based on the law of comparative costs. But to this law Mill added a law of international values, one of his important original contributions to economic analysis. Here again the elasticity of demand for goods entered into his theory.

Recall that Ricardo's international trade theory was incomplete; it failed to show how the gain from trade is divided among the trading countries. Mill showed that the actual barter terms of trade depend not only on domestic costs but also on the pattern of demand. More specifically, the terms of international exchange depend on the strength and elasticity of demand for each product in the foreign country.

Although the intricacies of Mill's theory are complex, the general notion is relatively straightforward.[19] He began by pointing out that the value of an imported good is the value of the commodity exported to pay for it. The things that a nation has available to sell abroad constitute the means for purchasing goods from other nations. Thus the supply of commodities made available for export could be thought of as the demand for imports. Mill referred to this idea as "reciprocal demand."

Mill explicitly assumed that under any given technological conditions, output could be changed without altering unit costs of production. Suppose that 10 yards of cloth made in England cost as much as 15 yards of linen but as many as 20 yards of linen in Germany. If there were no transport costs, the limits of the terms of trade between the two countries would be 10 yards of cloth for between 15 and 20 yards of linen.

Now suppose Germany increases the efficiency of producing linen by 50 percent, so that it produces 30 yards with the same effort that formerly produced 20. How will

---

[18] Mill, *Principles,* 277.

[19] Edgeworth and Marshall later depicted Mill's theory of reciprocal demand graphically. A concise presentation of their representation can be found in Robert B. Ekelund Jr. and Robert F. Hébert, *A History of Economic Theory and Method,* 4th ed. (New York: McGraw-Hill, 1997), 178–182.

these gains be divided between the two countries? If 10 yards of cloth formerly exchanged for 17 yards of linen, will they now exchange for 25.5 yards (also a 50 percent change)? This would hold only if the elasticity of demand for linen in England were unitary, so that it would spend the same portion of its income on linen as before. But if the demand for linen in England were *elastic* (a coefficient greater than one), England's increase in purchases would exhaust the higher output on linen before its price fell to reflect the full amount of its reduced cost of production. The ratio of exchange might settle at 10 yards of cloth for 21 of linen, and Germany would get most of the benefits of its increased efficiency in producing linen. If, however, the English demand for linen were *inelastic*, the price would have to fall considerably to induce England to buy the increased output that Germany could produce with its same effort. Germany would have to offer more than 25.5 yards of linen for 10 yards of cloth, and most of the gains would accrue to England.

Dynamics of the Economy

The first three books of his *Principles*, said Mill, cover the economic laws of a stationary and unchanging society in equilibrium, which he called Statics. In the final two books he added a theory of motion, of progressive changes and ultimate tendencies, which he called Dynamics. In Book IV, "Influence of the Progress of Society on Production and Distribution," Mill forecasted increasing production and population, continuing growth of society's mastery over nature, increasing security of person and property, and a growing role for corporations. Improvements in industrial production would be offset by diminishing returns in agriculture and mining as the population continued to grow.

Mill, like Smith and Ricardo, thought that the rate of profit would continue to fall. He agreed with Ricardo that a falling rate of profit was inevitable because of the increased cost of producing food for a growing population.

> The economical progress of a society constituted of landlords, capitalists, and labourers, tends to the progressive enrichment of the landlord class; while the cost of the labourer's subsistence tends on the whole to increase, and profits to fall. Agricultural improvements are a counteracting force to the two last effects; but the first, though a case is conceivable in which it would be temporarily checked, is ultimately in a high degree promoted by those improvements; and the increase of population tends to transfer all the benefits derived from agricultural improvements to the landlords alone.[20]

But Mill was more optimistic than Ricardo in showing why a falling rate of profit would be acceptable, thereby pointing to a more hopeful future.

> There is at every time and place some particular rate of profit, which is the lowest that will induce the people of that country and time to accumulate savings, and to employ those savings productively. This minimum rate of profit varies according to circumstances. It depends on two elements. One is, the strength of the effective desire of accumulation; the comparative estimate made by the people of that place and era, of

[20] Mill, *Principles*, 439.

> future interests when weighted against present. This element chiefly affects the inclination to save. The other element, which affects not so much the willingness to save as the disposition to employ savings productively, is the degree of security of capital engaged in industrial operations.[21]

Progress of society, Mill wrote, would tend to diminish the minimum acceptable rate of profit. More security, less destruction by war, reduced private and public violence, improvements in education and justice—all these would reduce the risk of investment and thereby reduce the minimum necessary rate of profit. In addition, people would tend to show more forethought and self-control in sacrificing present indulgences for future goals. This would increase the pool of savings, lower interest rates, and promote capital accumulation even though the profit rate was low.

The growth of capital would not cause a glut on the market, in that Say's law would keep the economy operating at full employment; but the rate of profit would decline. This tendency would be counterbalanced, however, by the waste and destruction of capital values during crises, improvements in production, the inflow of cheap commodities from abroad, and the outflow of capital into colonies and foreign countries.

The final result of progress, Mill thought, would be a stationary state. But why, he wondered, must we have a rapid rate of progress? Why not settle for a large output and a more equitable distribution of wealth?

> I cannot, therefore, regard the stationary state of capital and wealth with the unaffected aversion so generally manifested towards it by political economists of the old school. I am inclined to believe that it would be, on the whole, a very considerable improvement on our present condition. I confess I am not charmed with the idea of life held out by those who think that the normal state of human beings is that of struggling to get on; that the trampling, crushing, elbowing, and treading on each other's heels, which form the existing type of social life, are the most desirable lot of industrial progress. . . . It is only in the backward countries of the world that increased production is still an important object: in those more advanced, what is economically needed is better distribution, of which one indispensable means is a stricter restraint on population.[22]

As the working classes increase their intelligence, education, and love of independence, their good sense would grow correspondingly. Their habits of conduct would then lead to a population that would diminish in relation to capital and employment. Profit-sharing businesses and cooperative enterprises, operating within a competitive milieu, would further ameliorate conditions. This is preferable, Mill argued, to full-blown socialism, which by disparaging competition would promote monopoly.

On Government

In the final book, "On the Influence of Government," Mill defended the concept of minimal government:

[21] Mill, *Principles,* 441.

[22] Mill, *Principles,* 453.

> In all the more advanced communities, the great majority of things are worse done by the intervention of government, than the individuals most interested in the matter would do them, or cause them to be done, if left to themselves. The grounds of this truth are expressed with tolerable exactness in the popular dictum, that people understand their own business and their own interests better, and care for them more, than the government does, or can be expected to do.[23]

Mill then, however, introduced enough exceptions to smother the idea. He pointed out that individuals operating in a market economy are not necessarily the best judges of how much education society should provide. Child labor should be regulated. Municipal authorities should operate natural monopolies such as gas and water companies, or their rates should be regulated by the state. Where individuals are good judges of their own interest, the government may act to give effect to that judgment; for example, if the workers would gain from reducing the working day from 10 hours to 9, government action might be required to win this concession. If people are to receive charitable aid, it is desirable that such help come from public authorities rather than from uncertain private charity. Legislators should supervise and regulate colonization schemes.[24] Government should also do those things that serve the general interests of all people but that are not profitable to individuals, such as undertaking geographic or scientific exploration. Finally,

> . . . in the particular circumstances of a given age or nation, there is scarcely anything, really important to the general interest, which it may not be desirable, or even necessary, that the government should take upon itself, not because private individuals cannot effectually perform it, but because they will not. At some times and places there will be no roads, docks, harbours, canals, works of irrigation, hospitals, schools, colleges, printing presses, unless the government establishes them.[25]

Final Remarks on Mill

John Stuart Mill must appear prominently in any intellectual history. His importance was not limited to his being the last great economist of the classical school—the greatest of the orthodox economists during the two generations between Ricardo and Marshall. His first important book, *System of Logic* (1843), established him as a leading logician. The essays he published, including "On Liberty" (1859), "Considerations on Representative Government" (1861), and "The Subjection of Women" (1869), showed him to be an outstanding political scientist, social philosopher, and champion of the democratic way of life. Mill looms large as a man of courage and honesty in his trenchant criticisms of the status quo, his support of reforms that were radical in his day, and his concrete contributions to the discipline of economics. Cynics may scorn his belief in progress through the development of our intellectual and moral faculties, but it cannot be denied that he had a noble

[23] Mill, *Principles,* 571.

[24] Somewhat ironically, Mill was employed all his working life by the East India Company, which controlled British trade and colonization in India from 1600 to 1858.

[25] Mill, *Principles,* 590.

vision of the perfectibility of humanity. Mill's warmth, his humanitarianism, and his empathy for the poor and lowly were unusual for a leading theoretician in a science that had become known for its cold rationality and its sometimes dismal predictions.

We take leave of John Stuart Mill to turn to the socialists, who were less compromising in their ideas.

Questions for Study and Discussion

1. Briefly identify and state the significance of each of the following to the history of economic thought: Bentham, hedonism, utilitarianism, Say, law of markets, Senior, positive economics, abstinence, James Mill, John Stuart Mill, demand and supply as schedules, wages fund, law of international values, reciprocal demand, and Mill's stationary state.
2. Employ Bentham's principle of utility (pleasure-pain calculus) to explain each of the following: (a) lines at a specific fast food restaurant tend to be of equal length; (b) all else being equal, occupations characterized by high risk of on-the-job injury or death provide higher annual pay than safer jobs; (c) some college students "cut" one of their courses more than their other courses; and (d) when two products are of equal quality, consumers tend to opt for the lower-priced one.
3. Do you agree with Bentham that the interest of the community is simply the sum of the interests of the several members who compose it? If so, is it then accurate to say that whenever someone adds to his or her net pleasure, the interest of the community rises by that amount?
4. What is the law of markets? Identify which of the following people supported the notion and those who rejected it: Smith, James Mill, Say, Malthus, Ricardo, Senior, and John Stuart Mill.
5. Expand the following statement: The names Colbert, Turgot, and Say reflect the changing pattern of economic thought in France between 1650 and 1825.
6. Draw a contemporary supply and demand graph that incorporates the following information: vertical axis measures the interest rate (i); horizontal axis measures the quantity of savings (S) and investment (I); saving is a positive function of the interest rate, and investment is a negative function of the interest rate. Use the graph to explain (a) why saving will equal investment and (b) why an increase in saving (rightward shift of the curve) will not reduce total spending in the economy. Relate this to Say's law.
7. How did Senior and John Stuart Mill modify Malthus's theory of population?
8. Referring to Table 7-3 in the previous chapter, determine the limits of the terms of trade of wine for cloth. What, according to Mill, will determine the actual terms of trade within these limits?
9. Contrast Mill and Smith; Mill and Malthus; Mill and Ricardo.

Selected Readings

Books

Blaug, Mark, ed. *Ramsey McCulloch, Nassau Senior and Robert Torrens*. Brookfield, VT: Edward Elgar, 1992.

———, ed. *Jean-Baptiste Say.* Brookfield, VT: Edward Elgar, 1991.

———, ed. *Robert Malthus and John Stuart Mill.* Brookfield, VT: Edward Elgar, 1991.

Bentham, Jeremy. *The Collective Works of Jeremy Bentham.* Edited by J. H. Burns. Vols. 1 and 2, *The Correspondence of Jeremy Bentham.* London: University of London, The Athlone Press, 1968.

———. *An Introduction to the Principles of Morals and Legislation.* New York: Hafner, 1948. (Orig. pub. 1780.)

Bowley, Marion. *Nassau Senior and Classical Political Economy.* New York: Kelley, 1949.

Hollander, Samuel. *The Economics of John Stuart Mill.* 2 vols. Toronto: University of Toronto Press, 1985.

Mill, John Stuart. *Autobiography.* New York: Columbia University Press, 1924. (Orig. pub. 1873.)

———. *Dissertations and Discussions.* 2 vols. London: 1871. (Orig. pub. 1848.)

———. *Essays on Some Unsettled Questions of Political Economy.* London: The London School of Economics and Political Science, 1948. (Orig. pub. 1844.)

———. *Principles of Political Economy.* 7th ed. London: Longmans, Green, and Co., 1896. (Orig. pub. 1848.)

———. *Utilitarianism.* London: 1861.

Say, Jean-Baptiste. *A Treatise on Political Economy.* Translated by C. R. Prinsep. Philadelphia, PA: Claxton, Remsen & Haffelfinger, 1880. (Orig. pub. 1803.)

Senior, Nassau W. *Industrial Efficiency and Social Economy.* Edited by S. Leon Levy. 2 vols. New York: Holt, 1928. (Written 1847–1852.)

———. *An Outline of the Science of Political Economy.* New York: Kelley, 1951. (Orig. pub. 1836.)

Stark, W. *Jeremy Bentham's Economic Writings.* 3 vols. New York: Franklin, 1952–1954.

Journal Articles

Baumol, W. J. "Say's (at least) Eight Laws, Or What Say and James Mill May Really Have Meant," *Economica* 44 (May 1977): 145–162.

Bradley, Michael E. "John Stuart Mill's Demand Curves," *History of Political Economy* 21 (Spring 1989): 43–56.

de Marchi, Neil. "The Success of Mill's *Principles*," *History of Political Economy* 6 (Summer 1974): 119–157.

Hollander, Samuel. "The Wage Path in Classical Growth Models: Ricardo, Malthus, and Mill," *Oxford Economic Papers* 36 (June 1984): 200–212.

Thweatt, William O. "Early Formulators of Say's Law," *Quarterly Review of Economics and Business* 19 (Winter 1979): 79–96.

West, E. G., and R. W. Hafer. "J. S. Mill, Unions, and the Wages Fund Recantation: A Reinterpretation," *The Quarterly Journal of Economics* 92 (August 1981): 603–619.

Chapter 9

The Rise of Socialist Thought

The tenets and policy pronouncements of classical political economy drew criticism from several diverse groups of thinkers. We focus on the ideas of these groups in Chapters 9–11. This chapter provides an overview of socialism and examines the views of several early socialist critics of capitalism. Chapter 10 analyzes Marx's "law of motion" of capitalist society. In Chapter 11 we treat the reaction of the German historical school to the classical school's ideas.

OVERVIEW OF SOCIALISM

The Historical Background of Socialism

With the advent of large factories, the industrial revolution shattered the security of the old agricultural-village-handicraft economy. Around these factories sprang up crowded slums, where vice, crime, disease, hunger, and misery were a way of life. Industrial accidents brought scant or no compensation for the families of the maimed and the killed. Political rights for wage earners did not exist, and unions were illegal. Every ill wind that reduced production and employment compounded the misery of the workers, and every new triumph of industrialization—although ultimately creating more new jobs than it destroyed—threw tens of thousands of handicraft workers onto the labor market. The poverty of the masses seemed increasingly oppressive as great fortunes multiplied. As George Crabbe wrote in *The Village* in 1783:

> Where Plenty smiles, alas! she smiles for few.
> And those who taste not, yet behold her store.
> Are as the slaves that dig the golden ore.
> The wealth around them makes them doubly poor.

No wonder that a century after the beginning of the industrial revolution in England, John Stuart Mill believed that "hitherto it is questionable if all the mechanical inventions yet made have lightened the day's toil of any human being. They have enabled a greater population to live the same life of drudgery and imprisonment, and an increased number of manufacturers and others to make fortunes."

From this backdrop came calls for economic reform. But most owners of capital—often citing the pronouncements of Smith and the other classicists—held stubbornly to the concept that the best government is the one that interferes least in the economy. Some historians conclude that the rise of Marxian socialism was given additional force by the failure of earlier, more moderate socialists to persuade industrialists to join in humanitarian movements.

Types of Socialism

Those who advocated socialism often disagreed vehemently on the type of socialism to be sought. It is therefore imperative to delineate the several types of socialism before attempting the more difficult task of sorting out the common ideas. The major types of socialism include the following.

Utopian socialism. This dates from about 1800, with Henri Comte de Saint-Simon, Charles Fourier, and Robert Owen as key figures. They developed their ideas at a time when the industrial workers were still weak and unorganized, demoralized by the rapid changes of the industrial revolution, deprived of the franchise, and not yet aware of their latent power. The utopian socialists regarded the competitive market economy as unjust and irrational. They worked out concepts of perfect social arrangements and then appealed to the whole world to adopt them. They preached universal togetherness rather than class struggle and looked to the capitalists to cooperate with and even finance their schemes. Imaginary model cooperative communities were elaborated, and some were actually tried, usually unsuccessfully.

State socialism. This involves government ownership and operation of all or specific sectors of the economy for purposes of achieving overall social objectives rather than profit. The former Soviet Union is an example of a nation in which all of the major sectors were, until recently, state owned and operated. But state socialism also can occur within a capitalist framework. Examples within the United States are the federal Social Security system, the Tennessee Valley Authority, and the postal service. Historically, the state socialist considered the state to be an impartial power that could be influenced to favor the working class if the vote were extended and the workers educated and organized. Then the state could take over enterprises and become the employer; or it could foster and subsidize cooperatives (workers or consumers as owners). Louis Blanc was the chief early proponent of state socialism.

Christian socialism. This version of socialism developed in England and Germany after 1848, with Charles Kingsley being its leading advocate in England. It arose after the defeat of radical movements in both countries. The workers were offered the solace of religion to assuage their pain and to provide hope. The Bible was to form the manual of the government leader, the employer, and the worker; God's order was mutual love and fellowship. Property owned by the rich was to be held in trust for the benefit of everybody. This movement, repudiating violence and class struggle, advocated sanitary reform, education, factory legislation, and cooperatives.

Anarchism. With Pierre-Joseph Proudhon (1809–1865) as one of its earliest proponents, anarchism held that all forms of government are coercive and should be abolished. According to Proudhon:

> Experience, in fact, shows that everywhere and always the Government, however much it may have been for the people at its origin, has placed itself on the side of the richest and most educated class against the more numerous and poorer class; it has little by little become narrow and exclusive; and, instead of maintaining liberty and equality among all, it works persistently to destroy them, by virtue of its natural inclination toward privilege. . . . We may conclude without fear that the revolutionary formula cannot be *Direct Government*, not *Simplified Government*, [but rather] that it is NO GOVERNMENT. . . . Governing the people will always be swindling the people. It is always man giving orders to man, the fiction which makes an end of liberty.[1]

Anarchists did not advocate that society have no order but rather that society's order arise out of self-governing groups through voluntary or associate effort. Human nature, they contended, is essentially good if not corrupted by the state and its institutions. Private property should be replaced by collective ownership of capital by cooperating groups. Anarchists envisioned communities engaging in production and carrying on trade with other communities, with associations of producers controlling agricultural, industrial, and even intellectual and artistic production. Associations of consumers were expected to coordinate housing, lighting, health, food, and sanitation. Mutual understanding, cooperation, and complete liberty would characterize anarchist society. Individual initiative would be encouraged, and every tendency to uniformity and centralized authority would be effectively checked. Although the methods of achieving their goals differed, the ideal community of the anarchists resembled that of the utopian socialists.

Marxian socialism. As we will discover in Chapter 10, Marxian, or "scientific socialism," is based on a labor theory of value and a theory of exploitation of the wage earners by the capitalists. Although Marx and Engels passionately despised capitalism, they paid tribute to the great increase in productivity and production that it unleashed. But capitalism faced class struggles and contradictions that inevitably would lead to its being overthrown and replaced by socialism. The capitalist state oppresses the workers. The working class, in overthrowing the bourgeois state, will establish its own dictatorship of the proletariat to destroy the bourgeois class. Under the resulting socialism, private property in consumer goods is permitted, but the capital and land is publicly owned by the central government. Production is planned, as is the rate of investment, with the profit motive and the free market eliminated as the major guiding forces for the economy.

Communism. According to Marx, communism is the stage of society that eventually supersedes socialism. Under socialism, the slogan is "From each according to his ability, to each according to his work." Under communism the slogan becomes "From each according to his ability, to each according to his need." This presupposes a superabundance of goods relative to wants, the elimination of money payments based on work performed, and a devotion to society as selfless as a person's

---

[1] Pierre-Joseph Proudhon, *General Idea of the Revolution of the Nineteenth Century*, trans. John B. Robinson (London: Freedom Press, 1923), 108, 126. (Orig. pub. 1851.)

loyalty to his or her family. The state will wither away when antagonistic classes disappear, and government over people will be replaced by administration over things, such as large railway systems and coal-iron-machinery complexes.

The so-called communist countries today have actually established state socialism or are in the process of establishing it. Communism exists nowhere at present except in small cooperative communities, usually motivated by a common religious, or other crusading, fervor. Here people work together, pool their earnings, and draw the things that they need from the common fund.

Revisionism. In Germany revisionism was advocated by Eduard Bernstein (1850–1932). In England the Fabian socialists led by Sidney and Beatrice Webb (1859–1947; 1858–1943) were revisionists, but unlike the German left-wing movement they had never adhered to Marxism to any significant degree. Revisionism abjured the class struggle; denied that the state is necessarily an instrument of the wealthy class; and pinned its hopes on education, electioneering, and gaining control of government through the ballot. The government was to regulate monopolies, control working conditions in factories, take over some public utilities, and gradually extend its ownership of capital. Because the revisionists, especially the Fabian branch, favored municipal ownership of public utilities, revisionism has sometimes been called "gas and water socialism."

Syndicalism. Georges Sorel (1847–1922) promoted and popularized this form of socialism in labor circles in the Latin countries of Europe. Syndicalists were antiparliamentarian and antimilitarist. They believed that socialism deteriorates into bourgeois beliefs when it engages in political and parliamentary activity. If represented in parliament, the movement will degenerate into opportunism to gain political influence. What the workers require is one big union that will not play the bourgeois game of seeking social reform and the amelioration of conditions. The union must not dabble in strike and insurance funds, union contracts, union treasuries, or piecemeal reform. Strikes must be fomented to stir up the revolutionary consciousness and militancy of workers; sabotage frequently must be used as a weapon in the class struggle. Eventually the general strike of the one big union will overthrow capitalism; each industry will then be organized as an autonomous unit managed by the workers, and these units will be combined in a federation that will become the administrative center. The syndicalists expected coercive government to disappear.

Syndicalism differed from anarchism in that the former relied exclusively on revolutionary unionism and the general strike for the overthrow of government. But both favored the abolition of private property and extinction of political government. The Industrial Workers of the World (nicknamed "the Wobblies"), established in the United States in 1905, was an example of a syndicalist union.

Guild socialism. G. D. H. Cole (1889–1959), a professor of economics at Oxford University, was the major advocate of this type of socialism. It remained primarily a British movement, one of gradualism and reform, and reached its zenith around the time of World War I. The guild socialists accepted the state as a necessary institution for expression of the general interests of citizens as consumers. The actual management of industries was to be entrusted to the employees (the producers), organized in their industrial guilds, rather than to the government. But the government was to develop overall economic policy for the whole community, not merely for the workers. Every worker would be a partner in the enterprise for which he or she worked; this was the essence of the "industrial democracy" that guild socialists favored. The nation would no longer be divided into opposing camps of capital and labor; instead, it would be divided into producers and consumers, with each having its national association—the guild and the government. Thus producers and consumers would form a partnership of equals.

Commonalities of Socialism

The various strands of socialism had several features in common. First, they all repudiated the classicist notion of the harmony of interests. Instead they viewed society as being composed of distinct classes whose interests were often opposed to one another. Second, and following from the first, the socialists all opposed the concept of laissez-faire. With the exception of the anarchists, socialists viewed government as being potentially a progressive representative of the interests of the working class. Third, these people rejected Say's law of markets, claiming instead that capitalism is given to either periodic crisis or to general stagnation. Fourth, the socialists denied the concept of humanity upon which classical thought was erected, instead believing in the perfectibility of people. Capitalism produced self-interested behavior through its emphasis on making profits and accumulating wealth; with the proper environment, the nobler human virtues such as sharing with others would emerge. Fifth, each of the various socialist ideologies advocated collective action and public ownership of enterprise to ameliorate conditions of the masses. This ownership could be undertaken by the central government, local governments, or cooperative enterprises.

Whom Did Socialism Benefit or Seek to Benefit?

The more moderate groups (utopian, Christian, and guild socialists) claimed to represent everybody's interests, with primary emphasis on the needs and interests of workers. They did serve the workers by arousing the conscience of society and inspiring middle-class reformers, thereby promoting reform legislation. To the extent that they diverted workers from organizing unions and political parties to promote their own interests, they also served the employers and landowners. Christian socialism arose at a time when socialist doctrines were gaining ground among the workers. Its adherents felt that the radical movement must be Christianized or else Christianity would lose its appeal.

The more extreme socialist groups (Marxist, anarchist, and syndicalists) proclaimed class warfare against the rich. Their sole aim was to promote the interests of the working class. Through various trade union activity, parliamentary pressure, or the threat of revolts, their agitating and organizing helped win concessions from the capitalists.

How Was Socialism Valid, Useful, or Correct in Its Time?

Workers had legitimate grievances against laissez-faire capitalism as it developed in its early decades. In the early 1800s, utopian socialism expressed the disturbed conscience of humanity. Marxian socialism offered an involved theoretical dissection of contemporary society that exposed and exaggerated its alleged evils. But like other socialist criticisms, it had a certain validity in its time. Those speaking for the status quo had not squarely faced the two problems of poverty and recurring business depressions, and the socialists performed a service by concentrating their focus on these unresolved problems. Socialism played a historically useful role by promoting factory acts, sanitary reform, cooperative associations, workers' compensation laws, unions, pensions, and so forth.

Which Tenets of Socialism Became Lasting Contributions?

Many of the tenets of socialism have not stood the test of time. For example, we will discover in our assessment of Marx (Chapter 10) that his central forecast—the impoverishment of the working class—has not occurred. Nor has the reorganization of society along socialist lines brought about the hoped-for new flowering of freedom, increased collective activity for the common good, better standards of morality and justice, greater security for the individual, and subsequent cultural renaissance.

The socialist tenets have proved to present formidable problems in implementation. How does a society create a more equal distribution of income without impairing the incentives that lead to the production of output (and therefore the income itself)? If income payments become arbitrary, what prevents the government from using them to reward loyalists and punish people who have different ideas? How do you plan for and coordinate the allocation of productive resources in a large, industrialized economy? How much should go for consumption goods; how much for capital goods? Which consumption goods should be produced, and how many of each? What are the alternatives if the only supplier of a certain good offers shoddy wares? How can consumers make their wishes known to the top government planners who make decisions that vitally affect the humblest individual in the farthest corner of the land? Can political freedom exist in the absence of economic freedom; for example, can a free press exist when the government owns the printing presses? If production targets in the plan are stated in terms of *quantity*, how can product *quality* be assured? What forces will stimulate the search for new technology and new products in the absence of entrepreneurs?

The validity and usefulness of economic theories must ultimately be judged not by the degree of passion that they generate but rather by careful intellectual scrutiny and accumulated evidence. Neither intellectual scrutiny nor accumulated evidence has been kind to totalitarian Marxism, in particular. In the early 1990s this form of socialism dramatically collapsed in eastern Europe and the former Soviet Union. The remaining Marxist regimes are beset with tremendous problems that threaten their continued existence.

This is not to suggest that early socialists failed to make lasting contributions to the development of economic thought. In fact, they contributed in several important ways. First, these thinkers developed the foundation of contemporary socialist economic thought, which emphasizes state ownership of the means of production together with national planning and coordination. Many nations—such as India and Sweden—are still guided by democratic socialist aspirations. Also, large socialist voting blocs remain in some nonsocialist milieus, including Japan, Italy, and France. From these perspectives, it is clear that the socialist ideas did indeed have a lasting influence.

Second, several of the policy recommendations made by the socialists are now institutionalized within capitalist nations. Many of today's social programs—for example, social security, workers' compensation, unemployment compensation, minimum wage and overtime pay laws, occupational health and safety laws—were advocated in some form by the socialists and vehemently opposed by most supporters of classical economics. For a variety of reasons, society incorporated the policy proposals of the socialists and in so doing smoothed the rough edges of capitalism. As workers grew stronger as a group, many owners of capital decided that it was better that a little be given rather than having much be taken. Also, economic growth, to the surprise of most socialists, substantially increased the wages received by laborers. Workers, in essence, could afford to trade some of their direct wage payments for nonwage job amenities (shorter hours, pensions, health insurance) provided by their employers. They also could afford to pay taxes from which government could partially finance social security, job retraining programs, and so forth. In addition, middle-class reformers, who were more in the lineage of John Stuart Mill than Smith and Say, successfully championed the amelioration of unjust conditions while rejecting the socialists' demands for the elimination of private property.

A third lasting contribution of the socialists was their emphasis on and analysis of the growth of monopoly power, the problem of income distribution, and the reality of business cycles. This emphasis and analysis forced a reassessment of basic assumptions and accepted theories within the economics profession.

With these points in mind, let's examine the works of five leading early socialists: Saint-Simon, Fourier, Owen, Blanc, and Kingsley. These individuals, like their orthodox counterparts, asked and attempted to answer the three fundamental questions of economics: What should be produced? How should it be produced? For whom? The answers they provide were decidedly different from the classical ones! Therein lies the value of more closely probing their thinking.

HENRI COMTE DE SAINT-SIMON

Henri Comte de Saint-Simon (1760–1825) came from an impoverished family of the French nobility. He fought on the colonial side in the American Revolution as a regular officer, distinguishing himself in the Battle of Yorktown. During the early stages of the French Revolution he renounced his title. At the height of the Revolution he became a big speculator in the nationalized land of the church and of the *émigrés*, buying on credit and later paying in rapidly depreciating *assignats*. Saint-Simon served a term in prison but was later released after the fall of Robespierre.

Later, he abandoned the role of financier to become a philosopher and prophet. With reckless extravagance he entertained and subsidized promising young scientists, artists, and scholars, but this prodigality soon left him penniless, and he lived for several years at the home of a former servant. Upon the death of his mother, Saint-Simon surrendered his rights of inheritance in return for a small pension from his family. In 1823, due to a desperate financial position, he fired seven pistol bullets at his head but miraculously survived with only the loss of an eye.

Saint-Simon, a utopian socialist, developed his ideas before the political movement of the working class in France had taken shape. He therefore made no appeal to the workers to struggle against their employers. Regarding idleness as sin, he made a religion of work and industry. Saint-Simon alarmed the rich because he made production, not property, the basis for his proposed society. The line he drew separated producers from nonproducers.

An industrial parliament, he wrote, should consist of three chambers—invention, review, and execution. The first chamber, composed of artists and engineers, would design public works. The second chamber, run by scientists, would examine the projects and control education. The third chamber, consisting of the leaders of industry, would carry out the projects and control the budget. This was one of the earliest proposals for central planning undertaken by an educated elite.

Saint-Simon rejected the fundamental assumption of classical economists that the interests of the individual coincide with the general interest. He insisted that a new ethic was required to restrain the antisocial egotism of the rich and to prevent an anarchic uprising of the poor. Humanitarian concern for the working class was a dominant theme in his later writings.

Saint-Simon's attack on idlers led his followers to oppose the laws of inheritance and to urge the collective ownership of property. After his death, his disciples organized a school that became almost a religion. The Saint-Simonian enthusiasm for large-scale industry helped inspire big banks, railways, highways, the Suez Canal, and huge industrial undertakings.

A few excerpts from Saint-Simon's works will illustrate his ideas:

> The sole aim of our thoughts and our exertions must be the kind of organization most favourable to industry—industry understood in the widest sense, including every kind of useful activity; theoretical as well as practical, intellectual as well as manual. . . . Our desire is that men should henceforth do consciously, and with better direction and more useful effort, what they have hitherto done unconsciously, slowly, indecisively and too ineffectively. . . .
>
> Suppose that France suddenly lost fifty of her best physicists, chemists, physiologists, mathematicians, poets, painters, . . . engineers, . . . bankers, . . . businessmen, . . . farmers, . . . miners, . . . metal workers . . . ; making in all the three thousand leading scientists, artists, and artisans in France.
>
> These men are the Frenchmen who are the most essential producers, those who make the most important products, those who direct the enterprises most useful to the nation, those who contribute to its achievements in the sciences, fine arts and professions. They are in the most real sense the flower of French society; they are, above all Frenchmen, the most useful to their country, contribute most to its glory, increasing its civilization and prosperity. The nation would become a lifeless corpse as soon as it lost them. . . . It would require at least a generation for France to repair this misfortune. . . .

Let us pass to another assumption. Suppose that France preserves all the men of genius that she possesses in the sciences, fine arts and professions, but has the misfortune to lose in the same day Monsieur the King's brother [and other members of the royal household]. . . . Suppose that France loses at the same time all the great officers of the royal household, all the ministers (with or without portfolio), all the councillors of state, all the chief magistrates, marshals, cardinals, archbishops, bishops, vicars-general, and canons, all the prefects and subprefects, all the civil servants, and judges, and, in addition, ten thousand of the richest proprietors who live in the style of the nobles.

This mischance would certainly distress the French, because they are kindhearted, and could not see with indifference the sudden disappearance of such a large number of their compatriots. But this loss of thirty thousand individuals, considered to be the most important in the State, would only grieve them for purely sentimental reasons and would result in no political evil for the State.

In the first place, it would be easy to fill the vacancies which would be made available. There are plenty of Frenchmen who could fill the function of the King's brother as well as can Monsieur. . . . The ante-chambers of the palace are full of courtiers ready to take the place of the great household officials. . . . As for the ten thousand aristocratic landowners, their heirs could need no apprenticeship to do the honours of their drawingroom as well as they.

The prosperity of France can only exist through the effects of the progress of the sciences, fine arts and professions. The Princes, the great household officials, the Bishops, Marshals of France, prefects, and idle landowners contribute nothing directly to the progress of the sciences, fine arts and professions. Far from contributing they only hinder, since they strive to prolong the supremacy existing to this day of conjectural ideas over positive science. They inevitably harm the prosperity of the nation by depriving, as they do, the scientists, artists, and artisans of the high esteem to which they are properly entitled. They are harmful because they expend their wealth in a way which is of no direct use to the sciences, fine arts, and professions: they are harmful because they are a charge on the national taxation, to the amount of three or four hundred millions under the heading of appointments, pensions, gifts, compensations, for the upkeep of their activities which are useless to the nation. . . . Society is a world which is upside down. The nation holds as a fundamental principle that the poor should be generous to the rich, and that therefore the poorer classes should daily deprive themselves of necessities in order to increase the superfluous luxury of the rich.[2]

In 1819 Saint-Simon was arrested and tried for heresy for his expression of these controversial ideas, but he was acquitted. Indeed, Saint-Simon's ideas had revolutionary implications. He stated:

The richest and most powerful men have an interest in the growth of equality, since the means of satisfying their wants increases in the same proportion as the leveling of the individuals composing the community. . . . Scientists, artists and industrialists, and the heads of industrial concerns are the men who possess the eminent, varied, and most positively useful ability, for the guidance of men's minds at present time. . . . They . . . are the men who should be entrusted with administrative power. . . .

[2] F. M. H. Markham, ed., *Henri Comte de Saint-Simon, Selected Writings* (Oxford: Basil Blackwell, 1952), 70–74. Reprinted by permission of the publisher.

> The community has often been compared to a pyramid. I admit that the nation should be composed as a pyramid; I am profoundly convinced that the national pyramid should be crowned by the monarchy, but I assert that from the base of the pyramid to its summit the layers should be composed of more and more precious materials. If we consider the present pyramid, it appears that the base is made of granite, that up to a certain height the layers are composed of valuable materials, but that the upper part, supporting a magnificent diamond, is composed of nothing but plaster and gilt.
>
> The base of the present national pyramid consists of workers in their routine occupations; the first layers above this base are the leaders of industrial enterprises, the scientists who improve the methods of manufacture and widen their application, the artists who give the stamp of good taste to all their products. The upper layers, which I assert to be composed of nothing but plaster, which is easily recognizable despite the gilding, are the courtiers, the mass of nobles whether of ancient or recent creation, the idle rich, the governing class from the prime minister to the humblest clerk. The monarchy is the magnificent diamond which crowns the pyramid.[3]

Despite these extreme statements, Saint-Simon missed being a socialist in one respect: He did not advocate the appropriation of private property, although some of his disciples did.

CHARLES FOURIER

Charles Fourier (1772–1837) was an eccentric utopian socialist who slowly acquired a large and devoted following late in life and posthumously. He was by no means a revolutionary, and his appeals were usually addressed to the wealthy or to the king. The son of a middle-class merchant family that lost most of its possessions during the French Revolution, he was a clerk in various cloth houses and other businesses. A poor laborer all his life, he had to acquire his education in spare moments in library reading rooms. The titles of his books convey the unusual nature of his thought: *Theory of the Four Movements and the General Destinies* (1808), *The Theory of Universal Unity* (1829), and *The New Industrial and Social World* (1829).

Fourier was a critic of capitalism. Unlike Saint-Simon, he disliked large-scale production, mechanization, and centralization. Competition, he thought, multiplies waste in selling, and businessmen withhold or destroy commodities to raise prices. Commerce to him was pernicious and corrupt, and he laid bare the moral poverty of the bourgeois world. He denounced a society that "accords its high protection to the agents of famine and pestilence." And he criticized the "progress of financiering, systems of extortion, indirect bankruptcy, anticipations of revenue, [and] art of devouring the future," all of which he saw within capitalism. Under the terminology "progress of the mercantile spirit" he included "consideration according to commercial plundering and knavery. Stock-jobbing raised to a power which scoffs at law, encroaches upon all fruits of industry, shares in the authority of governments, and propagates everywhere the frenzy of gambling in the public funds."[4]

---

[3] Markham, ed., *Saint-Simon,* 77–80.

[4] Julia Franklin, trans., *Selections from the Works of Fourier* (London: Swan Sonnenshein, 1901), 93–94.

Fourier's solution to social problems was to remove the artificial barriers to the harmonious interplay of the twelve passions (five senses, four group passions [friendship, love, family feeling, and ambition], and three distributive passions [planning, change, and unity]). This could be accomplished by organizing cooperative communities called *phalansteries*, or *phalanxes*. His love of order, symmetry, and precision drove him to draw elaborate plans for these communities, down to the most insignificant details. Each association would combine 300 families, or 1,800 people, on nine square miles of land. Everybody would live in a palace-like dwelling three stories high, which he described minutely. Agriculture and handicraft production would predominate, and the output of wealth would increase tenfold over that of chaotic private industry. One large granary would be more economical to build and easier to guard against fire than 300 small ones. People's living together in honor and comfort would eliminate theft and the expense of guarding against it. Collective work would improve climatic conditions, and fewer clothes would be required. The economies of a common kitchen and apartments rather than separate dwellings were carefully calculated. The *phalanx* would solve the major problem, which was not the inequality of wealth, but rather its insufficiency.

Who would do the "dirty work" in this utopian colony? The children! Children love dirt, and they love to organize into gangs. Instead of thwarting these natural tendencies, they should be directed into useful social functions, such as doing the most disagreeable work. Meanwhile, children should learn a variety of trades, so that as adults they would not be overspecialized and limited to a single task.

Fourier advocated complete equality between the sexes. He asserted that confining women to housekeeping interferes with the proper development of natural talents.

After providing each member of the *phalanx* the minimum of subsistence, regardless of his or her contribution to the enterprise, the surplus would be divided as follows: 5/12 to labor, 4/12 to capital, and 3/12 to talent and skill. Therefore, an appeal could be made to capitalists to finance such a project on the basis of earning a satisfactory return on their investment. In fact, Fourier announced to the world that he would be at home every day at noon to await a capitalist who would underwrite an association. For the rest of his life he waited in vain, although his followers started many *phalanxes* throughout the world.

In the United States the movement was popularized before the Civil War by Albert Brisbane, Horace Greeley, George Ripley, and others. Of the forty Fourierist *phalanxes* organized in the United States, all of which failed, the best known were the North American Phalanx, located near Red Bank, New Jersey, and Brook Farm, which was organized in 1841 near Boston. Among the members and interested visitors to Brook Farm were Charles A. Dana, Nathaniel Hawthorne, Ralph Waldo Emerson, Amos Bronson Alcott, Margaret Fuller, Theodore Parker, Orestes Bronson, and William Henry Channing. A disastrous fire in 1846 ended the experiment.

Fourier showed much originality, and his ideas have remained influential, even though he is seldom credited with having reconnoitered new and uncharted ground. Cooperative living was central to his thinking as the way to change the environment in order to generate an entirely new and noble type of person. The phalanxes would provide cradle-to-grave, or womb-to-tomb, social security. For the early stages of his ideal society Fourier advocated "guaranteeism"—the assurance that every person would be given a minimum subsistence, security, and comfort. Fourier objected to overspecialization, warning that routine assembly line work warps and thwarts the individual, although it greatly expands output. The Fourierist *phalanxes,* although ultimately failures, influenced the labor movement at the time and inspired much thought on how to eliminate the wastes of private enterprise and promote a better economic system. The cooperative movement is in part a living monument to Fourier.

SIMONDE DE SISMONDI

Simonde de Sismondi (1773–1842) was a Swiss economist and historian of French descent. He and his family took refuge in England during the revolutionary disturbances of 1793–1794. On their return to Switzerland they sold most of their property and bought a small farm in Italy, which they worked themselves. Sismondi later returned to Geneva, where he wrote many scholarly works, among them a sixteen-volume *History of the Italian Republics of the Middle Ages* and a twenty-nine-volume *History of the French.*

Sismondi was among the first to launch a direct attack on classical economics, although he had been an ardent follower of Adam Smith in his earlier years. He was never a socialist in the modern sense, but he helped pave the way for socialist thought. In 1819, after viewing the appalling conditions in England following his absence of twenty-four years, he published *New Principles of Political Economy.* In this book he stated that unrestricted capitalistic enterprise, far from yielding the results that Smith and Say expected of it, is bound to lead to widespread misery and unemployment. His criticism of Say's law of markets and his denial that a free enterprise economy tends toward full employment were stated fairly early in the rise of modern industrial society: "Let us beware of this dangerous theory of equilibrium which is supposed to be automatically established. A certain kind of equilibrium, it is true, is reestablished in the long run, but it is after a frightful amount of suffering."[5] Recall that John Stuart Mill a half a century later was still proclaiming the impossibility of general gluts.

Sismondi, raising the possibility of overproduction and crises, was one of the early contributors to business-cycle theory. He thought that when wages are at the subsistence level, more capital funds become available for investment in machines. Bankers, by extending credit, add to the investment boom. The output of manufactured goods is thereby increased, while the demand for consumption is limited. The consequences are overproduction and periodic crises, the latter necessary to liquidate the excessive capital investment in large-scale industries. Widespread unemployment, of course, accompanies these crises. In addition, the increased concentration of wealth brought about by bankruptcies narrows the home market more and more. Hence industry is increasingly compelled to open up foreign markets, which necessarily results in nationalistic wars. Sismondi was thus one of the first people to formulate explicitly the now-familiar Marxist charge that economic imperialism is inherent in capitalism.

Only state intervention would ensure the worker a living wage and a minimum social security. Sismondi denied that the largest possible aggregate production

[5]Simonde de Sismondi, *New Principles of Political Economy,* vol. 1 (1819), 20–21.

necessarily coincides with the greatest happiness of the people. A smaller output, well distributed, would be preferable. In the general interest, therefore, the state should enact laws regulating distribution. Small-scale family farming, as opposed to tenant farming, would promote a more equitable distribution of income. He also urged small-scale production in the towns to avoid producing more than could be sold. Agriculture should be promoted at the expense of urbanization. He favored inheritance taxes; curbing new inventions by discontinuing patent rights so that "the zeal for discoveries will grow cold"; compelling employers to provide security for their workers in old age, illness, and unemployment; cooperation and solidarity between workers and employers; and profit sharing.

Sismondi stated that not every individual force is of equal strength and that individual self-interest need not coincide with the social interest. Peasants, he thought, try to increase their gross product, while large landowners are concerned only with net revenue. Suppose, he said, a well-cultivated piece of land produces a total output of 1,000 shillings, of which 100 go to the proprietor as rent. If the land were let out as pasture, it would yield, say, 110 shillings rent. The proprietor would therefore dismiss the tenants in order to gain 10 shillings, while the nation would lose 890 shillings' worth of output (1,000–110). The contemporary economist, of course, would reject this reasoning. If the land earns more rent as pasture, its contribution to society's well-being must be greater in this use than in alternative ones.[6]

Sismondi was the first to apply the term *proletary* to the wage laborer. The term had originally referred to the men in the Roman republic who had nothing, who paid no taxes, and who could contribute only their offspring—the proles—to the country.

Sismondi offered a relatively modern prescription for curing a glut in a particular industry:

> The government ought, in fact, to come to the assistance of men, and not of industry; it ought to save its citizens, and not business. Far from making advances to the master manufacturer, to encourage him to manufacture to a loss, it ought largely to contribute funds to take the operatives from an employment which increases the embarrassment of all their fellow citizens. It ought to employ them in those public works whose products do not bear upon the markets, and do not increase the general glut. Public edifices, town-halls, markets, public walks, are native wealth, though not of a kind that can be bought and sold. . . .
>
> But in assisting the workmen in any depressed industrial business by public works, government must adhere principally to the following rules:—not to compete with an existing business, and thus bring fresh disturbances into the markets; not to make of those works which it orders and pays for a permanent occupation, to which will be attached a new class of day-labourers—*proletarii*—but to make them perceive how long it will last, and where it will end, that they may not marry in this precarious state. . . .
>
> On whatever side we look, the same lesson meets us everywhere, *protect the poor* [the laboring class], and ought to be the most important study of the legislator and of the government. . . . Protect the poor, that they may keep . . . that share of the

[6] This assumes that there are competitive markets and no externalities.

> income of the community which their labour ought to secure to them; protect the poor, for they want support, that they may have some leisure, some intellectual development, in order to advance in virtue; protect the poor, for the greatest danger to law, public peace and stability, is the belief of the poor that they are oppressed, and their hatred of government; protect the poor, if you wish industry to flourish, for the poor are the most important consumers.[7]

Sismondi was less a socialist than a social critic and a dissenter from classical theory. His strong interest in the business cycle and his humanitarian views set him apart from the orthodox economists of his day and inspired the socialists, but he made no fundamental attack on the institution of private property, nor did he advocate communal existence.

ROBERT OWEN

Robert Owen (1771–1858) was the most spectacular and most famous of the utopian socialists. The son of a Welsh ironmonger and saddler, he attended school for only a few years. At nine he went to work in a neighboring store as a shop hand; later he was employed in dry-goods stores in London. At eighteen he borrowed 100 pounds and set up a partnership with a mechanic who could build the newly invented textile machinery. When his partner left him, Owen set himself up in business, using the machines he had on hand. Although he was successful, a better opportunity came his way. While still under the age of twenty, Owen became manager of one of the largest and best-equipped spinning mills in Lancashire. This mill employed 500 workers. Owen was the first spinner in Britain to use American Sea Islands cotton. His employer offered him a partnership, but instead he started a new company for the manufacture of yarn. Again highly successful, at twenty-eight he bought the New Lanark Mills in Scotland from David Dale, whose daughter he married soon afterward. Owen's spinning mills became the largest and best-equipped in Scotland.

By examining Owen's idea, we can see what led him to become a factory reformer, pioneer socialist, advocate of cooperatives, trade union leader, founder of utopian communities, and theorist in the field of education. His central thesis was that the environment molds human nature for better or worse. Human beings cannot form their own characters; their characters are without exception formed for them. Because character is made by circumstances, people are not truly responsible for their actions, and they should be molded into goodness instead of being punished for being bad. All of Owen's theories, dreams, and programs, like Fourier's, were based on the belief that providing better working conditions would produce better people. One should try to serve the community and thereby achieve one's own highest happiness. This concept reversed classical economics and Benthamite thinking, which held that self-interest would serve society.

In an essay published in 1813, Owen wrote:

---

[7] Simonde de Sismondi, *Political Economy and the Philosophy of Government* (London: Chapman, 1847), 220, 221, 223. (Orig. pub. 1826–1837.)

> Any general character, from the best to the worst, from the most ignorant to the most enlightened, may be given to any community, even to the world at large, by the application of proper means; which means are to a great extent at the command and under the control of those who have influence in affairs of men. . . .
>
> The happiness of self, clearly understood and uniformly practised . . . can only be attained by conduct that must promote the happiness of the community. . . .
>
> These plans must be devised to train children from their earliest infancy in good habits of every description (which will of course prevent them from acquiring those of falsehood and deception). They must afterwards be rationally educated, and their labour be usefully directed. Such habits and education will impress them with an active and ardent desire to promote the happiness of every individual, and that without the shadow of exception for sect, or party, or country, or climate. They will also ensure, with the fewest possible exceptions, health, strength, and vigour of body; for the happiness of man can be erected only on the foundations of health of body and peace of mind.[8]

Owen proceeded to convert the New Lanark Mills into a model community, a showplace inspected by distinguished visitors from all over the world. On arriving there, Owen found 500 pauper children living in a factory boardinghouse, serving seven- to nine-year apprenticeships. They had begun working at the age of six, and their working day, summer and winter, was twelve hours a day, six days a week. There was also a factory village to house the families of workers, who lived in poverty, crime, debt, sickness, and misery. Yet David Dale, the former owner, was far more humanitarian than most employers.

Owen introduced his reforms at New Lanark to prove that character could thereby be reshaped for the better. He discontinued the use of pauper children. Youngsters were allowed to work at age ten, but encouraged not to work until age twelve. Free schooling was offered to all ages. For preschool children he founded the Institute for the Formation of Character, the first infant school, or nursery, in Britain. There he wanted children to grow up happily, in a healthy environment. Comfortable houses were built for the families who worked at New Lanark. Food, fuel, and clothing were sold to the workers at cost. The working day was reduced to 10½ hours, and wages were relatively high. He paid his employees during slack times and sickness, gave them old age insurance, and provided recreational facilities. Fines and punishments, so characteristic of the time, were abolished, although workers were terminated for poor work.

Owen's employees worked hard, and Owen made good profits. In retrospect, New Lanark Mills was an early experiment with efficiency wages: purposeful above-market pay to enhance productivity and reduce turnover. Although Smith developed the seminal idea, Owen first put the idea into actual practice. Even though New Lanark Mills was profitable, his partners objected to Owen's extravagance. Twice he had to buy out his partners and find new ones. His third and last partnership, formed in 1814, included Jeremy Bentham. The partners agreed to limit their dividends to 5 percent on invested capital and to use all surplus revenue in the interests of the employees. Owen withdrew from his business in 1829 because of friction with some of his partners.

---

[8] Robert Owen, *A New View of Society and Other Writings* (London: Dent, 1927), 16, 17, 20. (Written 1813–1821.) Reprinted by permission of Dent and Everyman's Library.

This great textile manufacturer shocked the world when he denounced all established religions because they taught that people are responsible for their evil ways instead of correctly attributing evil to bad environment. He preached social rather than moral reformation. Even he himself was a mere product of forces over which he had no control:

> Causes, over which I have no control, removed in my early days the bandage which covered my mental insight. If I have been enabled to discover this blindness with which my fellow-men are afflicted, to trace their wanderings from the path which they were most anxious to find, and at the same time to perceive that relief could not be administered to them by any premature disclosure of their unhappy state, it is not from any merit of mine; nor can I claim any personal consideration whatever holding such truly pitiable objects around me, and witnessing the misery which they hourly experience from falling into the dangers and evils by which, in these paths, they were on every side surrounded,—could I remain an idle spectator?
>
> No! The causes which fashioned me in the womb,—the circumstances by which I was surrounded from my birth, and over which I had no influence whatever, formed me with far other faculties, habits, and sentiments. These gave me a mind that could not rest satisfied without trying every possible expedient to relieve my fellow-men from their wretched situation, and formed it of such a texture that obstacles of the most formidable nature served but to increase my ardour, and to fix within me a settled determination, either to overcome them, or to die in the attempt.[9]

Owen did things for people rather than encouraging people to use their own initiative to get things done. He pleaded with his fellow manufacturers to follow his example. He asked: Why not care for your living machines as well as you care for your inanimate ones? If you help the workers, he said, you will increase your own happiness and intellectual enjoyment. He appealed to the government to enact factory legislation and was mainly responsible for the Factory Act of 1819, although he denounced it as being far weaker than he wished. During the slump following the end of the Napoleonic wars, Owen urged the government to employ the poor in "villages of cooperation," modeled after his own establishment at New Lanark. Having failed to persuade either capitalists or government to follow his example, he himself promoted a model cooperative community to show the way. In 1825 he established the New Harmony colony on 30,000 acres in Indiana. He bought the property from the Rappites, a sect that did not have much of a future because its followers practiced celibacy. His type of organization, Owen thought, would sweep away capitalism and the competitive system. Whereas Fourier had allowed profit on the capital invested in utopian colonies, Owen favored only a fixed rate of interest until the owners of capital voluntarily gave it up, as he believed they would. Within three years the colony failed, and Owen had lost four-fifths of his $250,000 fortune. Other villages of cooperation, established later in Great Britain, also failed.

Owen then found himself leading a growing army of working-class disciples. The modification of the British antiunion laws in 1825 was followed by considerable growth of trade unionism. Workers also promoted cooperatives as the forerunners

---

[9] Owen, *New View,* 108.

of Owen's "villages of cooperation." Owen placed himself at the head of both movements. In 1832 he founded the National Equitable Labour Exchange as a market where products could be exchanged on the basis of notes representing labor time. His hope was to eliminate the twin social evils of money and profit by bringing producers and consumers into direct contact with one another. Although this experiment failed in two years, his followers founded the Rochdale Pioneers' Cooperative Society in 1844. This was the beginning of a highly successful consumers' cooperative (consumer-owned firms) movement in Great Britain, inspired by Owen but a far cry from the producers' cooperatives (worker-owned firms) he had hoped would replace capitalism.

Disappointment in the Reform Act of 1832, which left the workers voteless, led to an upsurge of unionism and later to the Chartist movement. Owen plunged into union activity in 1833 by promoting the Grand National Consolidated Trades Union, which soon recruited 500,000 members. Hasty strikes and bitter lockouts followed. There was internal dissension, with Owen opposing militant action, conflict, and strikes. He suddenly ordered the union dissolved in 1834, after six farm laborers were sentenced to deportation to Australia for seven years because they had administered secret oaths in organizing farm laborers in their district. But many of the constituent trade unions in the Grand National reorganized themselves as separate societies, living on to become the nuclei of the modern British union movement.

Owen had a significant impact on socialism as well as on cooperatives and unionism. The word *socialism* in the modern sense was first used in the Owenite *Co-operative Magazine* in 1827 to designate the followers of Owen's cooperative doctrines. It was formed from the word *social* as opposed to *individual,* applied to the ownership of capital. His sharp criticisms of capitalism and his dream of collective action to organize cooperative communities based on large-scale industry inspired a whole generation of socialists. He retained his devotion to social reform to the end of his life, at which time he also turned to spiritualism, which he used as an additional weapon to advance his many causes.

LOUIS BLANC

Louis Blanc (1811–1882), commonly regarded as a founder of state socialism, was a French social reformer, journalist, and historian who came from a royalist family. His grandfather, a prosperous merchant, was guillotined during the French Revolution, and the family was impoverished after Napoleon's fall. The publication of his *Organisation du Travail* (*Organization of Work*) in 1839 brought him fame and a position of leadership in the socialist movement. In the revolution of 1848 he was elected to the provisional government that overthrew the monarchy, the first avowed socialist to be elected to public office anywhere. Under pressure of Blanc and his followers over the issue of the right to employment, the government organized national workshops to give work to the unemployed. This make-work scheme, consisting mostly of common labor on public works, was deliberately mismanaged by Blanc's political enemies. To disperse the national workshops, the government gave the men employed in them the alternative of entering the army or leaving Paris for the provinces. The Paris workers threw up barricades in revolt, but the army blasted them with artillery. In four days of fighting at the end of June 1848, 16,000 people were killed on both sides. Blanc had to flee to England, but he returned to France in 1870. He was elected to the National Assembly, where he ended his days as a mild social reformer.

In Blanc's view, universal suffrage would transform the state into an instrument of progress and welfare. Uncompromising in his attacks on capitalism and competition, which he said would ruin both the laboring class and the bourgeoisie, he nevertheless was opposed to the doctrine of class war. He condemned even trade unionism, because he saw in strikes the futility of unprepared, isolated action. The solidarity of the entire community would promote state economic planning for full employment, the development of welfare services, government capital for getting national workshops started, and workers' cooperatives financed and promoted by the government. The state should become the "banker of the poor" by establishing a publicly owned bank to distribute credit to cooperatives. Capitalists could join the associations, receiving a fixed rate of interest on their capital, as guaranteed by the state. He believed that producers' associations aided by the state would attract the best workers and drive the capitalists out of business through superior competitive efficiency. Capitalism would simply fade away.

Blanc expressed his attitude toward the state succinctly as follows:

> Q.—How are we to pass from the present order of things to that which you contemplate?
> A.—By the intervention of Government.
> Q.—What is the Government or State?
> A.—It is a body of upright and distinguished men, chosen by their equals to guide us all on our way to liberty. . . .
> Q.—Does not the word Government or State imply an idea of tyranny?
> A.—Yes; wherever power is something distinct from the people.[10]

In his *Organization of Work,* Blanc wrote:

> Who would be blind enough not to see that under the reign of free competition the continuous decline of wages necessarily becomes a general law with no exception whatsoever? . . . The Population increases steadily; command the mothers of the poor to be sterile and blaspheme God who made them fruitful; for if you do not command it, the space will be too small for all strugglers. A machine is invented; demand it to be broken and fling an anathema against science! Because if you do not do it, one thousand workmen, whom the new machine displaces in the workshops will knock at the door of the next one and will force down the wages of their fellow-workers. A systematic lowering of wages resulting in the elimination of a certain number of laborers is the inevitable effect of free competition. . . .
>
> The government ought to be considered as the supreme regulator of production and endowed for this duty with great power. This task would consist of fighting competition and finally overcoming it. The government ought to float a loan with

[10] Louis Blanc, *A Catechism of Socialism* (1849).

the proceeds of which it should erect *social workshops* in the most important branches of national industry. . . . It would use competition as a weapon, not to destroy private industry without considerations, which would be to its own interest to avoid, but to guide them imperceptibly into the new system. Soon, indeed, workmen and capitalists would crowd to every industrial sphere where social workshops are opened, on account of the privileges they offer to their members. . . . Everybody, irrespective of position, rank or fortune, is interested in the creation of the new social order.[11]

CHARLES KINGSLEY

Charles Kingsley (1819–1875) was a clergyman, poet, novelist, and reformer. He was a chaplain to Queen Victoria, a professor of modern history at Cambridge, and a canon of Westminster. Early in his career he and the other Christian socialists sought to "socialize the Christian and Christianize the socialist." Kingsley was swept along by the Chartist movement when he went to London during the turbulent times of 1848. He shocked and angered the aristocrats when he announced at a public meeting, "I am a Chartist!" while the workers cheered.

Why was this vehement declaration so shocking to the respectable and the powerful? The Chartists had six demands: equal electoral districts, universal suffrage for both men and women, voting by secret ballot, parliaments elected annually, no property qualifications for serving in the House of Commons, and payment to members of parliament. By 1829 these demands—except for annual parliaments—had all been enacted into law. What, then, was all the excitement about in 1848?

First, reforms are dangerous when they are wrested from the ruling class by mass agitation and action; they are much safer when handed down from above. Revolutionary movements are unlikely to stop at the reforms they originally demand, and small victories simply spur them on. Second, large numbers of Chartists were striking and rioting, undertaking military training, and preparing for possible insurrection. Third, Chartists were threatening to elect a people's parliament to meet at Birmingham with half a million workers to protect it. No wonder Kingsley's declaration was shocking to many.

In 1848 the Christian socialists issued a weekly journal called *Politics for the People*. Kingsley wrote a series of "Letters to Chartists" over the signature of "Parson Lot." His second letter included a passionate defense of the poor:

My friends,—If I was severe on some of you in my last letter, believe me, it is not because I do not feel for you. There are great allowances to be made for most of you. If you have followed a very different "Reformer's Guide" than mine, it is mainly the fault of us parsons: we have never told you that the true Reformer's Guide, the true poor man's book, the true "God's Voice against Tyrants, Idlers, and Humbugs," was the Bible. Ay, you may sneer, but so it is; it is our fault, our great fault, that you should sneer—sneer at the

[11] Louis Blanc, *Organization of Work,* trans. Maria P. Dickoré (Cincinnati, OH: University of Cincinnati Press, 1911), 16, 51–53, 59. (Orig. pub. 1839.)

> very news which ought to be your glory and your strength. It is our fault. We have used the Bible as if it was a mere special constable's handbook—an opium-dose for keeping beasts of burden patient while they were being overloaded—a mere book to keep the poor in order. We have told you that the powers that be were ordained of God, without telling you who ordained the impotences and imbecilities that be, alas, sometimes! We have told you that the Bible preached to you patience, while we have not told you that it promised you freedom. We have told you that the Bible preached the rights of property and the duties of labour, when (God knows!) for once that it does that, it preaches ten time over the *duties of property* and the *rights of labour.* We have found plenty for texts to rebuke the sins of the poor, and very few to rebuke the sins of the rich. You say that we have not preached to you; really I think we have preached to you a great deal more than your fair share. For, for one wholesome rating that we have given the rich, we have given you a thousand. I have been as bad as any one, but I am sick of it.[12]

In his third letter Kingsley was more moderate and a more typical Christian socialist. He wrote:

> My friends,—and when I say friends, I speak honestly, and from the bottom of my heart, for you and I are after all, I believe, longing for the same thing—*to see all humbug, idleness, injustice swept out of England;* only I think you are going, if not the wrong road, yet certainly neither the shortest, the safest, nor the wisest road, to gain the good end.
>
> My friends, I have to tell you that in the Bible you will find what you long for, promised more fairly than any man in these days promised it you; that in that book you will find what you want to say, said for you; you will find how much of what you want to be done. Let me try if I cannot prove my words somewhat.
>
> What are the things which you demand most earnestly? Is not one of them, that no man shall enjoy wages without doing work?
>
> The Bible says, at once, that "*he that will not work, neither shall he eat*"; and as the Bible speaks to rich as well as poor, so is that speech meant for the idle rich as well as for the idle poor. . . .
>
> I entreat you, I adjure you, *to trust the Bible,* to trust my samples from it, and *to read it honestly for yourselves,* and see if it be not the true *Radical Reformer's Guide*—God's everlasting witness against oppression, and cruelty, and idleness.[13]

Elsewhere Kingsley wrote, "God will only reform society on condition of our reforming every man his own self—while the devil is quite ready to help us mend the laws and the parliament, earth and heaven, without ever starting such an impertinent and 'personal' request."

Kingsley repudiated mass meetings, physical violence, union strikes, and hatred of the rich by the poor. The rich are ignorant, not hostile. Kingsley's doctrines included love, religion, cooperative associations, sanitary reforms, and education. After a few years he abandoned his intense activities on behalf of Christian socialism, except for his continuing interest in the sanitary movement.

---

[12] Charles Kingsley, quoted in Charles W. Stubbs, *Charles Kingsley and the Christian Social Movement* (Chicago: Stone, 1899), 118–120.

[13] Kingsley, in *Christian Social Movement,* 121–123.

Questions for Study and Discussion

1. Briefly identify and state the significance of each of the following to the history of economic thought: utopian socialism, state socialism, Christian socialism, anarchism, Proudhon, revisionism, syndicalism, guild socialism, Saint-Simon, Fourier, *phalanxes,* producers' cooperatives, consumers' cooperatives, Sismondi, proletary, Owen, New Lanark Mills, Blanc, Kingsley, and the Chartist movement.
2. Discuss: The contributions of the early socialists to economic analysis are at best minor; it is questionable whether these people are of sufficient importance to deserve mention in a history of economic thought textbook.
3. Saint-Simon summarized his new philosophy as follows: "Everything by industry; everything for industry." What do you think he meant by this?
4. What are the contrasts between syndicalism and anarchism? Between Christian socialism and Marxian socialism?
5. Why, according to Sismondi, are economic crises and imperialism inherent to capitalism? What role do bankers play in this?
6. Assume perfect competition in the product market for yarn and in the resource market from which homogeneous, equally productive textile workers are hired (no efficiency wages). Next introduce a company run by Robert Owen and explain why Owen's firm cannot survive in the long run. Explain how efficiency wages might alter the outcome. Why might government succeed at accomplishing what Owen desired even though Owen individually could not?
7. Contrast Blanc's view of the proper role of the state with the view held by Adam Smith. With which of the two views, if either, would Proudhon agree?

Selected Readings

Books

Beer, Max A. *A History of British Socialism.* 2nd ed. London: Allen and Unwin, 1940.

Blanc, Louis. *Organization of Work.* Translated by Maria P. Dickoré. Cincinnati, OH: University of Cincinnati Press, 1911. (Org. pub. 1839.)

Blaug, Mark, ed. *Dissenters: Charles Fourier, Henri de Simon, Pierre-Joseph Proudhon, John A. Hobson.* Brookfield, VT: Edward Elgar, 1992.

Cole, G. D. H. *The Case for Industrial Partnership.* London: Macmillan, 1957.

Fourier, Charles. *Selections from the Works of Charles Fourier.* Translated by Julia Franklin. London: Swan Sonnenschein, 1901.

Hardach, Gerd, and Dieter Karras. *A Short History of Socialist Economic Thought.* Translated by James Wickham. New York: St. Martin's, 1978.

Johnson, Oakley C. *Robert Owen in the United States.* New York: Humanities Press, 1970.

Kingsley, Charles. *Works.* Edited by Mrs. Charles Kingsley. Vol. 7, *Letters and Memories.* Philadelphia: Morris, 1899.

Lichtheim, George. *The Origins of Socialism.* New York: Praeger, 1969.

Owen, Robert. *A New View of Society and Other Writings.* London: Dent, 1927. (Written 1813–1821.)

Proudhon, Pierre-Joseph. *General Idea of the Revolution in the Nineteenth Century.* Translated by John B. Robinson. London: Freedom Press, 1923. (Orig. pub. 1851.)

———. *What Is Property?* Translated by Benjamin R. Tucker. London: Reeves, no date. (Orig. pub. 1840.)

Raven, Charles E. *Christian Socialism,* 1848–1854. London: Macmillan, 1920.

Riasanovsky, Nicholas V. *The Teachings of Charles Fourier.* Berkeley, CA: University of California Press, 1969.

Saint-Simon, Henri. *Selected Writings.* Edited by F. M. H. Markham. Oxford: Blackwell, 1952.

Sismondi, Simonde de. *Political Economy and Philosophy of Government.* London: Chapman, 1847. (Orig. pub. 1826–1837.)

Journal Articles

Hansen, Niles. "Saint-Simon's Industrial Society in Modern Perspective." *Southwestern Social Science Quarterly* 47 (December 1966): 253–62.

Sowell, Thomas. "Sismondi: A Neglected Pioneer." *History of Political Economy* 4 (Spring 1972): 62–88.

Chapter 10

MARXIAN SOCIALISM

The socialist critics of classical economics preached dramatic reform; their objection to capitalism and its alleged evils was moral. Karl Heinrich Marx (1818–1883), the leading theoretician of "scientific socialism," dismissed that approach. He sought to show that capitalism had internal contradictions that would ensure its eventual demise. Marx believed that social revolution was inevitable within advanced capitalist countries, and he and his compatriot Friedrich Engels (1820–1895) advocated that the workers of the world unite to hasten this event.

Our objective in this chapter is to develop Marx's ideas in a systematic way. After examining biographical details and looking at intellectual influences, we develop Marx's theory of history. Then we take a detailed look at the components of his "law of motion" of capitalism. Finally, we critically assess his thinking.

BIOGRAPHICAL DETAILS AND INTELLECTUAL INFLUENCES

Biographical Details

Marx was born in Prussia to a Jewish family that converted to Protestantism during his childhood. He studied law, history, and philosophy at the universities of Bonn, Berlin, and Jena, and he received the degree of doctor of philosophy at the age of twenty-three. Two years later he married Jenny von Westphalen, the daughter of a baron who occupied a high government office. She was a devoted companion to Marx through all the vicissitudes of his career.

University positions were closed to Marx because of his radicalism. He therefore turned to journalism, was exiled from Germany, and went to Paris, where he studied French socialism and English political economy. While there he met Engels, who was on a brief visit. Engels became Marx's close friend, collaborator, and financial supporter, and together the two wrote the *Manifesto of the Communist Party* in 1848.

Marx was exiled to London in 1849. Except for brief visits to the Continent, he lived the rest of his life in England, where he spent days and years in the reading room of the British Museum exploring "the confounded ramifications of Political Economy." Tormented by illness, extreme poverty, and the death of three of his children in infancy, Marx continued to study, write, and organize. He wrote many articles for the *New York Tribune,* whose payments helped him subsist. He organized and led the International Working Men's Association, the "First

International," which lasted from 1864 to 1876. In 1867 he published the first volume of his magnum opus, *Das Kapital* (*Capital*). After Marx's death, Engels edited his manuscripts and published Volumes 2 and 3 of this work. After Engels died, the remaining manuscripts were left to the leading Marxist of the time, Karl Kautsky, who published another three volumes of Marx's writings under the title *Theories of Surplus Value.*

Intellectual Influences

Besides Engels, several other intellectuals influenced Marx. Chief among them were Ricardo, the early socialists, Darwin, Hegel, and Feuerbach.

The Ricardian influence. Marx studied the works of both Smith and Ricardo and was intrigued in particular by Ricardo's labor theory of value. He felt that Ricardo's theory had several shortcomings and proceeded to sketch his own labor theory—one that had revolutionary implications.

The role of the socialists. Marx was well aware of the pronouncements of several of the socialists discussed in the previous chapter. He shared their moral outrage against contemporary capitalism, their sharp criticism of classical political economy, and their socialist vision of future society. Marx felt, however, that socialism would not be forthcoming until the conditions of the working class deteriorated to the point of open rebellion. He sought to show why this deterioration was inevitable under capitalism.

The Darwinian connection. Charles Robert Darwin (1809–1882) was inspired by Malthus, and his own monumental work impressed Marx. Darwin stated that while reading Malthus on population, it suddenly occurred to him that in the struggle for existence that he had observed everywhere, favorable variations tended to be preserved and unfavorable ones destroyed. The result of this "natural selection" was the evolution of the species. Darwin formalized his theory in 1859 in his famous *On the Origin of Species by Means of Natural Selection.*

Marx read Darwin's book in 1860 and saw parallels in it with his own thinking on political economy. In a letter sent to Engels, Marx stated: "During the last four weeks I have been reading all kinds of things. Amongst others, Darwin's book on 'Natural Selection.' Even though it is developed in the clumsy English fashion, this is the book which contains the historico-natural basis for our views."[1] A month later in a letter to Lassalle, Marx wrote: "Darwin's book is very significant, and I like it as a scientific-natural basis for the historic struggle of the classes."[2] To Marx, the present organizational relationships in the economy, like present biological organisms, were consequences of past change and antecedents of changes still to come. Darwin thus influenced Marx by *reinforcing* Marx's perspective that dynamic, as opposed to static, analysis is the route to true understanding.

[1] Enrique M. Ureña, "Marx and Darwin," *History of Political Economy* 9 (Winter 1977): 549.

[2] Ureña, "Marx and Darwin," 549.

The Hegelian influence. Of far greater significance to Marx's thinking was the dialectical process developed by Georg Hegel (1770–1831). According to this eminent German philosopher, historical knowledge and progress occur through a process of conflict of opposing ideas. An existing idea, or *thesis,* gets confronted by an opposing idea, or *antithesis.* The ensuing struggle between the ideas transforms each into a new idea, or *synthesis,* which then becomes the new thesis. The process then begins again. Marx modified Hegel's notion of the dialectical process, using it to formulate his own theory of historical materialism.

Feuerbach's materialism. In common usage, the term *materialism* refers to the tendency of a person or society to overemphasize the pursuit of consumer goods. But this is not the definition of the term as used in the context of our discussion of Marx. Instead, philosophical "materialism" refers to an emphasis on "matter," "real things," or "the world of reality," as contrasted to "the realm of ideas" (idealism). Although Marx accepted Hegel's notion of a dialectical process within history, he replaced Hegel's idealism with a modified version of Ludwig Feuerbach's concept of philosophical materialism.

In his *Essence of Christianity,* Feuerbach distinguished between the idealized versus the real. People project idealized human attributes such as love for others, perfect knowledge and understanding, the power to effect change for the good of all, and so forth to "unreal" deities. Individuals then worship these deities as if they were supernatural or divine even though these gods, in reality, are the product of human imagination. To Feuerbach, history consists of the process through which people come to know and accept reality through use of their sense perceptions.

Marx subscribed to a somewhat similar view of religion. In 1844 he wrote: "Religion is the *opium* of the people. The abolition of religion as the *illusory* happiness of the people is required for [their] *real* happiness." More important, like Feuerbach, Marx emphasized materialism—the importance of material realities—as opposed to Hegel's idealism.

MARX'S THEORY OF HISTORY

Marx combined Hegel's dialectic with materialism to develop his theory of history. In every historical epoch, the prevailing methods or *forces of production* produce a set of *relations of production* that support them. But the material forces of production (technology, types of capital, skill level of labor) are dynamic; they are continuously changing. This is to be contrasted with the material relations of production (rules, social relations among people, property relations), which are static and reinforced by the superstructure. This superstructure consists of art, philosophy, religion, literature, music, political thought, and the like. All elements of the superstructure maintain the status quo. For Marx, history is a process through which the static relations of production (the thesis) come into eventual conflict with the dynamic forces of production (the antithesis). The result? Conflict revolutionizes the system so that new relations of production (synthesis and new thesis) permit the higher development of the forces of production. The mechanism for overthrowing old societies is the class struggle. Marx states this materialistic theory of history as follows:

> The general conclusion at which I arrived and which, once reached, continued to serve as the leading thread in my studies, may be briefly summed up as follows: In the social production which men carry on they enter into definite relations that are indispensable and independent of their will; these relations of production correspond to a definite stage of development of their material powers of production. The sum total of these relations of production constitutes the economic structure of society—the real foundation, on which rise legal and political superstructures and to which correspond definite forms of social consciousness. The mode of production in material life determines the general character of the social, political, and spiritual processes of life. It is not the consciousness of men that determines their existence, but, on the contrary, their social existence determines their consciousness. At a certain stage of their development, the material forces of production in society come in conflict with the existing relations of production, or—what is but a legal expression for the same thing—with the property relations with which they had been at work before. From forms of development of the forces of production these relations turn into their fetters [chains or restraints]. Then comes the period of social revolution. With the change of the economic foundation the entire immense superstructure is more or less rapidly transformed.[3]

Marx saw society evolving through six stages. In the earliest stage, which he called primitive communism, there were no antagonistic classes, no exploitation, and no class struggles. People held land in common ownership and jointly cooperated to wrest a meager living from nature. The efficiency of production was very low, and thus workers could not consistently produce a surplus beyond the subsistence needed by themselves and their dependents. Slavery and exploitation were therefore impossible, because they require the toilers to produce more than they must consume in order to survive. The society of American Indians before the arrival of the Europeans would be an example of primitive communism.

Gradually the efficiency of production rose to the level where the workers could produce more than their own subsistence. Then slavery became profitable, and exploitation and class conflicts arose. Here Marx meant the slavery of antiquity, such as that among the Hebrews, Egyptians, Greeks, and Romans; he did not mean the slavery that occurred in the United States, which he felt was an anachronism existing within a capitalist society. Slavery permitted a higher development of the productive forces of society, but eventually it became a barrier to further progress. Slaves were not the most highly motivated workers, and slave rebellions shook society and tore it apart. Eventually the system was overthrown and replaced by feudalism, a new set of relations of production that accommodated the new forces of production.

Feudalism is unique, said Marx, because the exploitation of the serf is most clearly visible. Under slavery the slaves appear to get nothing for their labor, even though they do receive subsistence. Under capitalism the workers appear to be paid for all the hours they work, even though the capitalist actually appropriates part of

[3] Karl Marx, *A Contribution to the Critique of Political Economy,* trans. N. I. Stone (Chicago: Kerr, 1913), 11–12.

the labor time without payment. In the feudal system serfs were allowed to work a few days per week on the land assigned to them but were forced to work the other days on the lord's land. This was obvious exploitation. Serfs had a greater incentive to work well than did the slaves, and feudalism brought a higher development of society's forces of production. But the system finally limited further progress, and it was overthrown and superseded by capitalism.

Although Marx passionately hated capitalism, he paid tribute to the great increase in productivity and production that it unleashed. But it, too, faced internal contradictions that would produce class struggle and its eventual overthrow. Under capitalism, said Marx, the techniques of production become increasingly concentrated and centralized, and the system of private ownership of capital becomes a barrier to further progress. An increasing amount of unemployment and "miserization of the working class" transpires, causing the workers to revolt. The state becomes an instrument of force used by capitalists against workers. But the working class prevails, overthrows the bourgeois state, and establishes its own dictatorship of the proletariat. Under this socialism, private property in consumer goods is permitted, but the capital and land are publicly owned by the central government, local authorities, or cooperatives promoted and regulated by the state. Production is planned, as is the rate of investment, with the profit motive and the free market eliminated as guiding forces for the economy. The dialectical process continues until finally the state withers away and pure communism prevails.

THE "LAW OF MOTION" OF CAPITALIST SOCIETY

Using this theory of history as the backdrop, Marx sought "to lay bare the economic law of motion of modern society." He did not draw a blueprint for socialism; this was not his objective. Rather, he sought to analyze the changing forces of production within a capitalist society. In other words, he wanted to determine the process through which the forces of production within capitalism would produce their antithesis and inevitable demise, just as had slavery and feudalism earlier.

Marx used six important interrelated concepts to construct his theory of capitalism: the labor theory of value, the theory of exploitation, capital accumulation and the falling rate of profit, capital accumulation and crises, centralization of capital and concentration of wealth, and class conflict. Each requires detailed elaboration.

Labor Theory of Value

Marx's starting point was the analysis of "commodities" in capitalist society. A commodity, said Marx, is something produced for profit and capable of satisfying human wants, whether the wants "spring from the stomach or from fancy." This commodity may satisfy these wants directly, as means of subsistence, or indirectly, as means of production. Use values constitute the substance of all wealth. Marx did not try to measure use values quantitatively, nor did he consider diminishing utility with increasing quantities of a commodity. He would therefore have said that a large wheat crop represents greater utility, and therefore greater wealth, than a small wheat crop. This would be true even though, if demand is inelastic, the more abundant crop might have lesser value in exchange.

In addition to use value, or utility, a commodity has exchange value, commonly abbreviated simply as "value." What determines the value of a commodity? Marx's important answer: the *socially necessary labor time* embodied in the commodity, considering normal conditions of production and the average skill and intensity of labor at the time. The socially necessary labor time includes the direct labor in producing the commodity, the labor embodied in the machinery and raw materials that are used up during the process of production, and the value transferred to the commodity during this process.

Suppose the average labor time contained in a pair of shoes is 10 hours. This average socially necessary labor determines the value of the shoes. If a worker is incompetent or lazy and takes 20 hours to produce a pair of shoes, its value is still only 10 hours. Suppose a worker or an employer leads the field in technology and efficiency, and a pair of shoes is produced with 5 hours of labor. Its value is nevertheless 10 hours, the average labor cost for society as a whole—that is, the socially necessary labor time.

A product's value is measured in units of simple average labor. Skilled work counts as multiple units of unskilled labor. Thus, one hour of an engineer's productive effort might contribute as much value to a commodity as five hours of simple labor. The marketplace equalizes the labor time of different skills to one common denominator of unskilled labor.

The market also determines the prices that are based on the underlying labor cost. One commodity, such as gold, becomes the universal equivalent that reflects all values. One coat will exchange for two ounces of gold because both require the same amount of socially necessary labor time in their production. If two ounces of gold are coined into two monetary pounds, then one coat will sell for two pounds. Temporary fluctuations of supply and demand will cause prices to deviate from true values, sometimes rising above value and sometimes falling below. The continual oscillation of prices allows them to compensate each other and reduce themselves to average prices that reflect the values of commodities.

Marx's labor theory of value differed from Ricardo's in an important way: To Marx, labor time determines the *absolute* value of goods and services; Ricardo believed that the *relative* values of different commodities are proportional to the labor time embodied within each. Marx believed that his labor theory stripped away the illusion (here again is his materialism) that owners of land and capital contribute to a commodity's value. His theory thus opened the door to a theory of exploitation of labor.

The Theory of Exploitation

Marx assumed in Volume 1 of *Capital* that all commodities sell at their value. How, then, does the capitalist receive a profit? According to Marx, the answer is by purchasing the one commodity that can create a value greater than its own. This commodity is labor power! Here we must distinguish carefully between Marx's concepts of labor power and labor time.

Labor power versus labor time. *Labor power* refers to a person's ability to work and produce commodities; *labor time* is the actual process and duration of work. Labor power is itself a *commodity* that is bought and sold in the market; it is what the capitalist needs to make profits. What determines the value of labor power? The answer, said Marx, is the socially necessary labor time required to produce the cultural necessities of life consumed by the laborers and their families. If these necessities could be produced in four hours per day, the value of the commodity labor power would be four hours of labor time per day. If the productivity of labor doubled, so that articles of subsistence could be produced in two hours per day, the value of labor power would fall 50 percent [(4 – 2)/4]. Two very important points require emphasis here. First, employers pay wages to workers equivalent to the workers' labor power; that is, they pay the going market wage. But, second, this market wage is sufficient only to purchase the cultural subsistence required for survival and perpetuation of the labor force. For Marx, the reason for this subsistence wage is not excessive population growth—he emphatically rejected Malthus's law of population. Rather, Marx felt that capitalism produces a large "reserve army of the unemployed" and that this excess supply of labor dictates that over the long run the average wage will remain near the cultural level of subsistence.

Surplus value. The exploitation of workers—the extraction of surplus value by capitalists—cannot occur when the productivity of labor is so low that the workers have to consume goods equivalent in value to their own output in order to survive. If that were the case, the value of a day's labor power would be a day's labor time. According to Marx, exploitation of labor arises only when workers can produce more in a day than they must consume in order to maintain themselves and their families. Then employers pay the workers the full market value of their labor power, but the daily pay equals only part of the value the laborers create. Through their ownership of capital, employers possess that which workers need to gain subsistence: jobs that pay wages. Hence, capitalists are in a position to set the length of the workday and in a sense say to workers, "Work the number of hours that we set or choose not to work for us at all." Necessity forces the workers to opt to work. But the labor time they spend during the workday creates a larger sum of values than the value of their own labor power, the costs of subsistence. The owners of the means of production garner a surplus value.

Marx illustrated these ideas with a numerical example that we summarize in Figure 10-1. Suppose that six hours of socially necessary labor time are embodied in the commodities that typical workers and their families must consume each day. Then half the labor of a twelve-hour workday (then customary) forms the value of a day's labor power. If half a day's average socially necessary labor time is also required to produce the gold contained in three shillings, then three shillings represents the value of a day's labor power. If this is the wage rate, workers receive the full value of the one commodity they sell: labor power.[4]

The capitalists employ the laborers, whom they supply with the required machinery and raw materials. Suppose that in 6 hours of labor time each worker

[4] In this illustration, the value imparted to a commodity by an hour of labor can also be represented by half a shilling; that is, an hour of labor will produce a quantity of gold worth six shillings in a twelve-hour workday.

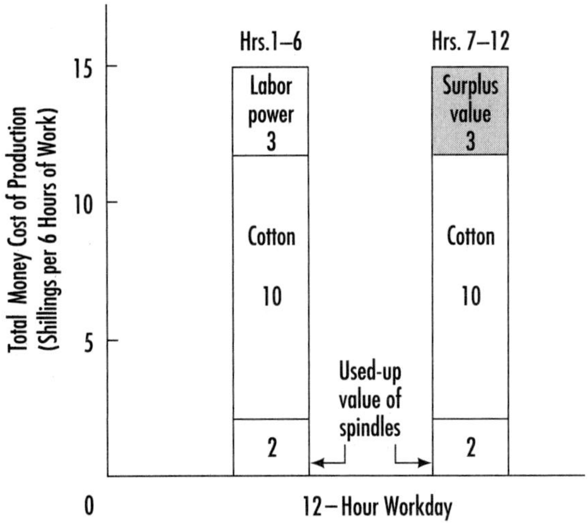

Figure 10-1 Marx's Theory of Exploitation
According to Marx, the capitalist pays the worker the market value of his or her labor power, which is 3 shillings in this example. But it takes only 6 hours of labor time to produce sufficient output to pay for this labor power. By working the employee 12 hours, the capitalist secures a surplus value of 3 shillings (the shaded area). This surplus value arises from the exploitation of labor. Here, the rate of exploitation is one (3 shillings of surplus value divided by 3 shillings paid to labor), or 100 percent.

converts 10 pounds of cotton into 10 pounds of yarn. Let us assume that the cotton used up during the 6 hours of labor has a value of 20 hours of labor, or 10 shillings. Finally, suppose that the wear and tear of the spindles amounts to 4 hours of labor, or 2 shillings, during the half-day of labor.[5] Thus, the total of the yarn produced in half a day is 30 hours of labor time: 6 for the labor power, 20 for the cotton, and 4 for the used-up value of the spindles. Note from the leftward bar in Figure 10-1 that the total *money* cost of production is 15 shillings: 3 for the labor power, 10 for the cotton, and 2 for the used-up value of the spindles. If profit does not arise from buying cheaply and selling dearly and if all commodities sell at their value, then the yarn must *sell* for 15 shillings.

> Our capitalist stares in astonishment. The value of the product is exactly equal to the value of the capital advanced [constant capital plus variable capital which includes labor]. . . . [He] exclaims: "Oh! but I advanced my money for the express purpose of

[5] To understand this assumption, suppose that all the spindles a worker operates will wear out after 10 days of working. Assume also that 80 hours were required to manufacture the spindles. These 80 hours are part of the socially necessary labor time required to manufacture yarn. As the spindles wear out, their value reappears in the yarn. In half a day, the worker uses up 1/20 of the value of the spindles (.5 days/10 days) and transfers it to the yarn; this is 4 hours of labor time (1/20 × 80 hours).

On the monetary side, assume that the spindles a worker uses cost 40 shillings each. Because they will last 10 days, 2 shillings will be transferred to the value of the yarn during each one-half day of use (4 shillings per day/.5).

> making more money." The way to Hell is paved with good intentions, and he might just as easily have intended to make his money, without producing it [yarn] at all. He threatens all sorts of things. He won't be caught napping again. In [the] future he will buy the commodities in the market, instead of manufacturing them himself. But if all his brother capitalists were to do the same, where would he find his commodities in the market? And his money he cannot eat. He tries persuasion. "Consider my abstinence; I might have played ducks and drakes with the fifteen shillings; but instead of that I consumed it productively, and made yarn with it." Very well, and by way of reward he is now in possession of good yarn instead of a bad conscience. . . . Our friend, up to this time so purse-proud, suddenly assumes the modest demeanor of his own workman, and exclaims: "Have I myself not worked? Have I not performed the labour of superintendence and of overlooking the spinner? And does not this labour, too, create value?" His overlooker and his manager try to hide their smiles. Meanwhile, after a hearty laugh, he re-assumes his usual mien. Though he chanted to us the whole creed of the economists, in reality, he says, he would not give a brass farthing for it. He leaves this and all such like subterfuges and juggling tricks to the professors of political economy, who are paid for it. He himself is a practical man; and though he does not always consider what he says outside his business, yet in business he knows what he is about.[6]

The answer to the capitalist dilemma is to extend the hours of work beyond the 6 used in the example. As seen in Figure 10-1, if the worker is required to work another 6 hours each day, 10 more pounds of yarn will get produced. These extra 10 pounds are also worth 15 shillings in the market, *but they cost the capitalist only 12 shillings* (0 for the labor + 10 for the cotton + 2 for the used-up value of the spindles). Hence the capitalist makes 3 shillings of profit, or surplus value. It does not matter that part of the industrial capitalist's profit is turned over to the banker in the form of interest, part to the landlord in the form of rent, and part to the merchant capitalist in the form of mercantile profits. *All* property income arises from the unknowing exploitation of labor in the productive process. Within capitalism, said Marx, the appearance that all labor is remunerated is an illusion. Capitalists are not evil people who rob the workers: "It is a cheap sort of sentimentality which declares this method of determining the value of labour-power, a method prescribed by the very nature of the case, to be a brutal method." Rather they pay workers the market wage but fail to understand the crucial truth that the source of their own profits is exploited labor.

The rate of surplus value. Marx designated the part of capital invested in machinery and raw materials as constant capital, c. The value of this capital is transferred to the final product without any increase. The capital that goes for wages, for the purchase of labor power, is variable capital, v. It produces a value greater than its own. The extra value it produces, which the capitalist takes without compensating the workers who produce it, is surplus value, s. The rate of surplus value, s', or the rate of exploitation, is given in Equation 10-1.

$$s' = \frac{s}{v} \qquad \textbf{(10-1)}$$

[6] Karl Marx, *Capital*, vol. 1 (Chicago: Kerr, 1906), 212–215. (Orig. pub. 1867.)

Note that the rate of surplus value is the ratio of the surplus value to the variable capital. It also can be thought of as the ratio of unpaid labor time to paid labor time. In the example used for Figure 10-1, $s' = 1$ or 100 percent, because $s = 3$ and $v = 3$ (3/3 × 100). Or, using the second definition, it is 6 hours divided by 6 hours. If the working day had been extended to 15 hours, the rate of surplus value would have been 150 percent (9/6 × 100). If it had been reduced to 9 hours, the rate would have been 50 percent (3/6 × 100).

What is the proper length of the working day? Marx stated:

> The capitalist maintains his rights as a purchaser when he tries to make the working day as long as possible, and to make, whenever possible, two working days out of one. On the other hand, the peculiar nature of the commodity sold implies a limit to its consumption by the purchaser, and the labourer maintains his right as seller when he wishes to reduce the working day to one of definite duration. There is here, therefore, an antinomy, right against right, both equally bearing the seal of the law of exchanges. Between equal rights force decides. Hence it is that in the history of capitalist production, the determination of what is a working day presents itself as the result of a struggle, a struggle between collective capital, i.e., the class of capitalists, and collective labor, i.e., the working class.[7]

Even if the working day were not lengthened, surplus value could be increased by raising the efficiency of production and thus reducing the value of the worker's labor power. If the worker's necessities could be produced in a shorter time, a larger share of the new value would go to the capitalist. Suppose the working day were shortened from 12 hours to 10; but instead of being divided into 6 hours of paid labor for the worker and 6 for the capitalist, it was divided into 4 for the worker and 6 hours for the capitalist. The rate of exploitation would rise from 100 (6/6 × 100) to 150 percent (6/4 × 100).

The rate of profit. The rate of profit (p') in Marx's formulation is the ratio of surplus value to the total capital invested, or:

$$p' = \frac{s}{c + v} \tag{10-2}$$

Again using the data in Figure 10-1, we find that in this example the rate of profit is 11.1 percent ($3/$27 × 100).

The transformation problem. Equation 10-2 helps clarify Marx's "great contradiction" or "transformation problem."[8] Consider the following propositions:

1. Marx assumed in Volume 1 of *Capital* that all commodities are sold at their values.
2. Labor, v, in Equation 10-2 is the sole source of value.

[7] Marx, *Capital*, 3: 190.

[8] Our purpose here is to outline the bare essentials of the transformation problem. A detailed, yet accessible, discussion of this topic is provided by Ronald L. Meek in chapter 5 of his *Smith, Marx, and After: Ten Essays on the History of Economic Thought* (London: Chapman & Hall, 1977).

3. Following from proposition 1, industries that employ a relatively large amount of machinery and raw materials, *c*, and a relatively small amount of labor, *v*, will have a lower surplus value, *s*, and profit rate on their capital, p', than industries that employ a small amount of constant capital, *c*, and a large amount of labor, *v*. This is the case because labor is the only commodity that can be exploited for profit.
4. Proposition 3 contradicts what Marx knew from his own observation: Mechanized industries, using much capital and little labor, have at least as high a rate of profit as industries using little capital and much labor. Like the classical economists, Marx knew that profit rates tend to equalize among industries.
5. If profit rates are *uniform* and capital-to-labor ratios *vary* among industries, then commodities will *not* sell at their values as Marx assumed in Volume 1. This appears to be a significant contradiction in Marx's analysis.

Marx recognized this problem even before writing Volume 1 and tried to deal with it in Volume 3 of *Capital*. He concluded that the selling prices of commodities produced in constant-cost, capital-intensive industries will sell *above* their values, whereas labor-intensive commodities will sell at prices *below* their true values. Thus, according to Marx, the labor theory of value still holds, but only for the capitalist system as a whole. Individual commodities will sell at prices above or below their values in order to equalize rates of profit for the whole economy. There is much debate over whether Marx successfully handled this transformation problem. There also is debate over the consequences of a faulty labor theory for his overall theory of capitalist development.[9]

Capital Accumulation and the Falling Rate of Profit

According to Marx, the rate of profit—p' in Equation 10-2—received by capitalists will tend to fall over the long run. The reason is the drive toward increasing efficiency through mechanization and labor-saving inventions. This raises what Marxists call the *organic composition of capital*, shown in Equation 10-3 as *Q*. Notice that this is the ratio of constant capital, *c*, to total capital, $c + v$.

$$Q = \frac{c}{c + v} \qquad \textbf{(10-3)}$$

An alternative profit rate equation, presented in Equation 10-4, can be derived from Equations 10-2 and 10-3.[10]

$$p' = s'(1 - Q) \qquad \textbf{(10-4)}$$

Notice that this new equation indicates that the rate of profit, p', varies directly with the rate of surplus value, s', and inversely with the organic composition of capital, *Q*. Therefore, as capitalists invest relatively more in machinery and less in labor power, *Q*

[9] For example, see Meek, *Smith, Marx, and After*, chapters 5–7. Also see Paul Samuelson, "Understanding the Marxian Notion of Exploitation: A Summary of the So-Called Transformation Problem between Marxian Values and Competitive Prices," *Journal of Economic Literature* 9 (June 1971): 399–431. Joan Robinson, Martin Bronfenbrenner, William Baumol, Michio Moreshima, and Paul Samuelson further address this topic in the December 1973 and March 1974 issues of this journal.

[10] Paul M. Sweezy provides the proof for this derivation in his *The Theory of Capitalist Development* (New York: Oxford University Press, 1942), 68.

rises and p' falls. This is of utmost importance to Marx. Recall that capitalism faces internal contradictions that hasten its demise. The drive toward the use of more capital reduces the rate of profit; *laborers* are the source of all value, including surplus value, and as relatively fewer workers are used, the profit rate falls! But if value and profit are produced only by labor, won't capitalists have an incentive to use more labor and less capital? For Marx, the answer was "No." He believed that the dynamics of capitalism inevitably lead to an increased organic composition of capital. There are two reasons. First, the enterprise that leads in promoting efficient production through the use of more and better constant capital will temporarily receive extra profits by lowering its costs of production. Eventually, product prices will fall to reflect the lower costs, and the employer who lags behind the trend toward mechanization in a particular industry will not survive. Second, the greater the efficiency of production, the lower the value of labor power—the number of hours required to produce the subsistence—and the greater the total amount of profit produced per working day.

The substitution of capital for labor has a second effect: The size of the industrial reserve army of the unemployed rises. Workers are thrown out of work by machinery or, stated in contemporary terms, become technologically unemployed. Also, the larger capital investments for each individual establishment lead to "a growing concentration of capital (accompanied by a growing number of capitalists, though not to the same extent)."

Marx perceived certain offsetting forces to the falling rate of profit. First, the intensity of exploitation, s' in Equation 10-4, can be raised by forcing the workers to increase their pace of work or by lengthening their working day. Second, wages temporarily may be cut below their value. Third, the constant capital may be cheapened. The ratio of constant capital to labor is a value relationship, and as machinery and raw materials become cheaper, the rise in the organic composition of capital and the fall in the rate of profit both become slower. Fourth, growing population in relation to jobs and increasing technological unemployment are conducive to setting up new industries that use much labor and little capital. The high rates of profits in such industries enter into the average rate of profit for the system as a whole. Fifth, foreign trade raises the rate of profit by cheapening the elements of both constant capital and the necessities of life. In addition, capital invested in colonies yields higher rates of profit because the ratio of constant to variable capital is lower and because the exploitation of colonial workers is more intense than the exploitation of wage labor at home.[11] Finally, the rate of exploitation is increased by reducing the value of labor power through increased efficiency of production.

Note that several of these factors that partially offset the falling rate of profit *increase* the rate of exploitation and further "immiserize" the proletariat. Hence class consciousness is heightened, and the probability of revolution is increased.

Capital Accumulation and Crises

The falling rate of profit, said Marx, is but one of the insoluble problems of capitalism. Another is the tendency for increasingly severe business crises.

[11] Lenin later emphasized this point. Contemporary Marxists view imperialism as a natural outgrowth of capitalism.

Marx attacked Say's law, stating that at best it applied only to simple commodity production. Self-employed small artisans, seeking to acquire use values, produce commodities in order to exchange them for others they wish to consume. The weaver of linen sells it and uses the money to buy food. The process can be represented by $C \rightarrow M \rightarrow C$, where the *C*s represent the commodities linen and food, respectively. These goods have equal exchange value and different use values. Money, *M*, is simply the medium of exchange.

But even under simple commodity production the possibility of crisis exists:

> Nothing can be more childish than the dogma, that because every sale is a purchase, and every purchase a sale, therefore the circulation of commodities necessarily implies an equilibrium of sales and purchases. If this means that the number of actual sales is equal to the number of purchases, it is mere tautology. . . . No one can sell unless some one else purchases. But no one is forthwith bound to purchase, because he has just sold. Circulation bursts through all restrictions as to time, place, and individuals, imposed by direct barter, and this it effects by splitting up, into the antithesis of a sale and a purchase, the direct identity that in barter does exist between the alienation of one's own and the acquisition of some other man's product. . . . If the interval in time between . . . the sale and purchase becomes too pronounced, the intimate connection between them, their oneness, asserts itself by producing—a crisis.[12]

Under large-scale capitalist production, the process of exchange becomes $M \rightarrow C \rightarrow M$, wherein people buy in order to sell, instead of selling in order to buy. Money is changed into commodities such as labor power, raw materials, and machinery. The products are then sold for money. This process does not make sense, however, if the two *M*s are equal. Therefore, the correct representation of the capitalist process is $M \rightarrow C \rightarrow M'$, where M' is larger than M by the amount of surplus value squeezed out of the productive workers. This is the process of expanding investment. "Accumulate, accumulate! That is the law of Moses and the prophets!"

Rapid investment in capital and labor temporarily increases the demand for labor and increases the wages that capitalists must pay. But these higher wages reduce the rates of surplus value and profit, ending the expansion and sending the economy in the opposite direction. The depression that results destroys the monetary value of fixed capital, enabling the larger capitalist to buy up smaller ones at bargain prices. Also, some factories close, prices of commodities fall, credit contracts, and wages fall. The rates of surplus value and profit thus get restored, and investment increases once again. "The present stagnation of production would have prepared an expansion of production later on, within capitalist limits." Each such business cycle, according to Marx, is of greater magnitude than the previous one, adding to the conditions that produce class struggle and social revolution.[13]

---

[12] Marx, *Capital,* 1: 127–128.

[13] The theory presented in this paragraph represents only one of the several theories of the business cycle sketched out by Marx in various parts of his writings.

The Centralization of Capital and Concentration of Wealth

The dynamics of capital accumulation and the tendency for recurring business crises centralize the ownership of capital and concentrate wealth in fewer hands.

> Capital grows in one place to a huge mass because it has in another place been lost by many. . . . The battle of competition is fought by cheapening of commodities. The cheapness of commodities depends, *caeteris paribus,* on the productiveness of labour, and this again on the scale of production. Therefore, the larger capitals beat the smaller. It will further be remembered that, with the development of the capitalist mode of production, there is an increase in the minimum amount of individual capital necessary to carry on a business under its normal conditions. The smaller capitals, therefore, crowd into spheres of production which Modern Industry has only sporadically or incompletely got hold of. Here competition rages in direct proportion to the number, and in inverse proportion to the magnitudes, of the antagonistic capitals. It always ends in the ruin of many small capitalists, whose capitals partly pass into the hand of their conquerors, partly vanish. Apart from this, with capitalist production an altogether new force comes into play—the credit system.
>
> In its beginning, the credit system sneaks in a modest helper of accumulation and draws by invisible threads the money resources scattered all over the surface of society into the hands of individual or associated capitalists. But soon it becomes a new and formidable weapon in the competitive struggle, and finally it transforms itself into an immense social mechanism for the centralization of capitals.[14]

Class Conflict

The concentration of wealth in the hands of fewer and fewer capitalists and the absolute and relative impoverishment of the workers together set the stage for class conflict. The growing "misery, oppression, slavery, degradation, exploitation" of the workers raise their sense of solidarity and will to revolt. "The knell of capitalist private property sounds. The expropriators are expropriated." The relations of production under capitalism come in conflict with the forces of production, and the former are "rapidly transformed." The workers overthrow the capitalists and establish a dictatorship of the proletariat. State ownership of the means of production replaces private ownership, the rate of capital expansion is stabilized, and the exploitation of workers is eliminated. The workers in a sense become owners of the capital.

THE LAW OF MOTION OF CAPITALISM: A SUMMARY

Figure 10-2 summarizes Marx's law of motion of capitalist development. As we indicated, his labor theory of value is the starting point for the entire theory. Workers are the source of all value, but as indicated by arrow *a,* labor does not get

[14] Marx, *Capital,* 1: 686–687.

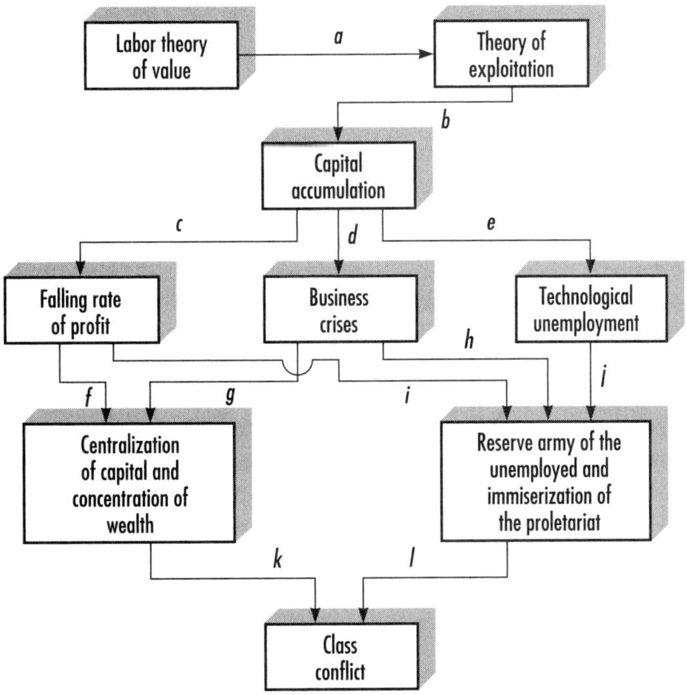

Figure 10-2 Marx's "Law of Motion" of Capitalism

According to Marx, because labor is the source of all value, surplus value and profits arise through exploitation of workers (arrow *a*). Competition among capitalists results in capital accumulation (arrow *b*), which causes a falling rate of profit, business crises, and technological unemployment (arrows *c*, *d*, and *e*). These outcomes produce centralization of capital and concentration of wealth (arrows *f* and *g*), as well as rising unemployment and poverty (arrows *h*, *i*, and *j*). The polarization of capitalists and workers leads to class conflict (arrows *k* and *l*) and the overthrow of capitalism.

all value. Instead, the capitalist pays labor the value of its labor power. This amount is less than the value of the output, the difference being surplus value expropriated by the capitalist in the form of property income. As shown by arrow *b*, surplus value is the source of capital accumulation. Arrows *c*, *d*, and *e* indicate, respectively, that capital accumulation produces a falling rate of profit, worsening business crises, and technological unemployment. All three bolster the size of the industrial reserve army of the unemployed and either directly or indirectly add to the immiserization of the proletariat (arrows *h*, *i*, and *j*). The declining rate of profit and worsening business crises also cause a centralization of capital and concentration of wealth (arrows *f* and *g*). As evidenced by arrows *k* and *l*, the eventual result of the process is class conflict.

This theory of capitalist development stands in clear contrast to that presented by Adam Smith. You are urged to compare Figure 10-2 with Figure 5-1 to confirm this fact.

ASSESSMENT OF MARX'S ECONOMICS

Marx contributed to the development of economic thought in several ways. His analysis, however, also was faulty in numerous respects.

Contributions

Some socialists consider Marx to be the single most important writer in the history of economic thought. Most economists, of course, do not share this view. But even economists who are critical of Marx agree that he contributed to economic analysis in several ways. First, Marx was an important participant in the struggle to establish a suitable theory of value in economics. The problems associated with the labor theory of value provided an incentive for economists to explore other routes for understanding exchange values.

Second, Marx was one of the first economists to note that business cycles are a normal occurrence in capitalist economies. Recall that Malthus had described the possibility of general gluts but did not develop the idea of business cycles. Marx, like Sismondi before him, addressed cyclical upswings and downswings in the market economy. These fluctuations occasionally burden capitalist economies today and remain the focus of intense scrutiny by economists worldwide.

Third, Marx accurately predicted the growth of large-scale enterprise and monopoly power. As these forms of enterprise arose, economists had to develop new theories of business behavior, resource allocation, and income distribution; economists could no longer assume a Smithian world of atomistic competitive enterprises in analyzing real-world markets and public policies.

Fourth, Marx highlighted the substitution effect as it applies to labor-saving capital. Indeed, in some circumstances, new capital can replace labor. He also discussed the idea of labor-saving innovation in more detail than had any of his predecessors. Finally, Marx contributed to economics through his emphasis on dynamic, rather than static, analysis. The dynamic approach was stressed later by institutional economists, growth theorists, and Austrian economists.

Analytical Flaws

Marx's analysis of the "law of motion" of capitalism has several shortcomings. Our discussion of them is organized around the major ideas of Marxian theory summarized in Figure 10-2.

Defects in the labor theory of value. There are several problems with Marx's labor theory of value. Contemporary economists dispute that workers are the source of all exchange value. Land and capital resources also are productive, independently of and beyond the value of the labor required readying them for production. Therefore, the owners of land and labor resources deserve a return that is sufficient to keep these resources employed in producing a particular commodity. It is true that capital in part is produced by past labor, but the past labor is paid in accordance with its contribution to producing the capital. The capital then becomes an independent resource that can be bought and sold. As such, it can create value beyond the value of the labor used to produce it.

A more technical criticism is the previously mentioned "transformation problem" associated with Marx's labor theory. Other technical problems allegedly exist. For example, in Volume 1 of *Capital*, Marx assumed a uniform rate of surplus value across all industries in order to contend that labor is the exclusive source of all value. As Edwin West has pointed out:

> But if this rate of exploitation is the same everywhere, hours of work have also to be uniform. Marx accordingly insisted that this was so and quoted contemporary evidence in support. A close examination of his sources (nineteenth-century factory inspectors' reports) fails, however, to confirm his prediction. Instead the data are more consistent with the competing neoclassical hypothesis, originating with Jevons, that work hours will vary because workers' labor and leisure preferences vary.[15]

Problems with Marx's theory of exploitation. According to Marx, the wages paid to workers tend toward the cultural subsistence because of the presence of a large reserve army of the unemployed. The worker is forced to work sufficiently long so as to create a surplus value for the capitalist. But no such reserve army has developed. People generally move into and out of unemployment; those in the unemployment "pool" are usually only temporarily unemployed. Periods of long-term massive unemployment have been the exception rather than the rule in capitalist nations. Under conditions of relatively full employment, employers must compete with one another to attract qualified workers, just as workers compete with one another to get the better jobs. Competition among employers raises wages, forces firms to improve their working conditions, causes employers to shorten hours, or some combination of the three. Historically, real wages have risen quite dramatically over the decades since Marx wrote, and labor's share of national income has either increased or been relatively constant in most industrial nations.

Shortcomings in Marx's analysis of capital accumulation. A glance at Figure 10-2 reminds us that Marx believed that capital accumulation causes a falling rate of profit, worsening business crises, and technological unemployment. Modern economists say that, although each of these outcomes is possible in theory, other outcomes also are theoretically possible and in fact often have resulted instead. It is true that capital deepening—the growth of capital at a rate faster than labor—in and of itself depresses the return on capital. But other forces also have been at work. Specifically, new technologies have increased the productivity of capital, offsetting the tendency of the rate of profit to fall. Historically, the rate of return on capital and the rate of profit have oscillated over the business cycle but have not trended downward.

What about capital accumulation and worsening business cycles? Again it is true that rapid expansion of capital can lead to overcapacity, followed by excessive inventories, curtailments of production, and increases in unemployment. As we indicated, Marx's contributions here are important. But investment booms are not the

[15] Edwin G. West, "Marx's Hypotheses on the Length of the Working Day," *Journal of Political Economy* 91 (April 1983): 266.

norm. During many periods, investment rises at a pace consistent with steady economic growth rather than impending economic crises.

Does capital accumulation cause unemployment, as Marx contended? The answer may be "Yes" if the capital simply is a substitute in production for labor. But even where this is the case, the lower production costs that result may expand the scale of an industry sufficiently to cause total employment to remain constant or even rise. Furthermore, many types of capital are complements in production with labor. For example, a new factory requires new employees, that is, results in an increase in the demand for labor and the number of available jobs. The point is that the accumulation of constant capital need not cause unemployment. Over the century since the publication of *Capital*, capital accumulation has been accompanied by rapid increases in total employment, although the relationship between additions to the capital stock and employment growth varies considerably by industry.

Problems with the idea of class conflict. Marx's prediction of the inevitability of class conflict rests on his theories of exploitation and capital accumulation, the latter causing a falling rate of profit, worsening crises, and technological unemployment. We have argued that these theories have serious shortcomings. History suggests that a polarization of workers and capitalists into two opposing classes has not occurred. Rather, a strong middle class has developed in most of the advanced capitalist nations. Members of this class include small business owners, self-employed professional people, salaried scientists, engineers, teachers, salespersons, advertisers, administrators, and so forth. Marx surely would have been surprised to learn that, thanks partly to capital accumulation, the collective earnings of workers is the major source from which the nation's savings arises. He also would have been surprised to discover that many wage earners have annual incomes that place them in the middle or even upper-middle "classes" in the society.

Marx felt that the state, acting as the executive committee of the bourgeoisie as a whole, would guarantee those conditions that would produce an oppressed proletariat. Marx failed to see that the state could be influenced to ameliorate economic conditions. He did not foresee welfare statism, public utility regulation, laws that establish the right of unions to organize and strike, fiscal and monetary policy, and the like.[16] Nor did he understand that the interests of the capitalist class as a whole do not necessarily coincide with those of each individual within it. For example, a single capitalist may resist to the utmost the granting of pensions. But when all employers have to grant them under identical terms, the burden is not so great as when only one must sacrifice a competitive position by incurring such a cost.

Refer to 10-1 PAST AS PROLOGUE

Somewhat ironically, successful Marxian revolutions did not occur in the advanced capitalist nations (such as England, France, and Germany) where Marx expected them. The nations in which they did occur (Russia, China) had a woeful lack of capital accumulation at the time of revolt. Moreover, the dramatic collapse of Marxism in eastern Europe and the Soviet Union exposed a disdain for Marxism, at least as it has manifested itself historically, even among the so-called proletariat. The historical evidence simply does not support Marx's theory of class conflict.

[16] Marx, of course, was not alone in failing to foresee these changes, but he is open to criticism because his theory spoke of the *inevitable* progression of capitalism to its demise.

10-1 PAST AS PROLOGUE

The Collapse of Marxism

Marx predicted that capitalism would collapse from internal contradictions and be replaced by socialism. Ironically, in the late 1980s and early 1990s just the opposite set of events took place. Internal difficulties in eastern European nations and the Soviet Union caused the collapse of Marxian socialism and gave rise to nascent capitalism. This collapse of Marxism is one of the truly remarkable events of the twentieth century.

Why did Marxian socialism fail? Although the reasons are many and complex, one is fundamental: Marxist regimes were built upon a flawed economic theory. From the start, Western economists had dismissed Marx's labor theory of value and his "law of motion" of capitalism. Eventually, even economists in the communist nations raised grave doubts about these theories. Although Marx himself said little about how the dictatorship of the proletariat would organize production, Marx's followers insisted that the centrally planned socialist economy was the logical, even necessary, successor to capitalism. This premise could not withstand mounting evidence to the contrary. While capitalist West Germany prospered, socialist East Germany languished. While capitalist South Korea boomed, communist North Korea remained a third-world country. While privatization, markets, and price reform in China greatly expanded food production, the system of collectivized farms in the Soviet Union increased its reliance on imported food.

Faced with the reality of the failing Soviet economy, President Mikhail Gorbachev introduced *perestroika* in 1986. This "restructuring of the economy" involved six interrelated elements: (1) the modernization of industry; (2) decentralization of decision making; (3) allowance for a limited private-enterprise sector; (4) improved worker incentives; (5) a more cost-based price system; and (6) an increased role in the international economy.

Accompanying *perestroika* was a campaign for *glasnost,* a greater openness of discussion and debate on economic and political matters. Although Gorbachev's *perestroika* was largely unsuccessful, *glasnost* delivered a stream of criticism of the existing political and economic system and engendered ever-bolder reform proposals. In eastern Europe and the Soviet Union, *glasnost* clearly revealed that the vast majority of people opposed the communist system of government and economics. This became apparent to the world in 1989 when the East Germans tore down the Berlin Wall, a wall their leaders had built decades earlier to keep East Germans from fleeing to the West. The destruction of the wall and the celebration that followed ended any remaining facade that the ideals of Marxism were shared by the people living under its regime.

The knell of Soviet Marxism sounded in 1991 when Russian President Boris Yeltsin stood on a tank in Moscow in defiance of a coup against Gorbachev. The coup quickly unraveled when the old-line coup leaders could not convince the

10-1 PAST AS PROLOGUE (continued)

military to act on their behalf. The Communist party and the Marxian theory it was based on disintegrated before the eyes of the world. The Yeltsin government then began the arduous task of dismantling centrally planned socialism and installing capitalistic institutions, such as free markets and private property.

The transition from Marxian socialism to capitalism has had mixed results. Capitalistic reforms in the former communist countries of Poland, Hungary, East Germany, and the Czech Republic have been quite successful, but privatization of Russian industry has been slow to improve general prosperity. Growth has been strong in recent years, thanks in part to export earnings from rising oil and gas prices. However, problems of corruption, poorly developed market institutions, and the prospect of increased state control over the economy all hinder capitalistic development in Russia. How the Russian transition from Marxism will eventually play out remains to be seen.

Questions for Study and Discussion

1. Briefly identify and state the significance of each of the following to the history of economic thought: Engels, *Manifesto of the Communist Party* (1848), *Das Kapital* (1867), Darwin, Hegel, Feuerbach, materialism, forces of production, relations of production, constant capital, variable capital, socially necessary labor time, labor power, surplus value, rate of exploitation, transformation problem, organic composition of capital, industrial reserve army, and proletariat.
2. Explain Marx's theory of history, relating it to the earlier ideas of Hegel and Feuerbach.
3. Explain each of these Marxian equations, relating them to his analysis of the "law of motion" of capitalism:
   a) Value $= c + v + s$
   b) $s' = s/v$
   c) $Q = c/(c + v)$
   d) $p' = s'(1 - Q)$
4. How do Marx's theory of history and his analysis of capitalism relate to Darwin's notion of evolution?
5. If workers are paid the value of their labor power, as Marx contended, then in what sense are they exploited?
6. Suppose that 3 hours of socially necessary labor time are embodied in the commodities that typical workers and their families must consume each day. Assume also that the capitalists employ these workers for 12 hours a day. What is the rate of surplus value? The rate of profit?
7. What is the transformation problem as it relates to Marx, and how did Marx attempt to deal with it?

8. Discuss the weakness in Marx's contention that the introduction of new machinery and new techniques of production would cause a growing reserve army of the technologically unemployed.
9. What role do business crises play in Marx's overall theory of capitalist development?
10. The reasoning fallacy "wishing it were so" occurs when someone so hopes a particular outcome will occur that it biases his or her analysis. Make a case that Marx fell prey to this reasoning fallacy.

Selected Readings

Books

Baran, Paul A., and Paul M. Sweezy. *Monopoly Capital.* New York: Monthly Review Press, 1966.

Blaug, Mark, ed. *Karl Marx.* Brookfield, VT: Edward Elgar, 1991.

Foley, Duncan K. *Understanding Capital: Marx's Economic Theory.* Cambridge, MA: Harvard University Press, 1986.

King, J. E., ed. *Marxian Economics.* 3 vols. Brookfield, VT: Edward Elgar, 1990.

Mandell, Ernest. *Marxian Economic Theory.* Translated by Brian Pearce. 2 vols. New York: Monthly Review Press, 1970.

Marx, Karl. *Capital.* Translated by Samuel Moore, Edward Aveling, and Ernest Untermann. 3 vols. Chicago: Kerr, 1906–1909. (Orig. pub. 1887–1895.)

———. *A Contribution to the Critique of Political Economy.* Translated by N. I. Stone. 2nd ed. Chicago: Charles Kerr, 1913. (Written in 1859.)

———. *The Economic and Philosophic Manuscripts of 1844.* Translated by Martin Milligan and edited by Dirk J. Struik. New York: International Publishers, 1964.

———. *Theories of Surplus Value.* Translated by G. A. Bonner and Emily Burns. London: Lawrence and Wishart, 1951. (Orig. pub. 1905–1910; written in 1862–1863.)

Marx, Karl, and Friedrich Engels. *Manifesto of the Communist Party.* New York: International Publishers, 1948. (Written in 1848.)

Meek, Ronald L. *Smith, Marx, and After: Ten Essays in the Development of Economic Thought.* London: Chapman & Hall, 1977.

Robinson, Joan. *Essay on Marxian Economics.* New York: St. Martin's Press, 1967.

Sowell, Thomas. *Marxism: Philosophy and Economics.* New York: William Morrow, 1985.

Sweezy, Paul M. *The Theory of Capitalist Development.* New York: Oxford University Press, 1942.

Tucker, Robert C., ed. *The Marx-Engels Reader.* 2nd ed. New York: W. W. Norton, 1978.

Journal Articles

Brue, Stanley L., and Craig MacPhee. "From Marx to Markets: Reform of the University Economic Curriculum in Russia," *Journal of Economic Education* 26 (Spring 1995): 182–194.

Dillard, Dudley. "Keynes and Marx: A Centennial Appraisal," *Journal of Post–Keynesian Economics* 6 (Spring 1984): 421–432.

Hutchison, T. W. "Friedrich Engels and Marxian Economic Theory," *Journal of Political Economy* 86 (April 1978): 303–320.

Minisymposium: Locating Marx after the Fall (papers and comments by E. Roy Weintraub, Anthony Brewer, John E. Elliot, Duncan K. Foley, Samuel Hollander, M. C. Howard, J. E. King, Takashi Negishi, Alessandro Roncaglia, Margaret Schabas, Ian Steedman). *History of Political Economy* 27 (Spring 1995): 109–206.

Ureña, E. M. "Marx and Darwin," *History of Political Economy* 9 (Winter 1977): 548–559.

West, Edwin G. "Marx's Hypotheses on the Length of the Working Day," *Journal of Political Economy* 91 (April 1983): 266–281.

Wolfson, Murray. "Three Stages in Marx's Thought," *History of Political Economy* 11 (Spring 1979): 117–146.

Chapter 11

THE GERMAN HISTORICAL SCHOOL

In this chapter we consider the German historical school, which arose in the 1840s with the publications of Friedrich List and Wilhelm Roscher and ended in 1917 when Gustav Schmoller died.[1] By then economists in general had absorbed some of the ideas of the school, and the school no longer existed as a distinct entity. Like the socialists, the German historical economists were generally critical of classical economics. Following an overview of the school, we develop the ideas of the school's main thinkers: List, Roscher, Schmoller, and Weber.

OVERVIEW OF THE GERMAN HISTORICAL SCHOOL

The Historical Background of the School

The peace treaty after the Napoleonic wars left Germany divided into thirty-nine separate states, most of them monarchical, almost all of them undemocratic. The victorious Great Powers of Europe manipulated Germany to promote their own ulterior purposes. Austria wanted to keep Germany weak and divided; Britain wished to see a strong Prussia to thwart a future resurgent France; Russia desired for itself the parts of Poland not yet seized by Germany or Austria.

The German struggle against Napoleon had aroused patriotic and nationalistic emotions. Many Germans demanded unification and constitutional reforms, but the quest for national unity was frustrated for half a century. The aspirations toward democracy remained unrealized for over a century and then were achieved only briefly under the most adverse conditions—under the stigma of losing World War I.

In 1815 the Holy Alliance of Prussia, Austria, and Russia was organized as a means of defeating revolution wherever it might threaten. Minor revolutionary outbursts in Germany from 1830 to 1832 were repressed, and the major upheavals of 1848 were crushed by Prussian and Austrian troops.

Prussia, the largest, richest, most militaristic, and most powerful state in Germany, dominated the country. Foreign countries wooed Prussia as a powerful ally. Foreign and native conservatives saw in Prussia a bulwark against democracy

[1] This chapter has benefited substantially from Jack C. Myles's unpublished doctoral thesis at Princeton University, "German Historicism and American Economics," 1956.

and socialism. Native nationalists relied on Prussia to forge a unified Germany. Prussia dominated the German government and armed forces. A series of successful wars further strengthened nationalism under Prussian hegemony. Advanced social legislation, enacted by Bismarck, expressed the paternalism of the monarchy and evoked loyalty and patriotism among the German workers. Bismarck bragged that in Germany the kings made the revolutions.

Because certain key economic institutions of nineteenth-century Germany differed substantially from those of Britain, it is not surprising that a different economic ideology arose. Mercantilist regulations persisted in Germany at least until the formation of the empire in 1871, long after they had disappeared from the British scene. Competition and freedom of enterprise, which the classicists took for granted in their economic analysis, were severely restricted in Germany. Because of the large bureaucracy that administered and regulated manifold phases of German economic life, the science of public administration was highly developed. British theories were obviously inapplicable to the German situation. The historical school defended and rationalized the German way of life by questioning the historical relevance of the British classical economic doctrines.

The Germany that gave birth to the historical school was divided, weak, and primarily agricultural. Nationalism, patriotism, militarism, paternalism, devotion to duty and hard work, and massive government intervention all combined to change the pattern and promote industrial growth. Because Germany of the mid-nineteenth century was far behind England in the development of industry, its economists reasoned that government assistance was required for it to catch up.

Major Tenets of the Historical School

Four principles were basic in the thinking of the German historical economists:

- Evolutionary approach to economics. The historical school applied a dynamic, evolutionary perspective in its study of society. It concentrated on cumulative development and growth. An analogy was sometimes drawn to Darwin's evolutionism in biology: The social organism is born, develops and grows, and finally decays and dies. Society is constantly changing. Therefore, what is relevant economic doctrine for one country at a particular time may be irrelevant for another country or another age. This relativistic approach was especially useful in attacking classical economics as being unsuitable for Germany.
- Emphasis on the positive role of government. The historical school was nationalistic, whereas classical economics was individualistic and cosmopolitan. If the social organism is the center of study, if it is the force for dynamic movement, then society and the state, rather than the individual, occupy the center of the stage. In Germany it was the state that fostered industry, transportation, and economic growth. In the process of defending a unified economy, it was easy to develop an ardent nationalistic glorification of the state. The historical school gave great prominence to the need for state intervention in economic affairs and emphasized that the community has interests of its own that are quite distinct from those of the individual.

- Inductive/historical approach. The economists of the historical school emphasized the importance of studying the economy historically, as part of an integrated whole. Because economic and other social phenomena are interdependent, political economy cannot be treated adequately except in combination with other branches of social science. The historical school criticized the abstract, deductive, static, unrealistic, unhistorical qualities of classical and marginalist methodology. It undertook massive inductive studies, using primary source material and studying changing social institutions. The school claimed that its historical method allowed it to study *all* the forces of an economic phenomenon, *all* the facets of economic behavior, not merely their economic logic. Some of the historical economists opposed nearly all forms of theorizing. They denied that there are any valid economic laws, with one exception: They believed that patterns of development are discernible in history and can be generalized into "laws of development."
- Advocacy of conservative reform. Political economy, said the historical economists, must not merely analyze motives that prompt economic activity but must weigh and compare the moral merit of these actions and their outcomes. It must determine a standard of the proper production and distribution of wealth so that the demands of justice and morality are satisfied. The historical economists thought the German state should be entrusted with the amelioration of conditions for "the common man." This would strengthen loyalty to the state while it safeguarded the health, well-being, and efficiency of the factory workers. Reforms, they hoped, would also divert the working class from socialistic ideology. The advocates of moderate social changes were dubbed "Socialists of the Chair," a reference to the academic positions they held.

Whom Did the Historical School Benefit or Seek to Benefit?

First, the members of the German historical school benefited themselves. They enjoyed close and friendly relations with government officials and rose to dominant positions in academic life. In fact, the German government controlled most universities, and Schmoller, known as the "professor maker," controlled a majority of the academic appointments in Germany through his influence at the Prussian Ministry of Education. His students and followers were placed in academic posts, whereas the German adherents of the Austrian marginalist school were excluded from university positions. The historical school also benefited the German imperial government by defending its role in a nationalistic state.

Second, the historical economists served the dominant business, financial, and landowning groups by promoting moderate reforms that frustrated the drive for a more radical democratization of society. Instead of the poor and lowly fighting and winning their own battles for improvements, concessions were given to them by a paternalistic state. As a result, servility, nationalism, and loyalty to the regime were more widespread in Germany than anywhere else.

How Was the Historical School Valid, Useful, or Correct in Its Time?

The evolutionary approach to society and to economic thought provided a useful antidote to the abstract thinking of the classical and marginalist schools. How else could one attempt to explain Great Britain's adherence to laissez-faire in the nineteenth century and its considerable departure from it in the twentieth century? The historical school was correct in its perspective that economists needed to familiarize themselves with changing history and changing environments, with economic and social evolution, in order to understand the present world. For this task, inductive factual studies were required. New theories and new ideas had to be evoked to understand new situations, and these new theories and ideas required careful testing through the use of empirical data.

Which Tenets of the Historical School Became Lasting Contributions?

The task of the German historical school was completed when economists of various persuasions agreed that historical empirical studies are required to explain the present, to test old theories, and to develop new ones. Today the historical inductive method has become generally accepted as complementary to the abstract deductive approach; changing times and methodological controversies have forced the two into an uneasy but tolerably placid marriage. For example, contemporary econometric analysis normally incorporates both abstract theorizing and empirical testing. The data for most of the empirical testing are historical as opposed to being derived directly from experiments. Today, however, economists generally search for the most *recent* historical data available to test their theories, as opposed to scrutinizing data gleaned from the distant past. If society is constantly changing and if new situations call for new analyses, then past experiences have only limited relevance. John Neville Keynes (the father of John Maynard Keynes) pointed out this fact as early as 1890:

> It is still more important to observe that just because of the evolution of industrial systems, and the shifting character of economic conditions, upon which the historical school of economics so much insists, the study of the past is rendered the less serviceable for the solution of present-day problems. Upon many of these problems extremely little light is thrown by economic history that relates to an earlier period than the nineteenth century. How indeed can generalizations based upon one set of circumstances be safely applied to quite another set of circumstances? Not only may the problems calling for solutions be novel in their character; there may even arise new industrial classes. With what classes in the fourteenth century, for example, are we to compare the modern factory operative and the modern capitalist employer? If, therefore, for no other reason than that institutions and habits and conditions change, another method of investigation than the historical must for very much of our economic work be essential. Political economy can never become a specifically historical science.[2]

[2] John Neville Keynes, *The Scope and Method of Political Economy,* 4th ed. (London: Macmillan, 1917), 327. (Orig. pub. 1890.)

Another lasting contribution of the school was its attack on laissez-faire. This theme was the trend of the future. The members of the historical school recognized that unrestricted free enterprise does not necessarily produce the best possible results for society as a whole. And they were right in their belief that reform can be a substitute for worse upheavals brought on by sharpening class distinctions.

A final word: The German nationalism advocated by the historical economists overreached itself as it evolved into a frenzied militarism. During the century ending in 1914, the hope was rising that the world could achieve peace, international cooperation, and universal harmony. The German historical economists struck a strident note of nationalism that jarred these internationalist sentiments of goodwill. Their ideas, perhaps unintentionally, contributed to the climate in Germany that led to World Wars I and II. In this respect, some of the ideas presented by the historical economists were detrimental to society's progress.

FRIEDRICH LIST

Life and Times

Friedrich List (1789–1846), a forerunner of the historical school, was inclined neither toward formal study in school nor toward his father's occupation as a tanner. He became a government clerk and by 1816 had risen to the post of ministerial undersecretary. A year later he accepted a professorship in administration and politics at the University of Tübingen, but his dissident political views caused his dismissal in 1819. He then became active in promoting a strong political and commercial union of the German states. In 1819 List presented a petition for a customs union to the Federal Assembly on behalf of an association of merchants and manufacturers that he had organized.

> Thirty-eight customs boundaries cripple inland trade, and produce much the same effect as ligatures [surgical ties] which prevent the free circulation of the blood. The merchant trading between Hamburg and Austria, or Berlin and Switzerland must traverse ten states, must learn ten customs-tariffs, must pay ten successive transit dues. Any one who is so unfortunate as to live on the boundary-line between three or four states spends his days among hostile tax-gatherers and custom-house officials; he is a man without a country.[3]

Elected to his state legislature in 1820, List advocated other administrative and financial reforms that were considered very radical in his day. He favored doing away with tolls on roads, tithes, state ownership of industries, feudal property taxes and limitations on productive land use, and excise duties. He advocated trial by jury, a reduction in the number of civil service officers, and a single direct income tax to meet the expenses of government. The government regarded the expression of these views as constituting treason and sentenced List to serve eight months in

[3] Friedrich List, as quoted in Margaret E. Hirst, *Life of Friedrich List and Selections from His Writings* (London: Smith, Elder, 1909), 139.

prison, after which he was deported. From 1825 to 1832 he lived in the United States, where he became a farmer, a journalist, and a business promoter, making and losing a fortune in coal mining. His protectionist ideas gained much more popularity in the United States than in Germany.

After returning to Germany, List became an ardent advocate of a railway network for Germany. The railway lines later built in Germany were to follow closely his sketch in a pamphlet published in 1833. His efforts to create a German customs union were realized in the establishment of the *Zollverein* in 1834. The plans he presented for a German postal system and a national patent law were realized more than twenty years after his death. Ill health, financial difficulties, and despair over the delay in German unification darkened his later days, and in 1846 he committed suicide.

Thoughts on Economic Development

In the introduction to his famous work, *National System of Political Economy,* List referred to himself in the third person:

> The author will begin, as theory does not begin, by interrogating History, and deducing from it his fundamental principles. . . . For greater clearness, we give here a cursory view of the principal results of his researches and meditations: The association of individuals for the prosecution of a common end, is the most efficacious mode toward ensuring the happiness of individuals. Alone, and separated from his fellow-creatures, man is feeble and destitute. The greater the number of those who are united, the more perfect is the association, and the greater and the more perfect is the result, which is the moral and material welfare of individuals. The highest association of individuals now realized, is that of the state, the nation; and highest imaginable, is that of the whole human race. . . .
>
> A nation may by war be deprived of its independence, its wealth, its liberty, its constitution, its laws, of its own special features, of that degree of culture and national well-being to which it may have attained; it may be wholly enslaved. Nations are thus the victims of each other, and selfish policy is continually disturbing and delaying the economical development of nations. To preserve, to develop, and to improve itself as a nation consequently, at present, and ever must be, the principle object of a nation's efforts. . . .
>
> In the economical development of nations, it is necessary to distinguish the following principle stages: the savage state, the pastoral state, the agricultural state, the agricultural and manufacturing state, and finally, the agricultural, manufacturing, and commercial state. . . . A nation that greatly values its independence and its safety, must make a vigorous effort to elevate itself as fast as possible, from an inferior to higher state of civilization, uniting and perfecting as quickly as possible, its own agriculture, manufactures, navigation, and commerce. . . . The elevation of an agricultural people to the condition of countries at once agricultural, manufacturing, and commercial, can only be accomplished under the law of free trade, when the various nations engaged at the time in manufacturing industry shall be in the same degree of progress and civilization; when they shall place no obstacle in the way of the economical development of each other, and not impede their respective progress by war or adverse commercial legislation.
>
> But some of them, favored by circumstances, having distanced others in manufactures, commerce, and navigation, and having perceived that this advanced state was

> the surest mode of acquiring and keeping political supremacy, have adopted and still persevere in a policy so well adapted to give them the monopoly of manufactures, of industry and of commerce, and to impede the progress of less advanced nations or those in a lower degree of culture. . . . The anterior progress of certain nations, foreign commercial legislation and war have compelled inferior countries to look for special means of effecting their transition from the agricultural to the manufacturing stage of industry, and as far as practicable, by a system of duties, to restrain their trade with more advanced nations aiming at manufacturing monopoly. . . .
>
> Experience teaches us, it is true, that the wind carries with it the seeds of one country to another, and that desert places have thus been changed into heavy forests. But would it be wise for the proprietor of waste land to wait for the wind to perform this office of planting and transformation during the lapse of centuries? Is it folly in him to force nature by planting his uncultivated lands, that he may attain his object in a score of years?
>
> The doctrine of Adam Smith in regard to international commerce, is but a continuation of that of the physiocrats. Like the latter, it disregards nationality; it excludes almost entirely politics and government; it supposes the existence of perpetual peace and universal association; it depreciates the advantages of national manufacturing industry, as well as the means of acquiring it; it demands absolute free trade.[4]

List advocated free trade within Germany while championing a high tariff against imports of manufacturing goods to protect newly emerging domestic industries. This position is now commonly called the "infant industry" defense of tariffs. He opposed protection for agriculture because this was an old, mature industry and because manufacturing required cheap food for labor and cheap raw materials. Besides, the development of large-scale industry through protection would enlarge the home market for agriculture. List severely condemned Adam Smith and classical economics for claiming universality for doctrines that were appropriate for England but inappropriate for underdeveloped countries. Heavy emphasis was placed on what history teaches us and the importance of the state. List popularized the idea of stages of economic growth and urged that the government actively assist a people who wished to pass from a lower to higher stage against the competition of more advanced nations. Only after a country reached industrial maturity could it revert to free trade.

Refer to 11-1 PAST AS PROLOGUE

List denied Smith's notion of the harmony of interest between the individual and society, arguing that the immediate private interests of certain members of the community do not necessarily lead to the highest good of the whole. A nation may suffer, for example, from an absence of manufacturing industry, but some people may flourish in selling foreign manufactures to domestic consumers. One person may grow rich by extreme parsimony, but if a whole nation follows that person's example, there will be no consumption and no support of industry. National unity, which is the result of past development, is necessary to the individual, whose interests should be subordinated to the preservation of this oneness.

List thought that manufacturing would develop only in the temperate zone, because only this climate would foster the necessary intellectual and physical effort.

[4] Friedrich List, *National System of Political Economy,* trans. G. A. Matile (Philadelphia, PA: Lippincott, 1856), 70–73, 181, 420. (Orig. pub. 1841.)

11-1 PAST AS PROLOGUE

List and Strategic Trade Theory

Aside from Thomas Malthus, classical economists agreed that free international trade can be beneficial to a nation. Smith and Ricardo stressed that specialization and exchange allow a country to reduce its opportunity cost of obtaining desirable goods.

Writing in 1841, Friedrich List disputed this support for free trade as it relates to manufacturing, stating:

> It is true that protective tariffs at first increase the price of manufactured goods; but it is just as true . . . that in the course of time, by the nation being enabled to build up a completely developed manufacturing power of its own, those goods are produced more cheaply at home than the price at which they can be imported from foreign parts. If, therefore, a sacrifice of *value* is caused by protective duties, it is made good by the gain of a *power of production*, which not only secures to the nation an infinitely greater amount of material goods, but also industrial independence in case of war. Through industrial independence and the internal prosperity derived from it the nation obtains the means for successfully carrying on foreign trade and for extending its mercantile marine; it increases its civilisation, perfects its institutions internally, and strengthens its external power.*

List applied his argument against free trade to *less-developed* nations, such as Germany in the 1840s, when it had only infant industries. But recently a variation of his argument has been heard in *advanced* industrial nations. Advocates of strategic trade policies contend that tariffs and import quotas should be used selectively

The tropics should remain on a free trade basis and continue to supply tropical products in exchange for manufactured goods. He saw this as the true foundation for the international division of labor and world trade. A country of the torrid zone would make a fatal mistake, he said, if it tried to become a manufacturing country. Nature did not invite it to that vocation. Tropical countries will therefore sink into dependence on those of the temperate zone. But competition among the manufacturing nations will provide manufactured goods at low prices, and it will also prevent any one nation from taking advantage, through its superiority, of the weaker nations of the torrid zone.

Military preparations, wars, and war debts, said List, may in certain cases immensely increase the productive powers of a country. He pointed to England as an example. War expanded its productive power so much that the increased values it received annually—that is, the increased output produced—far exceeded the annual interest on its enlarged war debts. In addition, spending money on supplying its armies meant shipping goods to the theater of war, which ruined foreign manufactures and ensured England's industrial supremacy.

to reduce the risk of product development borne by high-technology domestic firms. This trade protection in the home market will enable these firms to grow rapidly there. Rapid growth of sales at home and exports to unprotected markets abroad will permit these domestic firms to achieve economies of scale (lower average costs). The protected domestic firms therefore can eventually drive out higher-cost foreign producers and dominate world markets.

World market dominance will thus enable protected domestic firms to earn high profits abroad. These high profits supposedly will more than compensate for any earlier sacrifices resulting from the selective tariffs. In List's terminology, sacrifices of *value* are balanced by gains in the *power of production*. Also, the specialization in high-technology industries will likely spill over to other domestic industries, thus enhancing the powers of production in other areas of the domestic economy.

Some observers believe that Japan and South Korea successfully used tariffs, import quotas, and nontariff trade barriers as part of strategic trade policies in the 1980s and 1990s. However, strategic trade policies of this sort have a fundamental flaw. Nations placed at a disadvantage by these policies invariably retaliate with tariffs or import quotas of their own. For example, in the late 1980s the United States passed legislation permitting retaliatory tariffs against nations with unfair trade practices.

Thus, strategic trade policies are likely to backfire in the long run because they sacrifice world output that could have been achieved through specialization and trade. The final outcome of these policies may well be higher tariffs worldwide, reductions of world trade, and decreases in world output.

---

*Friedrich List, *National System of Political Economy* (New York: Kelley, 1966), 145. (Orig. pub. 1841.)

WILHELM ROSCHER

Wilhelm Roscher (1817–1894) was one of the founders of the "older historical school." This group wanted to supplement classical theory, whereas the younger school wished to supersede it entirely with historical studies and policy considerations. Roscher became professor of political economy at Göttingen and later Leipzig. His five-volume textbook, *Economic Science,* took forty years to complete (1854–1894) and was widely used in German schools. The first volume reached thirteen editions by 1878, when it was translated into English as *Principles of Political Economy.* Although Roscher repudiated the classical economics he had learned in his youth, he still built upon those ideas. This was the basis for the "younger historical school's" condemnation of the older forerunners. Schmoller, for example, held that Roscher and his associates had criticized classical economics and its methods effectively; but when it came to reconstructing economics, they had themselves lapsed into the methods that they had formerly condemned.

Roscher's ideas on the role of the state and on historical method follow:

> By the science of national, or Political Economy, we understand the science which has to do with the laws of the development of the economy of a nation, or with its economic life. . . . National life, like all life, is a whole, the various phenomena of which are most intimately connected with one another. Hence it is, that to understand one side of it scientifically, it is necessary to know all its sides. But, especially, it is necessary to fix one's attention on the following seven: language, religion, art, science, law, the state and economy. . . .
>
> If, by the public economy of a nation, we understand economic legislation and the governmental guidance or direction of the economy of private persons, the science of public economy becomes, so far as its form is concerned, a branch of political science, while as its matter, its subject is almost coincident with that of Political Economy. . . . Just as clear, is the close connection between politics and Political Economy, in the case of the science of finance, or of the science of governmental house-keeping, otherwise the administration of public affairs. . . . As the physiologist cannot understand the action of the human body, without understanding that of the head; so we would not be able to grasp the organic whole of national economy, if we were to leave the state, the greatest economy of all, the one which uninterruptedly and irresistibly acts on all others, out of consideration. . . .
>
> The thorough application of this [the historical] method will do away with a great number of controversies on important questions. Men are as far removed from being devils as from being angels. We meet with few who are only guided by ideal motives, but with few, also who hearken only to the voice of egotism, and care for nothing but themselves. It may, therefore, be assumed, that any view current on certain tangible interests which concern man very nearly, and which has been shared by great parties and even by whole peoples for generations, is not based only on ignorance or a perverse love of wrong. The error consists more frequently in applying measures wholesome and even absolutely necessary under certain circumstances, to circumstances entirely different. And here, a thorough insight into the conditions of the measure suffices to compose the differences between the two parties. Once the natural laws of Political Economy are sufficiently known and recognized, all that is needed, in any given instance, is more exact and reliable statistics of the fact involved, to reconcile all party controversies on questions of the politics of public economy, so far, at least, as these controversies arise from a difference of opinion. It may be that science may never attain to this, in consequence of the new problems which are ever arising and demanding a solution. It may be, too, that in the greater number of party controversies, the opposed purposes of the parties play a more important part even than the opposed views. Be this as it may, it is necessary, especially in an age as deeply agitated as our own, when every good citizen is in duty bound to ally himself to party, that every honest party-man should seek to secure, amid the ocean of ephemeral opinions, a firm island of scientific truth, as universally recognized as truth as are the principles of mathematical physics by physicians [physicists?] of the most various schools.[5]

---

[5] Wilhelm Roscher, *Principles of Political Economy*, trans. John J. Lalor, vol. 1 (New York: Holt, 1878), 87–88, 91–92, 112–113. (Orig. pub. 1854.)

Roscher added that the knowledge gained through the use of the historical method does away with feelings of self-sufficiency and that higher civilizations will not look down with contempt on lower ones. Societies are continually evolving from immature to mature forms, which may be considered the most perfect. The mature societies, however, eventually decline and decay.

Roscher showed his affinity for economic theory by including a simplified version of English classical price theory in his *Principles of Political Economy.* Instead of disdaining abstract theory, he sought to discover its historical basis. He asserted that the study of contemporary facts and opinions is an essential adjunct to the classical deductive method.

GUSTAV SCHMOLLER

Gustav Schmoller (1838–1917), the leading figure of the "younger historical school," was a professor of political science at Halle, Strasbourg, and Berlin. He taught many generations of students and administration officials and wielded great influence in academic and government circles. In addition to his work as a professor, Schmoller was an active member of the Academy of Sciences and also of the House of Lords of the Prussian Diet. He was one of the founders and a major leader of the *Verein für Sozialpolitik* (Association of Social Policy). This organization advocated social legislation and helped promote the idea of greater government activity in social and economic affairs.

The task of accumulating historical and descriptive factual materials is one that, Schmoller contended, should come prior to, and is far more important than, deductive theorizing. He and his followers castigated the separate study of small segments of economic phenomena and the assumption that everything else remained unchanged. They held that the essences of economic processes are lost once they are isolated and fragmented. Schmoller wanted to develop economics exclusively on the basis of historical monographs. In fact, Schmoller was so antagonistic to deductive economists that he declared publicly that members of the "abstract" school were unfit to teach in a German university.

The Methodenstreit

Schmoller engaged in a famous controversy with Carl Menger, founder of the abstract Austrian marginalist school, as to which is more fruitful—inductive or deductive analysis. This debate was named the *Methodenstreit,* or the "Battle of Methods." In 1883 when the method of historicism was nearing its high tide, Menger published a book on methodology that defended theoretical analysis and rated Schmoller's school as merely secondary in importance. Schmoller reviewed the book unfavorably in his *Jahrbuch,* and Menger replied in an angry pamphlet titled *Errors of Historicism,* in which he wrote: "The historians have stepped upon the territory of our science like foreign conquerors, in order to force upon us their language and their customs, their terminology and their methods, and to fight intolerantly every branch of enquiry which does not correspond with their special method."[6] When Schmoller received a copy of Menger's pamphlet for review in his *Jahrbuch*, he printed an announcement that he was unable to review it because he had returned it immediately to the author. Schmoller also printed the insulting letter to Menger that he had included with the pamphlet.

This controversy aroused bitter feelings and resulted in many publications on both sides. In the end the *Methodenstreit* seemed to resolve itself into the belief that both inductive and deductive methods are important and that they normally supplement each other. Restated, the gathering of information and the establishing of analytical tools with which to handle the accumulated information are both instrumental parts of sound economic science.

Schmoller's emphasis on historical research was repeated in his book, *Political Economy and Its Method*, in 1894.

> The historical sciences provide empirical material and data which transform the scholar from a mere beggar into a rich man as far as knowledge or reality is concerned. And it is this historical-empirical material which, like all good observation and description, serves to illustrate and verify theoretical conclusions, to demonstrate the limitations of the validity of certain truths, and more than anything else, to obtain inductively new truths. This applies particularly to the more complicated fields of political economy, in which it is possible to advance only on the basis of historical investigations. For example, purely abstract deductions are without value as regards the effects of machinery on wages and the influence of the production of precious metals on the value of money. This is even truer with respect to the evolution of economic institutions and theories, and the problem of economic progress in general. . . . To consult history belongs to the most appropriate methods of political economy. The most prominent opponent of the historical school, [Carl] Menger, admits that the most important economic institutions such as property, money, and credit have both an individual nature and a historical side to their existence; consequently "he who knows the essence of these phenomena only in one phase of their existence does not know them at all." If this is true with respect to money and credit it is even truer with respect to the family economy, the division of labor, the formation of social classes, different forms of business organization, the phenomena of the market and other institutions of trade, guilds, freedom of domestic trade, patterns of rural life and indeed, of all typical patterns and specific arrangements which are known as economic institutions and which, after having crystallized into law, tend to dominate either permanently or for centuries the economic process.[7]

Social Reform

Schmoller believed that ethical value judgments are to be encouraged. Justice in the economic system is to be realized through a paternalistic policy of social reform furthered by the state and all social groups. The guiding principle of social reform, he

[6] Keynes, *Political Economy*, 324.

[7] Contemporary Civilization Staff of Columbia College, *Introduction to Contemporary Civilization in the West: A Source Book*, vol. 2 (New York: Columbia University Press, 1946), 520–521.

said, is a more equitable distribution of income. Social science is to be the guide for the attainment of the objectives of social policy.

> What are economic institutions but a product of human feelings and thought, of human actions, human customs and human laws?
>
> If in the economic order we could recognize only the ruling of blind force, of selfish interests, natural masses and mechanical processes, it would be a constant battle, a chaotic anarchy. . . . No, harmony does not exist per se; selfish impulses combat each other, natural masses tend to destroy each other, the mechanical action of natural forces interferes relentlessly still to-day; the struggle for existence is to-day still carried on in the struggle of competition. . . . While struggle and strife never cease they do not preserve the same character throughout the course of history. The struggle which ended in annihilation, in subjugation, turns into a peaceful contest which is decided by an umpire. The forms of dependence grow milder and more human. Class government grows more moderate. Every brutal strength, every undue assertion of superior force is made punishable by law. Demand and supply, as they confront each other in the different systems of custom and law, are quite different in their results. . . .
>
> There is no worse delusion than that of the older English economists that there are a number of simple and natural legal and economic institutions which have always been as they are and will always remain so; that all progress of civilization and wealth is simply an individual or technical one; that this is simply a question of increased production or consumption which will and can be accomplished on the basis of the same legal institutions. This faith in the stability of economic institutions was the result of the naive overweening confidence of the older economists in the omnipotence of the individual and of the individual life. Socialism then has perhaps over-estimated the significance of social institutions. Historical economists and the modern philosophy of law have given them their due position by showing us that the great epochs of economic progress are primarily connected with the reform of social institutions.[8]

Schmoller accused the older historical school of attempting to apply the lessons of history too quickly. He called for much more historical study in order to establish an empirical basis for national economic theory. Yet despite the innumerable, massive historical studies he and his disciples published, they failed to produce an economic theory, and their major contribution lay in the area of economic history.

Protectionism

Late in life Schmoller changed his views on protectionism. In his younger years he had been an ardent advocate of free trade. By 1901 he favored a protective tariff for Germany, and he hailed Alexander Hamilton and Friedrich List as his teachers. He denied that the new era of protectionism had arisen because economists and statesmen had been unable to understand the beautiful arguments for free trade. He justified tariffs on the basis of List's "infant industry" argument, but he went

[8] Gustav Schmoller, *Idea of Justice in Political Economy* (Philadelphia, PA: American Academy of Political and Social Science, no date), 22, 26, 27, 37.

further than that. In addition, he felt that tariffs are international weapons that might benefit a country if used skillfully.

MAX WEBER

Max Weber (1864–1920) established himself in Berlin's legal profession. After publishing several scholarly works, he became a professor of political economy and sociology at Freiburg and later at Heidelberg and Munich. He considered himself an intellectual descendant of Schmoller.

Protestantism and the Rise of Capitalism

Weber aroused a lively controversy that has persisted through the years over the relationship between Protestantism and the rise of capitalism. He rejected the Marxian idea that religious doctrines are merely ideological manifestations of particular material economic conditions. Ideas for Weber were at least autonomous entities with the power to influence social changes. It seemed to him that capitalism was a *result* rather than a *cause* of the Reformation. He believed that Calvinist theology in particular, with its underlying notion that only some are "elected" for salvation, contained certain elements exceedingly conducive to rationalized, individualistic economic activity undertaken for profit. Speaking of Protestantism, Weber wrote:

> The religious valuation of restless, continuous, systematic work in a worldly calling, as the highest means to asceticism, and at the same time the surest and most evident proof of rebirth and genuine faith, must have been the most powerful conceivable lever for the expansion of that attitude toward life which we have called the spirit of capitalism. When the limitation of consumption is combined with this release of acquisitive activity, the inevitable practical result is obvious: accumulation of capital through ascetic compulsion to save. The restraints which were imposed upon the consumption of wealth naturally served to increase it by making possible the productive investment of capital.[9]

Criticisms of Weber's Thesis

R. H. Tawney and others have disputed Weber's analysis.[10] Religion, of course, has influenced people's outlook on society, but economic and social changes also have acted powerfully on religion. Weber, critics have argued, emphasized the first point but touched upon the second only in passing. Perhaps the rise of business enterprise induced the middle class to do away with Catholicism, which condemned usury, suspected economic motives, and took a dim view of private fortunes. Besides, as the largest feudal landowner, the Catholic Church sought to perpetuate such feudal institutions as the just price, primogeniture, entail, and mortmain.

[9] Max Weber, *The Protestant Ethic and the Spirit of Capitalism*, trans. Talcott Parsons (London: Allen and Unwin, 1930), 172. (Orig. pub. 1904–1905.)

[10] See R. H. Tawney, *Religion and the Rise of Capitalism* (New York: Harcourt, Brace & World, 1926).

Because the Reformation struck a powerful blow at authority, it loosened the hold of tradition on people's minds. Because it called into question ideas that had long held sway, it strengthened the temper of rationalism. It is true, Tawney argued, that Calvinism offered new sanctification to economic activities and the accumulation of wealth, but economic changes such as the great geographic discoveries and the expansion of commerce were ultimately responsible for the transformation of the Christian ethic from the sixteenth century onward. Both Calvinism and the spirit of capitalism, he said, were produced by the profound change in economic organization and social structure.

Several historical facts seem to support Tawney's thesis. First, contrary to Weber's paradigm, Luther's Protestant doctrines were surrounded by a feudal aura; note, for example, Luther's opposition to usury, while conversely, Catholicism was adaptable to the new world of business enterprise. Early capitalist manifestations were discernible in the late medieval cities in the Catholic countries of Italy and France before the Reformation. The threat of the Reformation apparently hastened Catholicism's adaptation. Second, a notably powerful motive for the revolt against Rome, especially among people who had no interest in business enterprise, was the prospect of plundering wealthy Church organizations. Third, peasants with grievances against their feudal overlords were swept into the Protestant movement. And, finally, the rising nationalist spirit in many countries conflicted with the Catholic internationalism centered in Rome.

In the complex interrelations of Protestantism and the rise of capitalism, it is difficult to disentangle cause from effect. Did Protestantism produce capitalism, as Weber implied? Or did rising capitalism produce Protestantism as a more suitable credo for its business activities, as some of Weber's opponents believed? Or is there some truth in both positions? Or is there no truth in either? For further discussion of the role of the Protestant Reformation in the development of economic thought, visit the text web site and read the chapter titled "Economic Thought from Biblical Times to the Protestant Reformation."

A POSTSCRIPT

Although the German historical school may be said to have ended with the death of Schmoller, its methodology and perspectives were carried on beyond that time by others, particularly by Werner Sombart (1863–1941). Sombart, an economic historian, questioned Weber's thesis that puritanism had a large share in forming the capitalist spirit of businessmen. Instead, he stated that "those parts of the Puritan dogma which appear to be of real importance for the formation of the spirit of capitalism are borrowed from the realm of ideas of Jewish religion." It was Jews, said Sombart, who gave capitalism its impersonal, rational, and materialistic qualities. But puritanism did help discipline the workers to the new way of life. To overcome the great difficulties of adapting workers to the technical and disciplinary requirements of capitalism, the workers had to be inspired with the desire to get ahead in the world through capitalist ideals. The desire for gain, instead of being an inborn trait of human nature, had to be deliberately inculcated in order that capitalism might flourish.

Sombart quoted the defense of the state made earlier by Lassalle:

> Ferdinand Lassalle . . . represented the idea of the state in eloquent words, when he explained: "The state is this unity of individuals in a moral whole, a unity which increases a millionfold the power of all individuals who are included within this union. . . . The purpose of the state is, therefore, to bring the human being to a positive development and a progressive development; in other words, to bring human determination, that is, the culture of which the human race is capable, into actual being."[11]

The nationalism that earlier members of the German historical school promoted reached its extreme in the writings of Sombart. By 1933 Sombart had become a full-fledged supporter of the Nazi philosophy. Germany under Hitler, he thought, was the new, dynamic system that would overcome capitalist decadence. He glorified racism and nationalism as welcome alternatives to the debilitated society that had been vanquished: "For us there is only one aim—Germany. For the sake of Germany's greatness, power and glory, we will gladly sacrifice every 'theory' and every 'principle,' whether it bears a liberal or any other stamp."[12]

Questions for Study and Discussion

1. Briefly identify and state the significance of each of the following to the history of economic thought: the Holy Alliance of 1815, List, infant industry argument, Roscher, Schmoller, *Methodenstreit,* Weber, Protestant ethic, R. H. Tawney, Sombart, and Socialists of the Chair.
2. Refer to the list of major tenets of the classical school in Chapter 4 and indicate which of these principles the historical economists would reject. Explain.
3. In what respect is most of the empirical research done by contemporary economists "historical"? Is this the type of research that the more extreme historical economists had in mind? Explain.
4. Debate: "The loss which a nation incurs by protection [tariffs and import quotas] is only one of *values,* but it gains *powers* by which it is enabled to go on producing permanently inestimable amounts of value. This loss of value should be regarded merely as the price paid for the industrial education of the nation." (Friedrich List, 1841)
5. Contrast David Hume's ideas about economic development (Chapter 4) with those expressed by List.
6. In what respect did the views of the older and younger historical schools differ regarding classical economics?
7. Cite the polar positions in the *Methodenstreit* (Battle of Methods). How did economists eventually resolve this issue?
8. What, according to Weber, is the Protestant ethic, and how does it relate to the growth of capitalism? Critically evaluate Weber's theory.
9. Cite possible reasons the historical school evolved mainly in Germany as opposed to other areas of Europe.

---

[11] Werner Sombart, *A New Social Philosophy,* trans. Karl F. Geiser (Princeton, NJ: Princeton University Press, 1937), 160.

[12] Sombart, *Social Philosophy,* 152.

Selected Readings

Books

Blaug, Mark, ed. *Gustave Schmoller and Werner Sombart.* Brookfield, VT: Edward Elgar, 1992.

Hirst, Margaret E. *Life of Friedrich List and Selections from His Writings.* London: Smith, Elder, 1909.

Lessnoff, Michael H. *The Spirit of Capitalism and the Protestant Ethic: An Enquiry into the Weber Thesis.* Aldershot, England: Edward Elgar, 1994.

List, Friedrich. *National System of Political Economy.* Translated by G. A. Matile. Philadelphia: Lippincott, 1856. (Orig. pub. 1841.)

Roscher, Wilhelm. *Principles of Political Economy.* Translated by John J. Lalor. 2 vols. New York: Holt, 1878. (Orig. pub. 1854.)

Schmoller, Gustav. *Idea of Justice in Political Economy.* No. 113. Philadelphia: American Academy of Political and Social Science, no date.

Tawney, R. H. *Religion and the Rise of Capitalism.* New York: Harcourt, Brace & World, 1926.

Weber, Max. *The Protestant Ethic and the Spirit of Capitalism.* Translated by Talcott Parsons. London: Allen and Unwin, 1930. (Orig. pub. 1904–1905.)

Journal Articles

Bostaph, Sam. "The Methodological Debate between Carl Menger and the German Historicists," *Atlantic Economic Journal* 6 (September 1978): 3–16.

Dorfman, Joseph. "The Role of the German Historical School in American Economic Thought," *American Economic Review* 45 (May 1955): 17–28.

Tribe, Keith. "Friedrich List and the Critique of 'Cosmopolitan Economy'", *Manchester School of Economic and Social Studies* 56 (March 1988): 17–36.

Veblen, Thorstein. "Gustav Schmoller's Economics," *Quarterly Journal of Economics* 16 (November 1901): 69–93.

Chapter 12

THE MARGINALIST SCHOOL—FORERUNNERS

The beginning of the marginalist school is dated at 1871, the year Jevons and Menger published their influential books on marginal utility theory. Several forerunners predated Jevons and Menger in the use of marginal analysis in economics. You may recall that the English economist David Ricardo employed the marginal approach in his theory of rent (Chapter 7). Subsequent contributions that fit within this analysis developed in several countries and through the efforts of numerous individuals largely working independently of each other. Among these forerunners were Antoine Cournot and Jules Dupuit in France and Johann von Thünen in Germany. In this chapter we develop an overview of the marginalist school and discuss the ideas of these three forerunners. Then in Chapters 13 and 14 we examine the writings of the individuals who brought the marginalist school to prominence. This school eventually became part of neoclassical economics, or contemporary microeconomics.

OVERVIEW OF THE MARGINALIST SCHOOL

The Historical Background of the Marginalist School

Serious economic and social problems remained unsolved even a hundred years after the beginning of the industrial revolution. Poverty was widespread, although productivity was increasing dramatically. The extremely uneven distribution of wealth and income created much dissatisfaction even though the general standard of living was rising. Business fluctuations affected many people adversely; individuals could no longer depend exclusively on their own initiative and ability to overcome conditions that were thrust upon them. Farmers and farm laborers had their difficulties; many drifted into cities, lured by the carrot of better opportunities and driven by the club of rural poverty. Industrial accidents often brought serious hardships to workers and their families before adequate workers' compensation laws were enacted. Long hours of labor, dangerous and unhealthy working conditions, the preponderant economic power of employers in bargaining with workers, the rise of monopolistic enterprises, and insecurity in old age were among the many problems that caused people to seek solutions beyond the narrow confines of classical economic thinking.

The trend of the nineteenth century in Europe was to develop three approaches of attack on pressing social problems, and all three flouted classical economic precepts. These approaches were to promote socialism; to bolster trade unionism; or to demand government action to ameliorate conditions by regulating the economy, eliminating abuses, and redistributing income. The marginalists opposed all three "solutions." They theorized with seemingly Olympian impartiality and concluded that, although the value and distribution theories of the classical economists were inaccurate, their policy views were correct. The marginalists defended market allocation and distribution, deplored government intervention, denounced socialism, and sought to discourage labor unionism as either ineffective or pernicious.

To the leading early marginalists, classical value and distribution theories erred in seemingly concluding that land rent is an unearned income and that exchange value is based on the labor time involved in the production process. The first idea was seized and expanded by the American economist Henry George, the second by Karl Marx. If classical economics could be made to say what its creators never intended—namely, that rent is immoral and labor creates all value—then the science of economics was overdue for a thorough revision.

Major Tenets of the Marginalist School

The basic ideas of the marginalist school are listed next and amplified later in the discussion of the forerunners and leading marginalist economists.

- Focus on the margin. This school focused its attention on the point of change where decisions are made; in other words, on the margin. The marginalists extended to all economic theory the marginal principle that Ricardo developed in his theory of rent.
- Rational economic behavior. The marginalists assumed that people act rationally in balancing pleasures and pains, in measuring marginal utilities of different goods, and in balancing present against future needs. They also assumed that purposeful behavior is normal and typical and that random abnormalities will cancel each other out. The approach employed by the marginalists had its roots in Jeremy Bentham, in that they assumed the dominant drive of human action is to seek utility and avoid disutility (negative utility).
- Microeconomic emphasis. The individual person and firm take center stage in the marginalist drama. Instead of considering the aggregate economy, or macroeconomics, the marginalists considered individual decision making, market conditions for a single type of good, the output of specific firms, and so forth.
- The use of the abstract, deductive method. The marginalists rejected the historical method (see Chapter 11) in favor of the analytical, abstract approach pioneered by Ricardo and other classicists.
- The pure competition emphasis. The marginalists normally based their analysis on the assumption of pure competition.[1] This is the world of small, individualistic, independent entrepreneurs; numerous buyers; many sellers; homogeneous products; uniform prices; and no advertising. No one person or firm has enough economic power to influence market prices perceptibly. Individuals can adapt their own actions to demand, supply, and price as

[1] There were exceptions here. We will discover later in this chapter that Cournot, a forerunner to the marginalist school, developed a theory of monopoly and duopoly, for example.

worked out in the market through the interactions of thousands of people. Each person is such a tiny operator relative to the size of the market that no one notices his or her presence or absence.

- Demand-oriented price theory. For the early marginalists, demand became the primary force in price determination. The classical economist emphasized cost of production (supply) as the significant determinant of exchange value. The earliest marginalists swung to the opposite extreme and emphasized demand to the virtual exclusion of supply. In Chapter 15 we will discover that Alfred Marshall synthesized supply and demand into what may be called neoclassical economics. This type of economics is basically marginalism with a judicious recognition of the surviving contributions of the classical school.
- Emphasis on subjective utility. According to marginalists, demand depends on marginal utility, which is a subjective, psychological phenomenon. Costs of production include the sacrifices and irksomeness of working, managing a business, and saving money to form a capital fund.
- Equilibrium approach. The marginalists believed that economic forces generally tend toward equilibrium—a balancing of opposing forces. Whenever disturbances cause dislocations, new movements toward equilibrium occur.
- Merger of land with capital goods. The marginalists lumped land and capital resources together in their analysis and spoke of interest, rent, and profits as being the return to property resources. This had its advantages analytically and also combated the conclusion drawn by some that land rent is unearned income and an unnecessary payment in order to ensure the use of land. Marginalists generally coupled the reward to the landowner with interest theory.
- Minimal government involvement. The marginalists continued the classical school's defense of minimal government involvement in the economy as the most desirable policy. In most cases, no interference with natural economic laws was in order if maximum social benefits were to be realized.

Whom Did the Marginalists Benefit or Seek to Benefit?

The marginalists sought to advance the interest of all of humankind through promoting a better understanding of how a market system efficiently allocates resources and promotes economic liberty. To a great extent the marginalists succeeded in this goal. By showing that, under competitive circumstances, the pay received by workers would be equal to their contribution to the value of the output, the marginalists helped counter the Marxian call for revolution by the proletariat. But marginalism—the economics of liberalism or political conservatism—also benefited those whose interests were simply in maintaining the status quo; that is, those who resisted change. This type of theory benefited employers (even though most of them did not really understand it) by opposing unions and by attributing unemployment to wages that were artificially high, inflexible on the downward side, or both. Marginalism also defended landowners against attacks based on Ricardian rent theory. This school also could be said to have benefited the wealthy, who generally opposed government intervention that might redistribute income.

How Was the Marginalist School Valid, Useful, or Correct in Its Time?

The marginalist school developed new and powerful tools of analysis, especially geometric diagrams and mathematical techniques. Thanks to these thinkers, economics became a more exact social science. Conditions of demand were given their rightful importance as one set of determinants for prices of both final goods and factors of production. The school emphasized the forces that shape individual decisions; this was valid in a world where such decisions were significant in determining the course of economic activities. The marginalists explicitly stated fundamental assumptions underlying economic analysis, as opposed to leaving them lurking in the background as did many of the classical economists. The methodological controversies that the marginalists aroused resulted in a separation of objective and verifiable principles that are based on stated assumptions from those principles that depend on value judgments and philosophical outlook.

The method of partial equilibrium analysis championed by many members of this school was useful for abstracting from the complexity of the real world. This approach—allowing one variable at a time to change while holding all other variables temporarily constant—enabled the investigators to dissect complex phenomena one step at a time. The problems of the immensely complicated society with its countless variables was thereby simplified and penetrated in an orderly and systematic manner. As the marginalists introduced successive variables, they eventually approached more realistic situations.

There is a certain virtue in not neglecting the individual economic unit or the small sectors of the economy; the microeconomic approach of marginalism complements the macroeconomic approach, which may overlook many problems by viewing the economy as a whole. As examples, we cite the following: (1) certain groups of people may become increasingly impoverished, although average real per-capita income for the nation may be rising; (2) the business cycle is of prime importance to the profitability of a large automobile company, but to the owner of a convenience grocery store, the business cycle is relatively less important than the opening of a competing store down the street; (3) aggregate analysis tells us that investments in some forms of human capital (for example, college education) pay higher returns than some investments in physical capital; yet a banker may be justified in not lending money to an individual to go to college unless the government guarantees the loan. In the case of the student, the banker simply has no collateral against which to make the loan. Clearly the microeconomic approach of marginalism has an important place in economic theory.

Which Tenets of the Marginalist School Became Lasting Contributions?

Several tenets of the marginalist school were subsequently challenged, and some were rejected. Keynes pointed to the alleged fallacy of composition associated with marginalist and neoclassical employment theory. If one firm were to cut wages, it could expand its market by selling more goods at lower prices. The decline in purchasing power among its own employees would not affect it, because they would normally buy only a negligible portion of its output. However, if all employers were to cut wages, they might find their markets shrinking rather than expanding. Also, critics argued that the assumption of pure competition was a reasonable abstraction looking backward from the 1870s, but it was too restrictive to be useful as competition declined after the 1870s. Today, pure competition can be found in only a few sectors of the economy. Institutionalist economists contended that historical and institutional factors dominated rational individual calculations in determining such things as length of the workday, consumer behavior, wage rates, and the like. The marginalist's view that the best government is the one that interferes the least became outdated as new events transpired and new economic theories developed. The analysis of these thinkers originally was static, timeless, and unsubstantiated with empirical evidence. There were few attempts at inductive verification of theories; in fact, hypotheses often were framed in ways that precluded testing. Business cycles were generally ignored in the firm conviction that supply creates its own demand and therefore that full employment is the rule. The school failed to explain economic growth, and its theory proved to be inadequate for slowly developing countries.

But despite these and other criticisms, many of the marginalist theories remained relatively unscathed, as attested to by the fact they can be found in contemporary textbooks on principles of economics and microeconomics. The school eventually was absorbed by the broader neoclassical school, which, together with variations of Keynesian macroeconomics, dominates economic analysis in Western counties and shares the international field with socialism. We will discover in the following discussion, and in the two chapters that follow, that these economists and their forerunners developed such lasting contributions as mathematical economics, the basic monopoly model, a theory of duopoly, the theory of diminishing marginal utility, the theory of rational consumer choice, the law of demand, the law of diminishing marginal returns as it applies to manufacturing enterprises, the concept of returns to scale, work-leisure choice analysis, the marginal productivity theory of factor returns, and so forth. In the past two decades this "choice-theoretic" approach introduced by the marginalists has experienced resurgence within economics.

ANTOINE AUGUSTIN COURNOT

Antoine Augustin Cournot (1801–1877) was a French mathematician who published treatises on mathematics, philosophy, and economics. He was the first economist to apply mathematics to economic analysis, but his pioneering work was neglected until after his death, when Jevons, Marshall, and Fisher continued his work. He was the first economist to develop concise mathematical models of pure monopoly, duopoly, and pure competition. In analyzing the demand for copper and zinc, both used to produce bronze, Cournot also developed the earliest complete model of what we now refer to as the derived demand for resources.

Cournot is considered to be a forerunner to the marginalist school because much of his analysis focused on the rates of change of total cost and revenue functions. Such rates of change—the mathematical derivatives—translate to what economists now refer to as *marginal cost* and *marginal revenue.* Unlike the present tendency to begin the analysis of market structures with pure competition and then introduce market imperfections, Cournot began his analysis with pure monopoly and then analyzed market circumstances wherein competitors existed. Of his several contributions to economic analysis, two in particular merit elaboration: his theory of pure monopoly and his theory of duopoly.

Cournot's Theory of Monopoly

Cournot is credited with being the first economist to derive the now-familiar proposition that a firm can maximize its profits by setting a price at which marginal revenue equals marginal cost. In 1838 he stated:

> Suppose that a man finds himself proprietor of a mineral spring which has just been found to possess salutary properties possessed by no other. He could doubtless fix the price of a *liter* of this water at 100 francs; but he would soon see by the scant demand [quantity demanded], that this is not the way to make the most of his property. He will therefore successively reduce the price of the liter to the point which will have him the greatest possible profit, i.e. if $F(p)$ denotes the law of demand [quantity demanded], he will end, after various trials, by adopting the value of p [price] which renders the product $pF(p)$ [total revenue] a maximum.[2]

Here Cournot is assuming that the total cost, and therefore the marginal cost, of obtaining the mineral water is zero. Because this is the case, total profits will be maximized at that quantity of output where total revenue (price × quantity) is the greatest. Using calculus, Cournot pointed out that this quantity is where the derivative of the total revenue function (marginal revenue) is zero.

Figure 12-1 shows Cournot's theory graphically. Notice in graph (a) that the proprietor of the mineral water faces a downward sloping demand curve, *D*. The marginal revenue curve, *MR*, lies below the demand curve because lower prices apply to all liters of the mineral water, not just the extra one sold. That is, each additional unit sold will add its own price to total revenue, but if that extra unit had not been offered for sale, the price received on the other liters would have been higher. The loss of this potential revenue must be subtracted from the gain in revenue received through the sale of the extra liter. Thus we see that marginal revenue is less than the price at all but the first unit of output *and* that the marginal revenue curve falls more rapidly than the demand curve. Note once again that the points on the marginal revenue curve in graph (a) represent the rates of change of total revenue shown by the *TR* curve in graph (b); marginal revenue is the derivative of the product $P \times Q$.

We see in Figure 12-1 (a) that the proprietor of the spring could charge 100 francs per liter, just as Cournot observed. At this high price, however, he would sell only 65 liters of mineral water. By dropping a vertical line downward from 65 liters to graph (b), we observe that the proprietor's total revenue would be 6,500 francs. Because costs are zero, total profit also would be 6,500 francs. But notice from graph (a) that marginal revenue is 80 at the 100-franc price. Clearly, marginal revenue (80) exceeds

[2] Augustin Cournot, *Researches into the Mathematical Principles of the Theory of Wealth*, trans. Nathaniel T. Bacon (New York: Macmillan, 1897), 56. (Orig. pub. 1838.)

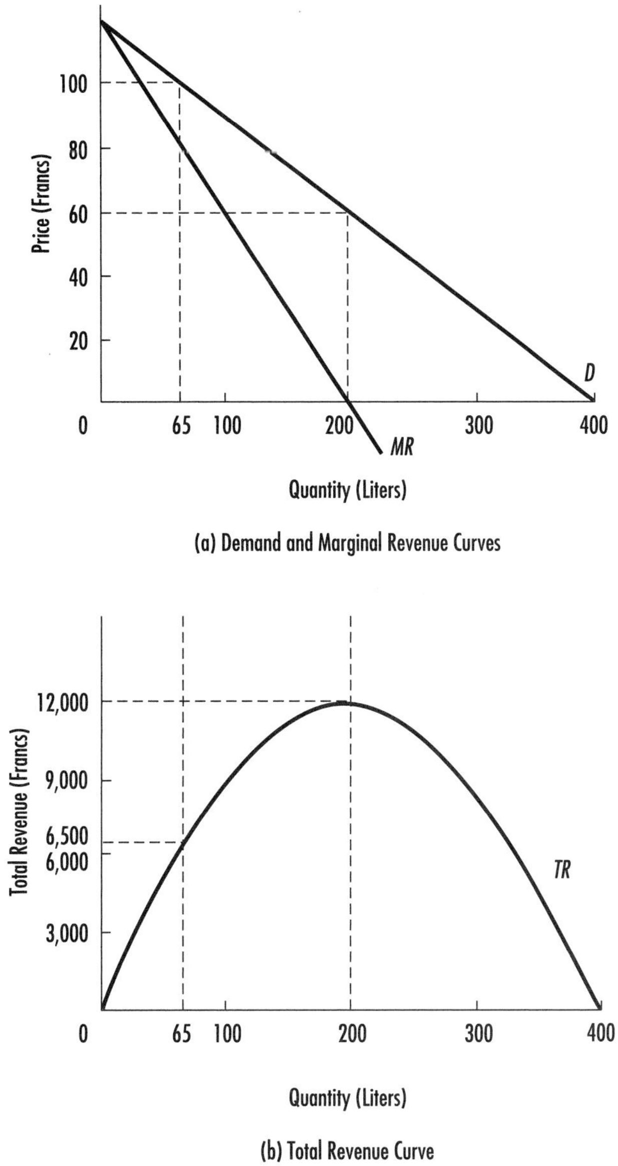

Figure 12-1 Graphical Representation of Cournot's Theory of Monopoly
In graph (a) Cournot's mineral water analysis assumes that costs are zero. The monopoly seller maximizes total revenue, and thus total profit, by selecting a price-output combination at which marginal revenue is zero. Here, that price-output combination is 60 francs and 200 liters of water. In graph (b) total revenue (total profit) is maximized where the slope of the *TR* curve (marginal revenue) is zero. At prices above 60 francs, consumers buy less than 200 liters of water; at prices below 60 francs, consumers buy more than 200 liters of water. In either case, total revenue (total profit) is less than 12,000 francs.

marginal cost (0). This is true for all units of mineral water up to the 200th liter. Instead of charging 100 francs per liter, the monopolist will use trial and error until the price settles at 60 francs. At 60 francs buyers will purchase 200 liters, and, as shown in graph (b), total revenue will rise to 12,000 francs. This is the monopolist's maximum total revenue. Because total costs are assumed to be zero, 12,000 francs is also the maximum profit. Observe that marginal revenue in graph (a) is zero at the profit-maximizing price and output of 60 francs and 200 liters. Because marginal costs are also zero, marginal revenue, *MR,* equals marginal cost, *MC;* that is, the profit-maximizing condition is fulfilled. We see in graph (b) that *any* price above or below 60 francs will reduce total revenue and, in this zero-cost case, total profit.

Cournot extended his theory to circumstances in which marginal costs are positive. The monopolist facing positive costs, he said, will also maximize profits—total revenue minus total cost—at that level of output where *MR* = MC. This rule also applies in situations where numerous competitors exist.

Cournot's Theory of Duopoly

Cournot's theory of duopoly, a market in which two firms compete, was the first formal attempt by an economist to analyze the conduct and performance of sellers in an oligopolistic market structure.

> To make the abstract idea of monopoly comprehensible, we imagined one spring and one proprietor. Let us now imagine two proprietors and two springs of which the qualities are identical, and which, on account of their similar positions, supply the same market in competition. In this case the price is necessarily the same for each proprietor. If p is this price, $D = F(p)$ the total sales, D_1 the sales from the spring (1) and D_2 the sales from the spring (2), then $D_1 + D_2 = D$. If so, to begin with, we neglect the cost of production, the respective incomes of the proprietors will be pD_1 and pD_2; and *each of them independently* will seek to make this income as large as possible.
>
> We say *each independently,* and this restriction is very essential, as will soon appear; for if they should come to an agreement so as to obtain for each the greatest possible income, the results would be entirely different, and would not differ, so far as consumers are concerned, from those obtained in treating of a monopoly.[3]

In formulating his theory of duopoly, Cournot assumed that buyers name the prices and that the two sellers merely adjust their output to those prices. Each duopolist estimates the total demand for the product and sets his own volume of output and sales on the assumption that the rival's output remains fixed. A stable equilibrium is achieved through a step-by-step adaptation of output by each producer, with the duopolists ultimately selling equal quantities of the good at a price that is above the competitive price and below the monopoly one.

Cournot worked out his duopoly case by way of mathematics and the geometrical representation shown in Figure 12-2. The horizontal axis represents the sales (D_1) by proprietor *1,* and the vertical axis the sales (D_2) by proprietor *2.* Curves m_1n_1 and m_2n_2 represent the maximum profit curves of proprietors *1* and *2,* respectively.

[3] Cournot, *Theory of Wealth,* 79–80.

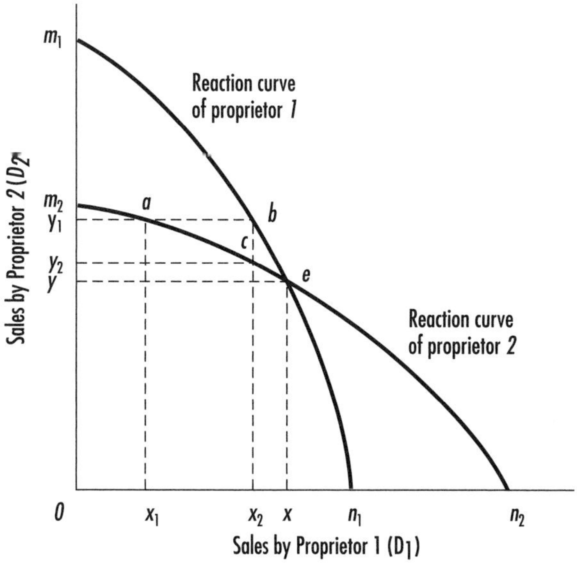

Figure 12-2 The Cournot Duopoly Model

Cournot's reaction functions show the output levels that each proprietor will select to maximize profit, given the assumption that the other proprietor's output (sales) will remain constant. Unequal levels of output, such as those depicted by points *a*, *b*, and *c*, are not sustainable. For example, at point *a*, proprietor *2* will produce output y_1, but proprietor *1* will react by expanding output from x_1 to x_2 (point *b*). Proprietor *2* will then react to proprietor *1*'s output of x_2 by reducing output from y_1 to y_2 (point *c*). Such reactions will generate successive changes in sales levels until equilibrium position e is reached. There, both duopolists have equal output ($x = y$), and no further output adjustment will occur.

Cournot derives these curves from his mathematical equations. Curve m_2n_2 shows the specific levels of proprietor *2*'s output that will maximize *2*'s profit, given the various levels of output offered by proprietor *1*. Point *a* on curve m_2n_2 is instructive. It tells us that if proprietor *1* sells x_1 units of mineral water, then proprietor *2* will discover that she can maximize her profits by selling y_1 units of the product. Curve m_1n_1, on the other hand, shows the maximum profit levels of output for proprietor *1* for the various levels of output offered by proprietor *2*. For example, point *b* on this curve indicates that if proprietor *2* offers y_1 units of output for sale, then proprietor *1* will choose to offer output level x_2 to maximize his profits. Because these curves establish the way each proprietor will *react* to the other's level of output, they are labeled *reaction curves.*

It is a rather simple matter to show that the output levels established by point *a* on the reaction curve of proprietor *2* and point *b* on the curve of proprietor *1* are not sustainable. If proprietor *1* sells x_1 units, proprietor *2* will sell y_1. How will proprietor *1* then react? He will react by selling x_2 liters of the mineral water (point *b*), because that gives him the maximum profit when proprietors *2's* output is y_1. Once proprietor *1* offers x_2 units, proprietor *2* then reacts by offering y_2 units (point *c* on m_2n_2). This process of trial and error will continue until an equilibrium is established at point *e*. Notice that at this intersection of the two reaction curves, the duopolists each sell the same amount of the product ($x = y$) and receive maximum profits, given the output of the other. This position, said Cournot, "is stable, i.e. if either of the producers, misled as to his true interest, leaves it temporarily, he will be brought back to it by a series of reactions, constantly declining in amplitude."

Cournot's Theories in Retrospect

Cournot's pure monopoly model is virtually that which appears in contemporary textbooks on principles of economics. Obviously, economists have found little fault with this model. The only thing worth noting in this regard is that Cournot did not recognize the possibility of price discrimination—the charging of different prices to different customers based on different elasticities of demand. This can occur in circumstances where the market can be segregated and where the buyers cannot resell the product. For example, if the owner of the mineral spring required that buyers consume the mineral water on the premises, it might be possible for the seller to charge individual buyers those prices that they are willing to pay rather than forgo the consumption. Under this pricing scheme marginal revenue would equal the price to each buyer, and the proprietor could garner even more revenue and profit than shown in Figure 12-1. We will see soon that fellow Frenchman Jules Dupuit understood this idea.

Cournot's theory of duopoly, on the other hand, has been criticized for making unrealistic assumptions and for omitting many alternative solutions of the duopoly case. In 1897, for example, Francis Y. Edgeworth, in his paper, "Pure Theory of Monopoly" (originally published in Italy), pointed out that a duopolist cannot be certain about how its rival will react. This uncertainty of mutual reactions renders the duopoly solution indeterminate. Edgeworth's advances in this area are discussed in Chapter 14.

In the 1920s economists began to broaden the possible reaction patterns of duopolists and oligopolists to include sales, costs, quality of product, and service competition. Cournot's assumption that firms set their level of output by assuming that the output of their rivals will remain constant was discarded. As soon as we admit that each firm considers its rival's potential reaction to its own policies, we have a whole range of possible outcomes, depending on what we assume about their behavior. Cournot was remarkable as a pioneer theorist of duopoly and oligopoly, but modern theory, naturally, has gone beyond his early efforts.

JULES DUPUIT

Engineer Arséne-Jules-Emile Dupuit (1804–1866) is a second important French forerunner to marginalism. Dupuit was born in Fossano, Piedmont, Italy, which in 1804 was a part of the French empire. He returned to Paris with his parents in 1814 and attended school at Versailles, Louis-le-Grand, and Saint Louis. Dupuit then earned a degree in engineering from the prestigious École des Ponts et Chaussées.

His studies and designs of roadways, water navigation, and municipal water systems won him wide acclaim within the engineering profession. In 1843 he was awarded the prestigious French Legion of Honor for his work. In 1850 Dupuit became the chief engineer in Paris, and in 1855 he ascended to the position of inspector-general of the French Corps of Civil Engineers.

While making his mark in engineering, Dupuit developed an ardent side-interest in theoretical and applied economics. Between 1844 and 1853, he published significant journal articles concerning diminishing marginal utility, consumer surplus, and price discrimination.[4] Central to each of these concepts was decision making at the "margin." Although Cournot also used this approach, there is no indication that Dupuit and Cournot were familiar with each other's work.

Marginal Utility and Demand

Dupuit stated that the value placed on a good (the water from the municipal water system) varies from individual to individual. Moreover, the amount of satisfaction or utility that an individual gets from a specific unit of water depends on how that particular unit is used. A person first uses water for highly valued uses, then, as the stock of water grows, for less valuable uses. Water used for drinking gives way to water used for gardening. In turn, water used for gardening gives way to water used for washing, and so on, culminating in its use for decorative purposes, such as water fountains.

We know that the ideas of subjective marginal utility and diminishing marginal utility were not new; recall that Bentham had discussed them sixty years earlier. But Dupuit surpassed Bentham by directly linking diminishing marginal utility to individual and market "curves of consumption." He observed that as the price of a good falls, people buy more of it to satisfy less pressing, lower marginal utility wants.

Dupuit constructed a diagram similar to Figure 12-3. If the price of water is 10 francs, said Dupuit, consumers buying 10 units of water must get a *minimum* of 10 francs' worth of utility from each of the 10 units. When the price of water falls to 5 francs, consumers will increase consumption of water to 18 units. This added consumption will end when the marginal utility of water has also declined to 5 francs. The 19th unit of water simply does not yield enough marginal utility to justify the 5-franc price.

In short, Dupuit established the concept of a demand curve: an inverse, or negative, relationship between a product's price and the amount of it people want to buy. In Dupuit's formulation, a demand curve is simply a marginal utility curve. Consuming successive units of a particular good yields increasingly less extra satisfaction. Thus consumers will not buy additional units of the good unless its price falls.

Later economists such as Walras (Chapter 18) criticized Dupuit for failing to distinguish between marginal utility curves and demand curves. Nevertheless, Dupuit is credited as being one of the first economists to draw a diagram showing an inverse relationship between price and quantity demanded. He also was one of the first economists to stress the marginal utility underpinnings of demand.

[4] The most important of these were "On the Measurement of the Utility of Public Works" (1844), "On Tolls and Transport Charges" (1849), and "On Utility and Its Measure" (1853).

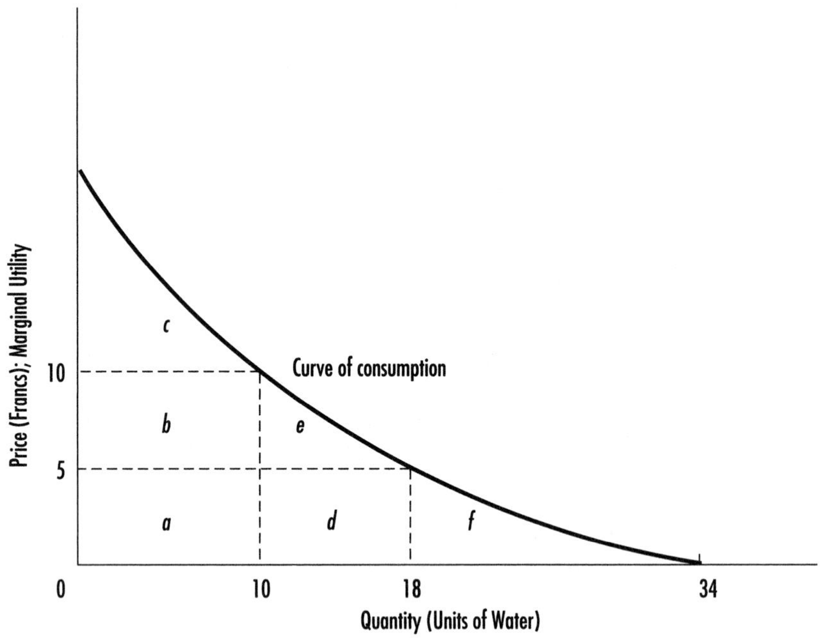

Figure 12-3 Dupuit's Curve of Consumption (Marginal Utility Curve and Demand Curve)

Dupuit's curve of consumption illustrates that marginal utility falls as consumption increases and that an inverse relationship exists between product price and quantity demanded. If the average cost per unit of water is 5 francs, the government seller could charge 5 francs and break even. But the seller could expand total utility through price discrimination. Specifically, it could charge 10 francs to those willing to pay that amount and obtain 50 extra francs of total revenue (5 francs × 10 units of sales). This added revenue would then enable it to charge less than 5 francs for those unwilling or unable to pay 5 francs. Total utility would rise to some amount greater than that shown by areas $a + b + c + d + e$, because purchases would increase beyond 18 units of water.

Consumer Surplus

Dupuit's curve of consumption led him to an important observation later stressed by Alfred Marshall (Chapter 15). Suppose the price charged by authorities is 10 francs, as shown in Figure 12-3. The implication is that consumers would be willing to pay more than 10 francs for all but the 10th unit of water; the marginal utility on all previous units exceeds 10 francs. Only on the last unit (unit 10) is price equal to marginal utility. On a per unit basis, the difference between each unit's marginal utility and its price is *utilité relative*, or surplus utility. The sum of all such differences between marginal utility and price is total consumers' surplus. At the 10-franc price in Figure 12-3, consumers' surplus is the triangle *c*. If the price were 5 francs, consumers' surplus would be the sum of areas *b*, *c*, and *e*.

Monopoly Price Discrimination

Many of the roads, bridges, and water systems that Dupuit engineered were government monopolies. Dupuit thus wondered what price, if any, the government should charge for these monopolized goods or services. If the goal was to maximize total utility, he said, then the price should be zero. In Figure 12-3 the area under any point on the marginal utility curve is the total utility associated with that output. Total utility obviously is greatest at a zero price (the sum of areas *a, b, c, d, e,* and *f*).

At a price above zero two things happen. First, some utility is transferred from the consumer to the seller. Net utility, however, does not decline as a result of this transfer. Second, some utility is lost; in today's terminology there is a deadweight loss. For example, if price is 10 francs rather than zero, quantity will be 10, not 34 units. Comparing the 10-franc and zero-franc prices, we see that the sum of areas *a* and *b* represents a transfer of utility from consumers to the seller. Meanwhile, the sum of areas *e, d,* and *f* delineates a loss of total utility.

Dupuit recognized the obvious: A zero price will not allow the provider to cover the cost of providing the good or service. He therefore suggested that the government seller set a price such that the costs of the service are recouped and the loss of total utility is minimized. One way to cover the costs of providing the good or service is to set a single price that yields total revenue ($P \times Q$) equal to total cost. For example, if the cost per unit of water is 5 francs, then the price could be set at 5 francs too. Eighteen units of water will be consumed, and total revenue will be 90 francs (5 × 18), enough to cover the 90-franc cost. Total utility in Figure 12-3 will fall by area *f*.

But Dupuit wondered if there could be an even better pricing scheme to cover the cost of provision. He concluded that a dual- or multiple-price scheme would reduce the loss of total utility to less than area *f*. Customers whose marginal utility was more than 5 francs might be charged more than the 5 francs per unit cost. In effect, some of the consumers' surplus of these buyers would be tapped for extra seller revenue. This above-cost pricing for these buyers would *not* result in a loss of total utility; it would simply transfer some consumer surplus to the seller. Most important, this extra revenue would allow the seller to charge less to those individuals whose marginal utility is under 5 francs. In Figure 12-3 a price below 5 francs for these customers would increase consumption beyond 18 units. As output expands beyond 18 units, the utility loss relative to the zero price shrinks to something less than area *f*. The dual- or multiple-price scheme therefore increases total utility relative to the single 5-franc price while continuing to meet the requirement that total revenue match total cost.

Today, we employ the term *price discrimination* to describe Dupuit's dual-price or multiple-price scheme. This idea was further developed and formalized by A. C. Pigou (Chapter 20) and Joan Robinson (Chapter 17). Price discrimination can occur only where it is possible to segregate buyers into identifiable groups and where resale of the product by customers is impossible or prohibitively expensive. It converts consumer surplus to higher revenues and, in the case of for-profit firms, higher profits. But, as indicated by Dupuit, price discrimination can also increase total output and enhance total utility. It is widely practiced by government enterprises and public utilities, precisely the forms of monopolies Dupuit had in mind.

Refer to 12-1 PAST AS PROLOGUE

12-1 PAST AS PROLOGUE

Gossen: Utility and Belated Fame

The works of still another forerunner of marginalism, Herman Heindrich Gossen (1810–1858), were not truly appreciated until after his death. Yet his thinking was so advanced that he deserves mention.

Gossen left his employment as a minor German government official to spend four years in seclusion writing a book, which was published in 1854. Very few copies of his *Laws of Human Relations and Rules of Human Action Derived Therefrom* were sold, perhaps because his treatment was highly mathematical. Very disappointed, he recalled the remaining printed copies and had them destroyed.

After William S. Jevons (Chapter 13) published the first edition of his acclaimed *The Theory of Political Economy* in 1871, he discovered a copy of Gossen's book and was amazed to learn that his theories of marginal utility had been nearly completely anticipated by another. Jevons gave full credit to Gossen in subsequent editions, and fame arrived posthumously to this pioneer theorist, whose book was reprinted in German in 1889.

Two laws stated by Gossen, in particular, foreshadowed the contributions of Jevons and other marginalists. Gossen's first law was the law of diminishing returns: The added utility of a good decreases as more of it is consumed. Among other things, this law explains how voluntary exchange produces mutual gains in utility. The farmer who raises livestock has more animals for slaughter than he personally desires to consume; independent of the money that he can receive for them, the marginal utility is low or negative. Likewise, the baker has so much bread that, beyond that consumed, the marginal utility of each loaf is low or even negative. Exchange of bread for meat allows both parties to obtain goods providing more marginal utility than their original stock.

Gossen's second law relates to the balancing of marginal utilities through rational consumption spending to secure maximum satisfaction. The rational person, said Gossen, should allocate his or her money income so that the last unit of money spent on each product bought yields the same amount of extra (marginal) utility. The marginal utility per unit of money spent on a product is marginal utility (*MU*) divided by the product's price (*P*). Therefore, symbolically, Gossen's condition for maximizing utility is:

$$\frac{MU_x}{P_x} = \frac{MU_y}{P_y} = \cdots, \qquad \textbf{(12-1)}$$

where MU_x and MU_y are the respective marginal utilities of two independent goods, *X* and *Y*, and P_x and P_y are their respective prices.

We will explore Jevons's and Carl Menger's formulation of this idea in more depth in the next chapter. We will find that this law of rational consumer behavior was the foundation of the demand analysis considered so important to marginalist value theory.

JOHANN HEINRICH VON THÜNEN

Johann Heinrich von Thünen (1783–1850), a third forerunner of marginalism, was born in Oldenburg, Germany. He studied briefly at the University of Göttingen and then purchased an estate in Mecklenburg. There he farmed and wrote his chief work, *The Isolated State*. In Volume 1 of this work, published in 1826, he developed a theory that considered the location of various forms of agricultural production in relation to the market in which the produce is sold. In this respect he is the founder of location theory and agricultural economics. In Volume 2 of *The Isolated State*, published in 1850, he expanded his analysis and in the process established a crude marginal productivity theory of wages and capital. Von Thünen was a forerunner to the marginalist John Bates Clark (Chapter 14), in particular.

Von Thünen's Location Theory

In developing his location theory, von Thünen first made several assumptions:

> Imagine a very large town, at the center of a fertile plain which is crossed by no navigable river or canal. Throughout the plain the soil is capable of cultivation and of the same fertility. Far from the town, the plain turns into an uncultivated wilderness which cuts off all communications between the State and the outside world.
>
> There are no other towns on the plain. The central town must therefore supply the rural areas with all manufactured products, and in return it will obtain all its provisions from the surrounding countryside.
>
> The mines that provide the State with salt and metals are near the central town which, as it is the only one, we shall in future call simply "the Town."[5]

Johann von Thünen then addressed his central question:

> The problem we want to solve is this: What pattern of cultivation will take shape in these conditions?, and how will the farming system of the different districts be affected by their distance from the Town? We assume throughout that farming is conducted absolutely rationally.
>
> It is on the whole obvious that near the Town will be grown those products which are heavy or bulky in relation to their value and hence so expensive to transport that the remoter districts are unable to supply them. Here too we shall find the highly perishable products, which must be used very quickly. With increasing distance from the Town, the land will progressively be given up to products cheap to transport in relation to value.
>
> For this reason alone, fairly differentiated concentric rings or belts will form around the Town, each with its own particular staple product.
>
> From ring to ring the staple product, and with it the entire farming system, will change; and in the various rings we shall find completely different farming systems.[6]

Figure 12-4 presents a slightly modified version of von Thünen's own representation of his theory. The innermost circle (I), labeled "Market Gardening and

[5] Johann H. von Thünen, *The Isolated State*, trans. Carla M. Wartenberg and ed. Peter Hall, vol. 1 (Oxford: Pergamon Press, 1966), 7.

[6] Johann H. von Thünen, *Isolated State*, 1: 8.

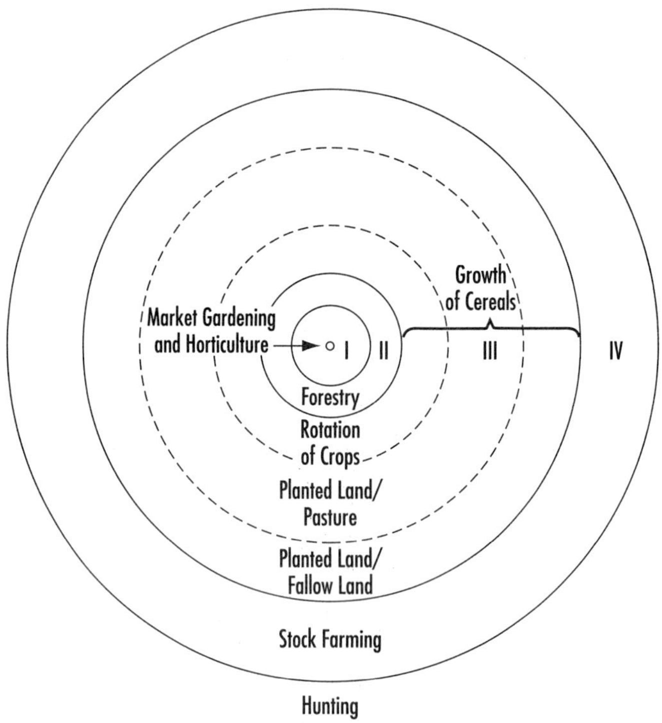

Figure 12-4 Johann von Thünen's Theory of Agricultural Location
In von Thünen's "isolated state," a series of concentric rings, each devoted to a particular type of agricultural use, develops around the central city. The farther the ring from the city, the less intensive is the production, the less perishable is the produce, and the greater is the ability of the commodity to bear the costs of transportation.

Horticulture," immediately surrounds the city. Here delicate products like strawberries, lettuce, cauliflower, and so forth will be grown. Additionally, farmers will raise barn-fed cows for the purpose of producing fresh milk, because its transport "is not only difficult and expensive, but milk becomes, particularly in time of great heat, unpalatable after a few hours."

The second ring (II) indicates the region in which intensive cultivation of forests occurs as a way to supply the city with fuel and building materials. These items need to be grown near the city because they are heavy in relation to their market value and costly to transport. Farmers will grow grain in the next three rings, which together constitute zone III, labeled "Growth of Cereals." In the innermost ring of this zone, landowners or their tenants will intensively plant grains and continuously rotate their crops to achieve the maximum yield from the soil. In the middle zone of ring III, said von Thünen, portions of the land will be planted and other parts used as pasture. The outermost ring within zone III will be characterized by some fields where grains are grown and others where the land is temporarily left fallow.

In the fourth ring (IV) outward in Figure 12-4, farmers will raise cattle and hogs. Although these animals are heavy, presumably they can be driven to town for slaughter at relatively little transport expense. Finally, all the land located beyond ring IV will be used only for hunting. The costs of transporting farm produce of any type to the city will simply be too great relative to the value of the commodities.

Johann von Thünen explained that, as the intensification of production in agriculture within the rings rises, diminishing returns cause what we now call marginal costs to rise. This leads to higher market prices, which in turn makes it profitable to cultivate new areas farther from the market. Restated, the intensification of agriculture widens the four major rings in Figure 12-4.

Johann von Thünen on Marginal Productivity

Johann von Thünen's careful thinking about the location of various types of agriculture led him to develop a marginal productivity theory of employment. He based this on the principle that added units of labor lead to successively smaller increases in total agricultural product. Recall that Ricardo also had used this same notion—the law of diminishing marginal returns—in his analysis of rent. Johann von Thünen further expanded the applicability of this law. He stated that, given this principle, the farmer must take care not to hire labor beyond that point at which the cost of the last addition of labor is matched by the value of the added agricultural yield. In contemporary terms, von Thünen was suggesting that the employer should add units of labor until the marginal revenue product of labor—the extra revenue accruing from the greater yield—equals the wage expense of hiring the worker. Furthermore, von Thünen understood that it is the marginal product of the last worker employed that establishes the "natural wage" received by all workers. This is sophisticated economic reasoning that foreshadowed the later contributions of John Bates Clark and Alfred Marshall. We will await a discussion of these economists to examine this theory in depth.

Questions for Study and Discussion

1. Briefly identify and state the significance of each of the following to the history of economic thought: Cournot, total and marginal revenue, duopoly, reaction function, Dupuit, diminishing marginal utility, curve of consumption, consumers' surplus, price discrimination, von Thünen, marginal productivity, Gossen.
2. Review the list of major tenets of marginalist thought discussed in this chapter and determine which of them apply to the writings of Cournot.
3. Recall from your previous economics the total revenue or total receipts test for elasticity of demand. Referring to the two graphs in Figure 12-1, determine whether demand is elastic or inelastic over the following ranges of output: (a) 0 to 200 range; (b) 200 to 400 range. Explain your answers.
4. Through specific reference to Cournot's monopoly model (Figure 12-1), explain why each of the following statements is erroneous: (a) "The pure monopolist charges the highest price per unit that it can obtain." (b) "The pure monopolist produces that level of output that maximizes its per unit

profit." (c) "Irrespective of its costs of production, a pure monopolist is assured of making an economic profit."

5. Draw a dashed horizontal line in Figure 12-2 (Cournot's duopoly model) such that it is slightly above the horizontal axis and extends rightward to the reaction function m_2n_2. What will be proprietor *2*'s initial level of output (sales)? Explain why. How will proprietor *1* then respond? Which levels of output will ultimately result given the assumptions of this model? Explain.
6. Use Dupuit's analysis of utility to explain why the amount of a product demanded falls as its price rises, other things being equal.
7. Cite several products that you buy that provide you with Dupuit's *utilité relative*.
8. Referring to Figure 12-1(a) (Cournot's monopoly model), identify the area of consumer surplus when price is 60 francs. Explain how price discrimination (Dupuit) could increase the monopolist's total revenue above 12,000 francs. Explain how multiple prices, rather than the single 60-franc monopoly price, could enhance total utility (assume as did Dupuit that the demand curve is the marginal utility curve).
9. Use the basic principles of von Thünen's location theory to explain why ready-to-pour concrete plants generally are located in or near cities in which their product is sold, whereas book publishers often are located far away from where the books are sold.
10. How, according to von Thünen, will a landowner determine the proper number of farm laborers to hire?
11. Use separate examples of your own choosing to explain each of Gossen's two laws.

Selected Readings

Books

Blaug, Mark, ed. *Johann von Thünen, Augustin Cournot and Jules Dupuit.* Brookfield, VT: Edward Elgar, 1992.

Black, R. D. C., A. W. Coats, and C. D. W. Goodwin, eds. *The Marginal Revolution, Interpretation and Evaluation.* Durham, NC: Duke University Press, 1973.

Cournot, Augustin. *Researches into the Mathematical Principles of the Theory of Wealth.* Translated by Nathaniel T. Bacon. New York: Macmillan, 1897, 1927. (Orig. pub. 1838.)

Ekelund, Robert B., and Robert F. Hébert. *The Secret Origins of Modern Microeconomics: Dupuit and the Engineers.* Chicago: University of Chicago Press, 1999.

Gossen, Herman H. *The Laws of Human Relations and the Rules of Human Action Derived Therefrom.* Translated by Rudolph C. Blitz. Cambridge, MA: MIT Press, 1983. (Orig. pub. 1854.)

Von Thünen, J. H. *The Isolated State.* Translated by Carla Wartenberg and edited by Peter Hall. Vol. 1. Oxford: Pergamon Press, 1966.

———. *The Isolated State.* In *The Frontier Wage,* translated by B. W. Dempsey. Vol. 2. Chicago: Loyola University Press, 1960.

Journal Articles

Clark, Colin. "Von Thünen's Isolated State," *Oxford Economic Papers* 19 (November 1967): 370–377.

Dupuit, Jules. "On the Measurement of the Utility of Public Works," in *Readings in Welfare Economics,* eds. Kenneth J. Arrow and Tibor Scitovsky. Homewood, IL: Richard D. Irwin, 1969: 255–283.

Ekelund, Robert B., Jr. "Price Discrimination and Product Differentiation in Economic Theory: An Early Analysis," *Quarterly Journal of Economics* 84 (May 1970): 268–278.

Fisher, Irving. "Cournot and Mathematical Economics," *Quarterly Journal of Economics* 12 (January 1898): 119–138, 238–244.

Liegh, Arthur H. "Von Thünen's Theory of Distribution and the Advent of Marginal Analysis," *Journal of Political Economy* 54 (December 1946): 481–502.

Theocharis, Reghinos D. "A Note on the Lag in the Recognition of Cournot's Contribution to Economic Analysis," *Canadian Journal of Economics* 23 (November 1990): 923–933.

Chapter 13

THE MARGINALIST SCHOOL—JEVONS, MENGER, VON WIESER, AND VON BÖHM-BAWERK

Although Cournot, Dupuit, von Thünen, and Gossen provided pathbreaking marginal analyses, marginalism as a more clearly defined school of economic thought originated with W. Stanley Jevons in England, Carl Menger in Austria, and Léon Walras at Lausanne, Switzerland. This is another interesting case of new ideas arising almost simultaneously in different places and from different people but stemming from a common dissatisfaction with old theories. Here, we will examine the contributions of Jevons, Menger, and two Austrians who followed in Menger's footsteps. We will defer discussing Walras until Chapter 18, which focuses on contributors to mathematical economics.

WILLIAM STANLEY JEVONS

William Stanley Jevons (1835–1882) was born in Liverpool, England. He spent five years in Australia as an assayer at the mint, where he earned enough to return to England to continue his studies. He was disappointed and bitter when he failed to win a prize in political economy at University College, London, and attributed this failure to the prejudice of his professors against the new ideas he was developing. Jevons published several books on logic and became professor of logic, political economy, and philosophy, first in Manchester and later at University College, London. He invented a logic machine, exhibited before the Royal Society in 1870, that could yield a conclusion mechanically from any given set of premises. Jevons was also famous as a historian of science, and he made outstanding contributions to the development of index numbers. Jevons was extremely introverted and did not have great influence on his immediate peers or students. At the age of forty-seven he drowned while swimming.

Jevons on Value Theory

Jevons called Ricardo "that able but wrong-headed man" who "shunted the car of Economic science on to a wrong line." Mill, he felt, pushed the car further toward confusion. The economic analysis presented by Senior was much more to Jevons's taste.

On the first page of *The Theory of Political Economy,* first published in 1871, Jevons stated:

> Repeated reflection and inquiry have led me to the somewhat novel opinion, that *value depends entirely upon utility.* Prevailing opinions make labour rather than utility the origin of value; and there are even those who distinctly assert that labour is the *cause* of value. I show, on the contrary, that we have only to trace out carefully the natural laws of the variation of utility, as depending upon the quantities in our possession, in order to arrive at a satisfactory theory of exchange, of which the ordinary laws of supply and demand are a necessary consequence. This theory is in harmony with facts; and, whenever there is any apparent reason for the belief that labour is the cause of value, we obtain an explanation of the reason. Labour is found often to determine value, but only in an indirect manner, by varying the degree of utility of the commodity through an increase or limitation of supply.[1]

Unlike Ricardo, who might say that pearls have value because people need to dive for them, Jevons is saying that pearls have value because buyers get utility from them and that people dive for pearls because pearls have such value. The specific level of utility associated with the pearls depends on the number of pearls people presently possess.

To explain Jevons's value theory, we must therefore begin with his theory of the law of diminishing marginal utility. Then our attention will turn to his related notions of rational consumer behavior, individual and market exchange, and the optimal amount of work.

Theory of diminishing marginal utility. Jevons's theory of diminishing marginal utility is similar to the earlier ideas of Gossen (Past as Prologue 12-1) and Dupuit. Jevons said that utility cannot be measured directly, at least with the tools at hand. This subjective pleasure or satisfaction can be estimated only by observing human behavior and noting human preferences. He also rejected any attempt to compare the intensity of pleasures and pains among different people.[2] But a single individual *can* compare utilities of successive units of a single good, said Jevons, and *can* compare the *marginal* utilities of several goods. With respect to the former, Jevons used graphical analysis to illustrate his "law of variation of the final degree of utility of a commodity." A contemporary version of his representation is shown as Figure 13-1.

The top graph in Figure 13-1 measures total utility on the vertical axis and the quantity of a particular commodity, say, good X, on the horizontal axis. Total utility, TU, rises as more of good X is consumed. Notice, however, that as more of X is consumed, total utility increases at a *diminishing rate.* Each successive unit of X adds less to total utility than did the previous unit.

---

[1] William Stanley Jevons, *The Theory of Political Economy,* 3rd ed. (London: Macmillan, 1888), 1–2. (Orig. pub. 1871.)

[2] Jevons, however, was inconsistent on this point. Later in his book he compared utilities among different people. More specifically, he extended the principle of diminishing marginal utility to money and gave a theoretical justification for the argument that redistributing income from the rich to the poor increases total happiness.

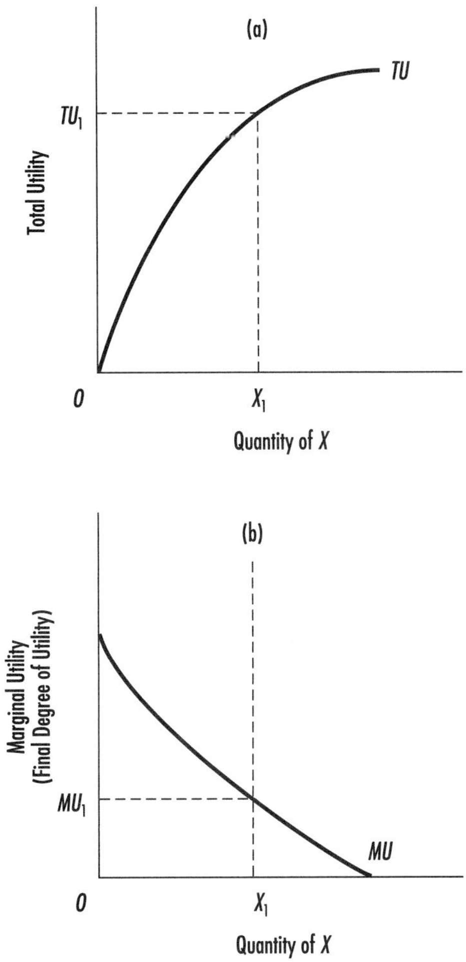

Figure 13-1 Jevons's Law of Diminishing Marginal Utility
The total utility that a consumer receives from each quantity of commodity X is shown by TU in the upper graph. The lower graph shows the marginal utility (MU), or the change in total utility, as each unit of the commodity is added. Marginal utility, which is equivalent to Jevons's final degree of utility, declines as more of commodity X is consumed. The total utility of quantity X_1 is TU_1; the marginal utility of unit X_1 is MU_1.

In the lower graph in the figure, the vertical axis measures the *change* in total utility, or marginal utility, *MU*. Marginal utility, equivalent to Jevons's "final degree of utility . . . varies with the quantity of [the] commodity, and ultimately decreases as that quantity increases. No commodity can be named which we continue to desire with the same force, whatever be the quantity already in use or possession." If the person having the marginal utility curve in Figure 13-1 decides to purchase

X_1 units of the commodity, said Jevons, then the total utility would be TU_1 and the final degree of utility (marginal utility) would be MU_1. Marginal utility in the lower graph is found by plotting the slope of TU (upper graph) at each of its points.

> We shall seldom need to consider the degree of utility except as regards the last increment which has been consumed, or, which comes to the same thing, the next increment which is about to be consumed. I shall therefore commonly use the expression *final degree of utility,* as meaning the degree of utility of the last addition, or the next possible addition of a very small, or infinitely small, quantity to the existing stock.[3]

Jevons's law of diminishing marginal utility solved the paradox of water and diamonds that puzzled some of the classical economists. Adam Smith believed that utility has nothing to do with the magnitude of exchange value because water is more useful than diamonds whereas diamonds are more valuable than water. The principle of diminishing marginal utility reveals that whereas the *total* utility of water *is* greater than the total utility of diamonds, the "final degree of utility" or *marginal* utility of diamonds is far greater than the marginal utility of water. We would rather have all the water in the world and no diamonds than the other way around; but we would rather have an additional diamond than an additional unit of water, given our abundant stock of the latter.

Rational choice: the equimarginal rule. Jevons employed his notion of final utility (marginal utility) to formalize a general theory of rational choice.

> Let s be the whole stock of some commodity, and let it be capable of two distinct uses ["barley may be used either to make beer, spirits, bread, or to feed cattle."] Then we may represent the two quantities appropriated to these uses by x_1 and y_1, it being a condition that $x_1 + y_1 = s$. The person may be conceived as successively expending small quantities of the commodity; now it is the inevitable tendency of human nature to choose that course which appears to offer the greatest advantage at the moment. Hence, when the person remains satisfied with the distribution he has made, it follows that . . . an increment of commodity would yield exactly as much utility in one use as in another. . . . We must in other words, have the *final degrees of utility* [marginal utilities] in the two uses equal.[4]

Notice that in this case the price of the two commodities is the same regardless of use. Hence, Jevons's example is simply a special case of Gossen's second law: The consumer wishing to maximize utility will allocate money income in such a way that the marginal utility of the last dollar spent on all commodities is equal. Symbolically this is stated as: $MU_x/P_x = MU_y/P_y \ldots = MU_n/P_n$. The role of diminishing marginal utility is important here. If the ratio of the marginal utility of X to its price is greater than that for other commodities, then the rational consumer will purchase more of X and less of other goods. As more of X is obtained, its marginal utility declines; as fewer units of goods such as Y and Z are consumed, their marginal utilities rise. Eventually the ratios of marginal utilities to the respective prices of the goods equalize and the consumer's total utility is maximized.

---

[3] Jevons, *Political Economy,* 51.

[4] Jevons, *Political Economy,* 59–60.

Theory of exchange. Jevons also used his principle of utility maximization to explain the gains from exchange. Suppose, said Jevons, that one party ("trading body") has only corn and another has only beef. How is it that exchange will benefit each, and at what point will exchange cease? Once again the equimarginal rule comes into play. Because party *A* has only beef, the ratio of the marginal utility of beef to its price will be low, whereas the ratio of the marginal utility of corn to its price will be high. The equimarginal rule correctly suggests that party *A* will benefit by obtaining corn and giving up beef. A similar situation exists for party *B*. The lost utility from sacrificing corn will be less than the gain in utility from the beef gained.

At which point will trade cease? The answer, said Jevons, is the point at which there are no further possibilities of utility gains from exchange. More specifically, trade will cease when, at the margin, a pound of beef has as much utility as, say, 10 pounds of corn *and* exchanges for 10 pounds of corn in the market. That is, if the price of a pound of steak is 10 times greater than the price of a pound of corn (for example, $10 versus $1) each person will consume both goods up to the point where the steak has 10 times the marginal utility of the pound of corn (for example, 100 versus 10 units of marginal utility). Or restated algebraically, exchange will cease when the ratio of marginal utilities of the two goods as seen by each trading party matches the ratio of prices (for example, 100/10 = $10/$1).

Jevons on labor. Recall that Jevons held utility to be the determinant of exchange value. At one place in his *Principles* he formulated his idea this way:

> Cost of production determines supply.
> Supply determines final degree of utility.
> Final degree of utility determines value.[5]

Why, therefore, does not cost of production determine value? Jevons, in refuting the labor theory of value, argued that labor cannot be the regulator of value because labor itself has unequal value; it differs infinitely in quality and efficiency. "I hold labour to be *essentially variable, so that its value must be determined by the value of the produce, not the value of the produce by that of the labour.*"

Labor itself is a subjective, psychological cost, a "painful exertion." The problem of economics is "to satisfy our wants with the least possible sum of labour." To accomplish this, the worker must compare the pain of work and the pleasure of earnings.

Jevons presented his theory of the optimal amount of work graphically as shown in Figure 13-2. The line *OX* represents the potential amount of product that the worker can earn in a working day, given some hourly wage rate. The height of points above the line *OX* measures pleasure (utility); the points below it measure pain (disutility). At the beginning of the working day, labor is usually more irksome than later in the day when the worker adjusts to it. Thus, there is neither pleasure nor pain at points *b* and *c* on the curve labeled MDU_w (marginal disutility of work), and there is actual pleasure from working—independently of the earnings—between those two points. Beyond *c*, however, the pain (marginal disutility) of additional work increases.

[5] Jevons, *Political Economy*, 166.

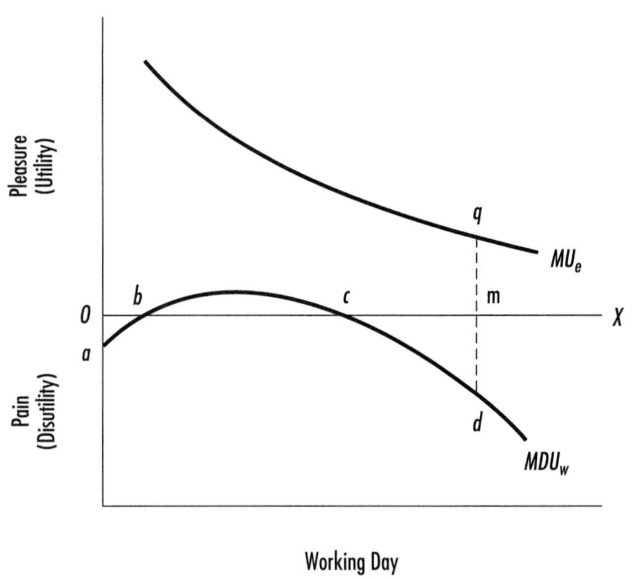

Figure 13-2 Jevons's Equilibrium between the Pain of Work and the Pleasure of Earnings

Jevons theorized that the worker compares the marginal utility of earnings from the job (MU_e) with the marginal disutility of work (MDU_w). The optimal amount of work is shown by *m*, where the marginal utility of earnings, *qm*, equals the marginal disutility of work, *dm*.

The marginal utility of the product, or more appropriately the marginal utility of the earnings, is shown by MU_e (marginal utility of earnings). Its downward slope reflects the law of diminishing marginal utility. At *m*, where *qm* equals *dm*, the pleasure gained from the earnings associated with the last unit of work is exactly equal to the pain of the labor endured ($MU_e = MDU_w$). The worker will choose to work and earn an amount represented by point *m*, because as seen by the two curves, hours of work beyond *m* will result in greater disutility from work than the gain in utility from the extra earnings. You should confirm that *m* is this person's optimal amount of work by scrutinizing points other than *m* along *OX*. It should be pointed out that Jevons did add some realism to his discussion by pointing out that "it is not always possible to graduate the [length of the workday] to the worker's liking."

A recapitulation of Jevons's thinking is in order. He believed that marginal utility is the determinant of exchange value. A change in exchange value may result from such factors as a change in people's relative preferences for commodities. When exchange value changes, the value of the labor used to produce the commodities also changes. Changes in the value of labor (wage rates) in turn cause changes in the optimal amount of work as viewed by workers in various industries. Therefore, asked Jevons, how can it be said that labor time is the cause of or even the measure of exchange value? Rather, the value of an hour of labor is determined by the final degree of utility of the product.

Other Topics Addressed by Jevons

Jevons discussed several additional topics that deserve discussion. First, although he did not fully develop a general theory of distribution based on marginal productivity, nor did he adequately explain the law of diminishing returns on which such a theory of distribution could be built, he did understand the rudiments of both ideas. Successive units of capital investment, he said, are less productive than preceding ones. Given a fixed number of workers in any industry, the amount of capital employed would determine the output per unit of capital. This output per unit of capital, said Jevons, would determine the interest payment to capital. Interest, he said, is one of three components of profits; the other two are wages of superintendence and insurance against risk.

Refer to 13-1 PAST AS PROLOGUE

Second, Jevons contributed to the theory of insurance and gambling. As detailed in Past as Prologue 13-1, he used his theory of diminishing marginal utility of money to show that gambling in a fair game does not pay.

Third, business cycles attracted Jevons's attention. He theorized that the sunspot cycle influences the weather, which affects the size of crops. Large crops occur when sunspots are at a minimum, and the resulting low prices of agricultural products stimulate the economy. The effects may manifest themselves internationally; a large crop and cheap food in India will leave wage earners surplus income that can be spent for clothing, thereby promoting prosperity for the cotton mills of Manchester. This sunspot theory of the business cycle, of course, did not stand the test of subsequent empirical testing and often is cited as a good example of the *post hoc, ergo proptor hoc* ("after this, therefore because of this") reasoning error.

Fourth, as mentioned earlier, Jevons contributed greatly to the development of index numbers. In particular he pioneered a method for constructing a general price index that would provide information on the extent of inflation or deflation from one period to the next. He then used his method to construct a general index of prices as well as price indexes for individual classes of commodities.

Jevons on Public Policy

Jevons favored free public museums, concerts, libraries, and education. He believed that child labor should be restricted by law and that health and safety conditions in factories should be regulated. He approved of trade unions as benefit, or friendly, societies because their insurance functions reduce the need for public relief. But unions should leave the wage rate to the operation of the natural laws. If they obtain wage increases, it is at the expense of other workers or of the population in general through higher prices. "The supposed conflict of labour with capital is a delusion. The real conflict is between producers and consumers." Profit sharing is preferable to union efforts to raise wages, and workers should save to improve their lot.

Jevons opposed regulating the hours of labor of adult males. He advocated excluding mothers with children below school age from factories and workshops for the sake of their children. But he deplored free hospitals and medical charities of all kinds because they "nourish in the poorest classes a contented sense of dependence on the richer classes for those ordinary requirements of life which they ought to be led to provide for themselves." He opposed government conservation

13-1 PAST AS PROLOGUE

Jevons: Is Gambling Rational?

Gambling has held a fascination for people since antiquity. Today, millions of gamblers each year crowd casinos in Las Vegas, Reno, Atlantic City, and other gambling meccas. Even government has become involved with gambling; people spend more than $40 billion a year on state lottery tickets in the United States.

In 1871 William S. Jevons used his theory of diminishing marginal utility to prove that gambling at a fair game is not economical. A fair game is one with a net expected value of zero. An example is a game where a $1 wager provides a .00001 percent chance of winning $100,000. The expected value of the $100,000 prize is $1, found by multiplying the amount of the prize by the probability of winning it. That is, $1 = .00001($100,000). This *plus* $1 of expected value of the prize equals the *minus* $1 expected value of the bet, making the net expected value of the game zero.

For purposes of analysis, Jevons assumed that people do not attach pleasure to gambling except for winning and that money is subject to the law of diminishing marginal utility. Under these assumptions, the potential prize from a fair game has a lower expected utility value than the amount of money bet. In our previous example, the marginal utility of the 99,999th, 99,998th (and so on) dollar won is less than the marginal utility of the first dollar bet. Although this is a fair *monetary* game, it is not a fair *utility* game. The expected utility value of the prize is some amount less than the bet.

If wagering on a fair game is irrational, then playing roulette, blackjack, or slot machines; buying lottery tickets; and betting on horses would seem to be even less rational. None of these games has sufficiently high odds of winning to make it fair, yet people still play them.

measures to check the waste of coal because such modes of interference "break the principles of industrial freedom, to the recognition of which, since the time of Adam Smith, we attribute so much of our success."

Jevons supported a cautious extension of legislation to improve public sanitation but was undecided about whether imprisonment for debt should be abolished. Moderate government regulation of railways won his approval. In his view, consumption taxes, such as the match tax, are most desirable because they do not affect industry adversely; besides, all people above the rank of actual paupers should contribute to the state in proportion to their incomes. Believing that people are essentially hedonistic, Jevons advocated Bentham's greatest-happiness principle. No laws, no customs, no rights of property, he said, are so sacred that they must remain if it can be proven that they stand in the way of the greatest happiness. But, he asked, how can we prove that a certain change will increase the sum of happiness? Without conclusive evidence, "the present social arrangements have the considerable presumption in their favour that they can at least exist, and they can be tolerated."

Two complementary explanations preserve the economist's perspective that most gambling is rational behavior. First, many people get utility from gambling, independently of any expected winnings. Jevons recognized that in fact, as opposed to theory, the playing of the game itself provides utility, just as does attending a sporting event, concert, or movie. For these people the utility of being part of the action augments the positive, but declining, marginal utility of money from potential winnings. These gamblers *do* act rationally; their expected gains in utility (playing *plus* potential winnings) exceed the negative utility of their wagers.

In an important 1948 article, Milton Friedman (Chapter 24) and L. J. Savage offered a second explanation for why some people gamble.* These economists challenged Jevons's assumption that marginal utility of money declines over all ranges of money income. The Friedman-Savage hypothesis is that the marginal utility of money declines over low ranges of money income, rises over higher ones, and then eventually falls. For many people the rising range of marginal utility of money income means that dollars from "big wins" (which greatly augment standards of living) have more marginal utility than the dollars bet. Where the odds of winning are low, a small wager provides the opportunity for a large win. Because dollars won in fair games provide more marginal utility than the dollars bet, the expected utility value of the prize exceeds the utility cost of the wager. People experiencing rising marginal utility of money income will therefore rationally participate in fair games. They may also gamble on less than fair games, such as lotteries, if their marginal utility of money is rising fast enough to compensate for these poorer gambles.

*Milton Friedman and L. J. Savage, "The Utility Analysis of Choices Involving Risk," *Journal of Political Economy* 41 (August 1948): 279–304.

CARL MENGER

Carl Menger (1840–1921), born in Galicia and the son of a lawyer, studied at the universities of Vienna and Prague and received his doctorate at the University of Cracow. As a professor at the University of Vienna, Menger published his pathbreaking treatise, *Principles of Economics.* This book appeared in 1871, the same year that Jevons's major work was published. Menger's long-range goal was to produce a systematic work on economics and a comprehensive treatise on the character and methods of the social sciences in general. His interests and the scope of his projects continued to expand, and in 1903 he resigned his professorship to devote himself entirely to his work. During the last three decades of his long life, he published very little because he was dissatisfied with his writing. On his death he left voluminous fragmentary and disordered manuscripts.

Table 13-1
Menger's Concept of Diminishing Marginal Utility

Unit Consumed	DEGREE OF MARGINAL SATISFACTION									
			(Food)			(Tobacco)				
	I	II	III	IV	V	VI	VII	VIII	IX	X
1st	10	9	8	7	6	5	4	3	2	1
2nd	9	8	7	6	5	4	3	2	1	0
3rd	8	7	6	5	4	3	2	1	0	
4th	7	6	5	4	3	2	1	0		
5th	6	5	4	3	2	1	0			
6th	5	4	3	2	1	0				
7th	4	3	2	1	0					
8th	3	2	1	0						
9th	2	1	0							
10th	1	0								
11th	0									

Menger's immediate and lasting impact on economics was substantial. Numerous later economists, collectively known as the Austrian school, championed and expanded his principles. Friedrich von Wieser and Eugen von Böhm-Bawerk, two of this school's more prominent early members, are discussed in this chapter. Later members of this group include such notable economists as Ludwig von Mises, Joseph Schumpeter, and Friedrich von Hayek. Two of Menger's more significant contributions were his theories of value and imputation.

Menger's Value Theory

Like Jevons, Menger based his value theory on the concept of utility. Contrary to Jevons, however, he deliberately made no use of mathematics in formulating his theory, and he avoided constructing it upon a Benthamite base. His exposition of diminishing marginal utility and the balancing of marginal utilities included an example reproduced here as Table 13-1. The table shows the hypothetical values of marginal utility for various numbers of units of 10 commodities, or classes of commodities (I through X). The successive figures down each column represent successive additions to total satisfaction resulting from increased consumption of the designated commodity. For example, notice that the most important item of consumption is food, and the first unit of food consumed is assumed to have a utility of 10, as shown in column I. If a second unit of food was consumed in the same day, its utility would be nine. With 10 units of food available, the last unit would give a satisfaction of one. Notice from column I that an 11th unit of food would add nothing to this person's total utility.

Tobacco, less urgently needed, is shown in column V. The first unit consumed gives a satisfaction of only 6, and beyond 6 units, higher levels of consumption do not increase utility. If an individual obtained 4 units of food, the person's utility per unit would fall from 10 to 7. She or he then would find that a 5th unit of food would afford the same satisfaction (6) as the 1st unit of tobacco (also 6). Suppose that this person wished to spend \$10 and that all units of all commodities cost \$1 per unit. How would the \$10 be allocated? You should draw on our previous discussion of the equimarginal rule to confirm that the answer is 4 units of I, 3 units of II, 2 units of III, and 1 unit of IV. At this combination, the entire \$10 will be expended, and the marginal utility/price ratios for each item will be 7/\$1.

An implicit assumption of Menger's table is that each unit of each commodity represents the same expenditure of money or effort or sacrifice (\$1 in our example). Otherwise, if a unit of tobacco could be obtained with \$.10 or 5 minutes of work, whereas a unit of food required \$1 or 50 minutes of work, the first unit of tobacco would be more desirable (6/\$.10) than even the first unit of food (10/\$1).

Another implicit assumption of Menger's table is that the economizing individual is able to rank satisfactions not only ordinally but cardinally as well. *Ordinal* ranking allows one to say that the first dollar spent on food in any one day gives more satisfaction than either the second dollar spent on food or the first dollar spent on anything else represented in the table. This is a *relative* statement indicating that one item is more or less highly ranked in terms of value than others. With *cardinal* values, one must say that the first dollar spent on food gives exactly twice as much utility as either the sixth dollar spent on food or the second dollar spent on tobacco. The validity of such precise comparisons is, of course, questionable. We will find that later economists substituted ordinal utility for cardinal utility in developing their theories of rational consumer choice.

Menger drew an interesting conclusion from his table. Suppose an individual could afford only 7 units of food. That individual would then satisfy only those food wants that ranged in importance from 10 to 4 units of marginal utility. The other food wants, ranging in importance from 3 to 1, would remain unfulfilled. What would be the usefulness of the 7 units of food to this person? Jevons would add the marginal utilities of each unit from the first through seventh to obtain an answer of 49 (10 + 9 + 8 + 7 + 6 + 5 + 4). Menger's answer, however, would be 28 (4 × 7), the marginal utility of the last unit times the number of units. Why? Menger answered that all units are alike; thus each has the same utility as the marginal unit. If a person had only 1 unit of food per day, his or her state of near starvation would attribute high utility to that unit. But if the person had 7 units, no single unit of food would give her or him more satisfaction than would the marginal unit.

Menger thereby equated exchange value with *total* utility, unlike Jevons, who equated exchange value with marginal utility. Jevons would have said that in column I of Table 13-1, 10 units of food have greater total utility than 5 units, but the 10th unit has a smaller marginal utility than the 5th unit. Similarly, a large wheat crop offers more total utility than a small wheat crop, even if the larger one sells for less money. According to Menger, on the other hand, 5 units of food offer more satisfaction for the individual (6 × 5 = 30) than do 10 units (1 × 10 = 10). Thus, Menger would say that a small wheat crop may be more satisfying to consumers than a large one. This would be the case where the smaller one sells for more money than the larger one, because the marginal utility of the larger crop is so low. Of the two formulations, contemporary economists generally accept Jevons's perspective on this matter.

The measure of value, said Menger, is entirely subjective. Therefore, a commodity can have great value to one individual, little value to another, and no value at all to a third, depending on the differences in the preferences of the three individuals and the amounts of income available to each. Thus, not only the nature of value but the measure of value are subjective. Value has nothing to do with cost of production:

> The value an economizing individual attributes to a good is equal to the importance of the particular satisfaction that depends on his command of the good. There is no necessary and direct connection between the value of a good and whether, or in what quantities, labor and other goods of higher order were applied to its production. A non-economic good (a quantity of timber in a virgin forest, for example) does not attain value for men if large quantities of labor or other economic goods were applied to its production. Whether a diamond was found accidentally or was obtained from a diamond pit with the employment of a thousand days of labor is completely irrelevant for its value. In general, no one in practical life asks for the history of the origin of a good in estimating its value, but considers solely the services that the good will render him and which he would have to forgo if he did not have it at his command. Goods on which much labor has been expended often have no value, while others, on which little or no labor was expended, have a very high value. Goods on which much labor was expended and others on which little or no labor was expended are often of equal value to economizing men. The quantities of labor or of other means of production applied to its production cannot, therefore, be the determining factor in the value of the good.[6]

The basis of exchange value, said Menger, is the difference in relative subjective valuations of the same goods by different individuals. He denied Smith's dictum that exchange value is due to the propensity to truck, barter, and exchange one thing for another, that trading is an end in itself because it is pleasurable. Menger argued instead that trading is undertaken to increase the satisfactions enjoyed by the parties to the exchange. Trade increases the total utility of both traders. "The principle which leads men to exchange is the same principle that guides them in their economic activity as a whole; it is the endeavor to ensure the fullest possible satisfaction of their needs."

The Theory of Imputation

Menger originated the idea of imputation in pricing factors of production. The marginalists emphasized the importance of consumer demand, especially in its subjective psychological aspects, in determining price. The concepts of marginal and total utility refer to consumer wants; therefore, they apply only to consumer goods

---

[6] Carl Menger, *Principles of Economics,* trans. and ed. James Dingwall and Bert F. Hoselitz (Glencoe, IL: Free Press, 1950), 146–147. (Orig. pub. 1871.) Reprinted by permission of the Institute for Humane Studies and the New York University Press.

and services. What governs the prices of "higher order" goods used in production, such as machinery, raw materials, land, and so forth? Menger, in his theory of imputation, held that such goods also yield satisfactions to consumers, though only indirectly, by helping to produce things that do satisfy consumer wants directly. The consumers' marginal utility for a piece of iron is governed by the marginal utility of the final product that is made from that iron, say, a thimble; the iron has usefulness *imputed* to it by the usefulness of the thimble. The principle of marginal utility is thereby extended to the whole area of production and distribution. The rent received by landowners, for example, is governed by the utility of the products grown on that land. The factors, or agents, of production are assigned use values that govern their exchange values. The present value of the means of production is equal to the prospective value (based on marginal utility) of the consumer goods they will produce, with two deductions: a margin subtracted "for the value of the services of capital" (interest) and a reward for entrepreneurial activity (profit).

The doctrine of imputation was an attack on the labor and real-cost theories of value. Menger said that it is a most fundamental error to argue that goods attain value *for us* because goods that have value *to us* were employed in their production. This false doctrine, he said, cannot explain the value of the services of land, the value of labor services, or the value of the services of capital. On the contrary, the value of goods used in production must, without exception, be determined by the prospective value of the consumer goods they help produce. Menger denied that the price of common labor is determined by the cost of minimum subsistence for the laborer and his family. The prices of labor services, like the prices of all other goods, are governed by their value. And their values are governed "by the magnitude of importance of the satisfactions that would have to remain unsatisfied if we were unable to command the labor services."

Conclusions

Menger's contributions to microeconomic theory are impressive. His writings are filled with numerous insights in addition to those we have discussed. One example is his discussion of monopoly, which characteristically suggested several important concepts that others later developed more fully:

> The monopolist is not completely unrestricted in influencing the course of economic events. As we have seen, if the monopolist wishes to sell a particular quantity of the monopolized good, he cannot fix the price at will. And if he fixes the price, he cannot, at the same time determine the quantity that will be sold at the price he has set. . . . But what does give him an exceptional position in economic life is the fact that he has, in any given instance, a choice between determining the quantity of a monopolized good to be traded or its price. He makes this choice by himself and without regard to other economizing individuals, considering only his economic advantage. . . .
>
> It would be entirely erroneous to assume that the price of a monopolized good always, or even usually, rises and falls in an exactly inverse proportion to the quantities marketed by the monopolist, or that a similar proportionality exists between the prices set by the monopolist and the quantity of the monopolized good that can be sold. If, for example, the monopolist brings 2,000 instead of 1,000 units of the

> monopolized good to market, the price of one unit will not necessarily fall from six florin, for example, to three florin. On the contrary, depending upon the economic situation, it may in one case fall only to five florin, for example, but in another to as little as two florin.[7]

This quotation indicates that Menger had a good understanding of the ideas of downward sloping market demand curves and differing elasticities of demand.

Our praise of Menger is not to suggest that his economic analysis was free of serious omissions or inaccuracies. For example, he did not adequately consider the role of rising marginal costs of production in helping to establish the relative values of commodities. Like Jevons, he seemed so intent on disproving the labor theory that he erred in a way similar to those he criticized. There can be no doubt, however, that he sufficiently advanced economic analysis to ensure his lasting place of honor in the history of economic thought.

FRIEDRICH VON WIESER

Friedrich von Wieser (1851–1926), a second member of the so-called Austrian trio, was born in Vienna into a distinguished aristocratic family whose sons usually entered the public service. He studied law at the University of Vienna, and after graduation he read Menger's book on economics. The ideas contained therein both captivated him and inspired him to study economics in German universities. Eventually he was appointed, with Menger's help, to a professorship of economics at the German University of Prague. He later taught at the University of Vienna, and he also held high posts in the Austrian government, serving at one time as minister of commerce. It was he who introduced the term *marginal utility* to the economic lexicon, although Dupuit, Jevons, and Menger had developed the concept before him.

Exchange Value versus Natural Value

Friedrich von Wieser, true to the marginalist doctrine, said that there is no "objective" exchange value, because "its roots are bedded in the subjective estimates of individuals, grouped to determine the result." We might well ask if the price offer at the margin really reflects the marginal utility for a good: A well-fed millionaire offers $20 for a steak dinner for which a starving beggar will not pay more than $1. But which of these two people associates the greater marginal utility with the dinner? Friedrich von Wieser was fully aware of this kind of problem.

> In order, however, properly to appraise the service of exchange value in economic life, it must be remembered that it does not contain exactly the same elements as does value in use in the self-contained economy. The latter simply depends upon utility; the former is besides dependent upon purchasing power. . . . Value in use measures utility; exchange value measures a combination of utility and purchasing power.[8]

[7] Menger, *Principles,* 211–213.

[8] Friedrich von Wieser, *Natural Value,* trans. Christian A. Malloch (London: Macmillan, 1893), 57. (Orig. pub. 1889.)

Therefore, said von Wieser, diamonds and gold are exceptionally high priced because they are luxuries, valued and paid for according to the purchasing power of the richest classes. Coarser foodstuffs and iron are low in price because they are common goods, whose prices depend primarily on the purchasing power and the valuation of the poor.

> Production is ordered not only according to simple want, but also according to wealth. Instead of things which would have the greatest utility, those things are produced for which the most will be paid. The greater the differences in wealth, the more striking will be the anomalies of production. It will furnish luxuries for the wanton and glutton, while it is deaf to the wants of the miserable and the poor. It is therefore the distribution of wealth which decides how production is set to work, and induces consumption of the most uneconomic kind.[9]

Von Wieser then introduced the concept of *natural value* as the sum of the marginal utilities of all goods obtained.

> In natural value goods are estimated simply according to their marginal utility; in exchange value, according to a combination of marginal utility and purchasing power. In the former, luxuries are estimated far lower, and necessaries, comparatively, much higher than in the latter. Exchange value, even when considered as perfect, is, if we may so call it, a caricature of natural value; it disturbs its economic symmetry, magnifying the small and reducing the great.[10]

From this distinction between natural and exchange value, von Wieser drew a conclusion that was more typically Germanic than marginalist: There is room for limited government intervention in the economy whenever the two types of value diverge significantly.

> People look for something better from government. This does not, however, in the least involve that the form of undertaking for profit be entirely rejected. It may be retained, but, with the endeavour to obtain the highest business return, must be conjoined, in some way or other, the endeavour to serve the interests of the public. In particular, where any considerable want is concerned while the power to pay is wanting, the service must be undertaken at limited prices,—that is to say, valuation according to exchange value must be replaced by valuation according to natural value. Thus emerges the "public enterprise."[11]

Friedrich von Wieser held that utility of each unit of the same type of goods equals the marginal utility of the last unit, because any one unit can be considered the marginal unit. In situations in which wants remain the same and supply increases, the marginal utility must fall; this is von Wieser's law of supply. His law of demand is shown when wants increase and supply remains the same, thereby increasing the marginal utility. Friedrich von Wieser agreed with Menger that the total value of a good is its marginal utility times the number of units available. This produces the

[9] von Wieser, *Value,* 58.

[10] von Wieser, *Value,* 62.

[11] von Wieser, *Value,* 225.

"paradox of value." Each additional quantity of goods brings with it a diminished increment of value. Value, and therefore utility, is zero when we have no goods or when goods become superabundant. At some point, marginal utility times the units of goods gives a declining total value. Although von Wieser did not so state it, this occurs where demand becomes inelastic. Do we therefore find a larger supply of goods less useful than a smaller supply where the demand is inelastic, because it will sell for a smaller sum of money? Should we convert superfluity into want, and want into a greater want, in order to create and increase value? "No," von Wieser replied. The highest principle of all economy is total utility (natural value). Where total value and total utility conflict, utility must conquer. He was confident, however, that human economies move almost entirely in the range where increasing supplies of goods increase both total value and total utility; that is, demands are elastic. "In most things we are so far from having a superfluity that almost every multiplication of goods shows a corresponding increase in total value," and "value is the form in which utility is calculated." Free competition prevents entrepreneurs from restricting output to raise prices significantly. If monopolies restrict output in order to raise prices, then government must take over, "but such cases are too few to call for socialist organization of society." The free economic order of society need only be "supplemented by suitable interference on the part of governments." He continued with the following:

> The assumptions of the simple economy are so framed as to demand the domination of the general interest. A paradox that arises in the opposition between personal power and social interest is therefore excluded. Yet even in the simple economy there are such glaring cases of this sort that the semblance of paradox is apt to arise. This mystery is most easily solved if we presuppose the extreme case in which a method of production makes possible an increase of stocks to the point of superabundance. Let us assume, for example, that by driving an artesian well or opening up a copious mountain spring it is possible to provide a town with pure water in superabundant quantities. If the principle of marginal utility were strictly adhered to, such an enterprise would never be started; a superabundant stock of free goods has a marginal utility of zero. But will such a consideration deter the public from incurring expenses for such an enterprise? Surely not. The undertaking guarantees the greatest possible benefit. The public will realize this benefit irrespective of the fact that the utility which results cannot be computed. It will be seen that the computation according to marginal utility does not simplify matters in this case, as it usually does in others. Rather it leads one astray. Hence the more complicated computation of total benefit will be resorted to.
>
> This is precisely the state of affairs where we examine all other cases of apparent paradox. Whenever the increase in supply, computed at the marginal utility, leads to a lower numerical expression [of total value], the reckoning by marginal utility ceases to simplify and the plan of production must be drafted on the basis of total utility.
>
> Marginal utility may be used as a basis for calculations where the larger stock still gives a larger product. It is inapplicable when the product is smaller. Cases of the first kind are altogether too general; the latter are exceptional.[12]

[12] Friedrich von Wieser, *Social Economics,* trans. A. Ford Hinrichs (New York: Adelphi, 1927), 128. (Orig. pub. 1914.)

That is, private enterprise serves society only when the demand for each firm's output is elastic. And demand will always be elastic under competitive conditions.

Opportunity Costs

Von Wieser is famous for the doctrine that came to be called the *opportunity-cost principle,* or the *alternative-cost concept.* This idea turned cost of production into a subjective psychological cost. The entrepreneur who produces something for a market gives up the opportunity to produce and sell alternative commodities:

> Whenever the business man speaks of incurring costs, he has in mind the quantity of productive means required to achieve a certain end; but the associated idea of a sacrifice which his efforts demand is also aroused. In what does this sacrifice consist? What, for example, is the cost to the producer of devoting certain quantities of iron from his supply to the manufacture of some specific product? The sacrifice consists in the exclusion or limitation of possibilities by which other products might have been turned out, had the material not been devoted to one particular product. Our definition in an earlier connection made clear that cost-productive-means are productive agents which are widely scattered and have manifold uses. As such they promise a profitable yield in many directions. But the realization of one of these necessarily involves a loss of all the others. It is this sacrifice that is predicated in the concept of costs: the costs of production or the quantities of cost-productive-means required for a given product and thus withheld from other uses. . . . The business man, comparing the profits of one product with its costs, compares two masses of utility.[13]

Economists agree that the opportunity-cost principle has wide applicability in economic affairs. Producing more automobiles may mean fewer houses. Building a school may mean giving up a hospital or giving up certain consumer or investment goods. Buying a personal computer may mean sacrificing a family vacation. Gaining more hours of leisure may mean smaller earnings from work. Opportunity costs are involved also when an entrepreneur considers his or her implicit wage, interest, and rent costs, because those factors could be earned in other employment. This principle therefore helps illuminate the basic economizing problems facing individuals, enterprises, and nations. Nevertheless, it is not at all clear that this idea explains anything *fundamental* about exchange value. It suggests that the value of a commodity is the value of the commodities forgone, but what determined the value of those alternative goods?

Refer to 13-2 PAST AS PROLOGUE

EUGEN VON BÖHM-BAWERK

Eugen von Böhm-Bawerk (1851–1914) was the third member of the early Austrian triumvirate (along with Menger and von Wieser). He was a professor of political economy at the University of Vienna and served in the Austrian government as minister of finance. He was married to von Wieser's sister.

[13] von Wieser, *Economics,* 99–100.

13-2 PAST AS PROLOGUE

Franklin and Bastiat on Opportunity Cost

Friedrich von Wieser is credited with articulating the concept of *opportunity cost*, but the idea is expressed earlier in the writings of both Benjamin Franklin (1706–1790) and Frédéric Bastiat (1801–1850). Franklin, the well-known American inventor and statesman, recognized opportunity costs in the use of both time and money.

> Remember, that *time* is money. He that can earn ten shillings a day by his labour, and goes abroad, or sits idle, one half of the day, though he spends but sixpence during his diversion or idleness, ought not to reckon *that* the only expense; he has really spent, or rather thrown away, five shillings besides.
>
> Remember, that *credit* is money. If a man lets his money lie in my hands after it is due, he gives me the interest, or so much as I can make of it during that time. This amounts to a considerable sum where a man has good and large credit, and makes good use of it.*

Bastiat was a French economist and journalist, well-known for his witty and engaging writing style. His notion of opportunity cost appears most prominently in his aptly named essay, *That Which Is Seen and That Which Is Not Seen,* in which he presents many examples of the unobserved (opportunity) costs that occur in both private and public economic activity. Perhaps the most famous of these examples is Bastiat's *Parable of the Broken Window,* in which he refutes the argument that destructive events are beneficial to the economy because of the commerce they create.

> Have you ever been witness to the fury of that solid citizen, James Goodfellow, when his incorrigible son has happened to break a pane of glass? If you have been present at this spectacle, certainly you must also have observed that the onlookers, even if there

Among von Böhm-Bawerk's contributions to economic analysis one stands out: his analysis of the element of time—not time in relation to systematic changes in the economy or in relation to economic growth, but time as a significant element in the normal course of economic affairs, influencing all values, prices, and incomes.

Theory of Interest

Eugen von Böhm-Bawerk's incorporation of time into economic analysis can clearly be seen in his famous *agio* (premium) theory of interest. Interest arises for three reasons, of which the first two are subjective:

are as many as thirty of them, seem with one accord to offer the unfortunate owner the selfsame consolation—"It's an ill wind that blows nobody some good. Everybody has to make a living. What would become of the glaziers if no one ever broke a window?"

Now, this formula of condolence contains a whole theory that it is a good idea for us to expose, *flagrante delicto,* in this very simple case, since it is exactly the same as that which, unfortunately, underlies most of our economic institutions.

Suppose that it will cost six francs to repair the damage. If you mean that the accident gives six francs' worth of encouragement to the aforesaid industry, I agree. I do not contest it in any way; your reasoning is correct. The glazier will come, do his job, receive six francs, congratulate himself, and bless in his heart the careless child. *That is what is seen.*

But if, by way of deduction, you conclude, as happens only too often, that it is good to break windows, that it helps to circulate money, that it results in encouraging industry in general, I am obliged to cry out: That will never do! Your theory stops at *what is seen.* It does not take account of *what is not seen.*

It is not seen that, since our citizen has spent six francs for one thing, he will not be able to spend them for another. *It is not seen* that if he had not had a windowpane to replace, he would have replaced, for example, his worn-out shoes, or added another book to his library. In brief, he would have put his six francs to some use or other for which he will not now have them.†

Bastiat wrote similar pieces regarding taxes, various forms of public spending, and free trade. To learn about Bastiat and Franklin's many other economic insights, visit the web site that accompanies the text.

---

*Benjamin Franklin, "Advice to a Young Tradesman," in *The Writings of Benjamin Franklin,* ed. Albert Henry Smith (New York: The Macmillan Company, 1907), 370 ("Advice" orig. pub. 1748.)

†Frederic Bastiat, "That Which Is Seen and That Which Is Not Seen," in *Selected Essays on Political Economy,* trans. by Seymour Cain, ed. George Huszar (Princeton: Van Nostrand, 1964), 2–3. (Orig. pub. 1850.)

- Present orientation. Goods are appreciated more highly in the present than in the future. "We systematically underestimate future wants, and the goods which are to satisfy them." This is a failure of perspective, the only irrationality that von Böhm-Bawerk introduced into his "economic man." People underestimate future needs because they have defective imaginations, because they have limited willpower and cannot resist present extravagance even when they are aware of future needs, and because they know that life is short and uncertain and therefore wish to enjoy life today rather than sacrifice for the future.
- Expectation of rising wealth. The second basis for interest, also subjective, derives from the idea that we are prepared to borrow and pay interest for

present rather than future consumption because we expect to have greater wealth in the future. Note that this basis for interest, like the first, focuses on consumption.

- Roundabout production. The third basis for interest involves production. The process of production is lengthened, or becomes more roundabout, when more and more capital goods are produced and used to make final products. For example, to fish more successfully one builds a boat; this lengthens the process of production, and the physical product—the number of fish caught—is greater than if all the time were spent fishing instead of building the craft. Until von Böhm-Bawerk's time, the length of the production period was regarded as a technological datum and therefore constant. Eugen von Böhm-Bawerk turned it into a variable.

From these three concepts followed the explanation of interest. It is an *agio*, or premium, placed on the value and price of present consumer goods. Workers and landowners receive the present value of their productive services. The increments in value, which are due to the more highly productive methods made possible by the passage of time, remain in the hands of the entrepreneur. Interest flows from the entrepreneur to the capitalist (financier) who made funds available for roundabout, or capital-using, production. Therefore, workers and landowners do receive the value of the product of their services, but the value is discounted to the present time.

To summarize: Interest *can* be paid by the entrepreneur, because the more roundabout the process of production, the more productive and efficient it becomes. Interest *must* be paid because people prefer present to future consumption.

Other Views

Eugen von Böhm-Bawerk agreed with the other two leaders of the Austrian marginalist school that the total utility of a good is its marginal utility times the number of units. He also agreed with them that the value of the means of production depends on the value of the final goods produced, which in turn depends on the marginal utility of the final goods. The value of the final product is greater than the value of the services that produce it by the amount of interest over the period of time that elapses.

Like the marginalists in general, von Böhm-Bawerk accepted Say's analysis that the economy normally tends toward full employment. He rebutted criticism of his belief that if all members of a community simultaneously save one-quarter of their incomes, production will remain unchanged:

> The fault of the reasoning [of my critic] is indeed not far to seek. It is that one of the premises, the one which asserts that a curtailment of "consumption for immediate enjoyment" must involve also a curtailment of production, is erroneous. The truth is that a curtailment of consumption involves, not a curtailment of production generally, but only, through the action of the law of supply and demand a curtailment in certain branches. . . . There will not, however, be a smaller production of goods generally, because the lessened output of goods ready for immediate consumption

may and will be offset by an increased production of "intermediate" or capital goods.[14]

Eugen von Böhm-Bawerk then quoted his critic as saying that the production of capital goods is called forth and guided only by the demand for consumer goods; if the demand for consumer goods is reduced by one quarter, why will more capital goods than formerly be demanded and produced? This is von Böhm-Bawerk's reply:

> The man who saves curtails his demands for present consumption goods but by no means his desire for pleasure-affording goods generally. This is a proposition which, under a slightly different title, has already been repeatedly and, I believe, conclusively discussed in our science both by the older writers and in contemporary literature. Economists are to-day completely agreed, I think, that the "abstinence" connected with saving is no true abstinence, that is, no final renunciation of pleasure-affording goods, but . . . a mere "waiting." The person who saves is not willing to hand over his savings without return, but requires that they be given back at some future time, usually indeed with interest, either to himself or to his heirs. Through saving not a single particle of the demand for goods is extinguished outright, but, as J. B. Say showed in a masterly way more than one hundred years ago . . . , the demand for goods, the wish for means of enjoyment is, under whatever circumstances men are found, insatiable. A person may have enough or even too much of a particular kind of goods at a particular time, but not of goods in general nor for all time. This doctrine applies particularly to saving. For the principal motive of those who save is precisely to provide for their own futures or for the futures of their heirs. This means nothing else than that they wish to secure and make certain their command over the means to the satisfaction of their future needs, that is over consumption of goods at a future time. In other words, those who save curtail their demand for consumption goods in the present merely to increase proportionately their demand for consumption goods in the future.[15]

Eugen von Böhm-Bawerk's emphasis on the productivity of capital, his defense of interest, and his support of Say's law of markets were probably partly a reaction to the growing influence of Marxism in his time. In 1896 he produced a famous criticism of Marx, which was published in English translation as *Karl Marx and the Close of His System.*

Questions for Study and Discussion

1. Briefly identify and state the significance of each of the following to the history of economic thought: Jevons, final degree of utility, equimarginal rule, sunspot theory of the business cycle, index numbers, Menger, Austrian school, imputation, von Wieser, opportunity-cost principle, von Böhm-Bawerk, and roundabout production.
2. Answer questions a–d using the data provided in the following table. Assume that the consumer has $65 to spend.

[14] Eugen von Böhm-Bawerk, "The Function of Saving," in *Annals of the American Academy of Political and Social Science,* publication no. 304 (May 1901): 62.

[15] von Böhm-Bawerk, "Saving," 62–64.

	PRODUCT X (PRICE = $5)		PRODUCT Y (PRICE = $10)	
Units of Product	MUx	MUx/Px	MUy	MUy/Py
1st	50		120	
2nd	45		110	
3rd	40		100	
4th	35		90	
5th	30		80	

a) Assuming *X* and *Y* are independent goods, determine the respective quantities of each that the person represented by these data will buy in order to maximize utility. Hint: It will be helpful to fill in the columns labeled MU_x/P_x and MU_y/P_y.
b) What would be this person's total utility according to Jevons? According to Menger? Explain the difference.
c) Suppose that the price of *X* rises to $10. How will this consumer respond?
d) Distinguish between cardinal and ordinal utility. Which of the two is assumed in this table?

3. Discuss the statement: Jevons and Menger resolved Smith's water-diamond paradox in one sense, but one could argue that they didn't fully resolve it because of their inadequate attention to the notion of supply.
4. Which of the major tenets of the marginalist school (listed in Chapter 12) apply to Jevons? To Menger?
5. What was Jevons's view on gambling? Relate the Friedman-Savage hypothesis (Past as Prologue 13-1) to Jevons's analysis. Friedman and Savage also used their analysis to explain why people with incomes at or near the point where their falling marginal utility of money begins to rise may choose to gamble and buy fairly priced insurance against large income losses. Explain the seeming paradox of gambling and buying insurance at the same time.
6. Explain how Menger's theory of factor imputation is consistent with the Austrian view that utility, not input cost, is the source of value.
7. According to Frank Knight, writing in 1921, an increase in hourly pay will lower a person's marginal utility of income from any given amount of production (or amount of work). Show this outcome on Figure 13-2. How will this affect the optimal amount of work? Can you think of reasons an increase in wages might have an effect opposite to this one on a person's optimal amount of work? Hint: Review Past as Prologue 2-1.
8. What does von Wieser mean when he says "exchange value measures a combination of utility and purchasing power"? How does natural value differ from exchange value? Should society be interested in maximizing exchange value or total utility?
9. What major contribution of von Wieser typically is discussed in the first week of a principles of economics course? How does this idea relate to the definition of economics itself?

10. How would Bastiat respond to the often-heard assertion that "war is good for the economy"?
11. On what three bases did von Böhm-Bawerk build his theory of interest? In what respect does his theory justify interest as an "earned" return to the lender?

Selected Readings

Books

Blaug, Mark, ed. *Carl Menger.* Brookfield, VT: Edward Elgar, 1992.

———, ed. *Eugen von Böhm-Bawerk and Friedrich von Wieser.* Brookfield, VT: Edward Elgar, 1992.

Caldwell, Bruce J., ed. *Carl Menger and His Legacy in Economics.* Durham, NC: Duke University Press, 1990.

Howey, Richard S. *The Rise of the Marginal Utility School, 1870–1889.* New York: Columbia University Press, 1989.

Jevons, William Stanley. *The Theory of Political Economy.* 3rd ed. London: Macmillan, 1888. (Orig. pub. 1871.)

Menger, Carl. *Principles of Economics.* Translated and edited by James Dingwall and Bert F. Hoselitz. Glencoe, IL: Free Press, 1950. (Orig. pub. 1871.)

Peart, Sandra J. *The Economics of W. S. Jevons.* London: Routledge, 1996.

Schabas, Margaret. *A World Ruled by Number: William Stanley Jevons and the Rise of Mathematical Economics.* Princeton, NJ: Princeton University Press, 1990.

Stigler, George J. *Production and Distribution Theories.* New York: Macmillan, 1941.

von Böhm-Bawerk, Eugen. *The Positive Theory of Capital.* Translated by William Smart. London: Macmillan, 1891(Orig. pub. 1888.)

von Wieser, Friedrich. *Natural Value.* Translated by Christian A. Malloch. London: Macmillan, 1893. (Orig. pub. 1889.)

Journal Articles

Alter, Max. "Carl Menger and *Homo Oeconomicus:* Some Thoughts on Austrian Theory and Methodology," *Journal of Economic Issues* 16 (March 1982): 149–160.

Bostaph, Samuel, and Yeung-Nan Shieh. "Jevons's Demand Curve," *History of Political Economy* 19 (Spring 1987): 107–126.

History of Political Economy 4 (Fall 1972). This entire issue is devoted to articles on the "marginal revolution" in economics.

Jaffé, William. "Menger, Jevons, and Walras Dehomogenized," *Economic Inquiry* 14 (December 1976): 511–524.

Jolink, Albert, and Jan Van Daal. "Gossen's Laws," *History of Political Economy* 30 (Spring 1998): 43–50.

Stigler, George. "The Development of Utility Theory. I," *Journal of Political Economy* 58 (August 1950): 307–327.

Symposium on Jevons and Menger (paper by Sandra J. Peart and comments by Robert Hébert, F. V. Comim, and Philippe Fontaine). *American Journal of Economics and Sociology* 57 (July 1998): 307–344.

White, Michael V. "Why Are There No Supply and Demand Curves in Jevons?" *History of Political Economy* 21 (Fall 1989): 425–456.

Chapter 14

The Marginalist School—Edgeworth and Clark

Several "second generation" marginalists developed ideas that expanded and advanced the microeconomic theories discussed in the previous two chapters. In this chapter we turn our attention to two such individuals: Francis Edgeworth and John Bates Clark.

FRANCIS Y. EDGEWORTH

Francis Y. Edgeworth (1845–1926) was born in Ireland, attended Trinity College in Dublin, and studied at Oxford University. He later became the Tooke Professor of Political Economy at Oxford, where he remained throughout his career. He was one of the founders of the Royal Economic Society, was editor of the *Economic Journal* for thirty-five years, served a term as president of the Statistical Society, and was a fellow of the British Academy. His contributions to economics are found in his *Mathematical Psychics,* written in 1881, and in numerous articles collected in 1925 under the title *Papers Relating to Political Economy.*

Edgeworth accepted Bentham's notion that every person is a "pleasure machine." Consumers, he said, seek to maximize the utility they can obtain from their limited income, workers seek to maximize the net gain from their labor, and entrepreneurs seek to maximize their profits by combining resources in ways that will minimize the costs of any particular level of output. According to Edgeworth, the most fruitful tool for analyzing this economic behavior is differential calculus. In supporting the mathematical approach, Edgeworth contrasted the precision of mathematical economics to the "zigzag windings of the flowery path of literature."

In general, then, one of Edgeworth's contributions to modern economics was his popularization of the use of mathematics within the discipline. Critics of this approach—for example, the Austrians and institutionalists—countered that a "zigzag path" that leads to new knowledge about economic phenomena or economic problems is clearly preferable to a "precise path" that leads only to endless refinement of what is already known. But this methodological debate aside, the importance of mathematics in formulating and testing theories in contemporary economics can hardly be questioned, and Edgeworth joins Cournot as one of the early pioneers in this area.

Of Edgeworth's various contributions to the content of economic thought, three in particular stand out. First, he originated the idea of an indifference curve, the importance of which will become increasingly evident as we progress through

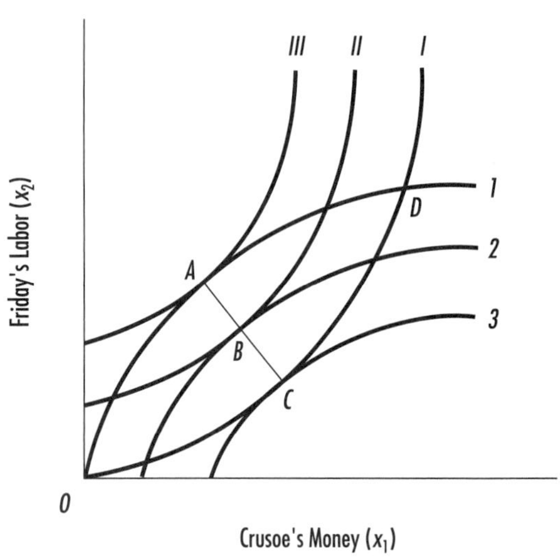

Figure 14-1 Edgeworth's Contract Curve
Edgeworth superimposed Crusoe's indifference map (*I, II,* and *III*) on Friday's map (*1, 2,* and *3*) and noted the points of tangency. The final terms of trade between the two will lie somewhere along the contract curve *ABC,* which traces out the loci of these tangency points. At all points off the contract curve (for example, *D*), one of the traders can move to a higher indifference curve without pushing the other trader to a lower one.

the history of economic thought. Second, he was one of the first economists to show the indeterminacy that we now generally associate with the pricing behavior of oligopolists. Finally, he elucidated the difference between average and marginal product, thus aiding in the development of the modern short-run production function and its numerous applications.

Indifference Curves and Exchange

In his *Mathematical Psychics,* Edgeworth introduced the notion of "curves of indifference," which he said show the various combinations of two items that will yield an equal level of utility to an individual. But unlike the modern representation that we will discuss in later chapters, Edgeworth drew his indifference curves essentially as shown in Figure 14-1. He used this graph to analyze an isolated exchange between two sole possessors of products, in this case Robinson Crusoe and his right-hand man Friday. Friday has labor, x_2, whereas Crusoe has money, x_1. Friday, of course, desires some of Crusoe's money, and Crusoe desires to have the use of some of Friday's labor.

To understand this somewhat unusual representation of indifference curves, it first will be useful to examine each set of indifference curves separately. The indifference curves *1, 2,* and *3* in the graph are lines showing equal levels of utility *for Friday,* much like a contour map shows lines of equal elevation. For example, all of the combinations of labor and money associated with points along curve *1* yield identical levels of utility to Friday. Curve *2*, however, yields greater total utility to Friday than curve *1*, and curve *3* more than *2*. This could be demonstrated by drawing a horizontal arrow through the curves and noting that its intersection with each successive curve denotes a larger amount of Crusoe's money for a specific amount of Friday's labor. If we think in terms of a map, we can say that Friday will prefer to be on indifference curves farther to the *east*. Although the graph shows only three of Friday's indifference curves, other such curves could be drawn on the indifference surface.

Curves *I*, *II*, and *III* represent Crusoe's indifference map. If we drew a vertical arrow through these curves, we would discover that those to the *north* yield higher levels of total utility to Crusoe. Each successive curve in this direction implies that Crusoe can obtain a larger amount of Friday's labor at that particular amount of Crusoe's money.

By overlaying Crusoe's indifference map on Friday's map, Edgeworth obtained a *contract curve*, which is the loci of tangency points of the two sets of indifference curves.[1] He concluded that the price of Friday's labor in terms of Crusoe's money is indeterminate, that it is subject to bargaining, but that it will lie somewhere along line *ABC*.[2] Why is this so? Edgeworth's answer is that at all points other than those on the line *ABC*, either Friday or Crusoe can add to his utility *without lessening the utility gained by the other party*. This can be seen by noting point *D* on Crusoe's indifference curve *I* and Friday's indifference curve *1*. Crusoe can attain curve *III*, rather than *I*, at *A* while still leaving Friday on his indifference curve *1*. Or looked at from Friday's perspective, Friday can achieve the higher utility associated with his indifference curve *3* at *C* without reducing Crusoe's utility—Crusoe remains on curve *I*. Hence the self-interests of the two traders will push them to the contract curve. Friday, of course, would prefer *C* on this curve because it would place him on indifference curve *3*, but Crusoe would prefer *A* because that would provide him more utility than at either points *B* or *C* (indifference curve *III* as opposed to *II* or *I*). To repeat: The final contract between the two traders in this case is indeterminate; any point on the contract curve is a possible point of equilibrium, and the final outcome will occur through bargaining.

Does this same indeterminacy occur under conditions of perfect competition? Edgeworth correctly noted that this is not the case; under such conditions all the parties to trade must accept the prices of goods and labor determined in the market. But in the bilateral monopoly situation—a circumstance where there are single sellers on each side of a transaction—the price is indeterminate.

The Italian economist Vilfredo Pareto (1848–1923), who is discussed in Chapter 20, reconstructed Edgeworth's indifference curves, positioning them in their modern form.[3] He also sought to derive them without resort to Edgeworth's implicit assumption of measurable utility. Pareto assumed that each of the two bilateral monopolists gained utility from the two goods being transacted, say, wheat

[1] Edgeworth drew only a single indifference curve for each individual but stated that a whole series of such curves exists.

[2] Jevons had wrongly contended that a determinate solution exists.

[3] A glance ahead to Figure 18-3 may be useful at this point if you are unfamiliar with the contemporary representation of indifference curves.

and linen, the quantities of which were shown on the two axes. In essence he constructed two separate graphs, one for each trading partner, in which the indifference curves for the two goods were convex to the origin. Then he repositioned one of the diagrams to overlay it on top of the other to form a box (one origin now being to the northeast). This diagram typically can be found in intermediate microeconomics textbooks and quite appropriately is referred to as the *Edgeworth box.* It simply is more sophisticated than Edgeworth's version in Figure 14-1. Like Edgeworth's representation, the Edgeworth box depicts the utility gains from exchange and the contract curve for two sole traders of two goods.

It will be discovered in Chapter 18 in our discussion of John Hicks that indifference curve analysis forms the basis for sophisticated theories of consumer choice and product demand. Thus Edgeworth's seemingly minor contribution in this regard assumed greater significance as the history of economic thought unfolded.

Duopoly Theory

Edgeworth's idea of indeterminacy is also present in his theory of duopoly. Recall from our previous discussion that Cournot theorized that, given certain restrictive assumptions, duopolists in the sale of a mineral water would each charge the same price and each garner one-half of the total sales. In Cournot's theory, the maximum profit or reaction curves of the two parties would produce a determinate equilibrium price (see Figure 12-2). Edgeworth altered Cournot's assumptions in two ways. First, he assumed that the sellers of the mineral water each have a limited capacity to meet consumer demand. Stated differently, at a price of zero the quantity demanded is greater than the amount that either seller singularly can produce. Second, Edgeworth assumed that in the short run the two sellers can charge different prices for the mineral water.

Figure 14-2 shows the essence of Edgeworth's theory.[4] The price per unit of mineral water is measured on the vertical axis that is common to both sellers. The output of duopolist *1* is measured from *0* rightward on the horizontal axis, whereas the output of duopolist *2* is measured from *0* leftward. Curves D_1 and D_2 are the demand curves faced by duopolist *1* and *2*, respectively. The assumption underlying these curves is that in the long run the two firms will share the market equally. The marginal revenue curves shown as MR_1 and MR_2 are positioned according to the relationship between price and marginal revenue set forth by Cournot in his pure monopoly model (Figure 12-1). These curves are relevant only if each firm considers itself a monopolist. We will find that once price cutting begins, these firms become competitors who see their marginal revenue equaling their product price. As in Cournot's model, marginal costs in Figure 14-2 are assumed to be zero; that is, they correspond with the horizontal axis.

Edgeworth states that each of these two sellers seeks to maximize its profits by varying its price (output) while assuming that the other party's price (output) will remain at its current level.

[4] This discussion is based on Francis Y. Edgeworth, *Papers Relating to Political Economy,* vol. 1 (London: Macmillan, 1925), 111–142.

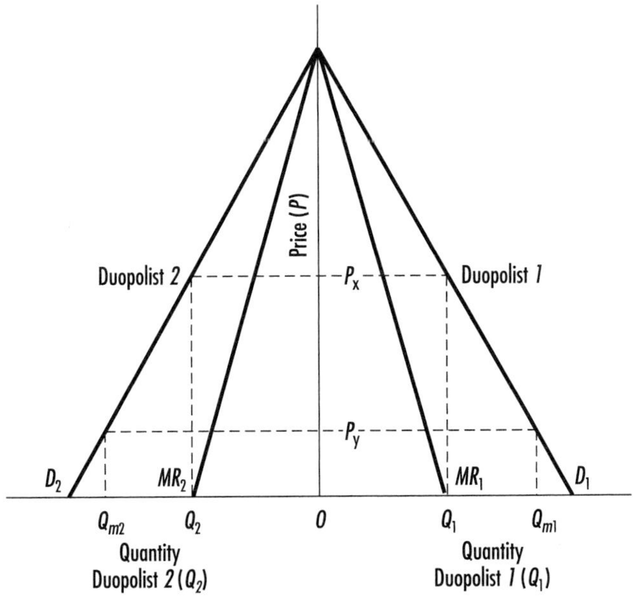

Figure 14-2 Edgeworth's Duopoly Model
In Edgeworth's duopoly theory, the price of the product is indeterminate. It could lie anywhere between P_x—the price that the duopolists would charge if they were separate monopolists—and P_y, the price that would enable them to produce at their maximum levels of output (assumed to be Q_{m1} and Q_{m2}). Furthermore, the price would likely gyrate between these two prices.

Suppose initially that duopolist *1* enters the market as a pure monopolist and therefore sets its price at P_x. Notice from the intersection of the marginal revenue curve MR_1 and the horizontal axis that at this price and output (Q_1) combination the condition for profit maximization is met: Marginal revenue equals marginal cost ($0 = 0$). Now suppose duopolist *2* enters the market. How will it respond? It could simply match duopolist *1*'s price and experience equal sales of Q_2. But seeing that duopolist *1* is charging P_x, and assuming that it will retain this price, duopolist *2* has an incentive to charge a price slightly below P_x, thereby taking business away from duopolist *1*. Stated technically, duopolist *2* sees that the marginal revenue of its extra units of output is no longer represented by MR_2 but is equal to the price that it charges. This price obviously exceeds the zero marginal cost of these units. Once this lower price (not shown) is set, however, duopolist *1*, believing that duopolist *2* will retain its price, observes that it can add to its profits by undercutting the price set by duopolist *2*. Price cutting continues in an attempt to secure additional sales and profit advantage until both duopolists are producing at their maximum levels of output (Q_{m1} and Q_{m2}). They therefore have no incentive to further reduce their prices. Notice that at these capacity levels of output, the price is P_y and that each firm is still making a profit. Price exceeds marginal cost for each seller, and each has total revenue ($P \times Q$) that exceeds its total cost (0).

Will the price therefore remain at P_y? According to Edgeworth, it will not! This somewhat surprising conclusion can best be understood by again focusing on the behavior of duopolist *1*. It will assume that duopolist *2* will retain the price-output combination P_y and Q_{m2}. Duopolist *1* consequently sees a way to increase its profits: reducing output below Q_{m1} and charging the corresponding higher price to the customers whom duopolist *2* cannot supply. That is, duopolist *1* sees it in its interest to behave as a monopolist in the portion of the market that remains. Its rise in price per unit will more than offset the loss of revenue on the reduced sales. Duopolist *2*, however, will note *1*'s higher price and follow suit, gladly giving up some sales to earn more total profit. This process will continue until P_x is reached, at which point one of the parties will again start a price war.

Conclusion? According to Edgeworth, no equilibrium price or output exists in situations where there are noncollusive duopolists. Any price between P_x and P_y in Figure 14-2 is possible, and the price may oscillate upward and downward.

Edgeworth's duopoly theory, like Cournot's, was later severely criticized. For example, Chamberlin pointed out that "in order for the price to descend, [the duopolist's] individual markets are completely merged into one, each drawing customers freely from the other by a slight reduction in price. But in order for it to rise again, their markets are completely separated [allowing each to have a portion of the buyers in isolation]."[5] Others criticized Edgeworth's unrealistic assumption that the duopolists fail to learn from the past reactions of their rivals and therefore do not anticipate their reactions in advance. Finally, the assumption of fixed capacity is unrealistic when viewed in the long run. Nevertheless, Edgeworth's contribution is of significance. It established the potential indeterminacy of pricing where mutual dependence is involved and stimulated further thinking on this important topic.[6]

Marginal versus Average Product

A final significant idea added by Edgeworth was his distinction between marginal and average product. The concept of a production function—the relationship between the various quantities of inputs and their corresponding output—was implied by Ricardo in his theory of rent. You may recall that Ricardo assumed the amount of land to be constant, added capital and labor, and observed diminishing returns. Also, von Thünen (Chapter 12) clearly had in mind a production function when he spoke of the marginal productivity of labor as it relates to agriculture. But a clear expression of the concept had to await Walras and Edgeworth. Of these two persons, it was Edgeworth who explicitly distinguished between the average and marginal products of a production function characterized by variable proportions of inputs.

To make his point, Edgeworth assumed that land was the fixed resource and that labor, together with tools, was the variable resource. He then constructed a table, the first two columns of which related various levels of the labor/tools input with

[5] Edward H. Chamberlin, *The Theory of Monopolistic Competition*, 7th ed. (Cambridge, MA: Harvard University Press, 1958), 40–41.

[6] In 1929, Howard Hotelling developed a theory of duopoly that challenged Edgeworth's view that instability of pricing and output levels is characteristic of duopoly. You can find out more in his "Stability in Competition," *Economic Journal* 39 (1929): 41–57.

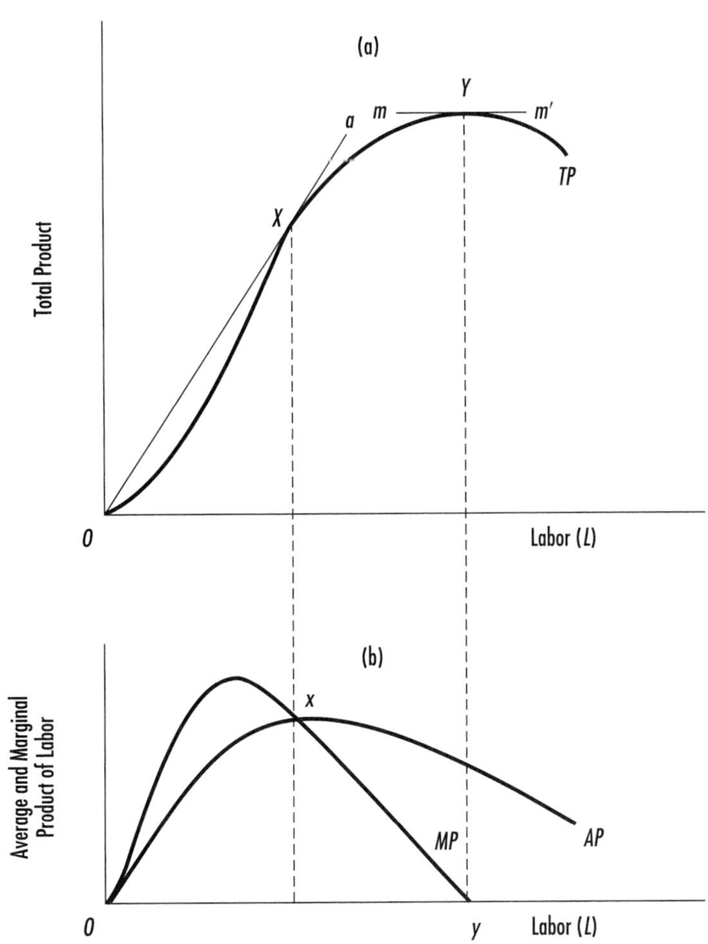

Figure 14-3 The Relationship between Total, Marginal, and Average Product
As shown in graph (a), as labor is added to a fixed amount of capital, total product first increases at an increasing rate, then at a diminishing rate, and finally declines. The marginal and average products of labor in graph (b) therefore rise for a time and then fall. When marginal product exceeds average product, average product rises; when marginal product is less than average product, average product falls.

the corresponding levels of total crops (total output or total product).[7] In a third column he then derived marginal product—the change in total product associated with each addition of the labor/tools input. In the fourth column he specified the average product, found by dividing total product by the labor/tool input. The values in the table showed the relationships between total, marginal, and average product.

Contemporary textbooks illustrate Edgeworth's distinctions graphically. Figure 14-3 shows the relationship between total, marginal, and average product

[7] This table is found in Edgeworth, *Political Economy,* 1: 68.

for a competitive firm operating in the short run. The underlying assumption here is that the production process entails only two inputs: the variable resource labor (*L*) and the fixed resource capital (*K*). Graph (a) in the diagram shows a short-run production function, and graph (b) shows the marginal and average products of labor that correspond with the total product curve shown in graph (a).

Marginal product (*MP*) is the change in total product associated with a change in the labor input. It can be found by using calculus or simply by drawing a straight line such as *mm′* tangent to the *TP* curve at any point and then determining the slope of the line. For example, note that the slope of *mm′* drawn tangent to *TP* at *Y* is zero, which is the value of the marginal product as shown at point *y* on *MP* in the lower graph. The other points on *MP* are found in a similar fashion. How then is the average product curve derived? Geometrically it can be found by drawing a straight line from the origin to any point on the total product curve and then finding the slope of the line drawn. One such line, O_a, is shown. Its slope (*TP/L*) is the average product (*x* on *AP*) associated with the labor input and total product represented by *X* on the total product curve.

Figure 14-3 thus helps us visualize Edgeworth's distinctions between total, marginal, and average product. Notice that when total product is rising at an increasing rate, marginal product is rising and is above the average product. Because *MP* > *AP*, average product is also rising. Whenever a number that is greater than the average is added to a total, the average must also rise. But once the total product rises at a decreasing rate, marginal product falls; that is, diminishing marginal returns occur. Eventually, marginal product falls below the average product, thus pulling the average down.

Refer to 14-1 PAST AS PROLOGUE

These relationships are of great importance in contemporary microeconomic theory. For example, they explain the shape of short-run cost curves for typical firms, are the basis for the marginal productivity theory of the demand for resources, and underlie the marginal productivity theory of income distribution. We discuss the first of these topics in Past as Prologue 14-1 and the other two topics in our discussion of John Bates Clark.

JOHN BATES CLARK

John Bates Clark (1847–1938) earned a worldwide reputation and represented America's great contribution to marginalist economics. He was born in Rhode Island, studied at Amherst and in Germany, and taught at Carleton, Smith, Amherst, Johns Hopkins, and Columbia. Thorstein Veblen (Chapter 19) was one of Clark's students at Carleton College, and his later fame was a source of great pride to Clark. The latter was undisturbed by the fact that much of Veblen's fame rested on criticisms of the kind of economic theory Clark had developed. In 1947 the American Economic Association initiated the coveted John Bates Clark Medal, awarded every other year to a promising young economist.

About 1880 Clark, quite independently, seemed to have thought out the concept of marginal utility and its influence on exchange value; apparently he had

14-1 PAST AS PROLOGUE

Jacob Viner's Cost Curves

Once economists established the production relationships shown in Figure 14-3, they began to explore the implications of the *TP*, *MP*, and *AP* curves for a firm's cost curves. In a significant 1931 article, Jacob Viner (1892–1970) illustrated the now-familiar short-run and long-run cost curves.*

In competitive labor markets, firms can hire as few or as many workers as they desire at the market wage rate. In the short run, then, the marginal cost of each added unit of output *falls* when the marginal product of each additional worker *rises*. This is true because marginal cost is the wage payment of an extra worker divided by his or her marginal product. A greater marginal product, accompanied by a constant wage payment, produces a lower marginal cost of output. Thus, the declining part of the marginal cost curve (*MC*) in Figure 14-4(a) directly corresponds to the increasing part of the marginal product curve (*MP*) shown in Figure 14-3.

But as diminishing returns set in, marginal product falls. Each extra worker produces less added output yet continues to receive an identical wage payment. The marginal cost of output thus *rises* and continues to rise as long as the marginal product of each additional (equally paid) worker *falls*. In Figure 14-4(a), the rising portion of the marginal cost curve corresponds to the falling part of the *MP* curve in Figure 14-3. Marginal cost rises because of the law of diminishing returns.

Viner distinguished between marginal cost (*MC*) and average total cost (*AC*). Average cost is found by dividing total cost by the quantity of output. Like the *MC* curve, the *AC* curve is *U*-shaped due to the influence of increasing and then diminishing returns. Viner's diagrams correctly illustrated that the *MC* curve cuts

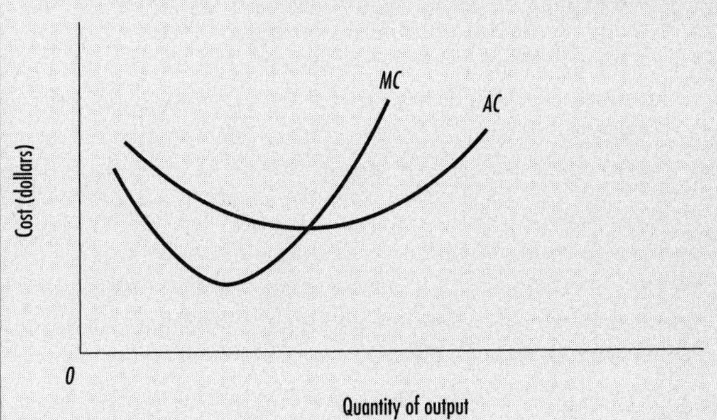

Figure 14-4(a)

14-1 PAST AS PROLOGUE (continued)

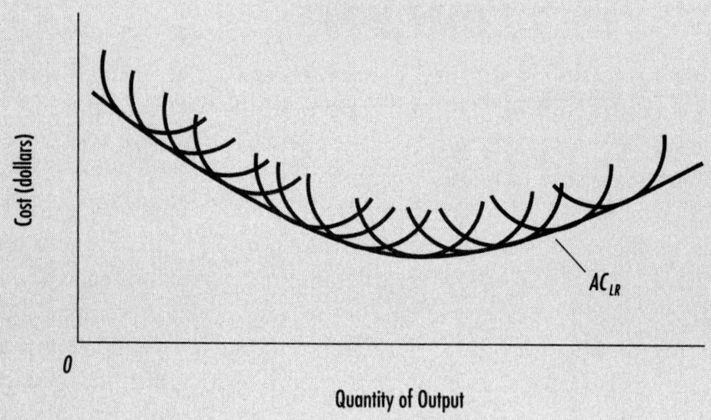

Figure 14-4(b)

the AC curve at its minimum point. When MC is less than average cost, AC falls, and thus the AC curve slopes downward; when MC is greater than average cost, AC rises, and thus the AC curve slopes upward. Only at the minimum point on the AC curve does MC equal AC.

Viner noted that in the long run a firm can alter its plant size, making capital a variable input. A firm's long-run average total cost curve reflects the least average cost at which any output can be produced after the firm has had time to make all appropriate adjustments to its plant size. As illustrated in Figure 14-4(b), the long-run AC_{LR} curve is the "envelope" of the short-run average cost curves, meaning that it comprises the points of tangency of the unlimited number of short-run average cost curves. The U-shape of the long-run AC_{LR} curve reflects economies and diseconomies of scale.

In a famous error, Viner's long-run AC_{LR} curve passed through the ***minimum*** points of each short-run AC curve, rather than connected the *tangency* points of the short-run curves. In reprinting his article in his collected works, Viner stated:

> Even the error is left uncorrected, so that future teachers and students may share the pleasure of many of their predecessors of pointing out that if I had known what an "envelope" was I would not have given my excellent draftsman the technically impossible and economically inappropriate assignment of drawing a [long-run] AC curve which would pass through the lowest cost points of all the sort-run *ac* curves.†

Ironically, this drafting error simply brought greater attention to Viner's article and greater general awareness of his significant contribution.

---

*Viner was a professor at the University of Chicago. His 1931 article "Cost Curves and Supply Curves" is reprinted in his *The Long View and the Short* (Glencoe, IL: The Free Press, 1958): 50–78.

†Viner, 79.

not read Jevons.[8] Much more significantly, he not only invented the term *marginal productivity* but also presented the clearest and best analysis up to his time of the marginal productivity theory of distribution. We will find that his theory was based on the law of diminishing returns, which Clark applied to all factors of production.

Marginal Productivity Theory of Distribution

In the opening paragraph of the preface to his most important book, *The Distribution of Wealth,* Clark summarized his analysis of distribution and his conclusions:

> It is the purpose of this work to show that the distribution of the income of society is controlled by a natural law, and that this law, if it worked without friction, would give to every agent of production the amount of wealth which that agent creates. However wages may be adjusted by bargains freely made between individual men, the rates of pay that result from such transactions tend, it is here claimed, to equal that part of the product of industry which is traceable to the labor itself; and however interest may be adjusted by similarly free bargaining, it naturally tends to equal the fractional product that is separately traceable to capital. At the point in the economic system where titles to property originate,—where labor and capital come into possession of the amounts that the state afterwards treats as their own,—the social procedure is true to the principle on which the right of property rests. So far as it is not obstructed, it assigns to every one what he has specifically produced.[9]

Clark's theory of distribution was based on the law of diminishing marginal returns, which he first presented in a paper at the third annual meeting of the American Economic Association in 1888. We know from our past discussion that this law originally was applied only to agriculture (even Edgeworth's table used an agricultural example). Clark generalized the idea to all factors of production. The underlying assumption is that all other things, especially technology, remain unchanged, while one factor is varied. Thus, if capital, land, and entrepreneurship are kept constant while units of labor are added, the marginal and average products of *labor* ultimately will fall even though total output may continue to increase. Similarly, if capital is added while the other factors remain constant, the marginal and average products of *capital* eventually will fall. It is important to realize that diminishing returns do *not* occur because the quality of the labor or capital inputs decline as more are added; all such units are homogeneous and therefore interchangeable. Rather, they occur because eventually the fixed factor becomes overused relative to the variable factor. In other words, at some point the variable factor becomes so abundant relative to the fixed factor that additional units of the variable factor cannot contribute much to output. For example, where labor is the variable factor, workers may have to wait in

[8] On this point Samuelson has commented: "To learn *for yourself* a new theory ten years or more after it has been widely published is to invite from the jury an indictment for negligence rather than an award for brilliance." Quoted by James Tobin, "Neoclassical Theory in America: J. B. Clark and Fisher," *American Economic Review* 75, no. 6 (December 1985): 30

[9] John Bates Clark, *The Distribution of Wealth: A Theory of Wages, Interest and Profits* (New York, 1899), v.

line to use machines. Where capital is the variable resource, machines and tools may stand unused because the workers needed to use them are unavailable.

Clark stated the law of diminishing returns as follows:

> The last tool adds less to man's efficiency than do earlier tools. If capital be used in increasing quantity by a fixed working force, it is subject to a law of diminishing productivity. . . . The diminishing productivity of labor, when it is used in connection with a fixed amount of capital, is a universal phenomenon. . . . The action of the general law . . . becomes the basis of a theory of distribution.[10]

Clark's marginal productivity theory of distribution under pure competition is illustrated in Figure 14-5. In graph (a), capital is assumed to be constant, and line *BC* represents the marginal productivity of labor. This is simply the downward sloping portion of the marginal product curve, labeled *MP* in our previous Figure 14-3. The first worker, *A,* will produce *AB* output or total product. But because of diminishing returns, subsequent workers will add less to output or total product than the worker added before. If *AD* workers are employed, the last worker produces an output of *DC,* and that establishes the wage rate for all of the workers (each of the workers could be considered the marginal one). We see then that curve *BC* is a demand for labor curve; it shows the number of workers who will be hired at each of several different wage rates. For example, if the wage rate exceeds *AE* (or *DC*), then employers would hire fewer than *AD* workers; some of the workers simply would not contribute an amount of output sufficient to justify the higher wage. Similarly, if the wage were lower than *DC,* more than *AD* workers would be hired. Even though the marginal product of added workers is falling, it would be above the new, lower wage. The equilibrium wage occurs where the marginal productivity of the variable factor—in this case, labor—is equal to the cost, or the earnings, of the factor.

Clark pointed out that in graph (a) of Figure 14-5 total wages are shown as the area *AECD* ($AE \times AD$). Because total output is the entire area under the curve, *ABCD,* the surplus of *EBC* accrues to capital as interest. This is the legitimate return to the fixed factor.

In Figure 14-5 (b) Clark holds the quantity of labor constant—at *AD* in graph (a)—and varies the amount of capital used in production. Line $B'C'$ represents the marginal productivity of capital and is therefore a demand curve for capital. At equilibrium each unit of capital gets as its reward the marginal output of capital, which is $D'C'$. Total interest is $A'E'C'D'$, and $E'B'C'$ is the residue that goes to labor. If the amount of capital were greater, other things being equal, the marginal productivity of capital and the rate of interest would be lower. If the amount of capital were smaller, the marginal productivity of capital and the rate of interest would be higher.

Clark considered land and capital to be one factor of production and thus merged rent, which is paid to land, with interest. He recognized that his distribution theory was a generalization of Ricardo's theory of rent:

> Ground rent we shall study as the earnings of one kind of capital-goods—as merely a part of interest. We are now able to see that wages and interest, though they are determined by the law of final productivity, are also capable of being measured exactly as

[10] Clark, *Distribution of Wealth,* 48–50.

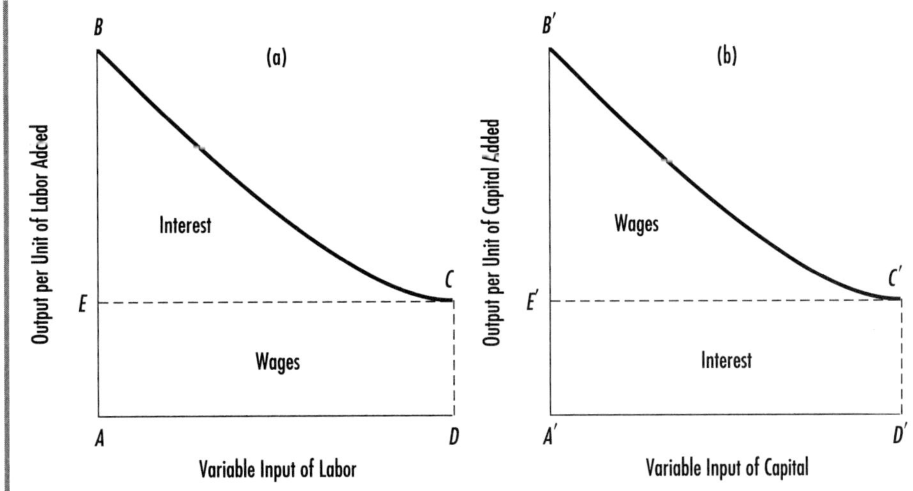

Figure 14-5 Clark's Marginal Productivity Theory
In graph (a), Clark assumed that capital is constant and that *BC* represents the marginal product of labor. If *AD* workers are hired, the wage rate for each worker will be *AE* or *DC*, and the total wage income will be *AECD*. The remaining product, *EBC*, will accrue to capital as interest. In graph (b), labor is constant and capital is variable. The interest rate will depend on how much capital is used. If *A′D′*, then the interest rate will be *A′E′*. Total interest will be *A′E′C′D′* and total wages *E′B′C′*. Both factors receive payments equal to their contributions at the margin.

> ground rent has been measured. That is to say, the Ricardian formula, which describes what is earned by a piece of land, may be used to describe what is earned by the whole fund of social capital: all interest may be made to take the form of a differential gain, or a surplus. Again, the Ricardian formula may be employed to describe the earnings of the whole force of social labor; for wages, in their entirety, are a differential gain. It is one of the most striking of economic facts that the income of all labor, on the one hand, and that of capital, on the other, should be thus entirely akin to ground rent. They are the two generic rents, if by that term we mean differential products; and the earnings of land constitutes a fraction of one of them.[11]

What about profit? "Profit has no place in such static conditions," said Clark. In a perfectly competitive economy, economic profits—those over and above the normal return to capital and entrepreneurship—tend to disappear at both ends of the productive process. "By bidding against each other in selling goods, employers make the prices smaller; and by bidding against each other in hiring labor and capital, they make wages and interest larger." In a no-profit economy, goods sell at cost of production. The businessperson receives wages for whatever labor she performs and interest for any capital she furnishes.

[11] Clark, *Distribution of Wealth,* 191.

It is possible, said Clark, for profits to exist temporarily as the economy moves toward equilibrium. Profits are then a residual. In Figure 14-5, if wages and interest do not exhaust the total output, the residual income is pure profit claimed by the entrepreneur. In graph (b) of that figure, $A'E'C'D'$ is interest, as directly determined, and $E'B'C'$ is the remainder left in the entrepreneur's hands for the payment of wages. The entrepreneur must pay the worker $AECD$ in graph (a) of Figure 14-5. If that is less than $E'B'C'$ of graph (b), there is a residuum, or economic profit, for the entrepreneur. If this occurred, however, firms would enter the industry, driving down the market price, which would eliminate the economic profit. In Clark's words, competition would "exclude such a profit by making these two areas equal."

Because Clark's marginal productivity theory is concerned with the demand for factors of production, it says little about factor supply. Alfred Marshall emphasized supply as well as demand for productive inputs, thereby showing how equilibrium in factor markets results in a price for each factor of production. Marginal productivity of a factor alone cannot determine its rate of reward unless the quantity of a factor supplied is assumed to be fixed. Take labor, for example. If the supply of labor is great relative to the demand for labor, then the wage *and* the marginal productivity of labor will be low; if supply is restricted, the wage *and* the marginal productivity will be high. It is therefore apparent that although Clark's wage theory was far superior to those provided earlier, it required considerable improvement by Alfred Marshall.

Clark recognized that his theory of income distribution is static, best suited to be a purely analytical instrument. The theory was designed to demonstrate the levels to which prices, wages, and interest tend if labor and capital remain fixed in supply, if improvements in methods of production cease, and if consumers' wants never change. We study such static laws separately in order to understand what goes on in a dynamic society, he said. The truth that the world is dynamic does not invalidate the conclusions of a static theory, because static laws are nevertheless real laws that reassert themselves after every dynamic change in the economy. Clark did not develop any sweeping dynamic (historical) theories. He relied almost exclusively on what is now known as the method of comparative statics, because he compared different stationary equilibria.

In the real world, said Clark, a legal monopoly may secure a permanent economic profit for an entrepreneur. Labor and capital are thus prevented from moving into the favored industry, despite the pull of natural economic forces. This condition, however, is not a true static state. Like a body of tranquil water, a static state has perfect fluidity but no flow; factors of production have perfect mobility but no motion. A monopoly represents an obstruction that prevents the working of static economic laws.

Capital is productive, and therefore interest exists. "Paying interest is but buying the product of capital, as paying wages is buying the product of labor." Interest furnishes a motive for abstinence. The motive for accumulating productive wealth is the desire for permanent income. Abstinence leads to new capital goods, but no additional abstinence is required to maintain the existing capital stock. Accumulation, said Clark, is a part of economic dynamics. In the real world capital increases faster than the supply of labor, and thus real wages rise and real interest rates fall.

Capital goods are employed in the order of their productivity, so far as people judge productivity correctly. The crudest hatchet will enormously increase people's power to get firewood, but better tools developed later will increase productivity by a smaller percentage:

> As accumulation proceeds, there are always made costlier machines, representing more capital; and the product that comes from using them is a smaller fraction of their cost. The straightening of the curves in railroads is one of the ways in which capital may find investment. This may cost as much as the first making of the corresponding parts of the road themselves; but it does not liberate as much labor in proportion to its costs, as did the building of the old and crooked road. . . . Everywhere do the forms of capital show differences in earning power; and the owners choose first the most productive forms, and later the less productive. To this fact is due the present low rate of interest. We are utilizing the opportunities for investment that stand late in the series and are low in the scale of productivity.[12]

Clark, however, was optimistic over the outcome of economic dynamics. He said five trends are helping to promote industrial progress: (1) Population is increasing, (2) capital is accumulating, (3) technical processes of industry are improving, (4) modes of organizing capital and labor are becoming more efficient, and (5) human wants are being multiplied and refined. Population is increasing less rapidly than capital, and therefore most of the benefits of progress will accrue to the wage-earning classes, said Clark.

In 1896 Clark seemed unconcerned about the rise of business monopolies.[13] Their high prices, he said, attract new competitors, and their large profits are reinvested, thereby promoting progress. The financial toll extracted from the public by the trusts works arithmetically. Progress, however, works geometrically through accumulation and reinvestment, which forever multiplies the fruitfulness of industry. As giant trusts invade one another's fields, they are driven to be efficient, and large firms are inherently more efficient than small ones.

In 1907, however, in his *Essentials of Economic Theory,* dealing with what he called economic dynamics, Clark became gloomy about the trust problem. Trusts are a product of economic dynamics. Fierce and costly strife among trusts induces them to take the final step in organization, thus bringing competition to an end. Goods become scarcer and more costly:

> No description could exaggerate the evil which is in store for a society given hopelessly over to a régime of private monopoly. Under this comprehensive name we shall group the most important of the agencies which not merely exist, but positively vitiate, the action of natural economic law. Monopoly checks progress in production and infuses into distribution an element of robbery. It perverts the forces which tend to secure to individuals all that they produce. It makes prices and wages abnormal and distorts the form of the industrial mechanism. . . . Prices do not conform to the standard of cost, and interest does not conform to the marginal product of capital.

---

[12] Clark, *Distribution of Wealth,* 185–186.

[13] John Bates Clark, "The Theory of Economic Progress," *Economic Studies,* American Economic Association, vol. 1 (April 1896), 11–15.

> The system of industrial relations is thrown out of balance by putting too much labor and capital at certain points and too little at others. Profits become, not altogether a temporary premium for improvement,—the reward for giving humanity a dynamic impulse,—but partly the spoils of men whose influence is hostile to progress.[14]

Clark favored government regulation of monopolies to preserve competition. In effect, he urged that we ride roughshod over laissez-faire to gain the goal of that doctrine—namely, to allocate resources to their highest valued uses and to accord the factors of production the value of their contributions.

Ethical Implications of Clark's Distribution Theory

In 1879 Henry George (1839–1897) published his *Progress and Poverty.* In it he argued that all economic rent is an *unearned* income, that it grows as society progresses, and that it impoverishes all other classes. The solution, according to George, is to tax away all such rent through a single tax on land. This way the "incentive thwarting" effects of taxes on capital would be removed. Although George opposed socialism, many economists suggested that the result of his tax proposal would be to nationalize land without compensation, with the land being rented to the highest bidder. Clark was well aware that his marginal productivity theory spoke directly to George's ideas. Also, as evidenced by the following statement, Clark was very mindful of Marx's theory that capitalism is a system based upon the exploitation of labor:

> The indictment that hangs over society is that of "exploiting labor." "Workmen" it is said, "are regularly robbed of what they produce. This is done within the forms of law, and by the natural working of competition." If this charge were proved, every right-minded man should become a socialist; and his zeal in transforming the industrial system would then measure and express his sense of justice. If we are to test the charge, however, we must enter the realm of production. We must resolve the product of social industry into its component elements, in order to see whether the natural effect of competition is or is not to give each producer the amount of wealth that he specifically brings into existence.[15]

Clark's overall conclusion from his marginal productivity theory was that the division of the social income into wages, interest, and profit is, in principle, equitable. Society is not at liberty to violate the "fixed laws of distribution." If all people receive all they create, the different classes of people who combine their forces in industry have no grievances against one another. Private property is ethically justified because it is based on an ethical distribution of income.

This view of economic justice did not go unchallenged. Critics pointed out that in the real world of monopoly and monopsony power, factor payments do not equate with marginal productivity. They also noted that much property is inherited,

---

[14] John Bates Clark, *Essentials of Economic Theory* (New York: Macmillan, 1907), 375, 377.

[15] Clark, *Distribution of Wealth*, 7.

rather than obtained through one's own productive effort. So even if *capital* is rewarded according to its contribution, this does not necessarily imply that the distribution that accrues to *individuals* is ethical. Stated bluntly, inheritance may render the notion of "to each according to his contribution" somewhat meaningless. Finally, critics pointed out that Clark's view of justice involves circularity of reasoning. The theory requires an assumption of an initial ethical distribution of income to make a case for the justice of the subsequent distribution. More specifically, that which gets produced—and hence the types and amounts of the factors of production demanded—depends upon the pattern of consumer spending. The distribution of income in place will shape this pattern of spending and hence shape the subsequent distribution of income. But can we be certain that the initial distribution is ethically derived? The philosophic consideration and complexities here become great. One is reminded of the dialogue between two people in a property dispute, both claiming ownership of a parcel of land. Said the first, "This land is mine!" The second person, however, countered, "No, it isn't; this land has been in my family for centuries. My great-grandfather fought the Indians for it." Replied the first person, "Fine. I'll fight *you* for it!"

Most contemporary economists conclude that the marginal productivity theory helps explain how income is distributed in a capitalist society but that it is greatly inadequate as an ethical justification for the observed distribution.

Refer to 14-2 PAST AS PROLOGUE

The "Adding-Up" Problem and the Returns to Scale

Clark's marginal productivity theory raised a theoretical debate, from which emerged the important economic idea of returns to scale. Clark's analysis implied that paying each factor of production its marginal product would normally exhaust all of the output. In terms of Figure 14-5 (a) and (b), the wage areas in the two graphs would be equal, and this would also be true of the two capital areas. Another way of saying this is that the sum of the wage and interest areas in *each* graph would just match the area of total output.

Philip H. Wicksteed (1844–1927) investigated this proposition in more depth. From his mathematics he concluded that the sum of the payments based on marginal productivity would "add up" to the total product only if there were perfect competition and constant returns to scale. Such returns are said to occur when all of the resources used in the production process are increased proportionately and as a result total product rises by the same proportion. More concretely, suppose that capital and labor are both increased by 100 percent (the size of an enterprise doubles). If total output or total product also rises by 100 percent, then the firm has experienced constant returns to scale.

Several prominent economists, among them Edgeworth, Pareto, and Walras, challenged Wicksteed's contention on various grounds. The details of this esoteric "adding-up" debate are of little modern importance, but the debate did produce a salutary outcome: a clearer understanding of the laws of returns to scale. Where the returns to scale are constant, the long-run average cost of producing a product will also be constant. This outcome is the case because total output rises at the same rate as total cost. Where all inputs are simultaneously increased by one proportion,

14-2 PAST AS PROLOGUE

Clark, Marginal Productivity, and Executive Salaries

Chief executive officers (CEOs) of many large American corporations earn multimillion-dollar salaries. For example, in 1998 the lowest-paid CEO among the ten highest-paid executives received more than $50 million of annual compensation (salary, bonuses, and stock options). Are these sky-high salaries justified on John Bates Clark's marginal productivity grounds? That is, do they reflect the CEO's contribution to the firm's output and thus to revenues?

There is much debate among economists as well as public officials on this question. Economists who believe that CEO salaries in general are justified by marginal productivity considerations make the following two arguments. First, they point out that decisions made by the CEOs of large corporations, for better or worse, affect the productivity of the entire organization—everyone from their immediate subordinates to entry-level workers. Good decisions enhance productivity throughout the organization; bad decisions do the opposite. Only executives who have demonstrated an uncanny ability to consistently make good business decisions attain the top positions in large corporations. Because their supply is limited and their marginal productivity great, top CEOs receive enormous salaries.

Second, some economists note that CEO pay may be like the prizes professional golfers and tennis players receive for winning tournaments. The purpose of these high prizes is to promote the productivity of all those who aspire to win. In corporations the top prizes go to the winners of the "contests" among managers to attain, at least eventually, the CEO positions. Thus high CEO pay may not derive solely from the CEO's *direct* productivity. Instead, it may exist because the

and total output rises by a larger proportion, increasing returns to scale are said to have occurred. Such returns result in a lower average cost of production, because total cost rises by a lesser amount than total output. Finally, decreasing returns to scale take place when the proportionate increase in inputs gives rise to a smaller increase in total product. Therefore, all else being constant, the average cost of production will rise.

The Swedish economist Knut Wicksell (Chapter 16), writing in the early 1900s, pointed out that a typical firm would likely experience increasing returns to scale over an early range of additions to its inputs, then constant returns, and finally decreasing returns to scale. When converted to average cost terms, this implied the now familiar *U*-shaped, long-run average cost curve previously shown in Past as Prologue 14-1. As the typical firm expands its plant size, it first experiences declining average cost and then eventually rising average cost. Today, we call the former *economies of scale* and the latter *diseconomies of scale.*

high pay creates incentives that raise productivity of hundreds of corporate "wannabes." In any event, note that the high CEO pay remains grounded on high productivity.

Critics of existing CEO pay acknowledge that CEOs deserve higher salaries than ordinary workers or typical managers, but they scoff at the arguments that existing exorbitant salaries of CEOs are justified economically. They point out that CEO pay in other industrial nations, including Japan and Germany, is far lower than CEO pay in the United States. Also, they note that the ratio of CEO salaries to average salaries in major American firms is much higher than in their foreign counterparts, many of which compete quite successfully with American corporations.

So why have multimillion-dollar salaries emerged in the United States? The answer, say critics, is based on the separation of corporate ownership and control. Corporations are owned by their stockholders but controlled by corporate boards and professional executives who are largely insulated from corporate owners. Because many board members are present or past CEOs of other corporations, they tend to exaggerate CEO importance and, consequently, overpay their own CEOs. In essence, the corporate boards convert some of the firms' profits into higher CEO pay—profits that rightfully belong to corporate stockholders. Disgruntled stockholders usually simply sell their shares of stock in a particular corporation rather than try to reshape corporate boards or to change corporate CEO pay scales. Also, excessive CEO compensation in a handful of corporations tends to beget excessive pay elsewhere, as other firms attempt to attract and retain CEO talent.

In short, critics believe that multimillion-dollar CEO pay bears little relationship to corporate productivity and revenue. It is clear from our discussion that this issue remains unresolved.

Questions for Study and Discussion

1. Briefly identify and state the significance of each of the following to the history of economic thought: Edgeworth, indifference curve, contract curve, marginal versus average product, John Bates Clark, marginal productivity theory of wages and interest, Wicksteed, constant, increasing, and decreasing returns to scale, and Henry George.
2. Discuss the following statement: In the case of economics, the precision of mathematics is far superior to the "zigzag windings of the flowery path of literature."
3. Answer the following questions by referring to Figure 14-1.
   a) In what respect do Edgeworth's indifference curves imply diminishing marginal utility?
   b) Explain why the self-interests of the two traders will push them to points on the contract curve, *ABC*.

4. Compare and contrast the duopoly theories of Cournot and Edgeworth. What do Edgeworth's theory of bilateral exchange (Figure 14-1) and his duopoly theory have in common?
5. Referring to Figure 14-3, explain why, over some ranges of input additions, the average product is rising even though the marginal product is falling.
6. How do Viner's short-run marginal and average cost curves relate to Edgeworth's marginal and average product curves?
7. In what respects are Clark's marginal productivity curves, in Figure 14-5 (a) and (b), labor demand and capital demand curves? Explain. Why must one know something about the supply of labor and capital to have a full theory of wages and interest?
8. What conditions would have to be met in Figures 14-5 (a) and (b) for the firm to earn an economic profit (refer to specific areas of the graphs)? Why would this profit vanish in the long run, according to Clark?
9. If you were asked to write an essay on the forerunners to John Bates Clark and his marginal productivity theory, who would you include? Explain why.
10. Contrast Clark's marginal productivity theory of the distribution of income with the distribution theory formulated by Marx.

Selected Readings

Books

Blaug, Mark, ed. *Alfred Marshall and Francis Edgeworth.* Brookfield, VT: Edward Elgar, 1992.

Clark, John Bates. *The Distribution of Wealth: A Theory of Wages, Interest and Profits.* New York: Macmillan, 1899.

———. *Essentials of Economic Theory.* New York: Macmillan, 1907.

Edgeworth, Francis Y. *Mathematical Psychics.* London: Routledge & Kegan Paul, 1881.

———. *Papers Relating to Political Economy.* Vol. 1. London: Macmillan, 1925.

Stigler, George J. *Production and Distribution Theories.* New York: Macmillan, 1941.

Journal Articles

Brue, Stanley L. "Retrospectives: The Law of Diminishing Returns," *Journal of Economic Perspectives* 7 (Summer 1993): 185–192.

Collier, C. F. "Henry George's System of Political Economy," *History of Political Economy* 11 (Spring 1979): 64–93.

Henry, John F. "John Bates Clark and the Marginal Product: An Historical Inquiry into the Origins of Value-Free Economic Theory," *History of Political Economy* 15 (Fall 1983): 375–389.

Humphrey, Thomas M. "The Early History of the Box Diagram," *Economic Quarterly* 82 (Federal Reserve Bank of Richmond, Winter 1996): 37–75.

Nichol, Archibald J. "Edgeworth's Theory of Duopoly Price," *Economic Journal* 45 (March 1935): 51–66.

Tobin, James. "Neoclassical Theory in America: J. B. Clark and Fisher," *American Economic Review* 75, no. 6 (December 1985): 28–39.

Chapter 15

The Neoclassical School—Alfred Marshall

The microeconomic thought of the marginalists discussed in the previous three chapters gradually was transformed into what we now call neoclassical economics. Because *neo* means "new," *neoclassicism* implies a new form of classicism. The neoclassical economists were "marginalists" in the crucial sense that they emphasized decision making and price determination at the margin. Nevertheless, at least three differences between the earlier marginalists and later neoclassical economists can be discerned. First, neoclassical thought stressed both demand *and* supply in determining the market prices of goods, services, and resources, whereas the earlier marginalists tended to stress demand alone. Second, several of the neoclassical economists—for example, Wicksell and Fisher—took a far greater interest in the role of money in the economy than did the earlier marginalists. Finally, neoclassical economists extended marginal analysis to market structures other than pure competition, pure monopoly, and duopoly.

The first of these differences is evident in the works of Alfred Marshall (1842–1924), the greatest figure in the neoclassical school and the subject of this chapter. The last two differences are addressed in Chapters 16 and 17.

MARSHALL'S LIFE AND METHOD

Marshall was the son of a cashier in the Bank of England. His father was a rather tyrannical gentleman, author of a tract called *Man's Rights and Woman's Duties.* He overworked Alfred at his studies, made him promise never to play chess because it was a waste of time, and tried to banish mathematics from the boy's life because it was irrelevant to the ministry, which the father had picked for his son's career. Young Marshall, however, rejected a scholarship at Oxford that would have led to the church, rejected the ministry, and rejected the study of "dead languages." Instead, he attended Cambridge, where he devoted himself to mathematics, physics, and later on, to economics. He was aided by a well-to-do-uncle, his father simply being too poor to pay for his tuition when he gave up the Oxford scholarship.[1]

Marshall was a hypochondriac about his health and hypercritical about his writing. He threw much of what he wrote into the wastebasket, and, in fact, many of

[1] According to Ronald Coase, "Marshall's father was completely convinced of the correctness of his own narrow views, had little regard for the feelings and wishes of others, and thought it right to control the actions of those in his power by 'an extremely severe discipline.' He was, as Alfred Marshall said, 'a bad educator.'" Ronald H. Coase, "Alfred Marshall's Mother and Father," *History of Political Economy* 16 (Winter 1984): 519–527.

his major ideas were worked out a decade or more before they appeared in 1890 in his *Principles of Economics.* In successive editions of that work, he introduced so many qualifications, exceptions, and hesitations into his system that he weakened the clear and definite principles on which many love to lean. Marshall criticized Jevons for rushing into print before he was ready. Marshall kept portions of his book *Industry and Trade* (1919) in printed proofs for fifteen years before publication. Because he was slow to publish his work, his ideas seemed commonplace by the time they appeared. Yet he was the most influential economic theorist of his day and undoubtedly the greatest of his generation. As early as 1888 it was being said that his former students occupied half the economic chairs in the United Kingdom.

Marshall popularized the modern diagrammatic approach to economics—the bane of beginning students—that helped elucidate certain fundamental principles. Although he was an expert mathematician who liberally placed mathematics in footnotes and appendixes, he was skeptical of the overall value of mathematics in economic analysis. In 1906 he wrote:

> [I had] a growing feeling in the later years of my work at the subject that a good mathematical theorem dealing with economic hypotheses was very unlikely to be good economics: and I went more and more on the rules—(1) Use mathematics as a shorthand language, rather than as an engine of inquiry. (2) Keep to them till you have done. (3) Translate into English. (4) Then illustrate by examples that are important in real life. (5) Burn the mathematics. (6) If you can't succeed in (4), burn (3). This last I did often.[2]

Marshall was the great synthesizer, seeking to combine the best of classical economics with marginalist thinking, hence producing "neoclassical" economics. Many of his footnotes and appendixes offer hints of ideas of which he was aware, but which others later worked out in greater detail.

Marshall defined his subject as follows: "Political Economy or Economics is a study of mankind in the ordinary business of life; it examines that part of individual and social action which is most closely connected with the attainment and with the use of the material requisites of wellbeing."[3]

Economists, he said, like other scientists, collect, arrange, interpret, and draw inferences from facts. They seek knowledge of the interdependence of economic phenomena, of cause-and-effect relationships. Every cause tends to produce a definite result if nothing occurs to hinder it. Economics is not a body of concrete truth, but rather an engine for the discovery of concrete truth.

We seek to discover economic laws. Any law is a general proposition, or statement of tendencies, more or less certain, more or less definite. Social laws are statements of social tendencies. Economic laws, or statements of economic tendencies, are those social laws that relate to human conduct in which the strength of the major motives can be measured by financial price. Economics is less exact than the natural sciences, but progress is being made toward greater precision.

The implications of Marshall's approach and definitions are interesting. Economic laws are not natural laws that are necessarily beneficent. It is not imperative, though

---

[2] Alfred Marshall, *Memorials of Alfred Marshall*, ed. A. C. Pigou (London: Macmillan, 1925), 427.

[3] Alfred Marshall, *Principles of Economics*, 8th ed. (London: Macmillan, 1920), 1. (Orig. pub. 1890.)

it may be desirable, that they be allowed to work themselves out without any restraining hand. The relationships among supply, demand, and price tend to produce certain results if they are allowed to work themselves out by themselves, but society can influence the outcome if it so desires. As just one example, society can increase the amount of higher education utilized by the general population by reducing the price (providing public universities, grants to private colleges). Marshall's thinking left room for cautious reform, that is, for modest departures from laissez-faire.

Marshall had little to say about business cycles, partly because of his microeconomic approach. He and others who developed theories of the behavior of individuals and the conduct of small representative firms found it easy to ignore fluctuations. It was left to later aggregate economics to grapple with such problems.

UTILITY AND DEMAND

Marginal Utility

According to Marshall, demand is based on the law of diminishing marginal utility. "The marginal utility of a thing to anyone diminishes with every increase in the amount of it he already has." Marshall introduced two important qualifications at this point. First, he pointed out that he was concerned with a moment in time, which is too short an interval to consider any changes in character and tastes of a particular person. With the passage of time one's tastes can change, so that, for example, the more good music one hears, the stronger one's taste for it is likely to become. This is not an exception to the law of diminishing marginal utility, because such long-range changes in tastes are excluded from the analysis; in a short moment of time dynamic changes such as these are imperceptible.

Marshall's second qualification of the law of diminishing marginal utility concerns consumer goods that are *indivisible.* "A small quantity of a commodity may be insufficient to meet a certain special want; and then there will be a more than proportionate increase of pleasure when the consumer gets enough of it to enable him to attain the desired end." Marshall cited the case of wallpapering a room. If twelve pieces of wallpaper are required to cover the walls, securing all twelve pieces will yield disproportionately much more pleasure than securing only ten pieces and thus being unable to finish the job. Or, in modern terms, securing the fourth tire for an automobile will yield more satisfaction than the first three together.

The utility approach of the Marshallian system dealt with pleasures and pains, desires and aspirations, and incentives to action. How can we measure the utility of such intangibles? Marshall boldly said, "with money." The earlier marginalists said that the strength of a person's preferences determines the amount of money the person is willing to spend to acquire some product or the amount of labor the person is willing to sacrifice to achieve some goal. Marshall, however, turned the relationship around so as to measure preferences according to the financial scale of payments. The earlier marginalists would say that if shoes are twice as useful to you as a hat, you are willing to pay twice as much for shoes—for example, \$40 versus \$20. Marshall would say that because you are willing to pay twice as much for shoes as for the hat, we can conclude that the shoes yield twice as much utility to you.

The precise money measurement of preferences or motives in business life makes economics the most exact of the social sciences. This measuring device of economics, rough and imperfect as it is, is the best device we have to gauge people's psychological drives as expressed in the marketplace.

We cannot directly compare the amounts of pleasure that two people derive from eating a hamburger. Nor can we compare the degrees of pleasure one person gets from eating a hamburger at two different times. But if we find a person who is in doubt as to whether to spend a set amount of money on a hamburger, a soft drink and candy bar, or whether to ride a bus rather than walk, we may say that the person expects equal pleasure from them. Money, said Marshall, measures utility at the margin—the point at which decisions are made:

> If then we wish to compare even physical gratifications, we must do it not directly, but indirectly by the incentives which they afford to action. If the desires to secure either of two pleasures will induce people in similar circumstances each to do just an hour's extra work, or induce men in the same rank of life and with the same means each to pay a shilling for it; we then can say that those pleasures are equal for our purposes, because the desires for them are equally strong incentives to action for persons under similar conditions.[4]

Two people with equal incomes will not necessarily derive equal benefit from its use. Take one pound or dollar from each of them, and the intensities of the satisfaction given up may not be equal at all. But when many people are involved, the idiosyncrasies of individuals tend to counterbalance one another. Then we can say that the amount of money that people of equal incomes give to obtain a benefit or avoid an injury is a measure of the extent of the marginal benefit or injury.

An increment of money, like an additional unit of goods, has a greater marginal utility to a poor person than to a rich person, because the poor person has less money initially. How, then, can we generalize about progress, happiness, and the effects of taxation if wealth and income have such wide differences of marginal utility? Here again the answer lies in large numbers. If we take whole cross sections of the income groups of society, money becomes an acceptable measuring rod of utility. Furthermore:

> By far the greater number of the events with which economics deals affect in about equal proportions all the different classes of society; so that if the money measures of the happiness caused by two events are equal, it is reasonable and in accordance with common usage to regard the amounts of the happiness in the two cases to be equivalent. And, further, as money is likely to be turned to the higher uses of life in about equal proportions, by any two large groups of people taken without special bias for any two parts of the western world, there is even some *prima facie* probability that equal additions to their material resources will make about equal additions to the fullness of life, and the true progress of the human race.[5]

Let us measure the strength of preferences or motives by money, said Marshall. Let us ascertain how much money a particular group is willing to pay as a measure of

[4] Marshall, *Economics,* 15–16.

[5] Marshall, *Economics,* 20.

the utility of something it desires. Or, alternatively, we can determine the disutility of something by measuring the amount of money that must be offered to induce a group to undergo a certain effort or to experience an abstinence it dislikes.

Rational Consumer Choice

Thus far we have established that Marshall subscribed to the notions of utility and diminishing marginal utility. His demand analysis also employed the idea of rational consumer choice. In a money economy, said Marshall, each line of expenditure will be pushed to the point at which the marginal utility of a shilling's (or dollar's) worth of goods will be the same as in any other direction of spending. Each person will attain this result "by constantly watching to see whether there is anything on which he is spending so much that he would gain by taking a little away from that line of expenditure and putting it on some other line." Thus, for example, the consumer who must decide whether to buy new clothes or to use the money for a vacation is weighing the marginal utilities of two different types of expenditures. Recall that Gossen (his second law), Jevons, and Menger described this process of rational choice earlier. Unlike these theorists, however, Marshall successfully tied this equimarginal rule directly to the contemporary law of demand.

Refer to 15-1 PAST AS PROLOGUE

Law of Demand

Marshall's law of demand follows directly from his notions of diminishing marginal utility and rational consumer choice. Suppose that a consumer's expenditures are in equilibrium such that the last dollar spent on each of several products yields identical marginal utility. That is, suppose that $MU_x/P_x = MU_y/P_y \ldots = MU_n/P_n$. How will this consumer react if the price of product *X* falls while the prices of the other goods remain constant? Marshall reasoned that the rational consumer would buy more of product *X*. Why is this so? The answer is that, following the decline in the price of *X*, the ratio MU_x/P_x will exceed the MU/P ratios for the other goods. To restore a balance of expenditures, the consumer will substitute more of *X* for less of *Y*, *Z*, and the like. As this substitution occurs, the marginal utility of *X* will fall, and the marginal utility of the other goods will rise. At some point the now-lower marginal utility of *X*, in relation to the lower price of *X*, will yield a ratio equal to the MU_y/P_y and the MU_z/P_z. Thus equilibrium will be restored. Therefore, in Marshall's words: "the amount demanded increases with a fall in price, and diminishes with a rise in price." This is the now-familiar law of downward sloping demand.

Marshall illustrated the law of demand with both a table and a demand curve. He drew his demand curve by assuming that the period of time is sufficiently short to justify a *ceteris paribus* assumption. We have already observed that he held tastes or preferences constant. Other variables that he held constant were the person's wealth, the purchasing power of money, and the price of substitute commodities. Today such "other things equal" constitute what we call the determinates of demand. In the long run these determinants can change, and when they do, the entire demand curve shifts either leftward or rightward. Thus Marshall had a clear conception of differences between changes in the quantity

15-1 PAST AS PROLOGUE

Rational Economic Behavior and Prospect Theory

Mainstream economic theory assumes that individuals are rational utility maximizers who have good information and, at least on average, process it accurately in pursuing their economic self-interests. This view of economic behavior traces its roots to classical economics, with Adam Smith's reference to the butcher, baker, and brewer, and later to Bentham's calculus of seeking pleasure and avoiding pain. Marginalists Gossen, Jevons, and Menger formalized rational choice in terms of equating the marginal utilities of the last dollars spent across commodities. Marshall further advanced the theory by integrating this equimarginal principle into the law of demand. Although these theoretical contributions are significant to economic theory, is the underlying premise of rational economic behavior valid?

Some recent developments challenge the idea that individuals accurately process information and the assertion that any errors in processing tend to cancel out. Daniel Kahneman (1934–) and Amos Tversky (1937–1996) argue that when faced with complex decisions and uncertain outcomes, people employ "rules of thumb" in decision making rather than incurring the costs of gathering better information. These rules of thumb are often biased by people's inability to accurately assess probabilities, which in turn leads to improperly estimated costs and benefits and, thus, to irrational decisions.

Kahneman and Tversky conducted a series of experiments that gave rise to *prospect theory,* which asserts that people will choose a guaranteed gain over a probable gain, even when the probable gain carries a greater expected value. Conversely, people will opt for an uncertain loss over a certain loss, even when the expected value of the uncertain loss is greater. Suppose that a person is offered \$500 or the chance to win \$1,500 on a coin toss. With a 50 percent chance of winning the coin toss, the expected value of the probable gain is \$750 (0.5 × \$1,500), greater than the guaranteed \$500. Suppose instead that the person can choose between a certain loss of \$500, or tossing a coin and having a 50 percent chance of paying nothing and a 50 percent probability of losing \$1,500. Again the expected value of the probable outcome (a \$750 loss) is greater than the certain outcome (a \$500 loss). Despite identical dollar amounts in the two situations, Kahneman and Tversky's experiments revealed that people tend to choose the guaranteed outcome in the face of a gain and the uncertain outcome when faced with a loss.

Does prospect theory contradict the economist's principle of rational economic behavior? Not necessarily, but it does challenge the idea that the rational action is

demanded (measured along the horizontal axis) and changes in demand (shifts of the entire curve).

In formulating his theory of demand, Marshall chose to ignore the inconsistency he introduced by assuming that the purchasing power of money is constant.

to choose the alternative with the greatest expected net value (probability of an outcome × the value of the outcome), an often-used criterion for assessing rational economic behavior.

There are many real-world instances of actual or seemingly irrational behavior caused by difficulties in processing probabilities or due to mental or emotional defect of the decision maker. Kahneman and Tversky suggest that irrational decisions are not simply random occurrences that we would expect to average out. In their view, sound economics needs to recognize and account for "irrationality."

If the assumption of rational behavior is invalid, does this invalidate the model upon which the assumption is based? In 1953 Milton Friedman (1912–) addressed the criticism of using invalid assumptions. He explained,

> The abstract methodological issues we have been discussing have a direct bearing on the perennial criticism of "orthodox" economic theory as "unrealistic" as well as on the attempts that have been made to reformulate theory to meet this charge. Economics is a "dismal" science because it assumes man to be selfish and money-grubbing, "a lightning calculator of pleasures and pains, who oscillates like a homogeneous globule of desire of happiness under the impulse of stimuli that shift him about the area, but leave him intact"; it rests on outmoded psychology and must be reconstructed in line with each new development in psychology; it assumes men, or at least businessmen, to be "in a continuous state of 'alert,' ready to change prices and/or pricing rules whenever their sensitive intuitions . . . detect a change in demand and supply conditions;" it assumes markets to be perfect, competition to be pure, and commodities, labor, and capital to be homogeneous.
>
> As we have seen, criticism of this type is largely beside the point unless supplemented by evidence that a hypothesis differing in one or another of these respects from the theory being criticized yields better predictions for as wide a range of phenomena. Yet most such criticism is not so supplemented; it is based almost entirely on supposedly directly perceived discrepancies between the "assumptions" and the "real world."*

Prospect theory suggests that, even on average, people sometimes violate the rational behavior assumption of mainstream economic theory. Friedman maintains that it does not matter so long as people act as if they are maximizing their utility and the model based on that assumption generates valid predictions about their behavior. If the models built on the rationality assumption remain the most accurate predictors of economic outcomes, Friedman would defend their continued use.

*Milton Friedman, *Essays in Positive Economics* (University of Chicago Press, 1953), 30–31.

When the price of a product such as *X* falls, two effects are at work that increase the quantity purchased. Marshall focused on the *substitution effect* (or the relative price effect). But when the price of *X* falls, an *income effect* also occurs; that is, the consumer experiences a gain in purchasing power. Some of this increase in real income is likely to be spent on *X*, thus contributing to the increase in the quantity of *X* demanded. The clear distinction between these two effects did not occur until later in the history of economic thought.

Consumer's Surplus

Unlike the Austrians, Marshall asserted that the total utility of a good is the sum of the successive marginal utilities of each added unit. Therefore, the price a person pays for a good never exceeds, and seldom equals, that which he or she would be willing to pay rather than go without the desired object. Only at the margin will price generally match a person's willingness to pay. Thus, the total satisfaction a person gets from purchasing successive units of a good exceeds the sacrifices required to pay for the good. Recall that Dupuit first noted this excess of utility over expenditure in 1844. Marshall, however, is credited for naming the concept "consumer's surplus" and systematically exploring it.

Marshall used the price and quantity data shown in Table 15-1 to illustrate consumer's surplus. Note from the table that the person for whom these data apply would buy one pound of tea annually if the price were 20 shillings. At 14 shillings he would buy two pounds, at 10 shillings three pounds, and so on. Suppose, said Marshall, that the market price was actually 2 shillings. This consumer would buy seven pounds of tea annually, pay 2 shillings for each pound, and spend 14 shillings. Notice, however, that the first pound provides 20 shillings' worth of utility, the second 14 shillings' worth of utility, and so forth. This person's total gain in utility from the purchase of the seven pounds of tea is thus 59 shillings (20 + 14 + 10 + 6 + 4 + 3 + 2). Because his expenditure is only 14 shillings, he receives a consumer surplus of 45 shillings (59 – 14). Looked at slightly differently, the consumer's surplus on the first pound of tea is 18 shillings (20 – 2), on the second 12 shillings (14 – 2), and so forth, for a cumulative total of 45 shillings. As a glance ahead to Figure 15-1 will show, consumer surplus is therefore the area below the demand curve and above the market price. The consumer's surplus increases significantly in a productive social environment in which the price of goods falls as they are produced more efficiently. As an individual reaches equilibrium at a lower point on his demand curve (because he will buy more goods as they become cheaper), his consumer's surplus grows. Referring again to the "paradox of value" discussed in detail by the Austrians, Marshall would say that a large wheat crop is more useful than a small one. If people pay less for the larger crop, the consumer's surplus of utility is larger. In this respect, Marshall would agree with Jevons as opposed to Menger.

Marshall purposely selected tea as an illustration to avoid a problem referred to previously. Because the amount a person spends on tea relative to his total expenditures is small, a decline in the price of tea leaves the consumer's real income or purchasing power relatively constant. But this is not the case for all goods in all situations. For example, suppose in a modern example that a person lives in an area that has frigid winters and heats her home with natural gas. Additionally, suppose the data in Table 15-1 represent the demand schedule for natural gas rather than for tea. Finally, assume that the per-unit price of natural gas falls dramatically, say, from 20 shillings to 2 shillings. Because this consumer spends a large portion of her budget on natural gas, this decline in price increases her real income (purchasing power of money income).

Table 15-1
Marshall's Idea of Consumer's Surplus

PRICE PER POUND (SHILLINGS)	QUANTITY PURCHASED (POUNDS)
20	1
14	2
10	3
6	4
4	5
3	6
2	7

At Price = 2*S*.: Total Utility = 59*S*.
Total Expenditure = 14*S*.
Consumer's Surplus = 45*S*.

But as her real income rises, its marginal utility, like that of other items, falls. Thus, not all of the units of money used to measure consumer surplus possess the same utility value. More specifically, the marginal utility of shillings differs when this consumer is buying one unit of natural gas at 20 shillings and seven units at 2 shillings. We therefore cannot conclude in this case that the *utility* surplus to this consumer is equivalent to the full 45 shillings. Marshall was aware of this problem and, along with choosing an example to minimize it, explicitly assumed that the marginal utility of income was constant. This assumption, however, conflicted with his other statements in his *Principles* that the marginal utility of money is less for those who have much income than for those who have little income.

A second problem associated with measuring a consumer's surplus becomes evident in dealing with *market* as opposed to *individual* demand schedules and curves. Market demand curves typically are aggregations of thousands or even millions of individual curves. The measurement of the total consumers' surplus requires adding together interpersonal units of utility. Most economists agree that the diversity of individual preferences and income levels make such comparisons and additions impossible. Nevertheless, Marshall's notion of consumer surplus has proved to be a valuable tool for analyzing several economic phenomena, for example, the "deadweight" or efficiency losses from taxes, monopoly, and tariffs.

Elasticity of Demand

Marshall was far superior to his predecessors in handling elasticity of demand, analyzing the subject verbally, diagrammatically, and mathematically. The only universal law pertaining to a person's desire for more of a commodity, Marshall said, is that, other things being equal, it diminishes with every increase in his supply of that commodity. It follows, therefore, that the lower the price, the more the consumer will buy. That is why the demand curve slopes downward to the right. Elasticity of demand tells us whether the diminution of desire (marginal utility) is slow or rapid as the quantity increases. It relates the percentage drop in price to the percentage increase in quantity demanded, which, of course, is based on diminishing marginal utility of the good. The numerical coefficient of the elasticity of demand (E_d) is the percentage change in quantity divided by the percentage change in price. Demand is *elastic* when the percentage change in quantity exceeds the percentage change in price; demand is *inelastic* when the percentage change in quantity is less than the percentage change in price; and demand is *unit elastic* when the percentage changes are equal. Stated in terms of absolute values, if $E_d > 1$, demand is elastic; if $E_d < 1$, demand is inelastic, and if $E_d = 1$, demand is unit elastic.

Marshall also discussed what we now call the determinants of the elasticity of demand. Elasticity of market demand tends to be great when a good has a high price relative to the size of the buyers' incomes. Marshall said that a lowering of the price results in many more buyers being able to afford the product. On the other hand, when the price of a product is low relative to people's incomes, a similar percentage change in price will not result in much of an increase in purchases. The great bulk of buyers already are in the market. Marshall also noted that the demand for a particular product will tend to be more elastic the more it can serve as a substitute for other goods. In terms of a contemporary example, a decline in the price of chicken is likely to produce a greater percentage increase in purchases than the percentage decline in price because consumers can easily substitute chicken for other items such as beef and pork whose prices remain unchanged.

The principle of elasticity of demand is useful for understanding a wide range of problems and policies. Governments, for example, tax commodities for which there are inelastic demands (cigarettes, alcohol) rather than those with elastic demands (chicken), because the revenue yield is greater. Monopolistic prices are likely to be set at higher levels where demand is generally less elastic (antibiotics) than where it is highly elastic (Frisbees). Restrictions of agriculture output result in greater gross revenue to farmers if the demand for the product is inelastic (wheat) and smaller revenue if the demand is elastic (strawberries).

SUPPLY

Supply, said Marshall, is governed by cost of production. Marshall conceived of supply not as a point or single amount but rather as a curve, like the one shown in Figure 15-1 later in this chapter. Supply is a whole series of quantities that would be forthcoming at a whole series of prices.

For purposes of exposition, Marshall divided time into three periods: (1) the immediate present, (2) the short run, and (3) the long run.

Immediate Present

Market prices refer to the *present,* with no time allowed for adaptation of the quantity supplied to changes in demand. The corresponding market period, which may be as short as one day, is defined as that period during which the quantity supplied cannot be increased in response to a suddenly increased demand. Nor can the quantity supplied be decreased immediately in response to a decline of demand, because it takes time for production to be curtailed and inventories reduced. If there were a run on shoes in a city, the messages to increase production and shipments would be flashed back to the distributors and the manufacturers. Shoes would not arrive in the retail stores, however, until a lapse of perhaps a day or two.

If a good is perishable, and if we assume that the seller is trying to maximize profits or minimize losses, the market supply curve is perfectly inelastic—a vertical straight line. The firm would rather sell its fresh fish for a small amount than let it spoil. If the good is not perishable, the sellers have reservation prices below which they will not sell. Some vendors, however, will sell at prices well below cost of production, perhaps because they have pressing bills to pay. The market supply curve therefore slopes upward and to the right until it encompasses the total quantity on the market. Then it becomes vertical, because no matter how high the market price, by definition no greater quantity can be supplied during the market period.

Short Run

To analyze the period that Marshall referred to as the short run, he divided costs into two types, which he called *supplementary costs* and *prime costs.* Supplementary costs are now known as *fixed costs;* prime costs are known as *variable costs.* Fixed costs, or overhead costs, such as top executive salaries and plant depreciation, are constant; they cannot be changed in the short run. In fact, the short run is defined as that period during which the variable inputs can be increased or decreased, but the fixed plant costs cannot be changed.

Variable costs—Marshall's prime costs—include those for labor and raw materials that change over the short run according to changing levels of output. In the short run, all variable costs must be covered, but some of the fixed costs need not be. For example, a railroad will continue to operate in the short run even if part of the fixed investment is never recovered through revenue. As long as it has fixed equipment and tracks, it must continue to pay its fixed costs. If these costs exceed the losses accruing from operating, the railroad will stay in business. In the short run the firm's supply curve is based on variable costs.

The short-run supply curve slopes upward and to the right—the higher the product price, the larger is the quantity supplied. Modern economics views the short-run supply curve as a marginal cost curve; recall from Past as Prologue 14-1 that these costs rise because of diminishing returns to the variable inputs. Therefore, higher market prices enable firms to profitably expand their output. Marshall's explanation was less satisfactory. He said that although the cost of production is measured in terms of money, behind these financial costs lie two psychological sacrifices—the irksomeness of working and the sacrifice of putting off consumption by saving. For the latter Marshall used the term *waiting* rather than Senior's *abstinence.*

The worker finds additional hours of labor each day to be increasingly irksome (recall Jevons on this point). Therefore, the longer the work day, other things being equal, the greater is the hourly remuneration required to induce workers to work the last hour. And even though the earlier hours do not represent as great a per-hour sacrifice, the workers get the same rate of wages for all hours worked.[6] Of course, the higher the wage rate, other things such as productivity being equal, the higher the marginal cost of production. Firms find it advantageous to increase their work-days or employ lesser-quality workers to increase their production only when the price they receive for their product rises. In contemporary language, the higher product price means that marginal revenue, which in pure competition equals the price, exceeds the marginal cost of the old quantity, and this entices the firm to expand output until marginal revenue and marginal cost are once again equal.

Long Run

In the long run, all costs are variable, and they must all be covered if the firm is to continue in business. If the price rises such that total revenue exceeds total cost of production, capital will enter the industry, typically through new firms, and market supply will increase. The entire supply curve will shift rightward. If the price falls below the average cost of production, capital will withdraw, probably by the exit of firms. Consequently, the market supply will decline (the supply curve will shift leftward).

EQUILIBRIUM PRICE AND QUANTITY

What determines market price? The classical economists said, "Cost of production," meaning objective labor-time cost, and the sacrifice of abstinence. "Demand," said the early marginalists. Marshall, the great synthesizer, said, "*Both* supply *and* demand." Behind supply lie both financial and subjective costs. Behind demand lie utility and diminishing marginal utility:

> We might as reasonably dispute whether it is the upper or the under blade of a pair of scissors that cuts a piece of paper, as whether value is governed by utility or cost of production. It is true that when one blade is held still, and the cutting is effected by moving the other, we may say with careless brevity that the cutting is done by the second; but the statement is not strictly accurate, and is to be excused only so long as it claims to be merely a popular and not a strictly scientific account of what happens.[7]

Marshall illustrated the idea of equilibrium competitive market price and quantity with both a table and a graph; his table is reproduced here as Table 15-2. Figure 15-1 shows his supply and demand analysis graphically.

Numerical Representation

Given a grain market, as illustrated in Table 15-2, the amount each farmer or other seller offers for sale at any price is governed by his or her own immediate need for money and estimate of future prices. Assuming equality of bargaining power between sellers and buyers, the "higgling and bargaining" of the market will result in a price close to 36 shillings. The price can therefore be called the true equilibrium

[6] Marshall pointed out that each worker therefore derives a worker's surplus, or economic rent, from all but the last hour of labor.

[7] Marshall, *Economics,* 348.

Table 15-2
Marshall's Determination of Equilibrium

COMPETITIVE MARKET PRICE AND QUANTITY		
PRICE (SHILLINGS)	AMOUNT HOLDERS ARE WILLING TO SELL (UNITS)	AMOUNT BUYERS ARE WILLING TO BUY (UNITS)
37	1,000	600
36	700	700
35	600	900

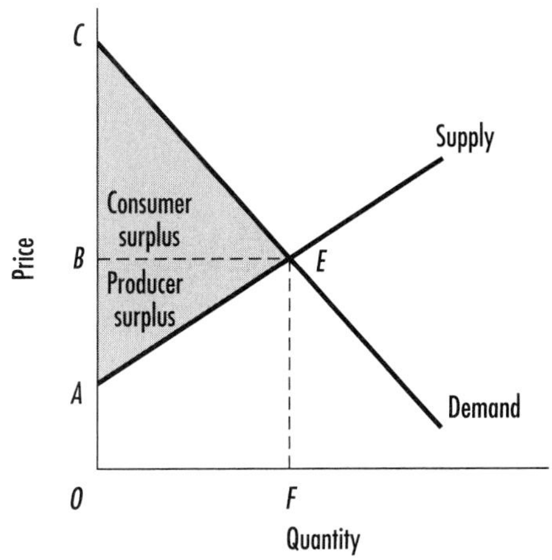

Figure 15-1 Marshall's Equilibrium Price and Quantity
"Higgling and bargaining" of sellers and buyers, said Marshall, result in an equilibrium price (here *B*) that equates quantity supplied and quantity demanded (both *F*). Buyers collectively receive consumer surplus of *BCE;* sellers collectively receive producer surplus of *ABE.*

price, because if it were fixed at the beginning and throughout, it would exactly equate the quantities demanded and supplied (700). Notice that if the price were 37 shillings, a surplus of 400 units (1,000 – 600) of wheat would occur, and this would push the price downward. On the other hand, if the price were 35 shillings, suppliers would be willing to sell 300 fewer units (600 – 900) of wheat than demanders desire. This shortage obviously would drive the price upward.

Graphical Representation

Figure 15-1 graphically shows Marshall's equilibrium price and quantity. Marshall placed quantity on the horizontal axis because he viewed it to be the *independent* variable. Today, economists view quantity as the *dependent* variable [$Q = f(P)$], yet they continue to place price on the vertical axis and quantity on the horizontal axis. In effect, they bow to Marshallian tradition rather than to mathematical convention.

Figure 15-1 not only shows the equilibrium price, *B*, and quantity, *F*, but also illustrates Marshall's previously discussed notion of consumer surplus. If we disregard the problems of interpersonal utility comparisons and diminishing marginal utility of income, we can say that area *BCE* measures consumer surplus. The demand curve indicates that some consumers would be willing to pay more than the market price, *B*, rather than go without the product. The price is established by the marginal utility received by the last unit of the good purchased, and because all units are priced at *B*, consumers collectively receive a utility surplus equal to *BCE*.

Marshall also presented the idea of a producer surplus, which is shown in the figure as *ABE*. Some sellers would be willing to sell their product at less than the market price rather than hold onto their goods. Because these producers receive the market price of *B*, however, they receive a surplus in a way analogous to consumers. Marshall pointed out that producer's surplus exists both for the worker (who gets a worker's surplus) and for the owner of accumulated wealth (who gets a saver's surplus). Recall that the irksomeness of the last hour worked in a day establishes the wage rate for all the hours; thus, for earlier hours workers get paid more than the minimum wages they would be willing to accept rather than not work those hours. Similarly, Marshall said that postponing consumption is a sacrifice, and the rate of interest has to be high enough to call forth the marginal supply of saving. As all savings receive the same interest rate, some savers are receiving more than the amount of their utility sacrifice. This is the saver's surplus.

Marshall's masterful handling of the element of time in discussing market price was one of his many significant contributions to economic thinking. As a general rule, he said, the shorter the period of time, the greater the influence of demand on value. The reason is that the influence of cost of production takes longer to work itself out than does the influence of changes in demand. Passing events influence market value, but in long periods these irregularities neutralize one another. In the long run, therefore, the cost of production is the most important determinant of price and value. In a stationary state, with monetary aberrations ruled out, cost of production would govern price and value. In a changing world, however, with adaptations to change that are imperfect and gradual, both demand and supply are important.

In the short run, an increase in demand increases the price, either because workers of lesser quality are used or because longer workdays are needed to increase output. In the long run, however, more factories can be built and more workers can be attracted to the industry and trained. Supply can then be increased without a rise in price, or perhaps with even a decrease in price, if there are certain economies of large-scale production. This latter possibility will be discussed later under the heading Increasing and Decreasing Cost Industries.

Marshall defined the long-run normal price as one that exactly balances the quantity supplied and demanded *and* that would be equal to the long-run average cost of production. The normal price changes with every change in the efficiency of production. Market prices tend to fluctuate around normal prices, but it is only by accident that they are ever equal. There are very gradual or secular movements of normal price caused by the gradual growth of knowledge, population, and capital and the changing conditions of demand and supply from one generation to another.

DISTRIBUTION OF INCOME

The distribution of income in a competitive economy is determined by the pricing of factors of production. Businesspeople, said Marshall, must constantly compare the relative efficiency of every agent of production they employ. They also must consider the possibilities of substituting one agent for another. Horsepower replaced handpower, and steampower replaced horsepower. At the margin of indifference between two substitutable factors of production, their prices must be proportionate to the money value they add to the total product. The most striking advantage of economic freedom is manifest when a businessperson experiments at his own risk to find the combination of factor inputs that will yield the lowest costs in producing the output. Entrepreneurs must estimate how much an extra unit of any one factor of production will add to the value of their total product. They will employ each agent up to that margin at which its net product would no longer exceed the price they would have to pay for it. Marshall based this analysis on the diminishing returns that result from the "disproportionate use of any agent of production."

Wages

Wages, said Marshall, are not determined by the marginal productivity of labor alone. Marginal productivity *is* the basis for the demand for labor, which is a derived demand depending on the demand by consumers for the final products. But wages, like the return to any factor of production, depend on both demand and supply. If the supply of labor increases, other things remaining constant, the marginal productivity of labor will fall (the labor supply curve will cut the labor demand curve further downward). Hence, the equilibrium wage rate will fall. If the supply of labor is reduced, the marginal productivity of labor will rise (the labor supply curve will cut the demand curve higher up), and the wage rate will rise. Marginal productivity by itself, therefore, does not determine wages, because varying the number of workers will produce many possible marginal productivities. It is correct, however, to say that wages measure and are equal to marginal productivity with a given supply of labor. For each employer the wage rate is fixed at the market wage; that is, the firm is a wage taker, so it varies the number of employees in order to reach the optimal level of employment. This optimum occurs where the wage rate (marginal resource cost) equals the extra revenue that the firm gains by selling the marginal product (marginal revenue product).

Marshall not only correctly identified the demand for labor as a derived demand but also discussed the determinants of the wage elasticity of labor demand. Pigou later summarized these as Marshall's four laws of derived demand. In modern terms these laws are:

1. Other things being equal, the greater the substitutability of other factors for labor, the greater will be the elasticity of demand for labor. For example, in some circumstances robotic machinery can be readily substituted for labor. A wage rate increase therefore will produce a disproportionate decline in employment.

2. Other things being equal, the greater the price elasticity of product demand, the greater will be the elasticity of labor demand. Suppose, for example, that the product demand is elastic (restaurant meals) and the wage rate rises. This will increase the costs of production and raise the product price. The higher product price will be met with a substantial decline in purchases, thus necessitating an equally substantial decline in the number of workers hired (cooks, cashiers, waitresses and waiters).

3. Other things being equal, the larger the proportion of total production costs accounted for by labor, the greater will be the elasticity of labor demand.[8] For example, where labor costs are 100 percent of total costs, a wage rate increase of 20 percent will increase total costs by 20 percent. But where labor costs are only 10 percent of total cost, the same 20 percent increase in the wage would result in only a 2 percent rise in total cost. The relatively high increase in costs in the first case could be expected eventually to cause a large rise in product price, a sizable decline in production and sales, and thus a large drop in employment.

4. Other things being equal, the greater the elasticity of the supply of other inputs, the greater the elasticity of demand for labor. To illustrate, let's suppose that the wage rate in a certain industry rises and that this prompts an attempt to substitute capital for labor. Will this increased demand for capital drive up *its* price and thus retard the substitution process? The answer is "Yes" if the supply of capital is highly inelastic, but "No" if it is highly elastic. The wage elasticity of labor demand will be greater when a supply of capital is elastic than when that supply is inelastic.

Interest

Another distributive share that Marshall considered is interest. A rise in the rate of interest diminishes the use of machinery, because the businessperson avoids the use of all machines whose net annual surplus is less than the rate of interest. Lower interest rates increase capital investments. The demand for the loan of capital is the aggregate of the demands of all individuals in all trades. As with final commodities, the higher the price, the less capital demanded; the lower the price, the more capital demanded. This relationship is based on diminishing marginal productivity associated with an increase in the quantity of the factor, just as the demand for consumer goods is based on diminishing marginal utility from successive quantities consumed.

The diminishing marginal productivity of capital as more units are acquired constitutes the demand for capital, with prices recorded in terms of rates of interest. The *quantity of saving supplied* depends on the rate of interest, and the rate of interest depends on the *supply* of saving. The supply of saving is the whole series of quantities that would be offered at different interest rates, just as demand is a series of quantities that would be taken at different prices. For saving, as for the supply

[8] In the 1930s John R. Hicks challenged Marshall's third law, showing that, for highly technical reasons, it is not valid in all situations. More precisely, Marshall's rule assumes that the product demand elasticity is greater than the elasticity of substitution between capital and labor. John R. Hicks, *The Theory of Wages,* 2nd ed. (New York: St. Martin's Press, 1966), 241–247.

of other items, the price (interest rate) settles at the point of intersection of the demand and supply curves. Thus, the price (interest rate) determines the quantity of the commodity supplied (saving).

The main motive for saving is the willingness of people to postpone consumption from the present in hopes of gaining a greater reward in the future:

> Human nature being what it is, we are justified in speaking of the interest on capital as the reward of the sacrifice involved in the waiting for the enjoyment of material resources, because few people would save much without reward; just as we speak of wages as the reward for labour, because few people would work hard without reward.
>
> The sacrifice of present pleasure for the sake of future, has been called *abstinence* by economists. But this term has been misunderstood: for the greatest accumulators of wealth are very rich persons, some of whom live in luxury, and certainly do not practice abstinence in that sense of the term in which it is convertible with abstemiousness. What economists meant was that, when a person abstained from consuming anything which he had the power of consuming, with the purpose of increasing his resources in the future, his abstinence from that particular act of consumption increased the accumulation of wealth. Since, however, the term is liable to be misunderstood, we may with advantage avoid its use, and say that the accumulation of wealth is generally the result of a postponement of enjoyment, or of a *waiting* for it.[9]

Marshall recognized that other motives for saving might also be important. He mentioned family affection, force of habit, miserliness, magnitude of income, and prudence in wishing to provide for the future. Some saving might therefore occur even if interest were zero or negative. If a person wanted a certain annuity for his old age, he might save less at a high rate of interest than at a low rate; the high rate would yield the same total sum of money with a lower amount of saving. But these are the exceptional cases. A fall in the interest rate will generally induce people to consume more in the present, and a rise will induce them to consume less. Thus, interest tends toward an equilibrium level that equalizes the aggregate demand for capital in a market with the aggregate supply forthcoming at that rate.

Profits, Rent, Quasi-Rent

According to Marshall, normal profits include interest, the earnings of management, and the supply price of business organization. Interest has already been discussed. The earnings of management are a payment for a specialized form of labor. The remaining portion of normal profits, the supply price of business organization, is a reward to entrepreneurship.

Marshall incorporated Ricardian rent theory into his system:

> The amount of . . . rent is itself governed by the fertility of land, the price of the produce, and the position of the margin: it is the excess of the value of the total returns which capital and labour applied to land do obtain, over those which they would have obtained under circumstances as unfavorable as those on the margin of cultivation. . . .

[9] Marshall, *Economics*, 232–233.

> The cost of production on the margin of the profitable application of capital and labour is that to which the price of the whole produce tends, under the control of the general conditions of demand and supply: it does not govern price, but it focuses the causes which do govern price.[10]

For the individual producer, said Marshall, land is merely a particular form of capital. There is not much difference between land and buildings; both are subject to diminishing returns as their owner tries to gain additional output from them. For society as a whole, however, the supply of land is permanent and fixed. If one person has land, there is less for others to have. In contrast, if one were to invest in improvements of land or in buildings on it, one would not appreciably curtail the opportunities of others to invest capital in similar improvements.

In the short run, Marshall wrote, land and manufactured capital goods are similar because the supplies of both are fixed. Therefore, the return to old capital investments is something akin to rent; Marshall called it "quasi-rent." Interest is the earnings of "free" or "floating" capital, or on new investments of capital; quasi-rent is the earnings on previous capital investments in the short run. Even if part of the economic rent of land is taxed away, landowners will continue to rent out land, assuming that they wish to maximize their returns instead of withdrawing the land from use in a fit of pique. Similarly, a tax on part of the earnings on fixed capital will not interfere with production in the short run, because it is better to lose part of one's normal profits than to lose everything except scrap value. The analysis assumes that the capital is specialized and has no alternative uses. In the long run, of course, quasi-rent disappears, because a normal return to the fixed capital investment is essential if the investment is to be renewed and business perpetuated.

This is another way of saying that only variable costs influence prices in the short run. Prices in turn determine the earnings of the fixed investment. In the long run, however, both variable costs and normal returns on the fixed investment must be covered, and they both affect price:

> To sum up the whole in a comprehensive, if difficult, statement:—Every agent of production, land, machinery, skilled labour, etc., tends to be applied in production as far as it profitably can be. If employers, and other business men think that they can get a better result by using a little more of any one agent they will do so. They estimate the net product (that is the net increase of the money value of their total output after allowing for incidental expenses) that will be got by a little more outlay in this direction, or a little more outlay in that; and if they can gain by shifting a little of their outlay from one direction to another, they will do so.
>
> Thus then the uses of each agent of production are governed by the general conditions of demand in relationship to supply: that is, on the one hand, by the urgency of all the uses to which the agent can be put, taken together with the means at the command of those who need it; and, on the other hand, by the available stocks of it. And equality is maintained between its values for each use by the constant tendency to shift it from uses, in which its services are of less value to others in which they are of greater value, in accordance with the principle of substitution.[11]

[10] Marshall, *Economics,* 427–428.

[11] Marshall, *Economics,* 521–523.

INCREASING AND DECREASING COST INDUSTRIES

A key analytic device for Marshall was his concept of the "representative firm," which for him was the typical nineteenth-century sole proprietorship. This abstraction served at least three major purposes in his analysis. First, in speaking of the normal cost of producing a commodity, he referred to the expenses of a representative producer who is neither the most efficient nor the least efficient in the industry. Second, this analytic device showed that an industry can be in long-period equilibrium even though some firms are growing and others declining; they simply neutralize each other. Third, even though the representative firm may not be increasing its internal efficiency, it can experience falling costs of production as the industry expands.

Refer to 15-2 PAST AS PROLOGUE

15-2 PAST AS PROLOGUE

Why Do Firms Exist?

Marshall's focus on the "representative firm" set the course that microeconomic analysis was to follow for many decades. Following Marshall, economists built precise models of representative firms operating under conditions of pure competition, monopolistic competition, oligopoly, and pure monopoly. With this emphasis on the firm, it is surprising that Marshall and early neoclassical economists did not ask why representative firms, or for that matter real-world firms, exist at all? If markets work effectively, why have hierarchical business organizations arisen to plan and coordinate large segments of economic activity? Conversely, if planning and coordination within firms confer economic advantages over market coordination, why isn't there a single business firm producing all of a nation's output? What limits the ultimate size of businesses?

London-born Ronald H. Coase addressed precisely these questions in his first publication. His 1937 article, "The Nature of the Firm," eventually established an entirely new field of economic inquiry based on transaction costs, property rights, and contracts.* For this work and a subsequent landmark article on externalities, Coase was awarded the 1991 Nobel Prize in economics. Upon accepting his prize, Coase stated:

> I was 21 years of age [when I first wrote the 1937 article]. I could never have imagined that these ideas would become some 60 years later a major justification for the award of a Nobel Prize. And it is a strange experience to be praised in my eighties for work I did in my twenties.†

Coase suggested that firms exist because selling and buying by individuals in markets involve *transaction costs*. These costs include the costs of identifying buyers and

15-2 PAST AS PROLOGUE (continued)

sellers, determining or negotiating prices, establishing contracts, monitoring the performance of the parties to any contracts, and enforcing contract compliance. Where transaction costs are low or moderate, market coordination, rather than firm coordination, may be the most efficient way to accomplish production and distribution. Farmers can directly buy their inputs from resource suppliers and bring their produce to market to sell directly to firms or individuals. A hierarchical firm may not be necessary to minimize the sum of production and transaction costs.

But in cases where transaction costs from market exchange are sufficiently large (say, building and selling an automobile), it would be economical to establish a centralized organization where production decisions can be planned and coordinated by command. Firms can raise capital, employ managers and workers, and secure raw materials. The actions of the thousands of automobile designers and manufacturing workers can be better planned and coordinated through the firm than through the individual market exchanges or contracts otherwise required.

However, the internal costs to the firm of coordinating production and distribution can rise as the organization grows and becomes more complex. Entrepreneurial incentives erode; bureaucracy emerges; and legal, accounting, and other support services need to be internalized. At some point, further expansion of the size and scope of the firm raises the transaction costs of securing and coordinating inputs above the transaction costs associated with market exchange.

According to Coase, competition will dictate that firms find their optimal sizes. Firms ("little planned societies") can continue to exist only if they perform their coordination function at a lower cost than could the market itself. If firms are too large, they will have higher costs than their smaller competitors and eventually will fail.[‡]

*Ronald H. Coase, "The Nature of the Firm," *Economica* 4 (November 1937): 386–405. Coase emigrated from England to the United States in 1951, eventually moving to the University of Chicago in 1964.

†Ronald H. Coase, "The Institutional Structure of Production," *American Economic Review* 82 (September 1992): 713–719.

‡Other well-known contributors to this field of research include Armen Alchian, Harold Demsetz, and Oliver E. Williamson. See Armen Alchian and Harold Demsetz, "Production, Information Costs, and Economic Organization," *American Economic Review* 62 (December 1972): 777–795; and Oliver E. Williamson, "Hierarchical Control and Optimum Firm Size," *Journal of Political Economy* 75 (April 1976): 123–138.

The Life Cycle of Business Enterprises

Marshall took a dynamic view of the growth and decline of business enterprises:

> We may read a lesson from the young trees of the forest as they struggle upwards through the benumbing shade of their older rivals. Many succumb on their way, and a few only survive; those few become stronger with every year, they get a larger share of light and air with every increase in their height, and at last in their turn they tower

above their neighbours, and seem as though they would grow on for ever, and for ever become stronger as they grow. But they do not. One tree will last longer in full vigour and attain a greater size than another; but sooner or later age tells on them all. Though the taller ones have a better access to light and air than their rivals, they gradually lose vitality; and one after another they give place to others, which, though of less material strength, have on their side the vigour of youth.

And as with the growth of trees, so was it with the growth of businesses as a general rule before the great development of vast joint-stock companies, which often stagnate, but do not readily die. Now that rule is far from universal, but it still holds in many industries and trades. Nature still presses on the private business by limiting even more narrowly that part of their lives in which their faculties retain full vigour. And so, after a while, the guidance of the business falls into the hands of people with less energy and less creative genius, if not with less active interest in its prosperity. If it is turned into a joint-stock company, it may retain the advantages of division of labour, of specialized skill and machinery: it may even increase them by a further increase of its capital; and under favourable conditions it may secure a permanent and prominent place in the work of production. But it is likely to have lost so much of its elasticity and progressive force, that the advantages are no longer exclusively on its side in its competition with younger and smaller rivals.

When therefore we are considering the broad results which the growth of wealth and population exert on the economies of production, the general character of our conclusions is not very much affected by the facts that many of these economies depend directly on the size of the individual establishments engaged in the production, and that in almost every trade there is a constant rise and fall of large businesses, at any one moment some firms being in the ascending phase and others in the descending. For in times of average prosperity decay in one direction is sure to be more than balanced by growth in another.[12]

Internal versus External Economies

Internal economies, said Marshall, are the efficiencies or cost savings introduced by the growth in size of the individual firm. As the firm grows larger, it can enjoy more specialization and mass production, using more and better machines to lower the cost of production. Buying and selling also become more economical as a firm's size increases. Larger firms can secure credit on easier terms, and they can use high-grade managerial ability more effectively.

On the other hand, *external economies* come from outside the firm; they depend on the general development of the industry. As the industry grows, suppliers of materials build plants nearby to serve the expanding industry; these supplies become cheaper both because transport costs are reduced and because they are mass produced in firms that are growing. Perhaps, in addition, providers of transportation services emerge to meet the special needs of the burgeoning industry, thus reducing the cost of delivering products to customers.

[12] Marshall, *Economics,* 315–317.

Marshall thought that an increased volume of production in an industry will *usually* increase the size and therefore the internal economies possessed by a representative firm; it will *always* increase the external economies to which the firm has access. Therefore, he said, the cost of production in terms of labor and sacrifice will fall if the volume of output expands.

External economies are available to all firms in an industry. However, if internal economies grow with the size of the firm, how can competition be maintained? If as a firm becomes larger it becomes more efficient, will this not mean that eventually there will be only a single firm in the industry (natural monopoly)? Marshall's concept of the representative firm provided the answer. The decline and death of the entrepreneur will lead to the decline and death of the firm. Individual businesses, Marshall thought, will typically not last long enough to realize all the benefits of an ever-increasing scale of production. New entrepreneurs will elbow their way into the business arena and renew the process of increasing the size and efficiency of their firms.

Increasing and Decreasing Returns to Scale

If all factors of production used in an industry expand, will the cost per unit of output rise or fall? Marshall thought that we generally have increasing returns to scale in industry; as labor and capital expand, organization and efficiency improve. Only when we rely heavily on nature, as in agriculture, do we have decreasing returns. Where the actions of the laws of increasing and decreasing returns to scale are balanced, we have the law of constant returns: Expanded output is obtained through a proportionate expansion of both labor and the sacrifice of waiting. With enlarged outputs of blankets, for example, the increasing cost of wool may be exactly counterbalanced by the growing efficiency of manufacturing blankets, and we will have constant costs. In most manufacturing, Marshall thought, the cost of raw materials counts for little, and the law of increasing returns to scale is almost unopposed.

Marshall drew an optimistic conclusion from this analysis. Although there may be disadvantages resulting from a rapid growth of population, the final outcome is likely to be favorable. The collective efficiency of people can be expected to increase more than proportionately to their increased numbers.

If an industry is governed by the law of constant returns, an increased demand for its product will in the long run not affect the price. If it is an industry with decreasing returns, an increase in demand will raise the product's price; more will be produced, but not so much more as would be produced if it was characterized by constant returns. If the industry conforms with the law of increasing returns to scale, increased demand will ultimately cause the price to fall, and more will be produced than if it were an industry of constant returns.

Welfare Effects of Taxes and Subsidies

Marshall's analysis of constant, increasing, and decreasing cost industries led him to the following novel policy conclusions: (1) Either a tax or a subsidy will reduce net consumer utility in a constant cost industry; (2) a tax may add to net consumer

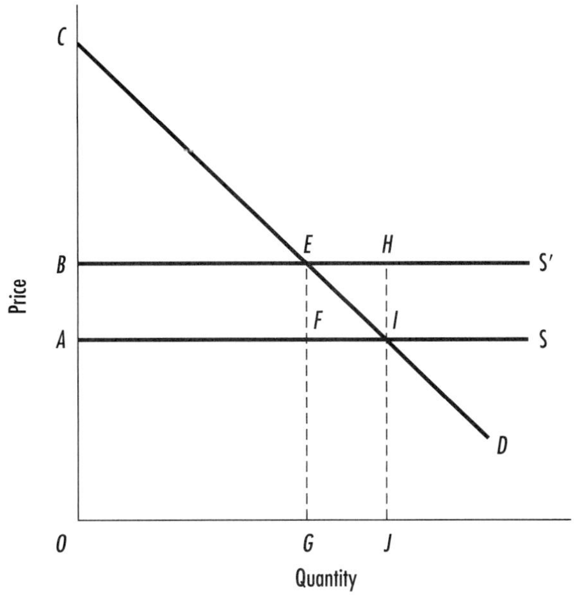

Figure 15-2 The Welfare Effect of a Per-Unit Tax in a Constant Cost Industry
According to Marshall, a per-unit tax on a constant cost industry reduces net consumer utility. A tax of *IH* shifts the supply curve upward from *S* to *S′* and increases the product price from A to B. Government gains tax revenue of the amount represented by ABEF, but consumers lose consumer surplus of the greater amount ABEI, which is area ACI minus BCE.

utility in an increasing cost industry; and (3) a subsidy may add to net consumer utility in a decreasing cost industry.

Figure 15-2 illustrates Marshall's thinking as it relates to the simplest situation: a constant cost industry. The horizontal supply curve *S* in the figure tells us that this is a constant cost industry. Another way of saying this is that changes in demand (shifts of the curve) will not alter the present equilibrium price *A*. Now suppose that a tax of *AB* is levied on each unit of this product and therefore that the cost per unit including the tax rises to $B(A + AB)$. How much revenue will this tax yield, and how much will the higher price reduce consumer surplus? Marshall answered that the tax will yield revenue to the government equal to *ABEF* (*AB*, the tax per unit, times *AF*, the new equilibrium quantity). Consumer surplus—originally *ACI*—falls to *BCE*. Hence the loss of consumer surplus is *ABEI*. Because the loss in consumer surplus exceeds the gain in tax revenue, *ABEF* (which when spent presumably will yield that amount of utility to consumers of public goods), net consumer utility declines. Marshall pointed out that the same outcome results from a subsidy to a producer in a constant cost industry; the amount of the subsidy exceeds the gain in consumer surplus. You should confirm this by assuming that the initial supply curve is *S′* in Figure 15-2 and that government provides a subsidy of *BA* per unit to the producers.

Marshall applied this same type of analysis to increasing and decreasing cost industries. In the former case his analysis showed that a tax would raise tax revenue by more than it would reduce consumer surplus. By restricting the output of firms in the increasing cost industry, unit costs would actually fall, exclusive of the tax. The revenue received should then be used to subsidize the industries experiencing decreasing costs. As the output of decreasing cost industries rises, their unit costs, exclusive of the subsidy, will fall. The gain in consumer surplus will exceed the subsidy.

The implication of this argument is that competitive prices and laissez-faire do not necessarily result in maximum satisfaction to the community. Marshall was well aware of this. If producers are very much poorer than consumers, he said, restricting supply and raising prices will increase aggregate satisfaction; conversely, if consumers are poorer than producers, expanding production and selling commodities at a loss (covered by a government subsidy) may increase total utility. Again, if an individual spends income in such a way as to increase the demand for the services of the poor and thereby increase their incomes, something more is added to the total utility than if an equal amount were added to the incomes of the rich. If a person spends income on things that are produced in increasing cost industries, those things become more expensive for the neighbors, thereby lowering their real incomes:

> These conclusions, it will be observed, do not by themselves afford a valid ground for government interference. But they show that much remains to be done, by a careful collection of the statistics of demand and supply, and a scientific interpretation of their results, in order to discover what are the limits of the work that society can with advantage do towards turning the economic actions of individuals into those channels in which they will add the most to the sum total of happiness.[13]

When Marshall died in 1924 John Maynard Keynes proclaimed him the "greatest economist in the world for a hundred years." Although this may be disputed, few would disagree that Marshall was the most influential economic theorist of his generation. His *Principles of Economics* introduced thousands of subsequent economists to economic analysis. The fact that this book attained its maximum circulation forty years after the publication of its first edition attests to its lasting importance. Nearly all contemporary economists would include Marshall with Adam Smith, David Ricardo, and John Stuart Mill as one of the four greatest figures of the classical and neoclassical schools.

Questions for Study and Discussion

1. Briefly identify and state the significance of each of the following to the history of economic thought: neoclassical thought, law of demand, consumer's surplus, elasticity coefficient, supplementary costs, prime costs, equilibrium price, rules of derived demand, quasi-rent, constant, increasing, and decreasing cost industry, internal economies, and external economies.
2. Is the standard neoclassical assumption of rational economic behavior valid? How would Kahneman and Tversky (Past as Prologue 15-1) answer that question?

[13] Marshall, *Economics,* 475.

Do you agree with Friedman's assertion that it doesn't matter whether the underlying assumptions of a model are valid? Explain.

3. What is Marshall's law of demand? How does it relate to (a) the equimarginal rule, (b) the law of diminishing marginal utility, and (c) consumer surplus?
4. Speculate on how you think Marshall would respond to the following question: Do pearls have value because people dive for them, or do people dive for pearls because pearls have value?
5. Contrast Marshall's distinctions between: (a) supplementary and prime costs; (b) immediate present, short run, and long run; (c) increasing and decreasing cost industries; and (d) internal and external economies.
6. Explain this statement: In the short run, a profitable firm focuses solely on its prime costs (variable costs) in deciding how much to produce. Supplementary costs (fixed costs) are irrelevant to this decision.
7. Compare and contrast the theory of wages presented by John Bates Clark (Chapter 14) with the one presented by Marshall.
8. Explain, through your own illustrations or examples, Marshall's determinants of the wage elasticity of derived demand. Given these determinants, why would we expect the wage elasticity of the demand for labor to be greater in the long run than in the short run?
9. Using the method of analysis employed in Figure 15-2, explain and show graphically Marshall's conclusions that a subsidy to a decreasing cost industry would increase consumer surplus by an amount greater than the subsidy.
10. Discuss the following quote from Phillip C. Newman: "Marshall's contribution to neoclassical economics was to reintroduce the classical concept of cost into economics."

Selected Readings

Books

Blaug, Mark, ed. *Alfred Marshall and Francis Edgeworth.* Brookfield, VT: Edward Elgar, 1992.

Maloney, John. *Marshall, Orthodoxy and the Professionalisation of Economics.* London: Cambridge University Press, 1985.

Marshall, Alfred. *Industry and Trade.* 4th ed. New York: Kelley, 1970. (Orig. pub. 1919.)

———. *Principles of Economics.* 8th ed. London: Macmillan, 1920. (Orig. pub. 1890.)

Pigou, A. C., ed. *Memorials of Alfred Marshall.* New York: Kelley, 1956. (Orig. pub. 1925.)

Reisman, David A. *The Economics of Alfred Marshall.* New York: St. Martin's Press, 1986.

Tullberg, Rita M., ed. *Alfred Marshall in Retrospect.* Brookfield, VT: Edward Elgar, 1990.

Journal Articles

Aldrich, John. "The Course of Marshall's Theorizing about Demand," *History of Political Economy* 28 (Summer 1996): 171–217.

Dooley, Peter C. "Consumer's Surplus: Marshall and His Critics," *Canadian Journal of Economics* 16 (February 1983): 26–38.

The Eastern Economic Journal 8 (January/March 1981). The entire issue is devoted to papers on Marshall.

Frish, Ragnar. "Alfred Marshall's Theory of Value," *Quarterly Journal of Economics* 64 (November 1950): 494–524.

Humphrey, Thomas M. "Marshallian Cross Diagrams and Their Uses before Alfred Marshall: The Origins of Supply and Demand Geometry," *Economic Review* (Federal Reserve Bank of Richmond) 78 (March/April 1992): 3–23.

Keynes, John M. "Alfred Marshall, 1842–1924," *Economic Journal* 34 (September 1924): 311–372.

Whitaker, John K. "Alfred Marshall: The Years 1877 to 1885," *History of Political Economy* 4 (Spring 1972): 1–61.

———. "Some Neglected Aspects of Alfred Marshall's Economic and Social Thought," *History of Political Economy* 9 (Summer 1977): 161–197.

Chapter 16

The Neoclassical School—Monetary Economics

There is no separate school of monetary economics as such, although some contemporary economists are called "monetarists" and some economic schools emphasize monetary phenomena more than others. Therefore, we see in the Time Scale of Economic Ideas that a white arrow emanates from the neoclassical school to monetary economics and from the latter back to the neoclassical school.

The classical and Marxist schools and the early marginalists regarded money merely as a veil that has to be pulled aside to examine the real world; they felt that money and prices are subordinate to more basic economic factors. Others, such as Wicksell and Keynes, combined monetary analysis with their study of fundamental economic processes. Money in economic theory was destined to increase in importance over the years with the growth of banking, credit, and economic fluctuations as well as the increasingly important monetary policies of central banks and governments.

Marshall devoted some attention to monetary analysis. Specifically, he stated a version of the equation of exchange called the *Cambridge equation*. This version is $M = kPT$, where M is the stock of money, k is the fraction of income that people collectively wish to hold in the form of cash balances, P is the general price level, and T is either the volume of trade or real income. Marshall's k is nothing more than the reciprocal of the velocity of circulation, V, in the more familiar equation of exchange, $MV = PT$. Fisher, one of the subjects of this chapter, developed this later version of the equation. So even though certain aspects of the theories presented by Wicksell, Fisher, and Hawtrey are more closely associated with macroeconomics than microeconomics, these economists are within the overall Marshallian neoclassical tradition.

Collectively, Wicksell, Fisher, and Hawtrey made a twofold contribution to economics. First, they explored an area that had been neglected but was growing in importance and therefore required emphasis. Second, they helped integrate monetary analysis into general economic theory. It is important to note, however, that they may have exaggerated the role of money; it is easy to overcompensate for past shortcomings by allowing the pendulum to swing too far in the opposite direction.

As we have suggested, the monetary economists of the neoclassical school differed noticeably from the nonmonetarists in the same school because the monetary theorists had to deal with aggregative analysis, such as total demand, total money supply, total saving, and total investment. A split within the neoclassical tradition ensued. The nonmonetary branch looked at the individual person's or firm's real sacrifices, income, consumption, saving, and investment. The monetary branch aggregated these categories for the whole economy, emphasizing monetary factors along with real factors. It remained for later economists to synthesize monetary and nonmonetary economics, although credit is due Wicksell as an important forerunner of these later economists.

JOHN GUSTAV KNUT WICKSELL

John Gustav Knut Wicksell (1851–1926) was born in Stockholm, Sweden, in a middle-class family. After studying mathematics, languages, literature, and philosophy as an undergraduate at the University of Uppsala, he took advanced degrees in mathematics and physics there. He was elected president of the student body of the university and became increasingly active in the philosophical, political, and literary debates and activities of student circles. As a popular lecturer and pamphleteer, he explored such social questions as the population problem, birth control, emigration, alcoholism and its causes, prostitution, the future of marriage, the right to universal suffrage, and the need for direct progressive income taxes. He was both a scholar and a social reformer—two pursuits that in his day were often considered incompatible.

Wicksell's interest in social problems and reform led him to a study of economics. From 1885 to 1890 he studied at universities in England, France, Germany, and Austria. His most memorable experience in the study of economic theory was his discovery in a Berlin bookshop of von Böhm-Bawerk's book on capital theory soon after its publication in 1888. This book had a profound influence on his own economic thinking.

Wicksell obtained a modest government subsidy in 1896 to begin his monetary studies in Berlin. Otherwise, his small irregular income depended on journalism and popular lecturing on social questions, as well as on occasional private tutoring and high school teaching. He received his first small academic appointment in 1896 and a professorship in 1901 at the age of fifty. In 1909 Wicksell served a brief prison term for making ironical remarks on church doctrine.

Wicksell made several major contributions to economics. For example, you may recall from Chapter 14 that he was one of the earliest economists to suggest that the typical firm will first experience increasing returns, then constant returns, and finally decreasing returns as it expands its size. As we will see later in this chapter, he anticipated the theory of monopolistic competition that was worked out later by Chamberlin and Robinson in the 1930s. But Wicksell's chief claim to fame lies in his contributions to monetary economics. These advancements include: (1) an analysis of the role of interest rates in achieving an equilibrium price level or in generating cumulative inflationary or deflationary movements; (2) recognition of the potential contribution of the government and the central bank in retarding or promoting price stability; and (3) an early statement of the saving-investment approach to macroeconomic equilibrium. This last contribution established Wicksell as the father of the so-called Stockholm school of economics.[1] In addition, his work became one of the sources of Keynesian economics; Keynes himself complimented Wicksell as an important precursor of his own ideas. Wicksell's overall objective was

[1] Other members of this school included Erik Lindahl, Gunnar Myrdal, and Bertil Ohlin.

to synthesize monetary theory, business-cycle theory, public finance, and price theory into one system. Although he was not totally successful, he advanced the state of economic thinking in this area.

Price Level Changes

To Wicksell, monetary theory turned on one main question: Why do prices collectively rise or fall? To answer this question, he turned to an analysis of interest rates. Here he distinguished between the normal or natural rate of interest and the bank rate.

The *normal* or *natural* rate of interest, he said, depends on supply and demand for real capital that is not yet invested. The supply of capital flows from those who postpone consuming part of their income and thereby accumulate wealth. The demand for capital depends on the profit that can be realized from its use, or its marginal productivity. The interaction of supply and demand determines the natural interest rate:

> The rate of interest at which the *demand for loan capital and the supply of savings* exactly agree, and which more or less corresponds to the expected yield on the newly created capital, will then be the normal or natural rate. It is essentially variable. If the prospects of the employment of capital become more promising, demand will increase and [quantity demanded] will at first exceed supply [quantity supplied]; interest rates will then rise and stimulate further savings at the same time as the demand from entrepreneurs contracts until a new equilibrium is reached at a slightly higher rate of interest. And at the same time equilibrium must *ipso facto* obtain—broadly speaking, and if it is not disturbed by other causes—in the market for goods and services, so that wages and prices will remain unchanged. The sum of money incomes will then usually exceed the money value of the consumption goods actually produced, but the excess of income—i.e., what is annually saved and invested in production—will not produce any demand for present goods but only for labour and land for future production.[2]

The normal or natural rate of interest applies only to credit between individuals. Banks, however, complicate matters, because unlike private persons, they are not restricted to their own funds in their lending or even to the funds placed at their disposal by savers. Because banks create credit, they can extend loans even at very low rates of interest. On the other hand, they need not lend out all of the funds placed at their disposal by savers. Hence the bank rate of interest may be either less than or greater than the normal or natural rate of interest. When either of these two situations occurs, the price level will eventually change. Let us examine each case.

- Bank rate < natural rate. If banks lend money at materially lower rates than the normal or natural rate as defined in the previous quotation, saving will be discouraged, and the demand for consumption goods and services will rise. Simultaneously, entrepreneurs will seek more capital investments because of

[2] Knut Wicksell, *Lectures on Political Economy*, trans. E. Classen, 2 vols. (London: Routledge & Kegan Paul, 1935), 2: 193. (Orig. pub. 1906.) Reprinted by permission of the publisher.

the greater net profits to be realized as the cost of borrowing money falls. As investment increases, more income accrues to workers, landowners, the owners of raw materials, and so forth. The prices of consumption goods therefore begin to rise. Juxtaposed with this increased demand for both consumption and investment goods, however, is an unchanged or even diminished supply of goods as saving diminishes, assuming that we start at a position of full employment. Anticipations of price increases will cause prices to rise even more. Equilibrium is disturbed, and a cumulative upward price movement begins. The fundamental cause is a bank or market rate of interest below the normal or natural rate that would bring into balance real saving and real investment at constant prices. Prices will rise without limit so long as the bank rate of interest is less than the natural rate.

- Bank rate > natural rate. Conversely, if the bank rate of interest is above the natural or normal rate, prices will fall. The reason? Saving will increase, and investment spending will decline. The decline in investment spending will reduce national income, which in turn will cause the prices of consumer goods to decline. With the prices of both capital and consumer goods falling, the general price level will obviously decline; that is, deflation will occur. Expecting further price declines, buyers will reduce their present expenditures even further, thus aggravating the deflation.

Implication for Public Policy

Wicksell's analysis of interest rates and his predilection for reform led him to emphasize the role of government and the central bank in promoting economic stability. In his *Interest and Prices,* published in 1898, he became the first economist to advocate stabilizing wholesale prices by controlling discount and interest rates.

The principal cause of cyclical fluctuations, he said, is the fact that technological and commercial progress has not maintained the same rate of advance as the increase in needs, especially of an expanding population. With demand rising, people seek to exploit the situation by increasing investment; but it takes time to increase the volume of output through new discoveries, inventions, and other improvements. The rush to convert large masses of liquid capital into fixed capital produces a boom. If, however, the technical improvements are already in operation and no new ones promise a profit in excess of the margin of risk, depression occurs.

Wicksell did not pursue these real causes of business fluctuations in great depth. He instead focused his attention on the monetary causes, which we discussed previously. To eliminate this latter cause he advocated that banks establish a rate of interest that neither raises nor lowers commodity prices; that is, one at which the bank rate of interest just equals the normal or natural rate of interest. This latter interest rate, remember, is the rate that supply and demand would determine if money did not exist and all lending were in the form of capital goods. The natural rate of interest itself, however, is not fixed. It fluctuates with all the real causes of swings in the economy, such as the efficiency of production, the supply of fixed and liquid capital, the supply of labor and land, and so forth. An exact coincidence of the market and natural rates of interest is, therefore, unlikely unless bankers do something about it. He wrote:

> This does not mean that the banks ought actually to *ascertain* the natural rate before fixing their own rates of interest. That would, of course, be impracticable, and would also be quite unnecessary. For the current level of commodity prices provides a reliable test of the agreement or diversion of the two rates. The procedure should rather be simply as follows: *So long as prices remain unaltered the banks' rate of interest is to remain unaltered. If prices rise, the rate of interest is to be raised; and if prices fall, the rate of interest is to be lowered; and the rate of interest is henceforth to be maintained at its new level until a further movement of prices call for a further change in one direction or the other.*
>
> The more promptly these changes are undertaken the smaller is the possibility of considerable fluctuations of the general level of prices; and the smaller and less frequent will have to be the changes in the rates of interest. If prices are kept fairly stable the rate of interest will merely have to keep step with such rise or fall in the natural rate as is inevitable.
>
> In my opinion, the main cause of the instability of prices resides in the inability or failure of the banks to follow this rule. . . .
>
> The objection that a further reduction in rates of interest cannot be to the advantage of the banks may possibly in itself be perfectly correct. A fall in rates of interest may diminish the banks' margin of profit more than it is likely to increase the extent of their business. I should like then in all humility to call attention to the fact that the banks' prime duty is not to earn a great deal of money but to provide the public with a medium of exchange—and to provide this medium in *adequate measure*, to aim at stability of prices. In any case, their obligations to society are enormously more important than their private obligations, and if they are ultimately unable to fulfill their obligations to society along these lines of private enterprise—which I very much doubt—then they would provide a worthy activity for the State.[3]

Wicksell feared that the growing production and stock of gold would inflate currency, thus causing interest rates to fall and prices to rise. Therefore, the free coinage of gold should be suspended, and the world should pass over to an international paper standard. Such a standard is usually regarded as a means of meeting a growing *scarcity* of gold, but it can just as well be used to correct an *overabundance:*

> In any case, such a prospect need not, on closer investigation, provide cause for consternation. On the contrary, once it had come into being it would perhaps be the present system which would sound like a fairy tale, with its rather senseless and purposeless sending hither and thither of crates of gold, with its digging up of stores of treasure and burying them again in the recesses of the earth. The introduction of such a scheme offers no difficulty, at any rate on the theoretical side. Neither a central bureau nor international notes would be necessary. Each country would have its own system of notes (and small change). These would have to be redeemable at par at every central bank, but would be allowed to circulate only inside the one country. It would then be the simple duty of each credit institution to regulate its rate of interest, both relatively to, and in unison with, other countries, so as both to maintain in equilibrium

[3] Knut Wicksell, *Interest and Prices*, trans. R. F. Kahn (London: Macmillan, 1936), 189–190. (Orig. pub. 1898.) Reprinted by permission of the publisher.

> the international balance of payments and to stabilize the general level of world prices. In short, the regulation of prices would constitute the prime purpose of the bank rate, which would no longer be subject to the caprices of the production and consumption of gold or of the demand for the circulation of coins. It would be perfectly free to move, governed only by the deliberate aims of the banks.[4]

Forced Saving

In discussing aggregate saving and investment, Wicksell analyzed the theory of forced saving. This was not a new idea. Bentham had presented this doctrine, which he had called "forced frugality," in his *Manual of Political Economy,* written by 1804 but published in 1843. In analyzing the role of government in increasing capital, Bentham had spoken of taxes and paper money as being forced frugality. Creating paper money, he had said, is a kind of indirect taxation, because it acts as an income tax on those people with fixed incomes. John Stuart Mill in "On Profits, and Interest" in his *Essays on Some Unsettled Questions of Political Economy,* written in 1829 or 1830, had stated that if bankers depreciate the currency, it operates to a certain extent as a forced accumulation. The higher product prices tax away some of the real income of consumers. Léon Walras clearly had stated the theory of forced savings in 1879, probably inspiring Wicksell and through him all the later German authors who dealt with the subject.

Wicksell hypothesized a case in which a new enterprise was financed through a bank loan—pure credit creation—without a corresponding accumulation of real capital. Assuming full employment at the outset, more land and labor would be employed in producing capital goods than if there were no credit creation to finance a new enterprise, leaving less credit available for turning out consumer goods. Nevertheless the demand for articles of consumption would increase rather than diminish, because entrepreneurs would bid up the prices of land and labor as they expanded investment. With the resulting rise in prices, entrepreneurs would acquire fewer capital goods than they originally contemplated based on the size of the loans they negotiated. At the same time consumption would be restricted as prices rose. This enforced restriction would, in fact, constitute the real accumulation of capital that must be achieved if capital investment is to increase. "The *real saving* which is necessary for the period of investment to be increased is in fact *enforced*—at exactly the right moment—on consumers as a whole."

Wicksell on Imperfect Competition

Wicksell recognized the inadequacy of the purely competitive model in retail markets, thus anticipating by several decades the theory of monopolistic or imperfect competition proposed by Edward Chamberlin and Joan Robinson (Chapter 17). It is remarkable that thirty-two years passed between Wicksell's statement of the problem and its further systematic development, but the idea of pure competition

[4] Wicksell, *Interest and Prices,* 193–194.

was central to much of the marginalist thinking, and its revision required overwhelming evidence of monopolistic tendencies in the economy.

In 1901 Wicksell wrote that retailers usually have a fixed circle of customers, and this enables them to have fixed rather than fluctuating prices. While retail prices do respond to changes in wholesale prices, they do so only after a time lag and in modified form:

> Practically every retailer possesses, within his immediate circle, what we may call an actual sales monopoly, even if, as we shall soon see, it is based only on the ignorance and lack of organization of the buyers. He cannot, of course, like a true monopolist, raise prices at will—only in places remote from trade centres can a considerable local rise in prices occur—but if he maintains the same price and quantities as his competitors, he can almost always count upon his immediate neighbourhood for customers. The result is not infrequently an excess of retailers, apparently for the convenience, but really to the injury, of the consumers. If, for example, two shops of the same kind are situated at different ends of the same street, it would be natural that their respective markets would meet in the middle of the street. Now if a new shop of the same kind is opened in the middle of the street each of the others will, sooner or later, lose some of its customers to the new shop, since the people living round the middle of the street believe that if they get the same goods at the same price they are saving time and trouble by making their purchases at the nearest shop. In this, however, they are mistaken, for the original shops which have now lost some of their customers without being able to reduce their overhead expenses to a corresponding degree will gradually be compelled to raise their prices [because they will no longer be operating on the lowest point of their average cost curve]—and the same applies to the new competitors who have been obliged from the beginning to content themselves with a smaller turnover. . . . The correct remedy, unless one of the competitors (such as a great store) manages to overshadow all the others, is clearly the formation of some form of organization among buyers. But so long as such an association does not exist—and between persons in different positions of life and without more intimate bonds it is extremely difficult to establish—the anomaly must remain that competition may sometimes raise prices instead of always lowering them, as one would expect.[5]

With respect to a complete monopoly, Wicksell followed the lead of Cournot and others by indicating that the volume of sales is artificially restricted to the point that yields maximum profits. Every rise in price reduces the quantity of goods demanded. "But so long as the falling off in demand [quantity demanded] is less than proportionate to the increased profit per unit of the commodity resulting from the higher price, the total net profit . . . will increase." Conversely, when the decrease in sales is more than proportionate to the increased profit per unit, further price increases are disadvantageous. It is important to note, said Wicksell, that fixed, or overhead, costs have no influence whatever in determining the most profitable monopoly price; only variable costs (marginal costs) are to be considered.

---

[5] Wicksell, *Political Economy,* 87–88.

IRVING FISHER

Irving Fisher (1867–1947), a Yale mathematician-turned-economist, was a man of many projects. In addition to his vast written output in economics, he published several highly successful mathematical textbooks. Having suffered from tuberculosis as a young man, he turned to diet and health fads and cultivated these interests all his life, writing several popular books on how to be healthy and live long. He advocated eugenics and joined the antiliquor and antitobacco crusades. Long before World War I he proposed a league of nations to preserve peace. He invented many mechanical gadgets, one of which was the visible card-index system that could be mounted on a rotary stand; eventually Fisher received about a million dollars for this, his only commercially successful invention. The fortune he and his wife possessed, which grew to about nine million dollars in the stock market, was lost in the crash of 1929.

Fisher's Theory of Interest

In his *The Rate of Interest*, published in 1906, Fisher first set forth his sophisticated theory of how interest rates are determined. He published a revised and expanded version of this theory in 1930 in his *The Theory of Interest*. Fisher perceived two factors interacting to establish the interest rate: the *impatience rate* and the *investment opportunity rate.*

The impatience rate is the extent of the community's willingness to obtain present consumption (income) by giving up future consumption (income). The community values both present as well as future consumption, and though it would prefer to have more of both, it is forced by scarcity at any point in time to trade off future consumption if it wishes to gain present consumption. The amount of future consumption it is willing to trade off for present consumption depends on how impatient it is. The less impatient, the more it is willing to save and invest, thereby gaining future consumption. The more impatient, the less it is willing to give up present consumption (to save) in order to obtain goods in the future. Of course, the more present consumption the society has relative to future consumption, the lower the relative value of present consumption, at the margin. That is, when society has much present consumption relative to future consumption, the relative value of *additional* amounts of present consumption is small.[6]

The second factor in interest rate determination, said Fisher, is the investment opportunity rate. Unlike the impatience rate, which involves subjective valuations, the investment opportunity rate is determined by real factors such as the quantity and quality of resources and the state of technology. At one extreme, it would be feasible to devote these resources to producing goods for present consumption alone. At the other extreme, society could use all of them to produce capital, such that present consumption was zero but future consumption would be large. However, as society moves from the first extreme (all present consumption) to the

[6] In today's terminology we would call the impatience rate the marginal rate of substitution of future goods for present goods. Fisher is referring to the slope of a "willingness" or indifference curve that is convex to the origin.

latter one (no present consumption), it experiences diminishing marginal returns. That is, as people cut back present consumption to increase investment and thereby to obtain greater future consumption, the rate of return on investment—the investment opportunity rate—falls. This simply is the previously discussed principle of diminishing marginal returns associated with additions to the capital stock.[7]

In Fisher's words, "The more we invest and postpone our gratification, the lower the investment opportunity rate becomes, but the greater the impatience rate; the more we spend and hasten our gratification, the lower the impatience rate becomes but the higher the opportunity rate." Restated, as society saves and invests, two things happen. First, it gets less and less future consumption from each additional unit of present consumption forgone. Diminishing returns to capital result in a declining rate of return on investment. Second, as present consumption declines and future consumption rises, the relative value of present consumption at the margin rises. In other words, society values present consumption relatively more than previously because it has less present consumption than before.

On the other hand, the less we save and invest as a society, the lower is the relative value of present consumption (Fisher's impatience rate) and the higher is the marginal rate of return on investment.

The equilibrium interest rate will occur where the rate of return on investment and the rate at which society is willing to trade off present for future consumption are equal. We see then that the interest rate depends on both the technological *ability* of society to gain greater future consumption by giving up present consumption and society's *willingness* to trade present for future consumption. This rate of interest, which normally will be positive, will exactly reflect the premium people are willing to pay for present rather than future consumption. Some individuals will decide that it is in their best interest to lend money (postpone consumption) at this interest rate, whereas others will decide to borrow money (consume now rather than later). The amounts people wish to borrow at the equilibrium interest rate will just match the amount people desire to lend. Furthermore, saving will just equal investment.

Fisher pointed out that this *real* rate of interest may or may not equal the observed *monetary* or *nominal* interest rate. The latter depends upon the expected rate of inflation. If, for example, the expected rate of inflation is 5 percent and the real rate of interest is 3 percent, then the nominal rate of interest will be approximately 8 percent. Lenders will demand 8 percent to ensure that borrowers return to them the full purchasing power of the principal lent out, *plus* the real interest rate. This effect of inflation on the nominal rate of interest has come to be known as the *Fisher effect*. A rapid increase in the stock of money may initially reduce interest rates, but, according to Fisher, it will also cause prices to rise. As a result of these higher prices, lenders will *increase* the nominal rate of interest by an amount equal to the rate of inflation expected over the lives of their loans. In this respect, high nominal interest rates may be caused by high expected rates of inflation, as opposed to real factors, such as time preferences and real rates of return on investment.

[7] In today's terminology Fisher is describing a production possibilities curve that is concave to the origin. Fisher, in fact, presented his theory graphically, using production possibilities and indifference curves.

The Quantity Theory of Money

Fisher restated and amplified the old quantity theory of money based on the equation of exchange. Fisher saw five determinants of the purchasing power of money, or its inverse, the price level: (1) the volume of currency in circulation, (2) its velocity of circulation, (3) the volume of bank deposits subject to check, (4) its velocity, and (5) the volume of trade. Monetary economics, the branch that handles these five regulators of purchasing power, is an exact science, Fisher said, capable of precise formulation, demonstration, and statistical verification.

Fisher's equation of exchange is shown as Equation 16-1:

$$MV + M'V' = PT \qquad \textbf{(16-1)}$$

where M is the quantity of currency, V is its velocity of circulation, M' is the quantity of demand deposits, V' is its velocity of circulation, P is the average level of prices, and T is the quantity of goods and services transacted or sold, with each unit being counted each time it is sold or resold.

Fisher's version of the equation of exchange differs from the Cambridge equation by stressing V, the rate at which the money stock turns over, while downplaying k, the fraction of income people wish to hold in the form of cash balances. The Cambridge k is simply $1/V$.

According to Fisher, prices vary *directly* with the quantity of money (M and M') and the velocity of circulation (V and V') and vary *inversely* with the volume of trade (T). The first of these three relations is the most important, said Fisher, because it constitutes the *quantity theory of money.*

Fisher assumed that M', the volume of demand deposits, tends to hold a fixed relation to M, the quantity of currency in circulation; that is, deposits are normally a relatively fixed, definite multiple of currency. There are two reasons for this. First, bank reserves are kept in fixed definite ratio to bank deposits. Second, individuals, firms, and corporations maintain fairly stable ratios between their currency and deposit balances. If the ratio between M and M' is temporarily disturbed, certain factors automatically come into play to restore it. Individuals will deposit surplus cash, or they will cash surplus deposits. Transition periods of rising or falling prices will also disturb the relation between M and M' but only temporarily. As long as the normal relation holds in the long run, the existence of bank deposits magnifies but does not distort the effect on the level of prices produced by the quantity of currency in circulation.

To propound a cause-and-effect relationship between the quantity of currency and the price level, Fisher also had to assume that the velocity of circulation and the volume of trade are constant. He recognized that both fluctuate over the business cycle, but they always tend to return to an equilibrium level. The tendency toward stability in T also depends on full-employment equilibrium, because with considerable unemployment an increase in M might very well increase T instead of P. The volume of trade also grows in the long run with the change in the population, efficiency of production, and so forth. Yet in the short run, with a fully employed economy, the quantity of currency in circulation normally determines the price level. He wrote:

> We come back to the conclusion that the velocity of circulation either of money or deposits is independent of the quantity of money or of deposits. No reason has been, or, so far as apparent, can be assigned, to show why the velocity of circulation of

> money, or deposits, should be different, when the quantity of money, or deposits, is great, from what it is when the quantity is small.
>
> There still remains one seeming way of escape from the conclusion that the sole effect of an increase in the quantity of money in circulation will be to increase prices. It may be claimed—in fact has been claimed—that such an increase results in an increased volume of trade. We now proceed to show that (except during the transition period) the volume of trade, like the velocity of money, is independent of the quantity of money. An inflation of the currency cannot increase the product of farms and factories, nor the speed of freight trains or ships. The stream of business depends on natural resources and technical conditions, not on the quantity of money. The whole machinery of production, transportation, and sale is a matter of physical capacities and technique, none of which depend on the quantity of money. . . . We conclude, therefore, that a change in the quantity of money will not appreciably affect the quantities of goods sold for money.
>
> Since, then, a doubling in the quantity of money: (1) will normally double deposits subject to check in the same ratio, and (2) will not appreciably affect either the velocity of circulation of money or of deposits or the volume of trade, it follows necessarily and mathematically that the level of prices must double. . . .
>
> We may now restate, then, in what causal sense the quantity theory is true. It is true in the sense that *one of the normal effects of an increase in the quantity of money is an exactly proportional increase in the general level of prices.*[8]

What is the "transmission mechanism" through which increases or decreases in M cause changes in P? According to Fisher, people desire to hold a specific quantity of cash balances in relationship to their expenditures (you may recall Marshall's k). The increase in the amount of cash in the economy disturbs this optimum ratio, causing individuals to readjust their cash-to-expenditure ratios by increasing expenditures. This added spending drives up product prices in the same proportion as the increase in cash in the economy. Hence there is a *direct* link, said Fisher, between increased currency and prices. Recall that Wicksell had stressed an *indirect* link: Money creation would cause changes in the bank interest rate that would set off changes in saving and investment that would eventually cause the price level to change.[9]

Monetary Policy

The quantity theory of money offers a way to stabilize the overall price level and thereby stabilize the economy: strictly control the quantity of currency in circulation. This might be achieved with irredeemable paper money, but Fisher took a dim view of the solution before the Great Depression of the 1930s. Paper money not redeemable in gold tends to arouse public distrust, be too easily overissued by the monetary authorities, provoke speculation, and align debtors in a campaign for inflation. The plan he advocated would make paper money redeemable on demand, not in any required weight or coin or gold, but rather in a quantity of gold that

[8] Irving Fisher, *The Purchasing Power of Money* (New York: Macmillan, 1911), 154–157.

[9] This is not to suggest that Wicksell failed to recognize this so-called real balance effect. See Wicksell's *Interest and Prices,* 39–40.

would represent constant purchasing power. The purchasing power of the dollar would thus remain constant. The more gold in a dollar, the more a dollar would buy and the lower prices would be, and vice versa.

According to Fisher's plan, we would first abandon gold coins and use only gold certificates—paper money redeemable in gold bullion. The government would vary the quantity of gold bullion it would give or take for a paper dollar; that is, it would vary the price of gold in order to maintain stability in the general price level. If the price index rose 1 percent, thereby indicating that the purchasing power index was too low, the weight of the gold dollar would be increased by 1 percent. If the price index fell 1 percent below par, the weight of the gold dollar would be reduced by 1 percent. If this weight change did not fully correct the undesirable price change, further changes in the same direction would be required.

If a flood of gold poured into our circulation from domestic or foreign sources, redundant gold certificates would cause a price rise, according to the quantity theory of money. Decreasing the price of gold would reduce the supply of gold certificates for two reasons: First, the deposit of gold with the government would be discouraged. Second, people would exchange their paper money for gold. The currency in circulation would thereby be reduced, and prices would be forced downward. If, alternatively, gold were being exported, prices would fall as money in circulation was reduced. Raising the price of gold would reverse the outflow and thereby restore the previous price level:

> The plan would put a stop, once and for all, to a terrible evil which for centuries has vexed the world, the evil of upsetting monetary contracts and understandings. All contracts, at present, though nominally carried out, are really tampered with as truly as though false weights and measures were used for delivering coal or grain.[10]

Fisher, like most monetarists, believed that price fluctuations cause rather than result from business fluctuations; therefore, stabilizing prices by controlling the quantity of money would eliminate the business cycle. In an article published in 1925 he concluded that "changes in price level almost completely explain fluctuations in trade, for the period 1915–23." He earlier stated:

> If I were to choose a physical analogue it would be not the swing of a clock pendulum but the swaying of the trees or their branches. If, in the woods, we pull a twig and let it snap back, we set up a swaying movement back and forth. That is a real cycle, but if there is no further disturbance, the swaying soon ceases and the twig becomes motionless again.
>
> Another objection to the theory of cyclical regularity in business is that it overlooks "friction." The twig, once deflected and then left to itself, soon stops swaying. So also a rocking chair, left to itself, will soon stop rocking; so also will a pendulum in a clock which has run down. Friction brings them to rest. To keep them going some outside force must be applied. So, in business we must assume that the effect of any initial disturbance would soon wear off, after a very few oscillations of rapidly diminishing amplitude. The resultant business cycle would speedily cease altogether if dependent only on its own reactions. To keep it up there must be applied some outside force. But, unless the outside force happens also to be cyclical and unless, in addition, the

[10] Irving Fisher, *Stabilizing the Dollar* (New York: Macmillan, 1920), 108.

> rhythm of said force or forces happens to be exactly synchronous with the business pendulum itself, these outside forces will not perpetuate, but obfuscate, the cycle, like the wind blowing on the trees. We cannot imagine anything analogous to the "escapement" in a clock which so nicely times the outside force as to keep up the natural swing of the pendulum.
>
> I, therefore, have no faith whatever in "the" business cycle. I do not doubt that, after any disturbance in one direction or the other business tends to swing back to normal (and a very little beyond) just as does the tree.[11]

After the crash of 1929 Fisher saw the greatest cause of deflation and depression as the growth of debts. Excessive debts lead to liquidation, with the dumping of goods on the market. Falling prices of goods lead to further pressure for liquidation of debts. Fisher came to believe that fluctuations in demand deposits are the greatest cause of business fluctuations. In other words, he lost faith in the stable relationship between currency and demand deposits. He also implicitly accepted a criticism of his earlier stabilization plan—that checking accounts, as means of payment, are so vast compared to the gold reserves behind them that small changes in the price of gold have little effect on the average price level.

Fisher's solution was to require 100 percent reserves behind demand deposits, thereby divorcing the process of creating and destroying money from the business of banking. First, a government currency commission would offer to buy liquid bank assets (up to 100 percent of the bank's checking deposits) for currency or lend currency to banks on those assets as security. Then all checkbook money would have to be backed 100 percent by currency reserves. In other words, demand deposits literally would be deposits, consisting of cash held in trust for the depositor. Banks could lend out only their own money or money put into savings accounts. This would eliminate runs on banks, bank failures, much of the government debt, and most bank earnings. Banks would have to levy service charges on deposits to compensate themselves for their loss of earnings when their power to create credit was destroyed. The biggest benefit of Fisher's policy would be the elimination of great monetary inflation and deflation, thereby mitigating economic booms and depressions.

To stabilize the purchasing power of the dollar, the currency commission would be required to buy securities when the index was below the official par and to sell when it was above. The now-familiar mechanism of open-market operations of the Federal Reserve System would be a substitute for gold price variations that Fisher had advocated earlier. The country had already departed from the gold standard when he began advocating this "100 percent money" plan, and he did not favor returning to it.

It is apparent that Fisher did not think that business cycles are inherent in the economy. He regarded their cause as almost entirely monetary and argued that their cure would be effected by stabilizing prices. As late as 1936, Fisher wrote:

> As explanations of the so-called business cycle, or cycles, when these are really serious, I doubt the adequacy of over-production, under-consumption, over-capacity, price-dislocation, mal-adjustment between agriculture and industrial prices, over-confidence, over-investment, over-saving, over-spending.

[11] Irving Fisher, "Our Unstable Dollar and So-Called Business Cycle," *Journal of the American Statistical Association* 20, n.s. (June 1925), 192–193. Reprinted by permission of the publisher.

> I venture the opinion, subject to correction on submission of future evidence, that, in the really great booms and depressions of the past, each of the above-named factors has played a subordinate role as compared with two dominant factors, namely (1) over-indebtedness (especially in the form of bank loans), to start with, and (2) deflation (or appreciation of the dollar), following soon after; also that, where any of the other factors do become conspicuous, they are often merely effects or symptoms of these two.
>
> Though quite ready to change my opinion, I have, at present, a strong conviction that these two economic maladies, which may be called the "debt disease" and the "dollar disease" are, in the great booms and depressions, more important causes than all others put together.[12]

Fisher did outstanding work in mathematical economics, statistics, and index numbers. He was a pioneer in developing the new field of econometrics (Chapter 18), which made statistical methods a part of economic analysis rather than simply a mere adjunct to it. He was honored for his contributions by being elected president of the American Economic Association, the American Statistical Association, and the Econometric Society.

RALPH GEORGE HAWTREY

Ralph George Hawtrey (1879–1975) was a British treasury official who found time to write many books about monetary economics. His main concern was business fluctuations, which he attributed largely to the instability of credit. There might be other causes of fluctuations, he admitted, but they are minor and can be controlled by monetary devices.

Monetary Theory of the Business Cycle

The key figure in Hawtrey's scheme is not the producer but rather the wholesale merchant or trader, and the key factor is the rate of interest. If the banks apply credit restrictions, the direct effect on production in agriculture, mining, and manufacturing is likely to be small. The producers' profit depends on output, and they cannot reduce working capital below a certain level without curtailing production. If producers rely on temporary borrowing, the interest charge, even at a high rate, will be a minor item among their costs.

Wholesalers, by contrast, are very sensitive to the rate of interest. They borrow money to hold inventories, and because their markup is quite small, interest charges are an important component of their costs. Higher interest charges will increase the cost of carrying goods, and they will have to reduce their inventories. Lower interest rates thus make it easier to carry large stocks of goods. Merchants take the initiative in production by increasing or decreasing orders. Their borrowing operations are influenced not only by the terms on which their banker is willing to lend but

[12] Irving Fisher, *100% Money,* 2nd ed. (New York: Adelphi, 1936), 120–121.

also by the level of demand and the prospects of price movements in the market. If they expect prices to rise, they will wish to increase inventories to make an extra profit. In doing this, they must consider the interest charge for the additional money they must borrow, because the extra charge for interest is certain, whereas the rise in prices is speculative.

Why do business fluctuations occur? Because of the inherent instability of credit working through the merchants to upset the rest of the economy in cumulative departures from an unstable equilibrium:

> If the banks increase their lending, there will ensue a release of cash and an enlargement of the consumers' income and outlay [on consumption and investment goods]. The increase in the consumers' outlay means increased demand for goods in general, and the traders find their stocks of finished products diminishing. There result further orders to producers; a further increase in productive activity, in consumers' income and outlay, and in demand; a further depletion of stocks. Increased activity means increased demand, and increased demand means increased activity. A vicious circle is set up, a *cumulative* expansion of productive activity.
>
> Productive activity cannot grow without limit. As the cumulative process carries one industry after another to the limit of productive capacity, producers begin to quote higher and higher prices. The vicious circle is not broken, but the cumulative growth of activity makes way for a cumulative rise of prices. The vicious circle of inflation is set up.
>
> Once an expansion of demand has been definitely started, it will proceed by its own momentum. No further encouragement from the banks to borrowers is required.
>
> A similar principle applies to a contraction of demand. Suppose that the banks take steps to reduce their lending. There will ensue an absorption of cash and compression of the consumers' income and outlay [on consumption and investment goods]. Demand falls off, traders' stocks of finished products accumulate, orders to producers are cut down. Decreased activity means decreased demand, and decreased demand means decreased activity.
>
> The vicious circle of depression is the counterpart of the vicious circle of activity, except that it does not encounter any definite limit such as productive capacity interposes in the way of increasing activity. But the decline in activity is certain to be accompanied by a fall in wholesale prices, for producers will make concessions, each of them endeavoring to get as big a share as possible of the limited amount of demand, in order to keep his plant at work. Here we see the vicious circle of deflation.[13]

Discretionary Monetary Policy

The central bank can regulate credit and thereby promote stability. Sometimes it merely has to modify a tendency to expansion or contraction; at other times it must reverse the tendency. Because the existing tendency possesses a certain momentum, significant force is required to reverse it. The greatest danger is that action will be too late and success therefore more doubtful. If, for example, a vicious circle of

[13] R. G. Hawtrey, *The Art of Central Banking* (London: Longmans, Green, 1932), 167–168. Reprinted by permission of the publisher.

inflation has taken hold, there may be such pressure to borrow that only a flat refusal to lend can counteract it. The central bank would thereby abrogate its function as the lender of last resort. Similarly, a depression may cause such pessimism among traders that they cannot be induced to borrow.

Hawtrey recommended several remedies for curbing the instability of credit and the ensuing instability of economic activity: central bank open-market operations, changes in the rediscount rate, and variations in the reserve requirements of commercial banks. If national income is to be kept steady, then both credit and currency must be allowed to vary. Raising interest rates and restricting bank reserves can curb inflation, because such policies can always be pushed to the point where they become effective. But the converse is not necessarily true. Cheap money and greater bank reserves may not stimulate a revival. When the demand for goods is low, wholesalers seek to reduce their inventories by cutting their purchases to a level below their sales. But if sales fall off more quickly than they expect, the goods in stock may actually increase. In such a situation wholesalers cannot be induced to borrow even at very low rates of interest in order to build up the goods on hand. The outcome is what Hawtrey called a complete credit deadlock, with economic stagnation and deep depression as in the 1930s. "A deadlock is a rare occurrence, but unfortunately in the nineteen-thirties it came to plague the world and raised problems which threatened the fabric of civilisation with destruction."[14]

The way to avoid deadlock, Hawtrey decided, is to take proper action during the previous boom. Early action must be taken to stop excessive monetary expansion. When the bank rate is raised sufficiently, the boom is reversed. After the reversal occurs, the bank rate must be reduced rapidly to avoid a cumulative and vicious deflation:

> When we assume that the high bank rate has done its work, that means that it has successfully overcome the vicious circle of expansion and started the vicious circle of deflation. In order to break the latter, it is essential to infuse into the traders a sufficiently concentrated tendency to increase their purchases. At a time when their purchases are still adapted to the restrictive tendencies of a high bank rate, a *sudden* transition to a low bank rate will have this effect. If the transition is delayed and spread over a longer interval, its power at any one time may be insufficient, and the vicious circle of deflation will go on gathering impetus till it becomes irresistible.[15]

Refer to 16-1 PAST AS PROLOGUE

Hawtrey's concept of the merchant as the crucial figure in economic life may have been more appropriate for England than elsewhere, because England was then the leader in world trade. Its declining position in world trade makes this view less tenable today. Hawtrey's uncritical faith in the efficacy of discretionary monetary policy by way of open-market operations made him quite popular in the United States during the 1920s, because the idea then prevailed that the Federal Reserve System could stabilize the economy with the device. His lucid identification of the tools of monetary policy is indeed a lasting contribution to economics. Hawtrey's early emphasis on the importance of inventories has received increasing recognition

[14] R. G. Hawtrey, *Capital and Employment,* 2nd ed. (London: Longmans, Green, 1952), 79.

[15] Hawtrey, *Capital and Employment,* 113.

16-1 PAST AS PROLOGUE

Hawtrey and Active Monetary Policy, 1982–Present

Ralph G. Hawtrey emphasized the need for timely monetary policy by the central bank to interrupt both the "vicious circle of inflation" and the "vicious circle of deflation," or depression. But, Hawtrey went on to say:

> Possible though it is to stop this [depression] by taking prompt measures to relax credit in time, far better would it be to regulate credit at all times in such a way that neither of the two vicious circles ever gets a serious hold. In quiet conditions credit responds easily to moderate upward and downward movements of the bank [interest] rate. If these movements were always initiated in time, the conditions need never be other than quiet in a monetary sense.*

In the mid- to late 1980s and early 1990s, activist monetary policy took center stage in the U.S. government's attempt to stabilize the economy. One reason for this primary role was that fiscal policy (changes in government spending and taxes to stabilize the economy) was largely dormant. Political polls and voters' choices made it clear that citizens disliked tax increases, no matter how they were rationalized.

Conversely, tax decreases were largely ruled out because of the enormous federal budget deficits. The record-high deficits also made increases in government spending economically untenable. Furthermore, vociferous opposition from concerned special interest groups often blocked proposed reductions in government spending. In short, the large U.S. budget deficits and political climate of the 1980s and early 1990s froze U.S. fiscal policy.

The task of stabilizing the economy therefore fell on the Federal Reserve (the "Fed"). For this reason the post-1982 period in the United States serves as a good case study of active monetary policy. Between 1982 and 1989 the Fed adroitly used this policy to nurture a noninflationary expansion. Whenever growth in the economy slowed, the Fed increased the money supply sufficiently to lower interest rates and stimulate business activity.

However, in the late 1980s the record-long peacetime expansion began to accelerate inflation. The Fed therefore sought to engineer a "soft landing" for the high-flying economy. Its goals included higher interest rates, a slight slowdown in the economy's growth, and a decline in inflation—all while avoiding a recession.

The economy landed according to its own script. High interest rates joined with high consumer debt to produce the economy's eighth post–World War II recession. The Fed reacted by easing interest rates, just as Hawtrey would suggest. After nine months of recession, the economy began slowly to recover. But this recovery was so anemic that a "double-dip" recession seemed possible. The Fed again took action, this time dramatically dropping interest rates. These lower interest rates aided the recovery; by 1993 the economy had begun a sustained expansion. The expansion was sufficiently vigorous to accommodate a major tax-rate

16-1 PAST AS PROLOGUE (continued)

increase in 1995. The tax-rate increase, together with strong economic growth, boosted tax revenue so much that the federal budget deficit reached surplus by 1999. All the while, the Fed adjusted interest rates to keep the expansion alive and inflation low.

In an effort to keep prices stable and curb excessive stock market speculation, the Fed raised interest rates steadily from January 1999 through June 2000. Its efforts were successful, as inflation remained low and stock prices leveled off. In January 2001, the Fed reversed course in an attempt to keep the economy from stalling. Despite the Fed's action, recession began in March and continued through most of 2001. During this time, revelations of corporate fraud (e.g., Enron) and the September 11 terrorist attacks further shook the confidence of consumers, businesses, and financial investors. The Fed responded with a series of interest rate cuts, resulting in market lending rates that reached forty-year lows.

Low interest rates continued throughout 2003. The dramatic easing of monetary policy over this period aided economic recovery but also weakened the U.S. dollar and increased the risk of inflation. At the same time, an initially weak expansion, large tax rate cuts, and increased expenditures on homeland security and military operations in Afghanistan and Iraq transformed the budget surpluses into record deficits. With the economy continuing to strengthen, in 2004 and 2005 the Fed raised interest rates in a series of 13 steps. The fourth consecutive increase came in February 2006, with many economists expecting the Fed to raise rates at least once more in 2006.

The experience of 2004–2005 reinforced the view that active monetary policy is useful for preventing "vicious circles" of inflation and depression. Nevertheless, modern economists agree that monetary policy remains an imperfect art. The current consensus is that it can help to smooth business cycles but not necessarily eliminate them.

---

*Ralph G. Hawtrey, *Capital and Employment*, 113.

by economists in recent decades. Some economists have identified fluctuations in stock of unsold goods as one of the key factors in understanding post–World War II expansions and recessions.

Postscript: Subsequent chapters will reveal that later economists refined, expanded, and in some cases reoriented the contributions of Wicksell, Fisher, and Hawtrey. Some of the major economic debates of our time are rooted firmly in the soil tilled by these three economists. Two examples of such debates are the disagreement on the causes of macroeconomic instability and the controversy over the relative effectiveness of discretionary monetary policy versus monetary rules.

Questions for Study and Discussion

1. Briefly identify and state the significance of each of the following to the history of economic thought: Wicksell, normal or natural rate of interest, bank rate of interest, forced savings, Fisher, impatience rate, investment opportunity rate, quantity theory of money, real balance effect, Fisher effect, Hawtrey, open-market operations, and credit deadlock.
2. Suppose that the natural rate of interest just equals the bank rate of interest. Will either inflation or deflation occur, according to Wicksell? Explain, relating your answer to investment and saving.
3. Discuss the following statement: Wicksell felt that the focus of monetary policy should be on the interest rate; Fisher believed that it should be on the stock of money.
4. Suppose that society becomes more impatient; its members desire to consume more goods today rather than wait to consume them in the future. What will be the impact on the equilibrium interest rate, according to Fisher?
5. Explain the distinction between real and nominal interest rates. To whom do we credit this distinction?
6. Suppose that a nation having a fractional reserve banking system decided to adopt, without warning or any other action, a 100 percent reserve requirement. What would you expect to happen to the price level? Explain your reasoning. How did Fisher's proposal for a 100 percent reserve requirement hope to eliminate this problem?
7. How, according to Hawtrey, might a central bank reduce the stock of money in the economy? Drawing upon knowledge gained from past economics courses, explain each of Hawtrey's three tools for monetary policy.
8. What commonalities exist among the economic theories of Wicksell, Fisher, and Hawtrey? What distinct differences are there?
9. Update Past as Prologue 16-1 by researching changes in output, inflation, and monetary policy since 2004. Does it appear that recent Fed efforts to smooth the business cycle have been successful?

Selected Readings

Books

Blaug, Mark, ed. *Irving Fisher, Arthur Hadley, Ragnar Frisch, Friedrich Hayek, Allyn Young, and Ugo Mazzola*. Brookfield, VT: Edward Elgar, 1992.

———, ed. *Knut Wicksell*. Brookfield, VT: Edward Elgar, 1992.

Conrad, J. W. *An Introduction to the Theory of Interest*. Chap. 4. Berkeley, CA: University of California Press, 1959.

Deutsher, Patrick. *R. G. Hawtrey and the Development of Macroeconomics*. Ann Arbor, MI: University of Michigan Press, 1990.

Fisher, Irving. *The Works of Irving Fisher*. Edited by William J. Barber. 14 vols. London: Pickering and Chatto, 1998.

———. *The Money Illusion*. New York: Adelphi, 1928.

———. *The Nature of Capital and Income*. New York: Macmillan, 1906.

———. *100% Money.* 2nd ed. New York: Adelphi, 1936.

———. *The Purchasing Power of Money.* New York: Macmillan, 1911.

———. *Stabilizing the Dollar.* New York: Macmillan, 1920.

Gorlund, Torsten. *The Life of Knut Wicksell.* Translated by Nancy Adler. Stockholm: Almqvist and Wiksell, 1958.

Hawtrey, Ralph George. *The Art of Central Banking.* London: Longmans, Green, 1932.

———. *Capital and Employment.* 2nd ed. London: Longmans, Green, 1952.

———. *Currency and Credit.* London: Longmans, Green, 1919.

Uhr, Carl G. *Economic Doctrines of Knut Wicksell.* Berkeley, CA: University of California Press, 1960.

Wicksell, Knut. *Interest and Prices.* Translated by R. F. Kahn. London: Macmillan, 1936. (Orig. pub. 1898.)

———. *Lectures on Political Economy.* Translated by E. Classen. 2 vols. London: Routledge, 1934–1935. (Orig. pub. 1901 and 1906.)

Journal Articles

Boianovsky, Mauro. "Wicksell on Deflation in the Early 1920s," *History of Political Economy* 30 (Summer 1998): 219–276.

Crockett, John H., Jr. "Irving Fisher on the Financial Economics of Uncertainty," *History of Political Economy* 12 (Spring 1980): 65–82.

Dimand, Robert W. "The Fall and Rise of Irving Fisher's Macroeconomics," *Journal of the History of Economic Thought* 20 (June 1998): 191–202.

Scandinavian Journal of Economics 80, no. 2 (1978). Contains several articles on the economic contributions of Knut Wicksell.

Tobin, James. "Neoclassical Theory in America: J. B. Clark and Fisher," *American Economic Review* 75, no. 6 (December 1985): 28–38.

Trescott, Paul B. "Discovery of the Money-Income Relationship in the United States, 1921–1944," *History of Political Economy* 14 (Spring 1982): 65–88.

Chapter 17

The Neoclassical School—The Departure from Pure Competition

Theories of imperfect competition are well within the scope and tradition of the marginalist or neoclassical school. Although these theories were not fully developed until the early 1930s, they have far deeper roots. For example, recall that Cournot developed models of pure monopoly and duopoly as early as 1838 and that Edgeworth and Wicksell analyzed situations in which the demand curves faced by competitors were less than perfectly elastic. The interest in imperfect competition arose because of the gap in economic theory between the pure models of competition and monopoly and because the theory of pure competition was becoming increasingly untenable. Pure competition applied most fully to agriculture, but even there the theory was becoming less suitable to modern conditions than it had in earlier times. Where only a few buyers offered to purchase farm products in a local market, as with tobacco, meat, grain, and milk, pure competition no longer reigned. In addition, although conventional analysis of price formation helped identify the secondary economic impacts of the growing government intervention in agriculture, such intervention reduced the general usefulness of the model of pure competition.

According to many economists, the neoclassical theory of pure competition had even less direct applicability to modern industrial production and trade than to agriculture. The theory presupposes that many buyers and sellers all dealing with a perfectly homogeneous product so that no individual has perceptible influence in the market. Buyers are therefore completely indifferent as to which seller they patronize. In such a world every seller can dispose of any quantity of goods at the market price, and no advertising, no brand names, and no salesmanship are required. This, said the critics, is obviously a rather abstract and simplified world! Today most economists would agree that the pure competition model provides important insights into the nature and outcomes of competition but does not accurately describe most national and international markets.

The methodology of the theories of imperfect competition discussed in this chapter shows all the characteristics of the neoclassical school. The methodology deals with marginalism and the microeconomic approach in an abstract, deductive, and subjective manner, and its economics assumes a rational, static, and momentarily unchanging world that tends toward equilibrium. Little in these theories is designed to explain fluctuations, growth, and change as a dynamic process.

By showing how monopolies can raise prices above the competitive equilibrium level to yield economic profits over the long run, the theories concerning departure from pure competition were influential in creating a greater willingness among economists to accept more vigorous government antitrust policies and government regulation of the profits of utility monopolies. The theories thus provided the rationale for government objectives that had been enacted almost half a century earlier. The hope persisted that vigorous government action to encourage competition would reverse the trend toward big business that dated back to the 1870s in the United States and even earlier in England. The supposed blessings of pure competition that some economists still hope to achieve represent a reaction to monopoly and an exercise in futility. We cannot win back an economy that resembles pure competition in an age of international competition, and even if we could, it would not be an economy of great stability, growth, and efficiency. In fact, pure competition as a goal has been replaced largely by "workable competition," which represents a compromise between pure competition and oligopoly.

From these additions to neoclassical theory we learn that under monopolistic competition, even in the absence of the power to realize a monopoly profit, prices are likely to be higher and output lower than under pure competition. Furthermore, under conditions of monopolistic competition and monopsony, the factors of production do not receive returns equivalent to the value of their marginal contributions. These new theories thus struck a blow to the widespread idea that a private enterprise system *necessarily* results in the best allocation of productive resources and *necessarily* rewards all factors of production appropriately.

It is remarkable that the new ideas were fully developed independently and almost simultaneously by Edward Chamberlin in the United States, Joan Robinson in England, and Heinrich von Stackelberg in Germany. Von Stackelberg's analysis led him to abandon all hope for economic order except as provided by the state. If the economic world disintegrates into a wasteful struggle of monopolies without an integrating force, then the force of the state must be called upon to impose order. No wonder von Stackelberg wholeheartedly embraced fascism. We will see that Chamberlin and Robinson drew far less radical conclusions.

Our central attention in the remainder of this chapter will be on Chamberlin and Robinson, whose collective contribution was to explore several situations that lie between pure competition and pure monopoly. But before addressing their theories, it will be useful to discuss briefly the early microeconomic ideas of Piero Sraffa.

PIERO SRAFFA

Piero Sraffa (1898–1983), an Italian who migrated to England, studied under Marshall, taught at Cambridge University, and was the editor of the definitive edition of Ricardo's collective works and correspondence. When France fell under the German blitzkrieg in 1940, he was interned by the British as an enemy alien. Keynes denounced the "fatheads" who were mistreating distinguished refugee scholars and wrote, "If there are any Nazi sympathizers still at large in this country, we should look in the War Office and our Secret Service, not in the internment camps."

We will find in Chapter 22 that Sraffa's *Production of Commodities by Means of Commodities* (1960) established him as a leading member of the Post–Keynesian school of economics. As such he was a critic of neoclassicism. Nevertheless, his earlier work was within the methodological tradition of neoclassicism and was seminal in generating the emerging critique of the theory of pure competition.

In the December 1926 issue of the *Economic Journal*, Sraffa published an important article. In it he pointed out that unit costs of production may very well fall as a firm increases its scale of production. Unit costs may decrease because of internal economies as the firm expands output or because overhead charges are distributed over a larger number of units produced. The falling unit costs are incompatible with pure competition (in the extreme this can lead to a *natural monopoly*). If the firm grows more efficient as its size increases, there will be fewer firms and less competition. Thus it is necessary to abandon the path of free competition and turn toward monopoly.

Sraffa presents a well-defined theory, but it is important to remember that both pure competition and natural monopoly are extreme cases. In industries with few firms, competitive forces can still prevail. Sraffa is correct, however, that two conditions can break up the purity of markets: (1) A single producer can affect market price by varying the quantity of goods it offers for sale; (2) each producer may engage in production under circumstances of individual decreasing costs.

Both conditions have more characteristics of monopoly than pure competition. A pure competitor is a "price taker" and faces a horizontal demand curve. Because it can sell all that it wants at the market price, it expands output so long as market price exceeds its rising marginal cost. Hundreds of firms exist because each achieves minimum average cost at relatively small scale. But a firm that has monopoly power must lower its price on all units of output to increase its sales. It therefore has an incentive to curtail its output to keep its price, revenue, and profit high. Also, because some firms experience declining rather than rising average costs, they can expand their scale of operations well beyond the small size that is consistent with pure competition.

Traditional theory holds that a firm's expansion of output is limited by rising costs. Sraffa said that this expansion of output is limited because of monopoly pricing.

> Everyday experience shows that a very large number of undertakings—and the majority of those which produce manufactured consumers' goods—work under conditions of individual diminishing costs. Almost any producer of such goods, if he could rely upon the market in which he sells his products being prepared to take any quantity of them from him at the current price, without any trouble on his part except that of producing them, would extend his business enormously. It is not easy, in times of normal activity, to find an undertaking which systematically restricts its own production to an amount less than which it could sell at the current price, and which is at the same time prevented by competition from exceeding that price. Business men, who regard themselves as being subject to competitive conditions, would consider absurd the assertion that the limit to their production is to be found in the internal conditions of production in their firm, which do not permit of the production of a greater quantity without an increase in cost. The chief obstacle against which they have to contend when they want gradually to increase their production does not lie in the cost of production—which, indeed generally favours them in that direction—but in the difficulty of selling the larger quantity of goods without reducing the price, or without having to face increased marketing expenses. This necessity of reducing prices in order to sell a

> larger quantity of one's own product is only an aspect of the usual descending demand curve, with the difference that instead of concerning the whole of the commodity, whatever the marketing expenses necessary for the extension of this market are merely costly efforts (in the form of advertising, commercial traveller, facilities to customers, etc.) to increase the willingness of the market to buy from it—that is, to raise that demand curve artificially.[1]

In general, each firm enjoys special advantages in its own protected segment of the total market. It would not lose all of its business if it raised its price, and it would not take away all of its rivals' business if it lowered its price. Therefore, the firm enjoys certain monopoly elements even in a market that appears competitive, and the demand curve it faces slopes down and to the right:

> We are led to ascribe the correct measure of importance to the chief obstacle which hinders the free play of competition, even where this appears to predominate, and which at the same time renders a stable equilibrium possible even when the supply curve for the products of each individual firm is descending—that is, the absence of indifference on the part of the buyers of goods as between the different producers. The causes of the preferences shown by any group of buyers for a particular firm are of the most diverse nature, and may range from long custom, personal acquaintance, confidence in the quality of the product, proximity, knowledge of particular requirements and the possibility of obtaining credit, to the reputation of a trademark, or sign, or name with high traditions, or to such special features of modelling or design in the product as—without constituting a distinct commodity intended for the satisfaction of particular needs—have for the principal purpose that of distinguishing it from the products of other firms. What these and the many other possible reasons for preference have in common is that they are expressed in a willingness (which may frequently be dictated by necessity) on the part of the group of buyers who constitute a firm's clientele to pay, if necessary, something extra in order to obtain the goods from a particular firm rather than from any other.
>
> When each of the firms producing a commodity is in such a position the general market for the commodity is subdivided into a series of distinct markets. Any firm which endeavours to extend beyond its own market by invading those of its competitors must incur heavy marketing expenses in order to surmount the barriers by which they are surrounded; but, on the other hand, within its own market and under the protection of its own barrier each enjoys a privileged position whereby it obtains advantages which—if not in extent, at least in their nature—are equal to those enjoyed by the ordinary monopolist.[2]

In a stable industry, said Sraffa, a firm can lower its price and thereby increase its sales and profits to the detriment of competing firms. If a firm raises prices, however, profits are increased without injuring competition; in fact, rival firms gain from the rise in prices because they are then free to raise their own prices. The second method of raising profits is therefore more acceptable to businesspeople

---

[1] Piero Sraffa, "The Laws of Returns under Competitive Conditions," *Economic Journal* 36 (December 1926): 543. Reprinted by permission of the publisher.

[2] Sraffa, "Laws of Returns," 544–545.

than the first, because the profits are regarded as more stable if they do not arouse retaliation by competitors.

Sraffa's widely read and discussed article touched off an outburst of thinking and writing about the shortcomings of then-current economic theory.

EDWARD HASTINGS CHAMBERLIN

Edward Hastings Chamberlin (1899–1967) was born in La Conner, Washington, received his undergraduate degree from the University of Iowa, and earned his doctorate at Harvard, where he later became a professor. He published his *The Theory of Monopolistic Competition* in 1933.[3] This important book fused the previously separate theories of monopoly and competition, and it sought to explain a range of market situations that are neither purely competitive nor totally monopolistic. Chamberlin held that most market prices are actually determined by both monopolistic and competitive elements.

The Theory of Monopolistic Competition

A key concept of the theory of monopolistic competition is that of product differentiation. Within a general class of goods, specific products are "differentiated if any significant basis exists for distinguishing the goods (or services) of one seller from those of others." This implies that each firm's demand curve slopes downward, and therefore its marginal revenue curve must lie below the demand, or average revenue curve. Chamberlin was among the first of many theorists in the late 1920s and early 1930s who applied the idea of marginal revenue implicit in Cournot's monopoly model.[4] As we know from previous discussion, marginal revenue is the addition to total revenue resulting from the sale of an additional unit of output. Under pure competition, with each firm able to sell all it produces at the going market price, the marginal revenue is equal to price, and the marginal revenue and demand curves are identical horizontal lines. Thus, if a farmer can sell all bushels of wheat at $5 per bushel, every additional bushel sold adds $5 to total revenue.

The situation is quite different in markets in which pure competition does not prevail. With a downward sloping demand curve, the marginal revenue curve slopes downward more steeply. For example, if an entrepreneur can sell one pair of shoes per day at a price of $20, two pairs at $18, and three pairs at $16, in each case except the first the marginal revenue is less than the price. The marginal revenue is $20 for the first pair, but only $16 for the second pair. This can be calculated in two ways: (1) Total revenue goes from $20 ($20 × 1) to $36 ($18 × 2), an increase of $16; (2) the additional pair of shoes sells for $18, but the price of the first pair had to be reduced $2 in order to sell a second pair (16 = 18 − 2). Similarly, the marginal revenue derived from selling the third pair of shoes is $12.[5]

[3] It had been submitted in an earlier version in 1927 as his doctoral thesis at Harvard.

[4] Joan Robinson, not Chamberlin, however, is credited for emphasizing the *importance* of marginal revenue in theories of the firm.

[5] If you are still confused on this point you may wish to review the explanation of Figure 12-1.

The cost curves facing a typical firm are those developed by Jacob Viner (review Past as Prologue 14-1). Marginal cost is the addition to total cost as a result of producing one more unit of output. The short-run marginal cost curve for a typical firm is shaped like the letter *U*. This general shape results from the law of increasing and diminishing returns; that is, familiar *U*-shaped cost curves derive from the short-run production function shown earlier as Figure 14-3.

Recall that when marginal cost is below average cost, average cost necessarily falls; when marginal cost is greater than average cost, average cost necessarily rises. Therefore, the marginal cost curve cuts the average cost curve at the latter's lowest point.

The profit maximizing output for each firm is determined at the intersection of the marginal cost and marginal revenue curves. As long as the addition to total revenue from producing one more unit exceeds the addition to total costs, adding to production adds to profit. If, on the other hand, marginal cost is rising and exceeds marginal revenue, it pays to reduce output. As Cournot had pointed out, maximum profit occurs only at the output where marginal cost and marginal revenue are equal. This single rule applies to both pure competition and monopoly, as well as to the range of situations in between.

According to Chamberlin, only where a firm enjoys significant monopoly will its price exceed average cost in both the short and long runs. Where many firms operate under monopolistic competition, free entry into the industry will eliminate monopoly profit in the long run. As more firms offer to sell goods that are close, although imperfect, substitutes for each other, each producer can sell fewer goods at each price than formerly. Long-run equilibrium occurs when each seller's total revenue just equals its total cost (or average revenue equals average cost). Because a normal profit is considered to be a cost, the firm is earning only a normal profit. Such a profit is one that does not attract further entry into the industry, nor causes firms to exit.

These ideas are illustrated graphically in Figure 17-1, which is based on Chamberlin's own representation. The firm's average cost curve, *AC*, includes the average rate of profit—or normal profit—required to keep the business operating in the long run. Goods can therefore be sold at average cost and still show a profit in the accounting sense. Marginal cost, *MC*, is derived from total cost.

To understand Chamberlin's thinking, let's first examine demand curve *D* and the corresponding marginal revenue curve *MR*. The demand curve slopes downward because the firm can increase its sales by lowering its price; if it raises its price, sales will decline. Even those customers who are devoted to a particular seller or the product's brand name will accept slightly differentiated products if the price becomes too high. The marginal revenue curve *MR* intersects the marginal cost curve at output level *B*. As seen by demand curve *D*, at this profit-maximizing level of output, the firm can charge price *M*. This price is also the average revenue of *B* units, and we see that it exceeds average cost by *NS*. Because *NS* is the profit per unit, total profit is area *LMNS* ($NS \times LS$).

If the firm enjoys long-run monopoly power—for example, if entry to the industry is blocked—this situation will represent the long-run equilibrium for the costs and demand depicted in Figure 17-1. The extra profit is monopoly profit of the type identified by a long list of earlier contributors to economic thought. If, however, other firms are free to enter the industry, they will do so in order to share in the above-normal profits. As firms enter, the demand curve confronting our firm will fall, eventually declining to *D′*. A glance at the new marginal revenue curve,

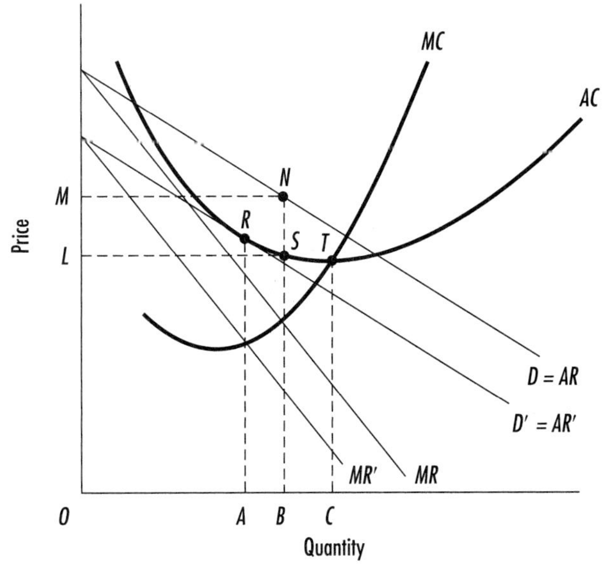

Figure 17-1 Chamberlin's Theory of Monopolistic Competition
Given demand curve *D* and marginal revenue curve *MR*, the monopolistic competitor produces quantity *B*, at which *MR* = *MC* and at which it earns an economic profit of *LMNS*. This economic profit attracts new entrants to the industry, resulting in a downward shift of the firm's demand and marginal revenue curves to *D′* and *MR′*. In long-run equilibrium, the firm maximizes profit by producing quantity *A*, earns only a normal profit (*P* = *AC*), produces less than the competitive output (*A* rather than *C*), and charges a price (*R*) that exceeds marginal cost and lowest average cost. The result is excess capacity and allocative inefficiency.

MR′, reveals that the firm will now produce output level *A* where *MR′* = *MC*, and charge price *R*. At this price and quantity, average revenue equals average cost, and therefore the economic profit has disappeared.

For a firm producing in a market of pure competition, the demand curve and the marginal revenue curve are horizontal and identical. In the long run *C* units would be produced, and the price per unit would be *T*. Thus Chamberlin's significant conclusion:

> The price is inevitably higher and scale of production inevitably smaller under monopolistic competition than under pure competition. . . .
>
> The common result of this assemblage of factors is excess productive capacity [horizontal distance *AC* in Figure 17-1], for which there is no automatic corrective. Such excess capacity may develop, of course, under pure competition, owing to miscalculation on the part of producers, or to sudden fluctuations in demand or cost conditions. But it is the peculiarity of monopolistic competition that it may develop over long periods with impunity, prices always covering costs, and may, in fact, become permanent and normal through a failure of price competition to function. The surplus capacity is never cast off, and the result is high prices and waste. The theory affords

> an explanation of such wastes in the economic system—wastes which are usually referred to as "wastes of competition." In fact, they could never occur under pure competition, and it is for this reason that the theory of pure competition is and must be silent about them, introducing them, if at all, as "qualifications," rather than as parts of the theory. They are wastes of monopoly—of the monopoly elements in monopolistic competition.[6]

To recapitulate: Chamberlin's model indicates that monopolistic competitive firms offer differentiated products, charge prices that exceed their marginal costs, and operate at levels of output at which their average costs are higher than the minimum. Consequently, society's scarce resources are not allocated to their highest valued uses; there is ***allocative inefficiency.*** Society values additional units of the goods that these firms produce more than the alternative products that are being produced instead. Also, *if* these additional units were produced, the average cost of the product would decline.

Qualifications

Many economists, following Chamberlin's lead, have reiterated that pure competition results in a larger output, more efficient production, and lower selling prices than occur under monopolistic competition. But this conclusion requires two qualifications.

First, Chamberlin's conclusions are built on the unrealistic assumption that cost curves are the same in each situation. If we were to have pure competition in the steel industry, we might have thousands of small firms producing steel. Each "steel mill" might be a little larger than a blacksmith's forge, and the price of steel would be much higher than it is at present, even with a few producers enjoying monopolistic power. All we can say is that under pure competition each producer in the long run tends to produce at the minimum point of its own average cost curve. Economies of scale are ***assumed*** to be achieved by all the firms.

If we depart from pure competition, total output decreases and prices rise because of the downward sloping demand curve. But there is no doubt that a modern steel mill is more efficient than a blacksmith's forge. The assumption that each firm has achieved economies of scale is unrealistic in this case. The cost curves of a small firm in pure competition in steel would lie far above those of modern firms. Thus pure competition would not necessarily provide the greatest volume of output and the lowest prices.

Second, contemporary economists note that a world of pure competition, with all products being standardized, would be a dull world indeed. Monopolistic competition results in a number of variations of each general product, thus enabling consumers to better fulfill their diverse tastes. Rather than a standardized hamburger, for example, the consumer has the choice of numerous variations of the same general product, and as is evident by buying patterns, different people tend to like one variation better than others. Thus, monopolistic competition provides positive benefits associated with product variety.

Refer to 17-1 PAST AS PROLOGUE

[6] Edward H. Chamberlin, *The Theory of Monopolistic Competition,* 5th ed. (Cambridge, MA: Harvard University Press, 1946), 88, 109.

17-1 PAST AS PROLOGUE

Principals, Agents, and X-Inefficiency

In his *Wealth of Nations* Adam Smith pointed out that the directors of joint-stock companies (corporations), being the managers of other people's money rather than their own, cannot be expected to watch over the owners' money with the same vigilance as would the owners in a private partnership. Smith asserted that negligence and lavish expenditures, therefore, must always prevail in the management of such companies.

Today, economists call this divergence of interests the ***principal-agent problem.*** Principals are the corporate owners; they are the firm's stockholders. These owners hire agents—executives, managers, and workers—to carry out profit-maximizing activity on the principals' behalf. The agents, however, tend to maximize their own utility, not necessarily the profits of faceless stockholders. They may be able to accomplish this through corporate expenditures that raise, not lower, their employer's costs. For example, they may build elaborate office buildings, buy executive jets, hire unnecessary subordinates, pay excessive wages, undertake unprofitable mergers, and so forth.

In an oft-cited 1966 article, Harvey Leibenstein (1922–1993) referred to the result of excessive costs as ***X-inefficiency,*** to distinguish it from ***allocative inefficiency*** (resource misallocation resulting from prices that exceed marginal cost).[*] X-inefficiency, said Liebenstein, occurs when a firm's actual cost of producing any output is greater than the lowest possible cost of producing it. In terms of Figure 17-1 (or Figure B in Past as Prologue 14-1), X-inefficiency would be shown as *MC* and *AC* curves lying above those shown.

Economists doubt there is room for X-inefficiency in competitive firms. In perfect competition, the long-run entry of firms equates product price with minimum *AC*. A firm whose cost curves are positioned above those of competitors will find that its minimum *AC* exceeds market price, resulting in a loss and eventual bankruptcy. Similarly, a monopolistic competitor would suffer a loss in the long run if its cost curves were above the lowest curve attainable (see Figure 17-1).

X-inefficiency is more likely, however, in monopoly and oligopoly, where entry barriers can shelter inefficient managers from competitive pressures to minimize cost. In fact, X-inefficiency may be on the order of 10 percent of costs for the typical monopolist and 5 percent for an average oligopolist in a highly concentrated industry.[†]

Most economists view X-inefficiency with less concern than a few decades ago. One reason for the suspected decline in X-inefficiency may be that firms have partly countered the principal-agent problem by tying pay to profit. Stock option plans and profit-sharing schemes tend to align the financial interests of executives, managers, and workers with the interest of principals (stockholders). By boosting profit, cost reduction thus aids the agents as well as the principals.

17-1 PAST AS PROLOGUE (continued)

Also, the emergence of a highly developed "market for corporate control" has undoubtedly reduced X-inefficiency. Firms that fail to minimize costs tend to have lower stock market valuations than if they were efficient. This enables other firms to offer to buy shares in X-inefficient corporations from stockholders at share prices above those existing in the stock market. Such "tender offers" may result in stockholders selling their shares, enabling the buyers to wrest corporate control from the existing executives. The new agents will then try to earn a positive return on their financial investment by replacing existing executives and managers with those who are more attuned to reducing costs and maximizing stockholder value. In this way, takeovers and the threat of takeovers reduce X-inefficiency.

*Harvey J. Leibenstein, "Allocative Efficiency vs. 'X-Efficiency'," *American Economic Review* 56 (June 1966): 392–415.

†William G. Shepherd, *The Economics of Industrial Organization,* 4th ed. (Englewood Cliffs, NJ: Prentice-Hall, 1997), 107.

JOAN ROBINSON

Joan Robinson (1903–1983), long-time professor of economics as Cambridge University, was a student of Alfred Marshall. Her book, *The Economics of Imperfect Competition,* was published a few months after Chamberlin's and covers substantially the same ground. In the decades following its appearance in 1933, Robinson expanded her activities and made important contributions in Keynesian and Post–Keynesian economics, economic development, and international trade. We will mention her again in Chapter 22 in our discussion of Post–Keynesian economics. In addition to her other contributions, Robinson offered a significant critique of Marxist economics, though her position was that of a friendly detractor. Robinson was known in her later years as a critic of conventional economics, and her overall works are difficult to fit within any particular school of thought. This fact must be kept in mind as we discuss her early neoclassical contributions.

Monopsony

To the concept of monopolistic competition Robinson added the idea of monopsony, a situation in which there is either a single buyer in a market or a group of buyers acting as one. She analyzed the outcomes of monopsony buying power in product and resource markets.

Product-market monopsony. When there are many buyers of a commodity, their aggregate demand curve slopes downward and to the right, because it is based

Table 17-1
Monopsony in a Product Market (Hypothetical Data)

(1) UNITS	(2) PRICE	(3) TOTAL COST	(4) MARGINAL COST	(5) MARGINAL UTILITY
1	$1	$1	$1	$7
2	2	4	3	6
3	3	9	5	5
4	4	16	7	4
5	5	25	9	3
6	6	36	11	2

on marginal utility. The more units of a good a person acquires, the lower its marginal utility and the less he or she offers for an additional unit.

If there is only a single buyer or if all the buyers form an agreement to act together, we can assume that the market demand curve remains unaltered. We can also assume that the supply curve remains unchanged, because it indicates how much all the sellers together will offer at each price. The supply price is based on the cost of producing each quantity, and this cost does not change in the presence of a monopsony.

Robinson stated two generalizations: (1) Under pure competition, the buyer will purchase successive units of goods at any one time up to the point where the *price* is equal to marginal utility; (2) under monopsony, the buyer will regulate purchases in such a way that the *marginal cost* to him (as distinct from the marginal cost of production) is equal to marginal utility. These important propositions are illustrated in Table 17-1.

First consider *pure competition* among buyers. Suppose the market price of some hypothetical product *X* is $4. No single buyer can influence the price, regardless of the amount that he purchases. We assume that the marginal utility data in column 5 is for a particular consumer who buys only this good. At any one time, ownership of the first unit of the product provides the consumer $7 of marginal utility. A second unit provides $6 of marginal utility to him, the third unit $5, the fourth unit $4, and so forth. At the market price of $4, the consumer will buy four units of the product. That is, he will buy units of the product up to the point where the price ($4 from column 2) is equal to marginal utility ($4 from column 5).[7]

Now suppose the same consumer is the *only* buyer of product *X* in this market. Acquiring the first through the fourth units of the product still provides a marginal utility for him of $7, $6, $5, and $4 (column 5). Assuming that firms can increase the production of this product only under conditions of increasing costs (upward

[7] Notice that our consumer receives a Marshallian consumer's surplus of $6 in this example.

sloping market supply), the more units our consumer wishes to buy, the higher will be the price. Because this monopsonist is the sole buyer, he must pay a higher per-unit price if he wishes to buy a larger number of units; greater output comes at higher per-unit production cost. We see from columns 1 and 2 in Table 17-1 that he can buy one unit of *X* for $1, but two units would cost him $2 each, for a total cost of $4. As shown in column 4, the marginal cost to him of the second unit is $3 ($4 – $1) rather than simply $2, the actual price of the second unit. This $3 marginal cost, however, is less than the marginal utility of the second unit ($6), and therefore the person will choose to buy it. We observe from the table that this consumer will decide to buy three units of the product, because at this amount his marginal cost ($5) is just equal to his marginal utility ($5).

Conclusion: Under normal conditions of an upward sloping product supply curve, the monopsonist will purchase fewer units of a product (3) than would competitive buyers (4) *and* will pay a lower-than-competitive price ($3 as opposed to $4). The monopsonist can control the product price by adjusting the quantity of purchases much like a monopolistic seller can control the same price by adjusting the level of output.

Robinson pointed out that in the presence of a perfectly elastic supply curve—that is, where marginal costs and average costs of production are equal—the supply price will be constant and the quantity purchased under monopsony will be the same as under pure competition. If an industry is working under a diminishing supply price, the marginal cost to the monopsonist will be less than the price of the commodity; he or she will buy more of the product than would pure competitors.

Resource-market monopsony. Robinson also analyzed monopsony in the market for resources, using the labor market as an illustration. The contemporary graphical representation of labor market monopsony, Figure 17-2, derives directly from Robinson's own presentation. To keep the explanation manageable, we will initially disregard the curve labeled *VMP* in the figure. Following Marshall's approach, Robinson declared that an employer's short-run labor demand curve is its marginal revenue product curve, *MRP*. This is true in both monopsonistic and competitive labor markets. Marginal revenue product is the increase in total revenue to the employer when it hires an additional worker; it is the extra revenue that the firm gets when it sells the greater output that the added worker helps produce. Where there is pure competition in the sale of the product, marginal revenue product declines as more workers are hired solely because of the law of diminishing returns. Each added worker contributes less to extra output, and therefore less to marginal revenue, than did the previously added worker.

The labor supply curve facing a monopsonist slopes upward and to the right. Because the monopsonist is the only employer of a particular type of labor, it faces the market labor supply curve. This curve also indicates the average wage cost, *AWC*, because it shows the wage rate that must be paid *per worker* to attract a particular number of workers. Under monopsony, the marginal wage cost—the extra cost associated with employing one more worker—exceeds the average wage cost, or wage rate. The monopsonist must increase the wage rate to attract additional workers away from alternative employment, household activity, or leisure, and it must pay this higher wage rate to *all* of the workers. The extra cost of employing

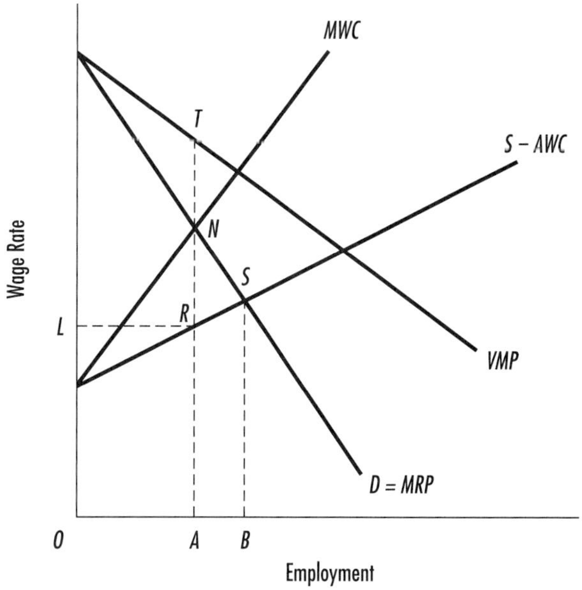

Figure 17-2 Robinson's Theory of Monopsony
The monopsonistic employer faces a marginal wage cost curve *MWC* that lies above the market supply curve *S*. To maximize its profit, it restricts its hiring (*A* rather than *B*) in order to pay a lower-than-competitive wage (*R* rather than *S*). According to Robinson, monopsonistic exploitation is *NR*, the difference between marginal revenue product *MRP* and the monopsony wage. When there is monopoly or monopolistic competition in the product market, the value of the marginal product *VMP* exceeds *MRP*, and monopoly exploitation is *TN*.

an additional worker is therefore more than the wage rate paid to that worker. It also includes the extra wage paid to workers who could have been attracted at a lower wage rate.

How many workers will the monopsonist represented in Figure 17-2 employ? The answer, said Robinson, is *A*, because this is the number at which the marginal revenue product of the last worker employed just equals the marginal wage cost (point *N*). If *MRP* were greater than *MWC*, it would be profitable for the firm to hire more workers; if *MRP* were less than *MWC*, the employer could add to his profits by reducing employment.

The monopsonist shown in Figure 17-2 will pay a wage rate of *L*. As seen by the supply curve, it can attract its profit-maximizing number of employees, *A*, at this wage rate.

This model enabled Robinson to draw several interesting conclusions. First, a labor-market monopsonist will employ fewer workers than would be hired by employers competing with one another for workers (*A* rather than *B*). The monopsonist reduces employment to avoid driving up the wage it must pay to all workers. Second, under monopsony the worker is exploited. Robinson cited one definition of exploitation of labor as a factor of production: being employed at a wage that is less than one's marginal revenue product (*R* rather than *N*). If the market for labor is perfect, so that each employer can hire all the labor needed at the market wage, the marginal wage cost of labor to the individual employer is equal to the wage rate. The employer will be impelled by self-interest to hire workers up to the point where the marginal revenue product is equal to the worker's wage rate. Exploitation of labor under this definition normally does not occur in a competitive labor market.

Exploitation under Monopolistic Competition

Robinson cited another definition of exploitation offered by A. C. Pigou (Chapter 20), her colleague at Cambridge. Exploitation occurs when the worker's wage is less than the value of the marginal product of labor (*VMP*). Accepting this definition, she said that exploitation might exceed *NR* in Figure 17-2. If there were monopoly or imperfect competition in selling the products turned out by labor, then the firm's marginal revenue curve would lie below the *VMP* curve, as illustrated in the figure. Under pure competition in the sale of the product the firm can sell all it produces at the market price; therefore, marginal revenue product is equal to the value of the marginal product, the latter calculated as marginal product times product price. When the firm has monopoly power and therefore faces a downward sloping product demand curve, however, it must lower the price of its goods if it wishes to increase sales (recall the monopoly model). Because the lower price will apply to *all* the firm's output, its marginal revenue will be less than price. Restated, the monopolist's sale of an additional unit of output does not add the full amount of the product's price to the monopolist's marginal revenue. Consequently, the marginal revenue that a firm takes in when it hires an additional worker and sells the resulting greater output will be less than the extra output (marginal product) times the price received for those units. The firm will have to sell all units at the lower price, even those it could have sold at a higher price had it not hired the extra worker. Marginal revenue product will be marginal product times marginal revenue, not times price. Under this definition, *TR* in Figure 17-2 measures total exploitation of labor: *NR* measures the exploitation due to monopsony; *TN* shows that resulting from monopoly or monopolistic competition in the sale of the product.

Remedies for Exploitation

To remedy exploitation of labor under monopsony, said Robinson, a trade union or a trade board should impose a minimum wage on the industry. Then the supply of labor to the industry becomes perfectly elastic at the imposed wage rate, and the marginal wage cost of labor is identical with the average wage cost. Referring to Figure 17-2, if a wage rate of *S* were imposed, the monopsonist would no longer be bidding up the price of labor as he increased employment. The new supply curve would be a horizontal line emanating from the vertical axis and going through point *S*, and employment would increase from *A* to *B*. The wage would equal the marginal revenue product, and exploitation from monopsony would disappear.

To eliminate exploitation under monopoly, the selling price would have to be controlled in such a way that it would equal marginal and average cost. To eliminate exploitation under monopolistic competition, the most common market type according to Robinson, markets would have to become perfect or purely competitive:

> When the market becomes perfect the firms will expand, and in the new position of equilibrium, when profits are once more normal, the firms will be of optimum size, costs will be lower, and the price of the commodity will have fallen.
>
> The removal of the imperfection of the market must therefore lower the price of the commodity. It is likely also to alter the marginal physical productivity of the number of men formerly employed in the industry, since the workers are now organized in optimum firms instead of sub-optimum firms. In the old position they were receiving less than what was then the value of the marginal physical product, and in the new position they will receive the value of their marginal physical product, but it does not follow that they will be better off in the new position than in the old, since the value of the marginal physical product may have diminished; the marginal physical product may have diminished, and the price of the commodity must have fallen.[8]

Economists have identified monopsony power in several real-world labor markets. For example, studies have shown monopsony outcomes in isolated labor markets such as those for some public school teachers, professional athletes (before free agency), nurses, newspaper employees, and so forth. But in most labor markets workers have alternative employers for whom they could work, particularly when these workers are occupationally and geographically mobile. In addition, strong labor unions have emerged to counteract potential monopsony power in several labor markets.

Refer to 17-2 PAST AS PROLOGUE

Criticisms

Chamberlin offered one criticism of Robinson's analysis of exploitation. He did not cover distribution theory in the first edition of his book, but did so in subsequent editions. His retort to Robinson's exploitation theory was that *all* factors, not merely labor, receive less than the value of their marginal products under conditions of monopolistic competition. The Pigou-Robinson definition of exploitation applies only to pure competition in the sale of the product, because it is impossible under other market conditions for all factors to get the value of their marginal products (recall the "adding-up" problem). According to the Pigou-Robinson view, all factors are exploited, and employers could avoid the charge of "exploitation" only by going into bankruptcy.

Two decades after her book appeared, Robinson herself criticized the type of economic theorizing she had helped pioneer:

> *The Economics of Imperfect Competition* was a scholastic book. It was directed to analyzing the slogans of the text-books of twenty years ago: "price tends to equal marginal cost" and "wages equal the marginal product of labour"; and it treated text-book questions, such as a comparison of the price and output of a commodity under conditions of monopoly and of competition, demand and costs being given.

[8] Joan Robinson, *The Economics of Imperfect Competition* (London: Macmillan, 1933), 284–285.

17-2 PAST AS PROLOGUE

Robinson, Monopsony, and Public Policy

The major policy implication of Joan Robinson's monopsony theory is that government may be able to enhance allocative efficiency by raising resource prices in monopsonized markets. In the mid-1930s the U.S. government enacted three important laws designed in part to accomplish this objective.

In 1935 Congress passed the National Labor Relations Act, or Wagner Act. This landmark law guaranteed the twin rights of labor: (1) the right of self-organization, free from interference by the firm and (2) the right to bargain with employers. Also, it listed and outlawed unfair labor practices by firms against unions and their members.

Union membership and bargaining power soared under the protection of the Wagner Act. Consequently, monopsonistic and oligopsonistic employers increasingly faced strong unions across the bargaining table. These negotiations eventually resulted in higher union wages, bearing no resemblance to the exploitive monopsony wages. In fact, the growing strength of labor unions required amendments to the Wagner Act limiting labor's bargaining power (the Taft-Hartley Act of 1947 and the Landrum-Griffin Act of 1959). Today, labor experts agree that unionism has successfully checked potential monopsony power in such oligopolistic industries as automobile manufacturing, steel, maritime trade, and domestic transportation.

A second policy manifestation of Robinson's theory of monopsony was the passage of the Robinson-Patman Act in 1936 (named for Arkansas legislator Joseph Taylor Robinson). This act amended Section 2 of the Clayton Act of 1914, which earlier had outlawed price discrimination that reduces competition. The 1936 amendment added specific details to the law. For example, volume discounts were limited, allowed only when they were justified by lower costs. Also, the act outlawed free advertising, promotional allowances, and phantom brokerage fees provided by

The assumptions which were adequate (or which I hoped were adequate) for dealing with such questions are by no means a suitable basis for an analysis of the problems of prices, production and distribution which present themselves in reality. . . .

In principle, it is possible to set out a system of simultaneous equations showing what combination of price, outlay on production costs and outlay on selling costs would yield the best profit for a particular commodity in a particular market, taking into account the reaction upon costs and sales of other commodities produced by the same firm. Even if he had the data, the business executive would need an electric, not a human, brain to work out from the equations the correct policy in time to put it into effect. And the data are necessarily extremely vague, since the consequences of a given policy cannot be isolated in ever-changing markets. The recent development of advertising is a witness to the difficulty which manufacturers have in knowing the consequences of advertisement, for firms to individual buyers but not their competitors. Thus, small businesses were protected from unfair cost advantages given to large competitors who could use their monopsony power to extract price concessions from suppliers.

Many economists are highly critical of the Robinson-Patman Act, claiming the law "protects competitors, not competition." That is, the law reduces healthy price competition and impedes the formation of efficient market structures, resulting in higher product prices and allocative inefficiency. Proponents counter that the law enhances competition by keeping large firms from unfairly driving out smaller competitors and acquiring monopoly power.

The Fair Labor Standards Act of 1938 is a third law directly related to Robinson's monopsony model. This law, which set a legal minimum $.25 hourly wage, sought to counteract monopolistic exploitation in low-wage labor markets. The goal here was to establish a "living wage" for full-time workers.

Over the years, Congress has increased the minimum wage from $.25 to $5.15 and extended its coverage. Although the minimum wage is popular with the general public, many economists criticize it. These critics observe that low-wage labor markets in advanced industrial societies usually are *not* those characterized by monopsony; workers in these markets usually have numerous employment options. Rather than reducing monopsony power, say these economists, the minimum wage raises wages above competitive levels in some labor markets. The result is higher unemployment, particularly among teenagers. Defenders of the minimum wage counter that low, and possibly monopsony, wages remain a potential reality in many low-wage labor markets. They cite the $.75 to $1.00 hourly wages paid to workers by U.S. firms in many developing countries.

In summary, Joan Robinson's monopsony model helped to initiate or support three major pieces of legislation in the United States: the Wagner Act, the Robinson-Patman Act, and the Fair Labor Standards Act. Of these, the last two are still somewhat controversial.

if they knew its effects there would be no scope for persuading them that it is greater than they think. In reality, evidently, an individual demand curve (for a particular product produced by a particular firm) is a mere smudge, to which it is vain to attribute elegant geometrical properties. . . .

In my opinion, the greater weakness of *The Economics of Imperfect Competition* is one which it shares with the class of economic theory to which it belongs—the failure to deal with time. It is only in a metaphorical sense that price, rate of output, wage-rate or what not can move in the plane depicted in a price-quantity diagram. Any movement must take place through time, and the position at any moment of time depends upon what it has been in the past. The point is not merely that any adjustment takes a certain time to complete and that (as has always been admitted) events may occur meanwhile which alter the position, so that the equilibrium towards which

> the system is said to be *tending* itself moves before it can be reached. The point is that the very process of moving has an effect upon the destination of movement, so that there is no such thing as a position of long-run equilibrium which exists independently of the course which the economy is following at a particular date.[9]

Alfred Marshall had anticipated this last objection of his illustrious pupil, although he had considered this tendency only a minor interference with the larger movement toward an equilibrium price in a market for a single good.

As indicated previously, in later years Robinson turned away from her early microeconomic theories and explored other economic fields in an effort to develop a more dynamic and more realistic analysis of the economic world.[10]

Questions for Study and Discussion

1. Briefly identify and state the significance of each of the following to the history of economic thought: Sraffa, Chamberlin, product differentiation, monopolistic competition, Robinson, monopsony, monopsonistic exploitation, marginal revenue product, and value of the marginal product.
2. What role did Sraffa play in the emergence of theories of less-than-perfect competition?
3. Draw a graph for a Sraffian firm experiencing declining average costs over the full range of output. What does this curve imply about the location of the marginal cost curve? Sketch in this marginal cost curve. Also draw a demand and marginal revenue curve. Show the firm's profit-maximizing price and quantity. Explain why this natural monopoly would go bankrupt if government forced it to charge a price equal to marginal cost (where the demand curve and marginal cost curves intersect).
4. The following characteristics of pure competition and pure monopoly typically are listed in current principles of economics textbooks: pure competition (very large number of competitors, standardized product, "price taker," free entry) and pure monopoly (single seller, no close substitutes, "price maker," blocked entry). Construct a similar list for monopolistic competition. Which of the characteristics tend to be more like monopoly? Which tend to be more like those for a competitive market?
5. Indicate which of the following propositions about monopolistic competition are true and which are false. For those that are false, explain why, referring to either Figure 17-1 or 17-2.
   a) Chamberlin's concern about monopolistic competition was focused on the short run; in the long run, monopolistic competitors earn only a normal profit, and therefore, the quantity of output and average cost are the same as they would be under conditions of pure competition.
   b) Monopolistic competitors tend to have similar, yet differentiated products.

[9] Joan Robinson, "Imperfect Competition Revisited," *Economic Journal* 63 (September 1953): 579, 585, 590. Reprinted by permission of the publisher.

[10] For a review of these other contributions, see Harvey Gram and Vivian Walsh, "Joan Robinson's Economics in Retrospect," *Journal of Economic Literature* 21 (June 1983): 518–550.

c) Robinson contended that no exploitation of labor exists under monopolistic competition as long as the market from which the firm hires workers remains competitive.

6. In the tables that follow, the production data on the left and the labor supply data on the right represent a monopsonist as described by Robinson. Suppose that this firm is selling its product for $2 per unit in a perfectly competitive product market (*MRP* = *VMP*).

UNITS OF LABOR	TOTAL PRODUCT	UNITS OF LABOR	WAGE RATE
0	0	0	—
1	13	1	$2
2	25	2	4
3	34	3	6
4	41	4	18
5	46	5	10
6	48	6	12

a) Determine the firm's total revenue product and marginal revenue product (*MRP*) for each unit of labor.
b) Determine the firm's total wage cost and marginal wage cost (*MWC*) for each unit of labor.
c) How many units of labor will this firm choose to employ, and what wage rate will it pay?
d) If a government wished to get a socially efficient minimum wage, which wage would it select?

7. Explain why the curve labeled *MWC* lies above the curve labeled *AWC* in Robinson's monopsony model (Figure 17-2). In what respect is this fact an *advantage* to the monopsonist?
8. Use Figure 17-2 to show how either a legal minimum wage or a union-negotiated wage might increase both the wage rate and employment in a monopsonized labor market.
9. In what respects are Chamberlin and Robinson clearly in the marginalist or neoclassical tradition? In what respects are they outside the mainstream of that tradition?
10. What is the principal-agent problem? How does it relate to X-inefficiency? Why is X-inefficiency more likely to occur in oligopoly and pure monopoly than in pure competition and monopolistic competition? Do you think X-inefficiency is a growing problem in the economy? Explain your reasoning.

Selected Readings

Books

Blaug, Mark, ed. *Edward Chamberlin*. Brookfield, VT: Edward Elgar, 1993.

Breit, William, and Roger L. Ransom. *The Academic Scribblers*. Rev. ed. Chap. 6. Chicago, IL: Dryden Press, 1982.

Chamberlin, Edward H. *The Theory of Monopolistic Competition*. 5th ed. Cambridge, MA: Harvard University Press, 1946. (Orig. pub. 1933.)

Feiwel, George R., ed. *Joan Robinson and Modern Economic Theory*. 2 vols. New York: New York University Press, 1989.

Rima, Ingrid, ed. *The Joan Robinson Legacy*. Armonk, NY: M. E. Sharpe, 1991.

Robinson, Joan. *The Economics of Imperfect Competition*. London: Macmillan, 1933.

Shackleton, J. R., and Gareth Locksley, eds. *Twelve Contemporary Economists*. Chaps. 11 and 13. New York: Wiley, Halsted, 1981.

Turner, Marjorie S. *Joan Robinson and the Americans*. Armonk, NY: M. E. Sharpe, 1989.

Journal Articles

American Economic Review 54 (May 1964). Several articles in this volume assess the historical impact of the theory of monopolistic competition.

Ekelund, Robert B., Jr., and Robert F. Hébert. "E. H. Chamberlin and Contemporary Industrial Organization Theory," *Journal of Economic Studies* 17, no. 2 (1990): 20–31.

Reinwald, Thomas P. "The Genesis of Chamberlin's Monopolistic Competition Theory," *History of Political Economy* 9 (Winter 1977): 522–534.

Robinson, Joan. "Imperfect Competition Revisited," *Economic Journal* 63 (September 1953): 579–593.

Sraffa, Piero. "The Laws of Returns under Competitive Conditions," *Economic Journal* 36 (December 1926): 535–550.

Chapter 18

MATHEMATICAL ECONOMICS

The term *mathematical economics* refers to those economic principles and analyses formulated and developed through mathematical symbols and methods. Of the economists we have discussed, Cournot, Dupuit, Jevons, Edgeworth, and Fisher, in particular, stated theories in mathematical terms. In fact, the use of mathematical symbols and graphs to supplement verbal explanations is common practice. Mathematical economics therefore does not constitute a separate school of economic thought but rather a distinct method. Theorists from several schools use mathematical language to express in a clear and consistent way the definitions, postulates, and conclusions of a theory. As stated by Paul Samuelson, "By 1935 economics entered a mathematical epoch. It became easier for a camel to pass through the eye of a needle than for a nonmathematical genius to enter into the pantheon of original theorists."[1] Of course, not all economic knowledge can be expressed in mathematical symbols, and not all economists favor the mathematical approach.[2]

This chapter unfolds as follows. First, we distinguish between the broad types of mathematical economics. Next, we scrutinize the economic ideas of Walras, Leontief, von Neumann, Morgenstern, and Hicks—all mathematically minded theorists who significantly advanced the discipline of economics. Finally, we briefiy discuss linear programming, which is an application of microeconomic production theory. Other contributions to mathematical economics, for example, those by Samuelson, are discussed in later chapters.

TYPES OF MATHEMATICAL ECONOMICS

Mathematics is used in economics in two general ways: (1) to derive and state economic theories and (2) to test economic hypotheses or theories quantitatively. Algebra, calculus, difference and differential equations, linear algebra, and topology are the major tools employed in the former, whereas mathematical techniques such as multiple regression analysis are used for the latter. Econometrics, which is the dominant tool of contemporary economics, combines these two types of mathematical economics. Before turning to that topic, however, it is useful to examine simple examples of each of the two general uses.

[1] Paul Samuelson, "Alvin Hansen as a Creative Economic Theorist," *Quarterly Journal of Economics* 90 (February 1976): 25.

[2] One prominent critic has stated, "The prestige accorded to mathematics in economics has given it rigor, but, alas, also mortis." Robert L. Heilbroner, "Modern Economics as a Chapter in the History of Economic Thought," *History of Political Economy* 11 (Summer 1979): 198.

Mathematical Theorizing

To illustrate as simply as possible how economic theories can be stated mathematically, let's express demand and supply relationships as algebraic equations.

In functional form the demand relationship can be stated as

$$Q_x = F(P_x, T, C, I, P_n, E) \tag{18-1}$$

where

- Q_x is the quantity of good X
- P_x is the price of X
- T is consumers' tastes
- C is the number of potential consumers
- I is the total income of consumers and its distribution
- P_n is the price of related goods (substitutes and complements)
- E is the expectations of the consumers

The equation of the demand curve for X is thus

$Q_x = f(P_x)$, or as formulated by Marshall,

$$P_x = g(Q_x) \tag{18-2}$$

where the other variables are held constant (determinants of demand). A linear demand curve takes the form

$$P_x = a - bQ_x \tag{18-3}$$

where a is the price at which zero units of X are demanded, and b is the rate at which Q_x rises as the price falls (a is the vertical intercept of a demand curve, and b is its slope).

The supply relationship, on the other hand, is given by equation 18-4:

$$Q_x = F(P_x, N, P_r, P_s, E, T_n), \tag{18-4}$$

in which

- Q_x is the quantity of good X
- P_x is the price of X
- N is the number of firms supplying X
- P_r is the price of the resources used to produce X
- P_s is the price of the substitute goods the firm could produce
- E is the expectations of producers
- T_n is the range of production techniques available

If we hold all these parameters constant except P_x and Q_x, then the supply relationship becomes

$$Q_x = f(P_x), \text{ or } P_x = g(Q_x) \tag{18-5}$$

A linear supply curve takes the form

$$P_x = c + dQ_x \tag{18-6}$$

where c is the price at which zero units of X are offered for sale, and d is the rate at which Q_x rises as P_x increases (c is the vertical intercept of a supply curve, and d is its slope).

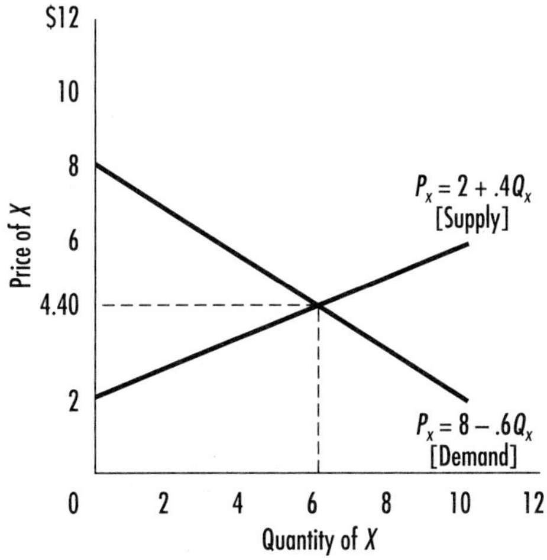

Figure 18-1 Supply and Demand Equations
Plotting the demand equation (18-7) and the supply equation (18-8) yields the familiar demand and supply curves. The intercept of the demand curve is 8, whereas its slope is –.6. The intercept of the supply curve is 2, and its slope is .4. The equilibrium price and quantity are $4.40 and six units, respectively.

To illustrate how we would then solve for the equilibrium price and quantity, suppose that we knew that the demand and supply equations were as follows:

$$P_x = 8 - .6Q_x \text{ (Demand)} \quad \textbf{(18-7)}$$
$$P_x = 2 + .4Q_x \text{ (Supply)} \quad \textbf{(18-8)}$$

Because we have two equations and two unknowns, we can solve for P_x and Q_x. More specifically, we know that in equilibrium there will be a single price, and because P_x in the demand equation will equal P_x in the supply equation,

$$8 - .6Q_x = 2 + .4Q_x \quad \textbf{(18-9)}$$

To solve for Q_x we first subtract 2 from both sides of the equation to eliminate it from the right-hand side. That gives us

$$6 - .6Q_x = .4Q_x \quad \textbf{(18-10)}$$

Next, we add $.6Q_x$ to both sides to eliminate it from the left-hand side. This leaves

$$6 = .4Q_x + .6Q_x, \text{ or } 6 = 1Q_x \quad \textbf{(18-11)}$$

Therefore, the equilibrium quantity is 6 (6/1). You are urged to determine the equilibrium price, P_x, by inserting the equilibrium quantity (6) into either the demand or supply equation (18-7 or 18-8) and solving for P_x. It turns out to be $4.40.

These demand and supply equations are plotted graphically in Figure 18-1. Note that the intercept of the demand curve is 8, and the slope is –.6. The intercept of the supply equation, on the other hand, is 2, and its slope is .4. The equilibrium price and quantity are $4.40 and six units.

Economists often use graphs to clarify their mathematical theories. These graphs are conspicuous features of nearly all undergraduate textbooks in economics. Each line in these graphs represents a mathematical equation.

Statistical Testing

Recall that the second general type of mathematical economics is that associated with statistical testing. To illustrate, let us consider one commonly used technique: regression analysis. Suppose we wish to test the theory that firms possessing larger market shares (S) will tend to have greater monopoly power and therefore higher rates of return on stockholders' equity (r) than firms that face considerable competition and thus have smaller market shares. These rates of return, r, are found by dividing a firm's after-tax profit by the value of the shareholders' equity, which in turn consists of (1) the money received by the firm when they issued the shares of stock and (2) the retained earnings reinvested by the firm over the years.

We know, of course, that parameters other than market share, for instance, advertising intensity (A) and degree of entry barriers (E), most probably influence a firm's rate of return. The researcher then chooses a particular algebraic form to summarize the relationships. The form is based upon the type of theorizing previously discussed. One such form is as follows:

$$r = \alpha_0 + \alpha_1 S + \alpha_2 A + \alpha_3 E + e \quad \textbf{(18-12)}$$

The α*s* are the parameters of the equation; they show how a particular change in the variable on the right-hand side affects the rate of return. The e is a random error, which is needed because not all the factors that influence r are observable.

Initially, let us ignore all the variables in the equation other than the rate of return and the market share.[3] This leaves

$$r = \alpha_0 + \alpha_1 S + e \quad \textbf{(18-13)}$$

The next step then is to identify a sample of firms for which one can get data on rates of returns and market share. Suppose that plotting these data provided a scatter diagram such as the one shown in Figure 18-2. Regression analysis is then used to "fit" a line through the scatter points. The technique is to find one that minimizes the sum of the squared vertical distances between these points and the points on the line. Notice that the regression line in the figure geometrically represents equation 18-13; α_0 is its intercept, and α_1 is the slope of the line. This line indicates that for our hypothetical data every 20 percentage points of additional market share increases the profit rate by 5 percentage points.[4]

How confident can we be that any given estimated parameter is the true one? Researchers use several statistical tests to determine the reliability of any given estimate.

[3] Omitting these variables will bias the estimates of α_0 and α_1, but we are doing this for expository reasons.

[4] These numbers conform in a general way to findings of several empirical studies done on the subject in the United States. If interested, you should see William G. Shepherd, *The Economics of Industrial Organization,* 4th ed. (Englewood Cliffs, NJ: Prentice-Hall, 1997), 99–104.

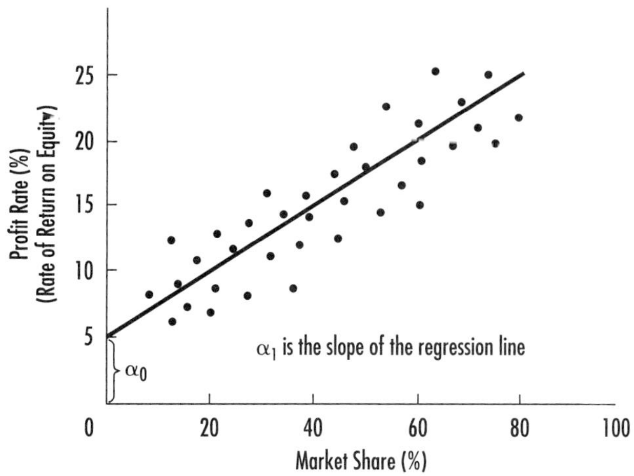

Figure 18-2 A Regression Line
Regression is the technique of fitting the best line through a set of data points. In this hypothetical example, profitability as measured by the rate of return on equity is positively related to market share. Regression analysis and other statistical techniques help economists verify the validity of economic theories.

It is not our purpose to explain them here, but rather only to indicate that they include the *standard error of the estimate* (the amount that the estimated parameter can vary from the true value, or the degree of dispersion of the scatter points) and the *t-statistic* (the ratio of the estimate to the standard error). In contrast, the reliability of the entire regression line is measured by the *coefficient of determination*, which is more commonly called R^2, the fraction of variation in the variable on the left-hand side (rate of return) that can be explained by the variation in the right-hand-side variable(s) (market share). The value of R^2 can vary between 1 and 0, and normally the higher the R^2, the better the fit of the model.

In drawing the regression line in Figure 18-2, we ignored two additional parameters: advertising effort (A) and degree of barriers to entry (E). Adding these parameters limits the ability to depict a regression line graphically, but the mathematical principles involved allow us to handle any number of variables so long as there are fewer variables than observations. Computers, of course, greatly aid actual calculations of estimates of the parameters. In the case of our example, studies indicate that greater advertising intensity and higher entry barriers *do* relate to profitability but *do not* have nearly as great an impact as does market share.

Can we conclude then that monopoly power increases with market share and therefore causes higher-than-normal profit? Although many scholars accept this interpretation, some economists strongly dissent. These critics argue that greater market share results in increasing returns to scale, which then reduce per-unit production and marketing costs. These lower costs, not the enhanced monopoly power gained from the larger market share, generate the observed higher profits. This controversy highlights the limitations of quantitative testing of economic theories:

Simple tests of the theories may still leave ambiguities. It also reveals why economists of goodwill often disagree, even after a substantial amount of empirical testing. But irrespective of the numerous limitations of empirical research, it is clear that this type of applied mathematics has contributed greatly in helping to distinguish valid economic principles from the hundreds of invalid theories advanced over the decades.

Econometrics

As we indicated earlier, econometrics combines the two types of mathematical economics just discussed. Typically, the econometrician develops a theory in mathematical terms, then gathers and statistically tests data that bear on the theory. The theory then is used to predict the impacts of changes in the variables. The roots of the econometric approach go back hundreds of years. Sir William Petty's follower, Charles Davenant, defined "Political Arithmetick" as the "art of reasoning by figures upon things related to government." Quesnay, the French physiocrat, did genuine econometric work.

The Norwegian economist and statistician Ragnar Frisch, who shared the first Nobel Prize in economics in 1969, introduced the term *econometrics* in 1926. He modeled the term on the term *biometrics,* which appeared late in the nineteenth century to denote the field of biological studies employing statistical methods. Econometrics, as a separate method of studying economic life, developed very rapidly just after World War I. The Econometric Society, which publishes the journal titled *Econometrica,* was founded in 1930. Today econometrics is the standard methodological approach used within the discipline.[5]

Econometrics developed in response to the growing professionalism in microeconomics and to the demand for forecasts of macroeconomic changes. Researchers began testing their abstract mathematical models using new econometric techniques and the numerous data sets that were becoming increasingly available. Econometric analysis became important to corporations as a method of conducting market studies, including estimating demand curves and elasticity of demand. The rise of large corporations, among other factors, made the study of macroeconomic fluctuations one of increasing usefulness both to private enterprises and to society as a whole. If, for example, a large enterprise could forecast business fluctuations with a reasonable degree of accuracy, it could to some extent insulate itself from their adverse effects. Also, a large corporation could employ the staff required to make such forecasts. In addition, society as a whole, operating through government and through private nonprofit research organizations, was interested in forecasting business trends in order to control, ameliorate, or counteract them. Growing government intervention in the economy stimulated econometric research, and national governments became the world's major agencies for gathering statistics.

Econometric analysis has been useful both in forecasting the future and in conducting policy analysis. Whereas forecasting involves a projection of likely events and consequences, policy analysis is important in analyzing the effects of government

[5] You are urged to browse through a current issue of a major economic journal such as the *American Economic Review* or the *Journal of Political Economy* to substantiate this fact.

programs and policies. With the proliferation of government in health care, education, urban problems, and a variety of other areas, the need has arisen to determine as accurately as possible what effects these programs have had on individuals and institutions. Econometric techniques provide the analytical framework for such determinations. Nearly all regulatory agencies use econometric analysis to assess economic impacts of private actions and their own policies.

Policy analysis has been proven to be much more accurate than the perilous art of forecasting. Forecasting has other merits, however, than mere prediction of GDP, investment, and so forth. The real advantage of forecasting models is that they force economists and planners to consider the intricate interdependencies in an economic system, thereby helping decision makers anticipate the types of positive and negative effects of alternative actions.

As the technology available to solve large arithmetic processes has become more sophisticated, econometric models have themselves grown in size and complexity. The Dutch were the originators of comprehensive macro models. In 1939 Professor Jan Tinbergen began a model for the Dutch economy to be used by government planners. For this work he shared the Nobel Prize in economics in 1969 with Frisch. In the United States, Lawrence Klein, a Nobel Prize winner at the University of Pennsylvania, is credited for taking a leading role in this area. Today, several major universities, private forecasting firms, nonprofit research institutes, and government agencies have large models (200 or more equations) through which they analyze changes in the U.S. economy.

Refer to 18-1 PAST AS PROLOGUE

LÉON WALRAS

Léon Walras (1834–1910) was born in Evreux, France. The early part of his life was largely unsuccessful. He failed the entrance exam to the Ecole Polytechnique twice, wrote a novel that went unnoticed, and founded a bank that failed. But his father was an economist, and the younger Walras had read Cournot's *Mathematical Principles of the Theory of Wealth.* This subject matter and approach to economics interested him, and he turned to economics. In 1870 he was appointed professor of political economy at Lausanne, Switzerland. There he founded the Lausanne School of Economics, which emphasized the application of mathematics to economic analysis. He was succeeded by another famous member of this school, Vilfredo Pareto, who, you may recall, helped pioneer the use of indifference curves.

Walras is considered to be one of the three originators of marginalism, the others being Jevons and Menger. In his *Elements of Pure Economics* published in 1874, Walras independently arrived at the basic marginalist principles. He also is credited with calling economists' attention to Cournot's earlier work in this area.

Walras developed and advocated general equilibrium analysis, which considers the interrelationships among many variables in the economy. This stood in contrast to the partial equilibrium analysis used by Jevons, Menger, and Marshall. Just as a rock dropped into a pond causes widening circles of ripples, any change in the economy causes further changes that radiate outward with gradually diminishing force. And just as these ripples sometimes reach shore and rebound eventually to affect the initial point of impact, so, too, are there feedback effects of initial

18-1 PAST AS PROLOGUE

Advances in Econometrics

Econometric models *prove* nothing. If they are properly specified, satisfy certain assumptions, and the data are good, these models can strengthen our confidence in certain economic relationships and often yield good predictions. When ideal conditions do not exist, "diseases" are introduced that threaten the validity of the results. Since Ragnar Frisch and Jan Tinbergen shared the first Nobel Prize in economics, econometricians have discovered new econometric diseases and their treatments, as well as techniques for investigating new types of questions. In 2000 and 2003, four new Nobel laureates were crowned, each for their advancements in econometrics. James Heckman (1944–) and Daniel McFadden (1937–) shared the award in 2000 for their contributions to *microeconometrics;* Robert Engle (1942–) and Clive Granger (1934–) were co-recipients in 2003 for advancing methods dealing with *time series analysis.*

The choice of econometric model depends on whether variables are continuous (such as variables measured in monetary terms) or discrete (variables with gaps, such as the choice between two cars or what grade to assign). McFadden's work focused on *discrete choice* (choosing between distinct alternatives), and he developed the method known as *conditional logit analysis* for dealing with discrete choice situations. A logit model can be used to estimate the probability that a group sharing a given set of characteristics (income, age, and so forth) will make the same choice or produce the same outcome. Two similar models, *probit* and *tobit models,* were used to predict medal counts at the 2000 and 2004 summer Olympic games. Using population and GDP as explanatory variables for thirty-six countries, economists Andrew Bernard and Meghan Busse correctly predicted the medal count for one nation, were within one medal for nine countries, and were within three medals for twenty-three nations.*

When data are analyzed, the sample must be drawn from the population at random to produce unbiased results. Samples not drawn at random are known as *selective samples,* and it is for his work in this area that Heckman received his Nobel Prize. *Selection bias* (another term for selective samples) usually occurs as a result of the data collection process. Surveys, a common method for gathering data, even if distributed randomly, may only be answered by certain types of people within the population. Even if those who do respond to a survey are truthful, the fact that only some choose to participate creates a *self-selection* problem, a particular form of selection bias.

Those using economic data frequently have no control over selection bias problems, as they have neither control over the collection procedure nor the resources to gather the information themselves. Fortunately, Heckman developed a procedure for handling the problem, aptly named the *Heckman correction.* Much of Heckman's own work applied to labor market issues (where the selective sample is that subset of the population that is employed), but his contributions have been used by others to investigate a wide range of questions.

Economists are often interested in seeing how variables are related over time, these relationships are investigated using *time series analysis*. Engle and Granger earned their Nobel Prizes for improving the methods available for time series analysis.

An econometric model requires an error term to reflect the effect of factors that cannot be measured and included in the model (see Equation 18-12). Basic econometric technique assumes that these errors are distributed randomly so that the average of these errors over time is zero (they have no long-run effect on the dependent variable, which is also expected to maintain a given long-run value). Unfortunately many error processes do not behave according to this assumption, and in a time series model a systematic error can cause a variable to move in such a way that the model would not accurately predict. Engel identified the problem of *time varying volatility*, where variables exhibit greater fluctuations in some periods than in others. Granger's work centers on models where errors are not random but, in fact, are related to past errors.

Suppose that Figure 18-2 represents the relationship between the market share and the profit rate for a company over time. A simple regression would reveal a positive relationship (α_1, the slope of the regression line, > 0). Suppose however, that for independent reasons, both market share and the rate of profit were rising for a firm. The regression line and α_1 would suggest that an increase in market share increases the rate of profit, but the opposite could be true. Both could be rising for reasons independent of each other, and yet from one period to the next they could be moving in opposite directions. Is this plausible from a theoretical perspective? If a company in one month aggressively pursues a greater market share by cutting prices, it could well experience a lower rate of profit for that month. Company growth over time may well increase market share and rate of profit, but certain strategies geared to increasing one variable might reduce the other. This problem is an example of *cointegration*. Granger is credited with identifying cointegration, and Engle and Granger (and many that have followed) collaborated on the development of techniques for detecting and correcting it.

As econometricians improve the toolkit, researchers return to old data sets and sometimes find that original conclusions were in error. Correcting for these newly identified deficiencies can effectively rewrite history. These advances in econometrics mirror the evolution of economic thought in other areas; one generation identifies the mistakes of its predecessors, usually leaving us with a better understanding.

---

*Andrew Bernard and Meghan Busse, "Who Wins the Olympic Games: Economic Resources and Medal Totals," *Review of Economics and Statistics* 86 (February 2004): 413–418.

changes occurring in single markets in the economy. This process of reverberation continues throughout the entire system until equilibrium is achieved simultaneously in all markets.

An increase in the price of oil provides a good illustration. According to the partial equilibrium approach, if we assume that everything else remains unchanged, a reduced quantity of oil will be bought at the higher price, and that is the end of the matter. But let us consider a few further ramifications explored using the general equilibrium perspective. The demand for substitute goods such as coal will rise, likely causing increases in their equilibrium quantities and prices. The increased price of oil will cause the price of gasoline to rise. Because reading a novel is in a sense a substitute for driving around town, the demand for books might rise. The demand for complementary goods such as automobiles and car washes, on the other hand, may fall as the price of gasoline rises. If the demands for oil and gasoline are relatively inelastic, the percentage of consumer income spent on petroleum products will rise relative to other products. This implies that the demand for numerous goods unrelated to oil and gasoline may decline somewhat. And, of course, transportation costs of goods shipped by truck will increase, causing prices of these items to rise. With all these changes in the markets for consumer goods, the derived demands for factors of production will shift, causing reallocations of resources. Less labor will be needed in some industries (for example, autos); more will be needed in others (for example, home insulation). Capital will also shift in response to differing rates of return on investment in differing industries. For example, producers will build more oil drilling rigs and offshore platforms and fewer new gasoline stations. At some point the changes brought about by the original disturbance will end; a general equilibrium will have been reached.

Walras's general equilibrium theory presents a framework consisting of the basic price and output interrelationships for the economy as a whole, including both commodities and factors of production. Its purpose is to demonstrate mathematically that all prices and quantities produced can adjust to mutually consistent levels. Its approach is static because it assumes that certain basic determinants remain unchanged, such as consumer preferences, production functions, forms of competition, and factor supply schedules.

Walras showed that prices in a market economy can be determined mathematically, taking cognizance of the interrelatedness of all prices. Rigorous proof of the existence of a solution using topology and set theory came later in the works of several economists, most notably John von Neumann, Kenneth Arrow, and Gerard Debreu.

The function for the quantity demanded of a good depends on the price. That is, price is the independent variable, said Walras, and the quantity demanded is the dependent variable. This formulation differed from that of Marshall, who said that the price is a function of the quantity demanded (see Equation 18-2). The quantity demanded of any one good, however, includes as variables the prices of all other commodities. A consumer will not decide how much of one good to buy without knowing the prices of all other goods. If there is a total of n commodities, the total amount demanded for any one of them is determined by the prices of all of them. The total quantity demanded for each commodity can be represented by $D_1, D_2 \ldots D_n$, and the prices by $p_1, p_2 \ldots p_n$. Hence, an equation can be established for each commodity showing the amount of it demanded as a function of all prices:

$$D_1 = F_1(p_1, p_2 \ldots p_n)$$
$$D_2 = F_2(p_1, p_2 \ldots p_n)$$
$$\ldots\ldots\ldots\ldots\ldots\ldots\ldots$$
$$D_n = F_n(p_1, p_2 \ldots p_n) \quad \textbf{(18-14)}$$

In a state of equilibrium the quantity demanded of any particular commodity equals the quantity supplied. Therefore, $D_1 = S_1$, $D_2 = S_2 \ldots D_n = S_n$. If supply is substituted for demand in the preceding three equations, we have:

$$S_1 = F_1(p_1, p_2 \ldots p_n)$$
$$S_2 = F_2(p_1, p_2 \ldots p_n)$$
$$\ldots\ldots\ldots\ldots\ldots\ldots\ldots$$
$$S_n = F_n(p_1, p_2 \ldots p_n) \quad \textbf{(18-15)}$$

We assume that the quantity supplied is given and fixed. With n commodities there are n prices that are unknowns. Because we have an equation for each commodity, there are n simultaneous equations that, under certain assumptions consistent with economic theory, are sufficient for determining a unique set of prices that will satisfy the system. As soon as all prices are known, the aggregate amount of any particular commodity demanded can be calculated. Because this amount demanded is satisfied at the prices so calculated, the problem of the distribution of the available commodities is solved.

Because general equilibrium concepts include many equations and thus many unknowns, the solution of such a system becomes exceedingly complex. In the example used previously, we simply do not know enough about the economy to predict the magnitude of the changed output of coal, automobiles, oil rigs, novels, car washes, and so forth that will result from, say, a 10 percent increase in the price of oil. The variables are too numerous, too changeable, and too uncertain to be worked out precisely, even with modern computers. Furthermore, the analysis typically assumes constant returns, the absence of externalities, perfectly flexible wages and prices, perfect competition in all markets, and so forth. Thus Walras's general equilibrium concept has largely been a theoretical tool helping us understand the blueprint of the economic system rather than an operationally useful statistical device.

Nevertheless, an awareness of the interdependence of economic phenomena is important, because without it we might go astray. For example, a person who loses a job because the industry involved is undermined by cheaper imported goods might reasonably conclude that imports reduce domestic employment; this is an example of partial equilibrium analysis—looking at domestic output and employment in a single industry. However, if we study the repercussions of increased imports and find that they increase employment in domestic seaports, that the lower prices on the imported goods leave consumers with greater income that then is spent on other domestically produced products, and that our exports increase because of our greater imports, then our conclusion may well be that imports do *not* cause a general reduction in domestic output and employment.

WASSILY LEONTIEF

Wassily Leontief (1906–1999), a Russian-born American economist, received his doctorate from the University of Berlin in 1928. He emigrated to the United States in 1931 and joined the faculty at Harvard. His chief contribution to economics is his input-output analysis, which is reminiscent of Quesnay's *Tableau Economique,* discussed in Chapter 3. This contribution won Leontief the Nobel Prize in economics in 1973. He originally sought to present the essence of general equilibrium theory in a simplified form suitable for empirical study. Thus input-output studies are a special form of general equilibrium analysis. This special form simplifies the presentation of production processes, for example, so that they are in linear form, thereby allowing for more direct conversion of such processes into empirical studies.

Input-Output Tables

Leontief published his first input-output table in the *Review of Economics and Statistics* in August 1936. His table depicted the economy of the United States in 1919 as a forty-six-sector system. Interest in his interindustry analysis spread as a result of World War II. The expansion of war industries created certain bottlenecks that made further growth more difficult. The increased output of airplanes, for example, required greater allocation of steel, aluminum, engines, and certain machine tools and other capital goods. Input-output analysis tried to anticipate these requirements and to plan for the expansion of these basic industries.

An input-output table describes the flow of goods and services among different sectors of a given national or regional economy and attempts to measure the relationship of a specific industry to other industries in the economy. For example, according to one of Leontief's tables, to produce an additional million dollars' worth of new automobiles, the industry would have to buy \$235,000 of iron and steel, \$79,000 of nonferrous metals, \$58,000 of chemicals, \$39,000 of textiles, \$32,000 of paper and allied products, \$10,000 of finance and insurance services, \$6,000 of telephone and telegraph services, and so forth.[6]

Leontief worked out an input-output grid that was later expanded by the Bureau of Labor Statistics. The grid sums up statistical information about the economy by showing the sources, the amounts, and the destinations of materials. This reveals the relationship of each segment of the economy to every other segment. Every *row* in an input-output table shows the *output* sold by one economic sector to every other sector; every *column* shows the *input* that each sector purchased from every other sector.

A portion of the grid is reproduced in Table 18-1 (several sectors are left out). We can see that in 1947, agriculture and fisheries sold \$10.9 billion of their output to themselves (feed, seed, breeding livestock, and so forth). Another \$15 billion was sold to food processors. These data provide the raw materials for computing how a change in one industry will affect all other industries. An expansion of the iron and steel industry, for example, will require an expansion of nonferrous metals, which in turn will

[6] Wassily Leontief, *Input–Output Economics* (New York: Oxford University Press, 1966), 71–73.

Table 18-1
Input-Output Relations in the United States in 1947 (in millions of dollars)

	INDUSTRY PURCHASING						
INDUSTRY PRODUCING	(1) Agricul-ture and Fisheries	(2) Food and Kindred Products	(3) Non-ferrous Metals	(4) Iron and Steel	(5) Motors and Generators	(6) Motor Vehicles	(7) Total
(1) Agriculture and Fisheries	10,856	15,048	11	—	—	—	44,263
(2) Food and Kindred Products	2,378	4,910	*	3	—	—	37,636
(3) Nonferrous Metals	—	—	2,599	324	366	176	6,387
(4) Iron and Steel	6	2	33	3,982	118	196	12,338
(5) Motors and Generators	—	—	—	—	317	—	1,095
(6) Motor Vehicles	111	3	*	*	—	4,401	14,265
(7) Total	44,263	37,636	6,387	12,338	1,095	14,265	769,248

* Less than $500,000.
Source: Wassily Leontief et al., *Studies in the Structure of the American Economy* (New York: Oxford University Press, 1953), 9. Reprinted by permission of Oxford University Press.

mean more purchases of agricultural and iron and steel products. The circular interdependence is resolved by solving the simultaneous equations implicit to the matrix.

Uses and Difficulties

Present national input-output tables divide the economy into more than 400 industries, producing an input-output matrix that has more than 400 columns and 400 rows. The rise of large corporations and the development of a significant government role in the economy have enhanced the usefulness of input-output tables for at least two major reasons. First, the government has become a vast buyer of goods and services. Therefore, both the government and its suppliers have to anticipate the effects of changes in the pattern of government buying. Second, the large corporation, in anticipating a growth of sales, has to plan for an expansion in the supply of inputs. A vertically integrated corporation can plan its own supply of some inputs. Others may indicate to their suppliers the extent to which they expect to increase their purchases of inputs. In either case input-output analysis will be useful.

Input-output analysis is even more relevant in less-developed counties, where economic planning is more pervasive. In a less-developed nation seeking economic growth, the construction of a large industry will require the expansion of supporting facilities; these are likely to be much scarcer than in highly developed nations. Suppose a meat canning plant is erected in a poor country. This enterprise will require expansion of electricity, water supply, transport facilities, workers' housing, cafeteria facilities, medical services, production of metal for cans, and so forth. These needs, and the further needs that they present, can be anticipated by way of input-output analysis.

The socialist economies have quite naturally put input-output analysis to use to a greater extent than the nations that rely mainly on private enterprise. Total economic planning requires that the planning body allocate materials and anticipate future needs. The planners must ensure that industries coordinate their expansions if serious bottlenecks are to be avoided. Because consumer preferences are subordinated to the overall plan, consumer whims and desires need not interfere with the preeminent goals for economic activity; in other words, in a completely socialized economy a sudden increase in consumer desire for automobiles will not divert steel away from, say, the machine-tool industry. Therefore, the complications that confront the use of input-output analysis for planning in a private enterprise economy do not occur to the same degree in a totally planned economy. The socialist economies have shown an active interest in mathematical economics in general and in Leontief's grid in particular. In fact, the former Soviet Union claimed that input-output analysis was a Soviet invention.

Input-output analysis is not without problems. This type of analysis is based on several simplifying assumptions. As one example, coefficients of production are assumed to be fixed; that is, constant quantities of each factor are necessary to produce a unit of output. As a second example, production functions are assumed to be linear, with no increasing or decreasing efficiencies as an industry expands or contracts; constant returns to scale are assumed. These assumptions are rather unrealistic. Increases in output frequently do not require proportionate increases in input, mainly because various factors are indivisible. For example, one might increase by 5 percent the ton-miles of freight hauled by a railroad without increasing the supply of locomotives and freight cars by 5 percent. The assumption of fixed production coefficients, on the other hand, precludes the possibility of factor substitution. But in the real world, we see many examples of such substitutions. For example, a reduction in the relative price of plastic has resulted in a substitution of plastic for glass in the bottle industry.

Technological changes make the grid obsolete rather quickly, and it is a tremendous task to revise the 160,000 entries that go into a table involving 400 industries. With the passage of time the input-output table for a given year becomes less and less accurate in predicting the input requirements for future years. Greater accuracy can be achieved, however, by extrapolating from trends observed in the past, thereby anticipating steady technological advances. For example, this method would allow us to predict the continuing reduction in the quantity of coal required to generate one kilowatt-hour of electrical energy.

JOHN VON NEUMANN AND OSKAR MORGENSTERN

John von Neumann (1903–1957) was born in Hungary and taught at the universities of Berlin and Hamburg. In 1930 he came to the United States, where he took a position at Princeton. There he wrote *Mathematical Foundations of Quantum*

Mechanics, a major work in physics, and met Oskar Morgenstern (1902–1977), an economist who first came to the United States from Vienna in 1925.[7] Together they wrote *Theory of Games and Economic Behavior* (1944), a book that contained several important contributions to economic theory, one of which was game theory.[8]

Game theory is applicable to situations analogous to games of strategy, such as chess and poker. Economists had pointed out earlier that duopolists are like chess players who carefully consider the likely moves of their opponent before moving themselves. In such situations there are conflicting interests, with each side using its ingenuity to outwit the other. If, for example, a firm is considering a cut in the price of its product, it makes considerable difference whether or not other producers of similar products will also reduce their prices. Some business decisions are made openly, such as publicly posted price changes, changes in advertising campaigns, and the manufacture of new products. These moves are analogous to chess, where all moves can easily be observed by both sides. Other decisions are secret, such as *sub rosa* price discounting, undertaking new research projects, and planning the invasion of new markets. Such moves are analogous to poker; one party does not know what cards the other party is holding until they are played out. If a company places a spy (such as a janitor) in its rival's business to ferret out secrets, this is like playing poker with a marked deck of cards. If businesses join monopolistic agreements, they must still plan strategy to outwit the public and the government's "trust-busters."

There is an implication in game theory that economic relations are based on a type of economic "warfare"—that one person's gain is another person's loss. But game theory also has been used to show that under many circumstances the best strategy is to cooperate with a rival as long as he cooperates with you (Past as Prologue 4-1).

The underlying logic of game theory can be seen by way of a highly simplified example. Among games of strategy we can distinguish between games of pure chance and games having strategic uncertainty. Shooting dice is a game of pure chance unless the dice are loaded; whether a player wins or loses, and how much, depends only on his own choices and on luck. In a game with strategic uncertainty, such as poker, an additional factor enters: What will the other party do?

Suppose there are only two major producers—*A* and *B*—of some slightly differentiated product and that each seller is considering three distinct business strategies to increase its market share: (1) increasing advertising, (2) offering an "improved" version of the product, or (3) reducing price. Presumably these firms believe that their long-term profitability is positively related to their market shares. We label *A*'s three strategies A_1, A_2, and A_3, whereas we label those for *B* as B_1, B_2, and B_3. For simplicity we assume that only pure strategies can be used; that is, each firm can select only a single strategy rather than some combination of all three.

Game theory rests on the assumption that the outcomes of each combination of the two firms' strategies can be set forth in a payoff matrix such as that shown in Table 18-2. Suppose that each party has knowledge of these outcomes but does

[7] John von Neumann was one of the three coinventors of the atomic bomb.

[8] Another contribution of particular note is the *N–M* index of utility. The authors showed that an individual's marginal utility curve for money could be derived by subjecting the person to a set of hypothetical decisions that involve risk (gambles). This is sometimes referred to as *modern cardinal utility analysis*. See William J. Baumol, *Economic Theory and Operations Analysis*, 2nd ed., chap. 22 (Englewood Cliffs, NJ: Prentice-Hall, 1965), or subsequent editions of Baumol's book.

Table 18-2
Game Theory: The Payoff Matrix

		A'S STRATEGIES			
		A_1	A_2	A_3	Row maximums
	B_1	+6	−8	+5	+6
B'S STRATEGIES	B_2	+10	−4	+3	+10
	B_3	−3	−10	+2	+2
Column minimums		−3	−10	+2	

not know what strategy the other party will take. All values in the table are gains or losses in market share *to firm A*. This is a zero-sum game, which means that *A*'s gain in market share exactly equals *B*'s loss, and *A*'s loss exactly equals *B*'s gain. The negative values in the table therefore represent *losses* to *A* but *gains* to *B*. The table tells us, for example, that if firm *A* uses strategy A_1—increased advertising—and firm *B* pursues the identical strategy, B_1, then the outcome will be a gain of 6 percentage points in *A*'s market share. Perhaps firm *A*'s present level of advertising is low, and additional advertising will have a disproportional impact on sales relative to the effect of *B*'s added advertising. Or, let's take another example. Suppose *A* uses strategy A_2—a product modification—while *B* cuts its price, B_3. We see that the outcome will be a 10 percentage point loss in market share for *A* and a 10 percentage point rise in market share for *B*.

What choices will these parties make? Let's assume that both parties are averse to risk and hence wish to avoid the worst possible outcome. Such worst-case outcomes are listed for *A* horizontally below the columns in the matrix (Column minimums). Note that if *A* selects strategy A_1, and *B* selects B_3, then *A* will suffer a loss of 3 percentage points of market share; this loss is the worst outcome possible from the choice of strategy A_1 (it will gain +6 and +10 if *B* selects B_1 or B_2). Similarly the worst-case outcomes for *A*'s strategies A_2 and A_3 are a loss of 10 percentage points and a gain of 2 percentage points, respectively. The numbers shown vertically at the far right of the matrix are the worst-case outcomes for each of *B*'s three strategies (Row maximums). If it chooses strategy B_1, for example, it could lose 6 percentage points of market share. (*A* might use strategy A_1 and gain 6 percentage points). If *B* goes with strategy B_2, the worst-case outcome is a loss of 10 percentage points of market share, and if it selects B_3 it may lose 2 percentage points of market share.

We see from these numbers that *A* will select strategy A_3, and *B* will select strategy B_3. The outcome is that *A* gains a 2 percentage point market share. This outcome is termed a *maximin* or *minimax* solution. *A* is maximizing the minimum gain from its various strategies. *B* is minimizing the maximum loss. Neither party has an incentive to change strategies as long as it remains averse to risk and the values in the payoff matrix remain accurate and known. This is not true for any other combination of strategies in the table. For example, suppose that A employs strategy A_1, hoping that B will use strategy B_2. Firm B, however, will respond to A_1 with strategy B_3. Firm A will now countermove to A_3, and the maximum equilibrium is achieved.[9]

An interesting and practical application of game theory can be seen in oligopolistic marketing behavior. Many companies test the market carefully before launching a new product or brand. Market tests in some industries resemble a poker game more than a scientific experiment. When player A places a new product on sale in a certain market, player B, who has a similar product in national distribution, may raise the stakes by greatly increasing its advertising budget in the area where player A is conducting the test. This confronts A with a difficult question: Does B intend to increase its national advertising budget greatly if A puts its new product on sale nationally? Or is B simply bluffing in an attempt to get A to underestimate potential national sales of its new product?

Refer to 18-2 PAST AS PROLOGUE

JOHN R. HICKS

John R. Hicks (1904–1989) was a professor at Oxford University and shared the Nobel Prize in economics in 1972 for his contributions to pure economic theory. In that year, *Business Week* described him as "neither a businessman's economist nor a public official's economist; he is the economist's economist." This was intended to mean that his contributions are highly abstract and technical, but part of the toolkit toted by most contemporary economists.

Hicks's contributions to economics are many and quite salutary. For example, he reevaluated and clarified Marshall's laws of derived demand for inputs; that is, he specified the determinants of the elasticity of the demand for labor and capital (Chapter 15, footnote 8). In 1937 he wrote an article titled "Mr. Keynes and the Classics," in which he helped devise what today is referred to in macroeconomics as the *IS-LM* model (Chapter 22). Other contributions of note include his refinements of Marshall's notion of consumer surplus, his improvements on Walras's general equilibrium analysis, and his theories concerning economic growth and development.

Of central interest to us in this chapter, however, is Hicks's recasting of the theories of demand and least-cost production.[10]

Demand Theory

To understand Hicks's theory of demand we must examine several interrelated ideas.

Indifference curves. You may recall that indifference curves originated with Edgeworth and Pareto. The aim of the idea was to avoid measuring utility quantitatively. According to the standard marginalist theories of Jevons and Menger, various

[9] A pure strategy maximin equilibrium need not always exist. But a mixed strategy one always does. A mixed strategy allows the players to use, say, 20 percent A_1 and 80 percent A_3.

[10] Other contributors to demand theory based on indifference curves include R. D. G. Allen, a collaborator with Hicks, and the Russian economist Eugen Slutsky.

18-2 PAST AS PROLOGUE

John Nash: Discovery, Despair, and the Nobel Prize

In the early 1950s several economists advanced von Neumann and Morganstern's pioneering work on game theory. The most prominent of these economists was John Nash (1927–), a brilliant mathematical economist.

Nash's story is unusual, even tragic. At the age of twenty-two he published two highly mathematical papers on game theory that established what is now called *Nash equilibrium*. Nine years later his promising academic career at MIT came to an abrupt end. Nash was involuntarily committed to a Boston-area hospital and diagnosed with paranoid schizophrenia. For the next thirty years he coped with his illness in relative obscurity in Princeton, New Jersey. Then, in 1994, he received the surprising news that he had won the Nobel Prize in economics for his youthful work on game theory.

As reported by *Time* magazine:

> When photographs of John Nash appeared in the press last week, a common reaction in and around Princeton, New Jersey, was a shock of recognition: "Oh, my gosh, it's him!" Nash, who shared the Economics Prize with John Harsanyi of the University of California and Reinhard Selten of the University of Bonn, is a familiar eccentric in the university town—a quiet, detached man who frequently spends his time riding the local "Dinky" train on its short hop between Princeton and Princeton Junction, reading newspapers discarded by other passengers. Some knew him as the author of the enormously complicated mathematical equations that appeared on [Princeton] classroom blackboards from time to time—the product of a splendid but troubled mind working out his thoughts when no one was around.*

Nash's personal struggles were documented by Sylvia Nassar in *A Beautiful Mind: A Biography of John Forbes Nash, Winner of the Nobel Prize in Economics, 1994* (New York: Simon and Schuster, 1998). Universal Studios adapted Nassar's book and turned Nash's story into the feature film *A Beautiful Mind*, winner of four Academy Awards, including Best Picture, in 2001.

Nash focused on the strategies within a game that lead to an outcome (a Nash equilibrium) in which neither party can increase its expected payoff by changing its current strategy.† That is, Nash equilibrium occurs when each party, acting independently, has exhausted all advantageous moves.

quantities of items could be assigned cardinal values, or *utils*, which could then be directly compared. For example, the first unit of ice cream consumed during a particular period might yield 10 utils of utility to a specific consumer, the second 5 utils, and so forth; the first unit of hamburger may yield 20 utils, the second 15 utils, and so forth. This implies that, for this person, the first unit of ice cream possesses exactly twice the utility value of the second one, but only one-half the utility of the first unit

In some games one or both parties have a *dominant strategy.* Such a strategy is one that, considering all options, produces the best result irrespective of the strategy chosen by the other party. Participants will obviously use dominant strategies when they are available, and such strategies will produce a Nash equilibrium.

In many games neither party has a dominant strategy, however, so the best strategy for each depends on the strategy used by the other. Each party adjusts its strategy to the other party's strategy until neither party can improve its payoff via further changes. For example, in Table 18-2 neither A nor B has a dominant strategy. But when A uses strategy A_3 and B uses strategy B_3, both have an incentive to "stand pat" with their current strategy. The Nash equilibrium is +2, shown in the bottom far right cell.

The game in Table 18-2 is a *noncooperative game:* Each party decides its strategy without collaboration with the other party. Such games are distinguished from *cooperative games,* in which rivals collusively coordinate their strategies to achieve a better outcome than either could expect without the cooperation. For example, two oligopolists might agree to set equal high prices so they each can obtain monopoly profit. Taken alone, these strategies are not a Nash equilibrium because both parties see an opportunity to increase profits further by offering secret price discounts to the other party's customers. This is the familiar prisoner's dilemma game (Past as Prologue 4-1) in which both parties confess because they assume the other party will confess.

But the parties to a price-fixing agreement may be able to turn their mutual high-price strategies into a Nash equilibrium through credible threats of retaliation against each other's price discounting. For instance, each firm may threaten the other with long-lasting, deeper price cuts should the other firm be detected selling below the collusive price. Because neither party wants a price war, these mutual threats may be credible. If so, the unstable high-price outcome will be converted to a Nash equilibrium, because neither firm dares cheat on the agreed-upon high-price strategy.

Today, some of the brightest minds in economics use mathematical game theory to gain insights on oligopoly, auctions, collective bargaining, international trade, monetary policy, and so forth. All owe a debt to the splendid but troubled mind of John Nash.‡

---

* *Time,* October 24, 1994.

† The idea traces back to Cournot. The equilibrium output outcome in his theory of duopoly is, in fact, a Nash equilibrium.

‡ Nash's key articles are reprinted in his *Essays on Game Theory* (Brookfield, VT: Edward Elgar, 1997).

of hamburger. Such precise measurement of the magnitude of utility seemed unrealistic and, therefore, was heavily criticized as a weak link in the overall theory of demand.

Hicks's indifference curve approach avoids the assumption that marginal utility can be cardinally measured. All that is required is that a consumer can rank preferences

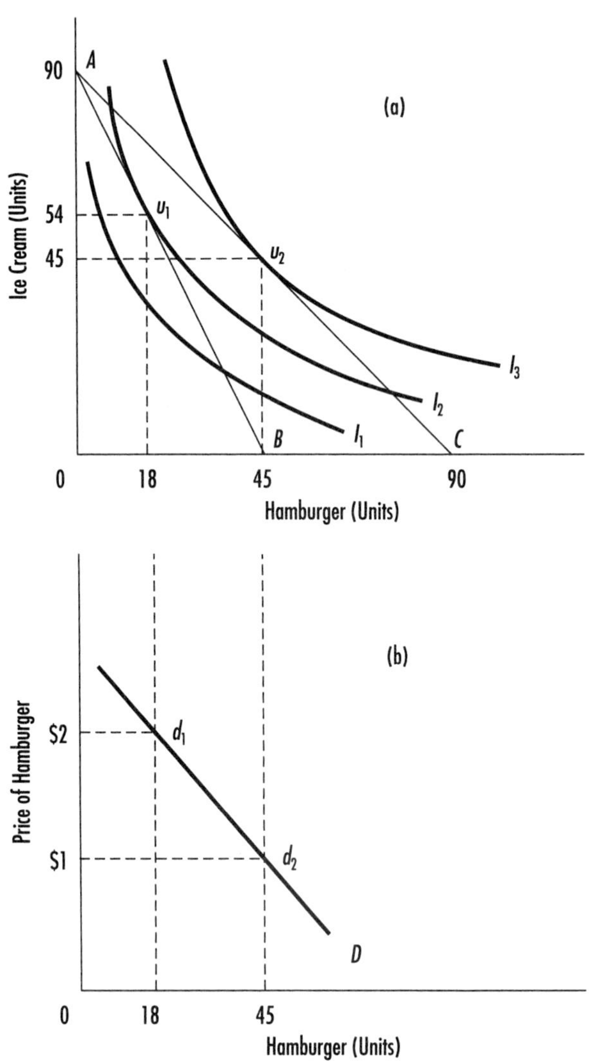

Figure 18-3 Deriving a Demand Curve from Indifference Curves
When the per-unit prices of ice cream and hamburger are $1 and $2, respectively, this consumer will maximize utility by purchasing 54 units of ice cream and 18 units of hamburger (point u_1). But when the price of hamburger falls to $1 per pound, the higher indifference curve I_3 can be attained by increasing purchases of hamburger. The demand curve for hamburger is determined in graph (b) by plotting the quantity of hamburger demanded before and after the decrease in price.

ordinally. In terms of our example, such ranking implies that the person need be able to say only, "I prefer the first unit of hamburger to the first unit of ice cream, or alternatively, I am indifferent between combination *A* (45 units of ice cream and 45 units of hamburger) and combination *B* (72 units of ice cream and 27 units of hamburger)." Hence, without resort to measuring utility, the consumer theoretically could determine the various combinations of hamburger and ice cream that would yield the same total satisfaction. All such combinations constitute an indifference curve, or equal-utility curve, such as the one labeled I_1 in Figure 18-3(a). As we noted earlier, an indifference curve is analogous to a line on a contour map that joins all points of equal elevation. Each indifference curve joins all points of equal total satisfaction to this consumer.

Indifference curves typically are convex to the origin because products are normally partial substitutes for one another. At their upper ends the indifference curves in the figure indicate that the person represented will give up a large quantity of ice cream to acquire a small quantity of hamburger and will still feel equally well off. The reason is that the former is relatively abundant and the latter relatively scarce. At the lower end of the curve, as hamburger becomes scarce relative to ice cream, this consumer will give up fewer units of hamburger to acquire another unit of ice cream.

The slope of an indifference curve indicates the *marginal rate of substitution* of hamburger (x) for ice cream (y); symbolically we state this as MRS_{xy}. The absolute value of the slope of an indifference curve is dy/dx. Note that the absolute value of the slope of each indifference curve declines as one moves down it. That is, the curve is convex to the origin.

Indifference curves farther to the northeast in Figure 18-3(a) signify higher levels of total utility. This can be verified by drawing an imaginary 45° line from the origin and noting that its intersection with each successive indifference curve denotes larger amounts of both ice cream and hamburger. The consumer would like to get to as high an indifference curve as possible.

Budget lines. The highest indifference curve this consumer can attain depends on her income and the prices of units of ice cream and hamburger. Two budget lines, or lines of attainable combinations, are shown in Figure 18-3(a). Let's initially disregard line AC. Suppose that the person's income is \$90, that these are the only two goods, and that the respective prices of ice cream and hamburger are \$1 and \$2 per unit. We see from budget line AB that the person could obtain 90 units of ice cream (\$90/\$1), 45 units of hamburger (\$90/\$2), or combinations of both, indicated by points such as u_1 on the line. The absolute value of the slope of this budget line is the ratio of the prices, p_x/p_y, which in this case is 2 (\$2/\$1).

Utility maximization. Given the budget line AB, this consumer chooses to purchase 54 units of ice cream and 18 units of hamburger during a particular period (point u_1). This combination, which occurs where AB is tangent to I_2, enables the consumer to "get to" the highest possible indifference curve or, in other words, to achieve the highest level of total utility. At the point of tangency, the rate at which the consumer is *willing* to give up ice cream to obtain hamburger (MRS_{xy}) equals the rate at which the market would *require* her to give up ice cream to obtain hamburger (p_x/p_y). To test your understanding of this model, you should explain (1) why combinations of the two goods to the northeast of I_2 are not attainable and (2) why the combinations of the two goods represented by points on the budget line other than u_1 are not as desirable as that shown at u_1.

A change in relative prices. Now suppose that the per-unit price of hamburger falls from \$2 to \$1. The new budget line becomes AC, because at the extreme the consumer can now purchase 90 units of hamburger (\$90/\$1) rather than the 45 units (\$90/\$2) that could have been purchased at the old price. The absolute value of the slope of the new budget line is 1 (\$1/\$1). This decline in the price of hamburger means that the consumer will now be able to achieve the higher indifference curve I_3. At the new point of tangency, u_2, the consumer buys 45 units of ice cream and 45 units of hamburger.

It is a relatively easy matter to trace out the demand curve for hamburger. At the initial per-unit price of \$2, this consumer will purchase 18 units; when the price falls to \$1, she buys 45 units. Notice that the horizontal axes in both the upper and lower graphs in Figure 18-3 measure the quantity of hamburger, whereas the vertical axis in the lower graph measures the price of hamburger. We locate the two prices of hamburger on the vertical axis of the lower graph and drop perpendicular lines from points u_1 and u_2 in the upper graph to the horizontal axis of graph (b). This allows us to plot points d_1 and d_2 in the lower graph. Connecting these points gives us a segment of this person's demand curve for hamburger, D. To reiterate the crucial point: The derivation of this demand curve does *not* require the cardinal measurement of utility.

Income and substitution effects. Hicks pointed out that the change in quantity that accompanies a price change is the result of two effects. First, there is a *substitution effect,* or relative price effect. That is, as the price of hamburger falls, our consumer redirects spending away from ice cream toward the now relatively lower-priced hamburger; an increase in the quantity of hamburger occurs because of substitution. Formally defined, the substitution effect is that part of the total change in quantity demanded that owes solely to the change in price, holding utility constant. Second, an *income effect* occurs, which is defined as that part of the change in quantity that results solely from the change in real income resulting from the change in price. When the price of hamburger fell, the real income of the consumer in our example rose. She now had greater purchasing power from her fixed \$90 money income than previously and used part of this added real income to buy more hamburger.

Although we have not done it here, Hicks showed how the total change in quantity could be separated into its two parts: that part resulting from the substitution effect and that part resulting from the income effect.[11] Among other things, this distinction between income and substitution effects was useful for contrasting normal, inferior, and Giffen goods. Robert Giffen earlier had argued through the use of data that low-income consumers had *upward-sloping* demand curves for some goods. This called into question the law of demand and became known as the "Giffen Paradox." Hicks's indifference curve apparatus helped to

[11] There are alternative ways to distinguish between these two effects graphically. In terms of Figure 18-3, one procedure is to draw a hypothetical budget line that is parallel to AC and tangent to the original indifference curve I_2. You may wish to draw such a line in the figure. This holds the utility of the consumer constant and thus isolates the substitution effect of the price decline. It is the horizontal distance between u_1 and the point of tangency between the hypothetical budget line and I_2. The remaining horizontal distance between u_1 and u_2 is the income effect of the price change.

solve this paradox. For *normal goods,* the substitution and income effects work in the same direction—both act to increase (reduce) quantity when price falls (rises). But for some unusual goods, termed *inferior goods,* the income effect, taken alone, tends to reduce (increase) purchases when product price falls (increases). A *Giffen good* is one for which this unusual income effect is so large that it swamps the normal substitution effect, causing purchases of the product to move in the same direction as the price changes. For example, a decline in the price of bread in a poverty-stricken nation allows low-income consumers to use their added real income to buy *less* of it, which might have been all they previously could afford, and instead buy *more* of other foods, such as meat and poultry.

Production Theory

Hicks's technique of maximizing a function subject to constraints also found applicability in production theory. For instance, he developed the idea of elasticity of substitution of one resource for another in the production process. Formally defined, this is a measure of the responsiveness of the ratio of the two resources to changes in their relative marginal productivities, or in the case of pure competition, to their costs. Microeconomists then refined what today we call *isocost-isoquant analysis.* Readers familiar with that analysis will readily see the similarity between the consumer's budget constraint or relative price line and isocost curves, or equal expenditure lines. The latter show the various combinations of two inputs that can be purchased with a specific dollar outlay, given the prices of the two resources. Isoquants, on the other hand, show the various combinations of two inputs that are capable of yielding a specific quantity of physical output. The least-cost combination of resources in producing any specific output is found at the tangency point of the isocost and isoquant curve. This theoretical construct gave rise to a technique that enables economists to solve problems in production, marketing, transportation, and inventory control. It is to this application of mathematical economics that we now turn.

LINEAR PROGRAMMING

Linear programming was developed during and after World War II, and one of the earliest applications was to the planning activities of the U.S. Air Force. Firms use linear programming in allocating scarce resources so as to maximize the attainment of a predetermined objective. It can be used to determine such things as the lowest-cost diet for animals, National Football League schedules, the cheapest way to ship goods to market, the most profitable product mix, and the best combination of factor inputs. Costs can thereby be minimized and profits maximized. Both mathematical and geometric techniques are used. Linear programming helps solve practical problems for businesses that marginal analysis cannot deal with effectively.

Two elementary examples will illustrate linear programming. Suppose a person needs at least 15 grams of an iodine salt and 15 grams of an iron salt per month to stay healthy. The person cannot buy either of these in a pure form but instead must buy them as trademarked patent medicines. There are two available: Nostrum 12 contains one gram of iodine and two grams of iron per ounce and costs $1 per ounce.

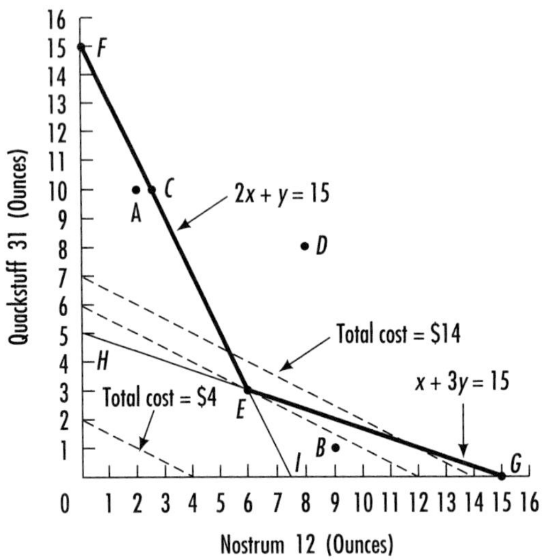

Figure 18-4 Linear Programming with Two Variables
The lowest-cost combination of Nostrum 12 and Quackstuff 31 that will provide 15 grams of both iodine salt and iron salt per month is six ounces of Nostrum 12 and three ounces of Quackstuff 31. The total cost will be \$12 [(6 × \$1) + (3 × \$2)].

Quackstuff 31 contains three grams of iodine per ounce and one gram of iron and costs \$2 per ounce. The consumer's problem is to determine what combination of the two preparations to buy to get the required medication at the lowest cost.

If the person takes x ounces of Nostrum 12 and y ounces of Quackstuff 31, he will get $x + 3y$ grams of iodine (there are three times as much iodine per ounce in Quackstuff 31 as in Nostrum 12) and $2x + y$ grams of iron. Because each element must total at least 15 grams, we get two equations:

$$x + 3y \geq 15 \text{ (Iodine)} \quad \textbf{(18-16)}$$

$$2x + y \geq 15 \text{ (Iron)} \quad \textbf{(18-17)}$$

These relationships can be plotted as areas bounded by straight lines. In the first equation, if $x = 0$, then $y = 5$; if $y = 0$, then $x = 15$. These two points locate line *HG* in Figure 18-4. In the second equation, if $x = 0$, then $y = 15$; if $y = 0$, then $x = 7.5$. The line *FI* can now be drawn.

The combinations of medicine lying to the left and below either line will not give the minimal requirements of iodine and iron. Point *A*, for example, with 2 ounces of Nostrum 12 and 10 ounces of Quackstuff 31, gives 32 grams of iodine (2 + 30) but only 14 grams of iron (10 + 4). Point *B*, showing 9 ounces of Nostrum 12 and 1 ounce of Quackstuff 31, gives 19 grams of iron (18 + 1) and only 12 of iodine (9 + 3). The proper combination of medicines will lie on or to the right of the heavy line *FEG*. Thus, at point *C*, with 3 ounces of Nostrum 12 and 10 ounces of Quackstuff 31, more than enough iodine and iron will be obtained. This is true also at point *D*, with eight ounces of each.

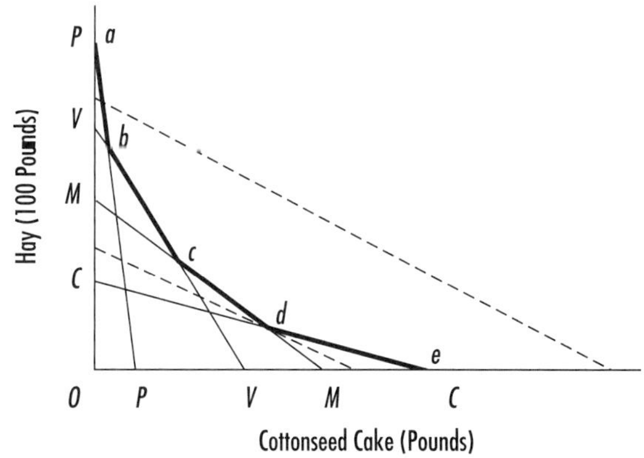

Figure 18-5 Linear Programming with Four Variables
The lowest-cost combination of hay and cottonseed cake that will meet the four nutritional requirements indicated by lines *PP, VV, MM,* and *CC* is found where the equal-cost line is tangent to the heavy line *abcde.*

Source: John F. Due and Robert W. Clower, Intermediate Economic Analysis, *4th ed. (Homewood, IL: Richard D. Irwin. ©1961), 472. Reprinted by permission of the publisher.*

Which of the acceptable combinations will cost the least? Suppose we could spend \$4 for the two medicines. If the whole sum were spent on Nostrum 12, four ounces could be bought at \$1 per ounce. If it were all spent on Quackstuff 31, two ounces could be bought at \$2 per ounce. A straight line connecting two ounces on the vertical axis with four on the horizontal axis will show all the combinations of the two products that could be bought with \$4. This is an equal-cost line, or isocost line. Its slope reflects the relative prices of the two products. If \$14 were available for spending on the two products, the equal-cost line would connect the 14 on the *X* axis with the 7 on the *Y* axis. All equal-cost lines are parallel. The lowest-cost line that will provide the required iodine and iron will go through point *E* where it is tangent to *FEG*, the equal-quantity (or isoquant) line. Twelve dollars is the lowest cost of acquiring 15 grams of each element. Three ounces of Quackstuff 31 and six ounces of Nostrum 12 will be bought. Any other combinations will give less than the minimal dosage of medicine or will cost more than \$12.

Let's examine another example of linear programming: A cattle producer wishes to fatten his steers in the most economical way. He can choose various mixtures of hay and cottonseed cake, both of which contain the four required nutrients: protein, minerals, vitamins, and carbohydrates.[12]

In Figure 18-5, any point on or to the right of line *PP* is assumed to satisfy the minimum protein requirement in the steers' ration; the slope of the line reflects the relative proportions of the protein in the two feeds. The minimum mineral requirement is met by diets represented by points on or to the right of line *MM.*

[12] This example is based on the presentation of John F. Due and Robert W. Clower, *Intermediate Economic Analysis,* 4th ed. (Homewood, IL: Richard D. Irwin, 1961), 471–473.

The minimum vitamin requirement is indicated by line *VV*, and the carbohydrate requirement by line *CC*. All points on or to the right of the heavy line *abcde* represent combinations of cottonseed cake and hay that simultaneously satisfy all four of the minimum nutritional requirements. Any point to the left of the heavy line indicates a combination of feeds that fails to provide one or more of the minimum requirements.

The parallel dashed lines are equal-cost lines, with each line representing the various combinations of the two feeds that can be bought with a given outlay. The lowest-cost combination of feeds is at point *d*. If cottonseed cake were to become more expensive, the equal-cost line would be steeper, and the lowest-cost combination might then be at *c* or *b*.

We see then that linear programming is a production-oriented descendant of the indifference curve approach to consumer behavior developed by Edgeworth, Pareto, Hicks, and others. The reduction in the cost of computation resulting from new computer technology has made linear programming increasingly important.

Questions for Study and Discussion

1. Identify and briefly state the significance of each of the following to the history of economic thought: econometrics, Walras, general equilibrium analysis, Leontief, input-output table, von Neumann and Morgenstern, game theory, zero-sum game, maximin equilibrium, Nash equilibrium, Hicks, marginal rate of substitution, budget constraint, substitution effect, income effect, Giffen good, elasticity of substitution, and linear programming.
2. Suppose that one of the determinants of supply changed such that the supply equation given as (18-8) became $P_x = 4 + .8Q_x$. If demand (18-7) remained unchanged, what would be the new equilibrium quantity and price? Use Hicks's notions of the substitution and income effects to explain the change in equilibrium quantity. Is this good a Giffen good? Explain why or why not.
3. As reflected by recent Nobel Prize awards, mathematics in general and econometrics in particular have grown in importance to the discipline of economics. How do you suppose Alfred Marshall (Chapter 15) would react to this development?
4. Contrast general and partial equilibrium analysis. What is the main advantage of each?
5. What do the rows show in an input-output table? What do the columns show? Suppose that economic planners in a command economy have decided that it is

		EMPLOYER'S STRATEGIES		
		E_1	E_2	E_3
UNION'S STRATEGIES	U_1	40¢	20¢	34¢
	U_2	50	28	16
	U_3	80	24	20

desirable to increase the output of automobiles by 40 percent over a five-year period. How might input-output analysis help them achieve this goal?

6. Suppose that the payoffs in the following game theory matrix are hourly wage gains as viewed by a union that is negotiating with an employer. The union's alternative strategies are U_1, U_2, and U_3; the employer's strategies are E_1, E_2, and E_3. Both parties are averse to risk. What will be each party's optimal strategy? Explain.
7. Contrast the "2-goods, 2-prices" model of utility maximization presented by Hicks with that associated with the equimarginal rule developed by Gossen, Jevons, and Menger.
8. Explain the statement: Linear programming is to economic production theory as input-output analysis is to general equilibrium theory.
9. Speculate as to the reasons mathematics appears to have made a greater inroad into the discipline of economics than into other social sciences, such as sociology and political science.

Selected Readings

Books

Chiang, Alpha. *Fundamental Methods of Mathematical Economics.* 3rd ed. New York: McGraw-Hill, 1984.

Dore, Mohammed, Sukhamoy Chakravarty, and Richard Goodwin, eds. *John von Neumann and Modern Economics.* New York: Oxford University Press, 1989.

Dorfman, Robert, Paul A. Samuelson, and Robert M. Solow. *Linear Programming and Economic Analysis.* New York: McGraw-Hill, 1958.

Hamounda, O. F. *John R. Hicks: The Economist's Economist.* Cambridge: Basil Blackwell, 1993.

Hicks, J. R. *The Theory of Wages.* 2nd ed. London: Macmillan, 1963. (First edition published 1932.)

———. *Value and Capital.* 2nd ed. Oxford: Oxford University Press, 1946. (First edition published 1939.)

Leontief, Wassily. *Input–Output Economics.* 2nd ed. New York: Oxford University Press, 1986.

Morgan, Mary. *The History of Econometric Ideas.* New York: Cambridge University Press, 1990.

Shackleton, J. R., and Gareth Locksley, eds. *Twelve Contemporary Economists.* Chaps. 7 and 9. New York: Wiley, Halsted, 1981.

von Neumann, John, and Oskar Morgenstern. *Theory of Games and Economic Behavior.* 3rd ed. Princeton, NJ: Princeton University Press, 1953. (Orig. pub. 1944.)

Walras, Léon. *Elements of Pure Economics.* Translated by William Jaffé. Homewood IL: Richard D. Irwin, 1954. (Orig. pub. 1874 and 1877.)

Wood, John C. *Léon Walras: Critical Assessments.* 3 vols. London: Routledge, 1993.

Journal Articles

Christ, Carl F. "Early Progress in Estimating Quantitative Economic Relationships in America," *American Economic Review* 75, no. 6 (December 1985): 39–52.

Dorfman, Robert. "Mathematical or 'Linear' Programming: A Nonmathematical Exposition," *American Economic Review* 43 (December 1953): 797–825.

Jaffé, William. "Léon Walras's Role in the 'Marginal Revolution' of the 1870's," *History of Political Economy* 4 (Fall 1972): 379–405.

Leonard, Robert J. "From Parlor Games to Social Science: von Neumann, Morgenstern, and the Creation of Game Theory 1928–1944," *Journal of Economic Literature* 33 (June 1995): 730–761.

Mirowski, Philip. "The When, the How, and the Why of Mathematical Expression in the History of Economic Analysis," *Journal of Economic Perspectives* 5 (Spring 1991): 145–157.

Schotter, Andrew, and Gerhard Schwödiauer. "Economics and the Theory of Games: A Survey," *Journal of Economic Literature* 18 (June 1980): 479–527.

Walker, D. A. "Léon Walras in the Light of His Correspondence and Related Papers," *Journal of Political Economy* 78 (July/August 1970): 685–701.

Chapter 19

The Institutionalist School

The institutionalist school, an American contribution to economic thought, began around 1900 and continues to the present. By 1900 its founder, Thorstein Veblen, had published his first book as well as many articles and book reviews.

In this chapter we focus on traditional institutionalism, not on the so-called new institutionalism discussed in Past as Prologue 19-2. After providing an overview of the traditional institutionalist school, we discuss Veblen, who critically dissected orthodox thinking and provided the theoretical approach of institutionalist economics; Wesley C. Mitchell, who stimulated empirical research with his own statistical studies; and John K. Galbraith, who popularized several institutionalist themes.[1]

OVERVIEW OF THE INSTITUTIONALIST SCHOOL

The Historical Background of the School

In the period between the Civil War and World War I, the achievements of American capitalism were impressive. Rapid growth made the United States the biggest and most powerful industrial system in the world. The improvements in living conditions of many wage earners, however, fell far short of their aspirations and of the possibilities created by the general rise in national income. Hours of labor were long; housing often was inadequate; security in times of sickness, unemployment, and old age was negligible; higher education was inaccessible for most workers' children; job security was virtually nonexistent; and health and safety regulations were inadequate. Frequently, employers organized company towns and dominated the workers, even in their personal lives; large-scale immigration tended to undermine wage rates; taxation was regressive; usury was widespread; and recurring recessions were devastating to those who lost their jobs.

The age of monopoly may be said to have begun in the 1870s, and this movement accelerated around the turn of the century. Conservative voices predominated in the schools, in the press, in the pulpits, and in government. The state and

[1] Two other traditional American institutionalists are John R. Commons (1862–1945), who helped persuade the nation of the need for reform through government legislation, and Clarence E. Ayres (1892–1972), a University of Texas professor who stressed the essential role of technology and technological change in determining the direction of the economy and of society. A third prominent American institutionalist, Douglass North, represents "new institutionalism" and is the subject of Past as Prologue 19-2.

federal governments, which proclaimed laissez-faire with respect to workers' interests, were quick to use the police and militia against labor in industrial disputes. They were also generous in establishing tariff protection for business and in granting large subsidies to railroads.

The American political and economic environment of the late nineteenth century led many economists to question the assumptions and conclusions of the neoclassical school. The doctrine that minimal government interference produces the maximum social well-being increasingly seemed untenable. There was much concern about monopoly, poverty, depression, and waste. The movement for social control and reform was gathering momentum, and it was in this milieu that institutional economics grew.

At the time two major methods of achieving social change were recognized: (1) reorganize society along socialist lines; and (2) undertake social reform, that is, ameliorate conditions through government intervention in the economy. The object of this second approach was to save capitalism by improving the conditions of the masses. Veblen was critical of social movements and favored a radical reconstruction of society. Nevertheless the institutionalist school he founded reflected the reformist approach. The changes wrought by the New Deal in the 1930s, for example, were greatly influenced by institutionalism.

The influence of the German historical school (Chapter 11) on American institutionalism is quite visible. Most of the leaders of the American Economic Association, which was founded in 1885, were familiar and friendly toward the German movement and its methodology. Some of Veblen's illustrious teachers had studied in Germany. John Bates Clark, who taught and encouraged Veblen at Carleton College, was one of these. Although Clark's marginalist theory had nothing in common with German historicism, he also formulated a creed of Christian reform that had much in common with German reformist thinking. Veblen was impressed with the lectures of George S. Morris at Johns Hopkins; Morris was the teacher of John Dewey and was one of the Hegelians trained in the German universities. Richard T. Ely of Johns Hopkins taught and worked with both Veblen and another institutionalist, John R. Commons. Ely had studied under some of the leading historical economists in Germany, and he became an ardent believer in the superiority of the inductive method of research over the deductive method. We should note, however, that despite certain similarities in methodology between the German historical school and American institutionalism, the latter was not nationalistic, and it was more liberal and democratic in its outlook.

Major Tenets of the Institutionalist School

The following describe seven key ideas of this school:

- Holistic, broad perspective. The economy must be examined as a whole, rather than examined as small parts or separate entities isolated from the whole. A complex organism cannot be understood if each segment is treated as if it were unrelated to the larger entity. Economic activity is not merely the sum of the activities of persons motivated individually and mechanically by the desire for maximum monetary gain. In economic activity there are also patterns of collective action that are greater than the sum of the parts. A union, for example, develops a character, an ideology, and a method of operation of its own. Its features cannot be deduced from the study of the individual members who belong to it.

Even the concept of economic activity is too narrow in the institutionalists' view. Economics, they assert, is intertwined with politics, sociology, law, custom, ideology, tradition, and other areas of human belief and experience. Institutional economics deals with social processes, social relationships, and society in all its facets.

- Focus on institutions. This school emphasized the role of institutions in economic life. An institution is not merely an organization or establishment for the promotion of a particular objective, like a school, a prison, a union, or a federal reserve bank. It is also an organized pattern of group behavior, well-established and accepted as a fundamental part of the culture. It includes customs, social habits, laws, modes of thinking, and ways of living. Slavery and a belief in slavery were institutions. Other examples are the beliefs in laissez-faire, or unionism, or a government social security system. Going out on New Year's Eve to raise a din and clatter is an institution. So was communist ideology in the Soviet Union and anticommunism in the United States. Economic life, said the institutionalists, is regulated by economic institutions, not by economic laws. Group social behavior and the thought patterns that influence it are more germane to economic analysis than is the individualism emphasized in marginalist theory. The institutionalists were especially interested in analyzing and reforming the institutions of credit, monopoly, absentee ownership, labor-management relations, social security, and the distribution of income. They advocated economic planning and the mitigation of the swings of the business cycle.
- Darwinian, evolutionary approach. The evolutionary approach should be used in economic analysis, because society and its institutions are constantly changing. The institutionalists disagreed with the static viewpoint that sought to discover eternal economic truths without regard for differences of time and place, without concern for changes that were occurring constantly. Instead of asking "What is?" the institutionalists asked "How did we get here, and where are we going?" The evolution and functioning of economic institutions should be the central theme in economics. This approach requires knowledge not only of economics but also of history, cultural anthropology, political science, sociology, philosophy, and psychology.
- Rejection of the idea of normal equilibrium. Rather than the idea of equilibrium, institutionalists emphasized the principle of circular causation, or cumulative changes that may be either salutary or harmful in seeking economic and social goals. Maladjustments in economic life are not departures from normal equilibrium but rather are themselves normal. Before World War II the outstanding maladjustment was the business slump. Then the problems of economic development became the center of attention. In the late 1970s the problem became stagflation, the simultaneous occurrence of inflation and unemployment, whereas in the mid-1980s, problems of trade deficits and federal budget deficits arose. The institutionalists are convinced that collective controls through government are necessary to continually correct and overcome deficiencies and maladjustments in economic life.

- Clashes of interest. Instead of the harmony of interests that most of their contemporaries and predecessors deduced from their theories, the institutionalists recognized serious differences of interests. People, said the institutionalists, are cooperative, collective creatures. They organize themselves into groups for the members' mutual self-interest, which becomes the common interest of the group. There are, however, clashes of interests between groups, such as big business against small business, consumers against producers, farmers against urban dwellers, employers against workers, importers against domestic producers, and the makers of goods against the lenders of money. Here, again, a representative and impartial government must reconcile or override clashing interests for the common good and for the efficient working of the economic system.
- Liberal, democratic reform. The institutionalists espoused reforms in order to bring about the more equitable distribution of wealth and income. They denied that market prices are adequate indices of individual and social welfare and that unregulated markets lead to the efficient allocation of resources and a just distribution of income. The institutionalists invariably condemned laissez-faire and favored a larger role for government in economic and social affairs.
- Rejection of pleasure-pain psychology. The institutionalists repudiated the Benthamite underpinnings of economic analysis. They reached out instead for a better psychology, and some of them incorporated Freudian and behaviorist ideas into their thinking.

Whom Did Institutionalism Benefit or Seek to Benefit?

The school embodied the middle-class desire for reform in an era of growing big business and banker capitalism. It represented the needs and interests of agrarian, small business, and labor groups. Government workers, reformers, humanitarians, leaders of consumers' organizations, and union members were attracted to the institutionalist ideas, which they hoped might alter the orientation of private business enterprise in favor of their own interests. Many academicians in fields other than economics praised the institutionalists' interdisciplinary focus and their advocacy of social change.

How Was the Institutionalist School Valid, Useful, or Correct in Its Time?

The institutionalists challenged the development of rigid orthodoxy in economic thinking. Many of their criticisms of orthodox theory were valid and helped to revise that type of theory to make it more tenable. The institutionalists' stress on looking at the economy as a whole as part of an evolutionary process and in an institutional setting added elements of realism to economic analysis.

The institutionalists roused belated, but deep and lasting, concern over business cycles and monopolies. They promoted a reform movement that effectively removed many of the rough edges of capitalism. In a world where knowledge was increasingly fragmented and compartmentalized, they urged closer integration of the social sciences. The emphasis of some of their members on inductive studies reduced the gap between economic theory and practice. Gathering and analyzing statistical data became popular in government circles, among private, nonprofit research organizations, in business and labor organizations, and among individual economists. The National Bureau of Economic Research, founded by Wesley C. Mitchell and others in 1920 and guided by him for many years, is a monument to this method

Which Tenets of the Institutionalist School Became Lasting Contributions?

The broader perspective that institutionalists advocated became a reality within the economic mainstream with the appearance and widespread acceptance of Keynesian macroeconomics. In fact, with their aggregate approach, their prescriptions for stabilizing the economy, and their attraction to political liberals, Keynesianism and post–Keynesianism tended to co-opt and supersede institutionalism.

The reform movements promoted by the institutionalists remain alive today. Modest steps toward national economic planning for limited objectives such as conservation, full employment, and international competitiveness are in line with institutionalist thought. Legal protection of unionism, social insurance, and minimum wage and maximum hour legislation all are legacies of the institutionalist challenge to orthodox economic thinking.

With the greatly expanded interest in problems of economic development, there has been new emphasis in this field of economics on the influence of the institutional environment on economic relations. By their nature the problems of economic development involve diverse cultural factors and are dynamic and evolutionary. Lasting contributions of institutionalists are also found in other fields, such as labor relations, law and economics, and industrial organization. Ironically, some of the more innovative *neoclassical* contributions of the past three decades consist of a new institutional analysis. For example, orthodox economists have analyzed such divergent institutions as property rights, seniority, retirement policies, and the family. But unlike the old-line institutionalists, these new theorists have sought to determine the economic rationality of institutions—the economic logic underlying their emergence and how their presence currently contributes to or detracts from economic efficiency.

Traditional institutional economics still has a presence within the United States today. The membership of the Association for Evolutionary Economics is largely composed of economists who are oriented toward institutionalist methods, policy perspectives, or both. The organization meets regularly and publishes the *Journal of Economic Issues*. Nevertheless, the overall penetration of institutionalism into the mainstream of economics remains modest. In this respect, R. A. Gordon's assessment is as true today as it was over three decades ago:

> It is clear . . . that what passes for orthodox economics is today more institutional than it was before, say, the Great Depression. . . . In an important sense, however, the central core of economic theory is about as "noninstitutional" as it was in Veblen's day. Samuelson's *Foundations* or Hicks's *Value and Capital* is developed in much more of an institutional vacuum than was Marshall's *Principles*. Theoretically inclined economists, with some exceptions, do not take kindly to the study of institutional arrangements or institutional development [they leave that to historians and sociologists]. Despite some

> of the new developments in the theory of the firm and of market behavior, micro economic theory is still concerned primarily with the kind of "equilibrium" which Veblen so severely criticized.[2]

We next turn to Thorstein Veblen, the brooding, enigmatic genius who is considered to be the founder of the institutionalist school.

THORSTEIN BUNDE VEBLEN

Thorstein Bunde Veblen (1857–1929), the son of Norwegian immigrants, was born on a frontier farm in Wisconsin and raised in rural Minnesota. He completed his undergraduate college education at Carleton College, Minnesota, where he was a student of J. B. Clark. His graduate work was done at Johns Hopkins, where he failed to obtain a scholarship, and at Yale, where he received a doctorate in philosophy. No academic position was available to him, however, largely because he held agnostic views at a time when a divinity degree was considered a desirable prerequisite for teaching philosophy.

Veblen received fellowships at Cornell and at the University of Chicago for postdoctoral work. He became the editor of the *Journal of Political Economy* at Chicago. Veblen never reached the rank of full professor, despite his eleven books and his lasting world reputation.

Because of marital troubles, indifference to most of his students, involvement with women, and poor teaching techniques, he had to move from college to college. After Chicago, he taught at Stanford, the University of Missouri, and the New School for Social Research. In 1918 he worked briefly for the Food Administration in Washington, D.C., and served as an editor of the journal *The Dial*. A former student aided him financially in his later years. He died in August 1929, a few months before the great stock market crash and the beginning of the depression he had been predicting.

Veblen was a bitter, skeptical, pessimistic, and lonely man. His books, though written somewhat ponderously and obscurely, are replete with wit, wisdom, and sardonic attacks on middle-class virtues. For example, in a footnote in *The Theory of Business Enterprise* he defined snobbery with a deft twist of his rapier wit:

> "Snobbery" is here used without disrespect, as a convenient term to denote the element of strain involved in the quest for gentility on the part of persons whose accustomed social standing is less high or less authentic than their aspirations.[3]

The Leisure Class

Veblen's first and most popular book was *The Theory of the Leisure Class*, published in 1899. The leisure class is characterized by conspicuous consumption, a propensity to avoid useful work, and conservatism.

---

[2] Quoted in Joseph Dorfman et al., *Institutional Economics: Veblen, Commons, and Mitchell Reconsidered* (Berkeley, CA: University of California Press, 1963), 136–137.

[3] Thorstein Veblen, *The Theory of Business Enterprise* (New York: Scribner's, 1904), 388.

Conspicuous consumption. Veblen held that the leisure class is engaged in the predatory seizure of goods without working for them. Those who accumulate wealth do so not merely to take care of their physical wants, or even their spiritual, esthetic, and intellectual wants. Rather, they wish to consume in a way that displays their wealth, because a show of wealth indicates power, prestige, honor, and success in our pecuniary (monetary) culture. To be reputable, such consumption must be wasteful. Poorer people must work in order to subsist, but even their pattern of spending includes an element of wasteful conspicuous consumption. Their outlook on life is imposed by the dominant leisure class.

According to Veblen, women can be especially useful in displaying the wealth and importance that men possess. Wearing expensive clothing and shoes that prevent them from doing useful labor, women advertise that they are supported by wealthy men. Hampered by long fingernails, cumbersome hairstyles, and delicate skin, some women give constant evidence that they are leisure-class women "kept" by leisure-class men.

The high gloss of a gentleman's hat or a patent-leather shoe, said Veblen, has no more intrinsic beauty than a similarly high gloss on a threadbare sleeve. Flowers that are difficult to grow and therefore expensive are not necessarily more beautiful than those that grow wild or with little care. For cropping lawns, pastures, and parks, cows are more useful than deer, but the latter are preferred because they are more expensive, less functional, and not vulgarly lucrative.[4]

One can amuse oneself in a Veblenese way with many modern evidences of conspicuous consumption. Annual parades of yachts, viewed in awe by thousands of landlubbers, are common in many coastal cities in the United States. A midwinter tan in the northern part of the nation suggests the possessor has spent idle time at an expensive desert or coastal resort (where presumably his $9,000 gold "oyster shell" watch is needed for swimming or scuba diving). For those who are not members of the leisure class, but would like people to think they are, tanning studios have emerged. Porsches and Mercedeses have become so common that members of the leisure class have had to step up to Rolls Royces and Bentleys.

Refer to 19-1 PAST AS PROLOGUE

Propensity to avoid useful work. Members of the leisure class must avoid useful, productive work. They must indulge only in wasteful or useless tasks if they are to remain reputable.

> These occupations are government, war, sports, and devout observances. Persons unduly given to difficult theoretical niceties may hold that these occupations are still incidentally and indirectly "productive," but it is to be noted as decisive of the question at hand that the ordinary and ostensible motive of the leisure class in engaging in these occupations is assuredly not an increase of wealth by productive effort. At this time as at any other cultural stage, government and war are, at least in part, carried on for the pecuniary gain of those who engage in them; but it is gain obtained by the

[4] This argument inspired H. L. Mencken to write, "Has the genial professor, pondering his great problems, ever taken a walk in the country? And has he, in the course of that walk, ever crossed a pasture inhabited by a cow? And has he, in making that crossing, ever passed astern to the cow herself? And has he, thus passing astern, ever stepped carelessly and—."

19-1 PAST AS PROLOGUE

Veblen Goods and Upsloping Demand Curves

Although Thorstein Veblen was a well-known critic of neoclassical economics, his theory that some consumers buy luxury goods mainly for their conspicuous consumption appeal has been integrated into neoclassical analysis. For example, some people buy expensive automobiles for the purpose of displaying their wealth. Owning these expensive cars apparently confers status, a source of utility independent of the cars' intrinsic utility.

In a classic 1950 article, Harvey Leibenstein (1922–1993) stated that "the utility derived from a unit of a commodity employed for purposes of conspicuous consumption depends not only on the inherent qualities of that unit, but also on the price paid for it."* That is, a "Veblen good" yields not only intrinsic utility but also conspicuous consumption utility, the latter directly related to price.

The accompanying figure shows the gist of Leibenstein's analysis. Downsloping demand curves D_1, D_2, and D_3 are derived by allowing product price to change while assuming that conspicuous consumption utility is constant along each curve. Curve D_2,

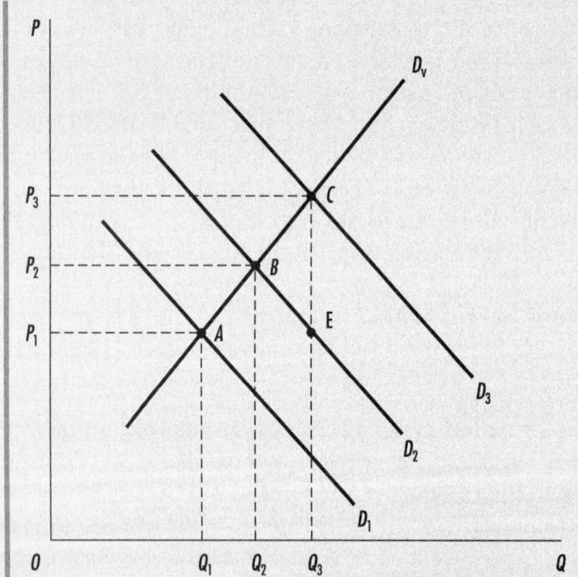

for instance, shows that this consumer will buy more of the product when the price falls, *if* the conspicuous consumption utility associated with curve D_2 does not change. Curve D_3 represents greater conspicuous consumption utility than D_2, but like curve D_2 is derived by holding that higher level of this utility constant as the price changes.

However, conspicuous consumption utility for Veblen goods is *not* constant as price changes; it falls as the price declines and rises as the price increases. For example, this utility might fall if the price of expensive automobiles were cut in half. In the figure a decline in price from P_3 to P_2 reduces conspicuous consumption utility and shifts the conventional demand curve leftward from D_3 to D_2. A price decline from P_2 to P_1 further reduces the good's conspicuous consumption utility, shifting the conventional demand curve leftward from D_2 to D_1.

In Leibenstein's analysis, a fall in product price produces both a standard price effect and a Veblen effect. Taken alone, the standard price effect (conspicuous consumption utility constant) of a P_2P_1 price decline is shown as the movement down demand curve D_2 from *B* to *E* and an increase in quantity demanded from Q_2 to Q_3. The Veblen effect is shown as the leftward shift of demand from D_2 to D_1 and a reduction in quantity demanded from *E* to *A* (or Q_3 to Q_1). In this case the Veblen effect of *EA* swamps the standard price effect of *BE;* a price decrease produces a net decrease in quantity demanded of *BA*. Other cases may produce quite the opposite results; thus a decline in price would increase quantity demanded, even for a Veblen good.

Note that price reductions of P_3 to P_2 to P_1 in the figure produce net reductions in quantity demanded from Q_3 to Q_2 to Q_1. Thus in this case *ABC* traces a positively sloped actual demand curve D_v. Lower prices lead consumers to reduce their purchases of this Veblen good. Presumably, consumers switch to other luxury goods whose prices and conspicuous consumption utility have not declined. Alternatively, an increase in price would increase this good's conspicuous consumption utility so much that consumers would purchase more of the good.

How realistic are upsloping demand curves for Veblen goods? *Individual* demand curves of this type may exist for some goods, but no positively sloped *market* demand curves for Veblen goods have been identified. Although certain consumers may reduce their purchases of some luxury goods when product price falls, many other purchasers enter the market to buy the good. For these new buyers the intrinsic utility value of the good exceeds its lower price. The net result is the standard one: Quantity demanded rises as product price falls. In the real world, the Veblen effect does not repeal the law of downsloping market demand.

Nevertheless, Veblen's discussion of conspicuous consumption and Leibenstein's utility analysis of this product appeal are important. Like the otherwise unrelated concept of a Giffen good (Chapter 18), the notion of a Veblen good explains why some individuals may have upsloping demand curves for specific products.

---

*Harvey Leibenstein, "Bandwagon, Snob, and Veblen Effects in the Theory of Consumer Demand," *Quarterly Journal of Economics* 62 (May 1950): 203.

> honorable method of seizure and conversion. These occupations are of the nature of predatory, not of productive, employment.[5]

Force and fraud are present today, Veblen said, as they were among barbarian peoples. We find them in modern warfare, in business, and in sports and games:

> Strategy and cunning is an element invariably present in games, as also in warlike pursuits and the chase. In all of these employments strategy tends to develop into finesse and chicane. Chicane, falsehood, browbeating, hold a well-secured place in the method of procedure of any athletic contest and in games generally. The habitual employment of an umpire, and the minute technical regulations governing the limits and details of permissible fraud and strategic advantage, sufficiently attest to the fact that fraudulent practices and attempts to overreach one's opponent are not adventitious features of the game. In the nature of the case habituation to sports should conduce to a fuller development of the aptitude for fraud; and the prevalence in the community of that predatory temperament which inclines men to sports connotes a prevalence of sharp practice and callous disregard for the interest of others.[6]

Conservatism. Veblen asserted that the evolution of social structure has been a process of natural selection of institutions. Progress can be attributed to the survival of the fittest habits of thought and the enforced adaptation of individuals to a changing environment. Institutions must change with changing circumstances. The development of these institutions represents the development of society. Unfortunately there is a conflict between current beliefs (ceremonial institutions) and current requirements (dynamic technological institutions) because of the cultural lag in the process of change:

> The situation of to-day shapes the institutions of tomorrow through a selective, coercive process, by acting upon men's habitual view of things, and so altering or fortifying a point of view or a mental attitude handed down from the past. The institutions—that is to say the habits of thought—under the guidance of which men live are in this way received from an earlier time. . . . Institutions are products of the past process, are adapted to past circumstances, and are therefore never in full accord with the requirements of the present. . . . At the same time, men's present habits of thought tend to persist indefinitely, except as circumstances enforce a change. These institutions which have so been handed down, these habits of thought, points of view, mental attitudes and aptitudes, or what not, are therefore themselves a conservative factor. This is the factor of social inertia, psychological inertia, conservatism. . . . The evolution of society is substantially a process of mental adaptation on the part of individuals under the stress of circumstances which will no longer tolerate habits of thought formed under and conforming to a different set of circumstances in the past.[7]

A portion or class of society that is sheltered from environmental forces will adapt its views more slowly to the altered general situation and will therefore retard the process

---

[5] Thorstein Veblen, *The Theory of the Leisure Class* (New York: Random House, Modern Library Edition, 1943), 40. (Orig. pub. 1899.)

[6] Veblen, *Leisure Class*, 273–274.

[7] Veblen, *Leisure Class*, 190–192.

of social change. The wealthy leisure class is in just such a sheltered position with respect to economic forces that make for change or readjustment. The characteristic attitude of this class is indicated in the maxim that, "Whatever is, is right." But the law of natural selection, as applied to human institutions, asserts that, "Whatever is, is wrong." That is, current institutions are wrong to some extent, from the evolutionary standpoint, because they do not change quickly enough to be in tune with the times.

Attacks on Neoclassical Economics

Veblen's theory of the leisure class constituted an attack on neoclassical economics, which assumed that consumers are sovereign. Through their "dollar votes" consumers determine the composition of commodities produced and therefore the allocation of society's resources that will maximize welfare. But if large portions of consumption are undertaken mainly to impress neighbors, who strive to retaliate by purchasing similar items to maintain their relative status, then government might be able to enhance overall well-being by restricting "wasteful" consumption by everyone. As pointed out by Breit and Ransom, "Thus Veblen, in making economic man into social man upset the [laissez-faire] policy implications of neoclassical consumption theory."[8]

Veblen also attacked neoclassical thought directly. For example, he declared John Bates Clark's system static and therefore useless and his "dynamics" essentially a deranged static condition. Veblen saw Clark's system as based on the preevolutionary view of normality and natural law—a view that prevents awareness of cumulative change. The hedonism of the dominant economic school would have

> a gang of Aleutian Islanders slushing about in the wrack and surf with rakes and magical incantations for the capture of shell-fish . . . to be engaged in a feat of hedonistic equilibration in rent, wages, and interest. And that is all there is to it. Indeed, for economic theory of this kind, that is all there is to any economic situation. The hedonistic magnitudes vary from one situation to another, but, except for variations in the arithmetical details of the hedonistic balance, all situations are, in point of economic theory, substantially alike.[9]

Hedonism presupposes rational, intelligent people who act quickly and smoothly according to their anticipation of pleasure or pain. They are clear-sighted and farsighted:

> The hedonistic conception of man is that of a lightning calculator of pleasures and pains, who oscillates like a homogeneous globule of desire of happiness under the impulse of stimuli that shift him about the area, but leave him intact. He has neither antecedent nor consequent. He is an isolated, definitive human datum, in stable equilibrium except for the buffets of the impinging forces that displace him in one direction or another. Self-imposed in elemental space, he spins symmetrically about his own spiritual axis until the parallelogram of forces bears down upon him, whereupon he

[8] William Breit and Roger L. Ransom, *The Academic Scribblers,* rev. ed. (Chicago, IL: Dryden, 1982), 39.

[9] Thorstein Veblen, *The Place of Science in Modern Civilization and Other Essays* (New York: Heubsch, 1919), 193.

> follows the line of the resultant. When the force of the impact is spent, he comes to rest, a self-contained globule of desire as before. Spiritually, the hedonistic man is not a prime mover. He is not the seat of a process of living, except in the sense that he is subject to a series of permutations enforced upon him by circumstances external and alien to him.[10]

Veblen in effect also accused the neoclassicists of supporting the present scheme of the distribution of wealth and income. Standard theory, he thought, is not truly a theory of anything, but merely folklore or theology used to justify private property and property incomes. Business economics has been developed to defend the business community, and the questions it asks and seeks to answer are not relevant to the population as a whole. Veblen was concerned with social economics instead of the business economics of price, profit, and ownership.

Finally, it is interesting to note that Veblen attacked the notion of perfect competition, which then dominated standard economic theory. He recognized that most businessmen had some monopolistic control over the prices they charged and that they used advertising to strengthen their market positions. This analysis, published in 1904, foreshadowed the rise of the theory of monopolistic competition in 1933 (Chapter 17).[11]

Instinct for Workmanship

Veblen believed that work is not generally irksome, or else the survival of the human race would be jeopardized. Humanity's greatest triumph over other species in the struggle for survival has been a superior ability to control the forces of environment. It is not people's proclivity for *effort* but for *achievement* that really matters. When not harassed by overwork, people have not an aversion to work, but instead an instinct for workmanship that conduces to the material well-being of the race and its biological success. People inherently want to do work and to do it well. They deprecate waste. Allied with the equally important instinct for parenthood, the instinct for workmanship impels the current generation to improve life for posterity. Basically we try to avoid greed and indolence, we educate and train our children, we improve technology, and we conserve our resources—all because of our instinct for workmanship and our wish to provide for our descendants. This instinct conflicts with the conventional antipathy to useful effort, but it is the dominant force, especially among the great mass of artisans, farmers, and technological experts.

Small-scale handicraft production and trade have gradually given way to large-scale capitalistic enterprises. Formerly the market was narrow, and business was managed with a view to earning a livelihood. The modern industrial system has as its dominant features the machine process and investment for profit. The growth of markets and investments has created new opportunities for shrewd manipulation. As the captains of industry enlarge their domain, their interests diverge more and more from those of the rest of the community. Instead of being interested in the production of goods, they are interested primarily in maximizing profits.

---

[10] Veblen, *Place of Science,* 73–74.

[11] A clear statement of Veblen's views on this matter is found in his *Business Enterprise,* 53–55.

> The business man's place in the economy of nature is to "make money," not to produce goods. The production of goods is a mechanical process, incidental to the making of money; whereas the making of money is a pecuniary operation, carried on by bargain and sale, not by mechanical appliances and powers. . . . The highest achievement in business is the nearest approach to getting something for nothing.[12]

Although the two objectives may coincide, the production of goods is merely a means to profit; and when the two goals conflict, the former is sacrificed to the latter. If necessary, coalitions of big businessmen, holding companies, and other types of monopolies are organized to restrict output and raise prices. When making money takes precedence over making goods, the instinct for workmanship is thwarted because production comes to be rated in terms of salability. The absentee owners, who are in control, hamper the increased output of goods that would otherwise occur. Their manipulations prevent prices from falling. They force workers and capital into the more competitive sectors of the economy, thus worsening the situation there. They profit from disturbances in the system that may hinder output. If the economy is unstable, the opportunities for profit increase. The shrewd operator can make money as a bull during the upswing of the business cycle and as a bear during the downswing. Progress is hampered by big business, which is more interested in the vendibility of goods than in their serviceability for the needs of society. Those interested in problems of price rather than in production include business entrepreneurs and their assistants—salespeople, accountants, advertisers, and so forth.

Credit and Business Cycles

Credit plays a special role in modern business, according to Veblen. Borrowing money can increase profits as long as the current rate of business earnings exceeds the rate of interest. Under competitive conditions, what is profitable for one businessperson to undertake becomes compulsory for all competitors. Those who take advantage of the opportunities afforded by credit are in a position to undersell those who do not. The recourse to credit therefore becomes widespread and typical. The competitive earning capacity of an enterprise comes to rest on the basis of the initial capital plus such borrowed funds as this capital will support. The competitive use of credit in extending business operations gives an enterprise a differential advantage against other competitors, but the credit expansion has no aggregate effect on earnings or on total industrial output. In fact, aggregate net profits from industry are reduced by the amount of interest that has to be paid to creditors outside the industrial process.

Why does the expansion of credit have no effect on total earnings or on industrial output? Is it not true that borrowed funds represent property? Won't this property be converted to productive use by drawing into the industrial process, directly or indirectly, the material items of wealth that these funds represent? "No," replied Veblen. While loans may be covered by property held by the lender, the property may be otherwise engaged. Real estate may support loans even though it cannot be converted to industrial use. Loans that are backed by corporate

[12] Thorstein Veblen, *The Vested Interests and the Common Man* (New York: Viking, 1946), 91–94. (Orig. pub. 1919.)

stock and industrial plants duplicate material items that are already a part of the industrial process.

Veblen neglected, of course, the fact that bank credit enables firms to mobilize a supply of labor from among those who are unemployed, underemployed, or self-employed (such as artisans and farmers). The drawing of labor into large industrial establishments increases the total output. Likewise, credit permits the mobilization of raw materials and capital equipment and the expansion of their supply. It widens the market and thereby stimulates greater production. Veblen's strictures on credit would be valid only if the supplies of the factors of production and final products were perfectly fixed and therefore could not be readily expanded.

Veblen's views on credit led him directly into his business-cycle theory. The extension of credit enables competing businesspeople to bid up the prices of the material capital goods used in industry. As their dollar value increases, these goods serve as collateral for the further extension of credit. The extension of loans on collateral such as shares of stock or real property has a cumulative character. Credit expands even more with the organization of monopolies, because the expected increase in the profits of monopolies and the imputed goodwill of the new corporations also are capitalized in the prices of the securities issued.

This cumulative extension of credit rests on a shaky foundation. Sooner or later a discrepancy will arise between the money value of the collateral and the capitalized value of the property computed on expected earnings. In other words, the rise in earnings will not keep pace with the rise of the nominal value of capital (capital plus loans). When this discrepancy becomes obvious, a period of liquidation begins. Along with liquidation, the industrial crisis is accompanied by credit cancellations, high discount rates, falling prices, forced sales, shrinkage of capitalization, and reduced output. The creditors take over business properties, thereby further consolidating ownership and control into fewer hands.

Workers benefit during prosperity not through higher rates of pay but through fuller employment. As the general price level rises, the increased cost of living reduces real rates of wages. Slowly money wages rise in response to increasing prices of goods, and this helps bring prosperity to an end, because profit margins shrink and capital values fall.

Veblen thought that the discrepancy between capitalization and earning capacity is chronic so long as no extraneous circumstances enter temporarily to set aside the trend of business affairs. Therefore chronic depression, more or less pronounced, is normal under the fully developed regime of machine industry. Depressions are temporarily overcome, however, by speculative increases of prices, new discoveries of precious metals, and credit expansion. The deliberate promotion of monopoly can restore the profitability of business by restricting output and raising prices, thereby bringing the accepted capitalization into line with the actual earning capacity. If successful, the monopoly will neutralize the cheapening of goods and services affected by current industrial progress.

The decline of profits and chronic depression can be remedied by an increase in the wasteful and unproductive consumption of goods as well as through monopoly. But private wasteful expenditure on a scale adequate to offset the surplus productivity of modern industry is nearly out of the question:

> Private initiative cannot carry the waste of goods and services to nearly the point required by the business situation. Private waste is no doubt large, but business principles, leading to saving and shrewd investment, are too ingrained in the habits of modern men to admit an effective retardation of the rate of saving. Something more to the point can be done, and indeed is being done, by the civilized governments in the way of effectual waste. Armaments, public edifices, courtly and diplomatic establishments, and the like, are almost altogether wasteful, so far as bears on the present question. . . . But however extraordinary this public waste of substance latterly has been, it is apparently altogether inadequate to offset the surplus productivity of the machine industry, particularly when this productivity is seconded by the great facility which the modern business organization affords for the accumulation of savings in relatively few hands.[13]

Solution: Soviet of Technicians

According to Veblen, then, there is conflict between industry, which produces goods, and business, which produces profits; between making goods and making money; between the instinct for workmanship and pecuniary considerations; between the community at large and the absentee owners, the captains of industry; between the need for stability and the extension of credit; between the buyers, who want more goods at lower prices, and the monopolists, who offer fewer goods at higher prices; between the need for social change and the conservatism of people's patterns of thought and action; between meeting the basic needs of people, which is possible, and meeting the desire for conspicuous consumption, which must leave the demand for goods unfulfilled as long as everyone tries to exceed others in wasteful consumption.

What is the solution to the difficulties raised by modern large-scale business enterprises? Veblen was simultaneously critical of and friendly toward socialism, but he was definitely not a socialist himself. He attacked Marx's labor theory of value as being at best tautological and at worst an unproven playful mystification. He denied the socialist claim that the rich are becoming richer and the poor poorer. The existing system, he said, has not made the workers poorer as measured absolutely; but it does tend to make them relatively poorer in terms of comparative economic importance. Modern society intensifies emulation and jealousy, which lead to unrest and make for socialism. With the abolition of private property, human nature might find nobler and socially more serviceable activities than emulating one another.

Veblen thought that the engineers—the technicians of society—might eventually lead the social revolution and operate industry for the common good. They are the ones to object to ownership, finance, sabotage, credit, and unearned income because these interfere with technological efficiency and progress. Engineers are the best representatives of the community at large, because capital and labor, bargaining over prices, have become a loose-knit vested interest that seeks its own benefit to the detriment of society. The outcome has been businesslike concessions and compromise between them. The two sides play a game of chance and skill, with the industrial

[13] Veblen, *Business Enterprise,* 255–257.

system becoming a victim of interference on both sides. Yet the material welfare of the community at large, and more specifically of the workers, depends on the smooth working of the industrial system without interference. This the engineers can achieve. Unlike the owners and workers, they are not motivated by self-interest. Because the technicians are more homogeneous and unified than the workers, they are the natural leaders, the officers of the line, the people with spirit of tangible performance and the most highly developed instinct of workmanship. Veblen asserted that a soviet of technicians could solve the nation's problems, but the chances of it happening are remote. At present the technical men are docile and harmless, generally well fed, and rather placidly content with the "full dinner-pail" allowed them by the vested interests.

Veblen did not base his hopes on reform—the amelioration of conditions under capitalism; in fact, he hoped to see capitalism superseded entirely. The idea that the engineers would make the social revolution was perhaps a fleeting thought for him. Toward the end of his life he looked quite favorably at the experiment in the Soviet Union, with its heavy emphasis on central planning. Because he died in 1929, Veblen knew nothing of the brutality of Stalinism that was to develop in the mid-1930s. Basically, however, he remained a pessimist, taking a dim view of human nature and the future prospects of humanity.

WESLEY CLAIR MITCHELL

Wesley Clair Mitchell (1874–1948) was Veblen's most brilliant student. Veblen was the great iconoclast who attacked with savage glee what he considered to be the absurdities of orthodox theory that defended the status quo; he gave institutionalism a philosophy and a theory. Mitchell was the great researcher whose most notable work centered on an analysis of business fluctuations; he gave institutionalism its empirical bent. He was too gentle and discreet to strike at the roots of neoclassicism with the ferocity of Veblen, but he did criticize its unrealistic abstractions and methodology. He felt that Veblen had progressed far beyond contemporary economists because of his more adequate view of human nature and his broader understanding of cultural processes. Yet Veblen relied too much on speculations that were not verified empirically. Mitchell believed that his statistical studies would provide a firmer foundation for Veblen's pioneering work.

Mitchell, who was born in Rushville, Illinois, received his Ph.D. from the University of Chicago in 1899. He took a position in the Census Office in Washington, D.C., then taught and did research again at the University of Chicago, as well as the University of California, Columbia University, and the New School for Social Research.

The Importance of Empirical Investigation

Economics, said Mitchell, is a science of human behavior. The future of the discipline, he contended, lies in moving toward more research and less theorizing. "Economics will develop more fruitfully in the future upon the quantitative side. The economists of today stand the best chances of improving upon the work of their predecessors if they rely more and more upon the most accurate statistical recording of observations."[14]

The National Bureau of Economic Research, which Mitchell founded in 1920 and directed for twenty-five years, is perhaps the greatest monument to his method. Under Mitchell's supervision it launched one of the first comprehensive studies of the amount and distribution of national income. Over the years it has published a vast bulk of statistical analyses. Today, its list of university research associates reads like a "who's who" in economic research in the United States. Ironically, most of these researchers are highly orthodox economists.

Mitchell's Study of Business Cycles

Mitchell's greatest contribution was in the study of business fluctuations. It is important to realize that his major work on the subject first was published over two decades before the Great Depression and Keynes's *General Theory*. Mitchell called his theory of business cycles a "working hypothesis" because it was tentative and subject to revision in light of additional evidence. In his hands, business-cycle theory approached a tested explanation of experience instead of an exercise in logic. The more intensively Mitchell sought the facts to explain fluctuations, the more his explanation broadened into a theory of how our economic system works. Instead of seeking a single decisive cause of the cycle as earlier economists had done, he explored the conditions that collectively produce the cyclical movements of the business system. If his ideas are commonplace now, it is because they have become so widely accepted.

Mitchell's empirical work on the business cycle led him to four major conclusions. Each merits elaboration, as follows:

- Business fluctuations arise in a *money* economy. Mitchell preferred to view crises and depression not as a disease of capitalism but rather as a problem arising in a society where economic activities are carried on mainly by making and spending money. This is a characteristic of capitalism, of course; but capitalism also has other features, such as how the means of production are owned. He stated, "It is not until the uses of money have reached an advanced stage in a country that its economic vicissitudes take on the character of business cycles."
- Business cycles are widely diffused throughout the economy. This is the case because enterprises are so interdependent. Business firms are bound to one another by industrial, commercial, and financial ties, so none prospers or declines without affecting others. The growth of credit has enhanced financial interdependence. The spread of corporate business organization, with all its interlocking relationships, organizes many nominally independent enterprises into communities of interest. The bonds are also channels through which the quickening or slackening of activity in one part of the economy can spread to other parts.

[14] Wesley C. Mitchell, *Types of Economic Theory from Mercantilism to Institutionalism*, ed. Joseph Dorfman, 2 vols. (New York: Augustus M. Kelly, 1967), 2: 749, 761.

- Business fluctuations depend on the prospects for profit. The prospects for profit, said Mitchell, are the clue to business fluctuations. A business enterprise can serve the community by making goods only if it makes a profit in the long run. The subordination of services to moneymaking is not grounded in the mercenary motives of businessmen but is a necessary result of a money economy. A public-spirited businessperson who disregards profits will be put out of business. Only government and philanthropic organizations can provide services without profit.

  Anticipated profits are more significant than past profits or losses, because business looks forward more than it looks backward. The prospect of future profits plays the decisive role in determining the direction of business expansion. Investment reaches its highest point at that stage of the cycle at which the anticipated profits are most attractive. Therefore an account of economic fluctuations in a business economy must deal primarily with the pecuniary aspects of economic activity.
- Fluctuations are systematically generated by the economy itself. Business cycles are not minor or accidental disruptions of equilibrium but rather an inherent part of the working of the economy itself. Permeating Mitchell's entire work is the evolutionary and dynamic approach. Thus, as each phase of the cycle evolves into its successor, the economy itself gradually undergoes cumulative changes. Therefore, believed Mitchell, the economists of each generation will probably have to recast the theory of business cycles that they learned as youths. According to Mitchell, cycles arise from forces within the economy, with each phase of the cycle generating the next:

  > An incipient revival of activity, for example, develops into full prosperity, prosperity gradually breeds a crisis, the crisis merges into depression, depression becomes deeper for a while, but ultimately engenders a fresh revival of activity, which is the beginning of another cycle. A theory of business cycles must therefore be a descriptive analysis of the cumulative changes by which one set of business conditions transforms itself into another set.[15]

Mitchell chose as his starting point that stage of the cycle in which activity begins to quicken after a period of depression. Once started, a revival of activity spreads rapidly over all or a large part of the economy through interconnecting enterprises. Rising wages and higher profits stimulate both consumption and investment demand. Inventories, which have been depleted during slack times, are replenished by retailers and wholesalers. An outbreak of optimism starts and spreads, thereby producing conditions that both justify and intensify it. In the late stage of a revival, prices begin to rise. Anticipations of further price increases stimulate orders for goods. Credit expands as business conditions improve. Profits increase, too, because wage and overhead costs lag behind rising prices. New investment in capital goods rises.

This, then, is the cumulative upward movement of revival. But why does it culminate in a crisis? Why does prosperity breed depression?

---

[15] Wesley C. Mitchell, *Business Cycles and Their Causes* (Berkeley: University of California Press, 1941), ix. (Orig. pub. 1913.)

Among the stresses that accumulate within the system during prosperity is the slow but sure increase in the costs of doing business. Overhead costs begin to rise as new capital is invested when the cost of goods is rising. New companies building new plants incur high costs in attempting to establish themselves, and sticky costs like rent and interest rise. Less efficient plants and machines, less capable management, and less efficient workers are employed during prosperity, thereby bidding up the prices of materials, labor, and so forth. By adding to the supply of goods sent to market, marginal firms make it more difficult to advance selling prices to offset rising costs. Labor costs rise, not only because less capable workers are employed but also because wages begin to catch up with rising prices. During prosperity the rising demand for goods increases the need for overtime labor, which is more expensive and less productive than normal labor. Labor discipline and productivity decrease because workers are less fearful of losing their jobs than in bad times. Waste in production increases as businesspeople grow careless, overly optimistic, and overly busy.

Rising production costs encroach on profits, especially because the prices of finished goods cannot be easily raised in the later stages of prosperity. The expansion of productive capacity, which promoted the growth of prosperity during the earlier period, adds to the supply of goods and services, increasing the difficulty of raising selling prices. Buyers ultimately resist rising prices because they cannot or will not continually pay more for goods. Certain prices fail to rise in line with costs because of public regulation, contracts, and custom. An actual or even a prospective decline in profits in a few important industries suffices to create financial difficulties in all industries.

The longer prosperity lasts, the more severe these stresses become, and they inevitably lead to crisis and depression. The pyramiding of credit ends when creditors become apprehensive. At the crisis point, demands are made on debtors to reduce or pay their debts in full. Vast liquidation occurs, with prices falling as goods are thrown on the market in desperate attempts to avoid bankruptcy. The expectation of falling prices further reduces the demand for goods and thereby makes this expectation come true. Because certain costs are sticky on the downward side just as they are with upward price movements, falling prices squeeze profit margins even more. Gloom spreads, investment spending declines, inventories are reduced, unemployment grows, consumer income and expenditures decline, and the economy sinks into a depression.

Given enough time, a depression generates within itself the forces that produce prosperity. Businesspeople cut waste and costs to the bone. Ultimately, wages, interest, rent, and other sticky costs fall to the point where they are in line with prices of goods. Labor costs also fall because overtime is eliminated, inefficient workers are discharged, and employed workers are driven to greater efforts by the fear of unemployment. As depression drags on, capital goods wear out and grow obsolete. Prices for new capital goods having fallen, the competitive struggle induces investment in new, more efficient, lower-cost machines that can be financed at low depression rates of interest. If it is at all possible, consumers must ultimately replace durable and semidurable goods that have worn out. Population continues to rise, thereby increasing the demand for all kinds of consumption goods. Inventories, which have been reduced to the barest minimum during depression, must be rebuilt as business expands. Optimism spreads, and the economy is once again on a cumulative upswing.

Social Planning

The frequent recurrence of economic crisis and depression, said Mitchell in 1935, is evidence that the automatic functioning of our business system is defective. Our difficulties have increased because of the widening markets, the growth of combinations, the increasing importance of semidurable goods that people can stop buying when times are bad, the movement of farm people to the cities, and farmers being increasingly dependent on markets instead of being self-sufficient as they once were. Business planning has not been able to counteract the growth of factors that make business cycles serious.

The task, then, is to promote careful social planning or national planning to overcome the worst features of business fluctuations while preserving economic liberty and increasing security. Mitchell's reliance on national planning to ameliorate the human condition was based partly on his pragmatic psychology. He defended social planning, denying that it is un-American. Our national history, he said, has been a history of planning, sometimes successfully, sometimes not. The U.S. Constitution embodied a plan for governing a country. Hamilton had a plan for economic recovery, and from 1917 to 1918 we planned economic mobilization to win the war. The greatest difficulty in social planning has been to agree on what we wish to accomplish. In fact, disunity over goals creates the most fundamental obstacle to planning in a democratic community, because unanimity of social aims is attained only on rare occasions.

A second difficulty in planning derives from the interdependence of social processes. Piecemeal planning, detail by detail, often brings unplanned and unwanted results, as illustrated by the establishment of Prohibition, which encouraged rum-running and the rise of rich, law-breaking syndicates. Wise social planning must consider both direct and indirect effects of social action. But certain results cannot be attained by individual action. Thus, said Mitchell, national planning is inevitable. The questions is, will it be fragmentary and unsound or systematic and technically thorough?

JOHN KENNETH GALBRAITH

John Kenneth Galbraith (1908–) was born in Canada and studied at the Universities of Toronto and California. His experience has included the post of chief economist for the American Farm Bureau Federation, high positions with the U.S. government during World War II, membership on the board of editors of *Fortune* magazine, ambassador to India during the Kennedy administration, professor of economics at Harvard University, and chairman of the Americans for Democratic Action. Galbraith is also a novelist and an expert on Far Eastern art.

Taken as a whole, Galbraith's major writings constitute both an attack on neoclassical economic thought and an analysis of modern capitalism. Nearly all of the characteristics of the institutionalist school apply to his many works.

The Conventional Wisdom

Galbraith is a critic of the neoclassical "conventional wisdom": a set of ideas that is familiar to all, widely accepted, but no longer relevant. His evolutionary approach explores changing conditions and examines the need to change our ideas to fit new situations. In a statement similar to that made by Veblen, Galbraith said, "Ideas are inherently conservative. They yield not to the attack of other ideas but to the massive onslaughts of circumstances with which they cannot contend." He is quick to point out that his attack is on the conventional wisdom, not on those who *originally* expounded the ideas:

> The reader will soon discover that I think very little of certain of the central ideas of economics. But I do think a great deal of the men who originated these ideas. The shortcomings of economics are not original error but uncorrected obsolescence. The obsolescence has occurred because what is convenient has become sacrosanct.[16]

And how is it that these obsolete neoclassical ideas have been able to survive? Galbraith answers as follows:

> The neoclassical system owes much to tradition—it is not implausible as a description of a society that once existed. . . .
>
> Additionally it is the available doctrine. Students arrive; something must be taught; the neoclassical model exists. It has yet another strength. It lends itself to endless theoretical refinement. With increasing complexity goes an impression of increasing precision and accuracy. And with resolved perplexity goes an impression of understanding.[17]

Within Galbraith's overall theory of modern capitalism, one can find several specific theories that challenge orthodox economics. Two theories of particular importance are his notion of the "dependence effect" and his theory of the behavior of the firm.

The Dependence Effect

According to Galbraith, modern capitalism is dominated by large enterprises and characterized by an abundance of contrived wants that are the product of corporate planning and massive advertising:

> As a society becomes increasingly affluent, wants are increasingly created by the process by which they are satisfied. . . . Wants thus come to depend on output. In technical terms, it can no longer be assumed that welfare is greater at an all-round higher level of production than at a lower one. It may be the same. The higher level of production has, merely, a higher level of want creation necessitating a higher level of want satisfaction. There will be frequent occasion to refer to the way wants depend on the process by which they are satisfied. It will be convenient to call it the Dependence Effect.[18]

It is not consumers who are sovereign in the modern industrial system, but rather the gigantic firms that produce and market goods and services. In Galbraith's "revised sequence," producers decide what shall be produced and then mold consumers' tastes so that they buy these products. Orthodox economics holds that initiative lies with the consumer, who buys goods and services in the market in response to

---

[16] John Kenneth Galbraith, *The Affluent Society* (Boston, MA: Houghton Mifflin, 1958), 4.

[17] John Kenneth Galbraith, *Economics and the Public Purpose* (Boston, MA: Houghton Mifflin, 1973), 27.

[18] Galbraith, *Affluent Society,* 158.

personal desires or demands. The neoclassical theories of consumer choice take wants as given. To say that consumers maximize their utility, says Galbraith, begs the important question of how consumers go about formulating those wants in the first place. And, if wants must be created through advertising, how urgent can they be? Furthermore, the neoclassical theory of consumer demand, with its emphasis on consumer sovereignty, implies that the market dictates the optimal composition of output and allocation of resources. This view, said Galbraith, makes little sense: "One cannot defend production as satisfying wants if that production creates the wants."

Galbraith's theory of consumer demand has an important policy implication: There will be an underallocation of resources to public goods. Galbraith called this circumstance "social imbalance." The creation of artificial wants through advertising and the propensity for emulation shifts resources toward private goods and away from public goods that have greater inherent value. New automobiles are seen as being more important than new roads; vacuum cleaners in the home are desired more than street cleaners. Alcohol, comic books, and mouthwashes take on a greater aggregate importance than schools, courts, and municipal swimming pools. One way to remedy this imbalance, said Galbraith, would be to impose sales taxes on consumer goods and services, using the proceeds to increase the availability of public sector goods and services.

Galbraith's Theory of the Firm

The neoclassical theory of the firm concludes that corporate behavior and performance can best be understood by assuming that firms attempt to maximize profits. According to Galbraith this may be true in the *market sector*, where owners of small firms actively manage their enterprises, but it does not describe the far more important *planning sector*—the 2,000 or so largest firms that produce over half of society's output. In the planning sector, ownership and control are divorced. The owners of the giant firms are the millions of holders of common stock who have no actual control over the operation of the corporation. Instead, control is exercised by the technostructure—a professional elite consisting of executives, managers, engineers, scientists, product planners, market researchers, marketing personnel, and so forth. The disgruntled stockholder who does not like the performance of a particular firm does not have the option of firing the management. The usual recourse is to sell the shares of the company and to buy shares of another company. It is naive, said Galbraith, to assume that the technostructure has an incentive to maximize the return to the millions of anonymous stockholders. The technostructure pursues much more complex purposes, which he categorized as protective and affirmative.

The central *protective purpose* of the firm is survival, which translates into the need to earn a profit sufficient to keep most stockholders relatively happy and to provide sufficient retained earning for investment and growth. One way that this less-than-maximum profit can be assured is by taking product price out of competition. Doing this can take the form either of direct price fixing or of informal price understandings within an industry. It is *not* the purpose of price fixing to restrict output and maximize joint profits as the neoclassical model implies. Instead, the purpose is to ensure that the rival firms earn a satisfactory level of profit, thus enabling them to meet their protective goals and to pursue their affirmative purposes.

The major *affirmative purpose* of the firm is corporate growth. Growth of output, sales, and revenues produces greater employment security and financial rewards to the members of the technostructure. In the orthodox theory of the firm, oligopolists restrict their production in order to boost their prices and enhance their profits: "No point is better accepted by the neoclassical model than that the monopoly price is higher and the output smaller than is socially ideal. The public is the victim. Because of such exploitation, oligopoly is wicked."[19] In Galbraith's theory, oligopolists fix prices at *low* levels—ones that achieve a minimum profit and permit expansion of total output and sales. Huge advertising outlays, campaigns to gain market share, unprofitable mergers between competitive and noncompetitive firms, and so forth all make perfect sense if the goal is growth. According to Galbraith, "The neoclassical model describes an ill that does not exist [high oligopolistic prices and restricted output] because it assumes a purpose that is not pursued [profit maximization]."[20]

Galbraith's theory of the firm has several interesting policy implications. For example, traditional antitrust efforts should be abandoned: "Nothing has yet happened to arrest the development and burgeoning power of the technostructure." Large firms have grown because of technological imperative. Their size owes to economies of scale, large research and development budgets, and the ability to incorporate new technology. It has been, and will continue to be, futile to try to arrest these forces through public policy, said Galbraith:

> Thus the [antitrust] remedy that emerges from the neoclassical model is harmless. It presents no threat to the power or autonomy of the technostructure or to its affirmative interest in growth. And since the remedy is thought to be comprehensive—since competition is considered the remedy for all industrial ills—it directs all complaints into an essentially harmless channel. What might be dangerous agitation for effective regulatory action or for public ownership or socialism comes out safely as a demand that the antitrust laws be enforced. . . . Best of all from the standpoint of the technostructure would be immunity from all attack. But the next best thing—and a very good thing—is a system of ideas that diverts all attack into channels that are safely futile.[21]

Should society then simply pursue a policy of laissez-faire, counting on these economic forces to produce the social good? Galbraith answered with a resounding "No." In the preface of his *Economics and the Public Purpose* he stated, "On no conclusion is this book more clear: Left to themselves, economic forces do not work out for the best except perhaps, for the powerful."

Although exploitation of consumers is not a problem of modern capitalism, there *are* other grave problems that arise from the exercise of power by the planning system. The public, through government, must wrest control of the planning sector of the economy from the technostructure, ensuring that it serves the public purpose. This control should take several forms. For example, a permanent public price and wage agency should control the prices of the largest firms in the economy and ensure that wage gains in the major collective bargaining agreements do

---

19 Galbraith, *Economics,* 119.

20 Galbraith, *Economics,* 120.

21 Galbraith, *Economics,* 121.

not exceed the growth of national productivity. A public planning authority needs to be established to join with the major corporations and unions to plan and coordinate economic activity. This planning authority will also have to coordinate economic plans with other industrial nations. Along with these reforms, Galbraith has called for government redistribution of income through public control of executive salaries, progressive taxation, an increase in the minimum wage, and a negative income tax plan. Firms in the market sector should be encouraged to merge so that they can compete more effectively with the firms in the planning sector. Like Veblen and Mitchell before him, Galbraith sees the need for a greatly expanded role for government in the modern economy.

Criticisms of Galbraith's Views

Galbraith's attack on conventional economics has produced many rejoinders. As just one example, critics have pointed out that, at the extreme, he seems to deny that the consumer has free will, that the buyer is able to determine his own interests and act on them. Orthodox economists reject this view and its implication that some undefined entity other than consumers themselves might best determine what is in the consumers' true interests. As another example, critics have stated that a firm that fails to maximize its long-run profits runs the danger of becoming a target for a corporate takeover. The price of the target firm's common stock, which reflects the discounted stream of its anticipated future earnings, will be lower for the nonprofit maximizer than it could be. By offering shareholders a price for their stock above the present market price, the acquiring firm can gain control of the target firm, replace the management, increase profits, and make a capital gain on their initial holdings.

In conclusion, Galbraith's volleys at economic orthodoxy, like those of Veblen before him, could be said to have forced neoclassicists temporarily to halt their march, to have required them to acknowledge and even engage the opposition. Galbraith elicited much return fire. This very fact—that he could not easily be ignored—is a testament to his powers of intellect, wit, and pen. Nevertheless, orthodox economics has experienced few casualties and even fewer defectors; put bluntly, it marches on. For institutionalism to reemerge as a major force in economic thought, it must win the minds of a future generation of economists. Its best hope for doing this is to develop a unified set of theories, readily understandable and teachable, that holds up to careful intellectual and statistical scrutiny. To date, say its detractors, it has not accomplished this.

Refer to 19-2 PAST AS PROLOGUE

Questions for Study and Discussion

1. Identify and briefly state the significance of each of the following to the history of economic thought: institutionalism, the Association of Evolutionary Economics, Veblen, *The Theory of the Leisure Class,* conspicuous consumption, instinct for workmanship, soviet of technicians, Mitchell, National Bureau of Economic Research, Galbraith, dependence effect, market versus planning sector, technostructure, and protective versus affirmative purposes of the firm.
2. Compare and contrast the characteristics of the German historical school listed in Chapter 11 with those of the institutionalist school.

19-2 PAST AS PROLOGUE

Douglass North and the New Institutionalism

The traditional institutionalism associated with Veblen, Mitchell, and Galbraith is generally critical of neoclassical economics and supportive of government intervention. In contrast, *new institutionalism* tends to be theoretical, market-oriented, and anti-interventionist.

There are several identifiable strands of this new institutionalist thought, each emphasizing the importance of institutions in understanding economic (or political) behavior and outcomes. One strand is the work of Harold Demsetz (1930–) on the role of property rights in promoting economic efficiency. A second strand is the analysis by Richard Posner (1939–) of the relationship between law and economics. A third is the focus of Ronald Coase (1910–) and Oliver E. Williamson (1932–) on transaction costs in explaining the organization and behavior of firms. A fourth is the work of James Buchanan (1919–) and Gordon Tullock (1922–) on public-choice theory, including analyses of rent seeking, interest groups, voting rules, and constitutional economics.*

The most sweeping strand of new institutionalism, however, is that associated with Douglass North (1920–), an American economic historian who won the 1993 Nobel Prize for his work. North criticizes neoclassical economics for its failure to recognize the importance of institutional constraints in economic decision making and its inability to explain the permanence of diverse economic institutions throughout the world. Unlike traditional institutionalists like Veblen, however, North embraces the neoclassicist's "choice theoretic" approach, which emphasizes rational economic decision making.

> The choice theoretic approach is essential because a logically consistent, potentially testable set of hypotheses must be built on a theory of human behavior. The strength of microeconomic theory is that it is constructed on the basis of assumptions about individual behavior. . . . Institutions are a creation of human beings. They evolve and are altered by human beings; hence our theory must begin with the individual. At the same time, the constraints that institutions impose on individual choices are pervasive.†

Institutions come into being because they minimize human interaction costs. They can be formal (for example, constitutions and laws) or informal (for example, unwritten codes of conduct). They can be specifically created (for example, the U.S. monetary system) or simply evolve over time (for example, the tradition of giving gratuities). Institutions are the formal and informal *rules* that govern economic and political behavior. In contrast, the *players* are individuals and organizations that exploit the opportunities provided within a particular institutional structure.

The form that institutions take owes much to the bargaining power of individuals and groups representing them. But once institutions are in place, the behaviors and outcomes from individual choices reinforce their continued presence. For example,

19-2 PAST AS PROLOGUE (continued)

worker stock ownership through pension plans reinforces support for capitalist institutions. As a result of reinforcement, a nation's institutions are *path dependent:* The institutional path first selected (or imposed) determines the path long taken. Institutions gradually evolve because the "players" sometimes succeed in getting the "rules" changed in their favor. Only when it is clear that a particular institutional path is a dead end to achieving desired objectives, or when the desired objectives themselves change, do societies radically alter their institutions.

Institutional constraints thus vary both through time and across countries. The institutions provide the incentive structures for various types of economic and political activity. Wealthy nations essentially are wealthy because their institutional constraints define a set of payoffs to political and economic activity that encourages education and skill acquisition, capital expansion, new technology, and thus economic growth. Poor nations are poor because their institutions define a set of payoffs to political and economic activity that discourages wealth creation. Property rights are poorly defined and enforced, the brightest minds enter government or emigrate, social and religious customs limit work and disparage material gain, and wealth redistribution is given more emphasis than wealth creation.

North's genius has been to wed traditional neoclassical analysis with the analysis of institutions. By so doing, he explains how institutions affect economic choices and how economic choices gradually alter institutions.

---

*Malcolm Rutherford, *Institutions in Economics: The Old and the New Institutionalism* (New York: Cambridge University Press, 1994), 2–3. We discussed Coase in Past as Prologue 15-2 and will discuss Buchanan and Tullock in Chapter 20.

†Douglass C. North, *Institutions, Institutional Change and Economic Performance* (New York: Cambridge University Press, 1990), 5.

3. As the classical school is to Isaac Newton, the institutionalist school is to whom? Explain.
4. Use Veblen's idea of conspicuous consumption to explain why a significant decline in the price of a particular product might lead to a reduction in the quantity demanded. How does this differ from a so-called Giffen good (Chapter 18)?
5. What is Veblen's distinction between making money and making goods? Use Cournot's monopoly model (Chapter 12) to explain how it might be possible to make more money by producing fewer goods.
6. Contrast Mitchell's views on the causes and nature of business fluctuations with the views expressed by Irving Fisher (Chapter 16).
7. True or false; if false, explain why: "Galbraith believes that firms in the planning sector are excessively large. They have gotten this way because of their incessant drive for monopoly power. To prevent monopolistic exploitation of the consumer, these firms need to be broken up into smaller competing firms."

8. Both Veblen and Galbraith have been described as *iconoclasts*. Find and state a dictionary definition of this word and explain why it is appropriate.
9. Suppose that price rises from P_2 to P_3 in the figure accompanying Past as Prologue 19-1. Draw appropriate lines and label the graph to show the standard price effect and the Veblen effect. Explain. Which effect dominates in this case?

Selected Readings

Books

Blaug, Mark, ed. *Thorstein Veblen*. Brookfield, VT: Edward Elgar, 1992.

———, ed. *Wesley Mitchell, John Commons, Clarence Ayres*. Brookfield, VT: Edward Elgar, 1992.

Breit, William, and Roger L. Ransom. *The Academic Scribblers*, 3rd. ed. Chap. 11. Princeton, NJ: Princeton University Press, 1998.

Dorfman, Joseph, et al. *Institutional Economics: Veblen, Commons and Mitchell Reconsidered*. Berkeley: University of California Press, 1963.

Galbraith, John Kenneth. *The Affluent Society*. Boston: Houghton Mifflin, 1958.

———. *Economics and the Public Purpose*. Boston: Houghton Mifflin, 1973.

———. *The New Industrial State*. Boston: Houghton Mifflin, 1967.

Gambs, John S. *John Kenneth Galbraith*. New York: Twayne, 1975.

Mitchell, Wesley C. *The Backward Art of Spending Money and Other Essays*. New York: Kelley, 1950. (Orig. pub. 1912–1936.)

———. *Business Cycles and Their Causes*. Berkeley: University of California Press, 1941. (Orig. pub. 1913.)

———. *Types of Economic Theory from Mercantilism to Institutionalism*. Edited by Joseph Dorfman. 2 vols. New York: Augustus M. Kelley, 1967 and 1969.

Samuels, Warren J., ed. *Institutional Economics*. 3 vols. Brookfield, VT: Edward Elgar, 1989.

Sharpe, Myron E. *John Kenneth Galbraith and the Lower Economics*, rev. ed. New York: International Arts and Sciences Press, 1974.

Veblen, Thorstein. *The Instinct of Workmanship*. New York: Huebsch, 1918. (Orig. pub. 1899.)

———. *The Place of Science in Modern Civilization and Other Essays*. New York: Huebsch, 1919.

———. *The Theory of Business Enterprise*. New York: Scribner's, 1904.

———. *The Theory of the Leisure Class*. New York: Random House, Modern Library Edition, 1934. (Orig. pub. 1899.)

Journal Articles

Gordon, Scott. "The Close of the Galbraithian System," *Journal of Political Economy* 76 (July–August 1968): 635–644. [Also, see Galbraith's "Professor Gordon on 'The Close of the Galbraithian System'," *Journal of Political Economy* 77 (July–August 1969): 494–503.]

Hayek, F. A. "The Non Sequitur of the Dependence Effect," *Southern Economic Journal* 30 (April 1964): 346–348.

Journal of Post–Keynesian Economics 7 (Fall 1984). [Contains several articles on Galbraith.]

Leibenstein, Harvey. "Bandwagon, Snob, and Veblen Effects in the Theory of Consumer Demand," *Quarterly Journal of Economics* 62 (May 1950): 183–207.

Rutherford, Malcolm. "Wesley Mitchell: Institutions and Quantitative Methods," *Eastern Economic Journal* 13 (January/March 1987): 63–73.

Walker, Donald A. "Thorstein Veblen's Economic System," *Economic Inquiry* 15 (April 1977): 213–236.

Chapter 20

WELFARE ECONOMICS

Welfare economics is the branch of economic analysis concerned with discovering principles for maximizing social well-being. It is not a distinct and unified system of ideas. Economics itself is often defined as the study of how society chooses to use its limited resources to achieve maximum satisfaction. Nearly every aspect of economics, therefore, has a welfare dimension. Nevertheless, several important contributors to economics have focused specifically on either or both of the following: (1) defining welfare optimality and analyzing how maximum welfare can be achieved; (2) identifying factors that impede the achievement of maximum well-being and suggesting ways that the impediments might be removed. We refer to these individuals as welfare economists.

This chapter explores the contributions of the following diverse theorists: Pareto, Pigou, von Mises, Lange, Arrow, and Buchanan. As indicated by the relevant dashed line in the full Time Scale of Economic Ideas, some of these individuals were supporters of the neoclassical school whereas others were antagonistic toward it.

The welfare economists addressed such heterogeneous topics as rules for achieving maximum welfare, the problem of external costs and benefits, income inequality, the potential for achieving maximum welfare under socialism, difficulties associated with majority voting, and decision making in the public sector.

VILFREDO PARETO

Welfare economics dates back to the classical economic ideas of Smith and Bentham. Several subsequent economists dealt with welfare considerations, including Marshall, who examined the welfare effects of taxes and subsidies in increasing and decreasing cost industries. Historians of economic thought, however, view Vilfredo Pareto (1848–1923) as the originator of the "new" welfare economics, which is rooted in Walras's principles of general equilibrium. Pareto was born in Paris to Italian parents, studied at the University of Turin in Italy, and later accepted the chair of economics at the University of Lausanne, Switzerland. There he continued and expanded the mathematical tradition established by his immediate predecessor, Walras. Pareto set forth his major ideas in his *Manual of Political Economy,* published in 1906.

Mention has previously been made of Pareto's important role in refining Edgeworth's notion of indifference curves. Edgeworth had assumed the existence of measurable utility and from this deduced his curves of indifference. Pareto wished to avoid the troublesome problems of measuring and comparing utility among individuals by constructing indifference maps showing various levels of *ophelimity*, or satisfaction. Pareto's indifference curves and his attention to the conditions for optimality are thus the direct antecedents to the modern indifference curve analysis discussed in Chapter 18.

Pareto Optimality

Of particular relevance to the topic at hand, Pareto refined Walras's analysis of general equilibrium and set forth the conditions for what we now call *Pareto optimality*, or maximum welfare. Other economists then established the more rigorous mathematical proof that perfectly competitive product and resource markets achieved Pareto optimality.

Maximum welfare, said Pareto, occurs where there are no longer any changes that will make someone better off while making no one worse off. This implies that society cannot rearrange the allocation of resources or the distribution of goods and services in such a way that it aids someone without harming someone else. The Pareto optimum thus implies (1) an optimal distribution of goods among consumers, (2) an optimal technical allocation of resources, and (3) optimal quantities of outputs. We can demonstrate these conditions by supposing the existence of a simple economy containing two consumers (Smith and Green), two products (hamburger and potatoes), and two resources (labor and capital). The conditions for a Pareto optimum in this simple economy are those that would exist in a realistic economy having numerous consumers, goods, and resources.

Optimal distribution of goods. The optimal distribution of goods—that is, the distribution that will maximize consumer welfare—occurs where Smith and Green each have identical *marginal rates of substitution* between the two goods. We express this symbolically as:

$$MRS_{hp}S = MRS_{hp}G \tag{20-1}$$

where $MRS_{hp}S$ and $MRS_{hp}G$ are Smith's and Green's respective marginal rates of substitution of hamburger for potatoes. Recall from our discussion of indifference curves in Chapter 18 that the marginal rate of substitution is the maximum amount of one product a consumer is willing to give up to get an additional unit of another product; it is the absolute value of the slope of an indifference curve at a particular point on the curve. Suppose that the marginal rates of substitution for the two goods differ for Smith and Green, or specifically that Smith has a MRS_{hp} of five, whereas Green has one of two. This means that Smith is willing to give up five units of potatoes to get an additional unit of hamburger (or one-fifth unit of hamburger to get one unit of potatoes), whereas Green is willing to give up only two units of potatoes to get the added unit of hamburger (or one-half unit of hamburger to get one unit of potatoes). At the margin, therefore, Smith values hamburger relatively more and potatoes relatively less than does Green. The basis for a Pareto improvement is thus established. Smith can trade some potatoes to Green—who values them relatively more—and in return receive hamburger, which Smith values relatively more. Because the exchange makes both parties better off and leaves neither worse off, total welfare in the two-person economy rises.

As Smith gets more hamburger and Green gets more potatoes, Smith's MRS_{hp} will fall and Green's MRS_{hp} will rise. Exchange will end when the marginal rates of substitution are equal; that is, when there are no further possibilities for an exchange that will make at least one of the parties better off without leaving the other worse off. Therefore, the Pareto optimal distribution of goods among consumers occurs where the consumers' marginal rates of substitution are equal.[1]

Optimal technical allocation of resources. In our two-goods, two-resources example, the optimum allocation of resources to productive uses will occur where the *marginal rates of technical substitution* between labor (l) and capital (k) in the production of hamburger and potatoes are equal. The marginal rate of technical substitution of labor for capital ($MRTS_{lk}$) is the maximum number of units of capital that could be substituted for a unit of labor without changing the level of output.[2] This second condition for Pareto optimality is shown symbolically as follows:

$$MRTS_{lk}H = MRTS_{lk}P \qquad \textbf{(20-2)}$$

where $MRTS_{lk}H$ and $MRTS_{lk}P$ are the marginal rates of technical substitution of labor for capital in the production of hamburger and potatoes.

If these rates differ between the two uses, then a Pareto improvement is possible. Suppose, for example, that the $MRTS_{lk}$ in producing hamburger is two, whereas in producing potatoes it is three. This means that we would need to substitute only two units of capital for one unit of labor to maintain a given output of hamburger, whereas to hold the output of potatoes constant, we would need to substitute three units of capital for the single unit of labor. Thus, at the margin, *capital* is relatively more efficient in producing hamburger than potatoes. Or, as viewed from the opposite perspective, *labor* has relatively greater productivity at the margin in producing potatoes than hamburger. By using more capital to produce hamburger, thus freeing some labor to be used to produce potatoes, we would achieve a higher level of total output from the same level of input use. The additions to output where resources were added would exceed the losses in output where they were removed. Because no one is worse off and someone is better off, this is a Pareto improvement.

At some point, the rearrangement of factor inputs would come to a halt because diminishing returns in each use would cause the marginal product of the added resource to fall and the marginal product of the deleted resource to rise. Once the marginal rates of technical substitution in producing the two goods became equal, no further reallocation of resources would help someone without hurting someone else.

Optimal quantities of output. If production and distribution meet the conditions of Pareto optimality, then optimum levels of output will be achieved where the marginal rate of substitution of hamburger for potatoes—the rate at which

[1] Pareto demonstrated this through what we now refer to as the Edgeworth box diagram. You can find out more about this in any of the standard textbooks in intermediate microeconomic theory.

[2] If you have had a course in intermediate microeconomics, you may recall that the marginal rate of technical substitution is the ratio of the marginal products of the two resources; it is the absolute value of the slope of an isoquant at a given point.

each of the two consumers is willing to give up potatoes to get hamburger—equals the *marginal rate of transformation* (*MRT*) of potatoes for hamburger. This is the rate at which it is technically possible to transform potatoes into hamburger. Symbolically,

$$MRS_{hp} = MRT_{hp} \tag{20-3}$$

Suppose, for example, that the MRS_{hp} and the MRT_{hp} are four and three, respectively. This means that the rate at which the two consumers are *willing* to give up units of potatoes for hamburger (four to get one) exceeds the rate at which it is *technically necessary* to give up potatoes to get an additional unit of hamburger (three to get one). Consequently, the welfare of each consumer will rise by increasing the output of hamburger and reducing the output of potatoes. At the margin, the gains to the consumers will exceed society's opportunity costs. Only where the marginal rate of substitution of one product for the other product equals the marginal rate of transformation will there be no further opportunity to increase one or more person's well-being while not reducing someone else's welfare.

Evaluation

Pareto's welfare theory is a significant contribution to economics. He did much to help economists better understand the conditions for, and the welfare significance of, economic efficiency. However, the central Pareto criterion, "Does a change make someone better off while making no one worse off?" is not always well suited for evaluating public policies.

Of the several criticisms of the Pareto standard, four seem particularly germane. First, some economists argue that it fails to address the important issue of distributive justice, or the fair distribution of income in society. Instead, it simply establishes the efficiency conditions for any *existing* distribution. Second, and closely related, many public policies that increase national output and overall welfare also redistribute income as a by-product of the policy. For example, although a policy of free foreign trade normally boosts a nation's total output and welfare, it may also injure specific individuals who lose their jobs because of imports. A strict interpretation of the Pareto criteria would block the enactment of such a policy. Similarly, under most circumstances, immigration of skilled workers increases total output in the destination nation. However, the increased supply of labor may depress the wages received by native workers in the skilled labor markets. Should the immigration be allowed? Because there is a net gain to society in both examples, gainers theoretically could fully compensate the losers, thereby converting the situation to one that is consistent with Pareto's criteria. But should government legislate such policies as free trade and open immigration, even if such compensating payments are not actually made?[3]

[3] Later welfare economists developed competing criteria for evaluating whether a proposed change in policy is an improvement. Three classic articles are Nicolas Kaldor, "Welfare Propositions in Economics and Interpersonal Comparisons of Utility," *Economic Journal* 49 (1939): 549–552; Tibor Scitovsky, "A Note on Welfare Propositions in Economics," *Review of Economic Studies* 9 (November 1941): 77–88; and Abram Bergson, "A Reformulation of Certain Aspects of Welfare Economics," *Quarterly Journal of Economics* 52 (February 1938): 310–334.

A third objection to the Pareto criteria is that they are based on a static view of efficiency. Short-run movements away from Pareto optimality conceivably could increase long-run or dynamic efficiency. For example, some contemporary economists contend that by focusing on static efficiency some of the provisions of antitrust laws may impede private actions—such as joint development of new technologies—that would increase the nation's long-run growth of output and welfare.

Finally, the moral judgments that the Pareto criteria purposely exclude are often legitimate and dominant factors in policy formulation. Some private transactions—for example, prostitution, the sale of babies, and the purchase of drugs—that *may* be Pareto optimal may also conflict with society's moral values. Such values often dwarf considerations of economic efficiency in debates on public policy.

ARTHUR CECIL PIGOU

Arthur Cecil Pigou (1877–1959) succeeded Marshall in the chair of political economy at Cambridge University in 1908 and held this position until his retirement in 1943. He was the leading neoclassical economist after the death of his predecessor, and like Marshall, he expressed humanitarian impulses toward the poor, hoping that economic science would lead to social improvement. In his own cautious way, Pigou was willing to go further than Marshall in allowing a role for the government in ameliorating certain undesirable features of society.

In his *The Economics of Welfare,* written in 1920, Pigou hoped to provide the theoretical basis for government to enact measures that promoted welfare. As an economist, he was concerned with *economic* welfare, defined as "that part of social welfare that can be brought directly or indirectly into relation with the measuring-rod of money." Unlike Pareto, who cast his theories in terms of general economic equilibrium, Pigou continued in the "old welfare" tradition of Smith, Bentham, and Marshall, relying mainly on partial equilibrium analysis. His contributions to welfare economics include his observations on income redistribution and the divergence between private and social costs. Two other topics that we will examine are his discussion of price discrimination and what today is called the *Pigou effect.*

Income Redistribution

Basing himself on Jevons and Marshall's principle that the marginal utility of money diminishes as more is acquired, Pigou asserted that greater equality of incomes under certain conditions could increase economic welfare. Pigou insisted that interpersonal comparisons of satisfaction *can* properly be made when dealing with people of the same background raised in the same environment. In this sense he was more of a reformer than those "purely scientific" economists who fastidiously avoided value judgments and proclaimed the impossibility of comparing satisfactions among different people. He stated:

> Any transference of income from a relatively rich man to a relatively poor man of similar temperament, since it enables more intense wants to be satisfied at the expense of less intense wants, must increase the aggregate sum of satisfaction. The old "law of diminishing utility" thus leads securely to the proposition: Any cause which increases

> the absolute share of real income in the hands of the poor, provided that it does not lead to a contraction in the size of the national dividend from any point of view will in general, increase economic welfare.[4]

Divergence between Private and Social Costs and Benefits

Pigou's most significant deviation from orthodox theory lay in his focus on the divergence between social and private marginal costs and benefits. The idea that such a divergence could occur was not original with Pigou. Henry Sidgwick (1838–1900), writing in 1883, discussed the same general topic, but in a less concise way.[5] The private marginal cost of a commodity or service is the expense the *producer* incurs in making one more unit; the social marginal cost is the expense or damage to *society* as the consequence of producing that unit of product. Likewise, the private marginal benefit of a commodity is measured by the extra satisfaction it provides the *buyer;* social marginal benefit is the extra satisfaction *society* gets from the production of the added unit.

These distinctions are significant because the acts of production and consumption may impose costs or benefits on parties other than the producer and consumer. These external costs and benefits, or externalities, spill over to other parties and are sometimes referred to as "spillover effects." For example, said Pigou, sparks from railway engines may do damage to surrounding woods or crops without their owners being compensated for the damage. Social costs (internal + external) therefore are greater than the private costs (internal) to the railway; the net private marginal product exceeds the social net product. Similarly, an entrepreneur who builds a factory in a residential district destroys much of the value of other people's property. The increased sale of intoxicating beverages is profitable to the distiller and the brewer, said Pigou, but external costs are incurred when more police and prisons become necessary.

There are opposite cases, Pigou said, in which some benefits of private actions spill over to society's benefit, but for which the person who renders the benefit is not compensated. Thus the social marginal net product exceeds the private marginal net product. For example, the expansion of one firm in an industry may give rise to external economies in the industry as a whole that will reduce the costs of production of other firms. Private investment in planting forests will benefit surrounding property owners. Preventing smoke from pouring out of factory chimneys will benefit the community at large much more that it will benefit the factory owner. Scientific research is generally of greater value to society than to the researcher and inventor, although the patent laws aim at creating a closer match between private and social marginal net products.

Pigou derived an important welfare implication from his analysis: Not all competitive markets produce levels of output that maximize society's total welfare. The fact is demonstrated in Figure 20-1, which represents Pigou's ideas.

---

[4] A. C. Pigou, *The Economics of Welfare,* 4th ed. (London: Macmillan, 1932), 89. (Orig. pub. 1920.)

[5] The relationship between Pigou's and Sidgwick's ideas are spelled out by Margaret G. O'Donnell in "Pigou: An Extension of Sidgwickian Thought," *History of Political Economy* II (Winter 1979): 588–605.

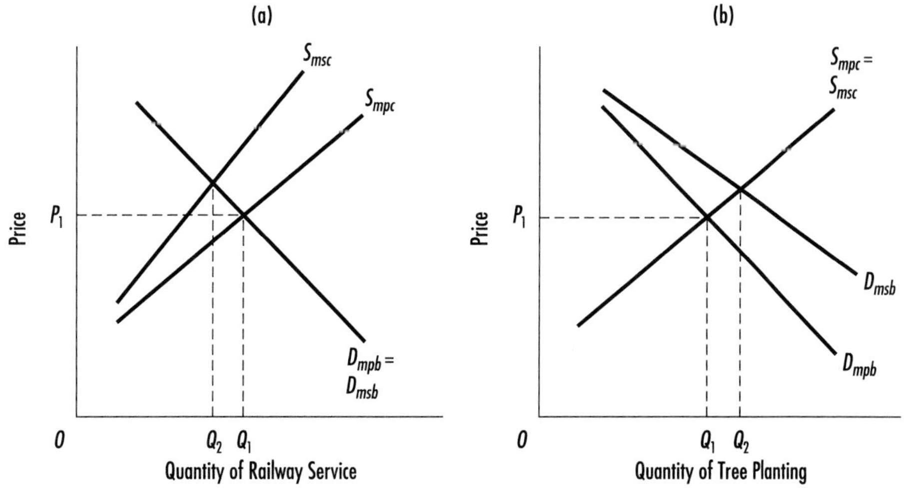

Figure 20-1 Pigou's Analysis of Externalities
(a) The presence of external costs (sparks from railways) means that marginal social costs are greater than marginal private costs. The market-determined quantity of output (Q_1) is too large to maximize society's welfare; marginal social cost exceeds marginal social benefit for units of output greater than Q_2. (b) The presence of external benefits (natural seeding of surrounding forest land) results in marginal social benefits that are greater than marginal private benefits. Thus equilibrium output (Q_1) is smaller than that which would be required to maximize society's welfare; marginal social benefit is greater than marginal social cost for all units of output less than Q_2.

Figure 20-1(a) shows a situation in which there are negative spillovers or externalities. Demand curve $D_{mpb} = D_{msb}$ reflects both the marginal benefits to consumers of railway services (internal benefits) *and* the marginal social benefits to society (no external benefits). Supply curve S_{mpc} shows the private or internal marginal costs of providing the services.

If there were *no* negative externalities in this market; that is, if all costs were internal to the railways and their users, the equilibrium price of railway service would be P_1 and the equilibrium quantity Q_1. This level of service would maximize the combined welfare of the railway and its users, and because no one else is affected, also maximize society's welfare.

Following Pigou's example, let's suppose, however, that railways transfer external costs to third parties. Thus we see in Figure 20-1(a) that a supply curve labeled S_{msc} lies above the curve that reflects marginal private costs (S_{mpc}). At each level of service, the railway not only incurs private costs such as labor and fuel but also transfers external costs to owners of woodlands and farmlands. The marginal social cost of any level of service or output is captured in S_{msc}; it consists of marginal internal costs plus the marginal external cost. The competitive market, responding to private costs and private benefits, results in price P_1 at which the quantity of the service supplied and demanded will be Q_1. But this is *not* the optimal quantity as viewed from a welfare perspective. Rather, the optimal quantity is Q_2, where marginal social cost equals marginal social benefit. At Q_1 the marginal social cost, shown by S_{msc}, exceeds the marginal social benefit, shown by D_{msb}. This is true for all quantities of railway service greater than Q_2; it costs society more to produce each of these units than the service adds benefits to society. Conclusion: Negative externalities result in an overallocation of resources (too much output) in those markets in which they occur.

In other markets, marginal social benefits exceed marginal private ones. The welfare results are shown in Figure 20-1(b). Again using one of Pigou's examples, we assume that D_{mpb} represents the marginal private benefit to a landowner from planting a forest, whereas D_{msb} represents the marginal social benefit. Presumably the reforestation benefits surrounding property owners through the natural seeding of those areas that will occur. The actual amount of private planting of trees will be Q_1, because at this output we see from D_{mpb} and S_{mpc} that marginal private benefit equals marginal private cost. But once again the competitive market does not produce maximum welfare. If the external benefits are considered, then the optimum level of planting would be Q_2, at which the marginal social benefit equals the marginal social cost. The market-determined level of output Q_1 is too small, and therefore too few resources are allocated to this use.

According to Pigou, the welfare task of government is to equalize (1) private and social marginal costs and (2) private and social marginal benefits. It can do this through the use of taxes, subsidies, or legal regulation. For example, government's options in the case of railways include legal prohibition against trains that emit sparks, laws that make the railways liable for their damages, taxes on railways or their users that would drive up the price of the service and reduce its level, or payments to the owners of woodlands and croplands who agreed not to plant so close to the tracks. Alternatively, government might pay people who plant forests a subsidy to reduce their expense of planting trees, thereby increasing the amount of the activity undertaken. Sidgwickian-Pigouvian analysis of social costs and benefits thus challenged the widely held perspective that we can always and everywhere rely on competitive markets to maximize society's economic welfare (produce Pareto optimality). There is a greater role for government in the economy, said Pigou, than that envisioned by advocates of laissez-faire.

Refer to 20-1 PAST AS PROLOGUE

Other Contributions

Several other theories presented by Pigou have had lasting relevance. His stress on the desirability of increasing savings in the economy—later out of vogue in the Keynesian era—found favor with many economists and government policymakers in the 1980s and 1990s. Pigou contended that people prefer present rather than future satisfaction of equal magnitude because the human telescopic faculty is defective; we therefore see future pleasure on a diminished scale. The bias contributes to far-reaching economic disharmony, because people distribute their resources between the present, the near future, and the remote future on the basis of a somewhat irrational preference. Consequently, efforts directed toward the remote future are sacrificed for those directed to the near future, while these in turn are given up to

20-1 PAST AS PROLOGUE

Pigou and Coase on Externalities

In 1959, when he was at the University of Virginia, Ronald Coase (Past as Prologue 15-1) published an obscure article on the Federal Communications Commission challenging Pigou's analysis of externalities. The article, published by the *Journal of Law and Economics,* intrigued its editor, Aaron Director, as well as other prominent Chicago economists, and they invited Coase to Chicago so he could present his ideas in more detail. The group of economists—including Martin Bailey, Milton Friedman, Arnold Harberger, Gregg Lewis, and George Stigler—met with Coase at Director's house one evening. Although the article excited their interest, the group still maintained that Pigou was correct and Coase was wrong. After his presentation and discussion, however, they had all changed their minds. As the economists left Director's house, many believed that they had witnessed a significant advance in economic theory.* A year later, Coase published "The Problem of Social Cost," an article that helped him garner the 1991 Nobel Prize.

In his 1960 article Coase stated that externalities are reciprocal:

> The [Pigou] approach has tended to obscure the nature of the choice that has to be made. The question is commonly thought of as one in which *A* inflicts harm on *B* and what has to be decided is: how should we restrain *A*? But this is wrong. We are dealing with a problem of a reciprocal nature. To avoid the harm to *B* would inflict harm on *A*. The real question that has to be decided is: should *A* be allowed to harm *B* or should *B* be allowed to harm *A*? The problem is to avoid the more serious harm.†

Coase proceeded to demonstrate what Stigler later dubbed the "Coase theorem." Coase explained that when either of two parties has property rights that are adversely affected by the action of the other, both parties will have an incentive to negotiate an acceptable outcome. Coase used the example of cattle from a ranch straying onto a neighbor's land and destroying crops.

If the property right is assigned to the farmer (the law assesses liability to the cattle-raiser), there will be an incentive for the cattle-raiser to offer a payment to the farmer to take some of the adjacent land out of farm production. But why would the farmer have an incentive to negotiate with the rancher? The answer from the farmer's perspective is that the foregone payment that could be obtained from the rancher is a cost of raising crops. Thus the farmer will want to see if he can receive a payment from the rancher that is greater than the loss of farm output on the adjacent land.

If the property right is assigned to the rancher (cattle can roam where they may), then the farmer has an incentive to offer a payment to the cattle-raiser to reduce the size of his herd. The rancher now has a new opportunity cost; if he increases the size of his herd, he loses the potential payment from the farmer. In

20-1 PAST AS PROLOGUE (continued)

either assignment of property rights, a negotiated settlement is likely and no intervention from government is necessary.

The upshot of the Coase theorem is that the clear assignment of property rights can eliminate the need for Pigouvian taxes and subsidies in circumstances where transaction costs are negligible. The problem, of course, is that many real-world externalities such as air and water pollution affect large numbers of people, making negotiation difficult. For example, the global warming problem involves thousands of firms and millions of individuals in various nations. In these cases, bargaining costs are substantial, and government intervention may prove to be optimal.‡

*Steven N. S. Cheung, "Ronald Coase," in *The New Palgrave: A Dictionary of Economics*, 4 vols. (London: Macmillan Press, 1987), 1: 455–457.

†Ronald H. Coase, "The Problem of Social Cost," *Journal of Law and Economics* 3 (October 1960): 1–44.

‡Coase's overall impact on economics is assessed in Steven G. Medema, ed., *The Legacy of Ronald Coase in Economic Analysis*, 2 vols. (Brookfield, VT: Edward Elgar, 1995).

enhance present consumption. The creation of new capital is checked, and people are encouraged to use up existing capital to such a degree that larger future advantages are sacrificed for smaller present ones. Natural resources are consumed more quickly and wastefully because future satisfactions are underrated.

Pigou concluded that economic welfare is diminished by government intervention that strengthens the tendency of people to devote too much of their resources to present use and too little to future use. Government should thus avoid any tax on saving, including property taxes, death duties, and progressive income taxes if it wants to maximize economic welfare. Heavy taxes on consumption are preferable because they encourage saving, but such taxes have the disadvantage of hurting low-income people disproportionately.

Pigou's desire to increase national saving to promote economic growth rested on his orthodox idea that economies tend toward full employment. In this connection he originated the idea that a decline in the general price level accompanying an economic downturn will increase the real value of people's assets. People, therefore, will decide to save less and consume more, thus increasing demand in the economy and pushing it back toward full employment. Economists have incorporated this idea into several contemporary economic models. For example, authors of textbooks on macroeconomics typically use this *Pigou effect*, or real balance effect, to help explain why the aggregate demand curve slopes downward and to the right (price level–real output model).

A final contribution of note is Pigou's discussion of price discrimination. It was he who classified price discrimination into three types: first degree, second degree, and third degree. First-degree price discrimination occurs when the monopolist charges each consumer the exact amount she or he would be willing to pay rather than go without the commodity. The monopolist, therefore, takes all of the consumer's surplus as revenue. Second-degree price discrimination is a cruder form of first-degree discrimination. The seller charges one price for each unit within an initial block of units and then charges lower prices for units within subsequent blocks. Electrical utilities commonly used this type of quantity discounting prior to the rate reforms of the 1970s and 1980s. Third-degree price discrimination involves separating groups of consumers into different classes and charging different prices based on the elasticity of demand for each group. One of many possible examples would be charging students and professors less than the general public for business newspapers and magazines.

Pigou's analysis of price discrimination extended the theory of monopoly pricing beyond that presented by Cournot and others. Joan Robinson, whom we have discussed already, in turn formalized Pigou's analysis in terms of marginal revenue and cost.

LUDWIG von MISES

Several ideas in welfare economics emerged from a long-running debate over whether economic welfare in both the Paretian and a broader sense of the term can be maximized under a system of socialism. An important early figure in this debate was Ludwig von Mises (1881–1973).

Biographical Information

Ludwig von Mises was an important member of the Austrian school of economic thought. He received his doctorate at the University of Vienna, where he studied with Schumpeter (Chapter 23) under von Wieser and von Böhm-Bawerk. The publication of his *Theory of Money and Credit* in 1912 earned him a nonsalaried appointment as "professor extraordinary" at the university. In 1940 he immigrated to the United States, where eventually he became a visiting professor at New York University. His emotion-charged style did not endear him to many economists who supported a nonideological, scientific approach to the discipline, yet in 1969 his colleagues named him a "Distinguished Fellow" of the American Economic Association.

Economic Calculation under Socialism

Ludwig von Mises touched off the welfare debate over socialism in his 1920 article, "Economic Calculation in the Socialist Commonwealth." He later expanded his antisocialist, pro-laissez-faire arguments in *Socialism* (original edition, 1922) and *Human Action: A Treatise on Economics* (1949). Von Mises contended that the same types of economic calculations that guide resources to their highest valued use under capitalism must be made by the socialist planner who desires to maximize consumer welfare. Without the private ownership of resources, free markets, and entrepreneurs, such calculations are impossible to make. Von Mises pointed out that contrary to the hopes of some socialists, markets and prices for *consumer goods* were inevitable under socialism so long as these goods were privately owned. The problem arises with *capital goods,* whose relative prices in a market economy reflect relative scarcities and productive values. Prices of capital quickly change in response to changes in consumer tastes, new technology, entrepreneurial expectations, and the like. But under socialism, where all capital is owned by the state, no such pricing mechanism exists. Thus the planner cannot accurately evaluate the relative scarcities and productive values of capital. "Where there is no free market, there is no pricing mechanism; without a pricing mechanism, there is no economic calculation."[6]

Change, said von Mises, is the central reality with which an economic system must cope: "In the world of reality there is no stationary state, for the conditions under which economic activity takes place are subject to perpetual alterations which it is beyond the human capacity to limit." Therefore, the problem of economic calculation is one of economic *dynamics*, not one of economic *statics*. In addition to the problems of minimizing costs and deciding on the proper allocation of goods, economic efficiency involves the problem of "dissolving, extending, transforming, and limiting existing undertakings, and establishing new undertakings."[7]

The economy is continuously generating new information, although this information is imperfect and subject to varying interpretations. Thus, according to von Mises, entrepreneurship is a central aspect in achieving dynamic economic welfare. Entrepreneurs attempt to anticipate the future; those who have greater anticipatory ability tend to reap rewards in the form of large profits, and their past successes enable them to command more resources for further anticipatory actions. The market "tends to entrust the conduct of business affairs to those . . . who have succeeded in filling the most urgent wants of consumers." The actions of these entrepreneurs create the prices upon which the more mundane static calculations—for example, minimizing costs—are constructed.

Profits and losses perform two important functions that cannot be duplicated under socialism: (1) they select out those who can best fulfill wants, and (2) they provide the incentive for entrepreneurs to avoid careless, audacious, and unreasonably optimistic decisions. Competition among entrepreneurs ensures that the benefits from their actions are widely shared by consumers, workers, and those who own the factors of production.

Socialism, said von Mises, cannot duplicate the functions of capital allocation and entrepreneurship required to channel resources efficiently in a dynamic setting. To those who contend that a socialist planning board can be instructed to take equivalent actions to those that would result under a competitive market system, von Mises replied:

> The cardinal fallacy implied in this and all kindred proposals is that they look at an economic problem from the perspective of the subaltern clerk whose intellectual horizon does not extend beyond subordinate tasks. They consider the structure of industrial production and the allocation of capital to the various branches and production aggregates as rigid, and do not take into account the necessity of altering this structure in order to adjust it to changes in conditions. . . .

[6] Ludwig von Mises, "Economic Calculation in the Socialist Commonwealth," in *Collective Economic Planning*, ed. F. Hayek (London: Routledge and Sons, 1935), 111.

[7] This interpretation and discussion of von Mises follow those of Peter Murrell in "Did the Theory of Market Socialism Answer the Challenge of Ludwig von Mises? A Reinterpretation of the Socialist Controversy," *History of Political Economy* 15 (Spring 1983): 92–105.

> The capitalist system is not a managerial system; it is an entrepreneurial system. . . . Nobody has ever suggested that the socialist commonwealth could invite the promoters and speculators to continue their speculations and then deliver their profits to the common chest. . . . One can not play speculation and investment. The speculators and investors expose their own wealth, their own destiny. This fact makes them responsible to the consumers.[8]

OSCAR LANGE

A second major contributor to the debate on socialism—and a significant figure in the broader history of welfare economics—is Oscar Lange (1904–1965). He was born in Poland and studied and taught at the University of Krakow. He received a Rockefeller fellowship that allowed him to visit several American universities, and in 1936 he became a lecturer at the University of Michigan. In 1943 Lange received a professorship at the University of Chicago. He returned to Poland in 1945 and was immediately appointed Poland's ambassador to the United Nations, a position that he served in for four years. From 1955 until his death in 1965 he was a professor at the University of Warsaw.

Economic Theory of Socialism

In an article entitled "On the Economic Theory of Socialism," published in 1937, Lange set forth a model of *market socialism*. If administered according to a fixed set of rules, said Lange, this form of socialism would result in economic efficiency and maximum social welfare. Market socialism is characterized by (1) private ownership of consumer goods and free choice of consumption from available goods, (2) free choice of occupation, and (3) state ownership of the means of production. There are markets and market prices for goods, services, and labor, but not for capital and intermediate goods (for example, component products that are brought together to make final products). But a price, said Lange, can take a form other than a market one; it also can be a *shadow price* or an index of the terms of exchange between two items. A central planning board, through a process of trial and error, can set the prices of capital goods by adjusting these prices to eliminate shortages and surpluses. This board pays all workers their market wage plus a share of the social dividend determined by the total yield of capital goods and natural resources. Through this control over shares of the social dividend, the central planning board can reduce the wide disparity of income that is characteristic of capitalistic economies.

The central planning board instructs the managers of state enterprises to act as if all prices are constant and to follow two rules. The first rule is to combine resources in the plant so that the average cost of production for any given level of output is at a minimum. Managers accomplish this by ensuring that the marginal

[8] Ludwig von Mises, *Human Action: A Treatise on Economics* (Auburn, AL: Ludwig von Mises Institute, 1998), 703–705. (Orig. pub. 1949.)

technical rates of substitution between resources are equal (recall the previous discussion of Pareto optimality). The second rule, said Lange,

> determines the scale of output by stating that output has to be fixed so that marginal cost is equal to the price of the product. . . . [This rule] performs the function which under competition is carried out by free entry of firms into an industry or their exodus from it, i.e. it determines the output of the industry.[9]

As long as accounting is done as if prices are constant, that is, as if they are independent of the decisions taken, said Lange, adherence to these rules will mean that prices that are set incorrectly from an equilibrium standpoint will create either shortages or surpluses of the commodities involved. Through trial and error the planners can adjust the prices to equilibrium levels. The trial and error procedure is much the same as that which occurs under capitalism, said Lange, but it can work better under socialism because central planners have access to a greater range of information about shortages and surpluses than do individual capitalists.[10]

Counterattacks

For several decades the conventional view among historians of economic thought was that Oscar Lange "delivered the *coup de grace* to the anti-socialist critics."[11] This interpretation is accurate in that Lange *did* establish that the static economic efficiency of the type envisioned by Pareto is theoretically possible under socialism. But it now seems ironic to have declared the debate over socialism won. The counterattack, led by Nobel prizewinner Friedrich von Hayek (1899–1992) and contemporary "neo–Austrians," increasingly won acceptance in academic circles. Their views have been bolstered by the collapse of the major centrally planned socialist nations and in developments in the economics of information. These counterarguments are of two types.

First, although it may be possible in theory to achieve economic efficiency through planning in a large economy, accomplishing this in actual practice is quite another matter. Central planning of the variety advocated by Lange—having the planning board serve as the auctioneer in solving Walras's equations—requires massive amounts of information. As pointed out by Samuelson and Nordhaus, "we don't have the tiniest fraction of the data needed to solve [such] a large general-equilibrium problem."[12]

The second counterargument is that the Lange approach fails to consider the need to give the participants in the economy sufficient *incentive* to allocate resources efficiently and to seek opportunities to increase output. Dynamic efficiency of the type envisioned by the Austrians requires the entrepreneurial function through which information is continuously and quickly discovered and utilized. In the competitive economy, the profit motive provides this incentive to entrepreneurs

[9] Oscar Lange, "On the Economic Theory of Socialism," in *On the Economic Theory of Socialism,* ed. Benjamin Lippincott (New York: McGraw-Hill, 1964), 76–77. (Orig. pub. 1938.)

[10] Other key contributors to the economic theory of socialism were Enrico Barone, Fred M. Taylor, H. D. Dickenson, Abba Lerner (Chapter 22), and Maurice Dobb.

[11] Philip C. Newman, *The Development of Economic Thought* (Englewood Cliffs, NJ: Prentice-Hall, 1952), 181.

[12] Paul Samuelson and William Nordhaus, *Economics,* 12th ed. (New York: McGraw-Hill, 1985), 685.

(who may be single individuals or groups of individuals within firms). Such incentives are lacking in a socialist economy, say these critics, and cannot be incorporated in a way that retains the system.

KENNETH ARROW

The history of economic thought shows a remarkable variety of thinkers. We have seen that some have been moral theorists, others political and social activists, still others developers and refiners of existing theory. It remains for a few, however, to straddle the area between economic theory and social philosophy. Such a theorist is Kenneth Arrow (1921–). Arrow completed his undergraduate work at City College of New York and did his graduate work at Columbia University. Upon receiving his degree, he accepted a position at Stanford University, where he was to transform the Economics Department into one of worldwide reputation.

Arrow not only displayed a rare talent for symbolic logic, mathematics, and statistics but also had an insight into new areas where such talents could be applied. His dissertation, *Social Choice and Individual Values*, became a classic in welfare economics. In this famous work he evaluated various criteria of social welfare and suggested inconsistencies in many of the previously held ideas.

Working at Stanford, Arrow continued his inquiry into the tenets of welfare economics. His numerous journal articles addressed questions such as these: How do we know if society is better off as a result of a policy choice? What is the logic of collective choice by members of a community with individual preferences? Is perfect democracy possible? What adjustments must be made if there is no possible way of maintaining a perfect democracy? Are there rules for determining what constitutes a just distribution of income?

Of particular interest to us is Arrow's *impossibility theorem*, or "the paradox of voting." To ascertain the relationship between individual preferences and social choices through democratic voting, Arrow first established four minimal conditions that social choices must meet if they are to accurately reflect the preferences of the individual voters: (1) Social choices must be transitive, that is, consistent, so that if *A* is preferred to *B* and *B* is preferred to *C*, then *C* cannot be preferred to *A*; (2) the group decision must not be dictated by anyone inside or outside the community; (3) social choices must not change in the opposite direction of individual choices (restated, a choice that society would otherwise have made must never be rejected simply because someone comes to like it more); and (4) a social preference made between two alternatives must depend only on preferences toward these two alternatives and not on people's opinions of other options.

Arrow then scrutinized majority voting schemes to see if democratic decision making could make choices among all sets of available alternatives without violating one of these conditions. After careful investigation, he reached a surprising conclusion: No majority voting scheme simultaneously respects the personal preferences of the voters, ensures maximum welfare, and does not depend upon the order that issues are voted upon.

For example, stated Arrow, suppose there is a community that consists of three voters (*1*, *2*, and *3*), and the community has three alternative policies from which

Table 20-1
Arrow's Paradox of Voting

POLICY	VOTER 1	VOTER 2	VOTER 3
A	1st choice	3rd choice	2nd choice
B	2nd choice	1st choice	3rd choice
C	3rd choice	2nd choice	1st choice

to choose: to disarm (*A*), to wage a cold war (*B*), or to wage a hot war (*C*). According to welfare theory, the community will arrange the order of the three alternatives according to its preferences and then, if possible, choose the alternative that stands highest on the list. This means that voters will state that they prefer alternative *A* to *B*, and so forth. The collective preference scale may then be established using the majority rule; that is, we could have a vote between *A* and *B* and between the winner and *C*.

Table 20-1 lists the three policies (*A*, *B*, and *C*) and the individual preferences of the three voters (*1*, *2*, and *3*). It tells us that voter *1* prefers policy *A* to *B* and *B* to *C* (implying a preference for *A* over *C*). Voter *2*'s first choice is policy *B*, her second choice *C*, and her third choice *A*. This means that she prefers *B* to *C* and *C* to *A* (implying a preference of *B* over *A*). Voter *3* prefers *C* to *A* and prefers *A* to *B*, and therefore prefers *C* to *B*.

Our next task is to ascertain the outcomes of several hypothetical paired-choice contests decided by majority vote. Let us conduct three such votes: *A* versus *B*, *B* versus *C*, and *A* versus *C*. *A* will win in the contest between *A* and *B*, because voters *1* and *3* each prefer *A* to *B*; the vote will be two to one in favor of *A*. We show this outcome in Table 20-2. If *B* is matched up against *C* in a vote, *B* will emerge as the winner, because policy *B* will be selected by voters *1* and *2*. We know then that the majority of this community prefers *A* to *B* and *B* to *C*. We therefore conclude that it must prefer *A* to *C*. Is our conclusion correct? To double check, let us conduct a vote between *A* and *C*. Here we discover that a majority of the voters (voters *2* and *3*) prefer *C* to *A*! We have violated the consistency, or transitivity, requirement: *A* is preferred to *B*, and *B* is preferred to *C*, but *C* is preferred to *A*. This majority voting scheme therefore fails to order the preferences of voters rationally.

Table 20-2
Vote Outcomes

ELECTION	WINNER
A vs *B*	*A*
B vs *C*	*B*
A vs *C*	*C*

Arrow's analysis showed that we need to design our decision-making process in a way that avoids the more obvious pitfalls. Perfect democracy is impossible, and we have to settle for second or third best. Achieving economic welfare in an economy that has a large public sector is no easy matter. Arrow's major contributions have been in challenging the assumptions on which political and economic systems of thought have been based. Since the eighteenth century, philosophers and political theorists have been grappling with how to perfect human institutions. Kenneth Arrow is their successor.

JAMES M. BUCHANAN

James M. Buchanan (1919–) is an unconventional economist who, like Kenneth Arrow, has greatly extended the boundaries of welfare economics. Specifically, Buchanan is the founder and one of the main contributors to *public-choice theory* (the economics of politics) and its subset, *constitutional economics* (the economics of rules).

Buchanan grew up in rural poverty in Tennessee. The realities of the Great Depression ended his dream to study law at Vanderbilt University. Instead, he enrolled at nearby Middle Tennessee State and stayed at home while attending college. For four years, morning and night, he milked dairy cows to help pay his way through school. Buchanan's modest, rural background most likely explains his well-known disdain for pretension and elitism.

Buchanan began graduate work in economics at the University of Chicago in 1945. There he was greatly influenced by the neoclassicism of Frank Knight (1885–1972) and, in Buchanan's own words, was converted into "a zealous advocate of the market order."[13] It was also at Chicago that, while browsing in the library, he discovered Knut Wicksell's obscure 1896 dissertation on taxes. In this essay Wicksell established the principle that only unanimity of collective choice can ensure justice and efficiency through public-sector action. For example, said Wicksell, if a government expenditure "holds out any prospect at all of creating utility exceeding costs, it will always be theoretically possible, and approximately so in practice, to find a distribution of costs such that all parties regard the expenditure as beneficial and may therefore approve it unanimously."[14] Buchanan has credited Wicksell's thinking for inspiring him to apply standard economic assumptions and principles to the analysis of political behavior and processes.

After he completed his graduate work at Chicago, Buchanan's academic career soon took him to the University of Virginia, where in 1962 he coauthored with Gordon Tullock the pathbreaking book, *The Calculus of Consent: Logical Foundations of Constitutional Democracy.* According to Buchanan:

> In retrospect, it is interesting to me that there was no sense of 'discovery' at any point in that book's construction, no moment of excitement. . . . Tullock and I considered ourselves to be applying relatively simple economic analysis to the choice

[13] James M. Buchanan, "Better than Ploughing," in *Recollections of Eminent Economists,* ed. J. A. Kregel, 2 vols. (New York: New York University Press, 1989), 2: 282.

[14] Knut Wicksell, "A New Principle of Just Taxation," translated by James M. Buchanan, in *Classics in the Theory of Public Finance,* eds. Richard A. Musgrave and A. T. Peacock (London: Macmillan, 1958), 89–90.

among alternative political decision rules, with more or less predictable results. We realized that no one had attempted to do precisely what we were doing, but the exercise was essentially one of 'writing out the obvious' rather than opening up wholly new areas of inquiry.

We were wrong. Public choice, as a subdiscipline in its own right, emerged in the early 1960s, in part from the reception of our book, in part from our own organizational-entrepreneurial efforts which later emerged in the Public Choice Society, in part from other works. Once the whole complex of political decision rules and procedures were opened up for economic analysis, the range of application seemed open ended.[15]

In the late 1960s Buchanan left the University of Virginia for the Virginia Polytechnic Institute, where he helped organize the Center for the Study of Public Choice and initiated the journal *Public Choice*. In 1983 Buchanan moved with the center to George Mason University, where he now resides. For his pioneering book and subsequent contributions to public-choice theory, Buchanan was awarded the Nobel Prize in economics in 1986.

The Public-Choice Perspective

Buchanan contends that only individuals know what gives them satisfaction or causes them dissatisfaction; no outside person or group of persons can determine this for them. Individuals have differing tastes, capacities, expectations, knowledge, and perspectives, but they possess one commonality: They pursue their self-interest in a purposeful way. This self-interested pursuit leads to *spontaneous order* through the process of exchange. Individuals seek out exchanges that enhance their well-being; they maximize their utility subject to constraints.

This perspective reflects the *homo economicus* (economic man) and market exchange viewpoints of the classical and neoclassical economists. However, Buchanan asks a fundamental question not fully pursued by earlier economists: If individuals seek their self-interest in the market, why would we expect them to pursue the social interest in or through government? For Buchanan, human nature is human nature; people maximize their utility subject to constraints whether operating in the marketplace, government service, or the political arena.

Put succinctly, Buchanan extended the convenient assumption of self-interested behavior and the idea of the exchange process "to the behavior of persons in their political or public-choice roles or capacities, either as participants in voting processes or as agents acting for the body politic."[16]

The theory of public choice took root only slowly within mainstream economics, but today it is found in nearly all public finance and principles of economics textbooks. This theory provides powerful insights, as several examples illustrate. First, public choice helps us understand the collapse of communism. Communist leaders and socialist managers promoted their own interest, not the idealized social good. Second, public choice helps us understand the rising public debt in many industrial nations. According to Buchanan, elected politicians will latch onto any

---

[15] Buchanan, in Kregel, *Recollections,* 286–287.

[16] James M. Buchanan, *Essays on the Political Economy* (Honolulu: University of Hawaii Press, 1989), 20.

rationale to create budget deficits. They stay elected by providing public goods and services at minimum short-term cost to taxpayers. Deficits disguise the true costs of public goods and therefore make politicians look better to their constituents.

Third, congressional representatives engage in logrolling, the exchange of votes, because this process gives them the power to obtain results that might not be accomplished individually. Fourth, businesses and labor groups engage in *rent-seeking behavior* (Past as Prologue 8-2). They attempt to persuade government to limit competition and create special rules that enhance private profit. Finally, the public-choice viewpoint explains why bureaucracy is endemic to government and tends to beget larger bureaucracy. Bureaucrats gain stature and secure salary increases by having more staff below them. Agencies also inevitably find more and more "problems" requiring larger budgets and more personnel to solve them.

Critique of Conventional Welfare Economics

Buchanan is critical of conventional welfare economics for attempting to compare private-sector real-world outcomes against theoretical social utility norms (such as Pareto optimality). In some welfare schemas, government officials are viewed as agents who can identify society's social welfare function, an aggregation of the utility preferences of the people. Government is "good"; it identifies and corrects the "bads" produced in the private sector and thereby enhances society's welfare.

Buchanan's objections to this line of reasoning are twofold. First, because utility can be known only individually, no one can discern a collective or social welfare function. Even individuals do not know their utility preferences until presented with real-world choices, and choices made today affect utility functions and choice tomorrow. It is not appropriate to attribute utility preferences or goals to society as such. Rather than trying to measure and weigh utility outcomes, welfare economics should focus on understanding and improving political and institutional rules.

Second, even if the social welfare function were known, the public sector is not a reliable institution for achieving it. This sector consists of people acting in their own best interests, and it is difficult to align these individual interests with the undefined social ideal. In brief, there is "government failure" as well as "market failure."

> There is no necessary presumption that simply because markets are imperfect, political processes will work better. On the contrary, as public-choice theory reminds us, there are very good reasons for doubting the capacity of political processes to achieve Pareto optimality. The normatively relevant comparison is between two imperfect institutions.[17]

Constitutional Economics

Although Buchanan is pro-individualist and suspicious of government, he is not an anarchist (Chapter 9). Without government to establish and enforce rules such as property rights and contracts, the pursuit of self-interest will degenerate into

[17] H. Geoffrey Brennan and James M. Buchanan, *The Reason of Rules* (London: Cambridge University Press, 1985), 116.

Hobbesian "warre" (the state of nature in which life for the individual is "solitary, poor, brutish, and short"). But Buchanan points out that although those seeking their own interests understand that the state is needed to constrain individual behavior, individuals also recognize the need for constitutional rules to constrain the *state*. Ideally, these ultimate rules should be derived through Wicksellian unanimous consent. Such consent may be possible, because at the writing of the constitution, no individuals can know with certainty how the constitutional rules will directly affect them in the future.

> The uncertainty that is required in order for the individual to be led by his own interest to support constitutional provisions that are generally advantageous to all individuals and to all groups seems likely to be present at any constitutional stage of discussion.[18]

Mutual consent (unanimity) may be possible and desirable in establishing ultimate constitutional rules, but efficiency considerations may mean that subsequent rule making may require less than unanimity, such as a majority voting rule. However, there is nothing sacrosanct about a majority rule. The optimal rule for passage of a measure may be some percentage greater or less than 50 percent. Percentages less than 100 percent impose costs on those opposed to the law, such costs rising as the percentage required for approval falls. On the other hand, achieving unanimity itself is costly because bargaining and decision-making costs rise rapidly with the increase of the percentage of the total vote needed for passage. An optimal voting rule is one that minimizes the sum of (1) the costs to those opposing the proposition and (2) society's bargaining and decision-making costs associated with gaining greater consensus.

Buchanan's public-choice perspective and work on constitutional economics have led him to conclude that government has grown too large. New constitutional constraints on government are needed to protect the original constitutional consensus. In this regard, he has supported a balanced budget amendment, which would require the federal government to balance its tax revenues and expenditures annually, and a monetary rule requiring the Federal Reserve Board to increase the money supply each year at a set percentage rate. He has also strongly supported tax limitation amendments to state constitutions.

These policy views have earned Buchanan a somewhat controversial reputation because the vast majority of contemporary economists do not share them. Buchanan and a rather tight-knit band of like-thinkers seem to welcome and enjoy this controversy. They are ardent advocates of their viewpoints and prolific researchers and writers. Public-choice theory having been interjected squarely into the mainstream of economics, it now remains to be seen whether Buchanan and his supporters will have further impact on the discipline.

AMARTYA SEN

Born on a university campus in Santiniketan, India, Amartya Sen (1933–) seemed destined for a life in academia. His father was a professor of chemistry at Dhaka University, and his grandfather taught Sanskrit and Indian culture at Tagore's

[18] James M. Buchanan and Gordon Tullock, *The Calculus of Consent* (Ann Arbor: University of Michigan Press, 1962), 78.

Vista-Bharati. After contemplating the study of Sanskrit, mathematics, and physics, Amartya Sen eventually chose, as he put it, "the eccentric charms of economics."[19]

Most of Sen's accomplished life has been spent on college campuses on three continents. He earned B.A. degrees from Calcutta University and Trinity College in Cambridge, and his Ph.D. from Cambridge, where Joan Robinson supervised his doctoral thesis. His thesis earned him a Prize Fellowship at Trinity College, which he used to support four years of study in philosophy. Sen's teaching positions have ranged from Presidency College in Calcutta, India, to Trinity College, to Harvard University in Cambridge, Massachusetts, including stops at Delhi University, the London School of Economics, Oxford University, U.C. Berkeley, Cornell, MIT, and Stanford.

Despite considerable time spent in academic circles, during his early years Sen witnessed poverty and famine, as well as the violence that resulted from people struggling to survive. Through early observation and later study, he concluded that problems such as famine were due less to a lack of food than to a lack of access, often resulting from income inequality, undemocratic institutions, and ineffective social policies. Sen's interest in these problems led him to work with the United Nations Development Programme (UNDP) to help improve measures of poverty and inequality.

Sen's major works include *Collective Choice and Social Welfare* (1970), and *On Economic Inequality* (1973). For his contributions to welfare economics, in 1998 he was awarded the Nobel Prize in economics. The combination of his theoretical work and humanitarian efforts led *Business Week* to refer to Sen as "The Mother Teresa of Economics."[20]

Sen's wife, Emma Rothschild, is an accomplished economic historian, having taught at MIT and Cambridge. Since 1991 she has served as the director of the Centre for History and Economics at the University of Cambridge and has held a number of research and policy board positions. Rothschild has also written numerous books and articles, including her 2001 work, *Economic Sentiments: Adam Smith, Condorcet and the Enlightenment.*

Social Choice

As we have seen, Kenneth Arrow concluded that no system of majority voting could simultaneously maximize social welfare and respect individual preferences independent of the ordering of votes. While accepting much of the work of his colleague, Sen attempted to refute the impossibility theorem and improve collective choice theory.

Sen thought that the impossibility theorem could be resolved by including two considerations that Arrow (and others) assumed away. Arrow's model of collective choice depends on a simple rank ordering (I like A more than B, and B more than C), but says nothing about the *intensity of preferences* (I like A much more than B, but B only a little bit more than C). Economists refer to this simple rank ordering as an *ordinal* measure—it puts items in order of preference but assigns no numeric value

[19] Amartya Sen, "Amartya Sen—Autobiography." The Nobel Foundation, 1998. http://nobelprize.org/economics/laureates/1998/sen-autobio.html (accessed February 4, 2005).

[20] *Business Week*, October 26, 1998, 44.

to their worth. *Cardinal* measures (*A* gives me 20 utils, *B* gives me 10) would make it easier to measure preference intensity, but they are generally rejected on the grounds that they are difficult to obtain and interpret (20 utils might be a lot on my scale, but hardly any on yours).

Why might intensity of preferences matter in collective choice? In a simple majority voting scheme it wouldn't, except to the extent that voters only slightly more in favor of policy *A* over *B* might decide that the cost of voting outweighs the benefits received from casting the deciding vote for *A*. In a decision-making framework where preferences could be more fully incorporated—for example, in a voting system through which voters distribute a fixed allotment of points—the paradox of voting is much less likely to occur. Those stronger preferences will carry more "voting weight" than they do in majority voting.

The other restriction imposed by Arrow (and many others) is that *interpersonal comparisons* are not allowed in the model. The rationale for this is that such comparisons are, at best, difficult to make and are most often useless. If two people determine that they will receive 20 utils from a proposed policy, this may indicate strong support from the first person and mild interest for the second. The problem is the lack of a commonly understood and accepted utility scale.

For Sen, however, interpersonal comparisons matter and are not prohibitively difficult. As he wrote,

> The use of interpersonal comparisons is widely thought to be arbitrary, and many people view these comparisons as "meaningless" in not being related to acts of choice. One way of giving meaning to such comparisons is to consider choices between being person *A* in social state *x* or being person *B* in social state *y*. For example, we could ask: "Would you prefer to be Mr. *A*, an unemployed laborer, in state *x*, or Mr. *B*, a well-paid engineer, in state *y*?" While the answer to the question does involve interpersonal comparisons, I should hazard the view that it is not entirely beyond our intellectual depth to be able to think systematically about this choice.[21]

Sen also suggested that people may make interpersonal comparisons in formulating preferences as they consider how policy options will affect not only themselves but those around them.

> The society in which a person lives, the class to which he belongs, the relation that he has with the social and economic structure of the community, are relevant to a person's choice not merely because they affect the nature of his personal interests but also because they influence his value system including his notion of "due" concern for other members of society. The insular economic man pursuing his self-interest to the exclusion of all other considerations may represent an assumption that pervades much of traditional economics, but it is not a particularly useful model for understanding problems of social choice.[22]

Sen's work reveals a deep concern for equity and justice in social choice—that outcomes not simply maximize total welfare but that the distribution of income also is

[21] Amartya Sen, *Collective Choice and Social Welfare* (San Francisco: Holden-Day, Inc., 1970), 4.

[22] Sen, *Collective Choice,* 6.

fair. Drawing from the philosophy of John Rawls, Sen suggests that one approach to generating equitable decisions is what he calls "maximin justice."[23] In such a scheme, individuals choose among alternative social states from an unknown starting position. In other words, maximin justice asks a person to choose the distributional arrangements for society under the assumption that they have not yet been born. Sen chose the word "maximin" because in choosing between different social states, people will select that set of arrangements that "maximizes their minimum welfare." Put another way, because of the risk of being the worst off person in society, one will choose a society where the worst off are still better off than in any alternative scenario.

Inequality

Sen argued that the traditional social choice framework, centered on the concepts of *utilitarianism* and *Pareto optimality*, often precludes a meaningful analysis of the equity effects of a policy. Jeremy Bentham's *utilitarianism*, the philosophy that society should pursue the greatest good for the greatest number, promotes the maximization of total social utility, but gives no consideration to equity. Furthermore, Sen demonstrated, using Figure 20-2 as an illustration, how application of the utilitarian framework may lead to less egalitarian outcomes.

The diagram represents a two-person society, with the horizontal axis measuring society's total income. Person *A*'s income is measured left to right, and person *B*'s from right to left, with society's total income equaling the sum of *A*'s and *B*'s income. Vertically Sen measured marginal utility of the income, so that any point on line A_1A_2 measures the marginal utility of an extra dollar of income for person *A* at that point. *A*'s total income will be the sum of the marginal utilities up to the income level that *A* receives, represented graphically as the area under the curve. Thus if *A* is receiving income *AC*, her total utility will be measured by the area AA_1EC. If her income rises to *AD*, although her marginal utility will fall, her total utility will increase to AA_1GD.

Sen began the example by assuming that *A* and *B* had identical utility functions, such that A_1A_2 and B_1B_2 are mirror images of each other. This implies that for any given dollar of income their marginal utilities would be equal, and using our earlier developed equimarginal rule, total welfare (utility) would be maximized if the two had equal incomes ($AC = BC$). Next suppose that *B*'s true utility function is B_3B_4, such that for any given level of income, *B*'s utility is half of *A*'s. (In Sen's example, *B* might represent someone physically or mentally challenged such that he is unable to obtain as much as *A* for any given dollar.) Starting from the original distribution of equal income ($AC = BC$), total social utility equals AA_1EC plus CFB_3B. If we redistribute income so that *A* receives *AD* and *B* receives *BD*, total social utility is increased by the area of triangle *EFG*. For Sen, this implied taking income away from someone who was already less fortunate (because of a disability) and giving it to the person with greater welfare. That defies social justice or fairness.

For Sen, *Pareto optimality* is also an unsatisfactory criterion for distribution. The condition of Pareto optimality only says that no one can be made better off without making someone else worse off. It says nothing about the distribution in society.

[23] Sen, *Collective Choice,* 135.

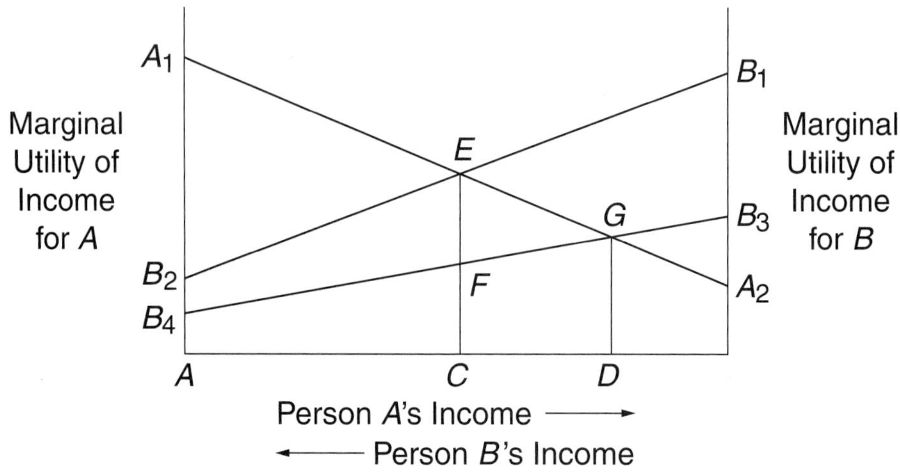

Figure 20-2 Sen's Critique of the Utilitarian Approach to Income Distribution
If two individuals, *A* and *B*, have identical utility functions, A_1A_2 and B_1B_2, respectively, then an equal distribution of income, $AC = BC$, will maximize total welfare, $AA_1EC + BB_1EC$. Redistribution of income from *B* to *A* (or vice versa) would reduce total welfare; the marginal utility of the last dollar received by *A* would be less than the marginal utility lost by B's reduction in income. Now suppose that *B* suffers from a condition such that *B* receives less enjoyment (marginal utility) from each dollar received, as shown by utility function B_3B_4. With an equal distribution of income, total utility is $AA_1EC + BB_3FC$, but *B* has lower total welfare than *A*. The egalitarian approach would redistribute income from *A* to *B* to equalize the total utility of each person. The utilitarian approach would do the opposite, redistributing income from *B* to *A* (so that *A* receives *AD* and *B* receives *BD*) to increase total welfare by *EFG*. Despite its reputation, the utilitarian approach is not egalitarian.

There could be multiple states that are Pareto optimal, each reflecting vastly different levels of income inequality, which Sen demonstrates with the following example:

> Suppose we are considering the division of a cake. Assuming that each person prefers to have more of the cake rather than less of it, every possible distribution will be Pareto optimal, because any change that makes someone better off is going to make someone else worse off. Since the only issue in this problem is that of distribution, Pareto optimality has no cutting power at all. The almost single-minded concern of modern welfare economics with Pareto optimality does not make that engaging branch of study particularly suitable for investigating problems of inequality.[24]

For Sen, traditional welfare economics was not up to the task of analyzing distributional issues. As Sen wrote,

---

[24] Sen, *On Economic Inequality* (New York: W.W. Norton, 1973), 7.

> To conclude, we do not seem to get very much help in studying inequality from the main schools of welfare economics—old and new. The literature on Pareto optimality . . . avoids distributional judgements altogether. The standard approach of 'social welfare functions' because of its concentration on individual orderings only (without any use of interpersonal comparisons of levels and intensities) fails to provide a framework for distributional discussions. . . . Finally, utilitarianism, the dominant faith of 'old' welfare economics, is much too hooked on the welfare *sum* to be concerned with the problem of distribution, and it is, in fact, capable of producing strongly anti-egalitarian results. As an approach to the measurement and evaluation of inequality it cannot take us very far. For the problem of inequality evaluation, the royal roads of welfare economics do look a trifle bleak.[25]

Sen's dissatisfaction with existing theory drove him to offer his own insights. Distributional concerns generally focus on extreme inequality, often implying that greater equality would improve society. Taking this premise to its logical conclusion would suggest total equality, but as Sen points out, equality is important to the extent that it reflects an equitable (fair) distribution. For Sen, that can take one of two forms.

> There are essentially two rival notions of the 'right' distribution of income, based respectively on needs and desert. It is easy to recognize the contrast between arguments of the kind: '*A* should get more income than *B* since his needs are greater', and those of the type: '*A* should get more income than *B* since he has done more work and deserves a higher reward'. Inequality can, therefore, be viewed not merely as a measure of dispersion but also as a measure of the difference between the actual distribution on income on the one hand and *either* (i) distribution according to needs, *or* (ii) that according to some concept of desert.[26]

Sen focuses most of his attention on the needs side of the argument as he examines how to maximize social welfare. Needs are often dismissed in the literature as an unsolvable problem because they involve interpersonal comparisons of utility functions that are difficult, if not impossible, to specify. Sen presented two cases supporting a more equal distribution, both acknowledging and embracing the incomparability of individual utility functions.

Probabilistic egalitarianism, built from the work of Abba Lerner (1903–1982), argues that precisely because of uncertainty, incomes should be equalized. Assuming that (1) there is a fixed amount of income to distribute, (2) that both society and individuals are subject to diminishing marginal utility, and (3) that everyone has equal probability of having a given utility function, Sen demonstrated that the expected total utility is maximized with an equal distribution. This does not mean that a completely equal distribution would necessarily maximize total welfare. In fact, the theory recognizes that individuals possess different welfare functions, suggesting that there is likely some unequal distribution that would yield higher welfare. However, given that we do not know the specifications and

[25] Sen, *On Economic Inequality,* 23.

[26] Sen, *On Economic Inequality,* 77.

distribution of those welfare functions, the best we can say is that, *on average,* welfare is maximized with an equal distribution of a fixed total output and income.[27]

Maximin egalitarianism, similar to maximin justice, argues that society should choose the distributional system that maximizes the gain to the least well-off person. Under circumstances of complete ignorance about people's needs, Sen demonstrates that the society's welfare is maximized with an equal distribution.[28]

Although he favored a more egalitarian, needs-based approach, Sen recognized that equalizing incomes is problematic from both a fairness and an efficiency perspective. He presents four approaches to the concept of desert.

1. *Incentives.* Desert-based systems create more incentives for work effort. To the extent that people are driven by their needs, the system can be defended on distributional grounds. Otherwise it must be defended on some other basis, such as the total amount of income generated.
2. *Merit.* People who accomplish more should receive more. Sen finds this approach particularly troublesome in that often those who accomplish more have been given an advantage, by genetics, cultural proclivities, or simply luck. He points specifically to those who, through no fault of their own, would receive less income because of their age, infirmity, or genetic defect. As Sen put it, "A system based on needs would seem to have greater use for the complex idea that we call humanity."[29]
3. *Marxist exploitation.* As we saw in Chapter 10, Marx's theory of exploitation argues that labor does not receive the full value of its contribution to output. As Sen points out, however, "Marx himself regarded this right to the 'fruits' of labour as a 'bourgeois right' to be supplanted by the principle of needs when the opportunity arose."[30]
4. *Neo-classical marginal productivity theory.* From Sen's perspective, J. B. Clark's marginal productivity theory of income distribution is less of a normative theory than the others, and to the extent that it is, offers little substance. The primary criterion is Pareto optimality, which offers little perspective on the optimal distribution.[31]

Sen finds none of these arguments for the proper distributional scheme as compelling as the needs argument.

In the sense that he builds on neoclassical theory, Sen is a mainstream economist. His efforts to integrate normative ("ought to be") considerations, however, set him apart from the rest of his cohort. His Nobel Prize vindicates his deviation from an exclusively positive ("what is") analysis.

---

[27]Sen, *On Economic Inequality,* 83–85.

[28]Sen, *On Economic Inequality,* 85–87.

[29]Sen, *On Economic Inequality,* 104–105.

[30]Sen, *On Economic Inequality,* 105.

[31]Sen, *On Economic Inequality,* 105.

Questions for Study and Discussion

1. Identify and briefly state the significance of each of the following to the history of economic thought: welfare economics; Pareto; Pareto optimality; marginal rate of substitution; marginal rate of technical substitution; marginal rate of transformation; Pigou; externality; first-, second-, and third-degree price discrimination; Pigou effect; von Mises; Lange; Arrow; impossibility theorem; Buchanan; unanimity rule; public-choice theory; rent-seeking behavior; Sen; intensity of preferences; interpersonal comparisons; Rawls; maximin justice; probabilistic egalitarianism.
2. Explain the following statement: Pareto's welfare analysis is in the tradition of Walras, whereas Pigou's welfare analysis is in the tradition of Marshall.
3. Recall from previous economics courses the notion of a production possibilities curve. Draw such a curve for two goods such that it is concave to origin. Explain the concept of the marginal rate of transformation (discussed in this chapter) as it relates to your curve. What does the concave shape of the production possibilities curve imply?
4. Explain why a negative externality in production results in too much of the good being produced from society's perspective, whereas a positive externality results in too little being produced. How, according to Pigou, might such over- and underallocations of resources be corrected?
5. State the Coase theorem (Past as Prologue 20-1). Why is the assumption of zero transaction costs crucial to this theorem?
6. Through direct reference to Cournot's monopoly model in Figure 12-1(a), explain how a monopolist might increase its profits above 12,000 francs by engaging in first-degree price discrimination, as defined by Pigou. (Hint: the marginal revenue curve in the figure now becomes coincident with the demand curve.) Contrast the quantity of mineral water sold in Cournot's model with that sold under the assumption of first-degree price discrimination.
7. Contrast the views of von Mises and Lange on the possibilities of achieving maximum welfare under market socialism.
8. Debate: Arrow's impossibility theorem is an interesting intellectual exercise, but it is of little practical importance. It dramatizes the extent to which economics has deteriorated into a science of the trivial.
9. Relate Buchanan's public-choice perspective to each of the following: (a) farm subsidies, (b) government budget deficits, (c) the growth of government bureaucracy, and (d) the resistance to privatization by many managers of state firms in China.
10. Summarize Buchanan's criticism of traditional welfare economics. Suppose that you were asked to rebut Buchanan's criticism. What line of reasoning would you employ?
11. Speculate as to why rules requiring a super majority (more than 60 percent in favor) are often in place for amending constitutions, whereas simple majority rules (50 percent plus) are normally specified for enacting laws within the constitutional framework.
12. According to Sen, how can Arrow's impossibility theorem be resolved?

13. How would Sen respond to Buchanan's statement that "there are very good reasons for doubting the capacity of political processes to achieve Pareto optimality"?
14. Suppose that a three-person economy produces $100,000 worth of income each year, and that there are two methods of distribution available to this society: The first method would distribute $30,000 each to two members of the economy, and $40,000 to the third. The second distribution scheme would allocate $80,000 to one person, and $10,000 each to the other two. How would Bentham (Chapter 8), Marx (Chapter 10), Pareto, and Sen answer the question: "Which distribution is most appropriate?"

Selected Readings

Books

Arrow, Kenneth J. *Social Choice and Individual Values.* New Haven, CT: Yale University Press, 1951.

Blaug, Mark, ed. *Arthur Pigou.* Brookfield, VT: Edward Elgar, 1992.

———, ed. *Vilfredo Pareto.* Brookfield, VT: Edward Elgar, 1992.

Buchanan, James M. *Economics: Between Predictive Science and Moral Philosophy.* College Station: Texas A&M University Press, 1987.

———. *Liberty, Market, and State: Political Economy in the 1980s.* New York: New York University Press, 1986.

———. *The Limits of Liberty: Between Anarchy and the Leviathan.* Chicago: University of Chicago Press, 1975.

Buchanan, James M., and Gordon Tullock. *The Calculus of Consent: Logical Foundations of Constitutional Democracy.* Ann Arbor: University of Michigan Press, 1962.

Butler, Eamon, ed. *Ludwig von Mises: Fountainhead of the Modern Microeconomic Revolution.* Brookfield, VT: Gower, 1988.

Lange, Oscar, and Fred M. Taylor. *On the Economic Theory of Socialism.* Edited by Benjamin E. Lippincott. New York: McGraw-Hill, 1964. (Orig. pub. 1938.)

Moss, Laurence S., ed. *The Economics of Ludwig von Mises: Toward a Critical Reappraisal.* Kansas City: Sheed and Ward, 1976.

Pareto, Vilfredo. *Manual of Political Economy.* Translated by Ann S. Schwier and edited by Ann S. Schwier and Alfred Page. New York: A. M. Kelley, 1971. (Orig. pub. 1906.)

Pigou, A. C. *The Economics of Welfare,* 4th ed. London: Macmillan, 1932. (Orig. pub. 1920.)

von Mises, Ludwig. *Human Action: A Treatise on Economics.* Chicago: Henry Regnery, 1966. (Orig. pub. 1949.)

Journal Articles

Murrell, Peter. "Did the Theory of Market Socialism Answer the Challenge of Ludwig von Mises? A Reinterpretation of the Socialist Controversy," *History of Political Economy* 15 (Spring 1983): 92–105.

O'Donnell, Margaret G. "Pigou: An Extension of Sidgwickian Thought," *History of Political Economy* 11 (Winter 1979): 588–605.

Sandmo, Agnar. "Buchanan on Political Economy: A Review Article," *Journal of Economic Literature* 28 (March 1990): 50–65.

Sen, Amartya. "Social Choice and Justice: Collected Papers of Kenneth J. Arrow—A Review Article," *Journal of Economic Literature* 23 (December 1985): 1764–1776.

Tarascio, Vincent. "Pareto: A View of the Present Through the Past," *Journal of Political Economy* 84 (February 1976): 109–122.

von Hayek, Friedrich. "The Competitive 'Solution'," *Economica* 7 (May 1940): 125–149.

Chapter 21

THE KEYNESIAN SCHOOL—JOHN MAYNARD KEYNES

The Keynesian system of ideas is one of the most significant schools of economic thought. The school began with the publication of Keynes's *The General Theory of Employment, Interest and Money* in 1936 and remains a major presence in orthodox economics today. It arose out of the neoclassical school, Keynes himself being steeped in the Marshallian tradition. Although Keynes sharply criticized certain aspects of neoclassical economics, which he lumped together with Ricardian doctrines under the heading of "classical economics," he used many of its postulates and methods. His system was based on a subjective psychological approach, and it was permeated with marginalist concepts, including static equilibrium economics. Keynes disassociated himself from attacks on the neoclassical theory of value and distribution.

In this chapter we provide a brief overview of the Keynesian school and discuss Keynes's major ideas. Then, in Chapter 22 we examine the ideas of several subsequent contributors to Keynesian economics.

OVERVIEW OF THE KEYNESIAN SCHOOL

The Historical Background of the Keynesian School

Keynes's ideas were given added impetus by the Great Depression of the 1930s, the worst the Western world had ever known. Yet the roots of his ideas can be traced back to before 1929. The work of many economists, including that of Mitchell and his associates in the National Bureau of Economic Research, was within the framework of aggregate economics, or macroeconomics, rather than the microeconomics of the neoclassical school. Keynes also adopted this macroeconomic approach. World War I and the economic controls enacted required an overall view of the economy. The growth of large-scale industrial production and trade made the economy more susceptible to statistical measurement and control, making the inductive, aggregate approach more feasible than in the past. In fact, this approach was increasingly necessary as the public became more eager for the government to deal actively with unemployment.

Keynesian thinking also had its roots in the spreading concern about secular stagnation, or a declining rate of growth. The mature private-enterprise economies of the Western world were less vigorous after World War I than before it. The rate of population growth was declining; most of the world had already been colonized;

there seemed to be no room for further geographic expansion; production appeared to outrun consumption as incomes and savings rose; and there were no new inventions like the steam engine, the railroad, electricity, and the automobile to stimulate new and vast capital investments. Also, the decline of vigorous price competition reduced the rate of replacement of old machinery with new and better machines, and the economy was dragged downward when the growing accumulated of depreciation funds from past investments were not spent quickly enough. These observations about secular stagnation, which became particularly important after 1929, were based in part on the works of Marx, John A. Hobson (1858–1940), Veblen, and others, and in part on actual observations and historical studies.

After the Great Depression began in the early 1930s, many economists in the United States advocated policies that later would be called Keynesian. It is interesting to note that these policies were presented before the publication of Keynes's *The General Theory.* Leading figures both inside and outside of the economics profession were urging public works programs, deficit budgets for the federal government, and the easing of credit by the Federal Reserve System. Many economists were aware of the multiplier effect that increased government spending could have on total spending and income. Some theorized that as the national income increased, consumption expenditures rose less rapidly than total income, and saving increased more rapidly. Wages were recognized as a source of demand for goods as well as a cost of production, and cutting wages was frequently opposed as providing no real remedy for unemployment; this was macroeconomic thinking. People derived these ideas independently of Keynes and widely discussed them in the United States. But it was Keynes who provided the analytical framework that integrated these ideas and touched off the "Keynesian revolution" in economics.

Major Tenets of the Keynesian School

The major characteristics and principles of Keynesian economics are listed next. We discuss them in more detail throughout this chapter and in Chapter 22.

- *Macroeconomic emphasis.* Keynes and his followers concerned themselves with the determinants of the *total* or *aggregate* amounts of consumption, saving, income, output, and employment. They were less interested, for example, in how an individual firm decides on its profit-maximizing level of employment than in the relationship between total spending in the economy and the aggregate of such employment decisions.
- *Demand orientation.* Keynesian economists stressed the importance of *effective demand* (now called aggregate expenditures) as the immediate determinant of national income, output, and employment. Aggregate expenditures, said these economists, consist of the sum of consumption, investment, government, and net export spending. Firms collectively produce a level of real output that they expect to sell. But sometimes aggregate expenditures are insufficient to buy all the output produced. As unsold goods accumulate, firms lay off workers and cut back output. That is, effective demand establishes the economy's *actual output,* which in some cases is less than the level of output that would exist if there were full employment (*potential output*).

- *Instability in the economy.* According to Keynesians, the economy is given to recurring booms and busts because the level of planned investment spending is erratic. Changes in investment plans cause national income and output to change by amounts greater than the initial changes in investment. Equilibrium levels of investment and saving—those that exist after all adjustments have occurred—are achieved through changes in national income, as opposed to changes in the rate of interest.

  Investment spending is determined jointly by the rate of interest and the *marginal efficiency of capital,* or the expected rate of return above the cost on new investments. The interest rate depends on people's preferences for liquidity and the quantity of money. The marginal efficiency of capital depends on the expectation of future profits and the supply price of capital. The expected rate of profit from new investment is unstable, and therefore one of the most important causes of business fluctuations.
- *Wage and price rigidity.* Keynesians pointed out that wages tend to be inflexible downward because of such institutional factors as union contracts, minimum wage laws, and implicit contracts (understandings between employers and their workers that wages will not be cut during downturns judged to be temporary). In periods of slack aggregate demand for goods and services, firms respond to lower sales by reducing production and discharging or laying off workers, not by insisting on wage cuts. Prices also are sticky downward; declines in effective demand initially cause reductions in output and employment rather than declines in the price level. Deflation occurs only under conditions of extremely severe depression.
- *Active fiscal and monetary policies.* Keynesian economists advocated that the government should intervene actively through appropriate fiscal and monetary policies to promote full employment, price stability, and economic growth. To combat recession or depression, government should either increase its spending or reduce taxes, the latter increasing private consumption spending. It also should increase the money supply to drive down interest rates in the hope that this will bolster investment spending. To counter inflation caused by excessive aggregate expenditures, government should reduce its own spending, increase taxes to reduce private consumption spending, or reduce the money supply to raise interest rates, which will dampen excessive investment spending.

Whom Did the Keynesian School Benefit or Seek to Benefit?

The great success of Keynesian economics came partly because it addressed a pressing problem of its day: depression and unemployment. Also, it offered something for almost everyone and rationalized what was already being done out of necessity. Society gains from full or fuller employment, and those individuals or groups who lose because of it (say, administrators of unemployment compensation programs) can be easily ignored. Although labor sometimes objected to specific Keynesian proposals, it strongly approved of Keynes's larger goals. Rising aggregate demand made for tight labor markets and permitted unions to negotiate improved wages and working conditions with less fear of unemployment. Business interests benefited from government contracts and government stimuli to get the economy out of depression or recession. When bankers had extensive excess reserves in the 1930s, they found a vast and profitable area for investment in government bonds, and government controls gave the banking system liquidity, security, and stability. Reformers and intellectuals enjoyed vastly increased employment in government service, and they could pursue with crusading zeal the mild, safe, and sane reforms that grew out of Keynesian thinking.

Farmers long had favored easy monetary policies and low interest rates. They also came to rely heavily on government spending programs for agriculture. In fact, their spokespersons had put forth a crude theory of the multiplier long before it was incorporated into the Keynesian system. In defending government intervention in order to raise farmers' incomes, they claimed that each dollar received by the farmer generated a seven-dollar increase in national income through the respending of the farmer's increased receipts.

In the 1960s and 1970s consumers in general looked favorably on tax cuts and supported politicians who suggested and voted for them. Such cuts, unaccompanied by overall reductions in government expenditures, were rationalized on the Keynesian principle that they were necessary to stimulate demand and economic growth. In the 1980s the rationale for tax cuts took on a "supply-side" orientation, but it was consistent with the Keynesian principles.

How Was the Keynesian School Valid, Useful, or Correct in Its Time?

Keynes geared economic theory to policymaking. World wars, worldwide depressions, and the growing complications of modern life undermined laissez-faire. Demands that something be done about business fluctuations grew more insistent, and Keynes provided both an explanation of fluctuations and a program to mitigate them. The role of economists and economic analysis in shaping the direction of government policy was thus greatly increased.

The Keynesian view that there are alternative means to reductions in nominal wages to achieve full employment was particularly timely. This policy prescription, which had emerged from neoclassical thinking, found little support as a politically practical solution to massive unemployment. More important, according to Keynes, a deep and general reduction of nominal wages makes for bad economic policy. He held that a single firm can increase sales and employment through wage cuts because the demand for its products will remain unaffected. A whole economy, however, cannot easily increase sales by cutting nominal wages (assuming it is isolated from international trade) because wages are a source of demand for goods as well as a cost of production. If wages begin to fall, people may come to expect them to fall still further; this may cause businesses to postpone investment spending, making the depression worse.

If falling wages result in falling prices, this again worsens matters, because the real burden of debts increases, transferring wealth from the entrepreneur to the *rentier.* In addition, profit margins become smaller, thus choking off new investments. Because wage cuts hurt wage earners who have high marginal propensities to consume and help employers who have low ones, the overall propensity to consume is diminished, and this further worsens the situation. A practical man, Keynes also objected to wage cuts because they would touch off labor troubles. He was quite successful in converting people to the idea that wage policy should be divorced from policies to counter depression. There are better ways to create full employment, Keynes said.

The Keynesian approach became immensely useful even to those who did not accept Keynes's policy conclusions. It established a new set of analytical tools through which to view the economy, encouraged the further development of national income accounting, stimulated a vast and fruitful effort at empirical studies of the real world, hastened the development of econometrics, and created a new liberalism on which reformers could pin their hopes for aiding those who benefited least from unfettered capitalism.

Which Tenets of the Keynesian School Became Lasting Contributions?

Numerous ideas developed by Keynes and his followers have become orthodox elements of contemporary macroeconomics. In fact, contemporary economics could be said to be a combination of neoclassical microeconomics and Keynesian-inspired macroeconomics. Keynesian concepts such as the consumption function; the marginal propensity to consume; the saving function; the marginal propensity to save; the marginal efficiency of capital; the transaction, precautionary, and speculative demands for money; the multiplier; *ex post* and *ex ante* saving and investment; fiscal and monetary policy; *IS-LM* analysis, and so forth are now standard fare in economics textbooks. Several of the earlier Keynesian precepts, such as the view that the economy can be "fine tuned" to a position of noninflationary full employment, have been largely discredited, but Keynesianism as an analytical method and as a system of ideas still dominates macroeconomics.

This is not to say that all of the ideas of Keynes and his followers proved to be correct. Some general criticisms of Keynes's thinking are discussed in the final section of this chapter. The critiques of Keynesian theories offered by contemporary monetarists and the "new classicists" are discussed in Chapter 24.

JOHN MAYNARD KEYNES

Biographical Details

John Maynard Keynes (1883–1946) was the son of eminently intellectual parents, both of whom survived him. His father was John Neville Keynes, outstanding logician and political economist. His mother, who was interested in public affairs and social work, was a justice of the peace, an alderwoman, and mayor of Cambridge. Among Keynes's teachers at Cambridge were Marshall and Pigou, both of whom recognized his brilliance. At twenty-eight, Keynes became editor of the *Economic Journal.* He also managed investments of its publisher, the Royal Economic Society, with unusual success. King's College of Cambridge University likewise made phenomenal profits under Keynes's financial guidance. His own considerable fortune of a half a million pounds was accumulated mainly through dealings in foreign currencies and commodities. He was, in fact, one of the speculators about whom he wrote:

> Speculators may do no harm as bubbles on a steady stream of enterprise. But the position is serious when enterprise becomes the bubble on a whirlpool of speculation. When the capital development of a country becomes a by-product of the activities of a casino, the job is likely to be ill-done. The measure of success attained by Wall Street, regarded as an institution of which the proper social purpose is to direct new investment into the most profitable channels in terms of future yield, cannot be claimed as one of the outstanding triumphs of *laissez-faire* capitalism—which is not surprising, if I am right in thinking that the best brains of Wall Street have been in fact directed towards a different object.[1]

Keynes was an important figure both in the world of practical affairs and academic life. He was chairman of the board of a life insurance company, he served as director of other companies, and he was a member of the governing body of the Bank of England. In addition to being a financier, he was a high government official, the author of many scholarly theoretical works, a journalist, a connoisseur and supporter of the arts, and a teacher at Cambridge University. He was a leading member of the "Bloomsbury Group," named after the section of London where the sisters Vanessa Bell and Virginia Woolf had their homes. This circle of brilliant artists, writers, critics, intellectuals, and conversationalists, lasting from 1907 to 1930, also included Leonard Woolf, Clive Bell, Lytton Strachey, E. M. Forster, and other notables. Keynes was the principal representative of the British Treasury at the peace conference after World War I, with power to speak for the chancellor of the exchequer. His experiences at the Paris negotiations and his strong opposition to the peace settlement forced upon Germany led him to resign his official position in 1919 and write his polemical *The Economic Consequences of the Peace*. In 1940 he rejoined the Treasury to guide Britain through the difficulties of war finance. He was his country's chief negotiator in organizing the International Monetary Fund and the International Bank for Reconstruction and Development and in obtaining the United States' postwar loan to Britain. He became a baron in 1942, and to those of his friends who criticized his accepting the title, his joking defense was "I had to do it in order to get servants."

In 1926 Keynes published a brief book entitled *The End of Laissez-Faire*, in which he stated that the evils of the day were the fruits of risk, uncertainty, and ignorance. Big business is often a lottery in which some individuals are able to take advantage of ignorance and uncertainty. The consequences are great inequalities of wealth, unemployment, disappointment of reasonable business expectations, and impairment of efficiency and production:

> Yet the cure lies outside the operations of individuals; it may even be to the interest of individuals to aggravate the disease. I believe that the cure for these things is partly to be sought in the deliberate control of the currency and of credit by a

[1] John Maynard Keynes, *The General Theory of Employment, Interest and Money* (New York: Harcourt, Brace and World, 1936), 159. Reprinted by permission of Harcourt Brace and Company.

> central institution, and partly in the collection and dissemination on a great scale of data relating to the business situation. . . . These measures would involve Society in exercising directive intelligence through some appropriate organ of action over many of the inner intricacies of private business, yet it would leave private initiative unhindered. . . .
>
> Devotees of Capitalism are often unduly conservative, and reject reforms in its technique, which might really strengthen and preserve it, for fear that they may prove to be first steps away from Capitalism itself. . . . For my part, I think that Capitalism, wisely managed, can probably be made more efficient for attaining economic ends than any alternative system yet in sight, but that in itself it is in many ways extremely objectionable. Our problem is to work out a social organization which shall be efficient as possible without offending our notions of a satisfactory way of life.[2]

Keynes did not depart from these views during the remaining two decades of his life.

The Keynesian System

The system of ideas that Keynes developed in *The General Theory* consists of several interrelated elements, the first of which is the consumption function.

Consumption function. Keynes pointed to a "fundamental psychological law" concerning the relationship between consumption and income:

> The fundamental psychological law, upon which we are entitled to depend with great confidence both *a priori* from our knowledge of human nature and from the detailed facts of experience, is that men are disposed, as a rule and on the average, to increase their consumption as their income increases, but not by as much as the increase in their income.[3]

Stated formally, (1) there is a positive functional relationship between consumption (C) and national income (Y), that is:

$$C = f(Y) \qquad \textbf{(21-1)}$$

and (2) the ratio of the change in consumption to the change in income—the marginal propensity to consume (MPC)—is positive and less than one.

$$MPC = \Delta C/\Delta Y \qquad \textbf{(21-2)}$$

This implies that saving (S) also rises with income; it, too, is a positive function of income.

$$S = f(Y) \qquad \textbf{(21-3)}$$

Like the MPC, the marginal propensity to save (MPS) is greater than zero and less than one.

$$MPS = \Delta S/\Delta Y \qquad \textbf{(21-4)}$$

---

[2] John Maynard Keynes, *The End of Laissez-Faire* (London: Hogarth, 1926), 47–58.

[3] Keynes, *General Theory,* 96.

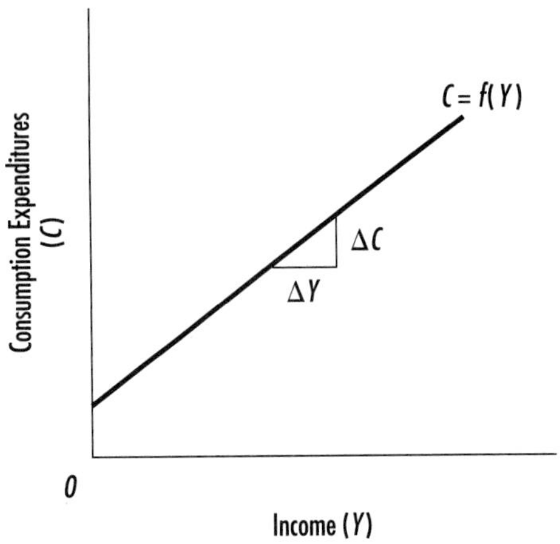

Figure 21-1 The Consumption Function
As national income increases, consumption also increases, but not by as much as the increase in income. The slope ($\Delta C/\Delta Y$) of the consumption function $C = f(Y)$ measures the marginal propensity to consume.

In Figure 21-1 we plot a short-run consumption function that shows the amounts that consumers will spend for goods and services at different income levels in a hypothetical economy. The curve's slope ($\Delta C/\Delta Y$) is the marginal propensity to consume.

Investment. Keynes defined economic investment as the purchase of capital goods. In addition, unintended investment occurs when sales decline and inventories of unsold goods rise. Note the distinction between *economic* investment and *financial* investment, which consists of the purchase of stocks, bonds, and other financial instruments. Financial investment is not investment in the Keynesian sense because it does not directly represent purchases of capital goods. For Keynes, financial instruments simply are alternative repositories for people's savings.

Businesses undertake investment on the expectation that the new capital will add to profits. When a business buys a piece of capital equipment, it "purchases the right to the series of prospective returns, which [it] expects to obtain from selling its output, after deducting the running expenses of obtaining that output, during the life of the asset."[4] The size of the expected income stream depends on (1) the productivity of the piece of capital, (2) the price at which the firm can sell the added output, and (3) the added wage and material expense that results from using the piece of capital.

A second consideration in the investment decision, said Keynes, is the *supply price* or the replacement cost of the asset. The supply price of the piece of capital is the price that would be just sufficient to cause the manufacturer of the capital to produce one additional unit. Keynes defined the *marginal efficiency of capital* as

[4] Keynes, *General Theory*, 135.

equal to that rate of discount that makes the present value of the series of expected returns just equal to the supply price of the capital asset. This is expressed mathematically as

$$K_s = \frac{R_1}{(1+r)} + \frac{R_2}{(1+r)^2} + \ldots + \frac{R_n}{(1+r)^n} \qquad \textbf{(21-5)}$$

where K_s is the supply price of capital, R is the expected return in a particular year, and r is the marginal efficiency of capital. For example, if the present cost of a capital asset is \$5,500, and it is expected to yield an annual return of \$1,000 for six years, with the assets worth nothing at the end of that time, the marginal efficiency of capital is 2.5 percent. Restated, \$1,000 per year for six years discounted to the present value using an interest rate of 2.5 percent would be worth \$5,500. Alternatively, \$5,500 invested at 2.5 percent would yield a return of \$1,000 each year for six years. The marginal efficiency of capital is its marginal productivity as a percentage of the original cost of the capital good, computed over the life of the capital investment and discounted for uncertainty as well as for futurity. Alternatively, it is the expected rate of profit of a new investment, not deducting depreciation or explicit and implicit interest costs.

Investments will continue to the point at which the marginal efficiency of capital is equal to the rate of interest—the cost of borrowing the funds with which to invest. For example, if the marginal efficiency of capital is 2.5 percent, an investment will not occur at an interest rate of 3 percent, but it will take place at an interest rate of 2 percent.

The marginal efficiency of capital is highly variable; it fluctuates with every change in people's expectations of future profits from contemplated investment. Increased investment in any given type of capital, said Keynes, reduces the marginal efficiency of that capital. There are two reasons. First, expected profits decline as increasing amounts of investment compete with one another. In terms of Equation 21-5, this implies that the values for R fall, and other things equal, a decline in these values causes a decline in the marginal efficiency of capital, r. Second, "pressures on the facilities for producing that type of capital will cause its supply price to increase." Notice that an increase in K_s in Equation 21-5, other things equal, also reduces the value of r. The principle that emerges, therefore, is that the amount of a particular type of investment in capital and its marginal efficiency are inversely related.

Keynes's ideas on the marginal efficiency of capital can be used to construct an investment demand curve such as the one labeled $I = f(i)$ in Figure 21-2. This curve shows the inverse relationship between the rate of interest (i) and the amount of investment (I) for an economy in which all the relevant investment projects have been arrayed in descending order of their marginal efficiencies of capital. If the market rate of interest is i_1, then the amount of investment will be I_1. For all investments up to I_1, the marginal efficiency of capital exceeds the cost of borrowing, whereas for all investments beyond I_1, the cost of borrowing exceeds the marginal efficiency of capital.

Keynes disagreed with the classical and neoclassical economists who thought that the rate of interest produces an automatic balance between the amount of saving businesses desire for new investment and the quantity of saving supplied. The rate of interest, he said, cannot be a reward for abstinence (Senior) or a reward

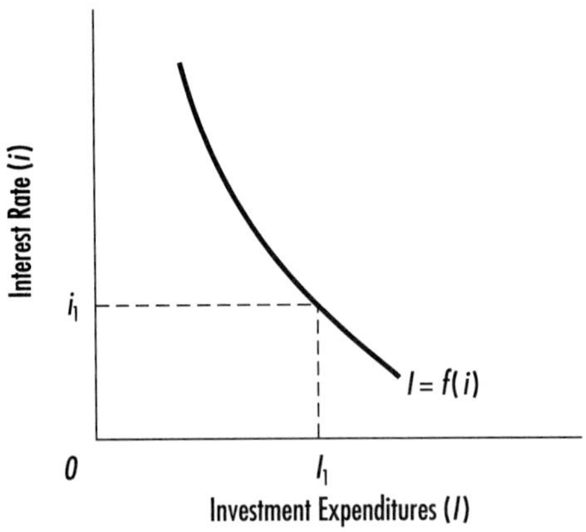

Figure 21-2 The Investment Demand Curve
The investment demand curve $I = f(i)$ for an economy is constructed by arraying all potential investment projects in descending order of their marginal efficiencies of capital. The curve is downward sloping, reflecting an inverse relationship between the interest rate, i (the financial "price" of each dollar of investing), and the quantity of investment demanded, I.

for waiting (Marshall). If a person hoards his savings in cash, he earns *no* interest. Saving depends much more on the *level of income* (recall our previous discussion of the savings function). The rate of interest is a reward for sacrificing liquidity—the ease with which an asset can be converted directly into goods and services without loss of its purchase price. The rate of interest depends on liquidity preference and the quantity of money, *money* being defined as currency plus demand deposits. A market interest rate is that price that equilibrates the individual's desire to hold wealth in cash with the available quantity of cash in the system.

Liquidity preference. Liquidity preference depends on three motives for holding money and the reluctance to part with it, except insofar as the rate of interest acts as an effective inducement. The first is the *transaction motive*—the need for cash to pay for current purchases for consumption and business needs. The second is the *precautionary motive*—the desire to keep some cash on hand for unforeseen emergencies. Finally, there is the *speculative motive,* the desire to hold cash while waiting for interest rates to rise, or stock and bond prices to fall, or the general price level to fall. Liquidity allows people to quickly seize financial and economic investment opportunities as they arise.

These motives for holding money translate into a demand for money curve such as L in Figure 21-3. The curve slopes downward, indicating that people will desire to hold more cash at lower interest rates. When the interest rate is low relative to some normal interest rate, people expect it to rise. When the interest rate rises, bond prices fall, and those who hold bonds experience losses. People therefore hold greater amounts of cash and fewer bonds when the interest rate is low. For the opposite reasons, they hold more bonds and smaller amounts of cash when the interest rate is high.

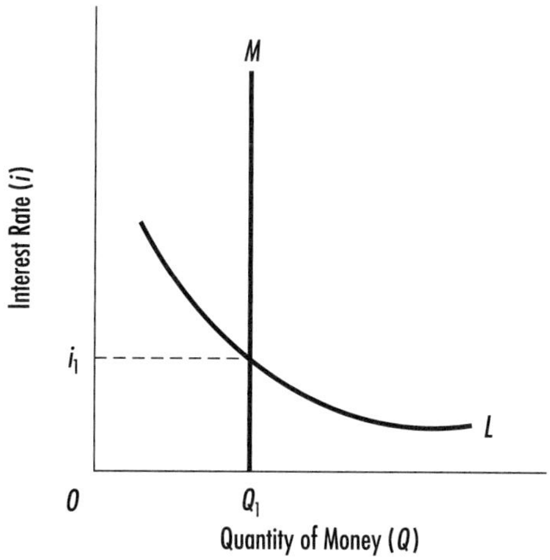

Figure 21-3 Liquidity Preference, Money Supply, and the Interest Rate
The demand for money curve (L) slopes downward because lower interest rates reduce the cost of "being liquid"—that is, of holding wealth as cash. The supply of money curve (M) is vertical, reflecting the specific amount of money provided by the central bank. The equilibrium interest rate (here i_1) is determined at the intersection of the liquidity preference curve (demand for money curve) and the supply of money curve.

The quantity of money supplied depends on the policy of the central bank. It can increase or decrease the money supply through changes in open market operations, reserve requirements, and the discount rate. The quantity of money supplied is assumed to be independent of the interest rate; hence, the money supply curve M in Figure 21-3 is vertical, or perfectly inelastic.

We see from the graph that the equilibrium rate of interest is i_1. An increase in the quantity of money—a rightward shift of M—would lower the interest rate, unless the public's liquidity preference was increasing more than the quantity of money. An important point emerges here: A lower rate of interest does not *reduce* saving, as the classical and neoclassical economists assumed. Instead it stimulates investment spending (Figure 21-2). If the economy was operating at less than full employment, national income would rise and saving would *increase.*

In summary, the level of investment in the economy depends on the interaction of (1) the marginal efficiency of capital, which defines the investment demand curve, and (2) the market rate of interest. The market rate of interest depends on the demand for money (liquidity preference) and the supply of money.

Equilibrium income and employment. Keynes assumed that there is a high correlation between national income and the level of employment. This is, of course, not necessarily true. Large investments in labor-saving capital, for example, can cause real domestic output and national income to rise more rapidly than employment. Keynes, however, was concerned mainly with the short run; he defended this emphasis with the quip, "In the long run we are all dead." In the short run we can

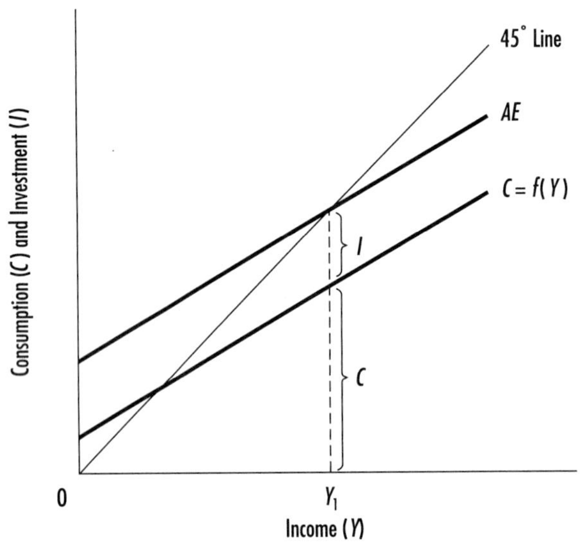

Figure 21-4 Equilibrium Income
Aggregate expenditures (*AE*) consist of *C* + *I* in the simplest Keynesian model. Equilibrium income occurs where the *AE* curve intersects the 45° line, because there planned expenditures (*C* + *I*) equal the level of income (Y_1). Also, in equilibrium planned investment *I* equals saving (the vertical distance between the 45° line and the consumption function).

neglect technological change; we can then agree that the level of income determines the level of employment, and the two variables can be used interchangeably.

If we ignore the government and international trade, the immediate determinants of income and employment are consumption and investment spending. These two spending components constitute the aggregate expenditures in the economy. Equilibrium national income occurs where the combined levels of consumption and investment spending equal the current level of income. Symbolically, this is where

$$Y = C + I \qquad \textbf{(21-6)}$$

Because saving is the difference between income and consumption, then

$$S = Y - C \qquad \textbf{(21-7)}$$

Solving the two equations provides an alternative condition for equilibrium income:

$$S = I \qquad \textbf{(21-8)}$$

The standard textbook presentation of the simple Keynesian model is shown as Figure 21-4. Paul Samuelson formalized this presentation, which is referred to as the Keynesian cross model. Thus, it might best be understood as "Keynesian economics" rather than the specific "economics of Keynes."[5]

[5] Axel Leijonhufvud made the distinction between "Keynesian economics" and the "economics of Keynes" in *On Keynesian Economics and the Economics of Keynes* (New York: Oxford University Press, 1968).

The aggregate expenditure curve AE shows the combined level of consumption and investment spending forthcoming at each level of income. The vertical distance between AE and the consumption function $C = f(Y)$ is the level of investment (I_1 in Figure 21-2). The vertical distance between the consumption function and the horizontal axis is the level of consumption. Equilibrium income is Y_1, because at this point the aggregate expenditures curve crosses the 45° line, indicating that $C + I$ equals the existing level of income, Y_1 (the height of the 45° line at Y_1 is equal to the horizontal distance OY_1).

We can also demonstrate that saving equals intended investment at Y_1. Recall from Equation 21-7 that the level of saving is found by subtracting the level of consumption from the level of income. In Figure 21-4, the level of saving at any level of income is therefore the vertical distance between the 45° line and the consumption function. Only at Y_1 is this vertical distance—saving (S)—equal to the level of planned investment (I).

How might a depression occur? asked Keynes. His answer is easily demonstrated through the simple model just developed. Suppose that the income level Y_1 in Figure 21-4 is the full employment level of income. Further assume that for some reason entrepreneurs become pessimistic about future business prospects and that this results in a downward revision of expected returns on a new investment. This translates to a decline in the marginal efficiency of capital and a leftward shift of the investment demand curve (Figure 21-2).

As shown in Figure 21-5, the decline in investment spending reduces aggregate expenditures from AE_1 to AE_2. In response to declining sales and rising inventories,

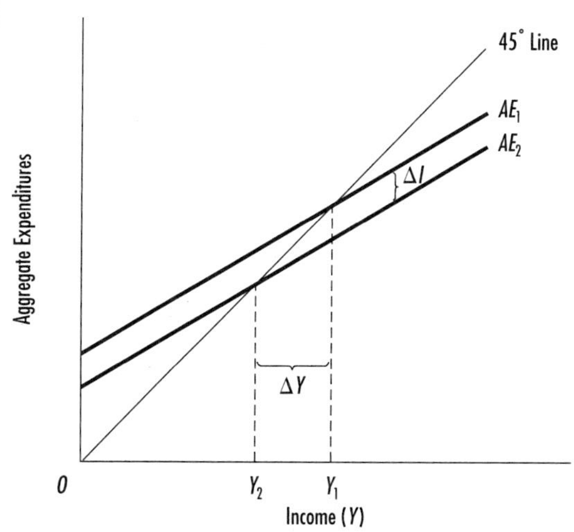

Figure 21-5 Changes in Equilibrium Income
A decline in aggregate expenditures from AE_1 to AE_2—in this case caused by a fall in investment spending—results in a decline of income from Y_1 to Y_2 and a rise in unemployment (not shown). The simple Keynesian multiplier is the ratio of the change in income (ΔY) to the initial change in investment spending (ΔI). Keynes said that government could counter the income decline by initiating an expansionary fiscal policy that would shift the aggregate expenditures curve from AE_2 back to AE_1.

firms reduce their employment and production. National income therefore declines from Y_1 to Y_2. We note that the equilibrium income declines by more than the drop in investment itself. The reason is the multiplier effect of an initial change in investment spending. Keynes borrowed this theory from R. F. Kahn, his Cambridge colleague, and incorporated it directly into his own model. The multiplier measures the ultimate effect on income of a change in spending; it is the change in income divided by the change in investment.

The size of the multiplier depends on the slope of the aggregate expenditures curve. Let's assume that the marginal propensity to consume—the slope of AE_1 and AE_2 in this particular case—is .6. That is, when people's income rises by $1, they spend 60 cents and save 40 cents ($MPS = .4$). Alternatively, when their income falls by $1, they reduce their consumption and saving by $.60 and $.40, respectively.

Suppose the reduction in investment spending in our example is $10 billion. This will immediately reduce income by $10 billion, because revenue to the sellers of capital goods will decline by an equal amount. Having experienced a decline in income of $10 billion, sellers will reduce their consumption spending by $6 billion [.6($10 billion)] and their saving by $4 billion [.4($10 billion)]. The decline in consumption spending of $6 billion will cause a *further* reduction of income of $6 billion, which in turn will reduce someone else's consumption spending by an *additional* $3.6 billion [.6($6 billion)]. Saving will decline by another $2.4 billion [.4($6 billion)]. This process will continue. Once the total decline in income reaches $25 billion, equilibrium will be restored. The $25 billion decline in income will reduce saving by an amount just equal to the initial $10 billion reduction in investment spending [.4($25 billion)]. The multiplier in this case is 2.5, which as shown by k in Equation 21-9 is the reciprocal of the marginal propensity to save.[6]

$$k = \frac{1}{MPS} \qquad \textbf{(21-9)}$$

Policies to promote full employment and stability. Keynes proposed a large government role to stabilize the economy at a full employment level of national income. To combat high unemployment such as that which would be associated with income Y_2 in Figure 21-5, Keynes suggested ways to increase aggregate expenditures. For example, the government should stimulate private investment during a depression by forcing down the rate of interest, which could be accomplished through a central bank policy. But there are limits to how low interest rates will fall. As a glance back to Figure 21-3 will reveal, the liquidity preference (demand for money) curve becomes perfectly flat at some low rate of interest. Any new money pumped into the economy by the central bank will be held by people as idle balances rather than used to buy bonds, and the interest rate will not fall. Because of this *liquidity trap,* monetary policy is not likely to be effective as a way to reduce interest rates and increase investment spending during a severe depression.

---

[6] In the U.S. economy the marginal propensity to save out of an increase in income perceived to be permanent is about .1, which would imply that the multiplier is 10(1/.1). We will discover in Chapter 22, however, that there are "leakages" other than savings in real-world economies and therefore that the estimated multiplier for the United States is between 2.2 and 2.7.

A second and more effective way to overcome depression is for the government to undertake an expansionary fiscal policy. Government spending, like private investment, serves as a source of aggregate expenditures. Such spending, declared Keynes, could be increased, thereby increasing aggregate expenditures and producing a multiple increase in national income. This would be shown in Figure 21-5 as an *increase* in aggregate expenditures from AE_1 to AE_2. If private investment is insufficient to absorb private saving at the full employment level of income, then government should borrow the excess saving and spend it on social investment projects.

The overriding problem, thought Keynes, is that the richer the society becomes, the more it saves and the more difficult it is to maintain full employment. A private enterprise economy may have difficulty maintaining adequate private investment. The government therefore may need to run budget deficits and "socialize" investment. This meant that the state would decide on the aggregate amount of private plus public investment required for full employment. Economic life as a whole need not be socialized because the existing system does not seriously misemploy the factors of production that are in use. The government should determine the volume, not the composition, of employment.

Refer to 21-1 PAST AS PROLOGUE

Criticisms

Keynes's short-run static thinking led him to exaggerate the trend toward secular stagnation. Like many economists before him, he thought that the profitability of new investment would decline as the most profitable projects were undertaken first, leaving less attractive projects for later exploitation:

> Ancient Egypt was doubly fortunate, and doubtless owed to this its fabled wealth, in that it possessed *two* activities, namely pyramid-building as well as the search for the precious metals, the fruits of which, since they could not serve the needs of man by being consumed, did not stale with abundance. The Middle Ages built cathedrals and sang dirges. Two pyramids, two masses for the dead, are twice as good as one; but not so two railways from London to York.[7]

Keynes underestimated the possibilities of technological change and the new capital investments it would stimulate.

Keynes was narrowly provincial with respect to both space and time. He seemed to think that unemployment might have become a problem in ancient Egypt and in the Middle Ages had it not been for the building of pyramids and cathedrals. His analysis of mercantilism strongly implied that the problems of 1636 were the same as those of 1936: "There has been a chronic tendency throughout human history for the propensity to save to be stronger than the inducement to invest." He thought that throughout history the weakness of the inducement to invest had been the key to the economic problem.

Keynes also can be criticized for his too-ready acceptance of wasteful government spending. To be sure, he preferred that the state finance useful, rather than

[7] Keynes, *General Theory,* 131.

21-1 PAST AS PROLOGUE

Keynes and the Stockholm School

The Stockholm school, based on Wicksell's analysis of the cumulative process, studied aggregative economic processes in a manner similar to Keynes. For years the English economists were unaware of the developments in Sweden, even though the Swedish economists paralleled and in some important ways anticipated the Keynesians. The Nobel prize-winning economist Gunnar Myrdal (1898–1987) chided Keynes for his "unnecessary originality." In 1913, as the result of worldwide depression, the Swedish government asked its leading economists to analyze different policies to combat unemployment. To do so, economists had to solve certain theoretical problems. How can output and investment expand from a depressed state when savings are very small? When investment expands without savers deciding to save more, in what sense does investment exceed saving? Investment ultimately requires saving; where does the saving come from?

Professor Myrdal in 1933 published an analysis that now seems to sharpen Keynes's concept of equilibrium income and changes in equilibrium income. Myrdal drew a distinction between forward-looking income, saving, and investment, which he called *ex ante,* and the backward-looking categories, or *ex post.* Thus, *ex ante* investment is planned investment for a future period based on *ex ante,* or planned, income. *Ex ante* saving is also based on expected future income and consumption. *Ex post* saving, investment, and income have been realized in some past period and thus can be examined in the statistical record.

To explain fluctuations, an *ex ante* analysis is required. One must examine expectations and plans for the future. Although future expectations and plans are

useless, projects. But he recognized that the business community might condemn useful public works if they competed with private enterprise. In such a situation wasteful spending was preferable to serviceable projects and was much better than doing nothing at all:

> Pyramid-building, earthquakes, even wars may serve to increase wealth, if the education of our statesmen on the principles of classical economics stands in the way of anything better. . . .
>
> If the Treasury were to fill old bottles with banknotes, bury them at suitable depths in disused coal-mines which are then filled up to surface with town rubbish, and leave it to private enterprise on well-tiered principles of laissez-faire to dig the notes up again (the right to do so being obtained, of course, by tendering for leases of the note-bearing territory), there need be no more unemployment and, with the help of the repercussions, the real income of the community, and its capital wealth also, would probably become a good deal greater than it actually is. It would, indeed, be more

to some extent based on present or past experiences and conditions, there is no mechanical straight-line connection between the two.

Because planned saving and planned investment are generally undertaken by different people possessing different motives, the two variables are unlikely to coincide except by accident. Discrepancies between them represent disequilibria in the economy that force changes toward a new equilibrium. The result is that income shifts to a new level at which *ex post* saving and investment are equal. Thus, if planned saving exceeds planned investment, income will fall until planned saving and investment are equal. If planned investment exceeds planned saving, perhaps through the expansion of bank credit, income will rise until planned saving and investment are equal. Equality of *ex ante* saving and investment produces equilibrium that normally manifests itself as an absence of gains or losses in saving and investment *ex post.*

Suppose because of optimistic anticipations investors decide to increase their investments in an economy that has some unemployment. Savers have not decided to save more than formerly. Total sales will rise, more goods will be produced, aggregate income will rise, and people will save more money. At the end of the period, realized incomes will exceed expected incomes, and realized saving will exceed planned saving.

When Keynes in his *Treatise on Money* (1930) wrote that the inequality between saving and investment causes changes in the level of income and employment, he meant *ex ante.* When in the *General Theory* (1936) he wrote that saving and investment always are equal, he meant *ex post.* At any level of income, *ex post* saving equals *ex post* investment because changes in inventories act as a balancing item that equates investment (purchases of capital goods *plus* changes in inventories) with the actual saving forthcoming. In his discussion of expectations and changes in income, however, Keynes obviously wove *ex ante* considerations into his theory.

> sensible to build houses and the like; but if there are political and practical difficulties in the way of this, the above would be better than nothing.[8]

Keynes was sympathetic toward private-wasteful-consumption spending as well as public waste. He defended Bernard de Mandeville's *The Fable of the Bees: or, Private Vices, Publick Benefits* (1705), which told of the appalling plight of a prosperous community that suddenly abandoned luxurious living and amusements in the interest of saving. Professor Calvin B. Hoover of Duke University reported Keynes's whimsy on this matter in a Washington hotel:

> While I was preparing to share dinner with Keynes in his hotel suite in Washington in 1934, he genially ridiculed my niceness in selecting a towel from the rack so as not to muss the others. He made a sweep with his arm and knocked two or three to the floor.

[8] Keynes, *General Theory,* 128–129.

> "I am convinced," he said, jokingly, "that I am more useful to the economy of the U.S.A. by stimulating employment through mussing up these towels than you are by your carefulness in avoiding waste."[9]

Of course, Keynes was not alone in the history of economic thought in overstating his case as a way to persuade his listeners and readers. And persuade his listeners and readers he did! His system of ideas gradually became the conventional macroeconomic wisdom in all of the industrial economies.

Questions for Study and Discussion

1. Identify and briefly state the significance of each of the following to the history of economic thought: John Neville Keynes; John Maynard Keynes; *The General Theory of Employment; Interest and Money;* consumption function; marginal propensity to consume; marginal propensity to save; marginal efficiency of capital; liquidity preference; equilibrium income and employment; Myrdal; *ex ante* versus *ex post* saving and investment; fiscal policy; and monetary policy.
2. Contrast the major tenets of the Keynesian school discussed in this chapter with those of the marginalist school presented in Chapter 12.
3. Explain the importance of Keynes's "fundamental psychological law" to his theory of equilibrium income and employment.
4. Use the information in the table to answer the following questions. Assume initially that no government spending or taxes occur in this hypothetical economy.

INCOME (Y)	CONSUMPTION (C)	SAVINGS (S)	INVESTMENT (I)
$000	$020	$–20	$40
100	100	00	40
200	180	20	40
300	260	40	40
400	340	60	40

   a) What is the marginal propensity to consume in this economy? What is the marginal propensity to save?
   b) What is the equilibrium level of income? Explain, using Equations 21-6 and 21-8.
   c) Suppose investment spending declined by $20. What would be the new equilibrium income and the new level of consumption? What is the size of the multiplier? Why would it be reasonable to assume that an increase in the unemployment rate would be associated with the decline in national income?
   d) What actions, according to Keynes, could the government take to restore the equilibrium level of income that you determined in part (b)?
5. Explain, using Keynes's concept of the marginal efficiency of capital, how it is possible for investment spending to decline, even though the market rate of interest remains unchanged.

[9] Calvin B. Hoover, "Keynes and the Economic System," *Journal of Political Economy* 56 (October 1948): 397.

6. Suppose that the following table reflects the investment demand schedule for an economy.

EXPECTED RATE OF RETURN	CUMULATIVE AMOUNT OF INVESTMENT HAVING THIS RATE OF RETURN OR HIGHER (BILLIONS)
12%	$10
10	20
8	30
6	40
4	50
2	60

a) Explain how the various expected rates of return shown in the first column would be determined according to Keynes.
b) If the interest rate in this economy is 8 percent, how much investment spending will be forthcoming? Explain.

7. Suppose that people in an economy want to hold for transaction purposes an amount of money equal to one-fourth of national income. The following table shows the combined amounts of money people want to hold for precautionary and speculative purposes.

INTEREST RATE	AMOUNT OF MONEY DEMANDED
12%	$ 80
10	100
8	120
6	140
4	160
2	180

a) If national income is $400 and the interest rate is 10 percent, what is the total amount of money people will want to hold?
b) If national income is $800 and the supply of money is $340, what is the equilibrium interest rate?

8. Discuss the following two quotations. With which, if either, do you agree?

> Up to a certain point it is possible to compare the influence of economic theories on society to that of grammarians on language. Languages are formed without the consent of grammarians, and are corrupted in spite of them; but their works throw light on the laws of the formation and decadence of languages. . . . [Cournot, 1838]

> The ideas of economists and political philosophers, both when they are right and when they are wrong, are more powerful than is commonly understood. Indeed the world is ruled by little else. Practical men, who believe themselves to be quite exempt

from any intellectual influences, are usually the slaves of some defunct economist. Madmen in authority, who hear voices in the air, are distilling their frenzy from some academic scribbler of a few years back. [Keynes, 1936]

Selected Readings

Books

Blaug, Mark, ed. *John Maynard Keynes.* 2 vols. Brookfield, VT: Edward Elgar, 1992.

Dillard, Dudley. *The Economics of John Maynard Keynes.* New York: Prentice-Hall, 1948.

Hansen, Alvin H. *A Guide to Keynes.* New York: McGraw-Hill, 1953.

Harcourt, G. C., ed. *Keynes and His Contemporaries.* New York: St. Martin's Press, 1985.

Harrod, R. F. *The Life of John Maynard Keynes.* New York: Harcourt, Brace and World, 1951.

Hazlitt, Henry, ed. *The Critics of Keynesian Economics.* Princeton, NJ: D. Van Nostrand, 1960.

Keynes, John Maynard. *The End of Laissez-Faire.* London: Hogarth, 1926.

———. *The General Theory of Employment, Interest and Money.* New York: Harcourt, Brace and World, 1936.

———. *A Treatise on Money.* 2 vols. London: Macmillan, 1930.

Leijonhufvud, Axel. *On Keynesian Economics and the Economics of Keynes.* New York: Oxford University Press, 1968.

Shaw, G. K., ed. *Schools of Thought in Economics: The Keynesian Heritage.* Brookfield, VT: Edward Elgar, 1988.

Skidelsky, Robert. *John Maynard Keynes: Hopes Betrayed, 1883–1920.* New York: Viking, 1986.

———. *John Maynard Keynes: The Economist as Savior, 1920–1937.* New York: Viking, 1993.

Journal Articles

Hansen, Bent. "Unemployment, Keynes, and the Stockholm School," *History of Political Economy* 13 (Summer 1981): 256–277.

Jensen, Hans E. "J. M. Keynes as a Marshallian," *Journal of Economic Issues* 17 (March 1983): 67–94.

Keynes, John Maynard. "The General Theory of Employment," *Quarterly Journal of Economics* 51 (February 1937): 209–223.

Lerner, Abba. "From *A Treatise on Money* to *The General Theory,*" *Journal of Economic Literature* 12 (March 1974): 38–43.

Salant, Walter S. "*Keynes and the Modern World:* A Review Article," *Journal of Economic Literature* 23 (September 1985): 1176–1185.

Tobin, James. "How Dead Is Keynes?" *Economic Inquiry* 15 (October 1977): 459–468.

Chapter 22

THE KEYNESIAN SCHOOL—DEVELOPMENTS SINCE KEYNES

Several important economists helped move their version of Keynes's approach to economics directly into the mainstream of macroeconomic theory. Prominent among them were Alvin Hansen and Paul Samuelson.[1] The first two sections of this chapter cover Hansen's and Samuelson's ideas. The third section looks at the ideas of "post–Keynesian economists" who contend that the contemporary *neoclassical synthesis* (synthesis between Keynesian macroeconomics and neoclassical microeconomics) is not only seriously flawed but also incompatible with Keynes's own ideas. Finally, we discuss the ideas of contemporary "new Keynesian" economists.

ALVIN H. HANSEN

Alvin H. Hansen (1887–1975) was born in Viborg, South Dakota, where he spent his early years of education in a one-room schoolhouse. He attended high school at Sioux Falls Academy and then enrolled at Yankton College, where he graduated in 1910. He received his Ph.D. from the University of Wisconsin in 1918 and from there went on to teach at Brown University and the University of Minnesota. At Minnesota he published *Business Cycle Theory* (1927), a book that earned him a reputation as being one of the nation's leading macroeconomic scholars.

In 1937, one year after Keynes's publication of *The General Theory,* Hansen joined the faculty at Harvard. He earlier had pointed out a mathematical error in Keynes's *Treatise on Money,* and his initial reaction to *The General Theory* was less than enthusiastic. But following deeper study of Keynes's system of ideas, Hansen soon changed his opinion. For several years he and his students at Harvard made Keynes's work and its policy implications the central focus of their Fiscal Policy Seminar. Several of those attending this seminar later became prominent contributors to economics and public policy. As pointed out by Richard Musgrave, one seminar attendee:

> The seminar left a deep impact on the future development of macroeconomics and public policy in the United States. The new insights of economic science and the plight of the depressed economy combined to give a sense of unique importance to

[1] Numerous other economists helped develop modern Keynesian economics, but space limitations preclude discussion of their ideas. Four of these persons won Nobel prizes for their efforts. They are James Tobin, Lawrence Klein, Franco Modigliani, and Robert Solow. Other important U.S. contributors to early Keynesianism include James Duesenberry, Arthur Okun, and Walter Heller.

> this venture. The new tools were at hand, and if properly used they would provide a solution to the key problem of unemployment.[2]

In addition to Musgrave, Hansen's students included such prominent economists as Evsey Domar, John Dunlop, Walter Salant, Paul Samuelson, Paul Sweezy, James Tobin, and Henry Wallich.

In 1941 Hansen published *Fiscal Policy and Business Cycles,* which supported Keynes's analysis of the macroeconomic problems of the 1930s and endorsed active and continuous policies by government to stabilize the economy. Hansen, noted for his always-present green visor, often testified before congressional committees on his policy views and on Keynesian principles. Because of his strong advocacy of government intervention to promote full employment, people called him "the American Keynes." But as pointed out by Paul Samuelson:

> Hansen was much more than the American Keynes, being an important creator in his own right. . . . When any schoolperson today uses the familiar . . . $C + I + G$ schedules of income determination, he is merely employing a watered-down version of what Hansen was creating in the late 1930s and what some of us in his circle formalized and packaged for educational use.[3]

Hansen's influence was international. Ten of his books were translated into one or more languages, totaling twenty-nine translations.[4] One of these, *A Guide to Keynes* became familiar to thousands of graduate students who used it in their struggle to understand the more esoteric sections of Keynes's *The General Theory.*

The Hicks-Hansen Synthesis

One year after the publication of *The General Theory,* John R. Hicks (Chapter 18) published an important journal article, "Mr. Keynes and the Classics: A Suggested Interpretation." Hicks pointed out that Keynes's theory of the interest rate—and therefore his theory of equilibrium income—was indeterminate. Figure 21-3 in the previous chapter shows us that Keynes viewed the interest rate as being determined by liquidity preference (the demand for money) and the supply of money. Once the market rate of interest is determined, then the level of investment becomes known (Figure 21-2). Together with consumption expenditures, investment determines aggregate expenditures and thus the level of national income and domestic output. But Hicks correctly noted that Keynes's liquidity preference schedule *itself* depends on the level of national income. At higher income levels, people desire to hold more money to buy the greater volume of goods and services available; they have a greater transaction demand for money. The level of income thus depends on the interest rate (through investment), but the interest rate depends on the level of income (through liquidity preference)!

[2] Richard A. Musgrave, "Caring for the Real Problems," *Quarterly Journal of Economics* 90 (February 1976): 5. For further information on Hansen's Fiscal Policy Seminar see Walter S. Salant, "Alvin Hansen and the Fiscal Policy Seminar," *Quarterly Journal of Economics* 90 (February 1976): 14–23.

[3] Paul A. Samuelson, "Alvin Hansen as a Creative Economic Theorist," *Quarterly Journal of Economics* 90 (February 1976): 25, 31.

[4] William Breit and Roger L. Ransom, *The Academic Scribblers,* rev. ed. (Chicago: Dryden, 1982), 84.

Hicks suggested a way to resolve this indeterminacy and in so doing developed a unified economic model that synthesized the Keynesian and neoclassical perspectives. Hansen elaborated on Hicks's article in his *Monetary Theory and Fiscal Policy* (1949) and in chapter 7 of *A Guide to Keynes*. Today we refer to the Hicks-Hansen synthesis as the *IS–LM* model. The *IS* symbolizes equality between investment (I) and saving (S) after multiplier adjustments have occurred; the *LM* symbolizes equality between the demand for money (L) and the supply of money (M). All values in the *IS–LM* model are in real, rather than nominal, terms.

The* IS *curve. The *IS* curve represents all the combinations of interest rates and levels of income at which planned investment equals planned saving. Alternatively defined, the curve represents potential points of equilibrium in the *goods market* (as distinct from the *money market*). The *IS* curve is derived in Figure 22-1. To demonstrate the derivation, we will begin with graph (a) in the figure and proceed clockwise

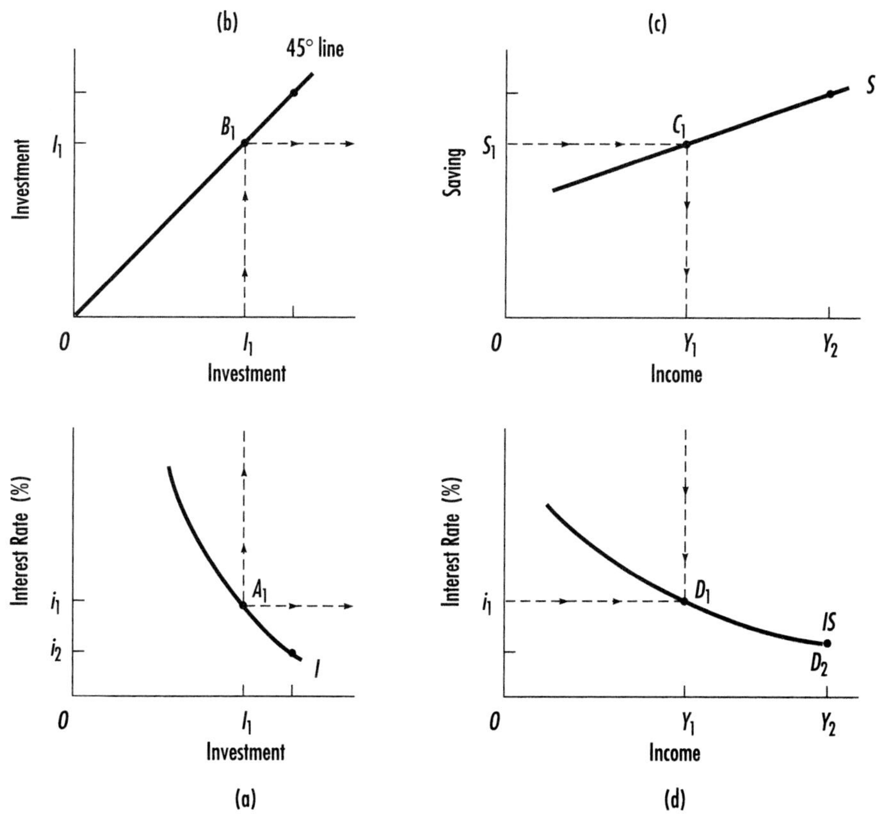

Figure 22-1 Deriving the* IS *Curve
The *IS* curve (d) shows all combinations of interest rates and income at which saving equals investment. It is derived from the investment demand function (a), a 45° line (b), and the saving function (c).

to (b), (c), and (d). Graph (a) shows the investment demand curve for a hypothetical economy, indicating the inverse relationship between the interest rate (i) and the amount of investment spending (I). Recall that the location of this curve depends on the marginal efficiency of capital. Suppose that the interest rate is i_1. Then as we see from A_1 on the curve, the level of investment will be I_1. In graph (b), which lies directly above the investment demand curve, the 45° line enables us to measure investment spending vertically as well as horizontally. By directing a line upward from A_1 in graph (a) to point B_1 on the 45° line in (b), we transfer the I_1 of investment from the horizontal axes in graph (a) to the vertical axis in (b).

Graph (c) shows the Keynesian saving function. As income (Y) increases, the level of saving (S) rises by a fraction. This fraction is the slope of the saving function and is Keynes's marginal propensity to save. A potential level of equilibrium income will occur at C_1 on the saving function, because at this point I_1 of investment is matched by an equal amount of saving, S_1. By dropping a vertical line downward from point C_1 on the saving function to the horizontal axis of graph (c) we discover that income is Y_1. Extending the line farther downward to graph (d), we establish point D_1. At an interest rate of i_1, the level of income that is consistent with equilibrium in the goods market is Y_1. By selecting other interest rates in graph (a) and following the procedure just outlined, other combinations of interest rates and income at which investment will equal saving are determined. At an interest rate of i_2, for example, investment and income are greater than at I_1. Our procedure thus establishes point D_2 in graph (d). Connecting all points such as D_1 and D_2 yields the *IS* curve. No single determinate level of income exists in this case. Depending on the rate of interest, income may be at any level represented by the *IS* curve.

The* LM *curve. The *LM* curve (Figure 22-2) shows potential points of equilibrium in the money market; it indicates all combinations of interest rates and levels of income at which money supplied and demanded are equal. The general technique for deriving this curve is similar to that for the *IS* curve. We begin with graph (a), which relates the interest rate (i) to the amount of money people desire to hold for speculative purposes (L_s). It is this element of the total demand for money that gives Keynes's liquidity preference curve its downward slope. At low interest rates people will hold large cash balances for speculative purposes and few bonds, because the expected rise in the interest rate will cause the price of bonds to fall. Such a rise would create a capital loss for those holding bonds. At high interest rates, on the other hand, people will economize on their holding of cash balances, because the opportunity cost of holding cash is thought to be large. We select a specific interest rate such as i_1 in graph (a) and observe that people will desire to hold L_{s1} for speculative purposes.

Graph (b) shows the total money supply. Increases in the money supply would be shown as parallel outward shifts of the line. In equilibrium the quantity of money supplied (M) must equal the amount of money demanded (L). The demand for money consists of money desired for speculative purposes (L_s), which in this case we have determined to be L_{s1}, and the amount people desire for buying goods and services (L_t). By extending a line upward from A_1 to B_1 we observe that the amount of money needed for transaction purposes is L_{t1} (M minus L_{s1}). These transaction balances will support national income of Y_1, as shown by C_1 in graph (c). Next, we drop a line

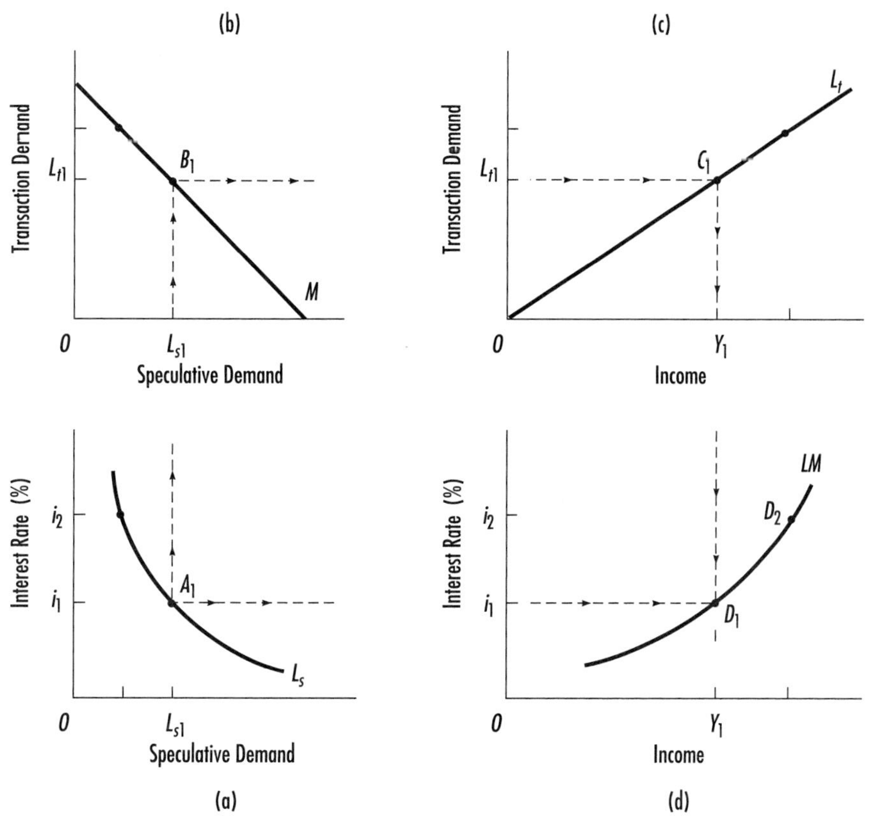

Figure 22-2 Deriving the* LM *Curve
The *LM* curve (d) shows all combinations of interest rates and income at which the demand for money equals the supply of money. It is derived from the speculative demand for money (a), the money supply (b), and the transaction demand for money (c).

vertically from C_1 and extend a line horizontally from A_1 to get point D_1 in graph (d). This point—as is true for all points on the *LM* curve—represents potential equilibrium between supply and demand in the money market. If the interest rate is i_1, the level of national income required for equilibrium in the money market is Y_1. Other points such as D_2 are similarly derived, and the locus of such points constitutes the *LM* curve.

The* IS–LM *equilibrium. Figure 22-3 combines the *IS* and *LM* curves. The equilibrium rate of interest and level of income are i_0 and Y_0. These are the only levels at which the goods market and money market are simultaneously in equilibrium; they are the only levels where both $S = I$ and $L = M$.

Hansen and others demonstrated that it is easy to add government spending and taxation to the *IS–LM* model and use it to analyze the interest rate and income effects of alternative fiscal and monetary policies. Government spending is added

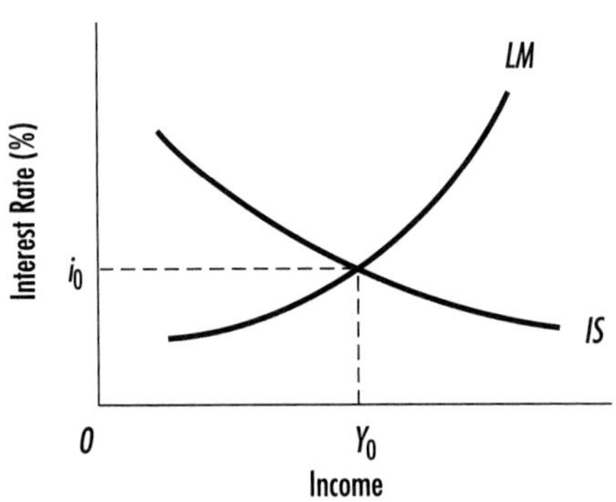

Figure 22-3 Equilibrium Interest and Income
The equilibrium interest rate and level of income are determined where the *IS* and *LM* curves intersect. This is the only combination of interest and income where there is equilibrium in both the goods market and the money market.

to the level of investment spending, and taxes are added to the level of saving. The model yields several interesting conclusions, only two of which we will list here.

Fiscal policy shifts the IS *curve.* This is the case because changes in spending change the level of income at each rate of interest. For example, an increase in government spending shifts the *IS* curve rightward, causing a rise in the interest rate and the level of income.[5] The size of the multiplier will be less than in the simple Keynesian case, however, because the rise in income will increase the amount of money needed for transactions. This translates to an increase in the demand for money and a higher interest rate, which crowds out a portion of the investment spending that otherwise would have occurred. The effectiveness of fiscal policy will depend on the elasticity of the *LM* curve. If it is highly elastic, a rightward shift of the *IS* curve will increase income without causing a substantial rise in the interest rate.

Monetary policy shifts the LM *curve.* For example, an increase in the supply of money, shown as a parallel outward shift of *M* in graph (b) of Figure 22-2, will shift the *LM* curve in Figure 22-3 rightward. The effectiveness of the increase in the money supply in increasing income will depend on (1) the extent to which the interest rate falls and (2) the elasticity of investment demand. If investment demand is highly inelastic, the *IS* curve also will tend to be inelastic, and a fall in the interest rate will have little effect on investment and income.

Refer to 22-1 PAST AS PROLOGUE

Stagnation Thesis

Hansen shared Keynes's concern that investment spending would increasingly be inadequate for the economy to reach its full potential. In *Full Recovery or Stagnation?* (1938), Hansen reasoned that the productive capacity of the economy increases with the addition of new capital and the use of improved technology.

[5] An increase in government spending can be shown by drawing a parallel line above the 45° line in Figure 22-1(b), with the vertical distance between the new line and the 45° line being the level of government spending.

22-1 PAST AS PROLOGUE

The Mundell-Fleming Contribution to *IS–LM*

The *IS–LM* model presented in Figure 22-3 assumes a closed economy—no international trade. Adding the foreign sector into the model is relatively simple. Following Samuelson's algebra (presented later in this chapter), the equation for the goods market becomes $Y = C + I + G + X - M$. So, instead of $S = I$, equilibrium in the goods market occurs where $S + T + M = I + G + X$.

The addition of international trade has two primary effects on the open-economy *IS–LM* model. The first is relatively simple: exports (X_0) and imports (M_0) become factors that can shift the *IS* curve. Increases in autonomous export spending shift the *IS* curve to the right, whereas increases in autonomous imports shift the *IS* curve to the left.

The second impact of the foreign sector on the *IS–LM* is based on the independent contributions of Robert Mundell (1932–) and J. Marcus Fleming (1913–1976) and is known as the Mundell-Fleming model.* Mundell, a Canadian citizen, did most of his work at the International Monetary Fund (IMF) and Columbia University in New York, and received the Nobel Prize in economics in 1999 for his contributions on the effects of monetary and fiscal policy under both fixed and flexible exchange rate systems. Fleming worked in the research department of the IMF, serving as Deputy Director for many years.

With the introduction of foreign trade into the model, exchange rates and the balance of payments become important considerations. From the perspective of the U.S. economy, the *exchange rate* measures how many U.S. dollars are required to buy one unit of another currency. If the exchange rate rises, more U.S. dollars are required to obtain the other currency. In other words, the dollar *depreciates.*

The *balance of payments accounts* record real and financial transactions that occur between nations. For a nation, the net flow of real and financial exchanges must equal zero. If, for example, the United States imports more goods and services than it exports (a trade deficit), then the extra U.S. dollars received by foreigners must eventually return to the United States in some form, such as through foreigners buying U.S.-owned financial (savings bonds) or real (office buildings) assets. For someone in the United States to purchase the foreign currency necessary to purchase the excess of imports, U.S. real or financial assets must be sold to the holders of the foreign currency.

What all this means for the *IS–LM* model is that, in addition to requiring equilibrium in the goods market (*IS*) and domestic money market (*LM*), general macroeconomic equilibrium also requires equilibrium in the balance of payments (*BP*). If the balance of payments is in disequilibrium, meaning that countries hold too many or too few foreign exchange reserves, then exchange rates, interest rates, or both must change to restore the balance. The Mundell-Fleming model applies to either fixed or flexible exchange rate systems, but for purposes of this discussion we will assume that the exchange rate is fixed.

22-1 PAST AS PROLOGUE (continued)

In the accompanying figure we introduce the *BP* curve, which reflects combinations of income and the interest rate consistent with balance of payments equilibrium. The *BP* curve is upward sloping: as income rises, so does the demand for imports. An increase in imports will cause a net outflow of dollars from the country. This will create balance of payments disequilibrium unless those foreign-held dollars return to the United States. Interest rates must rise to induce foreign holders to send back those dollars by investing in U.S. financial assets.

With the addition of the *BP* curve, the equilibrium interest rate (i_0) and level of income (Y_0) is determined by the intersection of the *IS, LM,* and *BP* curves.[†]

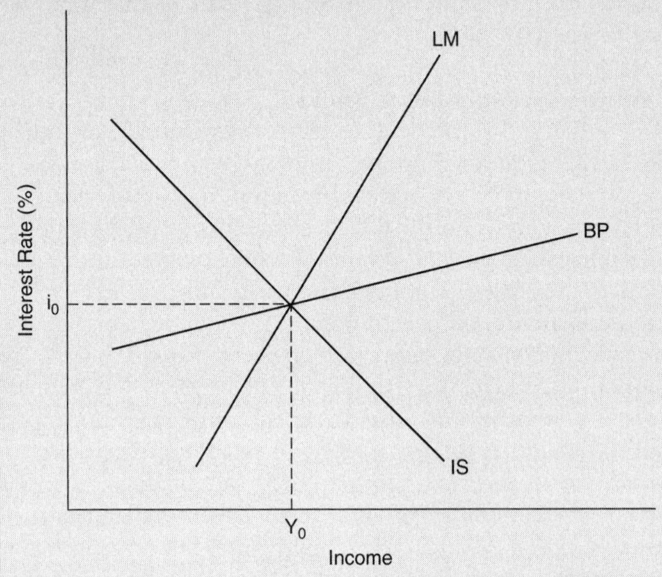

*Rudiger Dornbusch synthesized the independent work of Mundell and Fleming in 1976, integrating it with the *IS–LM* model. Dornbusch referred to the model as the Mundell-Fleming model, as it is most commonly known, but there is a minor controversy about whether Fleming deserves to be listed first. In particular, see James M. Boughton, "On the Origins of the Fleming-Mundell Model," *IMF Staff Papers* 50, 1 (2003), 1–6; and Robert Mundell, "On the History of the Mundell-Fleming Model: Keynote Speech," *IMF Staff Papers* 47, special issue (2002), 215–227.

†This assumes ***imperfect capital mobility*** (assets cannot move freely from one nation to another). If there is perfect capital mobility, the *BP* curve is horizontal. For an accessible explanation of this and other workings of the model, consult an intermediate level macroeconomics textbook.

In order for national income and output to rise at the same pace, new investment spending must grow, otherwise planned saving—which is a function of income—will exceed planned investment, causing the economy's actual level of output to fall below its potential. According to Hansen, it was unlikely that investment spending would expand sufficiently from one year to the next over the decades to keep the economy fully employed and growing at a healthy rate. Population no longer seemed to be expanding at the rate it had earlier, the pace of settlement of new areas had greatly slowed, technological change appeared in spurts as opposed to on a steady and reliable basis, and no new major industries such as railroads and automobiles were appearing on the scene. Consequently, increasingly greater amounts of investment spending were not probable.

It is important, however, to recognize that Hansen was not a pessimist in the sense of Malthus. Hansen believed that government could overcome the tendency toward secular stagnation through *compensatory finance*. In other words, by increasing its expenditures government could compensate for the inadequate investment and fill the gap between private-sector demand and potential output (income).

In retrospect Hansen's concern for secular stagnation, like Keynes's, appears to have been unfounded. The United States experienced strong economic growth in the decades following his expression of this thesis. In Hansen's defense, we might nevertheless note that government spending *did* increase as a percentage of GDP over these decades. Whether the rate of growth of GDP would have been as high without this relative growth of government demand is subject to much debate.

Refer to 22-2 PAST AS PROLOGUE

PAUL A. SAMUELSON

When Paul A. Samuelson (1915–) in 1970 was announced as the first American economist to be awarded the Nobel Prize, few were surprised at the selection. He is one of the best-known American economists, both to his fellow economists and to the public at large. He is recognized by countless professionals in the field, and his textbook, *Economics,* is familiar to millions of people who have taken college economics. Samuelson was born in Gary, Indiana, the son of Polish immigrants. His father was a pharmacist.

After receiving his B.A. from the University of Chicago, Samuelson enrolled in the Harvard graduate program in economics. At Harvard, Samuelson was caught up in the beginnings of the Keynesian revolution; Alvin Hansen was one of his professors. Already a brilliant mathematics student, Samuelson decided early to apply mathematics to the body of economic theory then described to him as "an Augean stable full of inherited contradictions, overlaps, and fallacies." The result of his early efforts was his doctoral dissertation, *The Foundations of Economic Analysis,* published as a book in 1947. In this work, which won him immediate academic acclaim, he used mathematics to set forth and prove the major propositions in economics.

Upon receiving his doctorate, Samuelson began searching for a university where he could teach and continue his research. Surprisingly to all who knew the young scholar, Harvard did not appoint him to a post, even though he had published eleven articles while still a graduate student. Undaunted, Samuelson took a position at neighboring Massachusetts Institute of Technology. MIT had long had

22-2 PAST AS PROLOGUE

Abba Lerner and the "Keynesian Steering Wheel"

Immediately upon Keynes's publication of *The General Theory* in 1936, Abba P. Lerner (1903–1982), then at the London School of Economics, recognized its significance and from that point forward turned his attention to exploring and extending Keynesian macroeconomics. He came from London to the United States in 1939 and published numerous articles and books while moving from one American university to another, including Columbia, Michigan State, and the University of California-Berkeley.

Lerner said that the economy is like an automobile without a steering wheel, traveling down a wide road that has curbs on each side. The car would hit one curb, then veer to the opposite side of the road, where it would hit the other, which in turn would send the car careening once again to the other side. To prevent business cycles—that is, to keep the economy on a steadier course—society must equip the car with a steering wheel. In *The Economics of Control* (1944) and *Economics of Employment* (1951), Lerner set forth the basic fiscal and monetary instruments for steering the economy between the extremes of depression and demand-pull inflation. According to Lerner, the government should adhere to three laws of functional finance.*

- *Adjust government spending and taxation so that aggregate demand in the economy is just sufficient to purchase the full-employment level of output at current prices.* Adherence to this law will ensure full employment and price stability. Because the goal is to balance the economy and not the budget, it should be of no concern to the government if this policy produces either a deficit or a surplus. Taxes should never be levied for the sole reason that government expenditures exceed tax revenues or reduced because tax revenues exceed government expenditures.
- *Borrow money or repay national debt only if it is desirable to change the rate of interest.* Borrowing money from the public reduces the money supply, whereas repaying national debt—buying Treasury bills and notes—increases

a reputation for engineering and science excellence but no parallel reputation in economics. Samuelson was soon to change that!

In 1948 Samuelson published his introductory economics text, *Economics*. It proved to be as innovative in teaching elementary micro- and macroeconomics as his *Foundations* had been in formalizing the propositions of economic theory. Since its first printing (a coauthored version was in its 17th edition in 2005), millions of students throughout the world have learned the principles of economics from it. Although it is no longer the dominant textbook in the field, nearly all the books that have exceeded it in popularity still employ the basic ordering of presentation that Samuelson first established.

it. Such actions should be undertaken only when it is necessary to change the interest rate and influence private investment and consumer installment spending. Printing money can best finance budget deficits designed to counter inadequate private spending. Budget surpluses created by fiscal policies designed to reduce inflation ought to be held by the government, rather than used to repay debt.

- *Place into circulation or withdraw from circulation the amount of money required to reconcile the policies undertaken to adhere to the first two laws.* Put simply, government must use monetary policy in coordination with fiscal policy to achieve its macroeconomic goals.

Lerner's laws for functional finance went beyond the policies advocated by Keynes in his *The General Theory*. In fact, Keynes initially objected to parts of Lerner's line of reasoning. In this regard Lerner wrote:

> [A]t a lecture to the Federal Reserve in Washington in 1944, [Keynes] showed concern that there might be "too much saving" after the war. When I pointed out that the government [by increasing its spending or reducing taxes] could always induce enough spending by incurring deficits to increase incomes, he at first objected that this would only cause "even more saving" and then denounced as "humbug" my suggestion that the deficits required to induce enough total spending could always be financed by increasing the national debt. (I must add here that Evsey Domar, at my side, whispered: "He ought to read the *General Theory*" and that a month later Keynes withdrew his denunciation.)[†]

As stated by Colander, "What eventually became known as textbook Keynesian policies were in many ways Lerner's interpretations of Keynes's policies. . . ."[‡]

---

*As summarized by Tibor Scitovsky, "Lerner's Contributions to Economics," *Journal of Economic Literature* 22 (December 1984): 1559–1560.

†Abba Lerner, "Keynesianism: Alive, If Not So Well," *Fiscal Responsibilities in a Constitutional Democracy*, ed. James Buchanan and Richard Wagner (Boston: Martinus Niijhoff, 1978), 67.

‡David C. Colander, "Was Keynes a Keynesian or a Lernerian?" *Journal of Economic Literature* 22 (December 1984): 1573.

Samuelson has published numerous, far-ranging articles in the most prestigious economic journals. Many of these articles are highly mathematical, and many are of major interest only to other experts in the field. Samuelson is not an empiricist; indeed he calls himself a generalist interested in expanding theory rather than testing it.

It is a difficult matter to fit Samuelson within a particular school of economics. He could just as appropriately have been placed in the chapter on mathematical economics or the one on welfare economics. His articles cover such diverse topics as consumer behavior, linear programming, capital and growth, economic methodology, the history of economic theory, welfare economics, public expenditure theory, national income determination, and fiscal and monetary policy. His collected papers are reprinted in five lengthy volumes.

The Multiplier-Accelerator Interaction

In 1939 Samuelson published two papers in which he identified and explored the interaction between the principles of the multiplier and accelerator. This interaction has become one of the foundations of modern business cycle theory. Neither idea taken singularly was new. We saw in the previous chapter that Kahn developed the notion of the multiplier and that Keynes used it as a central feature of his theory. John Maurice Clark (1884–1963), the son of John Bates Clark, discussed the *acceleration principle* as early as 1917.[6] He argued that fluctuations in the output and prices of capital goods are much greater than those for the consumption goods they produce. Even if the demand for consumer goods continues to grow, a change in the rate of growth will be transmitted back with intensified force or acceleration to the capital goods sector. A cessation of growth in the demand for final goods thus leads to a sharp decline in the demand for capital goods.

Hansen was aware there was an interaction between the two principles and suggested to Samuelson that he use his mathematical skills to explore the idea. Using difference equations, Samuelson demonstrated that changes in income (consumption) will depend on the size of the marginal propensity to consume and the size of the accelerator coefficient. The former determines the multiplier, and the latter is the change in investment spending induced by a change in the rate of income growth. Samuelson showed that, depending on the values of the multiplier and accelerator and whether an increase in investment is continuous, an initial autonomous increase in investment could produce a wide variety of outcomes, ranging from no lasting increase in income to an ever-increasing level of income.

The Simple Algebra of Income Determination

Much of the algebra of income determination found in intermediate macroeconomics textbooks originated with Samuelson (recall that the Keynesian cross diagram also was a Samuelson invention).

In order to illustrate the essence of Samuelson's approach, let's start with the basic Keynesian identity:

$$Y = C + I + G + X - M \qquad \textbf{(22-1)}$$

where Y stands for income, C for consumption, I for investment, G for government purchases, X for exports, and M for imports.

Consumption spending, tax revenues, investment spending (due to the acceleration principle), and imports all increase as income rises. The ratios of their rise to the increase in income are the marginal propensity to consume, the marginal propensity to tax, the marginal propensity to invest, and the marginal propensity to import.

[6] John M. Clark, "Business Acceleration and the Law of Demand," *Journal of Political Economy* 25 (March 1917): 217–235.

Government expenditures and the level of exports, on the other hand, are assumed to be *autonomous*—that is, determined independently of the level of income.

An equation can be formulated for each of the independent variables in the identity. The most complicated equation is the one for C, which we derive as follows:

$$C = a + bY \quad \textbf{(22-2)}$$

$$C = a + b(Y - T), \text{ or} \quad \textbf{(22-3)}$$

$$C = a + bY - bT \quad \textbf{(22-4)}$$

$$T = T_0 + tY \quad \textbf{(22-5)}$$

$$C = a + bY - b(T_0 + tY), \text{ or} \quad \textbf{(22-6)}$$

$$C = a + bY - bT_0 - btY \quad \textbf{(22-7)}$$

Equation 22-2 is the consumption function, where a is the amount of consumption spending that is independent of the level of income and b is the marginal propensity to consume. Total before-tax consumption, C, equals the autonomous level of consumption plus the consumption related to the level of income. The latter is found by multiplying Y by the marginal propensity to consume (b). But, as shown in Equation 22-3, income and therefore consumption will be lowered by taxes (T). In Equation 22-5, we see that taxes consist of those, if any, that must be paid irrespective of the level of income (T_0) and those that rise as income rises (tY). The marginal propensity to tax is t. By substituting Equation 22-5 into 22-4 we get Equation 22-6. Multiplying through Equation 22-6 yields Equation 22-7.

The other equations needed to formulate an income determination equation are as follows:

$$I = I_0 + zY \quad \textbf{(22-8)}$$

where I_0 is investment that is independent of income and z is the marginal propensity to invest. The term z then shows the change of investment that occurs when income rises. This is the accelerator notion. Other equations are:

$$G = G_0 \quad \textbf{(22-9)}$$

$$X = X_0 \quad \textbf{(22-10)}$$

$$M = M_0 + mY \quad \textbf{(22-11)}$$

where G_0, X_0, and M_0 are autonomous levels of government spending, export spending, and import spending, respectively, and m is the marginal propensity to import. Note that total import spending depends on the level of income.

By substituting each equation into the basic identity (22-1) and then manipulating the terms, we are able to derive the following complex income determination equation:

$$Y = \frac{1}{s + bt + m - z}(a - bT_0 + I_0 + G_0 + X_0 - M_0) \quad \textbf{(22-12)}$$

This equation is not as imposing as it first looks. Total income depends on aggregate spending, which in turn consists of two parts: that which does not depend on the level of income and that which does. The autonomous spending is captured by the terms in parentheses. The two negative terms simply subtract items (taxes and import spending) that do not contribute directly to demand for domestically produced goods. To repeat, the items within the parentheses sum to the total autonomous spending in the economy.

The fraction in Equation 22-12 is the complex multiplier. Recall that the simple multiplier was $1/MPS$. The terms in the complex multiplier are as follows: s is the marginal propensity to save $(1 - b)$, bt is the marginal propensity to consume times the marginal propensity to tax, m is the marginal propensity to import, and z is the marginal propensity to invest. Observe that all the terms in the denominator are positive, with the exception of z. We conclude that the multiplier will be smaller the higher are the marginal propensity to save, the marginal propensity to tax, and the marginal propensity to import. The reason is that savings, taxes, and imports are leakages from the income stream that occur when income rises. The complex multiplier will be larger the higher is the marginal propensity to invest, z, or the greater is the increase in investment that results from rising income. By multiplying the net autonomous spending by the value of the complex multiplier, we determine total equilibrium income, Y. You are urged to test your understanding of the model by ascertaining the impact of various changes in the terms in the equation on the value of Y.

Samuelson's mathematics of income determination helped clarify the intricacies of the Keynesian system. Other economists built similar models in which they greatly expanded the number of equations and inserted estimated values. As we indicated in Chapter 18, these econometric models are used to forecast changes in national income.

Samuelson's algebra also demonstrated that complex multipliers are less than those based solely on the marginal propensity to save. In the sophisticated present-day Keynesian econometric models, for example, the expenditure multiplier varies between 2.2 and 2.7.

The Phillips Curve

Recall that Lerner had identified the possibility of premature inflation, or inflation that would occur before the economy reached "high full-employment." In 1958 A. W. Phillips, of the London School of Economics, presented data showing the relationship between unemployment and the rate of change of money wage rates in the United Kingdom for the years 1861 through 1957. His graphic representation of the data came to be known as the Phillips curve. In 1960 Samuelson and Robert Solow plotted a Phillips scatter diagram for the United States from which they made a rough estimate of the Phillips curve facing the economy in 1960 (Figure 22-4). They wrote:

> All this is shown in our price-level modification of the Phillips curve [Figure 22-4]. The point *A*, corresponding to price stability, is seen to involve about 5 1/2 per cent unemployment; whereas the point *B*, corresponding to 3 per cent unemployment, is seen to involve a price rise of about 4 1/2 per cent per annum. . . . We have not here entered upon the important question of what feasible institutional reforms might be introduced to lessen the degree of disharmony between full employment and price stability. These could of course involve such wide-ranging issues as direct price and wage

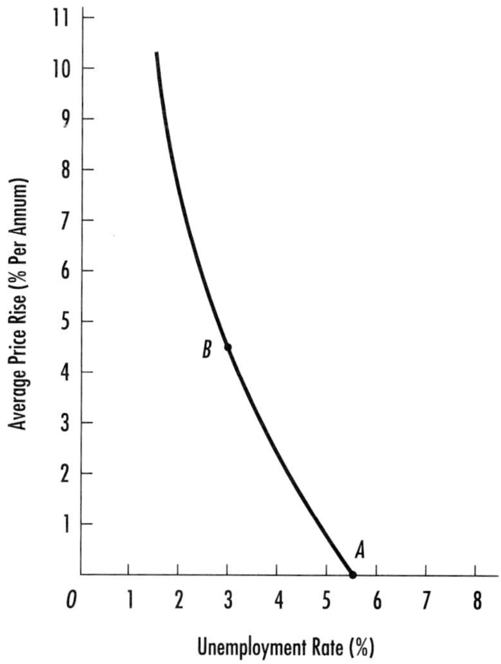

Figure 22-4 The Samuelson-Solow Phillips Curve for the United States, 1960
Writing in 1960, Samuelson and Solow stated, "This [curve] shows the menu of choices between different degrees of unemployment and price stability, as roughly estimated from [the] last twenty-five years of American data."

controls, antiunion and antitrust legislation, and a host of other measures hopefully designed to move the American Phillips curve downward and to the left.[7]

Samuelson once referred to the Phillips curve as one of the most important concepts of our time. What is its underlying economic logic? Which point on the curve should society set as its goal? What policies might shift the curve inward? Is the curve stable over time? What caused scatter points for the 1970s to lie far above and to the right of this curve? Is it possible that the long-run Phillips curve is perfectly vertical? These and related questions became the focal point of macroeconomic analysis during the 1960s and 1970s.

Other Contributions

Samuelson, either singularly or in conjunction with others, developed a plethora of additional ideas of importance to economics. The list that follows is far from exhaustive.

[7] Paul A. Samuelson and Robert M. Solow, "Analytical Aspects of Anti-Inflation Policy," *American Economic Review* 50 (May 1960): 192–193.

- *Comparative statics.* Economic theory is based on the idea of equilibrium. Given a set of forces, as in supply and demand models, a state will be achieved from which there is no tendency to move away. This is a static position. As soon as we allow the forces to change—say, people's income—then we have a dynamic situation. Eventually, a new equilibrium is reached. Samuelson's comparative statics method compares two states of equilibrium, without considering the path of adjustment. He was well aware in 1947 when he formulated the comparative static approach that an important part of the problem was left out—knowledge of the adjustment path. But the comparative static approach allows one to make inferences about the path of adjustment.
- *Revealed preference theory.* In developing an indifference map from which a demand curve was derived, Hicks and others postulated that a consumer is able to state preferences among all possible combinations of two commodities. Samuelson substituted an alternative approach that does not require that the consumer is able to provide information about her preferences. The approach permits the theoretician to reconstruct indifference curves solely by observing the consumer's actual purchasing behavior at different prices.
- *Efficient markets theory.* Along with others, Samuelson developed the notion that "properly anticipated prices fluctuate randomly." This idea has been dubbed the *efficient markets theory.*[8] An efficient financial market is one in which all new information is readily understood and therefore quickly incorporated into the market price. Thus any existing market price—say, the price of a share of IBM stock—already is based on all available information. Any subsequent change in the price of the asset will be unrelated to existing information or to past price changes. One interesting implication of this theory is that as a speculator, over the long haul, "You can't outguess the market. There are no easy pickings."[9]
- *Factor-price equalization theory.* Classical economists fully recognized that factors of production would flow toward areas where they could command the highest prices. Samuelson provided a mathematical proof to show that product mobility—buying and selling products in regions or nations other than where they were produced—is a substitute for factor mobility in diminishing differences in wages and other factor prices. Other contributors to this idea were Abba Lerner and Bertil Ohlin.
- *Public expenditures theory.* Along with Wicksell, Erik Lindahl, and Richard Musgrave, Samuelson is one of the major contributors to the theory of public expenditures. He defined a public good as "one that enters two or more persons' utility." The idea is that public goods have *consumption externalities*—their benefits are indivisible. Looked at differently, the marginal cost of providing additional consumers with the benefit would be zero, and it would be impossible to exclude nonpaying users from receiving the benefit. Because consumers will obtain the benefit from a public good whether or not they pay for it, potential buyers will have no incentive to reveal their true preferences. Consequently,

[8] Another major contributor to this idea was Franco Modigliani.

[9] Paul Samuelson and William D. Nordhaus, *Economics,* 12th ed. (New York: McGraw-Hill, 1985), 288.

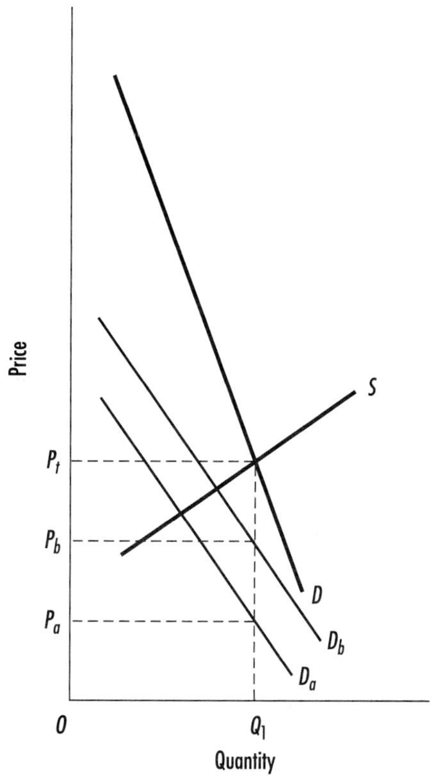

Figure 22-5 The Optimal Amount of a Public Good
Although the demand curve for a public good (D) does not reveal itself in the marketplace, we can find it theoretically by vertically summing individual willingness-to-pay curves (here, D_a and D_b) at each quantity. The optimal quantity of the public good represented is Q_1, because at that output, marginal social benefit (as shown by the relevant point on D) equals marginal social cost (as shown by the relevant point on S).

market demand will be insufficient to provide producers with adequate revenue to cover their costs. In short, the market will fail in the sense that it does not deliver goods for which the marginal social benefit exceeds the marginal social cost.

How might the optimal quantity of a public good be determined, at least in theory? Samuelson and others answered this question by developing the ideas underlying Figure 22-5. Suppose there are only two consumers, Avery and Baker, whose demand curves for a specific public good are D_a and D_b. These curves are *pseudo-demand curves,* because these consumers do not reveal them in the market. The pseudo-demand curve for the entire market is D. It is derived by summing D_a and D_b vertically, rather than horizontally as in the case of private goods. Both Avery and Baker consume the *full* amount of the public good, and the combined price they are willing to pay for it is the sum of the amounts they are *each* willing to pay. The optimal amount of the public good (Q_1) is determined by the intersection of the market demand and supply curves, D and S. The price that will cover costs is P_t, which is the sum of the prices of P_a and P_b. Quantity Q_1 is optimal from a welfare standpoint because the marginal social benefit (as shown by the relevant point on D) equals the marginal social cost (as shown by the relevant point on S). Government therefore should provide Q_1 units of the public good.

THE POST-KEYNESIANS

Thanks to Samuelson and others, mainstream economics came to include Keynesian principles of macroeconomics grafted upon neoclassical principles of microeconomics. Not all scholars of Keynes accepted this *neoclassical synthesis*. Some denied both the *IS–LM* interpretation of Keynes *and* standard microeconomics. Chief among these post–Keynesian critics was a group of economists at Cambridge, England, including Piero Sraffa (Chapter 17), Nicolas Kaldor (1908–1986), Joan Robinson (Chapter 17), and Luigi Pasinetti (1930–). John K. Galbraith (Chapter 19), Sydney Weintraub (1914–1983), and a handful of other economists contributed to this school of thought in the United States. Many of the post–Keynesians drew heavily on the work of Polish economist Michal Kalecki (1899–1970), who in 1933 had offered a "Keynesian-like" theory of total employment prior to *The General Theory*. Research by modern post–Keynesian scholars can be found in the *Journal of Post–Keynesian Economics*.

Major Tenets

The post–Keynesians are a small, yet diverse, group of economists. Some of the ideas of each individual within this paradigm differ from those expressed by others. Nevertheless, we can discern several basic tenets of this set of ideas.

- Neo–Ricardian view of production, value, and distribution. In 1960 Piero Sraffa published *Production of Commodities by Means of Commodities: A Prelude to a Critique of Economic Theory*, which reconstructed Ricardo's production and value theory in a modern form. According to Sraffa, the pattern of demand for various products does not affect the pattern of prices; rather, it affects only the scale of output in each industry. The real values (prices) of goods depend on the shares of other commodities necessary to produce them. Relative values (prices) and profits (if wages are given) are determined by the production techniques used to produce a composite standard commodity, which consists of the basic commodities in the economy. These basic commodities are goods that enter into the production of all other commodities; they are in essence "capital" goods that appear both as inputs and outputs. The key feature of the composite standard commodity is that a change in either wages or profits affects the inputs exactly the same way that it affects the output. Therefore, said Sraffa, the composite standard commodity is Ricardo's elusive invariable measure of value or of relative prices.

Of particular importance to the discussion at hand, Sraffa's theory produced a novel conclusion: The level of domestic output is entirely independent of how it is distributed between wages and profits. Any distribution of wages and profits is consistent with a particular level of output.

Robinson and other post–Keynesians expanded Sraffa's unconventional theme. The actual distribution of income between wages and profits, they said, will depend on the class struggle, on public policies that alter the distribution, and on the rate of investment (higher rates increasing the profit share). Robinson argued that it is desirable and possible for society to control the distribution of income. This can be done through the socialization of investment, public ownership of the means of production, or incomes policies (government policies to control wages and prices). Robinson believed these policies are firmly rooted in the proper interpretation of Keynes's *The General Theory.* In this respect she called herself a "left-wing Keynesian." She wrote:

> You might almost say that I am the archetypal left-wing Keynesian. I was drawing pinkish rather than bluish conclusions from the *General Theory* long before it was published. (I was in the privileged position of being one of a group of friends who worked with Keynes while it was being written.) Thus I was the first drop that ever got into the jar labelled 'Left-wing Keynesian.' Moreover, I am quite a large percentage of the contents of the jar today, because so much of the rest has seeped out of it meanwhile.[10]

- Markup pricing. Prices are set by oligopolistic corporations. These firms finance investment largely from retained profits. To achieve their desired levels of profits and therefore realize their investment plans, oligopolists set prices above current costs. Prices therefore "do not reflect current demand conditions; rather they reflect the funds requirements for the planned investment expenditure the firm considers necessary if it is to adjust its capacity sufficiently to meet expected future demand."[11] When costs rise, firms increase their prices to maintain their markups over their costs.
- Endogenous money. Contrary to the view held by Fisher (Chapter 16) and Friedman (Chapter 24), post–Keynesians regard the stock of money as being essentially endogenous to the economy, changing in response to changes in the level of wages. The needs of trade dictate the supply of money. Keynes himself pointed out that money "comes into existence along with debts."

  Inflation arises from the fight over the shares of the distribution of income. Wage increases cause production costs to rise, creating a greater demand on the part of firms for working capital to finance their more expensive goods-in-progress and inventories. Hence, business borrowing rises and the money stock increases.
- Pronounced cyclical instability. The economy is inherently unstable. Investment must grow sufficiently to keep national income and output growing at a steady rate. Because of periods of alternating environment of business optimism and

[10] Joan Robinson, *Collected Economic Papers,* 5 vols. (Cambridge, MA: MIT Press, 1980), 4: 264.

[11] Peter Kenyon, "Pricing," in *A Guide to Post-Keynesian Economics,* ed. Alfred S. Eichner (White Plains, NY: M. E. Sharpe, 1979), 40.

pessimism, it often does not. When investment is less than required to maintain the steady rate of growth, the economy recedes and unemployment rises.

- Need for an incomes policy. The "class struggle" for income shares and the markup pricing by oligopolists necessitate a permanent incomes policy:

> If there is perhaps one point on which economists with a post–Keynesian perspective are likely to agree, it is that inflation cannot be controlled through conventional instruments of fiscal and monetary policy. This is because they regard inflation as resulting, not necessarily from any "excess demand" for goods, but rather from a more fundamental conflict over the distribution of available income and output. The conventional policy instruments, by curtailing the level of economic activity, simply reduce the amount of income and output available for distribution, thereby heightening the social conflict underlying the inflationary process. . . . It is for this reason that post-Keynesian economists, instead of asking whether an incomes policy is necessary, have generally moved on to the question of how an incomes policy can be made to work effectively and equitably.[12]

THE NEW KEYNESIANS

Most modern Keynesians reject the neo–Ricardian value theory of the post–Keynesians. They also reject the post–Keynesians' call for incomes policies, citing the resource misallocations resulting from these policies and the poor historical success of wage and price controls in reducing inflation.[13]

Downward Price and Wage Inflexibility

Modern Keynesian macroeconomists have pursued a narrower line of inquiry than the post–Keynesians. The new Keynesian theorists have refocused attention on the traditional Keynesian question of why recessions occur. Their answer is that declines in aggregate demand produce declines in real output and corresponding increases in unemployment, because the price level and nominal wages are inflexible downward. The importance of this downward price and wage stickiness is demonstrated in Figure 22-6.

To illustrate, let's first suppose that prices and nominal wages are perfectly flexible. Suppose also that aggregate demand declines from AD_1 to AD_2 and aggregate supply remains at AS_1. The price level will therefore decline from P_1 at *a* to P_2 at *b*, and real output will temporarily fall from its full-employment level Q_f to less-than-full-employment output Q_1. This lower price level and greater unemployment will enable producers to reduce their nominal wages, so as to leave the real wage unchanged. As nominal wages fall, the aggregate supply curve will shift rightward, eventually from AS_1 to broken-line AS_2. At the *c* intersection of aggregate demand AD_2 and aggregate supply AS_2, real output returns to Q_f and the

[12] Eichner, *A Guide to Post-Keynesian Economics,* 17–18.

[13] See Alan Blinder, *Economic Policy and the Great Stagflation* (New York: Academic Press, 1979), chapter 6.

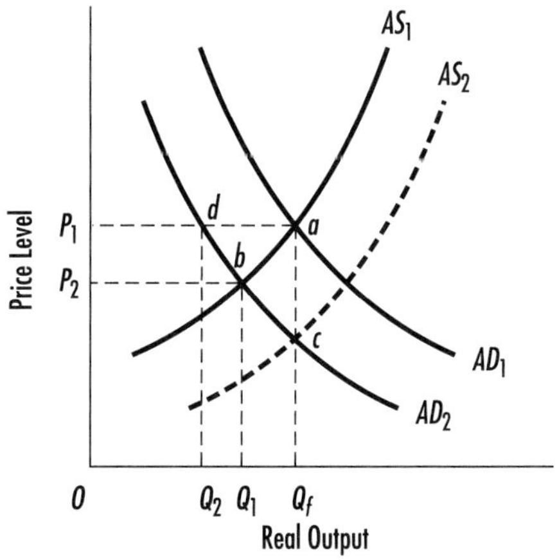

Figure 22-6 New Keynesianism: Inflexible Prices and Wages
According to new Keynesians, such factors as menu costs, formal and implicit contracts, efficiency wages, and "insider-outsider" relationships create downward inflexibility of prices and wages. Consequently, a decline in aggregate demand, as from AD_1 to AD_2, moves the economy from *a* to *d*, not from *a* to *b* to *c* as predicted by classical and new classical macroeconomics. Persistent, lasting low output and high unemployment, not an automatic rightward shift of the aggregate supply curve, may result unless government undertakes an expansionary fiscal and monetary policy to increase aggregate demand.

recession has automatically ended. This process simply describes the classical and new classical (Chapter 24) viewpoint. The economy is self-correcting, and thus government stabilization policies are unnecessary.

But the new Keynesians emphasize that the scenario is quite different if prices and nominal wages are for a time inflexible downward. Instead of moving the economy quickly from *a* to *b* to *c*, a decline in aggregate demand from AD_1 to AD_2 will move the economy from *a* to *d*, and real output will fall from Q_f to Q_2. Because wages are inflexible downward, the unemployment associated with real output Q_2 will persist until aggregate demand returns to AD_1. Active fiscal and monetary policy may be needed to effect this rightward shift of the aggregate demand curve.

New Keynesian economists such as Joseph Stiglitz of Stanford, Oliver Blanchard of Harvard, Stanley Fisher of MIT, George Akerlof of California-Berkeley, Assar Lindbeck of the University of Stockholm, and Robert Gordon of Northwestern have offered several possible explanations for downward price and wage rigidity.

Menu costs. Some firms must incur costs when they lower prices; for example, a restaurant must print a new menu. Similarly, other firms establish and print new price lists; communicate the lower prices to customers, perhaps through new advertising; print and mail new catalogs; and reprice items held in inventory. Where *menu costs* such as these are high, firms may be reluctant to lower their prices, even when faced with slack demand. Also, firms in oligopolistic industries must be concerned that a unilateral price reduction may set off deeper cuts by rivals. Thus, when aggregate demand in the economy declines, prices (at least for a time) may remain fixed while output and employment fall.[14]

Formal and implicit contracts. New Keynesians point out that unions often sign long-term contracts containing built-in nominal wage increases. Wage cuts simply are not an option when declines in aggregate demand unexpectedly occur; instead firms lay off workers. Even where contracts are being renegotiated, unions typically vigorously resist wage "givebacks." Union leaders, elected by the majority of members, often prefer layoffs for the few rather than wage cuts for the many.

Although many nonunion workers do not work under formal or explicit contracts, these workers may operate under implicit contracts, which are informal agreements or "invisible handshakes."[15] One common understanding may be that firms will maintain existing nominal wages during periods of slack product demand. Such "insurance" against wage cuts may benefit firms by allowing them to attract higher quality workers who require less supervision. In return for the pledge of no wage cuts, workers in effect pledge not to challenge the firm's right to lay off workers in response to declines in product demand.

If formal and implicit contracts permeate the workplace, then declines in wages are not forthcoming as aggregate demand declines. In terms of Figure 22-6, the economy moves from point *a* to *d*, and a recession occurs.

Efficiency wages. An efficiency wage is an above-market clearing wage that minimizes an employer's wage cost per effective unit of labor service employed. Normally, we would think that the market wage is the efficiency wage. However, when the costs of supervising and monitoring workers are high or worker turnover is great, firms may discover that an above-market wage will lower their labor costs. The higher pay raises the relative value of the job as viewed by each worker; it also raises the cost of being terminated or leaving. The higher opportunity cost (price) of shirking and being fired, or of voluntarily leaving the job, results in less shirking and reduced turnover, which together enhance productivity.

Firms paying efficiency wages will be reluctant to cut wage rates in response to declines in aggregate demand because these wage cuts will encourage shirking and increase the number of job quits, dampening productivity and increasing the firms' per-unit labor costs. In brief, the wage cuts will be self-defeating.[16] In this way efficiency wages may contribute to downward wage inflexibility and cyclical unemployment.

Insider-outsider theory. In Assar Lindbeck's "insider-outsider model" of sticky wages, "insiders" are employed workers who possess some market power; "outsiders"

[14] For more on menu costs, see N. Gregory Mankiw and David Romer, eds., *New Keynesian Economics* (Cambridge, MA: MIT Press, 1991).

[15] The major contributions to this literature are surveyed in Costas Azariadis and Joseph E. Stiglitz, "Implicit Contracts and Fixed-Price Equilibria," *Quarterly Journal of Economics* 98 (suppl. 1983): 1–22.

[16] For more on this subject, see George A. Akerlof and Janet L. Yellen, eds., *Efficiency Wage Models of the Labor Market* (Cambridge: Cambridge University Press, 1986).

are the unemployed who are unable or unwilling to underbid existing wage rates to gain employment.[17] Outsiders may be *unable* to underbid existing wages because employers may view the costs of hiring them as being too high. The employers may rightfully be concerned that the remaining higher-paid workers will view these replacement workers as "stealing" jobs. If the higher-paid "insiders" refuse to cooperate in team production with the new lower-paid workers, the firms' output and profits will suffer.

Even if firms are willing to hire "outsiders" at less than the existing wage, these unemployed people may not want to offer their services for less than the existing wage. That is, they may fear harassment from the higher-paid employees. Thus "outsiders" may remain unemployed, waiting for an increase in aggregate demand to regain employment, rather than undercutting existing wage scales. Wages will be inflexible downward in the presence of deficient aggregate demand and cyclical unemployment.

Questions for Study and Discussion

1. Identify and briefly state the significance of each of the following to the history of economic thought: Hansen, Fiscal Policy Seminar, *IS–LM* analysis, stagnation thesis, compensatory finance, Lerner functional finance, Samuelson, accelerator, Phillips curve, revealed preference theory, public expenditure theory, Sraffa, post–Keynesians, new Keynesians, menu costs, formal and implicit contracts, efficiency wages, and insider-outsider theory.
2. Comment on the following statement by Keynes: "I understand that Hansen is known in America as the American Keynes; I perhaps ought to be known as the English Hansen."
3. What motivated Hicks and Hansen to develop *IS–LM* analysis? Explain how fiscal policy could be used to shift the *IS* curve rightward. Explain how monetary policy could be used to shift the *LM* curve leftward. What would happen to equilibrium income and the interest rate in each case?
4. How does Lerner's theory of functional finance (Past as Prologue 22-2) relate to the statement that he expressed as follows:

   > "Of course we have no steering wheel!" says one of the [car's] occupants rather crossly. . . . "Suppose we had a steering wheel and somebody held on to it when we reached the curb! He would prevent the automatic turning of the wheel, and the car would surely overturn!"

5. In what way are saving, taxes, and import spending similar to one another? Explain why the complex multiplier tends to be smaller than the simple Keynesian one.
6. Explain why it is necessary to sum individual demand curves *vertically* to obtain a total demand curve for a public good, whereas the procedure for a private good is to sum them *horizontally*.

[17] Assar Lindbeck and Dennis Snower, *The Insider-Outsider Theory of Employment and Unemployment* (Cambridge: Cambridge University Press, 1988).

7. Critically assess the following contention of Eichner and Kregel: The purpose of post–Keynesian theory is "to explain the real world as observed empirically," while the purpose of neoclassical theory is "to demonstrate the social optimality if the real world were to resemble the model."
8. According to the new Keynesians, why isn't the economy self-correcting when faced with a decline in aggregate demand?
9. On what points do the new Keynesians disagree with the post–Keynesians?

Selected Readings

Books

Eichner, Alfred S., ed. *A Guide to Post-Keynesian Economics.* White Plains, NY: M. E. Sharpe, 1979.

Hansen, Alvin H. *Business Cycle Theory: Development and Present Status.* Boston, MA: Ginn & Co., 1927.

———. *Fiscal Policy and Business Cycles.* New York: W. W. Norton, 1941.

———. *Full Recovery or Stagnation?* New York: W. W. Norton, 1938.

———. *A Guide to Keynes.* New York: McGraw-Hill, 1953.

Lerner, Abba P. *The Economics of Control: Principles of Welfare Economics.* New York: Macmillan, 1944.

———. *Economics of Employment.* New York: McGraw-Hill, 1951.

Lindbeck, Assar, and Dennis Snower. *The Insider-Outsider Theory of Employment and Unemployment.* Cambridge: Cambridge University Press, 1988.

Mankiw, N. Gregory, and David Romer, eds. *New Keynesian Economics.* Cambridge, MA: MIT Press, 1991.

Samuelson, Paul A. *The Collected Scientific Papers of Paul Samuelson,* 5 vols. Vols. 1 and 2 edited by Joseph E. Stiglitz, vol. 3 edited by Robert Merton, vol. 4 edited by Hiroki Nagatani and Kate Crowley, vol. 5 edited by Kate Crowley. Cambridge, MA: MIT Press, 1966, 1972, 1977, 1986.

———. *Foundations of Economic Analysis.* Cambridge, MA: Harvard University Press, 1947.

Sraffa, Piero. *Production of Commodities by Means of Commodities: Prelude to a Critique of Economic Theory.* Cambridge: Cambridge University Press, 1960.

Journal Articles

Barber, William J. "The Career of Alvin Hansen in the 1920s and 1930s: A Study in Intellectual Transformation." *History of Political Economy* 19 (Summer 1987): 191–205.

Colander, David. "Was Keynes a Keynesian or a Lernerian?" *Journal of Economic Literature* 22 (December 1984): 1572–1575.

Gordon, Robert J. "What Is New-Keynesian Economics?" *Journal of Economic Literature* 28 (September 1990): 1115–1171.

Hicks, J. R. "Mr. Keynes and the Classics: A Suggested Interpretation." *Econometrica* 5 (April 1937): 147–159.

Quarterly Journal of Economics 40 (February 1976). This issue contains articles on Hansen by Richard A. Musgrave, Gottfried Haberler, Walter S. Salant, Paul A. Samuelson, and James Tobin.

Samuelson, Paul A. "A. P. Lerner at Sixty." *Review of Economic Studies* 31 (June 1964): 169–178.

———. "Interaction between the Multiplier Analysis and the Principle of Acceleration." *Review of Economics and Statistics* 21 (May 1939): 75–78.

Samuelson, Paul A., and Robert M. Solow. "Analytical Aspects of Anti-Inflation Policy." *American Economic Review* 40 (May 1960): 177–194.

Scitovsky, Tibor. "Lerner's Contributions to Economics." *Journal of Economic Literature* 22 (December 1984): 1547–1571.

Chapter 23

Theories of Economic Growth and Development

Adherents of several schools and eclectic thinkers alike have devoted much thought to economic growth and development. *Economic growth* is the increase of a nation's real output (GDP) that occurs over time. It results from (1) greater quantities of natural resources, human resources, and capital; (2) improvements in the quality of resources; and (3) technological advances that boost productivity.

A nation's real GDP per capita—that is, its standard of living—rises when its real output increases more rapidly than its population. *Economic development* is simply the process by which a nation enhances its standard of living over time. Specialists in economic development analyze the forces and policies that cause, or impede, the rise of standards of living in low- and moderate-income nations.

Especially since 1945, a vast outpouring of scholarship on growth and development has occurred. There are several reasons for this. The first is that economic growth is highly variable among nations. Why have some nations grown far more rapidly than others? The second reason is that the industrially advanced countries have overcome the worst excesses of business depressions through stabilization policies and more flexible markets. The emphasis has, therefore, turned to ways to achieve higher rates of growth. The third reason is that most poor countries, many of them colonies before World War II, are now politically free and are pursuing strategies to promote economic growth and development. Once called "backward" or "undeveloped," these nations are now called "developing" or "emerging." The fourth reason is that the collapse of Marxian socialism in eastern Europe and the Soviet Union has focused much attention on growth and development in these regions. Can the former communist countries transform their economies to capitalism and achieve more rapid economic growth? Finally, the rising standard of living in developing nations has become economically important to the industrially advanced nations in terms of direct investment, international trade, and international finance.

This chapter examines five divergent analyses of economic growth and development. We begin with a discussion of the Keynesian growth model established by Harrod and Domar. We then examine Solow's neoclassical growth model. Next, we look at Schumpeter's theory of economic development and institutional change. This is followed by discussions of Nurkse and Lewis, who both provide seminal ideas on economic development.

SIR ROY F. HARROD AND EVSEY DOMAR

Sir Roy F. Harrod (1900–1978) and Evsey Domar (1914–1997) separately contributed to what today is known as the Harrod-Domar analysis of growth. They established their theories within the Keynesian framework discussed in the previous two chapters and therefore are members of the broader Keynesian school. In 1947 Harrod, an Englishman, presented his ideas in a series of lectures at the University of London.[1] That same year Domar, who later was to hold positions at Johns Hopkins and MIT, published an article containing a similar theory in the *American Economic Review*.[2] Because the theories reach similar conclusions and are somewhat complex, we will discuss only Domar's growth model.[3]

The Capacity-Creating Effect of Investment

Domar noted that net investment spending adds to the nation's stock of capital, increases the economy's productive capacity, and raises its *potential* level of income. He said that the change in productive capacity, ΔY_q, will depend on the level of investment, I, and the "potential social average productivity of new investment," σ. Symbolically,

$$\Delta Y_q = I\sigma \qquad \textbf{(23-1)}$$

To demonstrate Domar's important point, let us suppose that the value of σ is .3. This tells us that each dollar of investment spending will increase the economy's capacity to generate future income by 30 cents. We also assume that the propensity to save (marginal = average) is .2. If equilibrium income is \$500 billion, then saving will be \$100 billion (.2 × \$500 billion). Net investment therefore must also be \$100 billion, because investment must match saving at the equilibrium level of income. This \$100 billion of investment will increase the economy's productive capacity and potential income by \$30 billion (.3 × \$100 billion). If income in the next period were to remain at \$500 billion, the economy would experience idle capacity and unemployment. Investment expands a nation's capacity to produce output and generate income.

The Demand-Creating Effect of Investment

Because the consumption function in the Keynesian model is assumed to be stable, added consumption expenditures are forthcoming only in response to expanding income. Consequently, investment spending is the source of increases in aggregate demand from one period to the next. Investment spending in the new period must

[1] R. F. Harrod, *Toward a Dynamic Analysis* (London: Macmillan, 1948).

[2] Evsey D. Domar, "Expansion and Employment," *American Economic Review* 37 (March 1947): 34–55. Also, "The Problem of Capital Accumulation," *American Economic Review* 38 (December 1948): 77–94.

[3] An excellent summary of Harrod's model is presented by Wallace C. Peterson in his *Income, Employment, and Economic Growth*, 5th ed. (New York: Norton, 1984). Harrod published a "tentative and preliminary" outline of a dynamic theory of growth in 1939. See "An Essay in Dynamic Theory," *Economic Journal* 49 (March 1939): 14–33.

exceed the amount in the previous period if the added potential income arising from that past investment is to be realized. The required increase in effective demand is given by Equation 23-2.

$$\Delta \Upsilon_d - \Delta I \times \frac{1}{\alpha} \qquad \textbf{(23-2)}$$

where $\Delta \Upsilon_d$ is the change in income, ΔI is the change in net investment spending, and α is the propensity to save. The fraction $1/\alpha$ is the simple Keynesian investment multiplier discussed in Chapter 21.

The Requirement for Balanced Growth

Domar defined balanced growth as a rate of income growth at which full employment of resources is maintained over time. It is achieved when changes in productive capacity ($\Delta \Upsilon_q$ in Equation 23-1) equal changes in effective demand ($\Delta \Upsilon_d$ in Equation 23-2).

$$\Delta \Upsilon_q = \Delta \Upsilon_d \qquad \textbf{(23-3)}$$

Substituting the previous values for $\Delta \Upsilon_q$ and $\Delta \Upsilon_d$ into Equation 23-3 provides Equation 23-4.

$$I\alpha = \Delta I \times \frac{1}{\alpha} \qquad \textbf{(23-4)}$$

By multiplying both sides of Equation 23-4 by α and then dividing by I, we obtain Equation 23-5.

$$\frac{\Delta I}{I} = \sigma\alpha \qquad \textbf{(23-5)}$$

Domar thus reached his major conclusions. The economy must grow in order to maintain full employment of its resources. To realize the rate of income growth required to match the growth of income capacity, investment must annually increase at a percentage rate equal to the product of the potential social average productivity of investment, σ, and the propensity to save, α.

In our previous example, income must rise from \$500 billion to \$530 billion (6 percent). Because the propensity to save is .2, the multiplier is 5 (1/.2). To achieve an increase in income of \$30 billion, investment must therefore rise by \$6 billion (\$30/5). Investment in the previous year was \$100 billion; in this year it must be \$106 billion. That is, it, too, must rise by 6 percent (\$6/\$100). We confirm this fact through Equation 23-5, where we see that this rate (.06) is equal to σ times α, or the product of the productivity of capital (.3) and the propensity to save (.2). The higher the values of each, the greater is the required rate of investment growth.

Domar and Harrod doubted that annual investment growth would *automatically* be sufficient to maintain full employment. Their models therefore reinforced the Keynesian conclusion that the economy is inherently unstable. In fact, their models implied that the economy is on a "knife edge." If investment did not grow at the required or warranted rate, the economy would recede. On the other hand, if the growth of investment spending exceeded the required or warranted rate, demand-pull inflation would result.[4]

ROBERT M. SOLOW

Robert M. Solow (1924–) was born in Brooklyn, New York, and earned his doctorate from Harvard University in 1951. He has spent his entire academic career at MIT, where he has occasionally collaborated with Paul Samuelson. In 1979 he was elected president of the American Economic Association, and in 1987 he won the Nobel Prize for his earlier work on economic growth.

Solow has contributed to several facets of economics, including linear programming, macroeconomic theory, environmental economics, and labor economics. Over the years he has defended the mainstream synthesis of neoclassical microeconomics and Keynesian-based macroeconomics, sparring intellectually with advocates of monetarism, post–Keynesianism, and more recently, new classical macroeconomics. In view of his self-described "eclectic Keynesian and new–Keynesian views," it is somewhat ironic that his macroeconomic growth theory is rooted in neoclassicism, not Keynesianism.

Solow's Growth Theory

In 1956 Solow published an influential analysis of economic growth. Unlike the Harrod-Domar theory, which implied that an economy's growth path is inherently unstable, Solow's theory supported the neoclassical view that the economy adjusts internally to achieve stable equilibrium growth. The Solow growth theory contains several key elements.[5]

Production, the labor force, and balanced investment. Solow begins his analysis by establishing an aggregate production function in which technology is constant and total output depends on the capital stock and the labor input. In the short run, an increase in labor, given a fixed stock of capital, yields diminishing returns, as does an increase in capital, given a fixed number of workers. In the long run, the production function exhibits constant returns to scale. If both capital and labor increase, say, by 1 percent, output (and income) will also rise by 1 percent.

Let's suppose that the growth of the labor force increases at a constant rate n each year. The labor force thus expands by nN, where N is the labor force size at the start of the year. For example, if n is .01 (or 1 percent) and N is 200 million, then the labor force will grow by 2 million (.01 × 200 million) over the year and will be 202 million at the start of the next year.

[4] Not all economists accept the "knife-edge" interpretation of Harrod's analysis. You may wish to see J. A. Kregel, "Economic Dynamics and the Theory of Steady Growth: An Historical Essay on Harrod's 'Knife-edge,'" *History of Political Economy* 12 (Spring 1980): 97–123.

[5] Robert M. Solow, "A Contribution to the Theory of Economic Growth," *Quarterly Journal of Economics* 70 (February 1956): 65–94. Our simplified discussion follows that of Robert E. Hall and John B. Taylor, *Macroeconomics,* 5th ed. (New York: W. W. Norton, 1997), 70–74. For a mathematically based treatment of the Solow growth model, see David Romer, *Advanced Macroeconomics* (New York: McGraw-Hill, 1996), 5–25.

If the amount of *capital per worker* is to remain constant, the rate of growth of the capital stock, K, must equal the rate of growth of the labor force, n. The growth of the capital stock, of course, is net investment (gross investment minus depreciation). Net investment must therefore rise by nK each year to equal the growth of the labor force nN. For example, if n is .01 as we have supposed, and the capital stock is \$30 trillion, then net investment is \$300 billion (.01 × \$30 trillion). The addition of \$300 billion to the capital stock is just sufficient to keep the amount of capital per worker constant. We label this required amount of investment *balanced investment* because it perfectly balances the growth of the labor force and the capital stock, ensuring a constant amount of capital per worker.

Saving and actual investment. Solow assumes that saving is proportional to income ($MPS = APS$). Each year the participants in the economy save a fraction of income, s, and consume a fraction of income, $1 - s$. The saving rate, s, and the level of income, Y, together determine total saving, sY. For example, if s is .2 (or 20 percent) and income is \$2 trillion, then total saving is \$400 billion (.2 × \$2 trillion). Because net investment absorbs all saving in the economy, *actual investment* is also sY. Actual investment is the amount of net investment actually forthcoming in a year and is always the same as the amount of saving.

The steady-state point. We combine the key elements of the Solow growth theory in Figure 23-1, in which all the variables are converted to a "per-worker basis." Saving per worker (equals investment per worker) is measured on the vertical axis, whereas capital per worker is measured on the horizontal axis. Because technology is constant, output per worker depends solely on the amount of capital per worker.

The straight line BI_w in Figure 23-1 represents balanced investment. It shows the amount of investment per worker that must occur to maintain each level of capital per worker. In contrast, the saving-per-worker curve, S_w, shows the actual investment per worker occurring at each amount of capital per worker. The shape of the S_w curve reflects diminishing returns. Saving per worker rises at a diminishing rate because each added unit of capital per worker contributes smaller added increments of output and income. Smaller increments of output and income, multiplied by a constant saving rate, mean smaller increases in saving. Because net investment equals saving, actual investment rises at a diminishing rate as capital per worker increases.

The intersection of the curves yields a *steady-state point* at which actual investment equals balanced investment. At this steady-state point, capital per worker is k^*, and the growth rates of output per worker, the labor force, total saving, and net investment are all equal. At k^* the economy is on an equilibrium steady-state growth path. The existing rate of growth of real output (not shown) will continue.

Solow acknowledged that actual investment initially could be either smaller or larger than balanced investment. If either, said Solow, the economy would adjust the relative amounts of capital and labor it uses until actual investment equals balanced investment. Such capital-labor and labor-capital substitutions were missing in the Harrod-Domar growth model.

To understand the adjustment process, first consider levels of capital per worker that are less than k^* in Figure 23-1. Observe that actual investment (as determined from curve S_w) exceeds balanced investment (as determined from line BI_w).

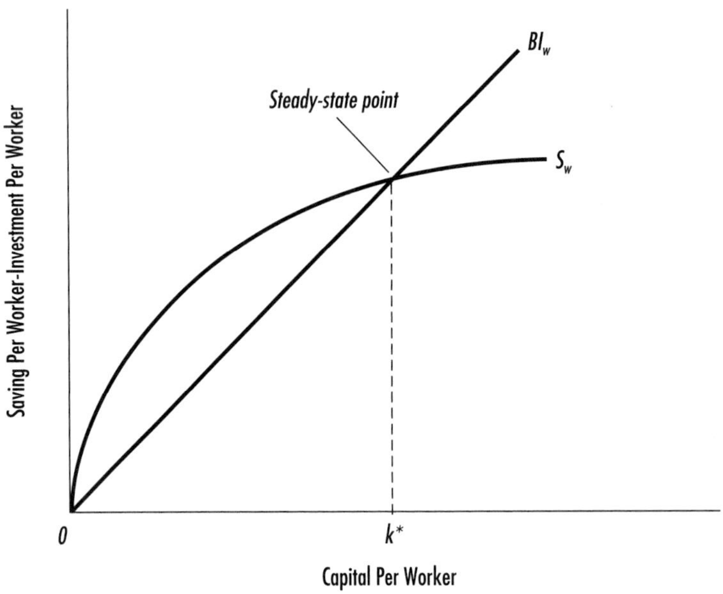

Figure 23-1 Solow's Growth Theory
According to Solow, the economy tends toward a steady-state point at which actual investment (as measured along S_w) equals balanced investment (as measured along BI_w). Balanced investment is that amount of investment needed to keep the capital stock growing at the same rate as the labor force. If actual investment exceeds balanced investment, capital per worker increases; if actual investment is less than balanced investment, capital per worker decreases. At capital per worker (k*), the growth rates of the capital stock, the labor force, and output are equal.

The capital stock therefore grows more rapidly than the labor force, and the amount of capital per worker rises. This process continues until the steady-state point is reached. There, actual investment is the same as balanced investment. And what if capital per worker is more than k*? Then actual investment is less than balanced investment, and the capital stock grows less rapidly than the labor force. Capital per worker falls until the steady-state point is reached. Solow thus shows that automatic changes in the relative uses of capital and labor enable the economy to achieve a stable growth path.

Solow on Technological Progress

Solow emphasized the importance of technological advance (held constant in Figure 23-1) to higher standards of living. For Solow, technological advance includes not only improved production techniques but also improvements in the *quality* of labor and capital. New technology is often embodied within capital; it is incorporated into new equipment and factories. When Solow introduces technological advance into his growth theory, the hypothetical economy achieves higher rates of output growth, independent of increases in the amount of capital per worker.

To test this prediction of the model, Solow developed new techniques for measuring the relative contributions of the factors causing economic growth. He found that increases in labor and capital inputs explain less than half of economic growth. The residual, he said, results from technological progress.[6]

JOSEPH ALOIS SCHUMPETER

Life and Influences

Joseph Alois Schumpeter (1883–1950), the son of a cloth manufacturer, was born in the Austrian province of Moravia (now a region in the Czech Republic) and educated in law and economics at the University of Vienna. He practiced law for several years, taught political economy, and in 1913 and 1914 was exchange professor at Columbia University. It was at this time that he and Wesley C. Mitchell began their long friendship. During World War I Schumpeter made no secret of his pacifist, pro-British, anti-German sentiments. He served briefly as minister of finance of the Austrian Republic in 1919. In 1921 he became president of a highly respected private banking house in Vienna. When the bank collapsed in 1924 after the great inflation in Germany, he returned to the academic world and accepted a professorship at the University of Bonn. From 1932 until his death he taught at Harvard, and he served as president of the American Economic Association, the first foreign-born economist to attain this distinction. His *The Theory of Economic Development* (1911), *Capitalism, Socialism, and Democracy* (1942), and his encyclopedic *History of Economic Analysis* (1954), edited by his wife after his death, are monuments to his gigantic scholarly achievements.

Two major intellectual influences in Schumpeter's life were Léon Walras and Karl Marx. From Walras, Schumpeter derived his emphasis on the interdependence of economic quantities. Schumpeter had a strong aversion to Marxism, but he admired Marx's understanding of the process of economic change. Schumpeter was deeply devoted to the institutions of capitalism, and he viewed with alarm the forces engendered by the very success of capitalism, because he thought that they would destroy the system. He agreed with Marx that capitalism would collapse, although for different reasons and with profound regret. A summary of Schumpeter's arguments can be found on the web site.

Economic Development and Business Fluctuations

Schumpeter constructed a theoretical system to explain both business cycles and the theory of economic development. The key process in economic change is the introduction of innovations, and the central innovator is the entrepreneur. Innovation is defined as changes in the methods of supplying commodities, such as introducing new goods or new methods of production; opening new markets, conquering new sources of supply of raw materials or semimanufactured goods; or carrying out a new

[6] Robert M. Solow, "Technical Change and the Aggregate Production Function," *Review of Economics and Statistics* 39 (August 1957): 312–320.

organization of industry, such as creating a monopoly or breaking one up. Innovation is much more than invention. Invention is not innovation if it is stillborn—that is, if it is not used. An invention becomes an innovation only when it is applied to industrial processes.

The entrepreneur is the person who carries out new combinations and who introduces innovations. Not all heads of firms or managers or industrialists are entrepreneurs; some may be running a business without trying new ideas or new ways of doing things. Nor are the entrepreneurs risk-takers. That function is left to the shareholders, who are typically capitalists but not entrepreneurs. Entrepreneurs may have only temporary connections with individual firms as financiers or promoters. But they are always pioneers in introducing new products, new processes, and new forms of business organization or in penetrating new markets. They are people with exceptional abilities who seize opportunities that others are oblivious to or who create opportunities through their own daring and imagination.

Without innovation, economic life would reach static equilibrium, and its circular flow would follow essentially the same channels year after year. Profit and interest would disappear, and the accumulation of wealth would cease. The entrepreneur, seeking profit through innovation, transforms this static situation into the dynamic process of economic development. This person interrupts the circular flow and diverts labor and land to investment. Because savings generated by the circular flow are inadequate, the entrepreneur relies on credit to provide the means for his enterprise. The resulting economic development arises from within the economic system itself, rather than being imposed from outside.

Innovations do not occur continuously, but rather occur in clusters. The activities of the most enterprising and venturesome entrepreneurs create a favorable climate in which others can follow. Credit expands, prices and incomes rise, and prosperity prevails. But not forever. The economic boom generates conditions unfavorable to its continued progress. Rising prices deter investment, and the competition of new products with old ones causes business losses. When businesspeople repay their debts, the deflationary process is intensified, and depression replaces prosperity. Business fluctuations therefore represent the process of adaptation to innovation. The system tends toward equilibrium, except that innovations always disrupt that tendency. The process that generates economic development also generates fluctuations, and every depression represents a struggle toward a new equilibrium.

Refer to 23-1 PAST AS PROLOGUE

Schumpeter in Retrospect

From today's perspective it is clear that Schumpeter, like Marx before him, was much too pessimistic about the near-term future of capitalism. Since the period in which Schumpeter wrote, capitalism has continued to expand and flourish in much of the world. Moreover, the collapse of communism led several former socialist economies to embrace capitalism as the ultimate goal of their reform efforts. Entrepreneurship recently has thrived throughout the world, as evidenced by highly successful startup firms and major innovations relating to personal computing, communications, genetic engineering, and the Internet.

Schumpeter's overall contribution to economics thus lies less with his views on the long-run fate of capitalism than with his emphasis on the importance of entrepreneurs

23-1 PAST AS PROLOGUE

Schumpeter, Creative Destruction, and Antitrust Policy

The standard neoclassical view of competition is that of numerous firms selling identical or similar products. When firms in a particular industry obtain high profits, new firms enter. This entry increases product supply, which reduces product price and drops profits to their normal levels. Competition, therefore, benefits consumers by producing prices that are just sufficient to cover producers' marginal and average costs of production, including normal profits. Competition benefits society by channeling society's resources to their highest valued uses.

In this neoclassical view of competition, monopoly is detrimental to consumers and society. Monopolists set higher-than-competitive prices, resulting in less-than-competitive output and an underallocation of resources to the monopolized product. For these reasons, nations have antitrust laws prohibiting dominant firms from engaging in such practices as pricing to eliminate rivals, requiring customers to exclusively buy from them, purchasing or merging with rivals, or stifling the entry of potential competitors. The United States has used antitrust laws to break up or restrict the practices of alleged monopolists such as Standard Oil (1911), Alcoa (1945), Xerox (1975), and AT&T (1982). In 1998 the government brought an antitrust suit against Microsoft, charging that it unfairly used its monopoly in the operating system market for personal computers to stifle competition in related markets.

Schumpeter took a much longer view of competition and monopoly. He emphasized that competition is a long-term process in which firms compete by developing entirely new products and processes. Monopoly cannot sustain itself over long periods because monopoly prices and profits create a powerful incentive for competing entrepreneurs to produce new products and discover new production methods. Such entrepreneurial innovation eventually results in *creative destruction;* it simultaneously *creates* new products and production methods while *destroying* existing monopoly power. As stated by Schumpeter:

> In capitalist reality . . . it is . . . competition from the new commodity, the new technology, the new source of supply, the new type of business organization—competition which commands a decisive cost or quality advantage and which strikes not at the margins of profits of the existing firms but at their foundation and their very lives. This kind of competition is . . . so . . . important that it becomes a matter of comparative indifference whether competition in the ordinary sense functions more or less promptly; the powerful lever that in the long run expands output and brings down prices is in any case made of other stuff.*

The policy implication of this long-run view of competition and monopoly differs from the neoclassical view. If creative destruction is an inevitable part of dynamic capitalism, then monopolization of an industry is of little concern. Eventually, new

23-1 PAST AS PROLOGUE (continued)

entrepreneurs will develop new products and methods rendering the old monopoly harmless. Historical examples: Airlines and trucks destroyed the monopoly of the railroads; movies brought new competition to live theater; and compact discs and cassettes replaced long-playing records. In the Schumpeterian view, government need not break up or restrict an existing monopoly because monopoly is a part of the dynamic long-run competitive process. All monopolies are temporary unless government itself protects them.

Most contemporary economists agree that creative destruction can, and occasionally does, occur. But they doubt that it is inevitable in all situations. Unimpeded by law, monopolists can "erect storm shelters . . . to shield themselves from the gales of creative destruction"[†] by taking actions to gain control over new and innovative products or prevent their development. One such action, for example, is buying out new rivals as quickly as they emerge. By preventing such anticompetitive actions, antitrust policy can contribute not only to short-run efficiency but also to the long-run process of creative destruction.

*Joseph A. Schumpeter, *Capitalism, Socialism, and Democracy,* 3rd ed. (New York: Harper & Row, 1950), 84–85.
†Walter Adams and James Brock, *The Structure of American Industry,* 9th ed. (Englewood Cliffs, NJ: Prentice-Hall), 310.

and innovation in achieving economic growth. New and improved technology, much of it commercialized by entrepreneurs, explains a large portion of the economic growth of the advanced industrial nations.

RAGNAR NURKSE

Ragnar Nurkse (1907–1959) was born in Estonia. In the early 1930s his family immigrated to Canada, and he studied at Edinburgh University and the University of Vienna. As an employee of the League of Nations, he published some distinguished studies in international economics. After World War II he accepted a professorship at Columbia University and remained there until his untimely death in Geneva while on leave of absence.

Nurkse gave renewed emphasis to external economies: The more investments made, the more viable each undertaking becomes. Therefore the low-income economies require progress on a broad front, with simultaneous expansion of industries that support each other and increase the chances of success. The great difficulty is that the poverty of countries has limited their capital formation.

The Vicious Circle of Poverty

Why do countries remain poor? asked Nurkse. His answer focused on the "vicious circle of poverty":

> The "vicious circle of poverty" . . . implies, of course, a circular constellation of forces tending to act and react upon one another in such a way as to keep a poor country in a state of poverty. Particular instances of such circular constellations are not difficult to imagine. For example, a poor man may not have enough to eat; being under-nourished, his health may be weak; being physically weak, his working capacity may be low, which means that he is poor, which in turn means that he will not have enough to eat; and so on. A situation of this sort, applying to a country as a whole, can be summed up in the trite proposition: "a country is poor because it is poor."
>
> The most important circular relationships of this kind are those that afflict the problem of capital formation in economically underdeveloped countries. The problem of economic development is largely, though by no means entirely, a problem of capital accumulation. The so-called underdeveloped areas, as opposed with the advanced, are underequipped with capital in relation to their population and natural resources.
>
> There are two sides to the problem of real capital formation: there is a demand side and supply side. The demand for capital is governed by the incentives to *invest;* the supply of capital is governed by the ability and willingness to *save*. In underdeveloped countries, a circular relationship exists on both sides of the problem. On the supply side, we have the small capacity to save, resulting from the low level of real income. But the low real income is a reflection of low productivity, which in turn is due largely to the lack of capital. The lack of capital is a result of the small capacity to save, and so the circle is complete.
>
> On the demand side, the inducement to invest may be low, because of the small buying power of the people, which is due to their small real income, which in turn is due to low productivity. The low level of productivity, however, is a result of the small amount of capital used in production, which in its turn is caused, to some extent, by the low inducement to invest.[7]

Nurkse said that it may seem surprising that there can be a deficiency in the demand for capital. "Is not the demand for capital, in most of these areas, tremendous?" he asks. His answer was "No." The incentive for private businesses to invest is severely limited by the small size of the domestic market. The size of the market is determined by the general level of productivity. Viewed in the aggregate, the "capacity to buy not only depends on, but is actually defined by, capacity to produce."

Balanced Development

Nurkse argued that if the poor countries are to advance, they must rely increasingly on industrialization instead of primarily on the production and export of raw materials. The nonindustrial countries, he said, are almost all in the low-income class, and they trade very little among themselves. The rich industrial countries show vigorous advances in real income per capita, yet they are not transmitting their own rate of growth to the rest of the world through a proportional increase in the demand for primary products. There are six major reasons for this: (1) In the advanced economies, industrial production is shifting from "heavy" to "light" industries (such

[7] Ragnar Nurkse, *Some Aspects of Capital Accumulation in Underdeveloped Countries* (Cairo: National Bank of Egypt, 1952), 1–3. Reprinted by permission of the publisher.

as engineering and chemicals) and therefore requires fewer raw materials relative to finished output; (2) as services become increasingly important in the richer countries, their raw-material demand lags behind the rise in their domestic product; (3) the income elasticity of consumer demand for many agricultural commodities tends to be low; (4) agricultural protectionism tends to reduce the imports of primary products into industrial countries; (5) substantial economies have been achieved in the industrial uses of natural materials through such developments as electrolytic tin-plating and systematic recovery and reprocessing of metals; and (6) the industrial countries have increasingly tended to displace natural raw materials with synthetics.

If primary production for export does not offer attractive opportunities for expansion, the alternative is industrialization. There can be two types of industrialization: that aimed at producing manufactured goods for export to the industrial countries and that catering mainly to domestic markets in the low-income countries. The second type generally requires a complementary advance in domestic agriculture, whereas the first does not. Neither type demands the abandonment or contraction of exports of the raw materials that a country is naturally adapted to produce.

The production of manufactured goods for export to the industrial nations offers little hope of success. Therefore low-income regions should expand the home market for finished goods. However, the size of the market depends on the volume of production. The difficulty is that the impoverished farm population cannot buy the manufactured goods offered for sale because of its own low productivity and incomes. Nor can the local economy supply the food required to sustain the new industrial workers. Therefore, industrial development for domestic markets requires a simultaneous rise of agricultural productivity on the home front.

The same principle applies within the manufacturing sphere. By itself a single industry cannot create sufficient demand for its own output because people working in new industries will not wish to spend all their income on their own products:

> Just as it is possible for manufacturing as a whole to fail if peasants can produce no marketable surplus and are too poor to buy anything from factories, so it is possible for a single branch of manufacturing to fail for lack of support from other sectors in industry as well as agriculture; that is, for lack of markets. . . . In short, while it is true that the active sectors will tend to pull the passive ones forward (and this is what some advocates of "unbalanced growth" have in mind), it is equally true that the passive sectors will tend to hold the active ones back. Would it not be better if every sector were in some measure "active" in the sense of advancing spontaneously, imbued with some expansive élan of its own instead of waiting for signals from others? Price incentives and restraints would then be needed merely to keep each sector's rate of advance in line with the community's pattern of demand. The principle of balanced expansion can be looked upon as a means of accelerating the overall rate of output growth.[8]

There are limits to the diversification of output. The need to maintain an efficient plant size is an important practical consideration that often limits the diversification of industry in any single country. Therefore manufacturing for home markets in the developing countries must also include production for export to one another's

[8] Ragnar Nurkse, *Patterns of Trade and Development* (Stockholm: Almqvist and Wiksell, 1959), 43.

markets. This is particularly important for countries with small purchasing power, which have much to gain from custom unions among developing nations.

Economic progress, said Nurkse, is not spontaneous or automatic. On the contrary, forces within the system tend to anchor it to a given level. Once the vicious circle of stagnation is broken, however, the circular relationships tend to make for cumulative advance. The synchronized investment of capital in a wide range of industries will enlarge the market for all of them, even though each industry, considered separately, would appear to be unattractive for investment. Most industries catering to mass consumption are complementary in the sense that they provide markets for each other. The social marginal productivity of capital is in essence higher than its private marginal productivity.

In low-income countries, Nurkse believed, the forces that would defeat the grip of economic stagnation must be deliberately organized through some central direction or collective enterprise. The actual investing could be undertaken by private enterprise, although the state might enforce compulsory saving and then coordinate investment. The deficiency of demand for capital arises only in the private sector of the economy. For the economy as a whole there is, of course, no such deficiency. Therefore, most developing countries will need a combination of private and government action in saving and investment. Each country must work out its own combination according to its particular needs and opportunities.

For the impoverished emerging countries today, balanced growth provides one possible path toward economic progress. The difficulty of this approach is that it requires large amounts of capital, which the poor countries have difficulty acquiring. Another option that has been proposed and implemented in some countries is promoting growth through import substitution. If a country already is importing manufacturing goods, it can erect import barriers and undertake the production of these goods at home without requiring balanced growth. Another option is to encourage foreign direct investment so as to increase the capital stock available for use by domestic workers.

W. ARTHUR LEWIS

In 1979 two prominent economists specializing in development economics shared the Nobel Prize in economics. One of these economists was Arthur Lewis (1915–1991); the other, Theodore Schultz. Lewis is the subject of our attention here.

W. Arthur Lewis was born in the British West Indies in 1915. He attended and then taught at the London School of Economics, later moving to Manchester University. In 1949 he published *The Principles of Economic Planning,* in which he warned of the impracticality of central planning and argued for planning through markets. This major work was followed in 1954 by his now-famous article on development, "Economic Development with Unlimited Supplies of Labour."[9] A year later Lewis published *The Theory of Economic Growth,* in which he emphasized the

[9] W. Arthur Lewis, "Economic Development with Unlimited Supplies of Labour," *Manchester School* 22 (May 1954): 139–191.

growth process in developing countries (as distinct from the growth theories of Harrod, Domar, and Solow, which focused on advanced capitalist countries).

Lewis held many distinguished positions during his career, including vice-chancellor of the University of West Indies, president of the Caribbean Development Bank, and president of the American Economic Association. From 1963 until his retirement, he was on the faculty of the Woodrow Wilson School of Public and International Affairs at Princeton University.

Lewis's Two-Sector Model

Lewis's dual model of economic development divides the economy into two sectors: a traditional *rural subsistence sector* and a modern *urban industrial sector*. The rural sector has so much surplus labor relative to capital and natural resources that much of this labor could be transferred to the urban sector without diminishing agricultural output. At the extreme, the marginal product of this redundant labor is zero.

The urban sector is industrialized and profitable. A portion of these profits is saved and invested in capital goods. Because of this expansion of plant and equipment, the urban sector has a growing demand for labor. It also has a substantially higher wage rate than the rural sector. Workers in the agricultural sector will, therefore, be attracted to the urban sector.

The mechanics of Lewis's model are depicted in Figure 23-2, which shows labor demand and supply in the urban industrial sector. Suppose that some fixed amount of real capital is available in this sector such that the demand for labor is D_1. This demand for labor curve is simply the marginal revenue product curve (MRP = marginal product × marginal revenue) deriving from the works of John Bates Clark (Figure 14-4a) and Alfred Marshall.

You will note that labor supply S to the urban sector in Figure 23-2 is perfectly elastic at the urban wage rate W_u. Lewis observed that the average urban wage rate in developing countries was about 30 percent higher than the average rural wage rate. Consequently, a vast supply of redundant rural labor is available to the urban industrial sector. At wage rate W_u urban employers can hire as few or as many workers as they desire.

In Figure 23-2, urban employers will choose to hire Q_1 workers because marginal revenue product at that employment level equals the wage rate (marginal resource cost). Recalling Clark, the total urban industrial output is the area under the labor demand curve D_1; it is area $a + b$. Of this amount, workers will receive area a as wages; capitalists will get the remaining area b as interest and profits.

Capitalists will reinvest a portion of their profits in new capital in the urban sector, raising labor productivity there. This increase in the marginal product of labor translates into a rightward shift in the labor demand curve, for example, from D_1 to D_2. With the new demand for labor D_2, firms in the urban sector will hire Q_2 workers. Total wages thus rise from area a to area $a + d$. Meanwhile, capitalist income increases from area b to area $b + c$. Q_1Q_2 rural workers are absorbed into the urban industrial sector, and because their marginal products were zero in the rural sector, the nation's total output jumps from area $a + b$ to area $a + b + c + d$. This process repeats itself: New reinvestment occurs, the stock of capital rises, the demand for labor increases, migration to the urban sector takes place, and national output expands.

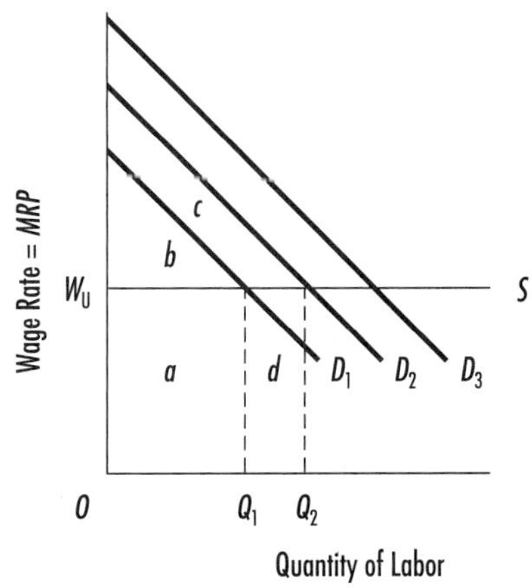

Figure 23-2 Lewis's Model of Economic Development: Unlimited Supply of Labor In the Lewis model, employers in the urban industrial sector face a perfectly elastic supply of labor curve because there is surplus labor in the rural agricultural sector (not shown) and the urban wage rate W_u exceeds the rural wage rate (not shown). If labor demand is D_1 in the urban sector, capitalists will employ Q_1 workers and earn interest and profit income shown by area *b*. Reinvestment of this income will expand the capital stock, increase labor productivity, and shift the labor demand curve rightward, say, to D_2. Thus urban employment will increase, as will total wages, capitalist income, and national output. The process will continue until the surplus labor in the rural sector is fully absorbed in the urban industrial sector.

Implications

Lewis's model helps explain how a developing nation that was previously saving and investing a small percentage of its national income converts itself into an economy voluntarily saving and investing large percentages of its national income. Once Lewis's process begins, expansion of national output and income happens rather automatically. For this reason, Lewis's two-sector model follows the tradition of Smith's classical economic theory. Nurkse's vicious circle of poverty is broken once surplus rural labor migrates to the urban industrial sector. This migration increases capitalist income, which in turn promotes greater saving and investment. The country experiences increased capital and national output without a direct shift of resources from consumer to investment goods.

Eventually, said Lewis, the entire surplus labor in the rural sector is absorbed into the urban industrial sector. The labor supply curve in Figure 23-2 then turns upward, because further expansion of demand in the urban sector will require higher wage rates to attract labor from the rural sector. At this stage of development, the neoclassical analysis of wage rates, with its downsloping labor demand curve and upsloping labor supply curve, comes to bear. Further increases in labor demand in the urban sector will increase both the wage rate and employment there.

Refer to 23-2 PAST AS PROLOGUE

Although the Lewis model has been criticized as being inapplicable to many present less-developed nations (Past as Prologue 23-2), the model roughly describes the

23-2 PAST AS PROLOGUE

The Todaro Criticisms of Lewis and Schultz

Lewis's positive view of rural-urban labor migration and Theodore Schultz's* emphasis on investment in human capital have come under fire by some development economists, particularly concerning the poorest of today's developing nations.

One prominent critic is Michael Todaro (1942–), who notes that Lewis's model does not square with the facts of development in many low-income nations. He observes that an unprecedented emigration of people from rural to urban areas has occurred in developing nations in Africa, Asia, and Latin America, yet the outcome has not been the self-sustaining growth implied by Lewis's model. Instead, the rate of rural-urban migration has swamped the capacity of urban areas to create jobs, increasing urban unemployment rates and producing urban squalor.

Lewis's model assumes that the urban wage rate will remain constant as capital expands. But Todaro notes that urban wage rates in developing countries have increased over time, both in absolute terms and relative to average rural incomes. A combination of trade-union pressure, high minimum wages (relative to average wages), and high-wage policies of multinational corporations has pushed wage rates upward in the urban sector, even in the presence of substantial unemployment stemming from rural emigration. Meanwhile, governments in developing nations have pushed the price of capital below its true costs through subsidized interest rates, favorable tax treatment, and other investment incentives. The result of overpriced labor and underpriced capital has been the widespread use of capital-intensive (labor saving), not labor-intensive (labor using), technologies. Says Todaro: "Gleaming new factories with the most modern and sophisticated automated machinery and equipment are a common feature of urban industries while idle workers congregate outside the factory gates."†

development process experienced historically by the United States and many other now-industrialized economies. Even those critical of Lewis's views recognize him as one of the most important figures in the emergence of development economics.

Questions for Study and Discussion

1. Identify and briefly state the significance of each of the following to the history of economic thought: economic growth, economic development, Domar, Domar's balanced rate of growth, Solow, steady-state point, Schumpeter, Schumpeterian innovation, Nurkse, vicious circle of poverty, Lewis, rural subsistence sector, and urban industrial sector.
2. Explain the following quote from Evsey Domar: "[I]t is not sufficient, in Keynesian terms, that savings of yesterday be invested today, or, as it is often

In brief, Todaro claims that the large increase in urban employment predicted by Lewis's model has not occurred. "For every new job created, two or three migrants who were productively occupied in rural areas may come to the city."‡ Todaro argues that the best policy for most developing countries is to reduce the flow of labor from rural to urban areas. Instead, governments of the slowly developing nations should pursue more balanced development between rural and urban sectors.

Todaro also questions Schultz's emphasis on investment in human capital in developing nations. High urban unemployment rates result in large queues of qualified workers for available jobs. At a specific market wage rate, employers typically hire those job applicants in the queue with the most advanced education. Thus workers are anxious to avail themselves of opportunities to improve their education. Responding to this demand, developing nations often allocate increasing amounts of society's scarce resources to education. However, the educational attainment and skill attainment acquired are actually above those needed for the jobs available in the developing countries. Thus investment in human capital is excessive; it simply raises the educational level of the unemployed.

Other economists in turn have countered Todaro's analysis. It is clear that substantial disagreement remains as to the character of labor markets in developing countries, the nature of rural-urban migration, and appropriate public policy. As stated by Lewis in 1984: "If conflict and disputes are indices of intellectual activity, our subject [development economics] seems adequately contentious."§

---

*Theodore Schultz's biography and contributions to human capital theory can be found on the text web site.

†Michael P. Todaro, *Economic Development in the Third World*, 3rd ed. (New York: Longman, 1985), 242.

‡Todaro, 262.

§W. Arthur Lewis, "The State of Development Theory," *American Economic Review* 74 (March 1984): 10.

expressed, that investment offset saving. Investment of today must always exceed saving of yesterday."

3. Suppose the relevant data for a no-government, no-foreign sector economy was as follows: (a) $\alpha = .25$, (b) $\sigma = .1$, and (c) equilibrium income in period 1 = \$600 billion. Use Domar's model to determine the percentage rate of growth of investment that would be required to maintain full employment. What would be the level of income in period 2? By how many millions of dollars would investment spending have to increase in period 3?
4. Distinguish between balanced investment and actual investment in Solow's growth theory. Explain: Each point on the BI_w curve in Figure 23-1 *could be* a steady-state point, but only one point on the curve *is* the steady-state point.
5. How would one show an increase in the saving rate in the Solow model (Figure 23-1)? Why will k^* no longer be the steady-state amount of capital per

worker? Explain the adjustment that will take place to achieve the new steady-state amount of capital per worker.

6. What does Nurkse mean when he says that a country is poor because it is poor? Why does the circular relationship implied by the previous statement offer hope for cumulative advance once a country breaks the grip of poverty?
7. What are the two sectors in Lewis's model? How are increases in labor demand explained in his model? Why does national output rise when labor migrates?
8. What are the major criticisms of the Lewis model?

Selected Readings

Books

Domar, Evsey D. *Essays in the Theory of Economic Growth.* New York: Oxford University Press, 1957.

Harrod, Roy F. *Toward a Dynamic Analysis.* New York: St. Martin's Press, 1966. (Orig. pub. 1948.)

Lewis, W. Arthur. *The Principles of Economic Planning.* London: Allen and Unwin, 1949.

———. *The Theory of Economic Growth.* Homewood, IL: Richard D. Irwin, 1955.

Nurkse, Ragnar. *Patterns of Trade and Development.* Stockholm: Almqvist and Wiksell, 1959.

———. *Some Aspects of Capital Accumulation in Underdeveloped Countries.* Cairo: National Bank of Egypt, 1952.

Rawls, John. *A Theory of Justice.* Cambridge, MA: Harvard University Press, 1971.

Schultz, Theodore W. *The Economic Value of Education.* New York: Columbia University Press, 1963.

———. *Transforming Traditional Agriculture.* New Haven, CT: Yale University Press, 1964.

Schumpeter, Joseph A. *Capitalism, Socialism, and Democracy,* 3rd ed. New York: Harper, 1950. (Orig. pub. 1942.)

———. *History of Economic Analysis.* Edited from manuscripts by Elizabeth B. Schumpeter. New York: Oxford University Press, 1954.

———. *The Theory of Economic Development.* Translated by Redvers Opie. New York: Oxford University Press, 1961. (Orig. pub. 1911.)

Seidl, Christian, ed. *Lectures on Schumpeterian Economics: Schumpeter's Centenary Memorial Lectures, Graz 1983.* New York: Springer, 1984.

Sen, Amartya K. *Collective Choice and Social Welfare.* San Francisco: Holden-Day, 1970.

———. *On Inequality.* New York: Oxford University Press, 1973.

Journal Articles

Bowman, Mary J. "On Theodore W. Schultz's Contributions to Economics," *Scandinavian Journal of Economics* 82, no. 1 (1980): 80–107.

Domar, Evsey D. "Expansion and Employment," *American Economic Review* 37 (March 1947): 34–55.

Findlay, Ronald. "On W. Arthur Lewis' Contributions to Economics," *Scandinavian Journal of Economics* 82, no. 1 (1980): 62–76.

Lewis, W. Arthur. "Economic Development with Unlimited Supplies of Labour," *Manchester School* 22 (May 1954): 139–191.

———. "The State of Development Theory," *American Economic Review* 74 (March 1984): 1–10.

Parayil, Govindan. "Schumpeter on Invention, Innovation and Technological Change," *Journal of the History of Economic Thought* 13 (Spring 1991): 78–89.

Schultz, Theodore W. "Investment in Human Capital," *American Economic Review* 51 (March 1961): 1–17.

Sen, Amartya K., and Prasanta K. Pattanaik. "Necessary and Sufficient Conditions for Rational Choice under Majority Decision," *Journal of Economic Theory* 1 (August 1969): 178-202.

Solow, Robert M. "A Contribution to the Theory of Economic Growth," *Quarterly Journal of Economics* 70 (February 1956): 65–94.

———. "Technical Change and the Aggregate Production Function," *Review of Economics and Statistics* 39 (August 1957): 312–320.

Chapter 24

THE CHICAGO SCHOOL—THE NEW CLASSICISM

The modern phase of the Chicago school of economics began in 1946 when Milton Friedman joined the faculty at the University of Chicago.[1] He and George Stigler, who arrived in 1948, firmly established the school's unique identity. Gary Becker, Robert Lucas, and several other prominent economists at Chicago have continued the tradition, as have economists holding widely scattered positions in academia, business, and government. Thus the ideas associated with the Chicago school are no longer exclusively confined to the university that gave the school its name.

We will discover that the tenets of the Chicago school fit within the broader classical-neoclassical tradition. The Chicago perspective is a variant of neoclassicism and is referred to as the "new classicism."

After providing an overview of the modern Chicago school, we discuss the works of three of its main figures: Friedman, Lucas, and Becker. In Past as Prologue 24-1, we discuss the economics of information associated with Stigler. Also, Ronald Coase (Past as Prologue 20-1) and Theodore Schultz (Past as Prologue 23-2) taught at Chicago.

OVERVIEW OF THE CHICAGO SCHOOL

The Historical Background of the Chicago School

Many of the important developments in economic thought since the time of Marshall stimulated, or at least rationalized, greater government involvement in the economy. Pigou's idea of externalities implied that government could improve the allocation of resources through selective taxes and subsidies. Robinson's theory of monopsony suggested that government should establish a minimum wage and promote labor unionism. The theories of imperfect competition and monopoly power led many to conclude that government's regulatory role in the economy ought to be expanded. Natural monopolies were to be regulated as public utilities, and unnatural monopolies broken up through antitrust actions. Because of a lack of competition, regulators need to monitor the conduct of firms in order to prevent outcomes inconsistent with the nation's efficiency and equity goals. The economic theory of

[1] Frank Knight (1885–1972), who along with Coase challenged Pigou's theory of social cost, and Henry Simons (1900–1946), who was a strong proponent of laissez-faire, were earlier contributors to what has become the Chicago tradition. So, too, was Jacob Viner (Past as Prologue 14-1). A good summary of their contributions is found in William Breit and Roger L. Ransom, *The Academic Scribblers,* rev. ed., chaps. 12 and 13 (Chicago: Dryden, 1982).

market socialism convinced many that the state could just as efficiently allocate resources and produce goods and services as could private enterprises. Widely accepted theories of economic development implied that government was the only available instrumentality for breaking the vicious cycle of poverty in developing countries. The Keynesian revolution had firmly taken root. Its basic premise that the government should use fiscal, monetary, and incomes policies to stabilize the economy became the new conventional wisdom. Rationales for government redistribution of income had emerged from both marginalist and Keynesian analyses.

Members of the Chicago school opposed this entire line of reasoning. In the earlier years of this school, its adherents made little progress in convincing others. The proponents of the Chicago perspective were advancing against a strong intellectual and historical tide. But the economic experience of the 1970s cast doubt on the validity of several aspects of the new economic orthodoxy. The tide ebbed and turned, placing the adherents of the Chicago view at the forefront of a new surge of intellectual ideas, with numerous younger economists following their lead.

Major Tenets of the Chicago School

The main principles and characteristics of the Chicago school may be summarized as follows:

- Optimizing behavior. Members of the Chicago school stress the neoclassical principle that people attempt to maximize their well-being; that is, they engage in optimizing behavior at the time of their decisions. The basic economic unit is the individual. Individuals combine into larger units—families, political interest groups, business organizations—as a way to achieve gains from specialization and exchange. Preferences tend to be stable and independent of prices. People make rational choices, although such choices do not always produce the results expected. Benefits and costs are uncertain. To reduce this uncertainty, the decision maker seeks information, but only to the point where the marginal benefit from the extra information equals the marginal cost of obtaining it. Consumers, workers, and firms respond to monetary incentives and disincentives.
- Observed prices and wages in general tend to be good approximations of their long-run competitive ones.[2] Prices and wages reflect opportunity costs to society at the margin. Divergences between actual and competitive prices caused by monopoly or monopsony are in general inconsequential. Monopoly prices persist in the long run only in instances where government blocks competitive entry. Even in those instances, competition will eventually generate new products and technologies that will undermine the monopolist's position. Establishing clear property rights and encouraging private negotiations can minimize externalities. Institutional arrangements—seniority pay, large executive salaries, union contracts, and so forth—that on the surface appear to set wages and prices independently of market forces usually exist because the parties involved see them as being efficient.

[2] This characteristic of the Chicago school is stressed by Melvin W. Reder in "Chicago Economics: Permanence and Change," *Journal of Economic Literature* 20 (March 1982): 1–38. This is the single best article on the Chicago school.

- Mathematical orientation. The Chicago school relies heavily on mathematical theorizing (unlike the neo–Austrians, for example), using both the Marshallian partial equilibrium method and the Walrasian general equilibrium approach. Empirical verification is stressed but sometimes left to others.
- Rejection of Keynesianism. The economy is self-adjusting and regulating, with minor fluctuations being self-limiting. Severe recessions and depressions result from inappropriate monetary policy, not from autonomous changes in spending. Changes in the money stock cause direct changes in the nominal gross domestic product, rather than operating exclusively through financial interest rates. Fiscal policy is generally ineffective, unless accompanied by changes in the money supply, and even in the latter case is impotent in the presence of rational expectations. The theory of seller's or cost-push inflation is erroneous because inflation is always and everywhere a monetary phenomenon.
- Limited government. Government is inherently inefficient as an agent for achieving objectives that can be satisfied through private exchange. Government officials have their own objectives that they seek to optimize and therefore inevitably divert a portion of the resources at their disposal to purposes other than those that benefit taxpayers. Rather than being in the public interest, government regulation normally benefits those who seek the regulation or those who learn to marshal it to their private advantage.

Whom Did the Chicago School Benefit or Seek to Benefit?

Advocates of the Chicago view helped convince the general population and elected officials that the competitive market system, left relatively free of government interference, produces maximum economic freedom, which in turn yields maximum individual and collective economic well-being. To the extent that this proposition is valid, the Chicago view benefits society at large.

Many corporate interests have benefited from the broader acceptance of Chicago views. Indeed some have championed and helped disseminate these ideas. The new classical economists have helped make the case for less government regulation and paperwork. They have also claimed, much to the delight of many corporations, that monopoly is inconsequential or short-lived, that corporate mergers are a necessary element in the "market for corporate control," and that advertising helps produce the competitive outcome by providing information about the alternatives from which consumers can choose. One also could argue that, by making the case that the tax system should be used to raise revenues and not to redistribute income, the Chicago economists have benefited high-income groups.

The Chicago school tenets, however, "cut two ways." For example, they preclude government actions such as providing loans for firms going bankrupt or imposing import quotas on foreign goods. Likewise, they oppose artificial barriers such as unnecessary licensures that increase remuneration in some occupations by making it difficult for new practitioners to enter.

On the other hand, groups and individuals who rely on government for subsidy, employment, regulation, or special legislation stand to lose by the political acceptance of Chicago school policies. For example, farm interests that advocate government price supports and subsidies have opposed the Chicago perspective. Unions or professional groups that represent government employees also have strongly voiced their displeasure with Chicago-style economics. Government officials who derive their personal employment and income from government regulations of economic activity also resist these ideas.

Although many of the more recent economists of the Chicago school are apolitical, the school as a whole served the cause of political conservatism in the United States. As stated by Melvin W. Reder, himself a member of the Chicago school:

> The remarkable success of the Chicago School during the third quarter of this century was due in large part to the fact that it was able to take a leading role both in scientific research and in providing for political conservatism. That it could fill this dual role was due to the fortunate combination of scientific talent and expository skill possessed by both Friedman and Stigler, but perhaps even more to the bankruptcy of intellectual conservatism at the end of World War II.
>
> The combined effect of the Great Depression in discrediting laissez-faire capitalism, and of Hitler in rendering suspect every type of nationalistic-conservative doctrine, was to leave the political right with very little intellectual support. While there were other spokesmen for laissez-faire (e.g., the Mises group), the professional esteem and academic positions of [the Chicago economists], as well as their skill in non-technical communication, gave them a tremendous advantage in competing for attention and support from the conservative public during the decades following 1945.[3]

How Was the Chicago School Valid, Useful, or Correct in Its Time?

The Keynesian revolution tended to put the advancement of microeconomics on hold, many of the best scholars in the profession directing their attention toward expanding the Keynesian system of ideas. Included were such prominent earlier microeconomists as Joan Robinson and John R. Hicks. The Chicago school, in a sense, maintained and strengthened the marginalist tradition at a time when it had diminished popularity. It helped preserve the long legacy of classical and neoclassical economics, while the Keynesian revolution was dominating the intellectual scene. This is not to suggest that the Keynesian revolution has ended. But it is to suggest that economists have once again turned to microeconomic analysis to expand their insights into the issues of the day, including those that previously seemed to be the exclusive domain of macroeconomic theorists. For example, the analysis of unemployment now includes emphasis on the microeconomic theories of job search and intertemporal substitution between work and leisure.

The Chicago school was also useful in its time by keeping alive the monetary views of Fisher during a period when they easily could have become permanently buried by the weight of Keynesian ideas. The rapid inflation of the 1970s and early 1980s turned the nation's attention away from the main concern of Keynesianism—unemployment—to the concern of Fisher and Friedman—inflation. The simultaneous

[3] Reder, "Chicago Economics," 35.

inflation and unemployment of this same period led many Keynesians to call for incomes policies, although they acknowledged that such policies would likely produce negative side-effects on efficiency. The new classicists, arguing that the long-run trade-off between inflation and unemployment was illusory, preserved the optimistic classical perspective that economic efficiency, price stability, and a natural rate of full employment are mutually attainable.

Which Tenets of the Chicago School Became Lasting Contributions?

Because of the recent vintage of several of the ideas associated with the new classical school, it perhaps is premature to judge which, if any, will become lasting contributions to economics. For example, monetarism lost much of its support during the 1980s and 1990s. Suffice it to say, however, that the new classical ideas have already penetrated deeply into the curriculum of U.S. universities. For example, the major textbooks on principles of economics all have chapters on the new classical macroeconomic perspective, including discussions of a natural rate of unemployment, rational expectations, a long-run vertical Phillips curve, and short-run versus long-run aggregate supply. The Chicago theories of human capital, household production, job search, and discrimination all are discussed within textbooks on contemporary labor economics. The case for flexible foreign exchange rates is standard fare in international economics textbooks. The Coase theorem of externalities (Past as Prologue 20-1), although still controversial, is treated in textbooks on public finance and environmental economics. In short, several of the ideas presented by members of the Chicago school, broadly defined, appear likely to be of lasting value. Nevertheless, a final assessment of these contributions must await the scrutiny of our children and grandchildren.

MILTON FRIEDMAN

Milton Friedman (1912–), the leading figure of the Chicago view, completed his undergraduate work at Rutgers University and received his graduate degrees from the University of Chicago and Columbia University. While at Chicago as a student he was greatly influenced by Frank Knight. In 1948 Friedman joined the faculty at Chicago and remained there until his retirement in 1977. Upon leaving Chicago, he served as a senior fellow at the Hoover Institution at Stanford University. He was president of the American Economic Association in 1967 and won the Nobel Prize in economics in 1976. Friedman's ideas are known to a wide spectrum of the American public. He has served as a columnist for *Newsweek,* written popular books, participated in an educational television series, and delivered addresses to numerous groups.

Consumption Function

In 1957 Friedman published *A Theory of the Consumption Function,* in which he suggested that the Keynesian consumption function is too simplistic:

> Consider a large number of men all earning $100 a week and spending $100 a week on current consumption. Let them receive their pay once a week, the pay days being staggered, so that one-seventh are paid on Sunday, one-seventh on Monday, and so on. Suppose we collected budget data for a sample of these men for one day chosen at random, defined income as cash receipts on that day, and defined consumption as cash expenditures. One-seventh of the men would be recorded as having an income of $100, six-sevenths as having an income of zero. It may well be that the men would spend more on pay day than on other days but they would also make expenditures on other days, so we would record the one-seventh with an income of $100 as having positive savings, the other six-sevenths as having negative savings. . . . These results tell us nothing meaningful about consumption behavior; they simply reflect the use of inappropriate concepts of income and consumption. Men do not adapt their cash expenditures on consumption to their [short-term] cash receipts.[4]

Friedman pointed out that lengthening the period of observation from a day to a week would eliminate the error in this simple example. But in terms of actual consumption-income data, the use of a period of even one year fails to correct the problem.

According to Friedman, a household's consumption is determined by *permanent* income rather than *current* income, where permanent income is defined as the average income that people expect to receive over a period of years. People attempt to maintain a reasonably stable standard of living from one year to the next, and changes in income that are considered to be temporary or transitory will neither greatly increase nor decrease people's present consumption. Stated differently, consumption does *not* respond to every change in income caused by changes in investment or government spending; it responds only to changes in income that people view to be permanent and long-lasting. The implication is that the marginal propensity to consume out of changes in current income is smaller than the Keynesian theory would suggest. This means that the investment multiplier is small, which in turn implies that the alleged internal instability in the economy is overstated.[5]

Monetary Theory

Friedman is best known for his ideas on the role of money in the economy. In this regard he has discussed several interrelated topics, including the demand for money, the quantity theory of money, the causes of the Great Depression, the ineffectiveness of fiscal policy, the long-run vertical Phillips curve, and the "monetary rule."

The demand for money. Friedman views the demand for money as the demand for cash balances. People demand cash balances because they provide utility to the holder. Unlike Keynes, Friedman made no distinction between types of money, that is, between idle versus active balances or transaction versus speculative balances. There are

[4] Milton Friedman, *A Theory of the Consumption Function* (Princeton, NJ: Princeton University Press, 1957), 220.

[5] In 1963 Albert Ando of the University of Pennsylvania and Franco Modigliani of MIT developed a similar theory in which consumption is related to income over people's entire lifetime. Like Friedman's hypothesis, this "life-cycle" theory implies that consumption in a given period may be less sensitive to changes in current income than some Keynesians suggested. Albert Ando and Franco Modigliani, "The 'Life Cycle' Hypothesis of Saving: Aggregate Implications and Tests," *American Economic Review* 53 (March 1963): 55–84. Modigliani won the Nobel Prize in economics in 1985 for his work.

three major determinants of the amount of money households and enterprises will desire to hold at any given time. These determinants are independent of factors that influence the supply of money.

- Total wealth. Total wealth in all forms, including human capital, can best be measured by permanent income. As wealth, or permanent income, increases, the amount of money people desire to hold as cash balances also increases.
- Cost of holding money. The second major determinant of money demand is the cost of holding money. Higher costs will result in less money being held. These costs vary with the interest rate, the expected rate of inflation, and the price level.

  One cost of holding money consists of the direct "interest rate" foregone on other forms of wealth that could be held. If the returns on nonmoney assets such as stocks and bonds rise, the opportunity cost of holding money rises, and less money is demanded. In general, however, the quantity of money demanded is insensitive to changes in the interest rate. The yield spread between returns on transaction (money) and nontransaction (stocks, bonds) forms of wealth is relatively stable. For example, when interest rates in general increase, banks compete to maintain their checkable accounts either by offering higher interest on these accounts or by increasing noncash benefits (quality of service, convenience, "no cost" safe deposit boxes). Consequently, the relative opportunity cost of holding money does not change significantly with changes in the interest rate in the economy, and the demand for money is interest inelastic.

  Another cost of holding money relates to the expected rate of inflation. This is the opportunity cost of foregone capital gains on real assets; it is the "return" sacrificed on assets that appreciate in value. Higher expected rates of inflation enhance the prospects for capital gains and thus increase this cost of holding money. Therefore, people reduce their present cash balances when they expect higher inflation.

  A final cost of holding money relates to the price *level* (as distinct from the expected rate of inflation). The higher the price level, the less the nominal cost of holding money because each dollar held will buy less. Increases in the price level, say, as measured by the Consumer Price Index, cause proportionate increases in the amount of money demanded. People will desire to increase their cash balances to keep them constant in real terms; that is, they will want to hold more cash to buy the higher-priced goods.
- Preferences. Preferences, or basic attitudes, about holding and using cash are the third major determinant of money demand. Friedman asserts that these preferences remain relatively constant "over significant stretches of space and time."

In summary, Friedman says that the amount of money demanded varies directly with permanent real income and the price level, inversely with the expected rate of inflation, and insignificantly with changes in the rate of interest.

The modern quantity theory of money. According to Friedman, the demand for money is relatively stable in the short run. The Federal Reserve System controls the supply of money. An increase in the supply of money will leave people holding cash balances in excess of amounts they want. They will attempt to rid themselves of these excess transaction assets by spending cash and writing checks. But the community as a whole cannot rid itself of excess cash balances; one person's spending leaves more cash in someone else's billfold or checkbook. Thus the attempt by people to rid themselves of cash balances will drive up the demand for goods and services and increase output, prices, or some combination of each. In circumstances wherein the economy is operating at its natural levels of employment and output, only prices will rise over the long run. As the price level rises, the demand for money increases (recall our previous discussion) because the community desires to hold additional money to buy the higher-priced goods. Eventually, equilibrium between the quantity of money supplied and demanded is restored, but at a higher price level.

Thus, according to Friedman, the modern quantity theory of money is established. It does not assume that velocity is a constant as did the older quantity theory, but rather that the demand for money is "highly stable—more stable than functions such as the consumption function that are offered as alternative key relations." Inflation, stated Friedman, "is always and everywhere a monetary phenomenon, produced in the first instance by an unduly rapid growth in the quantity of money."[6] This relationship between the money stock and prices, said Friedman, is confirmed by empirical evidence. Referring to studies done by others, he stated in 1956:

> There is perhaps no other empirical relation in economics that has been observed to recur so uniformly under so wide a variety of circumstances as the relation between substantial changes over short periods in the stock of money and in prices; the one is invariably linked with the other and is in the same direction; this uniformity is, I suspect, of the same order as many of the uniformities that form the basis of the physical sciences.[7]

In 1963 Friedman and Anna Schwartz published *A Monetary History of the United States, 1867–1960,* in which they presented their own empirical findings linking the growth of the money stock and the rate of inflation. Friedman considers this to be his most important book.

The cause of the Great Depression. In Chapter 7 of their book, Friedman and Schwartz reached the controversial conclusion that monetary policy was largely responsible for causing the Great Depression of the 1930s.[8] Later, Friedman expressed his position as follows:

> Keynes and most other economists of the time believed that the Great Contraction in the United States occurred despite aggressive expansionary policies by the monetary authorities—that they did their best but their best was not good enough. Recent studies have demonstrated that the facts are precisely the reverse: the U.S. monetary authorities followed highly deflationary policies. The quantity of money in the United States fell by one-third in the course of the contraction. And it fell not because there were no willing borrowers—not because the horse would not drink. It fell because the Federal Reserve System forced or permitted a sharp reduction in the monetary base,

[6] Milton Friedman, *Dollars and Deficits* (Englewood Cliffs, NJ: Prentice-Hall, 1968), 18.

[7] Milton Friedman, "The Quantity Theory of Money—A Restatement," in *Studies in the Quantity Theory of Money,* ed. Milton Friedman (Chicago: University of Chicago Press, 1956), 20–21.

[8] This chapter was published separately as the central portion of Friedman and Schwartz's *The Great Contraction* (Princeton University Press, 1963).

because it failed to exercise the responsibilities assigned to it in the Federal Reserve Act to provide liquidity to the banking system. The Great Contraction is tragic testimony to the power of monetary policy—not as Keynes and so many of his contemporaries believed, evidence of impotence.[9]

The long-run vertical Phillips curve. Recall that Wicksell had differentiated between the actual and natural rates of interest. Friedman said there is a similar distinction between the actual and natural rates of unemployment: "I use the term 'natural' for the same reason Wicksell did—to try to separate the real forces from monetary forces."[10] The natural rate of unemployment, said Friedman, is the one that will occur when the actual rate of inflation and the expected rate of inflation are equal. Authorities can push the actual rate of unemployment temporarily below the natural rate only by generating a level of inflation that is greater than expected. But once people adjust their expectations to the new higher rate of inflation, the natural rate of unemployment will return.

Friedman's analysis is formalized in Figure 24-1.[11] Our expository approach first will be to establish a short-run Phillips curve and then to explain how such short-run curves can shift upward to produce a vertical long-run curve.

Initially, let's focus on the short-run Phillips curve $SRPC_1$ in Figure 24-1. Suppose that the rate of inflation is P_1 and unemployment is at the natural rate U_n (point *a*). Next suppose that the monetary authorities desire to peg the actual rate of unemployment at U_1, in a sense indicating a willingness to trade off higher inflation (P_2 rather than P_1) for a lower rate of unemployment. Suppose that the monetary authorities increase the stock of money to accomplish this. This eventually raises the rate of inflation to P_2, and temporarily reduces unemployment to U_1 (point *b*). The reasons? Firms discover that their product prices are rising faster than their unit labor costs. The labor contracts under which many employees are working were set on the expectation that inflation would continue to be P_1. Because prices rise and nominal wages remain unchanged, real wage rates fall and employers respond by increasing employment. In addition, unemployed workers seeking jobs begin to receive higher nominal wage offers as firms bid for new employees. If workers mistake these nominal wage increases for better real wage offers, they will shorten the length of time they search for jobs. The result will be a lower rate of frictional unemployment. Conclusions: (1) When the actual rate of inflation exceeds the expected rate (P_2 rather than P_1), unemployment will fall (U_n to U_1); and (2) points on a short-run Phillips curve (for example, $SRPC_1$) show the various rates of unemployment associated with rates of actual inflation that differ from the expected rate.

The economy will not stay at *b* on $SRPC_1$, said Friedman. People adjust their expectations to the higher rate of inflation, P_2, and expect it to continue. Once such

[9] Milton Friedman, *The Optimum Quantity of Money and Other Essays* (Chicago: Aldine, 1969), 97. Be aware that this view remains controversial; Peter Temin tested the Friedman view empirically and concluded that monetary forces did *not* cause the Great Depression. See his *Did Monetary Forces Cause the Great Depression?* (New York: Norton, 1976).

[10] Milton Friedman, "The Role of Monetary Policy," in *The Optimum Quantity of Money and Other Essays* (Chicago: Aldine, 1969), 105. This paper was presented as the Presidential Address to the American Economic Association in 1967.

[11] Friedman developed the ideas underlying this figure in his Nobel lecture reprinted as "Inflation and Unemployment," *Journal of Political Economy* 85 (June 1977): 451–472.

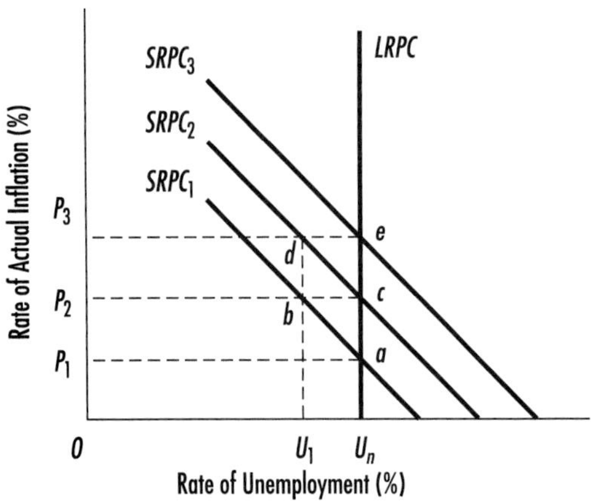

Figure 24-1 Friedman's Long-Run Vertical Phillips Curve
Each short-run Phillips curve shows the combinations of inflation and unemployment that are possible when the actual rate of inflation diverges from the expected rate. When inflation is greater than expected, such as P_2 rather than P_1, unemployment temporarily falls below its natural rate (from U_n to U_1, as shown at *b*). But once P_2 becomes the new expected rate, the short-run Phillips curve shifts from $SRPC_1$ to $SRPC_2$ and the rate of unemployment returns to its natural level (point *c*). In the long run, said Friedman, there is no trade-off between inflation and unemployment. The long-run Phillips curve is vertical, indicating that any one of several rates of inflation is compatible with the natural rate of unemployment.

an adjustment has taken place, the short-run Phillips curve shifts upward to $SRPC_2$. Higher rates of expected inflation translate into higher locations of the short-run Phillips curve. As old contracts expire, wages rise, real labor costs rise to their former levels, firms discharge workers, and the natural rate of unemployment gets reestablished (point *c*). The natural rate now is associated with a higher actual and expected rate of inflation.

Suppose that the monetary authorities try to reestablish the U_1 rate of unemployment. By increasing the money supply, they can once again temporarily achieve this (point *d*). But the employment gains are short-lived. The short-run Phillips curve shifts upward to $SRPC_3$, and the economy moves to point *e*. In the long run there is no trade-off between inflation and unemployment. The Phillips curve (*LRPC*) is perfectly vertical at the natural rate of unemployment. Monetary authorities can reduce unemployment below its natural rate in the long run only by continuously increasing the rate of inflation. In Friedman's words:

> To state the conclusion differently, there is always a temporary trade-off between inflation and unemployment; there is no permanent trade-off. The temporary trade-off comes not from inflation *per se*, but from unanticipated inflation, which generally means, from a rising rate of inflation. The widespread belief that there is a permanent trade-off is a sophisticated version of the confusion between "high" and "rising" that we all

> recognize in its simpler forms. A rising rate of inflation may reduce unemployment, a high rate will not.[12]

The monetary rule. Recall that Lerner had likened the economy to a car without a steering wheel (Review Past as Prologue 22-1). To avoid bouncing off one curb and then the other, the car needed a steering wheel—functional finance—used by a skillful driver. Friedman countered as follows:

> What we need is not a skillful monetary driver of the economic vehicle continuously turning the wheel to adjust to the unexpected irregularities of the route, but some means of keeping the monetary passenger who is in the back seat as ballast from occasionally leaning over and giving the steering wheel a jerk that threatens to send the car off the road.[13]

The car will get down the road just fine, as long as the government does not destabilize it. The Federal Reserve should abandon its use of discretionary monetary policy and adhere to the monetary rule: Increase the money supply annually at a steady rate roughly corresponding to the long-run rate of growth of capacity. There are four reasons such a rule is needed.

- The past performance of the Fed. According to Friedman, "Throughout its history, the Fed has proclaimed that it was using its powers to promote economic stability. But the record does not support this claim. On the contrary the Fed has been a major source of instability."[14]
- Limitations of economic knowledge. There are time lags between changes in the money stock and changes in output and prices, and these time lags are themselves variable and unpredictable. Attempts to fine tune the economy are just as likely to add to instability as to correct for it.
- Confidence. A monetary rule would enable businesses, consumers, and workers to make contracts with the confidence that the Fed was not going to later surprise them.
- Neutralization of the Fed. "A monetary rule would insulate monetary policy both from the arbitrary power of a group of men not subject to control by the electorate and from the short-run pressures of partisan politics."[15]

Economic Liberalism

Friedman has described himself as a nineteenth-century liberal. He is referring, of course, to the economic liberalism that we associate with the classical economists who emphasized economic freedom. Thus over the years he has advocated a series of reforms that would place less reliance on government and more reliance on the market. The market system protects not only *economic* freedom, said Friedman, but

[12] Friedman, "Monetary Policy," 104.

[13] Milton Friedman, *A Program for Monetary Stability* (New York: Fordham University Press, 1959), 23.

[14] Milton Friedman, *An Economist's Protest: Columns in Political Economy* (Glen Ridge, NJ: Thomas Horton, 1972), 65.

[15] Friedman, *Economist's Protest,* 66.

also *political* freedom. "Can a nation truly have political freedom where the printing presses are owned by the state and where workers are employed by the state?" asked Friedman. His answer was "No."

Several of Friedman's reforms have been enacted; others are still the subject of public debate. Examples of his proposals include an international system of flexible, market-determined foreign exchange rates; a U.S. all-volunteer army; less strict interpretation of the antitrust laws; the end to the nation's experiments with incomes policies; a negative income tax; educational vouchers that would give parents a choice as to the schools to which they send their children; a flat rate income tax; legalization of recreational drugs; and "privatization" of numerous public services.

Refer to 24-1 PAST AS PROLOGUE

Friedman's admirers and critics alike agree that he has helped establish that money "matters" in the economy. They also would agree that Friedman himself has "mattered," or made a difference, in both the history of economic thought and the course of public policy. As stated by Samuelson: "If Milton Friedman had not existed, it would have been necessary to invent him."

ROBERT E. LUCAS JR.

Robert E. Lucas Jr. (1937–) was born in Yakima, Washington, and earned his B.A. and Ph.D. degrees at the University of Chicago. During his early graduate studies he was influenced by Friedman, who taught first-year microeconomics in the graduate program, and by Samuelson's *Foundations of Economic Analysis.* Lucas has commented: "*Foundations* says, 'Here is the way you do it [economic analysis].' It lets you in on the secret of how you play the game, as opposed to cutting you off with big words. I think the combination of Samuelson's book and Friedman's class was what got me going."[16]

Lucas spent the first eleven years of his career at Carnegie-Mellon and then in 1974 returned to Chicago. In 1995 he was awarded the Nobel Prize in economics for his contributions to macroeconomics. In an ironic twist, his ex-spouse received one-half of his $1 million prize because seven years earlier she had inserted a clause in the divorce agreement to cover just such a possibility. The clause was set to expire in 1996.

Rational Expectations

Friedman's theory of the inflation-unemployment relationship (Figure 24-1) is based on the assumption of *adaptive expectations.* People determine their expectations about future inflation on the basis of past and present inflation and change their expectations only as new events unfold. Lucas goes beyond Friedman's analysis, saying that economic agents form *rational expectations* about future outcomes of current stabilization policy. Although the idea of rational expectations was not original, it was Lucas who developed its implications for macroeconomic theory and policy.[17]

[16] Arlo Kramer, *Conversations with Economists* (Totowa, NJ: Rowman & Allanheld, 1983), 30.

[17] John J. Muth originated the idea of rational expectations in his "Rational Expectations and the Theory of Price Movements," *Econometrica* 29 (July 1961). Lucas's contributions are compiled in *Studies in Business-Cycle Theory* (Cambridge, MA: MIT Press, 1981) and *Models of Business Cycles* (Oxford, England: Basil Blackwell, 1987). Thomas Sargent and Neil Wallace also contributed significantly to the rational expectations theory.

24-1 PAST AS PROLOGUE

From Stigler to "Lemons"

In the early 1960s Chicago-school economist George J. Stigler (1911–1992) pointed out that information is an economic good. Consumers decide how much of it to obtain by comparing marginal benefit and marginal cost.*

Consider an example of a consumer in the market for a new car. The marginal benefit (MB) of more information includes the utility associated with locating a particular brand and style that matches one's wants, as well as that associated with discovering a low price. Although the total benefit rises as more information is obtained, the marginal benefit of additional information declines. In contrast, the marginal cost (MC) of additional information generally rises as consumers obtain more of it. Such costs include transportation and other search expenses, the opportunity cost of time, and the utility sacrificed by delaying the purchase.

The consumer seeks out all units of information for which marginal benefit exceeds marginal cost, and the search process ends when MB = MC. There, said Stigler, the consumer has obtained the optimal amount of information. Thus a distribution of prices, not a single retail price, exists for new automobiles of the same brand. The extra information needed to eliminate the price variability entails a greater marginal cost than marginal benefit. Other things equal, the higher the marginal cost of information, the greater is the dispersion of prices in a market.

In 1970 George A. Akerlof (1940–) of the University of California at Berkeley extended Stigler's analysis of information. Akerlof asked a rather simple question: "Why does a new car lose so much value when the buyer drives it off the sales lot?" If physical depreciation is the culprit, then why can the same new car sit for weeks or even months on the lot and not lose value? Akerlof's answer, which earned him a share of the 2001 Nobel Prize in economics, was that some markets contain *asymmetric information*.†

Sellers of used cars have better information about the condition of their cars than do prospective buyers; information is not symmetrical on both sides of the market. Because buyers lack important information about used cars, an *adverse selection problem* emerges. Owners of defective cars ("lemons") wish to sell their cars, but most owners of high-quality cars of the same make, year, and model do not. The result is that most used cars on the market are of poorer quality than the same models that are not for sale. Because prospective used-car buyers know this, the demand for used cars is reduced, as is the market price. This low price of used cars further reduces the incentive of people owning good used cars to offer them for sale. Poor-quality cars, therefore, tend to drive out high-quality cars, and many potential welfare-enhancing transactions do not occur. When a buyer drives a new car away from the dealership, the car immediately assumes the value assigned it in the "lemon's market," even though the new car may be in perfect condition.

Contemporary economists have discovered several markets in which there is asymmetric information, including restaurant meals, motel rooms, physician services,

24-1 PAST AS PROLOGUE (continued)

electronic equipment, and some insurance and labor markets. They also remind us, however, that many private-sector arrangements have emerged that help reduce the asymmetry of information. Examples include transferable product warranties, franchising, and the establishment of brand names. Also, the problem is reduced because such private information providers as firms issuing consumer reports, producers of travel guides, credit bureaus, bonding agencies, brokers, and other intermediaries profit by providing information. Finally, the inexpensive access to information provided through the Internet may also reduce the problem of asymmetric information.

---

*George J. Stigler, "The Economics of Information," *Journal of Political Economy* 69 (June 1961): 213–225.

†George A. Akerlof, "The Market for Lemons: Qualitative Uncertainty and the Market Mechanism," *Quarterly Journal of Economics* 84 (August 1970): 488–500.

Lucas said that market participants reflect on their past errors, use and process all available information, and succeed in eliminating regularities in errors in predicting future price level changes. Because people understand that expansionary fiscal and monetary policies produce inflation, they immediately adjust their inflation expectations upward when government undertakes these policies. Resource and financial markets immediately adjust such that workers receive higher nominal wages, sellers of raw materials and other capital goods receive higher prices, and lenders receive higher nominal interest rates.

These reactions to expected inflation render expansionary fiscal and monetary policies ineffective. Instead of the temporary increases in profits, output, and employment implied by the move from *a* to *b* in Figure 24-1, the economy moves directly from *a* to *c*. That is, the expansionary fiscal and monetary policies directly and immediately boost the rate of inflation from P_1 to P_2 upward along the vertical long-run Phillips curve.

Lucas's Aggregate Supply Analysis

Lucas's analysis distinguished between short-run and long-run aggregate supply. In Figure 24-2(a) and (b) the vertical axes measure the price level, not the rate of inflation, and the horizontal axes measure real output, not the unemployment rate. In the new classical model represented by the figures, an ***unanticipated*** change in aggregate demand *does* affect the level of real output, but only temporarily. In contrast, an ***anticipated*** change in aggregate demand has no effect on real output and employment.

Suppose the economy is initially at point *a* in Figure 24-2(a) and that an unexpected surge in investment spending increases aggregate demand from AD_1 to AD_2. Producers immediately experience rising prices and conclude that these prices

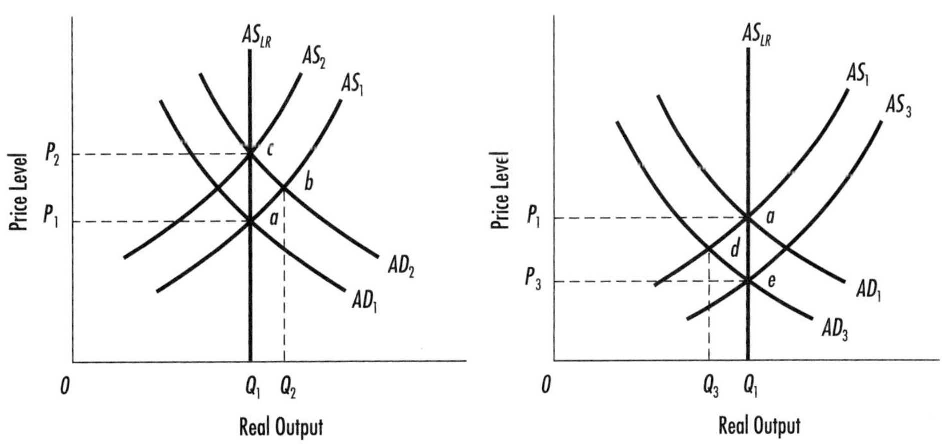

Figure 24-2 Lucas's New Classical Macroeconomics
(a) An unanticipated increase in aggregate demand from AD_1 to AD_2 temporarily moves the economy from *a* to *b*. The economy then moves to *c* because of rising nominal wages and other input prices that shift the short-run aggregate supply curve leftward from AS_1 to AS_2. An anticipated increase in aggregate demand moves the economy directly from *a* to *c* along long-run aggregate supply curve AS_{LR}. (b) An unanticipated decrease in aggregate demand from AD_1 to AD_3 temporarily moves the economy from *a* to *d*. Declines in nominal wages and other input prices shift the short-run aggregate supply rightward from AS_1 to AS_3, and the economy moves to e. An anticipated decrease in aggregate demand moves the economy directly from *a* to e along long-run aggregate supply curve AS_{LR}.

are rising relative to other prices (and to prices of labor). Expecting higher profits, they increase employment and output, moving the economy from *a* to *b*. Observe that the short-run aggregate supply curve AS_1 is upsloping; the unanticipated price-level increase from P_1 to P_2 expands real output from Q_1 to Q_2.

But in fact all prices, including the price of labor and other inputs, are rising due to the general increase in aggregate demand. Firms collectively experience rising costs, causing the short-run aggregate supply curve eventually to shift leftward from AS_1 to AS_2. The economy moves from *b* to *c*, reversing the previous increase in output. In the long run, the economy's aggregate supply curve is simply a vertical line (AS_{LR}) emanating upward from Q_1 through points such as *a* and *c*.

An unanticipated *decrease* in aggregate demand, as from AD_1 to AD_3 in Figure 24-2(b), works in the opposite way. Initially, firms misperceive that their falling prices are confined to their own products. Anticipating lower profits, they reduce employment and output, and the economy moves from *a* to *d*. Firms soon recognize, however, that *all* prices are falling, including wages and other input prices. As nominal costs fall, the short-run aggregate supply curve shifts rightward from AS_1 to AS_3. The economy moves from *d* to *e*, real output expands from Q_3 to Q_1, and the recession automatically ends. The economy is self-correcting, says Lucas, just as the classical economists thought. For this reason, his theory is known as *new classical macroeconomics.*

When changes in aggregate demand are anticipated, real output stays constant. For example, suppose in Figure 24-2(a) that the central bank increases the money supply in order to expand aggregate demand from AD_1 to AD_2. Because the Fed's action is public and the inflationary outcome is anticipated, firms immediately recognize that the higher prices being received for their products are part of the general inflation they had anticipated. They understand that the same forces that are raising their prices are raising their costs, leaving their profits unchanged. The short-run aggregate supply curve shifts leftward from AS_1 to AS_2 simultaneously with the rightward increase in aggregate demand from AD_1 to AD_2. The economy moves directly from *a* to *c* on long-run aggregate supply curve AS_{LR}. Real output remains unchanged at Q_1, and only inflation occurs. The long-run aggregate supply curve is the only relevant aggregate supply curve when increases in aggregate demand are anticipated. This is also true for the anticipated *decreases* in aggregate demand, such as from AD_1 to AD_3 in Figure 24-2(b). In that case, the economy moves directly downward along AS_{LR} from *a* to *e*.

Evaluation

Nobody who has seriously studied Lucas's theories looks at the macroeconomy quite the same as before. And, in fact, the idea of rational expectations is now very much a part of mainstream macroeconomics. Nevertheless, most macroeconomists reject the new classical propositions of automatic self-correction and policy ineffectiveness. Most economists contend that prices and wages are not perfectly flexible, particularly in a downward direction. Thus, the swift, automatic correction to recessions implied by Figure 24-2(b) is not forthcoming, and fiscal and monetary policy may be needed to move the economy from recession. (You may want to review Figure 22-6.) Mainstream economists also dispute the basic new classical premise that expansionary fiscal and monetary policies are always inflationary. If economists disagree on this point, they ask, why would we expect the general public to equate these policies with impending inflation and act on that expectation? Lucas has, in effect, extended the microeconomic theories of perfect competition, rational behavior, and Walrasian equilibrium to macroeconomics. There is considerable debate, however, on how closely his theory describes the true workings of modern, real-world economies.

GARY S. BECKER

Gary S. Becker (1930–) was born in Pottstown, Pennsylvania, did his undergraduate work at Princeton, and received his doctorate from the University of Chicago. Between 1957 and 1969 he was a professor at Columbia University. In 1970 he joined the faculty at Chicago, where he currently is a professor of economics and sociology. He was president of the American Economic Association in 1986 and, according to one historian of economic thought, "is one of the most original minds in modern economics."[18] The consummate theoretician, Becker seems more comfortable presenting

[18] Mark Blaug, *Great Economists since Keynes* (Totowa, NJ: Barnes and Noble, 1985), 15.

his positive theories of economics than championing the policy perspectives associated with Friedman and the Chicago school. In the mid-1980s, however, he began contributing columns for *Business Week,* which has increased his exposure to the broader public. In 1992 Becker was awarded the Nobel Prize in economics.

Becker has been referred to as an "intellectual imperialist." By this is meant that he has extended the economic approach, with its combined assumptions of maximizing behavior, stable preferences, and market equilibrium, into the traditional domains of sociology, political science, law, social biology, and anthropology. His strong belief in the relevance of the economic approach to a broad range of topics will become evident as we survey several of his ideas.

Discrimination

In 1957 Becker published *The Economics of Discrimination,* which was a revised version of his 1955 doctoral dissertation. He later pointed out that, "It was my first published effort to apply the economic approach to a problem outside of conventional fields of economics, and was greeted with indifference or hostility by the overwhelming majority of the economics profession."[19]

By the mid-1970s, however, the Becker model of discrimination, although still controversial, received prominent discussion in most of the major textbooks on labor economics. Becker views discrimination as a preference or "taste" for which the discriminator is willing to pay:

> Individuals are assumed to act as if they have "tastes for discrimination," and these tastes are the most important immediate cause of actual discrimination. When an employer discriminates against employees, he acts as if he incurs non-pecuniary, psychic costs of production by employing them . . .
>
> The discrimination coefficient of an employer against an employee measures the value placed on the non-pecuniary cost of employing him, since it represents the percentage difference between the money and the true or net wage rate "paid" to him. If π is the money wage rate paid, then $\pi(1 + d)$ is the net wage rate, with d being the discrimination coefficient.[20]

A concrete example will help clarify these ideas. Suppose that the market wage rate is \$6 and that the employer's d is .50. Then from this employer's perspective the wage rate for the group discriminated against is \$9[$\pi(1 + d) = \$6(1 + .50)$]. This implies that the prejudiced employer would be willing to pay a premium of up to \$3 per hour in hiring preferred workers as opposed to the group targeted by prejudice. Higher values of d suggest a stronger taste for discrimination. If d is zero, on the other hand, the employer is unprejudiced.

If discrimination coefficients are positive in the overall economy, then the demand for preferred workers will be greater than it would be without the taste for discrimination. As a result, the market wage rate for preferred workers will exceed

[19] Gary S. Becker, *The Economic Approach to Human Behavior* (Chicago: University of Chicago Press, 1976), 15.

[20] Gary S. Becker, *The Economics of Discrimination,* 2nd ed. (Chicago: University of Chicago Press, 1971), 153–154.

that for equally productive unpreferred ones. This fact has an important implication: Discriminating employers will have higher wage costs than those who do not discriminate. Those firms that discriminate will have to pay a wage premium, or "price," for their tastes. Firms that do not have this taste for discrimination, or whose taste is low relative to the wage differential, will hire the equally productive unpreferred workers at the lower wage and thereby gain a cost advantage over their discriminating competitors. Theoretically, only least-cost producers can survive in the long run in a competitive market economy; discriminators will have average costs that exceed the market-determined price; that is, they will suffer losses.

Becker's theory, therefore, is consistent with the broader new classical view: In the long run, the competitive market system will impose costs on discriminators, which will reduce the amount of discrimination, whether it be by gender, race, or religious preference. Government's role in hastening this process should be to resist pressure by interest groups to block free occupational choice.

Investment in Human Capital

In *Human Capital* (1964) Becker presented the theory of investment in human capital in its modern, generalized form. This book greatly extended the work done earlier by Becker's Chicago colleague, Theodore Schultz (see the book's web site). Figure 24-3 shows the theory as it applied to a hypothetical individual deciding whether or not to go to college. The decision to attend college for investment purposes depends upon the expected return on one's investment. Without college, the individual for whom the information in the figure applies could expect the annual earnings shown by line *HH*. With college, the earnings line becomes *CC*. Attending college for four years involves *direct* costs (1) such as tuition and books, and *indirect* costs (2), which take the form of foregone earnings during the investment period. Once the college graduate enters the labor force, she or he will earn more than would have been earned with only a high school diploma. The difference between the two earning streams is shown as (3). The investment decision requires a comparison of the present value of the annual increments to earnings (3) with the present value of the direct and indirect costs (1 and 2). If the former exceeds the latter—that is, if the *net* present value is positive—the investment will take place. The basic principle underlying Figure 24-3 applies to all human capital investment decisions, such as a decision by a worker to move to a new location to work, a decision by a firm to provide on-the-job training to its workers, or a decision by a developing nation to use resources to improve the general health of its workforce. In each case, the decision maker weighs future gains against present sacrifices.

Becker was the first to distinguish between general and specific training. *General training* increases the marginal productivity of workers not only in their present employment but also in any other employment in which they might engage. *Specific training* increases marginal productivity only within the firm providing it. Hence, some of our skills are specific to a particular firm or situation (*specific capital*), whereas others can be broadly applied to various situations or work settings (*general capital*).

Becker pointed out that the theory of human capital helps explain "a wide range of empirical phenomena that have either been given *ad hoc* interpretations or have baffled investigators." Such phenomena include evidence that (1) earnings typically

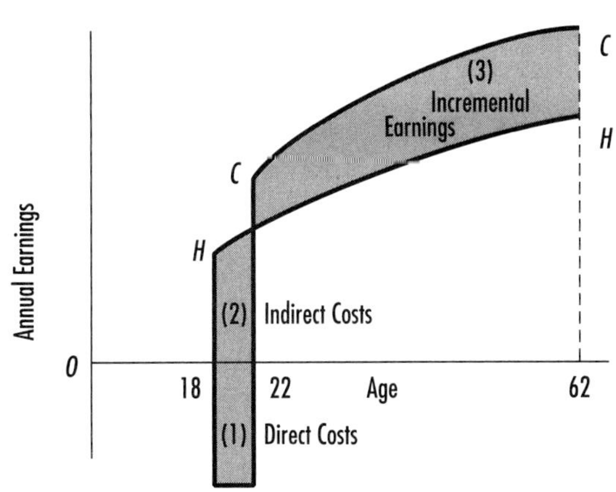

Figure 24-3 Investment in Human Capital: College Education
Investment in a college education requires present sacrifices in order to obtain a larger flow of lifetime earnings (*CC* rather than *HH*). The costs of four years of college consist of direct costs such as tuition and books (1) and the indirect costs of foregone earnings during college (2). The present value of these costs is compared to the present value of the expected incremental earnings (3) that result from the college degree. If the present value of (3) exceeds the present value of (1) and (2), the investment will take place.

increase with age at a decreasing rate, and the rate of increase tends to be positively related to the level of skill; (2) unemployment rates tend to be lower for those who have greater levels of skill; (3) younger persons change jobs more frequently and receive more schooling and on-the-job training than do older persons; and (4) people possessing more ability receive more education and on-the-job training over their lifetimes than others.

In the last sentence of *Human Capital,* Becker stated: "I would venture the judgement that human capital is going to be an important part of the thinking about development, income distribution, labor turnover, and many other problems for a long time to come." He was prophetic. Over the last two decades, human capital has been the subject of scores of books and hundreds of journal articles.

Refer to 24-2 PAST AS PROLOGUE

Theory of the Allocation of Time

The neoclassical theory of consumer behavior assumed that consumption is instantaneous. Becker argued that consumption takes time and that time is scarce and has value. The time used to consume a good is not available for an alternative use, for example, to earn income. Some consumer goods take more time to consume than others. Thus, said Becker, people take into account the "full cost" or "full price" of goods in making buying decisions. The full price of a good consists of its market price plus the value of the time needed for its consumption.

24-2 PAST AS PROLOGUE

Human Capital Formation? Or Screening and Signaling?

The work of Theodore Schultz (1902–1998) and Gary Becker (1930–) implies that the formation of human capital through education enhances productivity and earnings. The effect of education on earnings is well documented, with college graduates in 2001 earning 89 percent more than those with only a high school diploma.* Similarly, pay differentials can be significant between graduates of the most prestigious universities and those from lesser-known programs. But the effect of college education on productivity, independent of pre-education ability, is less clear.

Do the higher incomes of Ivy League graduates reflect greater acquisition of human capital, or is some other process afoot? The work of Michael Spence (1943–) and Joseph Stiglitz (1943–), corecipients of the Nobel Prize in economics in 2001 (along with George Akerlof), offers alternative explanations. Sellers of labor have more information about their abilities than do prospective employers. Because detailed information about each applicant is often costly to acquire, employers look for less expensive ways to assess quality differences between job candidates. One filtering mechanism is the school attended by the applicant. If an academic institution has a reputation of turning out high-quality graduates, employers will deem it less risky than hiring someone from an unfamiliar school. *Screening*, as Stiglitz calls it, allows employers to sort out high-ability applicants based on place of degree. Stiglitz developed the notion of

This important insight led Becker to suggest a reconstruction of the theory of choice. The household, being the basic decision unit, should be thought of as a producer as well as a consumer of utility-producing "commodities." Production of commodities takes place by combining goods (goods and services) bought in the market with time. To get the income necessary to buy the goods used to produce commodities, the household needs to expend labor market time. To produce and consume the commodity in the household, it must expend production and consumption time. An example is the production and consumption of a meal, say, a breakfast. It is produced and consumed by combining goods (eggs, bread, juice, bacon) with production time (the length of time required to prepare the meal) and consumption time (the time it takes to eat the meal).

The household must decide what commodities it wishes to consume and how it will go about producing these commodities. These decisions are made every day. A complicating factor is that some commodities require a lot of time and not many goods to produce, whereas others demand many goods and little time.

screening within the context of the insurance industry, but the concept applies to labor markets as well.

Knowing that prospective employers use screening mechanisms, job candidates may choose their education to *signal*, as Spence puts it, their greater ability. Assuming that more prestigious schools send a better signal but are also more costly to attend, a student must decide whether the potential income gains from the signal exceed the higher cost.

The underlying question is what is being screened and signaled? Do the top universities actually create more human capital than other institutions, or do they simply attract those of already higher ability? Screening and signaling occur earlier in the process as well, with strong institutional reputation attracting the best applicants, while discouraging those of lesser ability. High school students planning to attend college can signal their abilities through enrollment at highly regarded preparatory schools. Meanwhile, college admissions boards screen applicants by, among other things, the perceived quality of the high school attended.

To the extent that higher incomes reflect greater productivity, college graduates from more prestigious programs tend to be more productive. But the question raised by the contributions of Spence and Stiglitz remains: Does that greater productivity result from a better educational process or from students bringing in a higher quality set of inputs to their schools? Is more human capital development occurring in prestigious schools, or are those schools and their students merely signaling higher-quality, higher productivity potential workers?

---

*U.S. Bureau of the Census, Current Population Survey, Table-PINC-4, March 2002. In 1981, those with a college degree earned only 57 percent more than those with only a high school diploma.

An example of a *time-intensive commodity* is a natural suntan gained over several days at the beach. An example of a *goods-intensive commodity* is a fast food meal.

Becker pointed out several interesting implications of his model, and others have cited additional ones. Three examples will help demonstrate the types of insights that the model illuminates. The first is the implication that a rise in earnings from labor market time will likely cause people to shift their consumption patterns away from time-intensive commodities and toward goods-intensive ones. The reason is that the opportunity cost of household production and consumption time rises. A person may acquire a tan by spending short periods of time at a tanning salon rather than lying for hours on a beach, or eat at a restaurant rather than produce and consume a homegrown, garden-fresh meal. The second is that an increase in the productivity of household production time, say, through the development of microwave ovens, trash compactors, and washers and dryers, frees up either consumption time (watching soap operas, attending exercise classes), labor market time (part- or full-time employment), or some combination of each. The third is that, where both spouses have abilities to earn high incomes in the labor market, families are likely to have fewer children and produce more goods-intensive family experiences than families in which one spouse has low earnings potential and chooses not to work.

On the Family

In the preface to his *A Treatise on the Family* (1981), Becker wrote:

> This volume uses the assumptions of maximizing behavior, stable preferences, and equilibrium in implicit or explicit markets to provide a systematic analysis of the family. I build on my research during the past decade to analyze the allocation of time to children and to market work, marriage and divorce in polygamous as well as monogamous societies, altruism in addition to selfishness in families, intergenerational mobility, and many other aspects of the family. Although not all are considered, the systematic, unified treatment of the important aspects perhaps justifies the old-fashioned title "treatise."[21]

Theory of marriage. Marriage allows for a division of labor that enables partners to maximize their joint production and consumption of "commodities," which provide economic well-being. Reproducing and raising children are central "commodities" that marriage facilitates. In other words, partners form a household out of economic self-interest. Skill variations that enable gains from partnership result from different past experiences and other investments in human capital. The individual commanding the highest market wage opportunity most likely will engage in market work, whereas household production will be performed by the individual having the greatest relative productivity in those endeavors. Traditionally, married women have specialized in childbearing and other domestic activities. As a result,

> they have demanded long-term "contracts" from their husbands to protect them against abandonment and other adversities. Virtually all societies have developed long-term protection for married women; one can even say that "marriage" is defined by a long-term commitment between a man and a woman.[22]

Even relatively small differences in productive capacities between marriage partners imply large differences in allocation of time among labor market time, household production time, and consumption time. The reason is that engaging in an activity increases one's stock of specific human capital, which in turn increases productivity in that activity. This does not always result in complete specialization, however. In some cases, for example, one of the partners may opt to work part-time.

Marriage usually involves "positive sorting" between "high-quality" males and females. One reason is complementarity in production. The positive traits possessed by one partner increase the marginal contribution of the other in producing "full income," broadly defined to include "commodities."

Fertility. The family produces children ("durable capital"), which add to the family's full income, or economic welfare. But families do not produce as many children as

[21] Gary S. Becker, *A Treatise on the Family* (Cambridge: Harvard University Press, 1981), ix–x.

[22] Becker, *Family,* 14–15.

would be biologically possible because children are costly. In this respect, said Becker, they have a "price." This price involves direct costs such as expenditures for food, shelter, clothing, health care, day care, education, and so forth, and indirect costs in the form of opportunity costs of time. Young children in particular are time-intensive commodities. Fertility will depend on the price of children, parental income, and the trade-off that parents perceive between the quantity of children and their quality. As wage opportunities increase for women, the price of each child increases (the opportunity cost rises), and parents opt to have fewer, but "higher-quality" (healthier, better-educated) children.

Rural families in the past had more children than did urban families because the costs of raising children were lower in rural areas. Welfare programs, said Becker, reduce the cost of having children and increase fertility.

Altruism. Altruism, which is defined in terms of linked utility, is an important feature of a family. A person is altruistic when her or his utility increases because someone else's utility rises. Altruism adds to the potential gains from marriage, because consumption of a commodity enables utility to rise by more than the rise in utility to the consumer. One family member's joy adds to the other family member's joy.

In what Becker colorfully referred to as the "rotten kid theorem," he established that altruism in the family will tend to overcome selfishness. Becker states this theorem roughly as follows: Each beneficiary, no matter how selfish, maximizes the family income of his benefactor. Translated: Even the most troublesome children won't want to do anything that could reduce their potential inheritance.[23]

The idea here is that an action that reduces the family's full income will result in the altruistic head of the family having less full income to transfer to each of the benefactors. Selfish kids recognize that harming the family comes at the expense of harming themselves. This principle is general, in that it applies to interactions between all altruists and beneficiaries. But the restraining effect of altruism on self-interest diminishes with the number of benefactors, that is, with the size of the family or organization.

Divorce. Marriage partners search for information about prospective mates, but

> time, effort, and other costly resources must be spent on search, and the longer the search, the longer the gains from marriage are delayed. A rational person would continue to search on both the "extensive margin" of additional prospects and the "intensive margin" of additional information about serious prospects until the marginal cost and marginal benefit on each margin are equal.[24]

As a consequence, people often get married even though they have incomplete information about their partner. As such information reveals itself through the marriage, divorce may become a new optimal decision. Divorces are more likely early in the marriage than later, because the accumulation of information occurs during the

[23] Becker, *Family*, 183.

[24] Becker, *Family*, 220.

first few years of the marriage. Unexpected good or bad fortune (becoming a movie star; suffering infertility) increases the likelihood of divorce because it may turn an optimal match into one that one party may no longer judge to be optimal. The increase in the market productivity of women reduces the gains from specialization and increases the probability of divorce.

It is clear that Becker's work in this area is pioneering, provocative, and profound. As you might suspect, it is also controversial. As stated by Ben-Porath:

> So when all is said and done, the marriage of economics and the family is interesting; it may not be happy and it is certainly not peaceful, but it is unlikely to end in divorce. Will it also yield a progeny of verifiable knowledge? That remains to be seen.[25]

Questions for Study and Discussion

1. Identify and briefly state the significance of each of the following to the history of economic thought: Chicago school of economics, Friedman, permanent income, modern quantity theory, *Monetary History of the United States, 1867–1960,* long-run vertical Phillips curve, natural rate of unemployment, the monetary rule, Lucas, rational expectations, Stigler, information as an economic good, Akerlof, "lemons" problem, Becker, discrimination coefficient, specific versus general training, Spence, signaling, Stiglitz, screening, and "commodities."
2. Contrast the major tenets of the Chicago school with those of the marginalist school and the institutionalist school.
3. Relate the following quote from Sir Dennis Robertson to the place of the new classicism in the history of economic thought: "Highbrow opinion is like a hunted hare; if you stand long enough, it will come back to the place it started from."
4. What are the major determinants of the demand for money, according to Friedman? Is this demand stable or unstable in the short run? How does an increase in the supply of money that exceeds the long-run growth of output cause a rise in the general price level?
5. Explain this quote by Friedman: "A rising rate of inflation may reduce unemployment, a high rate will not."
6. Explain Lucas's distinction between short-run and long-run aggregate supply. Relate these ideas to Friedman's distinction between short-run and long-run Phillips curves.
7. What is "classical" about Lucas's new classical macroeconomics? Based on your understanding of his theory, do you think Lucas would favor the active fiscal and monetary policy championed by Lerner (Past as Prologue 22-2) or monetary and fiscal rules such as those proposed by Friedman and Buchanan (Chapter 20)? Explain your reasoning.
8. Briefly summarize Stigler's theory of information (Past as Prologue 24-1). Relate his theory to Becker's theory of marriage and divorce.

[25] Yoram Ben-Porath, "Economics and the Family—Match or Mismatch? A Review of Becker's *A Treatise on the Family,*" *Journal of Economic Literature* 20 (March 1982): 62–63.

9. How do the problems of asymmetric information and adverse selection (Past as Prologue 24-1) relate to the processes of signaling and screening (Past as Prologue 24-2)?
10. Use Becker's theories to explain each of the following:
    a) Discrimination will be costly to a firm operating in a competitive environment.
    b) Young people on average receive more schooling and on-the-job training than older people.
    c) The number of meals consumed at restaurants in the United States has increased more rapidly than the number consumed at home.
    d) Altruism adds to the potential gains from marriage.
11. With which, if either, of the following two statements do you agree? Explain your reasoning.

> There is no more important prerequisite to clear thinking in regard to economics itself than recognition of its limited place among human interests at large. [Frank Knight]

> The heart of my argument is that human behavior is not compartmentalized, sometimes based on maximizing, sometimes not, sometimes motivated by stable preferences, sometimes by volatile ones, sometimes resulting in an optimal accumulation of information, sometimes not. Rather all human behavior can be viewed as involving participants who maximize their utility from a stable set of preferences and accumulate an optimal amount of information and other inputs in a variety of markets. [Gary Becker]

Selected Readings

Books

Becker, Gary S. *The Economic Approach to Human Behavior.* Chicago: University of Chicago Press, 1976.

———. *The Economics of Discrimination,* 2nd ed. Chicago: University of Chicago Press, 1971. (Orig. pub. 1957.)

———. *Human Capital: A Theoretical and Empirical Analysis with Special Reference to Education.* New York: National Bureau of Economic Research, 1964.

———. *A Treatise on the Family.* Cambridge: Harvard University Press, 1981.

Friedman, Milton. *Capitalism and Freedom.* Chicago: University of Chicago Press, 1962.

———. *Essays in Positive Economics.* Chicago: University of Chicago Press, 1953.

———. *The Optimum Quantity of Money and Other Essays.* Chicago: Aldine, 1969.

———, ed. *Studies in the Quantity Theory of Money.* Chicago: University of Chicago Press, 1956.

———. *Theory of the Consumption Function.* Princeton, NJ: Princeton University Press, 1957.

Friedman, Milton, and Anna J. Schwartz. *A Monetary History of the United States, 1867–1960.* Princeton, NJ: Princeton University Press, 1963.

Hirsh, Abraham, and Neil de Marchi. *Milton Friedman: Economics in Theory and Practice*. Ann Arbor: University of Michigan Press, 1990.

Lucas, Robert E. *Studies in Business-Cycle Theories*. Cambridge, MA: MIT Press, 1981.

———. *Models of Business Cycles*. Oxford, England: Basil Blackwell, 1987.

Samuels, Warren J., ed. *The Chicago School of Political Economy*. East Lansing, MI: Michigan State University, 1976.

Shackleton, J. R., and G. Locksley, eds. *Twelve Contemporary Economists*. Chaps. 2 and 4. New York: Wiley, Halsted, 1981.

Stigler, George J. *The Economist as Preacher and Other Essays*. Chicago: University of Chicago Press, 1982.

Wood, John Cunningham, ed. *Milton Friedman: Critical Assessments*. 4 vols. London: Routledge, 1990.

Journal Articles

Ben-Porath, Yoram. "Economics and the Family—Match or Mismatch? A Review of Becker's *A Treatise on the Family*," *Journal of Economic Literature* 20 (March 1982): 52–64.

Chari, V. V. "Nobel Laureate Robert E. Lucas, Jr.: Architect of Modern Macroeconomics," *Journal of Economic Perspectives* 12 (Winter 1998): 171–186.

Hannan, Michael T. "Families, Markets, and Social Structures: An Essay on Becker's *A Treatise on the Family*," *Journal of Economic Literature* 20 (March 1982): 65–72.

Reder, Melvin W. "Chicago Economics: Permanence and Change," *Journal of Economic Literature* 20 (March 1982): 1–38.

"Symposium on the Chicago School," *Journal of Economic Issues* 9 (December 1975) and 10 (March 1976).

Thygesen, Niels. "The Scientific Contributions of Milton Friedman," *Scandinavian Journal of Economics* 79, no. 1 (1977): 56–98.

Chapter 25

CONCLUDING THOUGHTS

What conclusions, if any, can we draw from our study of the history of economic thought? Other observers will likely draw varying conclusions. Here are ours.

- Economics is a dynamic discipline. Our understanding of the principles of economics and the working of the economy has progressed over the years and is still emerging. New ideas and developments in the field have tended to be followed by yet other ideas and developments. Some of the subsequent thinking has extended, amplified, and improved the existing base of knowledge; other theories and studies have challenged the new ideas. Thus we again note the white versus black lines in the Time Scale of Economic Ideas (inside front cover). Recall that the white lines indicate schools mainly friendly to predecessors, whereas black lines indicate schools of thought mainly antagonistic to predecessors. This expansion and competition of ideas has not always produced "truth" in the scientific sense of that word, but they have generated a widespread, nearly universally accepted body of basic principles of economics. Such principles are still emerging in the field.
- Neither current events nor increased professionalization alone explains the development of economic theory. In some instances, it has been the critical issues of the day that have stimulated new developments in economic theory. One example is the debate on the corn laws and the birth of the classical theories of diminishing returns and land rent. In other cases, current events and problems have turned the profession's and the public's attention to theories—long before advanced—that suddenly have new relevance. An example is the renewed attention to the quantity theory of money during the historically high inflation of the 1970s. But in still other situations, the advancement of new theories came quite independently of the current issues. Increased professionalism among economists, along with the heightened interest in understanding unresolved paradoxes and improving existing theories, has been a major factor in the advance of the discipline. A prime example is the development of general equilibrium analysis.
- Individual economists have "mattered." Economic thinkers do economic thought. We have seen that individual economists have made a difference in the history of economic theory and method. Smith, Ricardo, Marx, Marshall, Walras, and Keynes, to name but a few, are to economics as Newton and Einstein are to physics and Darwin is to biology. This obviously is not meant to imply that the development of economics owes fully to those we have discussed in this book. For every economist studied there have been hundreds of

Refer to 25-1 PAST AS PROLOGUE

25-1 PAST AS PROLOGUE

The Nobel Laureates in Economics

In his 1895 will, Swedish industrialist Alfred Nobel established five large monetary prizes to be given annually for specific outstanding achievements in physiology or medicine, chemistry, physics, literature, and peace. In 1968 the Central Bank of Sweden added the Nobel Memorial Prize in economics.*

The table below lists the Nobel winners in economics, their nationalities, and their areas of principal achievement. A quick glance at the table reveals many of the economists we have discussed in this book. Also, note that their areas of contribution are diverse, involving both microeconomics and macroeconomics. Finally, observe that the United States has been a particularly fertile ground for advancements in economics.

YEAR OF AWARD	NAME (NATIONALITY)	PRINCIPAL CONTRIBUTIONS
1969	Ragnar Frisch (Norway)	Econometric studies
	Jan Tinbergen (Netherlands)	Econometric studies
1970	Paul Samuelson (USA)	Mathematical and Keynesian economics
1971	Simon Kuznets (USA)	National income accounting
1972	Kenneth Arrow (USA)	Welfare economics
	John R. Hicks (UK)	Microeconomic theory
1973	Wassily Leontief (USA)	Input-output analysis
1974	Gunnar Myrdal (Sweden)	Macroeconomics and institutional economics
	Friedrich von Hayek (UK)	Monetary theory and political economy
1975	Leonid Kantorovich (USSR)	Linear programming
	Tjalling Koopmans (USA)	Linear programming
1976	Milton Friedman (USA)	Monetary theory; political economy
1977	Bertil Ohlin (Sweden)	International trade theory
	James Meade (UK)	International trade policy
1978	Herbert Simon (USA)	Administrative behavior; rationality
1979	W. Arthur Lewis (UK)	Development economics
	Theodore Schultz (USA)	Agriculture; human capital
1980	Lawrence Klein (USA)	Econometric forecasting
1981	James Tobin (USA)	Macroeconomics and financial economics
1982	George Stigler (USA)	Industrial organization; information theory
1983	Gerard Debreu (USA)	Welfare economics
1984	Richard Stone (UK)	National income accounting
1985	Franco Modigliani (USA)	Theory of saving
1986	James Buchanan (USA)	Public choice

1987	Robert Solow (USA)	Growth theory
1988	Maurice Allais (France)	Public-sector pricing
1989	Trygve Haavelmo (Norway)	Econometrics
1990	Harry Markowitz (USA)	Financial economics
	William Sharp (USA)	Financial economics
	Merton Miller (USA)	Financial economics
1991	Ronald Coase (USA)	Property rights; organizational theory
1992	Gary Becker (USA)	Human capital; discrimination; family behavior
1993	Robert Fogel (USA)	Economic history
	Douglass North (USA)	Economic history; institutional analysis
1994	John Harsanyi (USA)	Game theory
	John Nash (USA)	Game theory
	Reinhard Selten (Germany)	Game theory
1995	Robert Lucas Jr. (USA)	Macroeconomics
1996	James Mirrlees (UK)	Microeconomics
	William Vickrey (USA)	Microeconomics
1997	Robert Merton (USA)	Financial economics
	Myron Scholes (USA)	Financial economics
1998	Amartya Sen (India)	Welfare economics; development economics
1999	Robert Mundell (Canada)	Open economy macroeconomics
2000	James Heckman (USA)	Microeconometrics
	Daniel McFadden (USA)	Microeconometrics
2001	George Akerlof (USA)	Asymmetric information
	A. Michael Spence (USA)	Asymmetric information
	Joseph Stiglitz (USA)	Asymmetric information
2002	Daniel Kahneman (Israel/USA)	Decision-making under uncertainty
	Vernon Smith (USA)	Experimental economics
2003	Robert Engle (USA)	Econometrics
	Clive Granger (UK)	Econometrics
2004	Finn Kydland (Norway)	Dynamic macroeconomics
	Edward Prescott (USA)	Dynamic macroeconomics
2005	Robert Aumann (Israel)	Game theory
	Thomas Schelling (USA)	Game theory

*For a discussion of the criteria for the prize and the selection process, see Assar Lindbeck, "The Sveriges Riksbank (Bank of Sweden) Prize in Economic Sciences in Memory of Alfred Nobel 1969–2000," in *The Nobel Prize: The First 100 Years,* Agneta Levinovitz and Nils Ringertz, eds. (London: Imperial College Press and World Scientific Publishing Co., 2001). Also of interest is Bernard S. Katz, ed., *Nobel Laureates in Economic Science: A Biographical Dictionary* (New York: Garland, 1989). Finally, William Breit and Roger W. Spencer, eds., have assembled interesting autobiographical lectures by thirteen Nobel winners in *Lives of the Laureates: Thirteen Nobel Economists,* 3rd ed. (Cambridge, MA: MIT Press, 1997).

others who have contributed greatly to the development of the discipline. Each book and journal article written on the subject adds directly or indirectly to the development of economic thought.

- New ideas seldom lead to the total abandonment of the existing heritage. New scholarship in economics normally is connected to a previous body of thought, and although it may alter or transform the older tradition, it rarely replaces it. Keynes, for example, drew heavily from the neoclassical scholarship and methodology. As revolutionary as they were, the Keynesian ideas did not supplant the neoclassical tradition. Recall that Keynes himself had no major quarrel with the main body of Marshall's microeconomic theory. Likewise, although the theory of monopolistic competition developed by Robinson and Chamberlin at first seemed to challenge economic orthodoxy, over the long haul it simply became a part of it. As stated by Stigler, "One of the prominent lessons of the history of human thought is that new ideas do not lead to the abandonment of the previous heritage; the new ideas are swallowed up by the existing corpus, which is thereafter a little different. And sometimes a little better."[1]
- Economics has become increasingly specialized. As the general body of economic knowledge has increased, individual economists have found it increasingly necessary and useful to specialize in a single or limited number of fields of the discipline. This specialization has become particularly noticeable in the last several decades. Not only is there specialization within economics (international economics, welfare economics, economic growth and development, labor economics, and so forth), but also there are specializations within the fields of economics (human capital theory and mobility and migration, both within labor economics).

  Table 25-1 shows the classification system used by the *Journal of Economic Literature* for new books in economics. The listings A, B, C, and so forth indicate major fields of economics, whereas the parentheses include the number of subcategories in each major field. Notice that the history of economic thought, for example, is B. During the past few decades, those specializing in one or two areas of economics have had the greatest aggregate impact on the discipline. "Big think"—the positing of broad, all-encompassing theories—still occurs but tends to be within specific subareas of economics rather than the entire subject matter of economics. A great deal of attention is focused on "little think," which attempts to place a small missing piece in the broader economic puzzle. Our study of the history of economic thought suggests that there is some optimal allocation of effort between "big" and "little" think for the maximum production of economic knowledge.
- Both positive economic thought and normative economic thought have been important in economics. Over the centuries, the discipline of economics has moved away from "political economy," with its emphasis on advocacy and "what ought to be," toward "positive economics," which eschews value judgments and focuses on discovering and stating uniformities among economic

[1] George J. Stigler, *Five Lectures on Economic Problems* (London: Longmans, Green, 1949), 24.

Table 25-1
***Journal of Economic Literature's* Classification System for Books: Major Headings (Number of Subheadings)**

A	General Economics and Teaching (3)
B	Methodology and History of Economic Thought (6)
C	Mathematical and Quantitative Methods (10)
D	Microeconomics (10)
E	Macroeconomics and Monetary Economics (7)
F	International Economics (5)
G	Financial Economics (4)
H	Public Economics (9)
I	Health, Education, and Welfare (4)
J	Labor and Demographic Economics (9)
K	Law and Economics (5)
L	Industrial Organization (10)
M	Business Administration and Business Economics; Marketing; Accounting (6)
N	Economic History (10)
O	Economic Development, Technological Change, and Growth (6)
P	Economic Systems (6)
Q	Agricultural and Natural Resource Economics (6)
R	Urban, Rural, and Regional Economics (6)
Z	Other Special Topics (2)

phenomena ("what is"). Examples of positive economics are value or price theory, theories of the firm, principles of the gains from specialization and trade, theories of the consumption function, and so forth.

But our study likewise reveals that "political economy," or normative economics, has contributed to the public awareness of economic principles and has helped advance the discipline of economics itself. This is true even in the most recent past, as evidenced in the works of such persons as Buchanan, Samuelson, Galbraith, Friedman, and Sen.

- Economics increasingly has incorporated mathematics and statistics into its basic methodology. Several important economists such as Cournot, Walras, and Pareto were self-described mathematical economists. Others such as Jevons and Wicksell used mathematics extensively. Within the past few decades, econometrics has become standard fare within the neoclassical and Keynesian traditions. As early as 1952, Samuelson wrote:

> Indeed as I look back over recent years, I am struck by the fact the species of mathematical economists pure and simple seems to be dying out and becoming extinct. Instead, as one of my older friends complained to me: "These days you

> can hardly tell a mathematical economist from an ordinary economist." I know the sense in which he meant the remark, but let me reverse its emphasis by concluding with the question: Is that bad?[2]

Increasingly, economists have answered in the negative. The danger is that the tools at hand often dictate which jobs are undertaken. Stated differently, a person adept at using a hammer may tend to think only of projects requiring use of nails. Mathematics, claim some, is better suited for "little think" than "big think," and therefore has tilted the discipline too far toward the former. Mainstream economists counter that there is nothing inherent about the mathematical approach to preclude using it to formulate broader theories. Becker's theory of marriage and the family is a case in point.

- Future developments in economics and the economy are difficult to predict. At any single point in the Time Scale of Economic Ideas, it would have been nearly impossible to predict with any certainty the course of subsequent events and developments both in economics and in the economy. Our study reveals that we ought to be extremely wary of economic theories that predict utopia, doom, or other "inevitable" outcomes. People and the economic systems in which they function have displayed remarkable resiliency in the face of changing economic circumstances. We also must resist the temptation to conclude that the wave of today necessarily is the wave of tomorrow. Just three decades ago, the participant-observer in economics might have falsely concluded that neoclassical ideas were permanently on the wane. Today we might just as easily—and just as prematurely—conclude the opposite: that economics *is* neoclassical economics. Keynesian, institutionalist, and socialist ideas are still very much alive and well may dominate economics in the future.

  Furthermore, there is activity today on several fronts by groups of economists dissatisfied with the current orthodoxy. These include the neo–Austrians, who reject the mathematical orientation of the discipline and the static definition of efficiency that pervades much of mainstream thought. There also are the supply-side economists, who advocate policies to increase production and stimulate productivity growth and who reject strict monetarism. There are traditional institutionalists and socialists, now on the defensive, but still working to formalize and popularize their ideas. There are the "post–Keynesians," discussed in Chapter 22, who are working to develop models in which prices and wages are "fixed" through the exercise of power, as opposed to being determined freely in the marketplace. One simply cannot predict which, if any, of these lines of reasoning will result in scholarship of sufficient importance to dictate its inclusion in the next chapter of the history of economic thought. But our review of the historical record demonstrates one thing clearly: New developments in economics *will* occur. What we know today about economics will not be enough to last us our lifetimes. Somewhat ironically, the study of the past in economics teaches us the importance of staying current. It also implores us to keep an open, yet discerning, mind.

[2] Paul A. Samuelson, "Economic Theory and Mathematics—An Appraisal," *American Economic Review* 42 (May 1952): 56–67.

Questions for Study and Discussion

1. Briefly identify and state the significance of each of the following to the history of economic thought: positive economics, normative economics, "big think," and "little think."
2. Comment on the following 1955 quote from C. R. McConnell:

> The entire question of advocacy versus analysis in economics may be a variation of the resource allocation problem. It is reasonable to expect that some balance in the allocation of economists [or their time] between policy and positive economics and the various hybrids thereof will lead to an optimum rate of development in economics itself.

3. Discuss this quote from Samuelson: "Obviously, you can become a great [economic] theorist without knowing the mathematics. Yet it is fair to say that you will have to be that much more clever and brilliant."
4. Do you think that all economics majors in college should be required to take a course in the history of economic thought? Explain your reasoning.

Selected Readings

Books

Blaug, Mark. *Great Economists since Keynes.* Totowa, NJ: Barnes and Noble, 1985.

Klamer, Arjo. *Conversations with Economists.* Totowa, NJ: Rowman & Allanheld, 1984.

Reder, Melvin. *Economics: The Culture of a Controversial Science.* Chicago: University of Chicago Press, 1999.

Robinson, Joan. *Economic Heresies: Some Old-Fashioned Questions in Economic Theory.* New York: Basic Books, 1973.

Shackelton, J. R., and Gareth Locksley, eds. *Twelve Contemporary Economists.* New York: Wiley, Halsted, 1981.

Shand, Alexander H. *The Capitalist Alternative: An Introduction to Neo-Austrian Economics.* New York: New York University Press, 1984.

Spiegel, H. W., and W. J. Samuels. *Contemporary Economists in Perspective.* Greenwich, CT: JAI Press, 1984.

Szenberg, Michael. *Eminent Economists: Their Life Philosophies.* Cambridge: Cambridge University Press, 1992.

Journal Articles

Anderson, Gary M., David M. Levy, and Robert D. Tollison. "The Half-Life of Dead Economists," *Canadian Journal of Economics* 22 (February 1989): 174–183.

Bordo, David Michael, and Daniel Landau. "The Pattern of Citations in Economic Theory 1945–68: An Exploration towards a Quantitative History of Thought," *Journal of Political Economy* 11 (Summer 1979): 240–253.

Franklin, Raymond S., and William K. Tabb. "The Challenge of Radical Political Economy," *Journal of Economic Issues* 8 (March 1974): 124–150.

Heilbroner, Robert L. "Analysis and Vision in the History of Modern Economic Thought," *Journal of Economic Literature* 28 (September 1990): 1097–1114.

———. "Modern Economics as a Chapter in the History of Economic Thought," *History of Political Economy* 11 (Summer 1979): 192–198.

Rima, Ingrid H. "The Role of Numeracy in the History of Economic Analysis," *Journal of the History of Economic Thought* 16 (Fall 1994): 188–201.

Walker, Donald A. "The Relevance for Present Economic Theory of Economic Theory Written in the Past," *Journal of the History of Economic Thought* 21 (November 1999): 7–26.

Name Index

Subject Index

Selected Classics

Gerard Malynes. *Lex Mercatoria: or, The Ancient Law-Merchant,* 1686 [Written in 1622].

Thomas Mun. *England's Treasure by Forraign Trade,* 1630.

Dudley North. *Discourses upon Trade,* 1691.

Charles Davenant. *Discourses on the Publick Revenues, and on the Trade in England,* 1698.

Adam Smith. *The Theory of Moral Sentiments,* 1759.

Anne Robert Jacques Turgot. *Reflections on the Formation and the Distribution of Riches,* 1766.

Richard Cantillon. *Essai sur la Nature du Commerce en Général,* 1775.

Adam Smith. *An Enquiry into the Nature and Causes of the Wealth of Nations,* 1776.

Jeremy Bentham. *An Introduction to the Principles of Morals and Legislation,* 1780.

Thomas Robert Malthus. *An Essay on the Principle of Population,* 1798.

J. B. Say. *A Treatise on Political Economy,* 1803.

David Ricardo. *Principles of Political Economy and Taxation,* 1817.

Thomas Robert Malthus. *Principles of Political Economy,* 1820.

Nassau William Senior. *An Outline of the Science of Political Economy,* 1836.

Augustine Cournot. *Researches into the Mathematical Principles of the Theory of Wealth,* 1838.

John Stuart Mill. *Principles of Political Economy,* 1848.

Wilhelm Roscher. *Principles of Political Economy,* 1854.

Herman H. Gossen. *The Laws of Human Relations and the Rules of Human Action Derived Therefrom,* 1854.

Karl Marx. *Capital,* 1867.

William Stanley Jevons. *The Theory of Political Economy,* 1871.

Carl Menger. *Principles of Economics,* 1871.

Léon Walras. *Elements of Pure Economics,* 1874.

Francis Y. Edgeworth. *Mathematical Psychics,* 1881.

Eugen von Böhm-Bawerk. *The Positive Theory of Capital,* 1888.

Friedrich von Wieser. *Natural Value,* 1889.

Alfred Marshall. *Principles of Economics,* 1890.

John Knut Wicksell. *Interest and Prices,* 1898.

J. B. Clark. *The Distribution of Wealth: A Theory of Wages, Interest and Profits,* 1899.